International Journal on Advances in Intelligent Systems

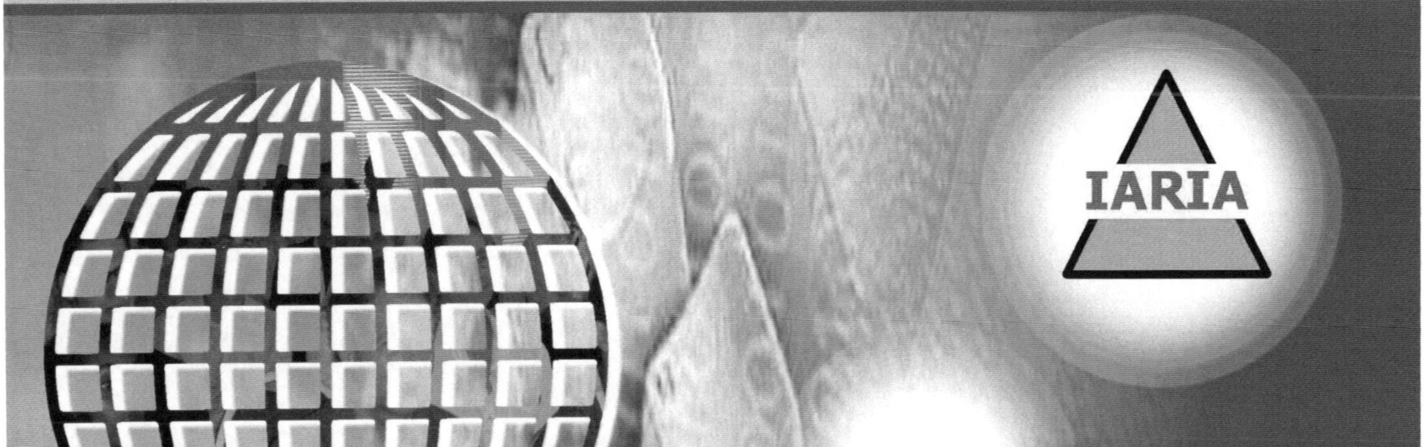

2017 vol. 10 nr. 3&4

Printed from e-media with permission by:

Curran Associates, Inc.
57 Morehouse Lane
Red Hook, NY 12571

CURRAN ASSOCIATES INC.
proceedings
.com

Some format issues inherent in the e-media version may also appear in this print version.

Printed by Curran Associates, Inc. (2018)

International Academy, Research, and Industry Association (IARIA)
412 Derby Way
Wilmington, DE 19810

Phone: (408) 893-6407
Fax: (408) 527-6351

petre@iaria.org

Additional copies of this publication are available from:

Curran Associates, Inc.
57 Morehouse Lane
Red Hook, NY 12571 USA
Phone: 845-758-0400
Fax: 845-758-2633
Email: curran@proceedings.com
Web: www.proceedings.com

The *International Journal on Advances in Intelligent Systems* is Published by IARIA.
ISSN: 1942-2679
journals site: http://www.iariajournals.org
contact: petre@iaria.org

Sponsored by IARIA
www.iaria.org

International Journal on Advances in Intelligent Systems
Volume 10, Number 3 & 4, 2017

Enn Õunapuu, Tallinn University of Technology, Estonia
Jeffrey Junfeng Pan, Facebook Inc., USA
Hervé Panetto, University of Lorraine, France
Malgorzata Pankowska, University of Economics, Poland
Harris Papadopoulos, Frederick University, Cyprus
Laura Papaleo, ICT Department - Province of Genoa & University of Genoa, Italy
Agis Papantoniou, National Technical University of Athens, Greece
Thanasis G. Papaioannou, École Polytechnique Fédérale de Lausanne (EPFL), Switzerland
Andreas Papasalouros, University of the Aegean, Greece
Eric Paquet, National Research Council / University of Ottawa, Canada
Kunal Patel, Ingenuity Systems, USA
Carlos Pedrinaci, Knowledge Media Institute, The Open University, UK
Yoseba Penya, University of Deusto - DeustoTech (Basque Country), Spain
Cathryn Peoples, Queen Mary University of London, UK
Asier Perallos, University of Deusto, Spain
Christian Percebois, Université Paul Sabatier - IRIT, France
Andrea Perego, European Commission, Joint Research Centre, Italy
Mark Perry, University of Western Ontario/Faculty of Law/ Faculty of Science - London, Canada
Willy Picard, Poznań University of Economics, Poland
Agostino Poggi, Università degli Studi di Parma, Italy
R. Ponnusamy, Madha Engineering College-Anna University, India
Wendy Powley, Queen's University, Canada
Jerzy Prekurat, Canadian Bank Note Co. Ltd., Canada
Didier Puzenat, Université des Antilles et de la Guyane, France
Sita Ramakrishnan, Monash University, Australia
Elmano Ramalho Cavalcanti, Federal University of Campina Grande, Brazil
Juwel Rana, Luleå University of Technology, Sweden
Martin Randles, School of Computing and Mathematical Sciences, Liverpool John Moores University, UK
Christoph Rasche, University of Paderborn, Germany
Ann Reddipogu, ManyWorlds UK Ltd, UK
Ramana Reddy, West Virginia University, USA
René Reiners, Fraunhofer FIT - Sankt Augustin, Germany
Paolo Remagnino, Kingston University - Surrey, UK
Sebastian Rieger, University of Applied Sciences Fulda, Germany
Andreas Riener, Johannes Kepler University Linz, Austria
Ivan Rodero, NSF Center for Autonomic Computing, Rutgers University - Piscataway, USA
Alejandro Rodríguez González, University Carlos III of Madrid, Spain
Paolo Romano, INESC-ID Lisbon, Portugal
Agostinho Rosa, Instituto de Sistemas e Robótica, Portugal
José Rouillard, University of Lille, France
Paweł Różycki, University of Information Technology and Management (UITM) in Rzeszów, Poland
Igor Ruiz-Agundez, DeustoTech, University of Deusto, Spain
Michele Ruta, Politecnico di Bari, Italy
Melike Sah, Trinity College Dublin, Ireland
Francesc Saigi Rubió, Universitat Oberta de Catalunya, Spain
Abdel-Badeeh M. Salem, Ain Shams University, Egypt
Yacine Sam, Université François-Rabelais Tours, France
Ismael Sanz, Universitat Jaume I, Spain
Ricardo Sanz, Universidad Politecnica de Madrid, Spain
Marcello Sarini, Università degli Studi Milano-Bicocca - Milano, Italy
Munehiko Sasajima, I.S.I.R., Osaka University, Japan
Minoru Sasaki, Ibaraki University, Japan
Hiroyuki Sato, University of Tokyo, Japan

Jürgen Sauer, Universität Oldenburg, Germany
Patrick Sayd, CEA List, France
Dominique Scapin, INRIA - Le Chesnay, France
Kenneth Scerri, University of Malta, Malta
Rainer Schmidt, Austrian Institute of Technology, Austria
Bruno Schulze, National Laboratory for Scientific Computing - LNCC, Brazil
Ingo Schwab, University of Applied Sciences Karlsruhe, Germany
Wieland Schwinger, Johannes Kepler University Linz, Austria
Hans-Werner Sehring, Namics AG, Germany
Paulo Jorge Sequeira Gonçalves, Polytechnic Institute of Castelo Branco, Portugal
Kewei Sha, Oklahoma City University, USA
Roman Y. Shtykh, Rakuten, Inc., Japan
Robin JS Sloan, University of Abertay Dundee, UK
Vasco N. G. J. Soares, Instituto de Telecomunicações / University of Beira Interior / Polytechnic Institute of Castelo Branco, Portugal
Don Sofge, Naval Research Laboratory, USA
Christoph Sondermann-Woelke, Universitaet Paderborn, Germany
George Spanoudakis, City University London, UK
Vladimir Stantchev, SRH University Berlin, Germany
Cristian Stanciu, University Politehnica of Bucharest, Romania
Claudius Stern, University of Paderborn, Germany
Mari Carmen Suárez-Figueroa, Universidad Politécnica de Madrid (UPM), Spain
Kåre Synnes, Luleå University of Technology, Sweden
Ryszard Tadeusiewicz, AGH University of Science and Technology, Poland
Yehia Taher, ERISS - Tilburg University, The Netherlands
Yutaka Takahashi, Senshu University, Japan
Dan Tamir, Texas State University, USA
Jinhui Tang, Nanjing University of Science and Technology, P.R. China
Yi Tang, Chinese Academy of Sciences, China
John Terzakis, Intel, USA
Sotirios Terzis, University of Strathclyde, UK
Vagan Terziyan, University of Jyvaskyla, Finland
Lucio Tommaso De Paolis, Department of Innovation Engineering - University of Salento, Italy
Davide Tosi, Università degli Studi dell'Insubria, Italy
Raquel Trillo Lado, University of Zaragoza, Spain
Tuan Anh Trinh, Budapest University of Technology and Economics, Hungary
Simon Tsang, Applied Communication Sciences, USA
Theodore Tsiligiridis, Agricultural University of Athens, Greece
Antonios Tsourdos, Cranfield University, UK
José Valente de Oliveira, University of Algarve, Portugal
Eugen Volk, University of Stuttgart, Germany
Mihaela Vranić, University of Zagreb, Croatia
Chieh-Yih Wan, Intel Labs, Intel Corporation, USA
Jue Wang, Washington University in St. Louis, USA
Shenghui Wang, OCLC Leiden, The Netherlands
Zhonglei Wang, Karlsruhe Institute of Technology (KIT), Germany
Laurent Wendling, University Descartes (Paris 5), France
Maarten Weyn, University of Antwerp, Belgium
Nancy Wiegand, University of Wisconsin-Madison, USA
Alexander Wijesinha, Towson University, USA
Eric B. Wolf, US Geological Survey, Center for Excellence in GIScience, USA
Ouri Wolfson, University of Illinois at Chicago, USA
Yingcai Xiao, The University of Akron, USA

International Journal on Advances in Intelligent Systems
Volume 10, Numbers 3 & 4, 2017

CONTENTS

SoNA: A Knowledge-based Social Network Analysis Framework for Predictive Policing

Michael Spranger*, Hanna Siewerts*, Joshua Hampl*, Florian Heinke* and Dirk Labudde*†
*University of Applied Sciences Mittweida
Faculty Applied Computer Sciences & Biosciences
Mittweida, Germany
Email: {*name.surname*}@hs-mittweida.de
†Fraunhofer
Cyber Security
Darmstadt, Germany
Email: labudde@hs-mittweida.de

Abstract—**Major incidents can disturb the state of balance of a society and it is important to increase the resilience of the society against such disturbances. There are different causes for major incidents, one of which are groups of individuals, for example at demonstrations. The ideal way to handle such events would be to prevent them, or at least provide information to ensure the appropriate security services are prepared. Nowadays, a lot of communication, even criminal, takes place in social networks, which, hence, provide the ideal ground to gain the necessary information, by monitoring such groups. In the present paper, we propose an application framework for knowledge-based social network monitoring. The ultimate goal is the prediction of short-term activities, as well as the long-term development of potentially dangerous groups, based on sentiment and topic analysis and the identification of opinion-leaders. Here, we present the first steps to reach this goal, which include the assessment of the risk for a major incident caused by a group of individuals based on the sentiment in the social network groups and the topics discussed.**

Keywords–forensic; opinion-leader; topic mining; expert system; text analysis; classification; sentiment analysis

I. INTRODUCTION

The representation and communication of individuals, companies and organizations, using the Internet, especially social networks, has become the standard in our society. Even though social networks are successful and have progressed throughout these past years, they have also contributed to the formation of new criminal energy. As already mentioned in [1], in particular, the provision of an infrastructure for rapid communication and the possibility to exchange ideas, pictures etc. in private and protected environments, which are difficult to control by investigators - if at all - enables radical or extreme political groups, criminal gangs or terrorist organizations to use Social Networks as a tool to plan, appoint and execute criminal offenses. These groups often use large-scale events with a high degree of group dynamics to promote their ideas. Events, such as sporting events, demonstrations or festivals, cause high expenses on security personnel. The inherent group dynamics cause a great uncertainty and unpredictability concerning the development of such events and make it difficult to estimate how much security personnel is needed. For example, in 2014 the police officers spent more than two million working hours just on securing soccer games in Germany [2]. Targeted and automated monitoring of social networks, taking into account the applicable legal provisions, can particularly support strategic security planning as well as the development of effective prevention strategies. As a positive side effect, the subjective sense of security of the users is strengthened. Authorities of the federal office for the protection of the constitution, as well as intelligence services, are aware of the importance of social networks as a source for important information and increasingly focus on extracting and analyzing this information. However, at this point the extraction and evaluation of the information is done manually. Taking into account the increasing number of users worldwide – currently, for example, approximately 40 % of the population worldwide uses social networks – it has to be noticed that there is an enormous amount of potential profiles or communication to be monitored. This demonstrates the need for an automated solution that is capable of handling this amount of data and the resulting complexity.

Consequently, the design of an application framework, namely Social Network Analyzer (SoNA), for monitoring groups and organizations in Social Networks as key elements of critical events is presented to assist decision-makers. A prototype implementing parts of this framework for monitoring publicly accessible Facebook data is discussed.

The paper is segmented in six sections. The first two sections following the introduction discuss the concept of predictive policing as well as give a short overview about the language characteristics in Social Networks. These sections are followed by an outline of the framework, which is still under development, including how the dangerous militant profiles can be selected, how the risk of an event can be assessed and the opinion-leaders can be identified. In Section V, a prototypical implementation including its architecture and currently available features is presented. Finally, the paper ends with a conclusion, also discussing the progress of the work and its future development.

II. PREDICTIVE POLICING AS A TOOL FOR RESILIENCE ENGINEERING

A major incident includes a great number of casualties and/or severe property damage [3]. At large-scale events, such as described above, there is always a possibility for a major catastrophic event to happen. However, whether or not it will happen is usually difficult to predict. Resilience is the ability of a socio-ecological system to recover from disturbances, for example a major catastrophic event, and retain or regain its identity, functions, structures and its ability to respond [4]. In a study about resilience the German Academy of Technical Sciences (acatech) developed a resilience cycle based on the Social Resilience Cycle by Edwards [5], which includes the following five stages: prepare, prevent, protect, respond and recover [6]. In order to return quickly to the defined secure state of balance [7] it becomes necessary to apply resilience engineering [8] in the sense of a technical support system, which allows to anticipate the disaster situation [6]. Crime that arises from dynamic groups at large-scale events as well as organized and especially political motivated crime regularly disturb the state of balance. Information gained from monitoring activities of such groups in the Internet and especially Social Networks can be used to predict the probability of such catastrophic events beforehand. Accordingly, the National Institute of Justice in the USA defined Predictive Policing as follows:

> "Predictive policing, in essence, is taking data from disparate sources, analyzing them and then using the results to anticipate, prevent and respond more effectively to future crime." [9]

The knowledge gained from the monitoring of suspicious groups in Social Networks directly contributes to an increase in resilience in the stages Prepare and Prevent of the resilience cycle [5] [10]. Therefore, the development of an automated solution to monitor Social Networks is an important step of resilience engineering.

III. Characteristics of Social Media Language

While the language used in chat rooms is one of the most researched topics [11], language used on the social media site Facebook seems to be one of the least researched, which is evident in the small amount of literature covering that topic [12]. Zappavigna [12] suggests that one reason might be the combination of several genres on one social media site, making the analysis very complex. Even though it is impossible to generalize the language found on the Internet [11], studies about language use for example in chat rooms or on microblogging sites, combined with the scarce literature covering some linguistic aspects on Facebook gave a starting point for an analysis. The focus of this paper is on posts and comments and, therefore, excludes messages written on the instant messenger.

In order to get a first impression of the language used in Facebook groups, a small corpus was created using posts and comments from different Facebook groups, relevant to the application of SoNA (see Table I). The structure of a "conversation" in a Facebook group is very different to the structure for example of a chat conversation. The starting point for a "conversation" on a group wall on Facebook is always a post, often written by the group itself. Afterwards, users can write a comment or reply to an already existing comment. In comparison to a chat conversation the user is not expected to write a comment immediately after a post was posted or write a reply to a comment from another user. In fact, they do not have to reply at all. This leads to the fact that "conversations" in Facebook groups are not almost-synchronous as in a chat conversation, yet clearly asynchronous [13] [14]. Therefore, it might be questioned whether to talk about "conversations" at all. Nonetheless, whenever users start a discussion on a group wall and reply to each other's comments within minutes, these conversations look very similar to chat messages. Overall, this "conversation" structure on Facebook leads to a highly complex way of communication, which makes the analysis of the language used and the meaning created difficult.

Furthermore, the wall on Facebook allows the users to include multimodal communication, by posting pictures or videos, either with a comment or with words included for example in the picture. Additionally, often posts include references to other websites or users simply repost a post from someone else. Another aspect that makes the automated analysis of meaning difficult is the language itself. Characteristics taken from studies on other Internet-based communication were used as features in an annotation with the UAM corpus tool of the small corpus mentioned above [11] [15] [16] [17] [18]. The results show clearly that there seems to be a difference between posts and comments. For example, orality, especially colloquial language, typing errors and lower case spelling of nouns seem to be more common in comments. In comparison, hashtags seemed to be used more often in posts than in comments. Furthermore, comments and posts can be distinguished by their length. While the length of posts varies between zero words (e. g., pictures) up to 892 words, the length of comments varies from 1 word up to 92 words. Moreover, these numbers show that in comments one can often find incomplete sentences. Even though, it seems that the typical features found in chat conversations are not used as often in comments and posts on Facebook, they are still present and create a challenge for the automated analysis used in SoNA. Especially, emoticons make the analysis of meaning difficult, because the way in which they are used to create meaning is complex and they can also be used to create irony [19]. This is why, so far, the sentiment analysis used in SoNA is based on word and not sentence level.

TABLE I: Summary of the corpus created under this work including different types of Facebook groups.

		subcorpus posts		subcorpus comments	
type	# groups	posts	words	comments	words
right-winged	5	46	4539	97	1559
left-winged	5	48	5003	94	1618
soccer ultras	2	20	1211	40	323
total	12	114	10753	231	3500

IV. Outline of a Framework

The analysis of social networks from the point of view of security policy pursues two main objectives. The first one is the identification and estimation of potential dangers, including their scope and location. The second one is to enable security forces to plan in the long-term. In order to do so, it is of special interest how a group is developing in terms of their size growth, their orientation or radicalization and the increase

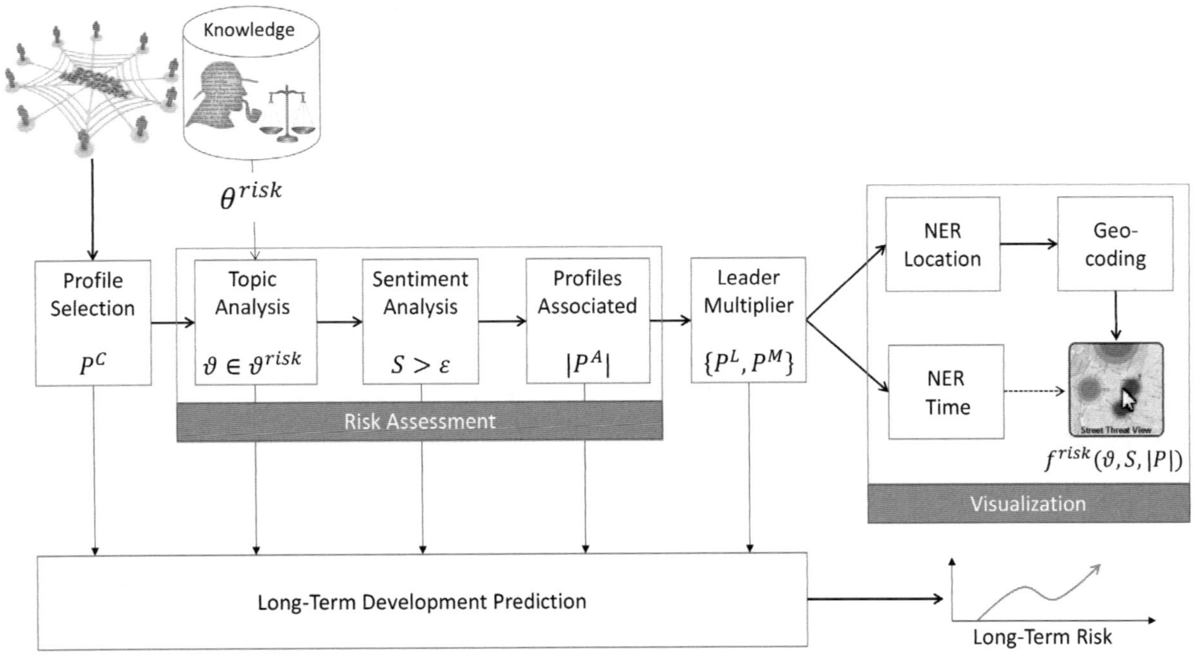

Figure 1: The proposed process chain for monitoring social networks.

in their propensity to violence. This section discusses basic concepts of a framework that addresses these tasks.

The proposed framework allows decision-makers of security forces, for example in the police's management and control centers, to identify and predict areas with high levels of crime. As a result, it is possible to deploy forces more efficiently depending on the specific situation. Thus, if, for example during a debate about the policy regarding refugees on publicly accessible pages of a social network, users loudly advocate arson attacks on refugee homes, decision-makers can now put security forces and specialized investigators on standby. If, on the other hand, before a soccer games, violent fans or fans in general do not seem to plan any riots, it may be sufficient to return to the minimum number of necessary staff to secure the event.

Another goal is to predict the long-term development of potentially violent groups. Such a prediction may include statements about the expected development of their membership, but also evidence of a possible increase in radicalization in the future. With this information, executives will be able to plan resources and make infrastructural decisions in the long term. If, for example, a district becomes, in the future, a point of attack for various, growing and violent political groups, due to certain circumstances, this information could lead to the construction of an additional police station or the expansion of the forces of an existing one. The development of a framework for the automated analysis of data from social networks with the aim of more effective crime prevention and defense in the long and short term, makes it an application from the field of predictive policing as defined in Section II.

In particular, the following tasks must be addressed by the framework:

1) selection of potential profiles of dangerous militants,
2) assessment of the probability that the danger occurs,
3) determination of location and time of risks.

In order to meet the special needs and challenges of forensics, especially with regard to the dynamics of language in social networks, it is necessary to resort to expert knowledge. This knowledge can be represented in the form of a Forensic Topic Map (FoTM) as explained in detail in [20]. In particular, abstract threats are modeled here, which form the basis for the assessment and evaluation of the communication content. Figure 1 shows the entire process chain for the proposed framework. All process steps except for the long-term prediction, which will be covered in future work, are explained in more detail in the following subsections.

A. *Selection of dangerous militants profiles*

The selection of so-called dangerous militants profiles ensures that profiles are not arbitrary selected and is thus essential to the observance of data privacy protection regulations. Furthermore, it focuses the monitoring on those profiles and thus regulates the limitation of the analysis effort. Even though the monitoring is limited to public profiles, and therefore all information publicly available, it is important not to violate the individual feeling of freedom, especially the freedom of speech as regulated in the legal framework of the respective legislature. The concept of the potential attacker was defined by a German working group, consisting of the heads from the State Offices of criminal investigations and the Federal Criminal Police Office, for the scope of German law as follows:

> "A dangerous militant is a person in whom certain facts justify the assumption that they will commit politically motivated offenses of considerable importance..." [21, translated by H. S.]

The extent to which this definition can be extended to other areas of organized crime and gangs, without a political motivation, remains to be legally clarified. Based on that concept, a dangerous militant profile can now be defined as follows:

> A dangerous militant profile is the profile of a dangerous militant in a social network. All profiles associated with this profile are part of the extended dangerous militant profile.

Traditionally, the selection of profiles to be monitored has been carried out manually. Appropriate candidates are selected, for example through research on the Internet or other investigations. In this way, however, new or short-term profiles are hardly detected. Here, automated approaches can help in the long-term.

For example, the task of automatically identifying a dangerous militant profile, associated with a certain crime area, given a group of profiles can be interpreted as a classification task. Let P be the set of all profiles of a particular social network, and R the set of risk classes, corresponding to an area of crime. Then the selection of potential militants profiles is a surjective mapping $f : R \rightarrow P$. An overview of classification techniques (supervised learning methods) is given, for example, in [22] [23]. However, as already emphasized by [24], a large amount of training data is needed to train classifiers with sufficient accuracy. This problem can be addressed, for example, by the use of semi-supervised learning methods, such as self-training or co-training. An overview of methods is described, e. g., in [25]. Whichever method is chosen, the performance depends on the choice of appropriate features. These should generally have sufficient discrimination power and should be as independent as possible.

Particularly in the context of social networks, the use of techniques for recommender machines is often used (push-mode) instead of classification (pull mode). Typically, such systems use Collaborative Filtering [26] [27], Content-based Filtering [28] [27], or a combination of both. In recent years, a whole series of studies have been devoted to the creation of friendships in social networks using these classic approaches [29] [30]. More recent approaches are based on social graphs [31] [32] or semantic analyzes, especially LDA, which attempt to produce recommendations based on lifestyles [33] [34] [35] [36]. However, the inclusion of structured data is more reliable than the analysis of latent topics and is therefore more suitable for classifying threats. Naruchitparames et al. presented a recommender system based on genetic algorithms [37]. As a feature (social genome), they propose the following Facebook feature:

- common friends,
- location,
- age range,
- common interests (likes and music),
- photo tags,
- events,
- groups,
- movies,
- education,
- religious and political attitude.

Manca et al. criticize earlier approaches because they do not take into account a mutual interest which is, however, necessary for friendship. They suggest a similarity-based recommender as a basis for friendships using so-called Social Bookmarks, i. e., shared bookmarks on the Internet [38]. Tags of shared images are the basis for the recommender system proposed by Cheung et al. and are another interesting feature to generate recommendations in social networks [39]. In a similar manner, a general classifier can be trained based on the profiles of known dangerous militants or offenders. For example, by means of corresponding known profiles, a classifier or a recommendation system could be implemented for detecting profiles of the hooligan scene or radical political groupings. Adapting this approach, a classifier can be trained in the sense of supervised learning, which can automatically detect such dangerous militants profiles. We can use a social feature vector $\vec{f^s}$ for each profile (see Equation (1)) as a basis for the computational task of the classification and recommendation of dangerous militants.

$$\vec{f^s} = \begin{pmatrix} friends \\ location \\ age \\ interests \\ \dots \end{pmatrix} \tag{1}$$

Considering this as a binary classification task, we need to assign each profile $\vec{f^s}$ either to the class of potential dangerous militants profiles or not. Assuming the features f_i^s are independent, we can use the Bayes theorem for computation (see 2).

$$\hat{y} = \arg \max_{c_i \in \{0,1\}} p(c_i) \prod_{j=0}^{|\vec{f^s}|} p(f_j^s | c_i) \tag{2}$$

Although we know that this assumption is not true, experiences have shown that this approach still produces good results [40]. In general, supervised approaches need a sufficiently large set of training examples which is a problem in many cases. To overcome this, we can use a bootstrapping approach, as shown in [41].

B. Assessment of the risk of dangers

After the potential dangerous militants profiles have been selected, the content analysis of the communication takes

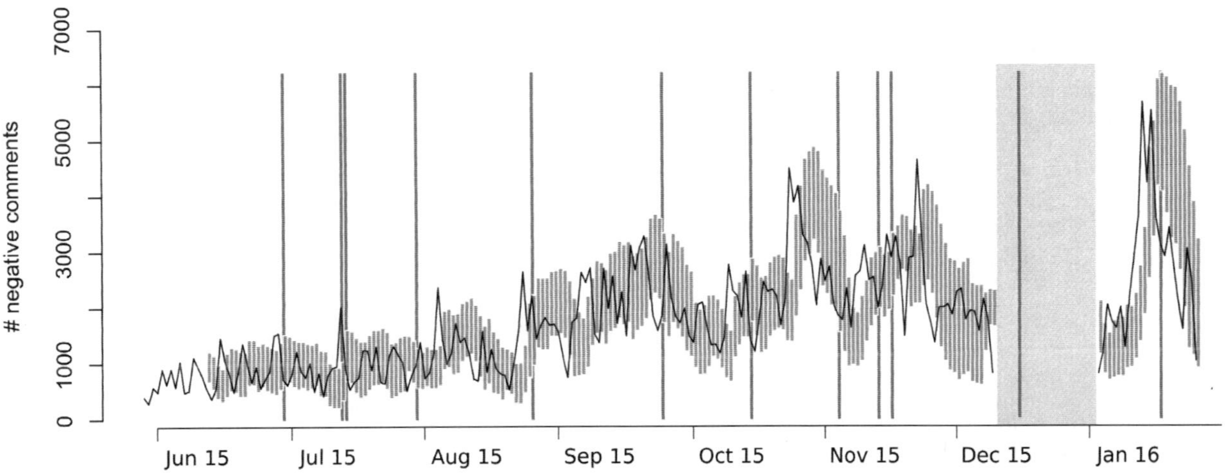

Figure 2: Results of a short-term study on the development of sentiment on the Facebook page of Pegida e. V. between June 2015 and January 2016. The blue areas mark the $95\,\%-$prediction interval. Red lines denote actual incidents during this period of time. The gray area marks a period with missing data.

place. This step is necessary to determine whether the extraction of further information is necessary to elucidate various modalities (location, time, participants, etc.) of possible events.

A prerequisite for the assessment of the probability that the danger occurs is once again the experience-based knowledge of the investigator, which must be available for each individual risk type, for example, in the FoTM as discussed in [20] [41].

After defining the risk classes $risk_1, ..., risk_n$ which should be monitored, the explicit definition of the corresponding danger topics is made: $\Theta^{risk} = \vartheta_{risk_1}, ..., \vartheta_{risk_n}$. A risk class describes the amount of all offenses belonging to a defined group, for example, left or right-winged politically motivated crimes. A risk topic includes all the terms and associations that characterize such a risk class. Afterwards, the selection of potential or known dangerous militants profiles leads to a set of candidate profiles for each risk class $P_i^c = p_{i1}, ..., p_{ik} \in P, i = 1, ..., n$ from the set of available profiles of the investigated social network is carried out taking into account a particular risk class to limit the scope of observation and analysis. Subsequently, the topics $\Theta^{com} = \vartheta_{com_1}, ..., \vartheta_{com_n}$ of the communication between these profiles must be extracted and it must be then analyzed to what extend they overlap with the risk topics. Afterwards, they are evaluated. In the simplest case the overlap can be represented binarily as shown in Equation (3).

$$f(\Theta^{com}) = \begin{cases} 1 & if\ \Theta^{com} \cap \Theta^{risk} \neq \emptyset \\ 0 & otherwise \end{cases} \tag{3}$$

In order to quantify the degree of correspondence of Θ^{com} and Θ^{risk}, a corresponding metric is needed to compare probability distributions over the terms t of a topic. Niekler and Jähnichen examined the suitability of the Jensen-Shannon divergence, the cosine similarity, and the dice coefficient as a measurement of similarity for various topics [42]. As a result, it was found that the best results were obtained on the basis of the cosine similarity $sim(\vartheta_{com}, \vartheta_{risk})$. Adapted to the present application, $sim(\vartheta_{com}, \vartheta_{risk})$ is thus defined as:

$$sim(\vartheta_{com}, \vartheta_{risk}) = \frac{\vartheta_{com} \cdot \vartheta_{risk}}{\|\vartheta_{com}\| \|\vartheta_{risk}\|} \tag{4}$$

If $f(\Theta^{com}) = 1$, i. e., $\exists \vartheta_{com_i} | \vartheta_{com_i} \in \Theta^{risk}$, the analysis of the sentiment S in the network is carried out. Approaches are found in the literature, especially for Twitter messages [43] [44]. In principle, these approaches can also be applied to other social networks such as Facebook. If the sentiment exceeds a threshold value ε, an increased risk can be assumed.

To evaluate this hypothesis the communication on the Facebook page of "Pegida e. V." (a mostly right-winged organization in Germany) was analyzed over a period of eight months, between June 2015 and January 2016. The extracted textual communication data was divided into individual sentences (tokenization). Subsequently, one out of three polarity classes pol: positive $(+)$, negative $(-)$ or neutral (0) was assigned to each sentence s using a probabilistic language model. Equations (5) and (6) show the associated likelihood function and the derived scoring function.

$$\log_2 P(s, pol) = \log_2 P(s|pol) + \log_2 P(pol) \tag{5}$$

$$\text{score}(s, pol) = \frac{\log_2 P(s, pol)}{|s| + 2} \tag{6}$$

The polarity class with the highest score is assigned to the respective sentence. The "Multi-Domain Sentiment Encyclopedia for the German Language", which was developed at the Darmstadt University of Applied Sciences, formed the basis for the training. It contains extracted mood-bearing terms from the MLSA-A corpus [45], the pressrelations dataset [46], and the

"German Sentiment Vocabulary" (SentiWS) [47], all annotated with the average polarity values in the range $[-1, 1]$.

The sentiment of a message $m = \{s_1, ..., s_n\}$ (post, comment) is decided in the simplest case by the number of its positive sentences $s+$ and/or negative sentences $s-$. The sentiment that dominates the constituent sentences also determines the sentiment of the whole message (see Equation (7)). In case of equality, the message is considered to be neutral m^0.

$$\mathrm{S}(m) = \begin{cases} m^+ & \text{if } |s^+| > |s^-| \\ m^- & \text{if } |s^+| < |s^-| \\ m^0 & \text{otherwise} \end{cases} \tag{7}$$

This approach, of course, is only a rough estimate of the sentiment, since it does not take into account the connection between meaning (semantic) and sentiment of a sentence. The accuracy, however, appears sufficient for a first check of the hypothesis, since the messages themselves were filtered in advance by the topic analysis. The results are presented in a histogram (see Fig. 2), with only negative messages (comments) m^- being taken into account.

Comparing the development of the sentiment of the comments in the network with the events during this period (marked by red lines), it was found that there is a possible correlation between these two. For example, on January 11th, 2016 serious riots lead by the right-winged scene occurred during the demonstration of the sister organization Legida e. kV. in Leipzig (Germany). Members in the Pegida network were also encouraged to attend this event. Similar to most of the cases, it can be clearly seen that the peak of negative communication is situated immediately before the incident. The sudden reduction in conversations at the time of the event can be explained by the active participation of the members in the event. The 95%-prediction interval (blue lines) supports the assumption that incidents mostly occur after a local or global peak.

Even if this short study is not considered representative and a random correlation between the occurrence of the incident and the discussion in the network cannot be ruled out, it still shows the potential of the presented approach. At this point, additional long-term studies with larger data sets considering different networks are necessary.

C. Detection of Leaders and Multipliers

Leaders and multiplier in the context of the intended analysis of social networks are individuals, who exert a significant amount of influence on the opinion and sentiment of other users of the network through their actions. In social sciences the term 'opinion leader' was introduced before 1957 by Katz and Lazarsfeld's research on diffusion theory [48]. Their proposed two-step flow model (see Fig. 3) retains validity in the digital age, especially in the context of social media.

Katz et al. assume that information disseminated in the Social Network is received, strengthened and enriched by opinion-leaders L_i in their social environment. Since opinion-leadership is strongly knowledge-driven and thus topic-dependent, this model must be supplemented by various thematically limited opinion-leaders L_{ϑ_i}. Each individual is then influenced by a variety of heterogeneous opinion leaders in his opinion as illustrated in Fig. 3. This signifies, that the opinion of an individual is mostly formed by its social environment. In 1962, Rogers references these ideas and defines opinion leader as follows:

> "Opinion leadership is the degree to which an individual is able to influence informally other individuals' attitudes or overt behavior in a desired way with relative frequency." [49, p. 331]

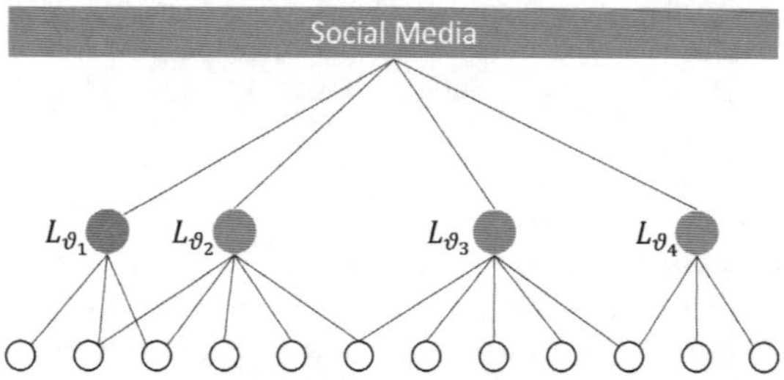

Figure 3: Extended two-step flow model adapted from [48]. Information is spread throughout social media. Individuals with a high level of competence at strategic local positions receive and amplify this information according to their competence (opinion-leader $L_{\vartheta_1}, ..., L_{\vartheta_4}$) and spread it to its followers and friends. This means, each individual's opinion is influenced by different opinion leaders depending on the topic (different colors) discussed in the network.

For the present study, the most important question to answer is what influence means, or rather how to identify an opinion leader or how the influencer can be distinguished from those being influenced. Katz defined the following features [48]:

1) personification of certain values
2) competence
3) strategic social location

One approach to identify opinion-leaders is to extract and analyze the content of nodes and edges of networks to mine leadership features. For instance, the sentiment of communication pieces can be analyzed to detect the influence of their authors, as shown by Huang et. al., who aim to detect the most influential comments in a network this way [50]. Another strategy is to perform topic mining to categorize content and detect opinion-leaders for each topic individually, as opinion-leadership is context-dependent [48] [51]. For this purpose, Latent Dirichlet Allocation (LDA) [52] can be used, as seen in the work of [53]. We considered the implementation of content-based methods problematic, as texts in social networks lack correct spelling and formal structure, which impairs such methods' performance.

Another approach to identifying leaders is to analyze the flow of information in a network. By monitoring how the interaction of actors evolves over time, one can identify patterns and individuals of significance within them. To achieve this, some model of information propagation is required, such as the

Markov processes used by [54] and the probabilistic models proposed by [55]. These interaction-based methods consider both topological features and their dynamics over time. However, the latter are not yet considered by our framework and are reserved for future developments.

We utilized methods, which are solely based on a network's topology, therefore, consider features, such as node degree, neighborhood distances and clusters, to identify opinion leaders. One implementation of this is the calculation of node centrality. The underlying assumption is, that the more influence an individual gains, the more central it is in its network. Which centrality measure is most suitable is dependent on the application domain. We judged eigenvector centrality to be most adequate, specifically Google's PageRank algorithm [56], which functions in a similar fashion. It recursively assigns a rank R to each node A, based on the rank of the nodes of its incoming edges T_i and its total number of links C_i. The value of an edge is strongly dependent on the score of its originator (see Equation (8)).

$$R(A) = \frac{1-d}{N} + d \sum_{i=1}^{n} \frac{R(T_1)}{C(T_1)}, 0 \leq d \leq 1 \quad (8)$$

With the damping factor d, normalized over the number of all nodes of the network N, a part of the resulting rank can be subtracted and distributed to all nodes. The application of PageRank for the purposes of opinion leader detection has seen merely moderate success [57] [58]. With LeaderRank, Lü et al. advocate further development and optimization of this algorithm for social networks, and have achieved surprisingly good results [59]. Users are considered as nodes and directed edges as relationships between opinion leaders and users. All users are also bidirectionally connected to a ground node. At time step t_0, all nodes receive the score $s_i(0) = 1$ except for the ground node initialized with $s_g(0) = 0$. Equation (9) describes the process of probability flow through the network, where $s_i(t)$ indicates the LeaderRank score of a node i at time step t.

$$s_i(t+1) = \sum_{j=1}^{N+1} \frac{a_{ji}}{k_j^{out}} s_j(t) \quad (9)$$

Depending on whether or not there exists a directed edge from node i to node j, the value 0 or 1 is assigned to a_{ij}. k_i^{out} describes the number of outgoing edges of a node. The final score is obtained as the score of the respective node at the convergence time t_c and the base node score at the same time, as shown in Equation (10).

$$S_i = s_i(t_c) + \frac{s_g(t_c)}{N} \quad (10)$$

The advantage of this algorithm compared to PageRank is that the convergence is faster and above all that nodes, that spread information faster and further, can be found. In later work, for example, by introducing a weighting factor, as in [60] or [61], susceptibility to noisy data has been further reduced and the ability to find influential distributors (hubs) of information has been added.

However, there might be cases in which LeaderRank would assign high scores to individuals, which are not relevant for the present application. When a user attained a significant audience, while also actively following many opinion leaders, we argue that their influence is based on their activity in the network and not their opinion, as their presence makes them more likely to be followed. We propose an approach to eliminate such hybrid leaders from the top ranks, which punishes the LeaderRank score $LR(\vartheta_i)$ of users with many interactions in the network, meaning, those users who follow many leaders. This way the top ranked users are pure leaders, whose influence is purely based on their opinions.

$$PSC(L_{\vartheta_i}) = \frac{LR(L_{\vartheta_i})}{1 + \frac{k_i^{out}}{k_{total}^{out}} * LR_{total}} \quad (11)$$

One way to calculate the PureScore of a particular topic-specific opinion leader $PSC(L_{\vartheta_i})$ is shown in Equation (11). The PureScore of a certain topic-specific opinion-leader is calculated by dividing its original LeaderRank score $LR(L_{\vartheta_i})$ by a percentage of the maximum score (equal to the number of users) defined by the node's share of network activity, k^{out} being the number of outgoing links. However, this approach needs to be evaluated in later work.

D. Visualization

If, with the approach described above, a risk greater than a threshold value ε was determined, further information such as locations, times and people involved are extracted from the text and subsequently transferred to a corresponding map with the help of geographical coordinates. An additional score $f_{risk}(\vartheta, S_\vartheta, |P|_\vartheta)$ provides information about the extent of the expected risk, estimated from the risk class, the sentiment score associated with it and the number of people involved in that particular discussion. This value can, for example, be used to color the geo location on a map, corresponding to a heat-scale. The obtained result directly supports the short-term strategic planning of security forces as proposed at the very beginning of this section.

V. Prototypical Implementation

The aim of the prototype's architecture is to implement the frameworks described in [20] as well as the sections above. It was programmed with Java and built as an Eclipse Rich Client Platform (RCP). Its OSGi implementation Equinox allows for a service-oriented architecture, consisting of three tiers:

1) *Persistence*: Data is fetched from the various social-network databases and put into *EMF* models. The models are stored into a, as for now, local *EMF Store* server. Thus, the databases and the *EMF Store* server form this tier. Any annotations and meta-data are also held by the models.
2) *Logic-Tier*: This tier contains various linguistic services, e. g., for topic modeling, used for annotation and querying. The modeling service, which provides CRUD-operations (Create, Read, Update, Delete) for models in the *EMF Store* server, also resides here.

Furthermore, all data retrieval services, which communicate with corresponding social-network APIs, are part of this tier.

3) *Access*: The high-level services, usually directly controllable by the UI, define this tier. At the current state of the development, this is the retrieval service, which initializes data fetching from the social networks, the query-service, used for data retrieval from the *EMF Store* server and the annotation services, which use the linguistic services to enrich models.

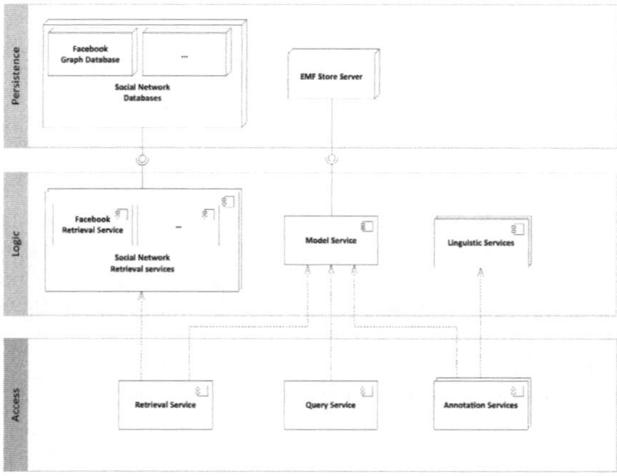

Figure 4: SoNA architecture overview with the respective services.

Figure 4 provides a visual representation of these tiers. When developing this application further, efforts will be made to make the prototype more closely resemble the SoNA framework described in this work. Permission services can be realized through user profiles in the *EMF Store* server.

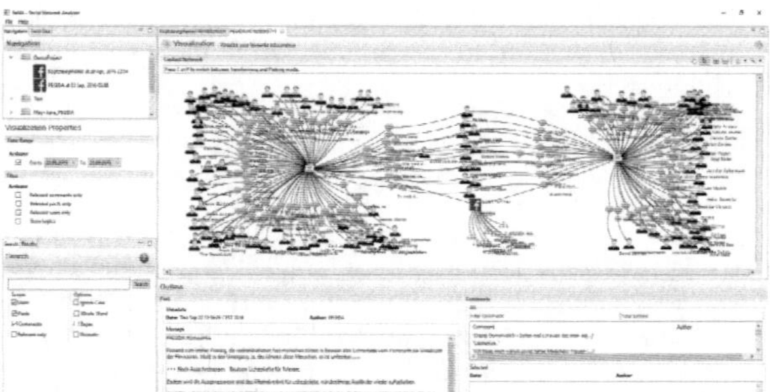

Figure 5: The user interface of the prototype. Shown is a downloaded Facebook page visualized in a graph. The Facebook logo node represents the page, which is connected to posts, which in turn are connected to their comments. The outermost nodes are users, which are associated to the comments they created.

The prototype provides a user interface to retrieve data from Social Networks, currently Facebook, and visualizes it in a 2D graph, as shown in Figure 5. Several filter options are available in order to reduce the output network to the most relevant nodes depending on the investigator's needs. Data can be retrieved from a specific part of the social network for a certain period of time or a certain amount of content (i. e., posts and comments), before being stored in models. Created models can then be annotated following the process chain as discussed in the former sections.

VI. Conclusion and Future Work

In this paper the theoretical framework SoNA was presented, which allows investigators of law enforcement agencies as well as intelligence services to monitor social networks in order to gather information about potentially dangerous activities. This information can support the long- and short-term planning of the deployment of security forces. It was shown that the knowledge gained by applying this framework can directly increase the resilience of a society in the first two stages of the resilience cycle. Furthermore, given the complexity of the language used in Social Media it was necessary to apply a knowledge-based and word-based approach. In this respect, a process chain for analyzing social networks was proposed and the main steps were discussed in detail. These include the selection of dangerous militant profiles, the assessment of the risk and the detection of leaders and multipliers. We presented a prototype of the SoNA framework, which aims to implement these aspects. Future work will include the remaining steps of the process chain as well as the evaluation of the entire framework. In order to do so, it is fundamental to create an appropriate test environment in collaboration with law enforcement agencies.

References

[1] M. Spranger, F. Heinke, S. Grunert, and D. Labudde, "Towards predictive policing: Knowledge-based monitoring of social networks," in Proceedings of the Fifth International Conference on Advances in Information Mining and Management (IMMM 2015), IARIA, Ed. ThinkMind Library, 2015.

[2] ZIS, "Jahresbericht 2013/14," 2014, [Online] https://lzpd.polizei.nrw/sites/default/files/2016-12/13-14_Jahresbericht.pdf, last accessed 2017-11-29.

[3] Deutsches Institut für Normung, "Begriffe im Rettungswesen," April 2015.

[4] J. Walker and M. Cooper, "Genealogies of resilience from systems ecology to the political economy of crisis adaptation." Security Dialogue, vol. 42, no. 2, 2011, pp. 143–160.

[5] C. Edwards, Resilient Nation. London: Demos, 2009.

[6] K. Thoma, Ed., Resilien-Tech: Resilience-by-Design; Strategie für die technologischen Zukunftsthemen, ser. acatech STUDIE. München: Utz, 2014.

[7] S. L. Pimm, The balance of nature? Ecological issues in the conservation of species and communities, 2nd ed. Chicago u.a.: Univ. of Chicago Press, 1992.

[8] C. S. Holling, "Engineering resilience versus ecological resilience," Engineering within ecological constraints, 1996, pp. 31–44.

[9] B. Pearsall, "Predictive policing: The future of law enforcement?" NIJ Journal, no. 266, 2009.

[10] K. Thoma, "Resilien-Tech. Resilience-by-Design: Strategie für die technologischen Zukunftsthemen," acatech Studie, 2014.

[11] C. Dürscheid, F. Wagner, and S. Brommer, Wie Jugendliche schreiben: Schreibkompetenz und neue Medien, ser. Linguistik - Impulse & Tendenzen. Berlin u.a.: de Gruyter, 2010, vol. 41.

[12] M. Zappavigna, Discourse of Twitter and social media: [how we use language to create affiliation on the web], ser. Continuum discourse series. London u.a.: Continuum Publ, 2012.

[13] C. Dürscheid, "Medienkommunikation im Kontinuum von Mündlichkeit und Schriftlichkeit. Theoretische und empirische Probleme," Zeitschrift für Angewandte Linguistik, vol. 38, 2003, pp. 37–56.

[14] S. Hintze, Emotionalitätsmarker in Kommentaren auf der PEGIDA-Facebook-Seite, ser. Networx, 2015, vol. 71.

[15] M. Beißwenger, Kommunikation in virtuellen Welten: Sprache, Text und Wirklichkeit ; eine Untersuchung zur Konzeptionalität von Kommunikationsvollzügen und zur textuellen Konstruktion von Welt in synchroner Internet-Kommunikation, exemplifiziert am Beispiel eines Webchats. Stuttgart: Ibidem-Verl., 2000.

[16] K. Luckhardt, "Stilanalysen zur Chat-Kommunikation: Eine korpusgestützte Untersuchung am Beispiel eines medialen Chats," Ph.D. dissertation, TU Dortmund, 2009.

[17] M. O'Donnell, "The UAM CorpusTool: Software for corpus annotation and exploration," in Bretones Callejas (Hg.) 2009 – Applied linguistics now, pp. 1433–1447.

[18] C.-V. Schnitzer, "Linguistische Aspekte der Kommunikation in den neueren elektronischen Medien SMS-E-Mail-Facebook," Doktor, Ludwig-Maximilians-Universität, München, 2012.

[19] E. Dresner and S. C. Herring, "Functions of the Nonverbal in CMC: Emoticons and Illocutionary Force," Communication Theory, vol. 20, no. 3, 2010, pp. 249–268.

[20] M. Spranger, S. Schildbach, F. Heinke, S. Grunert, and D. Labudde, "Semantic tools for forensics: A highly adaptable framework," in Proc. 2nd. International Conference on Advances in Information Management and Mining (IMMM). ThinkMind Library, 2012, pp. 27–31.

[21] B.-D. 16/3570, "Schriftliche Fragen mit den in der Woche vom 20. November 2006 eingegangenen Antworten der Bundesregierung," Drucksache des Deutschen Bundestages 16/3570 vom 24. November 2006, 2006.

[22] S. B. Kotsiantis, "Supervised machine learning: A review of classification techniques," in Proceedings of the 2007 Conference on Emerging Artificial Intelligence Applications in Computer Engineering: Real Word AI Systems with Applications in eHealth, HCI, Information Retrieval and Pervasive Technologies. Amsterdam, The Netherlands, The Netherlands: IOS Press, 2007, pp. 3–24.

[23] J. Han, M. Kamber, and J. Pei, Data Mining: Concepts and techniques, 3rd ed., ser. The Morgan Kaufmann series in data management systems. Waltham Mass.: Morgan Kaufmann, 2012.

[24] M. Ikonomakis, S. Kotsiantis, and V. Tampakas, "Text classification using machine learning techniques," WSEAS Transactions on Computers, vol. 4, no. 8, 2005, pp. 966–974.

[25] O. Chapelle, B. Schölkopf, and A. Zien, Semi-supervised learning, ser. Adaptive computation and machine learning, 2006.

[26] D. Goldberg, D. Nichols, B. M. Oki, and D. Terry, "Using collaborative filtering to weave an information tapestry," Communications of the ACM, vol. 35, no. 12, 1992, pp. 61–70.

[27] F. Ricci, L. Rokach, and B. Shapira, "Introduction to Recommender Systems Handbook," in Recommender Systems Handbook, F. Ricci, L. Rokach, B. Shapira, and P. B. Kantor, Eds. New York: Springer, 2011, pp. 1–35.

[28] R. van Meteren and M. van Someren, "Using content-based filtering for recommendation," in Proceedings of the Machine Learning in the New Information Age: MLnet/ECML2000 Workshop, 2000, pp. 47–56.

[29] L. Bian and H. Holtzman, "Online friend recommendation through personality matching and collaborative filtering," Proc. of UBICOMM, 2011, pp. 230–235.

[30] V. Agarwal and K. K. Bharadwaj, "A collaborative filtering framework for friends recommendation in social networks based on interaction intensity and adaptive user similarity," Social Network Analysis and Mining, vol. 3, no. 3, 2013, pp. 359–379.

[31] N. B. Silva, R. Tsang, G. D. C. Cavalcanti, and J. Tsang, "A graph-based friend recommendation system using genetic algorithm," in Evolutionary Computation (CEC), 2010 IEEE Congress on, 2010, pp. 1–7.

[32] F. Akbari, A. H. Tajfar, and A. F. Nejad, "Graph-based friend recommendation in social networks using artificial bee colony," in Dependable, Autonomic and Secure Computing (DASC), 2013 IEEE 11th International Conference on, 2013, pp. 464–468.

[33] N. M. Eklaspur and A. S. Pashupatimath, "A friend recommender system for social networks by life style extraction using probabilistic method-friendtome," International Journal of Computer Science Trends and Technology (IJCST), vol. 3, no. 3, 2015.

[34] Z. Wang, J. Liao, Q. Cao, H. Qi, and Z. Wang, "Friendbook: A semantic-based friend recommendation system for social networks," IEEE Transactions on Mobile Computing, vol. 14, no. 3, 2015, pp. 538–551.

[35] T. R. Kacchi and A. V. Deorankar, "Friend recommendation system based on lifestyles of users," in Advances in Electrical, Electronics, Information, Communication and Bio-Informatics (AEEICB), 2016 2nd International Conference on, 2016, pp. 682–685.

[36] D. M. Jadhavar and V. R. Chirchi, "Friend recommendation system for online social networks," International Journal of Computer Applications, vol. 153, no. 12, 2016.

[37] J. Naruchitparames, M. H. Güne, and S. J. Louis, "Friend recommendations in social networks using genetic algorithms and network topology," in 2011 IEEE Congress of Evolutionary Computation (CEC), 2011, pp. 2207–2214.

[38] M. Manca, L. Boratto, and S. Carta, "Producing friend recommendations in a social bookmarking system by mining users content," in The Third International Conference on Advances in Information Mining and Management (IMMM 2013), IARIA, Ed. IARIA, 2013, pp. 59–64.

[39] M. Cheung and J. She, "Bag-of-features tagging approach for a better recommendation with social big data," in Proc. 4th. International Conference on Advances in Information Mining and Management. ThinkMind Library, 2014, p. 83 to 88.

[40] I. Rish, "An empirical study of the Naïve Bayes classifier," IJCAI 2001 Workshop on Empirical Methods in Artificial Intelligence, vol. 22, no. 3, pp. 41–46.

[41] M. Spranger and D. Labudde, "Semantic tools for forensics: Approaches in forensic text analysis," in The Third International Conference on Advances in Information Mining and Management (IMMM 2013), IARIA, Ed. IARIA, 2013, pp. 97–100.

[42] A. Niekler and P. Jähnichen, "Matching Results of Latent Dirichlet Allocation for Text," in Proceedings of the 11th International Conference on Cognitive Modeling, ICCM 2012, 2012.

[43] X. Wan, "Co-training for cross-lingual sentiment classification," in Proceedings of the Joint Conference of the 47th Annual Meeting of the ACL and the 4th International Joint Conference on Natural Language Processing of the AFNLP: Volume 1-volume 1, 2009, pp. 235–243.

[44] S. M. Mohammad, S. Kiritchenko, and X. Zhu, "NRC-Canada: Building the state-of-the-art in sentiment analysis of tweets," arXiv preprint arXiv:1308.6242, 2013.

[45] S. Clematide, S. Gindl, M. Klenner, S. Petrakis, R. Remus, J. Ruppenhofer, U. Waltinger, and M. Wiegand, "MLSA-A Multi-layered Reference Corpus for German Sentiment Analysis," in LREC, 2012, pp. 3551–3556.

[46] T. Scholz, S. Conrad, and L. Hillekamps, "Opinion mining on a german corpus of a media response analysis," in International Conference on Text, Speech and Dialogue, 2012, pp. 39–46.

[47] R. Remus, U. Quasthoff, and G. Heyer, "SentiWS-A Publicly Available German-language Resource for Sentiment Analysis," in LREC, 2010.

[48] E. Katz, "The two-step flow of communication: An up-to-date report on an hypothesis," Public Opinion Quarterly, vol. 21, no. 1, Anniversary Issue Devoted to Twenty Years of Public Opinion Research, 1957, p. 61.

[49] E. M. Rogers, Diffusion of innovations. New York: The Free Press, 1962.

[50] B. Huang, G. Yu, and H. R. Karimi, "The finding and dynamic detection of opinion leaders in social network," Mathematical Problems in Engineering, vol. 2014, 2014, pp. 1–7.

[51] P. Parau, C. Lemnaru, M. Dinsoreanu, and R. Potolea, "Opinion leader detection." in Sentiment analysis in social networks, F. A. Pozzi, E. Fersini, E. Messina, and B. Liu, Eds., 2016, pp. 157–170.

[52] D. M. Blei, A. Y. Ng, and M. I. Jordan, "Latent Dirichlet Allocation," J. Mach. Learn. Res., vol. 3, 2003, pp. 993–1022.

[53] X. Song, Y. Chi, K. Hino, and B. Tseng, "Identifying opinion leaders in the blogosphere," in Proceedings of the sixteenth ACM conference on Conference on information and knowledge management - CIKM '07, M. J. Silva, A. O. Falcão, A. A. F. Laender, R. Baeza-Yates, D. L. McGuinness, B. Olstad, and Ø. H. Olsen, Eds. New York, New York, USA: ACM Press, 2007, p. 971.

[54] B. Amor, S. Vuik, R. Callahan, A. Darzi, S. N. Yaliraki, and M. Barahona, "Community detection and role identification in directed networks: Understanding the Twitter network of the care.data debate," CoRR, vol. abs/1508.03165, 2015.

[55] M. Richardson and P. Domingos, "Mining knowledge-sharing sites for viral marketing," in Proceedings of the eighth ACM SIGKDD international conference on Knowledge discovery and data mining, Za&iuml and O. R. ane, Eds. New York, NY: ACM, 2002, p. 61.

[56] S. Brin and L. Page, "The anatomy of a large-scale hypertextual web search engine," Comput. Netw. ISDN Syst., vol. 30, no. 1-7, Apr. 1998, pp. 107–117.

[57] C. Egger, "Identifying Key Opinion Leaders in Social Networks: An Approach to use Instagram Data to Rate and Identify Key Opinion Leader for a Specific Business Field," Master Thesis, TH Köln - University of Applied Sciences, Köln, 2016.

[58] M. Z. Shafiq, M. U. Ilyas, A. X. Liu, and H. Radha, "Identifying leaders and followers in online social networks," IEEE Journal on Selected Areas in Communications, vol. 31, no. 9, 2013, pp. 618–628.

[59] L. Lü, Y.-C. Zhang, C. H. Yeung, and T. Zhou, "Leaders in social networks, the Delicious case," PLoS One, vol. 6, no. 6, 2011, p. e21202.

[60] Q. Li, T. Zhou, L. Lü, and D. Chen, "Identifying influential spreaders by weighted LeaderRank," Physica A: Statistical Mechanics and its Applications, vol. 404, no. Supplement C, 2014, pp. 47–55.

[61] Z. H. Zhang, G. P. Jiang, Y. R. Song, L. L. Xia, and Q. Chen, "An improved weighted leaderrank algorithm for identifying influential spreaders in complex networks," in 2017 IEEE International Conference on Computational Science and Engineering (CSE) and IEEE International Conference on Embedded and Ubiquitous Computing (EUC), vol. 1, 2017, pp. 748–751.

Efficient ASIC Design of Digital Down Converter for Mobile Applications

Rajesh Mehra
ECE Department
NITTTR
Chandigarh, India
rajeshmehra@yahoo.com

Shallu Sharma
ECE Department
NITTTR
Chandigarh, India
shallu.ece@nitttrchd.ac.in

Akanksha Jetly
ECE Department
NITTTR
Chandigarh, India
akankshajetly@yahoo.com

Rita Rana
ECE Department
NITTTR
Chandigarh, India
er.ritarana@gmail.com

Abstract— **This paper presents ASIC design of digital down converter using 90nm technology for software defined applications. Computationally efficient multistage design technique is used to provide optimized solution for Third Generation Mobile Communications. Parks McClellan algorithm is used to minimize the filter order along with efficient polyphase decomposition technique. Multiplier based partially serial algorithm is used to enhance the performance in terms of area and power consumption. Multipliers and adders are optimally placed and routed to reduce the silicon area. The proposed Digital Down Converter ASIC has consumed 601 mm^2 area by consuming 3169.607 nW power to provide high performance optimized solution to software defined radios.**

Keywords-3G mobile communication; asic; base stations; radio transceivers; reconfigurable logic.

I. INTRODUCTION

The highly competitive nature of the wireless communications market and constantly evolving communication standards have resulted in short design cycles and product lifetimes. The talking point is to provide area and power efficient integrated design for Digital Down Converter (DDC) for 3G Applications [1]. In the recent past, telecommunications techniques have achieved a wide popularity, mainly due to the huge diffusion of cellular phones and wireless devices. The request for more complex and complete services, such as high speed data transmission and multimedia content streaming, has moved many research groups in the electronic field towards the study of new and efficient algorithms, codes and modulations. In Software Defined Radios (SDR), most radio receiver processing functions to be run on a general purpose (GP) programmable processor rather than being implemented strictly on non programmable hardware. The functionality of SDR receiver processor can be changed via "software reprogramming." The concept of SDR is now an IEEE Standard, i.e., IEEE P1900 [2]. These radios are reconfigurable through software updates. For high end digital signal processing where the highest possible performance is needed at low power consumption, ASICs are still the processors of choice. However, ASICs are very expensive and require long time in design and development. ASICs are inherently rigid and unsuitable to the applications that are constantly evolving. For these reasons, Programmable Logic Devices like Field Programmable Gate Arrays (FPGAs) have been emerged as an alternative to ASICs in wireless communication systems. FPGAs are mainly used for the flexibility they provide. The FPGAs suffer from the drawbacks of inefficient resource utilization, high cost and power consumption [3]. The cost factor can be improved by using less expensive FPGAs for system design and by efficient utilization of FPGA resources. The power factor can be improved by optimal usage of SRAM which can be taken care during FPGA manufacturing by using various techniques [4].

ASIC is an integrated circuit that is used for a particular application. It is composed of series of circuits that are taken from the technology dependent library to generate gate – level net list to implement the required functionality [5]. ASICs provide an advantage of high speed as compared to other programmable devices like PLDs, PALs and FPGAs since they are designed to perform a specific task. ASICs can be made compact by incorporating significant amounts of circuitry onto a single chip, which results in minimum power utilization [6]. By reducing inter-package interconnections, ASICs help in reduction of noise. ASICs provide increased performance at relatively low power consumption and comparatively less area-delay product (ADP). Besides, it consumes less energy per sample (EPS) and gives cost effective and reliable solutions [7]. Hence, ASICs are mainly used to increase the performance and power efficiency of the circuits but inability to reconfigure is the major drawback associated with these devices. The FPGA based DDC design [1] is extended to DDC ASIC to improve the performance in terms of area and power. FPGA's though providing the advantage of flexibility still leads to improper utilization of resources. So, having an integrated solution, i.e., a dedicated ASIC design for the proposed DDC will lead to further reduction of resources in terms of area and power. This results in cost effective solution for wireless communication applications.

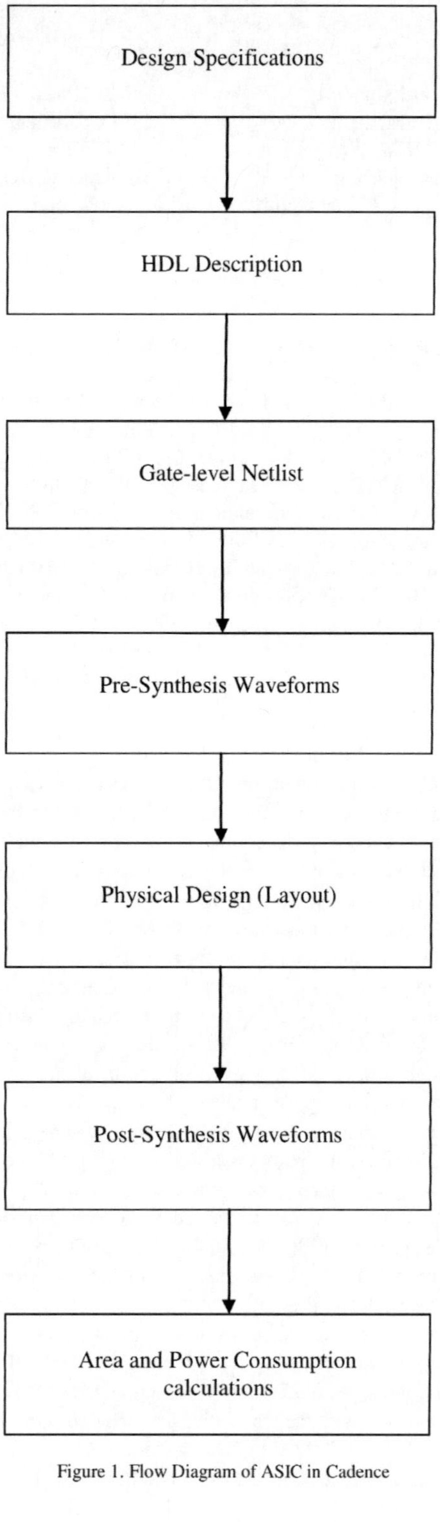

Figure 1. Flow Diagram of ASIC in Cadence

Figure 1 depicts the flow of ASIC in Cadence environment. In the present paper, the proposed design is implemented in technology dependent 90 nm foundry at 1.2 V. Firstly, the design is coded in Verilog hardware description language and then the gate level netlist is synthesized and the results are verified using pre-synthesis waveforms. Then the physical design implementation is done to find the total number of cells, area and power consumption and the results are verified using post-synthesis waveforms.

II. DIGITAL DOWN CONVERTER

The Software Defined Radio system can change its radio functions by swapping software instead of replacing hardware, seems to be the best solution given that mobile standards are springing up like mushrooms [8]. SDR thereby makes it possible to reprogram cell phones to operate on different radio interface standards. But that's not all. Putting much of a radio's functionality in software opens up other benefits. A mobile SDR device can cope with the unpredictable dynamic characteristics of highly variable wireless links [9]. SDRs use a single hardware front end but can change their frequency of operation, occupied bandwidth, and adherence to various wireless standards by calling various software algorithms. Such a solution allows inexpensive, efficient interoperability between the available standards and frequency bands [10]. Figure 2 illustrates SDR BS receiver that consists of two sections – a front-end high-data rate processing section and a back-end symbol rate or chip-rate processing section.

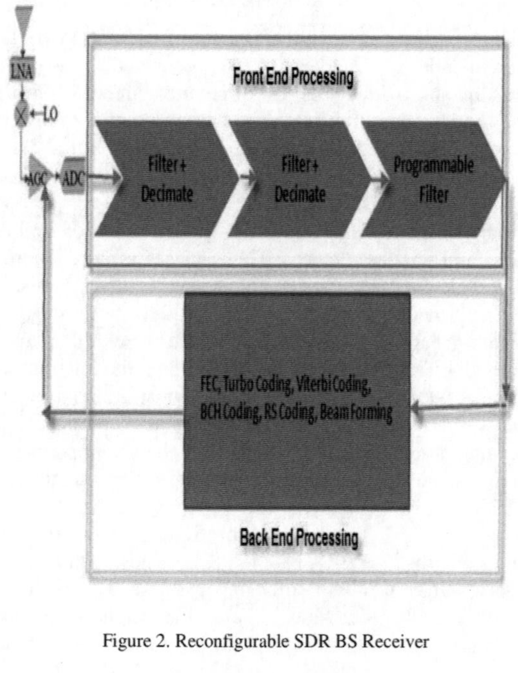

Figure 2. Reconfigurable SDR BS Receiver

Reconfigurable architectures provide flexible and integrated system-on-chip solutions that accommodate smooth migration from archaic to innovative designs, allowing recycling of hardware resources across multiple generations of the standards [11]. Software defined radio (SDR) technology enables such functionality in wireless devices by using a reconfigurable hardware platform across multiple standards. Sampling rate converters play important role in SDR systems [12]. Digital up-converters (DUCs) and digital down-converters (DDCs) are important components of every modern wireless base station design. DUCs are typically used in digital transmitters to filter up-sample and modulate signals from baseband to the carrier frequency [13]-[15]. DDCs, on the other hand, reside in the digital receivers to demodulate, filter, and down-sample the signal to baseband so that further processing on the received signal can be done at lower sampling frequencies. They are more popular than their analogue counterparts because of small size, low power consumption and accurate performance [16]-[22].

DDC performs decimation and matched filtering to remove adjacent channels and maximize the received signal-to-noise ratio (SNR) [23]. For the reference WCDMA DDC design, the carrier bandwidth is = 5.0 MHz, Number of carriers is = 1, IF sample rate is = 61.44 MSPS, DDC output rate 7.68 MSPS, Input precision is = 14 bits, Output precision is = 16 bits and Mixer resolution 0.25 Hz approximately and SFDR up to 115 dB is required. The DDC input is assumed to be real, directly coming from the ADC. The mixer translates the real band pass input signal from intermediate frequency to a complex baseband signal centred at 0 Hz. Mathematically, the real input signal is multiplied by a complex exponential as shown in Eq. (1) to produce a complex output signal with real and imaginary components Eq. (2) and Eq. (3) respectively. The sinusoidal waveforms required to perform the mixing process is obtained by using the Direct Digital Synthesizer (DDS). The decimators in the DDC need to down sample the IF data from 61.44 MHz back to 2x chip rate. The factor of 61.44/7.68 = 8 can be partitioned using different possible configurations. The down sampling by eight at once will result in an extremely long filter length and result in an inefficient hardware implementation. The use of shaping filter with decimation factor of 2 allows the remaining stages to be implemented as either one half band filter with decimation factor of 4 or two half band filters with decimation factor of 2 each. The second configuration is more suitable for hardware implementation because of less hardware consumption [24]-[26].

$$e^{-jw_o n} = \cos(w_o n) - j\sin(w_o n) \tag{1}$$

$$Y_r = X(n)\cos(w_o n) \tag{2}$$

$$Y_i = -X(n)\sin(w_o n) \tag{3}$$

III. DESIGN SPECIFICATIONS

An efficient DDC is designed for WCDMA Applications. The proposed DDC design is using three decimator stages. The input sample rate of first decimator is 61.44 MSPS, and the output sample rate is 30.72 MSPS. The pass band frequency is 2.34 MHz and the pass band ripple is 0.002 dB. It results in a digital filter of order 10 whose magnitude and phase response is shown in Figure 3.

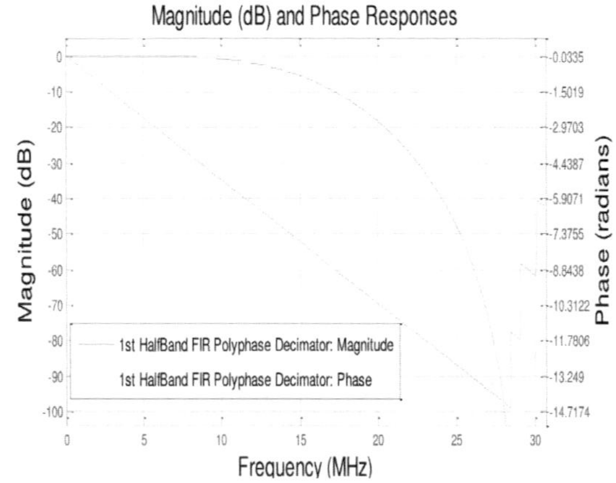

Figure 3. First Stage Half Band Decimator Response

The proposed partially serial pipelined MAC algorithm design technique based stage 1 decimator is shown in Figure 4. The 11 coefficients of first stage decimator have been processed by using 3 multipliers in partially serial style using MAC algorithm to optimize both speed and area factor simultaneously. The input pipeline registers are used to store the new coefficient values required for processing in the next cycle to further enhance the speed. The CE delays are used to make synchronization between stage 1 and stage 2.

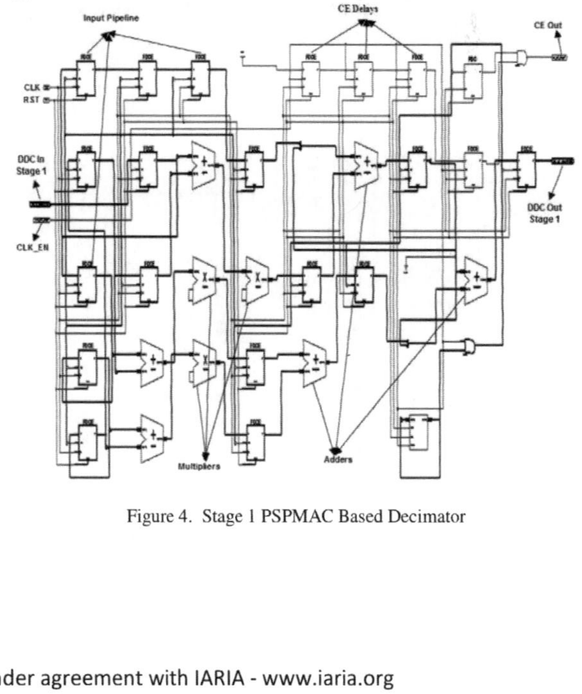

Figure 4. Stage 1 PSPMAC Based Decimator

The pass band edge of second decimator is 2.34 MHz and pass band ripple is 0.0001 dB. It results in digital filter with order 18 whose response is shown in Figure 5. The second stage decimator requires 27 coefficients for its hardware implementation.

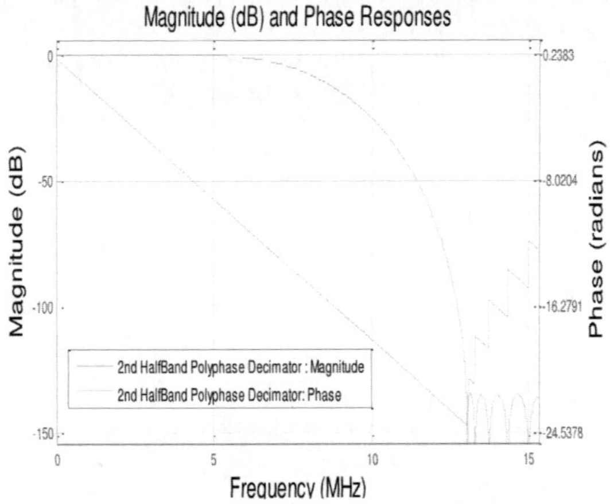

Figure 5. Second Stage Half Band Decimator Response

The second stage decimator requires 27 coefficients for its hardware implementation. To design the required decimator partially serial pipelined in partially serial pipelined MAC (PSPMAC) style 5 multipliers have been used as shown in Figure 6. The input pipeline registers are used to store the new coefficient values required for processing in the next cycle to enhance the speed further. The CE delays are used to make synchronization between stage 2 and stage 3.

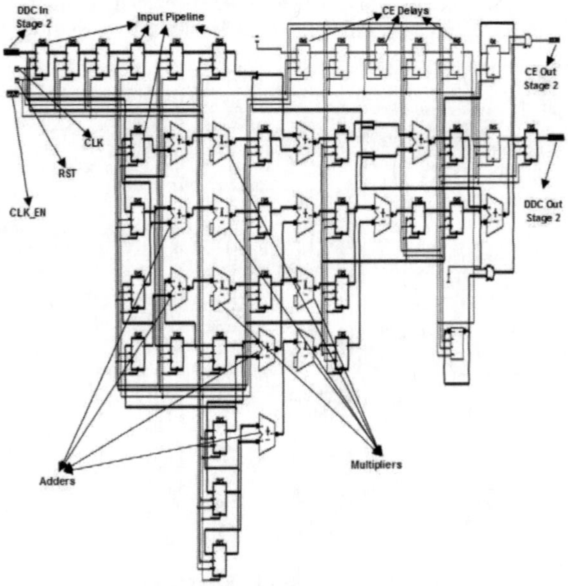

Figure 6. Stage 2 PSPMAC Based Decimator

The next stage RRC filter is used for sampling rate conversion from 15.36 MSPS to 7.68 MSPS. This 2x over-sampling rate is needed in the timing recovery process to avoid the signal loss due to the sampling point misalignment. The response of the filter is shown in Figure 7.

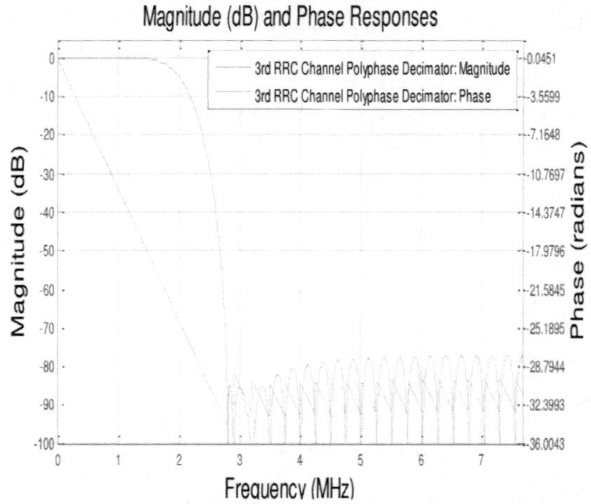

Figure 7. RRC Channel Filter

RRC filter is designed with 1.92 MHz cut off frequency, 0.22 MHz roll-off factor and 50 dB side lobe attenuation using Chebyshev window whose filter response is shown in Figure 6. The DDC is designed by cascading these three stages with 16 bit coefficients as shown in Figure 8.

Finally, the third stage RRC decimator has also been designed using partially serial architecture and only first section of it is shown in Figure 9. The 61 coefficients required to design this RRC filter have been processed using 38 multipliers to improve both area and speed. The delay pipelining and output registers are used for synchronization. The cascade of all optimized stages zoomed view is shown in Figure 10.

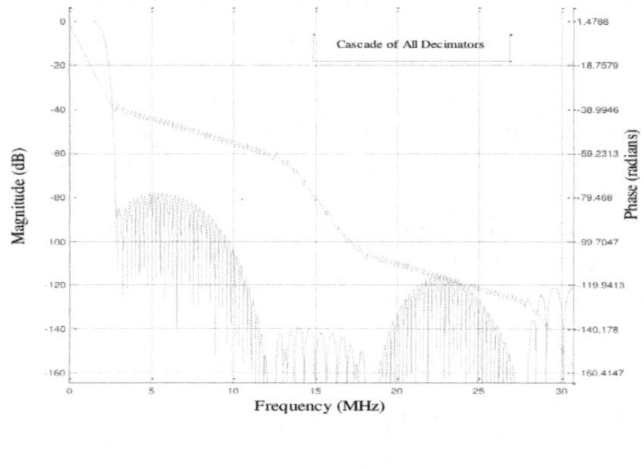

Figure 8. WCDMA DDC Output Response

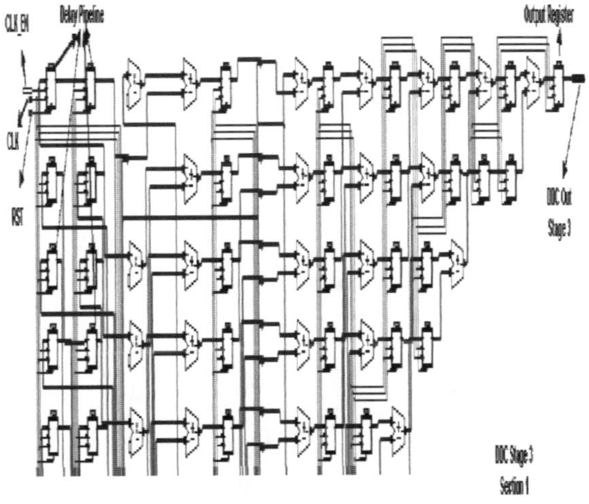

Figure 9. Stage 3 PSPMAC Based RRC Decimator

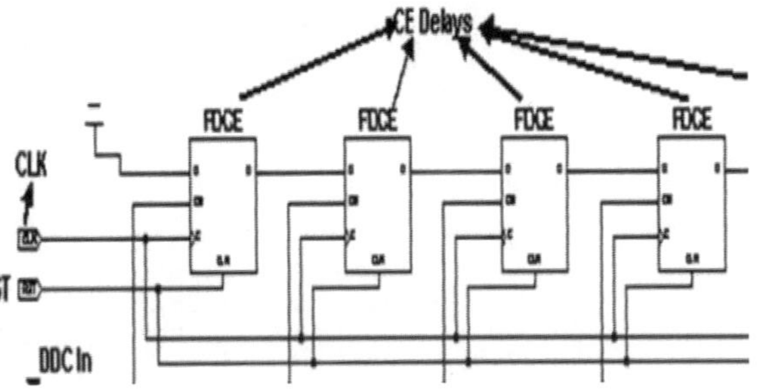

Figure 10. Proposed WCDMA DDC

IV. Hardware Synthesis And Simulation

In the proposed DDC designs CORDIC algorithm based optimized DDS design is used in place of DDS compiler block to generate sinusoidal waveform needed for frequency translation [27]. The FIR Compiler blocks of existing designs are replaced by equiripple techniques based decimators for optimal filter length to reduce the hardware requirement. It is further supported by the half band filter concept to improve the computational complexity for enhanced speed. Finally, Poly-phase decomposition technique is utilized in hardware implementation of proposed design to optimize both speed and area together by introducing the partially serial pipelined MAC architecture. The third stage of decimation has been developed using efficient RRC filter [28] design. All the decimators are implemented using MAC Algorithm with optimal number of embedded multipliers of target FPGA along with pipelined registers to enhance the speed performance and resource utilization. The Virtex-II Pro FPGA device is used for implementation that contains 136 embedded multipliers [29].

Two designs have been developed using different input output precisions. DDC is implemented using input precision of 14 bits and output precision of 16 bit and DDC 2 is implemented using input and output precision of 12 bits. The developed DDCs are simulated using Modelsim Simulator. The output response of DDC1 is shown in Figure 11 and output response of DDC 2 is shown in Figure 12. It can be observed from the simulated waveforms that the output response of both the designs is similar but speed performance of DDC2 is better as compared to DDC1.

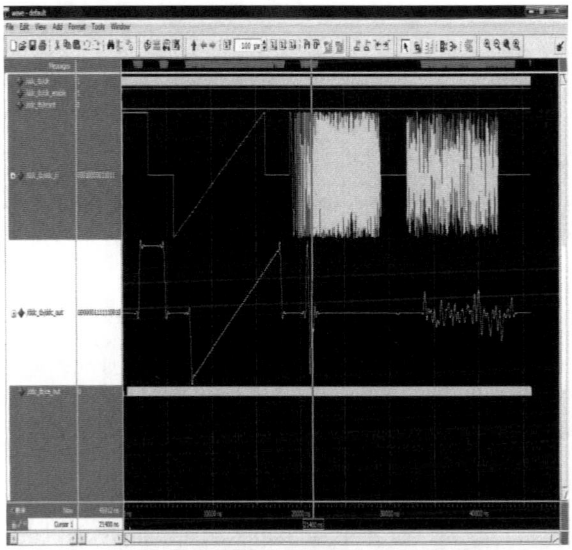

Figure 11. Optimized WCDMA DDC 1 Response

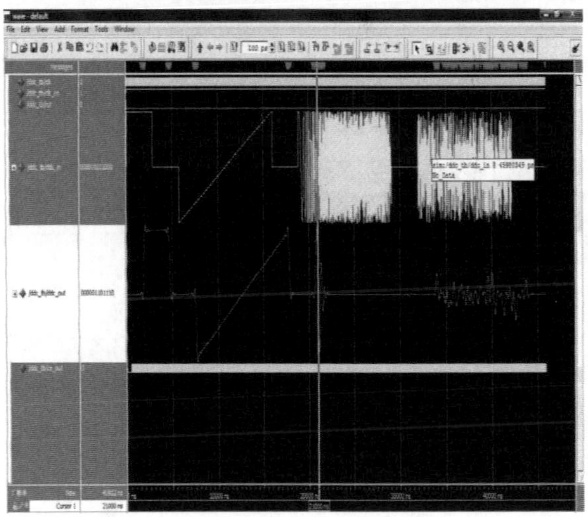

Figure 12. Optimized WCDMA DDC 2 Response

The optimized DDC designs are finally mapped for hardware implementation and synthesised on Virtex-II Pro based xc2vp30-7ff896 target device. The resource consumption of proposed DDC design on specified target device is shown in Table I.

TABLE I. RESOURCE UTILIZATION

Logic Utilization	DDC Design 1	DDC Design 2
Number of Slices	1477	1462
Number of Flip Flops	2535	2533
Number of LUTs	1429	1366
Number of I/Os	34	28
Number of MULT	46	46

The proposed optimized DDC 2 can operate at a maximum frequency of 146.36 MHz and DDC 1 can operate at 119 MHz as compared to 122.88 MHz in case of [23]. So the proposed DDC 2 provides an improvement of 19% in speed and DDC 1 provide almost same speed as that of existing DDC design. The developed DDC designs have shown better resource utilization as compared to DDC design of [24] which is shown in Table II. Bar graph of the above resource utilization of the proposed DDC design results is shown in Figure 13.

TABLE II. RESOURCE UTILIZATION COMPARISON

Logic Utilization	DDC Design [26]	Proposed DDC Designs
Number of Flip Flops	4.93%	9%
Number of Slices	7.9%	10%
Number of MULT	3.8%	33%

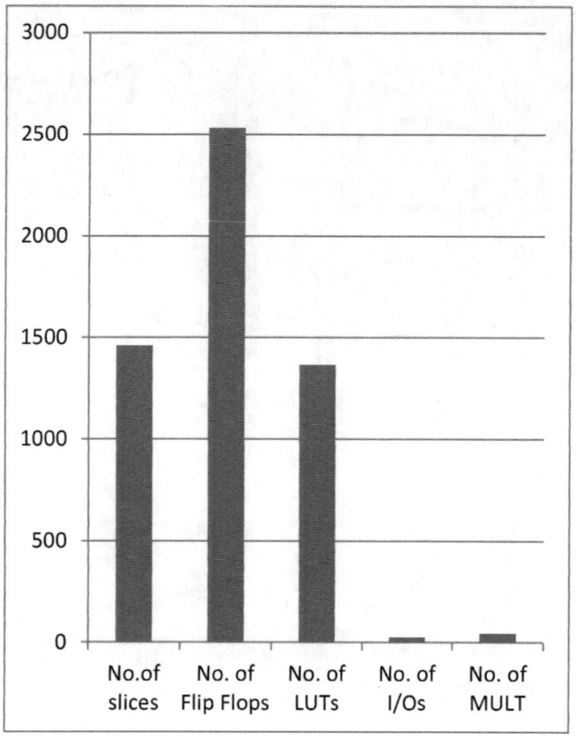

Figure 13. Resource Utilization Bar Graph

V. ASIC DESIGN ANALYSIS

An application-specific integrated circuit (ASIC), is an integrated circuit (IC) customized for a particular use, rather than intended for general-purpose use. A chip designed to run in a specific environment is an ASIC. ASICs use a hardware description language (HDL) to describe the functionality of ASICs such as Verilog or VHDL. The design is coded in Verilog hardware description language (HDL) [30, 31]. Here, ASIC implementation is done to calculate the power, delay, total no. of cells and area. The proposed filter is designed and simulated using 90nm technology cadence environment. Initially, RTL is developed from Verilog file as shown in Figure 14 which is verified using Pre synthesis simulation as shown in Figure 15. Physical design implementation is performed using optimized placement and routing as shown in Figure 16. Finally placed and routed DDC is validated using Post synthesis waveforms as shown in Figure 17. The performance of developed DDC was evaluated for different parameters as shown in Table III. It can be observed from result analysis that proposed DDC require 601mm^2 area and consume 3169.61 nW power.

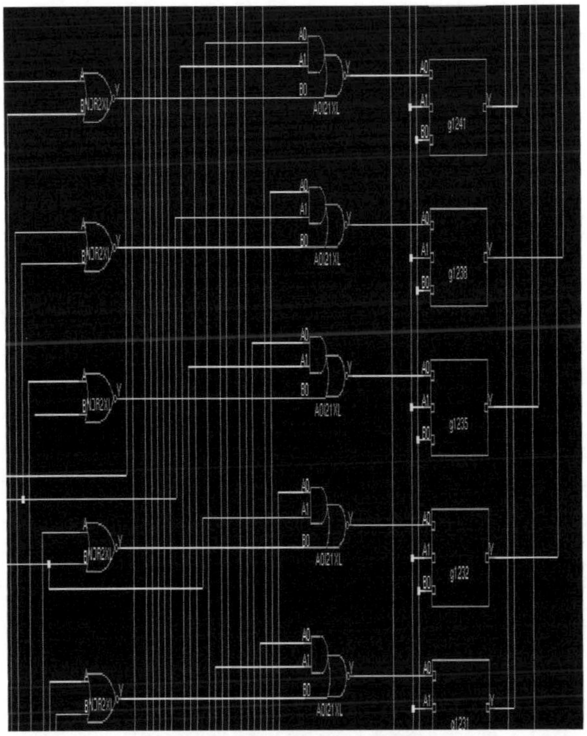

Figure 14. Gate level Netlist of DDC Design

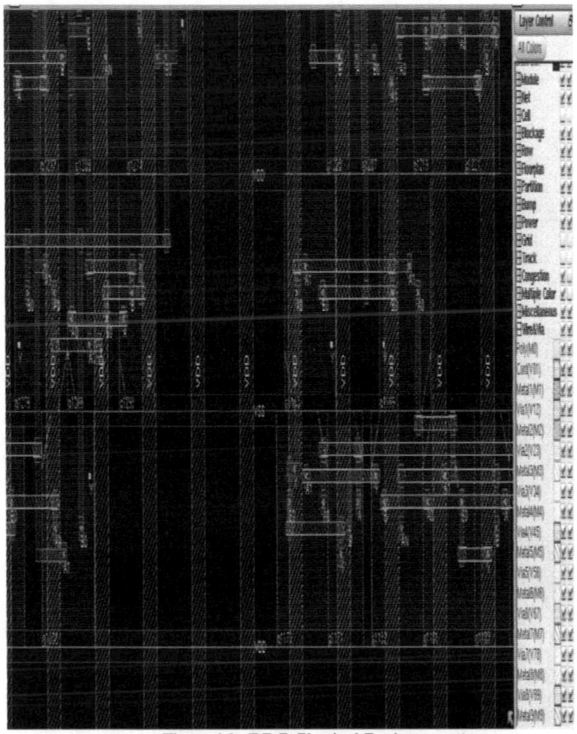

Figure 16. DDC Physical Design

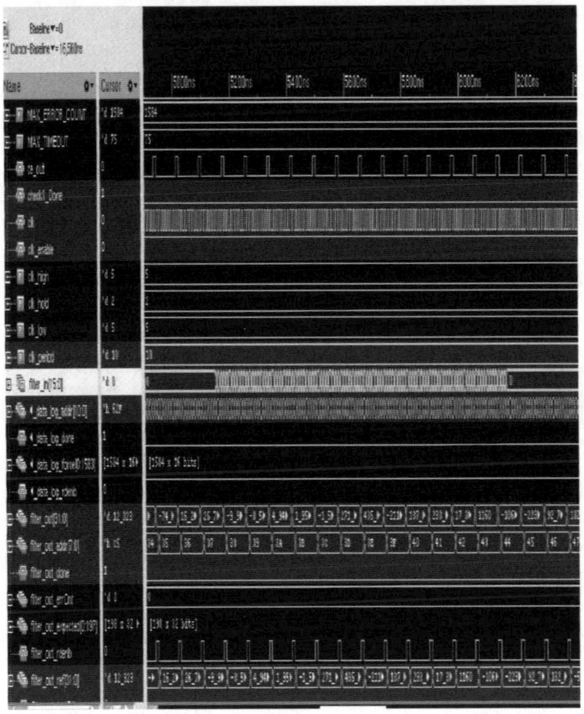

Figure 15. Pre-Synthesis Waveform of DDC

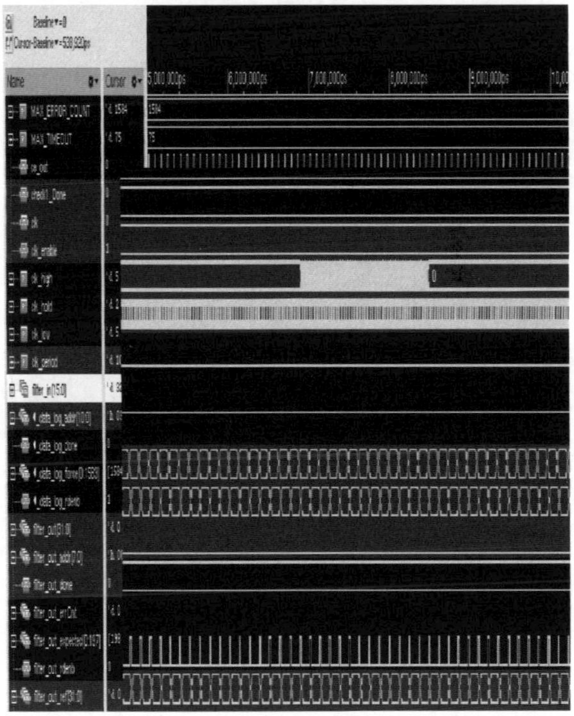

Figure 17. Post-Synthesis Waveform of DDC

Various parameters of DDC design after ASIC realization has been studied and summary of the results obtained are listed in Table III showing operational power supply, technology, total number of cells obtained, total cell area, leakage power, dynamic power and total power. Finally, the area and power consumption of DDC [1] and the proposed DDC ASIC are compared in Table IV. Bar graph of the above obtained results in shown in Figure 18.

TABLE III. DDC ASIC PARAMETERS

Parameter	Value
Power Supply	1.2 V
Technology	CMOS 90 nm
Total No. of Cells	138
Total Cell Area	601mm^2
Leakage Power	2347.455 nW
Dynamic Power	822.151 nW
Total Power	3169.607 nW

TABLE IV. AREA AND POWER COMPARISON

PARAMETERS	DDC[1]	PROPOSED DDC ASIC
Area	1462 Slice Registers	601 mm^2 Silicon Area
Power	-	3169.607 nW

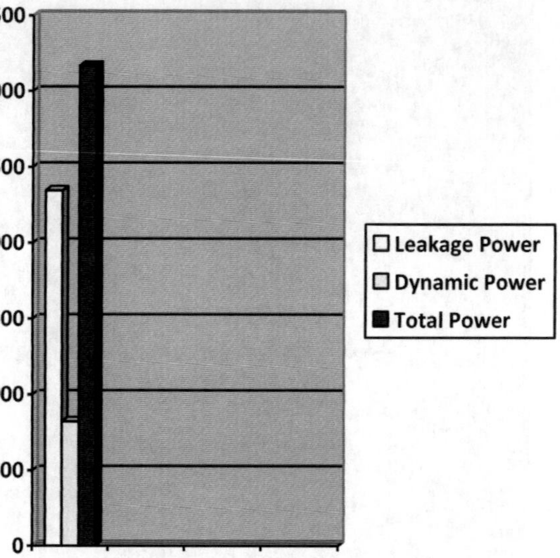

Figure 18. DDC ASIC Power Bar Graph

VI. CONCLUSION

This paper presents an efficient and cost effective DDC design for software defined radios. The proposed DDC designs are developed and implemented on multiplier based Virtex II Pro target FPGA using optimized MAC algorithm. Three decimator stages are optimized separately and then cascaded together. The optimized DDC has been developed using partially serial pipelined MAC algorithm for area and speed optimization. The ASIC realization of the proposed design is done to find the power consumption of the DDC circuit. From the results, it is concluded that the proposed design obtained has low power consumption, i.e., 3169.61 nW and reduced area utilization, i.e., 601mm^2. The DDC designs are efficiently floor planned and routed to achieve the desired timing constraints. The developed DDCs have shown improved resource utilization to provide cost effective solution for software radios in terms of low power consumption and reduced area.

ACKNOWLEDGMENT

The author would like to thank Dr. S.S Pattnaik, Director National Institute of Technical Teachers' Training & Research, Chandigarh, India and for constant motivation and support throughout this research work.

REFERENCES

[1] R. Mehra, "Prototype Design of Computationally Efficient Digital Down Converter for 3G Applications," The Tenth International Conference on Advanced Engineering

Computing and Applications in Sciences (ADVCOMP), pp. 52-57, 2016.

[2] V. Bhargav Alluri, J. Robert Heath, and M. Lhamon, "A New Multichannel, Coherent Amplitude Modulated, Time-Division Multiplexed, Software-Defined Radio Receiver Architecture, and Field-Programmable-Gate-Array Technology Implementation," IEEE Transactions on Signal Processing, Vol. 58, No. 10, pp. 5369-5384, October 2010.

[3] A. Beygi, A. Mohammadi, and A. Abrishamifar, "An FPGA-Based Irrational Decimator for Digital Receivers," IEEE International Symposium on Signal Processing and its Applications (ISSPA), pp. 1-4, 2007.

[4] P. Upadhyay, R. Mehra, and N. Thakur, "Low Power Design of an SRAM cell for Portable Devices," IEEE International conference on Computer and Communication Technology (ICCCT), pp. 255-259, 2010.

[5] K. K. Sharma and A. Samad, "Application Specific Integrated Circuit Implementation of Discrete Fractional Fourier Transform," International Journal of Information and Electronics Engineering, Vol. 3, No. 5, pp. 444-447, 2013.

[6] S. Yoon Park and P. Kumar Meher, "Efficient FPGA and ASIC Realizations of a DA-Based Reconfigurable FIR Digital Filter," IEEE Transactions on Circuits and Systems—II, Vol. 61, No. 7, pp. 511-515, 2014.

[7] A. A. AlJuffri, M. AlNahdi, A. Hemaid, O. A. AlShaalan, M. S. BenSaleh, A. M. Obeid, and S. M. Qasim, "ASIC Realization and Performance Evaluation of Scalable Microprogrammed FIR Filters using Wallace Tree and Vedic Multipliers," IEEE International Conference on Environment and Electrical Engineering (EEEIC), pp. 1995 – 1998, July 2015.

[8] T. Shono, Y. Shirato, H. Shiba, K. Uehara, K. Araki, and M. Umehira, "IEEE 802.11 Wireless LAN Implemented on Software Defined Radio with Hybrid Programmable Architecture," IEEE Transactions on Wireless Communications, Vol. 4, No. 5, pp. 2299-2308, September 2005.

[9] F. Rivet, Y. Deval, J. Baptiste Begueret, D. Dallet, P. Cathelin, and Didier Belot, "A Disruptive Receiver Architecture Dedicated to Software-Defined Radio," IEEE Transaction on Circuits and Systems-II: Express Briefs, Vol. 55, No. 4, pp. 344-348, April 2008.

[10] P. Cruz, N. Borges Carvalho, and Kate A. Remley, "Designing and Testing Software Defined Radios," IEEE Microwave magazine, pp. 83-94, June 2010.

[11] N. Lashkarian, Ed Hemphill, H. Tarn, H. Parekh, and C. Dick, "Reconfigurable Digital Front-End Hardware for Wireless Base-Station Transmitters: Analysis, Design and FPGA Implementation," IEEE Transactions on Circuits and Systems-I: Regular Papers, Vol. 54, No. 8, pp. 1666-1677, August 2007.

[12] V. Singh and R. Mehra, "Rational Rate Converter Design Analysis using Symmetric Technique," International Journal of Computer Trends and Technology, Vol. 27, No. 2, pp. 116-120, September 2015.

[13] G. Swathi and M. Revathy, "Design of a Multi-Standard DUC Based FIR Filter using VLSI Architecture," International Journal of Scientific Engineering and Research, Vol. 3, No. 11, pp. 41-44, November 2015.

[14] R. Verma and R. Mehra, "FPGA Implementation of FIR Interpolator for IEEE 802.11n WLAN," International Journal of Engineering Science and Technology, Vol. 8, No. 7, pp. 121-127, July 2016.

[15] R. Verma, and R. Mehra, "Design of Low Pass FIR Interpolator for Wireless Communication Applications," International Journal of Advanced Research in Computer and Communication Engineering, Vol. 6, No. 7, pp. 355-362, July 2016.

[16] F. Wang, "Digital Up and Down Converter in IEEE 802.16d," 8th international Conference on Signal Processing, pp. 16-20, 2006.

[17] R. Mehra and R. Arora, "FPGA-Based Design of High-Speed CIC Decimator for Wireless Applications," International Journal of Advanced Computer Science and Applications (IJACSA), Vol. 2, No. 5, pp. 59-62, May-2011.

[18] R. Mehra and S. Devi, "Efficient Hardware Co-Simulation of down Convertor for Wireless Communication Systems," International Journal of VLSI design & Communication Systems (VLSICS), Vol. 1, No. 2, pp. 13-21, June 2010.

[19] R. Mehra and R. Arora, "FPGA-Based Design of High-Speed CIC Decimator for Wireless Applications," International Journal of Advanced Computer Science and Applications, Vol. 2, No. 5, pp. 59 – 62, 2011.

[20] R. Mehra and L. Singh, "FPGA based Speed Efficient Decimator using Distributed Arithmetic Algorithm," International Journal of Computer Applications, Vol. 80, No. 11, pp. 37-40, 2013.

[21] X. Xu, X. Xie, and F. Wang, "Digital Up and Down Converter in IEEE 802.16d," IEEE International Conference on Signal Processing (ICSP), Vol. 1, pp. 17-20, 2006.

[22] S. Mahboob, "FPGA Implementation of Digital Up/Down Convertor for WCDMA System," IEEE International Conference on Advanced Communication Technologies (ICACT), pp. 757-760, 2010.

[23] K. Chunli, F. Xiangning, X. Zhiyuan, and Z. Hao "Design and Simulation of Two-channel DDC in Satellite Cellular Integrated System," IEEE International Conference on Wireless Communication networking and Mobile Computing (WiCoM), pp. 1-4, 2010.

[24] R. Mehra, "Reconfigurable Optimized WCDMA DDC for Software Defined Radios," Journal of Selected Areas in Telecommunications (JSAT), Cyber Journals: Multidisciplinary Journals in Science and Technology, Ontario, Canada, pp. 1-6, December Edition, 2010.

[25] H. Tarn, K. Neilson, R. Uribe, and D. Hawke, "Designing Efficient Wireless Digital Up and Down Converters Leveraging CORE Generator and System Generator," Application Note on Virtex-5, Spartan-DSP FPGAs, XAPP1018 (v1.0), pp. 8-44, October 2007.

[26] L. Fei-yu, Q. Wei-ming, W. Yan-yu, L. Tai-lian, F. Jin, and Z. Jian-chuan, "Efficient WCDMA Digital Down Converter Design Using System Generator," IEEE International Conference on Space Science and Communication, pp. 89-92, 2009.

[27] B. Kamboj and R. Mehra, "Efficient FPGA Implementation of Direct Digital Frequency Synthesizer for Software Radios," International Journal of Computer Applications, Vol. 37, No. 10, pp. 25-29, January 2012.

[28] R. Mehra and S. Devi, "FPGA Implementation of High Speed Pulse Shaping Filter for SDR Applications," Springer International Conference on Recent Trends in Networks and Communications, Communication in Computer and

Information Science (CCIS), Vol. 90, No. 1, pp. 214-222, 2010.

[29] Xilinx User Guide, "Virtex-II Pro and Virtex-II Pro X FPGA User Guide," UG012 (v4.2), pp. 178-185, November 2007.

[30] V. A. Pedroni, Circuit Design with VHDL, MIT Press Cambridge, Massachusetts London, England, pp. 364, 2004.

[31] K. Priya and R. Mehra, "Area Efficient Design of Fir Filter Using Symmetric Structure," International Journal of Advanced Research in Computer and Communication Engineering, Vol. 1, No. 10, pp. 842-845, 2012.

Intelligent Agents to Efficient Management Industrial Services and Resources

Antonio Martín-Montes
Higher Polytechnic School
Seville University
Seville, Spain
toni@us.es

Mauricio Burbano, Carlos Leon
Technical High School of Computer Science
University of Seville
Seville, Spain
aryburcen@us.es, cleon@us.es

Abstract— **Increasing product and process complexity combined with rapidly changing markets and dynamic competition are daily challenges faced by industries. Current industrial platforms need to evolve in order to support different advanced capabilities including semantic interoperability, self-optimization between edge and cloud, sensor fusion and processing, and edge-aware stream processing, among others. Companies can benefit greatly from of Internet of Things as a tool for finding growth in unexpected opportunities. In this area an enormous quantity of heterogeneous and distributed information is stored in databases, web sites and digital storehouses. In the traditional search engines, the information stored in Digital Industry Repository (DIR) is treated as an ordinary database that manages the contents and positions. The present search techniques based on manually annotated metadata and linear replay of the material selected by the user do not scale effectively or efficiently to large collections. This can significantly reduce the accuracy of the search and draw in irrelevant documents. This paper describes semantic interoperability problems and presents an intelligent architecture to address them. We concentrate on the critical issue of metadata/ontology-based search and expert system technologies. Our approach for realizing content-based search and retrieval information implies the application of the Case-Based Reasoning technology and ontologies. The objective here is thus to contribute to a better knowledge retrieval in the industrial domain. We have developed a prototype, which suggests a new form of interaction between users and digital enterprise repositories, to support efficient sharing of distributed knowledge.**

Keywords-Case base Reasoning; Ontology; jColibri; Semantic Interoperability; Artificial Intelligence.

I. Introduction

Currently, industrial information provides even more granular information through unit and equipment databases, which provide details about installed equipment, including models, designed capacity, throughput, and start up/shutdown dates for turbines, generators, and refining equipment. This data and information are stored in digital repositories, digital archives, and business Web sites. Digital Industry Repository (DIR) presents centralized hosting and access to content. DIRs provide the ability to share digital objects or files, the permissions and controls for access to content, the integrity, and intellectual property rights of content owners and creators. A primary research goal thereby is the development of concepts for semi-automatic service composition to support flexibility in re-tooling knowledge and quick adaptation to failures in the automation chain.

Digital repositories are online databases that provide a central location to collect, contribute and share knowledge resources to use in the industrial domain. In order to remain competitive, companies must be able to develop products and services quickly and manage data and knowledge efficiently. Access to these collections poses a serious challenge. Mechanisms to retrieve information and knowledge from digital repositories have been particularly important. Artificial Intelligence (AI) and Semantic Web provide the common framework to allow knowledge to be shared and reused in an efficient way. Results generated by the current searches are a list of results that contain or treat the pattern. Although search engines have developed increasing efficiency, information overload obstructs precise searches. Thus, it is necessary to develop new intelligent and semantic models that offer more possibilities [1]. In this paper, we propose a comprehensive approach for discovering information objects in large digital repositories based on analysis of recorded semantic metadata and the application of Case Based Reasoning technique. We suggest a conceptual architecture for a semantic search engine.

There are researchers and related field works that include intelligent techniques to share information such as [2] that describes the application of intelligent systems techniques to provide decision support to the condition monitoring of nuclear power plant reactor cores. An intelligent image agent based on soft-computing techniques for color image processing is proposed in [3]. Huang et al. [4] propose an intelligent human-expert forum system to perform more efficient knowledge sharing using fuzzy information retrieval techniques. Yang et al. [5] present a system to collect information through the cooperation of intelligent agent software, in addition to providing warnings after analysis to monitor and predict some possible error indications among controlled objects in the network. Gladun et al. [6] suggest a Semantic Web technologies-based multi-agent system to allow automatically controlling students' acquired knowledge in e-learning frameworks.

The meta-concepts have explicit ontological semantics, so that they help to identify domain concepts consistently and structure them systematically. The architecture presented differs from other reference architectures and we include it here due to its widespread use and importance in designing Internet of Things (IoT) systems capable of handling the tremendous amounts of data and knowledge generated by the sensors. In [7], the authors propose the construction of an ontology to formalize the industrial management knowledge. Bertola et al. [8] present the building blocks for creating a semantic social space to organize artworks according to an ontology of emotions, which takes into account both the information two ancestral terms share and the probability that they co-occur with their common descendants. In [9], the authors present an approach, which allows users to semantically query the building information modeling design paradigm using a domain vocabulary, capitalizing on building product ontology formalized from construction perspectives. Zhang et al. [10] propose a framework to quantify the similarity measure beneath a term pair, which takes into account both the information two ancestral terms share and the probability that they co-occur with their common descendants. In [11], the authors present a method for selecting a semantic similar measure with high similarity calculation accuracy for concepts in two different Computer-aided design model data ontologies.

In addition, the advancing development of integrated intelligent management systems has motivated to researchers to address the specific problem of integrating knowledge management. Many researchers have suggested that intelligent sensor network technologies could improve the effectiveness and efficiency of real-time management. In [12] authors have developed a distributed information management system to integrate and manipulate the heterogeneous, distributed information resources in the Iranian power industry. Mehrpoor et al. [13] describe an intelligent service to improve knowledge and information accessibility by personalizing the knowledge and information based on the stakeholder's situation in their working life, which is known as a recommender system. In [14], the authors study a grid-based infrastructure, which adopts the semantic Web and the Grid to share information in the press industry chain. Chen et al. [15] address the important issues in developing domain-specific ontology for manufacturing used in Industrie 4.0 demonstration production lines. For this purpose a generic ontology is developed considering all the aspects about the product from customized order to resulting production.

There is a lot of research on applying AI and semantic techniques to share knowledge. In this work we focus upon the latter tasks, which are intended to guarantee the desired quality of network services to the industry and to collect and evaluate the associated knowledge. Information has to be gathered for the purposes of accounting and for gaining information for future industrial services design. In this paper, we present a full integration of AI technologies and semantic methods during the whole life cycle from the industrial point of view. Our work differs from related projects in that we build ontology-based contextual profiles and we introduce to an approach using metadata-based ontology search and expert system technologies [16]. More specifically, the main objective of this research is to search possible intelligent infrastructures based on the construction of decentralized public repositories where no global schema exists. For this reason, we are improving representation by incorporating more metadata from within the information. The objective has focused on creating technologically complex to environments in the industrial domain and incorporates Semantic Web and AI technologies to enable precise location of industrial resources.

The remaining paper is organized as follows: In Section II reports a short description of important aspects in Industrial domain, the research problems and current work. Section III describes the systems and services interoperability requirements. Section IV studies the role of semantic and artificial intelligence in industrial domain. Section V y Section VI concern the design of a prototype system for semantic search framework, in order to verify that our proposed approach is an applicable solution. Section VII and Section VIII demonstrate the proposed intelligent architecture can successfully control an industrial domain. Finally, Section IX concludes chapter and outlines the future work.

II. TRANSFORMING INDUSTRIAL VALUE CREATION

Industrie 4.0 is currently one of the most frequently discussed topics by researches. Its aim deals with intentions between science and industry with continuous improvements of the general conditions for innovations. Industrie 4.0 is a strategic initiative to take up a pioneering role in industrial Information Technology (IT), which is currently revolutionizing the manufacturing engineering sector. Industrie 4.0 covers science and technology-based solutions in different specific fields like climate and energy, health and nutrition, mobility, security, and communication. Industrie 4.0 represents the coming fourth industrial revolution, which connects embedded system production technologies and smart production process to pave the way to a new technological age. In other words, industrial production machinery no longer simply processes the product, but the product communicates with the machinery to tell it exactly what to do. In more depth, we recognize six design principles of Industrie 4.0:

- Interoperability: it means that it is crucial to set up standards in order to rule the communication between Cyber-Physical Systems (CPS) of various manufacturers.
- Virtualization: necessary for an overall monitoring of physical processes, thus enables us to use it for simulations of models.
- Decentralization: it enables the different systems to make their decisions separately.
- Real-time capability: collecting of data in each step of the process should be in real-time.
- Service orientation: reliable service must be considered as well.
- Modularity: Modularity brings up flexibility to in terms that each individual model must be designed in such a way that it is easy to replace or apply new innovations.

In the age of Industrie 4.0, products have barcodes or Radio Frequency Identification (RFID) chips on the surface to pass information to machines, which communicate with and control each other. The physical and virtual worlds merge into cyber-physical systems. Not only intelligent machines and products, but also all entities involved in production, including suppliers and customers along the entire value chain are networked with Information Communications Technology (ICT), from logistics to production and marketing to service. They may have a need to know any information to provide efficient services: What product belongs in which packaging? What transport container is where? What processing step comes next? What machine requires maintenance or replacement parts, and when? Where can unrealized cost reduction potential be found in the logistics process?

The reason why researches have been investing so much effort in this project is that technology is the main building block for innovations and innovations shape the future. An important aspect is the connection between the physical and the knowledge of resource management and this connection can be established due to DIRs. DIRs contain data and knowledge of management about physical resources, which conform IoT. Embedded computer and networks monitor and control the physical processes, usually with feedback loops where physical processes affect computations and vice versa. This demonstrates why efficient knowledge retrieval is important to monitor physical processes, to create a virtual copy of the physical world and then make decentralized decisions.

For example, a machine at step 3 of a production process could alert other machines from steps 4 and onward that the production will be delayed a bit because there's an urgent fix that needs to be done on the machine at step 3. Of course, there will still be humans interacting with the machines in this manufacturing process. A production plant manager will still manage the plant, but s/he will have more data coming from all the machines, therefore enabling a better use of resources, better scheduling of maintenance and delays. Based on current technology, the manager located in the middle of the plant, with a tablet in hand, looking at all the data coming in from the machines, taking in all the information coming in verbally from the employees, and making decisions based on this data can therefore be: adjusting the production schedule, ordering supplies and adjusting employee assignments all according to the current plant conditions.

The knowledge and information data volumes produced in this complex system are permanently available and evaluated in real time. Not only do employees have mobile access to this data, they can also intervene in the processes using mobile devices. In this sense, the efficient knowledge retrieval is becoming increasingly important. The benefits for participants along the entire value chain are varied. Waste is reduced, the ability to respond to individual customer wishes is improved, and the production of one-offs, and very small quantities becomes more cost-effective. Faster, more reliable decisions can be made, business processes become more flexible and dynamic, new business models are created. Downstream services complement the traditional portfolio of manufacturing companies.

To reach these goals we need the capacity of different information systems, applications and services to retrieve, communicate, share and interchange knowledge in an effective and precise way, as well as to integrate with other systems, applications and services in order to deliver new products and services.

III. Systems and Services Interoperability Requirements

Connectivity and interoperation among computers, among entities, and among software components can increase the flexibility and agility of industrial systems, thus reducing administrative and software costs for industry. This capacity expands the industrial processes to automatically work together in an eficency way [17]. It is clear that the ability to interoperate is key to reducing industrial integration costs and inefficiencies, increasing business agility, and enabling the adoption of new and emerging technologies.

Interoperability is the ability of two or more industrial assets like hardware devices, communications devices, or software components, to easily or automatically work together. ISO/IEC 2382 Information Technology Vocabulary defines interoperability as "the capability to communicate, execute programs, or transfer data among various functional units in a manner that requires the user to have little or no knowledge of the unique characteristics of those units". An interoperability framework can be described as a set of standards and guidelines, which describe the way in which organizations have agreed, or should agree, to interact with each other.

In this context, interoperability is the ability of information and communication technology systems and of the business processes they support to exchange data and to enable sharing of information and knowledge. Technical dimension of interoperability includes uniform movement of industrial data, uniform presentation of data, uniform user controls, uniform safeguarding data security and integrity, uniform protection of industrial confidentiality, uniform assurance of a common degree of service quality (Figure 1).

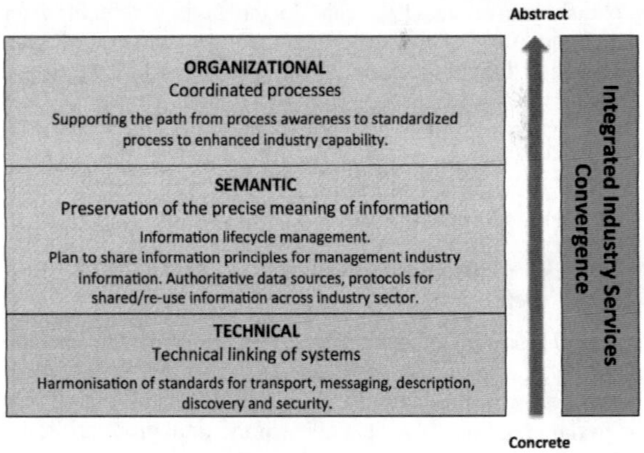

Figure 1. Levels of interoperability

Specifically, organizational interoperability is defined as the state where the organizational components of the industrial system are able to perform seamlessly together. The goal of semantic interoperability is to improve communication on industrial related knowledge both among humans and machines. In order to achieve this, a two-pronged approach is necessary: achieving a unified ontology and tackle concrete and clearly delineated issues. The functional goal is to allow data to be exchanged between different projects in multiple corporations using different equipment and software. From multiple manufacturers or vendors. Technical interoperability consists in being able to communicate and interact between two systems coming from different manufacturers.

Furthermore, achieving semantic and organizational interoperability requires strictly agreeing on the meaning of information and aligning business processes across enterprises/industries. At one level, general cross-industry frameworks and software infrastructure approaches can be, and are being, developed for semantics and business processes. For example, general semantics for major business transactions, such as purchase orders and invoices, are outlined through standards such as Universal Business Language (UBL), UN/CEFACT Core Components, and Open Applications Group Integration Standard (OAGIS).

Different efforts are being leveraged by many standards efforts to address semantic and organizational interoperability and are proving to be a model for addressing semantic and organizational interoperability like ebXML, RosettaNet, the new UN/CEFACT work on aligning its global business process standards work with Web and other services. In June 2002, European heads of state adopted the Europe Action Plan 2005 at the Seville summit. They call on the European Commission to issue an agreed interoperability framework to support the delivery of European Digital services to enterprises. This recommends technical policies and specifications for joining up public administration information systems across the European Union. This research is based on open standards and the use of open source software. These aspects are the pillars to support the European delivery of Digital services of the recently adopted European Interoperability Framework (EIF) [18] and its Spanish equivalent [19]. This document is a reference for interoperability of the new Interoperable Delivery of Pan-European Digital Services to Public Administrations, Business and Citizens program (IDAbc). Member States Administrations must use the guidance provided by the EIF to supplement their national Interoperability Frameworks with a pan-European dimension and thus enable pan-European interoperability [20].

IV. Implementation of Industrie 4.0 with Ontologies and Artifical Intelligence

In the current industry it is a need to disperse real time data, which can spread the effort and resources more accurately. So, productivity is increased and the use of raw material is optimized. The quality of the final product should also be improved; if the data coming from design process shows that the real value used always has an offset from the set point, then the design plans can be adjusted accordingly and the simulations as well. This will enable a simulation that actually corresponds to reality, and eventually a product that is closer to its original design. Adaptability is a big plus in Industrie 4.0. So, intelligent management of huge amounts of resources and associated data are areas that need a rapid development.

In practice, it is apparent that some companies have only a rudimentary grasp on Industrie 4.0 and so a basic automation and IT infrastructure must first be created. Even more advanced companies generally have a conventional system environment according to the classic automation pyramid with relatively rigid and outmoded systems that were installed for a specific task. These systems are usually based on proprietary and therefore inflexible data structures. Consequently, modifications and expansions are very time consuming and costly. This makes it possible to achieve enormous cost savings and economies of scale. Management has genuine real-time information for its decision-making processes. The results of any action taken can be directly measured, identified and then corrected as needed.

The Industrie 4.0 vision assumes the secure communication and cooperation of all participants across companies in real time for the entire lifetime of the product. The first step towards Industrie 4.0 for most companies is the complete vertical integration and digitization of the systems involved in the manufacturing process via a Manufacturing Execution System (MES), which allows real-time transparency. A horizontal integration of individual functionalities is also necessary. In this context, MES, the information hub, is the central element that collects, analyzes, processes and provides the other systems with the big data. The information that Industrie 4.0 provides together with, for example, big data, social media, and cloud computing, make it possible to optimize the decision-making process, secure design decisions early on and respond flexibly to disturbances, as well as optimize all the resources across more than one site.

In the industry domain levels of service provision can be influenced by different operations and parameters that affect the bottom-line results:

- Do you need to know in real time the status of many different components and devices in a large complex system?
- Do you need to measure how changing inputs affect the output of your operations?
- What gear must you to control, in real time, from a distance?
- Where are you lacking accurate, real-time data about key processes that affect your operations?

This has a variety of benefits along the entire value chain. It improves the ability to respond to individualized customer needs and makes it more profitable to manufacture individual units and small quantities. The flexibility is progressing through the dynamic design of business processes via the Internet in various dimensions as well as agile engineering processes. Intelligent monitoring and control increases efficiency and maximizes profitability. Here are few of the things you can do with the information and control capabilities you get from an intelligent system:

- Detect and correct problems as soon as they begin.
- Measure trends over time.
- Discover and eliminate bottlenecks and inefficiencies

- Control larger and more complex processes with a less specialized staff.

Industrie 4.0 is actually a concept, which has the strength of focusing the development efforts in the right places. Once the concept is defined, we can see where the system fails to perform, and this is where the effort for improvement can be concentrated. Using a simple analogy, we can compare the industrial paradigm with Formula One racing where the cars are going around a track with thousands of sensors monitoring the cars. Every time a car goes past the pit wall, the systems downloads data, and the race engineers tell the driver how to drive in response to that data. That is what is needed in our factories. There needs to be the equivalent of the pit wall somewhere to make sure that the factory machinery is working better than that of the competitors.

We propose a modern factory with all the steps automated and interrelated, with operators on their tablets tracking on going production. In industry it is important to stay aware of the global strategies of Industrie 4.0, and think of Industrie 4.0 when you acquire new equipment; a sensor with an Ethernet connection will eventually be useful to connect to the rest of the factory.

Thus, considerable effort is required in creating meaningful metadata, organizing and annotating digital documents, and making them accessible. This work concerns applications of the semantic technology for improving existing information search systems by adding semantic enabled extensions that enhance information retrieval from information systems.

Industrial repositories contain a large volume of digital information, generally focusing on making their knowledge to improve associate decision-support systems. Within a pool of heterogeneous and distributed information resources, users take site-by-site searching. Quality of search results varies greatly depending on quality of the search query from too limited set of results to a too large number of irrelevant results. For certain cases specifying a couple of keywords can be enough, if they are really specific and no ambiguity is possible. Currently, electronic search is based mainly on matching keywords specified by users with sought information web pages that contain those keywords. Ambiguity of most word-combinations and phrases, which are used for searching web resources, and poor linguistic features of available web-content indexing and matching mechanisms severely affect the results of most internet searchers.

Essentially, most Industrie 4.0 experts agree that a number of norms and standards already exist. Use of ontologies can provides the following benefits:

- Share the knowledge domain that can be communicated between agents and application systems.

- Explicit conceptualization that describes the semantics of the data.

In our work we analyzed the relationship between both thecniques ontologies and expert systems. We have proposed a method to efficiently search the target information on a digital repository network with multiple independent information sources. The use of AI and ontologies as a knowledge representation formalism offers many advantages in information retrieval. This scheme is based on the principle that knowledge items are abstracted to a characterization by metadata description, which is used for further processing. This characterization is based on an ontology that allows sharing the relevant information domains sources. This motivates researchers to look for intelligent information retrieval approach and ontologies that search and/or filter information automatically based on some higher level of understanding what is required. We make an effort in this direction by investigating techniques that attempt to utilize ontologies to improve effectiveness in information retrieval.

V. Implementation Intelligent Agents

Nowadays there are many platforms and tools available for the retrieval information and data. Although these tools are powerful in locating matching terms and phrases, they are considered passive systems. Intelligent Agents (IAs) may prove to be the needed instrument in transforming these passive search and retrieval systems into active, personal user assistants. In this sense, IAs are currently used to improve the search and knowledge retrieval from online databases and repositories. Software agents function in a particular environment, i.e., an agent platform, which is often populated by other agents and processes. While there are obvious similarities, there are also significant differences between agents and objects. The first is in the degree to which agents and objects are autonomous.

A model uses multiple agents, which deliver personalized search engine results. An IA is a data-processing entity, which carries out in an autonomous way tasks delegated by a user, but also a part of software, which can operate on behalf of another entity. In our context, intelligent software agents may be provided with a user-friendly interface, which is used to acquire user specifications of industry domain. In the context of this research, however, the tasks that we are primarily concerned with include reading, filtering and sorting, and maintaining information.

In the industry environment, IAs can be used to recommend actions, or distribute searches of the users among available multi-agents. The IA platform hosts several IAs, each of them having local knowledge and which may move autonomously in form of mobile intelligence to other agent platforms. An intelligent software agent has characteristics like mobility, ability to interact and to cooperate, learn and even reason, based on certain knowledge representations. These skills can be used for personalization or information filtering, motivating the usage of intelligent software agents in the context of educational systems to improve the knowledge retrieval. Each IA contains a list of knowledge storage registries to find additional content, and a list of other known IA platforms, which may belong to other institution. IAs can update their lists by communicating with other agents using a predefined communication protocol.

The agent knowledge acquisition can happen through experience problem solving, and inductive/deductive reasoning. In our proposal the IA intelligence consists of two components: semantic intelligence and rational intelligence. These two parts have different purpose and characteristics (Figure 2).

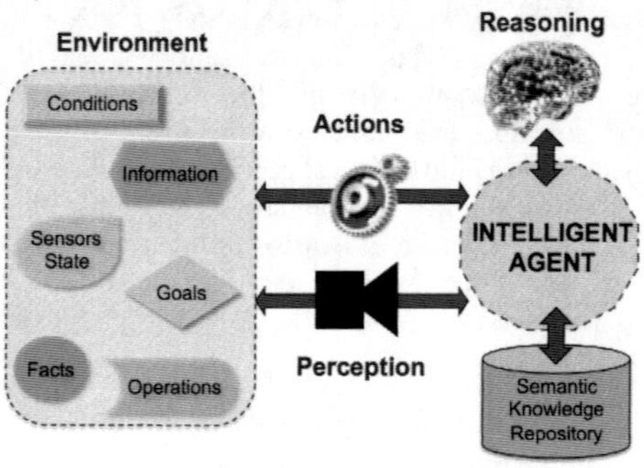

Figure 2. Intelligent Agent components

Rational intelligence depends on insight, which is the ability to detect, establish, forecast, and modulate relationships between problems and solutions. A high rational intelligence degree is usually not enough to produce proper behaviors and efficient results in the search engine. An engine with a high rational intelligence also needs to have a high semantic intelligence to thrive. Semantic intelligence improves productivity and effectiveness in making meaning connections. Semantic intelligence links knowledge through conceptual constructs (ontologies) connecting pieces of knowledge critical to achieve the integration of the data meaning. Thus, semantic reflects the knowledge in a general work domain, but rational intelligence decides how wisely these abilities are engaged, directed, and applied.

A. *Ontology Development*

Interoperability is the ability of two or more systems or components to exchange data and uses of information. Semantic interoperability is achieved when the interacting system attributes the same meaning to an exchanged piece of data, ensuring consistency of the data across systems regardless of individual data format. The semantics can be explicitly defined using a shared vocabulary as specified in an ontology. Semantic interoperability can be applied to all parts of an IoT system, i.e., on IoT platforms in the cloud, but also reaching to edge components and IoT devices. An important area to study IAs communication, collaborative, problem solving, and interaction in industry environments are the IA. These objects must have work area knowledge to solve domain-specific problems. In industry domain semantic interpretation of the information plays an important role in knowledge communication and transferring between the plant sensors and the control center. Considering the similarities and divergences in the different knowledge representation kinds we have chosen ontology. Ontology is a formal and explicit specification of shared conceptualization of a domain of interest. IAs must have common shareable ontology to share knowledge with each other and this common sharable ontology must be represented in a standard format so that all software agents can understand and thus communicate with.

Ontology is the knowledge structure, which identifies the concepts, property of concept, resources, and relationships among them to enable share and reuse of knowledge that are needed to acquire knowledge in the specific search domain. The ontology index comprises a plurality of relationships between the plurality of terms and sub-category terms of the ontology and a plurality of documents residing on the network. One or more search results that describe the one or more documents are presented to the user. The one or more documents contain the one or more search terms, or one of plurality of sub-category terms of the one or more search terms. The search request comprises one or more search terms of ontology. The ontology includes a plurality of terms.

Ontology models can be used to relate the physical world, to the real world, in the line-of-business and decision makers. The objective of our system is to improve the modeling of a semantic coherence for allowing the interoperability of different modules of environments dedicated to the industrial area. We have proposed to use ontology together with Case-Based Reasoning (CBR) in the acquisition of an expert knowledge in the specific domain. We need a vocabulary of concepts, resources and services for our information system described in the scenario, which requires definition about the relationships between objects of discourse and their attributes. The primary information managed in the domain is metadata about industrial resources, such as guides, digital services, alarms, and information. ReasInd project contains a collection of codes, visualization tools, computing resources, and data sets distributed across the grids for, which we have developed a well-defined ontology using Resource Description Framework (RDF) language [21] (Figure 3).

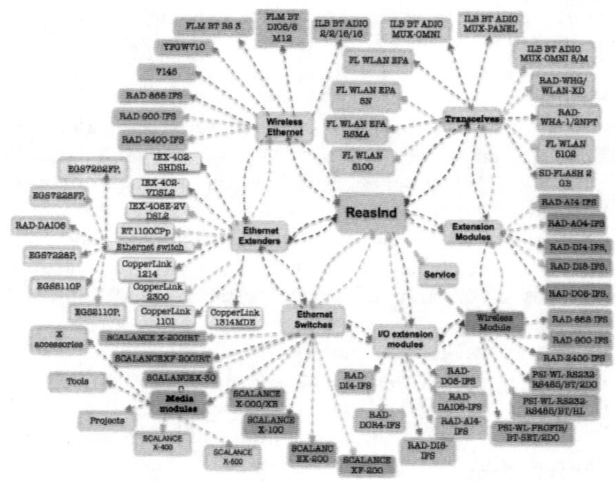

Figure 3. Class hierarchy for the ReasInd ontology

The total set of entities in our semantic model comprises the taxonomy of classes we use in our model to represent the real world. Together these ideas are represented by ontology. This provides the semantic makeup of the information model. The vocabulary of the semantic model provides the basis on which user-defined model queries are formed. Our ontology can be regarded as quaternion ReasInd:={caller, resources, properties, relation}, where caller represents the user kinds, resources cover different information sources like electronic services, web pages, databases, and guides. Also, properties contain all the characteristics of the services and resources and a set of relationships intended primarily for standardization across ontologies. We integrated three essential sources to the system: electronic resources, a catalogue of documents, and personal database.

We choose Protégé as our ontology editor, which supports knowledge acquisition and knowledge base development. It is a powerful development and knowledge-modeling tool with an open architecture [22]. Protégé uses OWL and RDF as ontology language to establish semantic relations [23]. For the construction of the ontology of our system, firstly we determine the domain and scope of the ontology: electronic services, web pages, DD.BB, and guides. Also it is also necessary to adapt the ontology to the user kinds needs. Second, we enumerate important terms in the ontology. It is useful to write down a list of all terms we would like either to make statements about or to explain to a user. Then we define the classes and the class hierarchy. Based on RDF Schema we describe the relations between classes, currently implemented 10 classes and about 175 properties. The ontology and its sub-classes are established according to the taxonomies profile. As mentioned in previous sections, relations among ontologies can be composed as a form of declarative rules, which can be further handled in inference engines.

The last step is to provide a conversational CBR system to retrieve the requested metadata satisfying a user query. We need to add enough initial instances and item instances to the knowledge base. Thirteen thousand cases were collected for user profiles and their different resources and services. This is sufficient for our proof-of-concept demonstration, but would not be sufficiently efficient to access large resource sets. Each case contains a set of attributes concerning both metadata and knowledge. However, our prototype is currently being extended to enable efficient retrieval directly from a database, which will enable its use for large-scale sets of resources.

VI. SYSTEM ACHITECTURE AND KEY ELEMENTS

The proposed architecture is based on our approach to share information in an efficient way by means of metadata characterizations and domain ontology inclusion. The system works by comparing items that can be retrieved across heterogeneous repositories and capturing a semantic view of the world independent of data representation. It implies to use ontology as vocabulary to define complex, multi-relational case structures to support the CBR processes [24]. The goal is achieved from a search perspective, with possible intelligent infrastructures to construct decentralized industrial repositories where no global schema exists. This goal implies the application of CBR technique.

In order to support the semantic shared knowledge in industrial repositories, a prototype CBR and ontology-based techniques have been development. The architecture of our system is shown in Figure 4, which mainly includes four elements: the acquire engine, ontology, knowledge base, and graphical user interface.

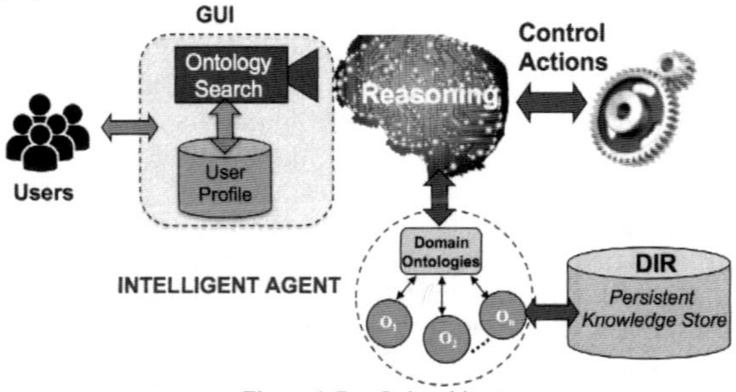

Figure 4. ReasInd architecture

A. The Acquire Engine - Case Based Reasoning

Our architecture itself is separated into three layers: DD.BB capable of storing, managing and controlling the extensive sets of knowledge; the CBR layer for indexing the knowledge for efficient retrieval and retain knowledge set; and GUI to provide low-latency functionality and access to recent data. CBR is a problem-solving architecture that solves a new problem, by remembering a previous similar situation and by reusing knowledge of that state. In the CBR application, problems are described by metadata concerning desired characteristics of an industry resource, and the solution to the question is a pointer to a resource described by metadata. A new difficulty is solved by retrieving one or more previously experienced cases, reusing the case, revising, and retaining. When a user introduces a description request to the system the reasoning cycle may be described by following processes (Figure 5).

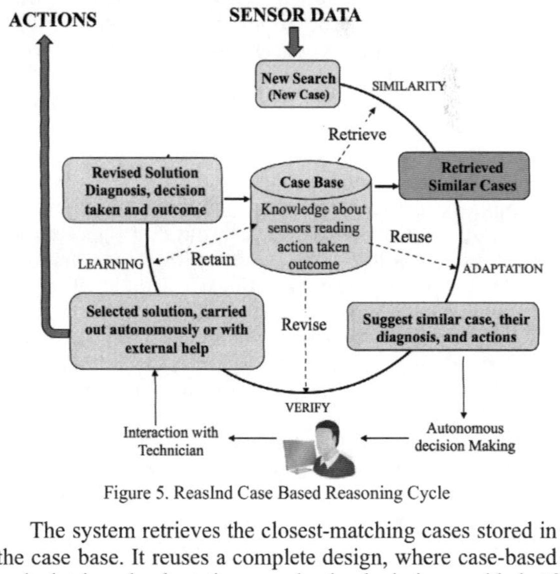

Figure 5. ReasInd Case Based Reasoning Cycle

The system retrieves the closest-matching cases stored in the case base. It reuses a complete design, where case-based and slot-based adaptation can be hooked, is provided. If appropriate, the validated solution is added to the case for use in future problem solving. It then checks out the proposed solution if necessary. Since the proposed result could be inadequate, this process can correct the first proposed solution. The system retains the new solution as a part of a new case. This process enables CBR to learn and create a new solution. The solution is validated through feedback from the user or the environment.

Implementing a CBR application from scratch remains a time-consuming software engineering process and requires a lot of specific experience beyond pure programming skills. This involves a number of steps, such as: collecting case and background knowledge, modeling a suitable case representation, defining an accurate similarity measure, implementing retrieval functionality and implementing user interfaces. In this work, we have chosen framework jColibri to develop the intelligent search.

JColibri is a java-based configuration that supports the development of knowledge intensive CBR applications and helps in the integration of ontology in them [25]. This way the same methods can operate over different types of information repositories. The Open Source JColibri system provides a framework for building CBR systems based on state-of-the-art software engineering techniques. JColibri is an open source framework, which affords the opportunity to connect easily by ontology in the CBR application to use it for case representation and content-based reasoning methods to assess the similarity between them. Nevertheless, at the same time, it ensures enough flexibility to enable expert users to implement advanced CBR applications.

B. Knowledgebase

The understanding provided through semantic models is critical to being able to properly drive the correct insights from the monitored instrumentation, which ultimately can lead to optimizing business processes or, in this case, industry services. As a result, semantic models can greatly enhance the usefulness of the information obtained through operations integration solutions. In the physical world a control point such a valve or temperature sensor is known by its identifier in a particular control system, possibly through a tag name like 103-AA12.

CBR case data could be considered as a portion of the knowledge, i.e., metadata about resources. The metadata descriptions of the resources and objects (cases) are abstracted from the details of their physical representation and are stored in the case base. Every case contains both a description of the problem and the associated solution. The information model provides the ability to abstract different kinds of data and provides an understanding of how the data elements relate. A key value of the semantic model then is to provide access to information in context of the real world in a consistent way.

Semantic models allow users to ask questions about what is happening in a modeled system in a more natural way. As an example, an oil production enterprise might consist of five geographic regions, with each region containing three to five drilling platforms, and each drilling platform monitored by several control systems, each having a different purpose. One of those control systems might monitor the temperature of extracted oil, while another might monitor vibration on a pump. A semantic model will allow a user to ask a question like, "What is the temperature of the oil being extracted on Platform 5?", without having to understand details such as, which specific control system monitors that information or, which physical sensor is reporting the oil temperature on that platform. Within a semantic model implementation, this information is identified using "triples" of the form "subject-predicate-object"; for example:

Tank1 <has temperature> Sensor 7
Tank 1 <is part of> Platform 4
Platform 4 <is part of> Plant1

These triples, taken together, make up the ontology for Plant1 and can be stored in the model server. This information, then, can be easily traversed using the model query language more easily than the case without a semantic model to answer questions such as "What is the temperature of tank 1 on Platform 4".

C. Evaluating a Set of Maching Cases

The inference engine contains the CBR component that automatically searches for similar queries-answer pairs based on the knowledge that the system extracted from the questions text. The retrieval process identifies the features of the case with the most similar query. It treats the RDF query schema and the RDF query instance as a tree then tries to match all possible interpreting paths of a query instance with annotated pictures and finally ranks the similarity match and finds the best answer. Based on the proposed representation model, we have developed a retrieval scheme for the intelligent retrieval system. Given a new case and a large precedents database, we develop the following scheme to identify those relevant precedents step by step. When a new case arises, users always want to find the factually relevant precedents that are similar in all or most representation elements. However, it is impossible to find an identical precedent with the new case due to the factual diversity of actual cases. In that case, those precedents sharing one or more representation elements with the new case are desired as they are potentially useful for making legal arguments [26].

The use of structured representations of cases requires approaches for similarity assessment that allows a comparison of two differently structured objects, in particular, objects belonging to different object classes. Retrieval strategy used in our system is cosine approach. Cosine similarity is a measure of similarity between two vectors by measuring the cosine of the angle between them [27]. The system relies on cosine similarity distance metrics when computing distance between symbolic vectors representing the retrieved cases. First, let us take an instance and break it down into features, in the simple case features can be just important attributes. Then we count the times a particular word appears in the document. What we end up with is a term vector or vector of terms and frequencies:

$$a_j = (a_{1,j}, a_{2,j}, \ldots, a_{t,j})$$
$$x = (x_1, x_2, \ldots, x_t)$$

$$similarity = Cos(\theta) = \frac{a_j \cdot x}{\|a_j\|\|x\|} = \frac{\sum_{i=1}^{n} a_{ij} \cdot x_i}{\sqrt{\sum_{i=1}^{n} (a_i)^2} \cdot \sqrt{\sum_{i=1}^{n} (x_i)^2}}$$

The attributes are used as a vector to find the normalized dot product of the two cases. By determining the cosine similarity, the system is effectively to find cosine of the angle between the two objects (Figure 6).

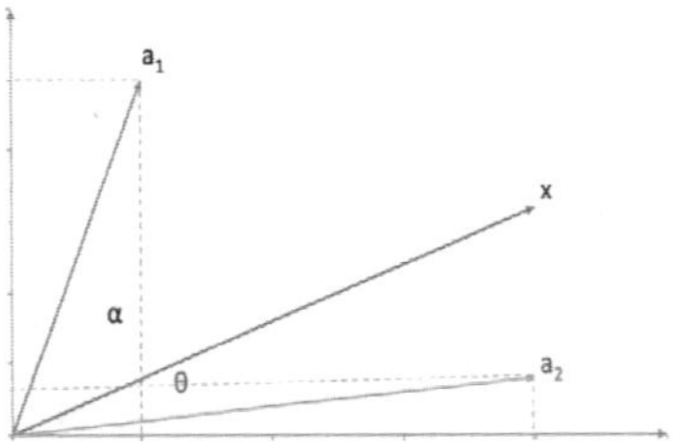

Figure 6. Similarity between documents

We can use the cosine similarity between the query vector and a document vector as a measure of the score of the document for that query. The resulting scores can then be used to select the top-scoring documents for a query. The result of cosine function is equal to 1 when the angle is 0, and it is less than 1 when the angle is of any other value. Calculating the cosine of the angle between two vectors thus determines whether two vectors are pointing in roughly the same direction. For cosine similarities resulting in a value of 0, the documents do not share any attributes because the angle between the objects is 90 degrees.

D. graphical user interface.

ReasInd is a platform, which is an intermediate link between users and search engine. Keeping in mind that our final goal is to reformulate requests in the ontology to queries in another with least loss of semantics. We come to a process for addressing complex relations between ontologies. By using ReasInd, the user can tune the query in accordance with his needs, excluding answers from an inappropriate domain and add semantically similar results. Advanced conversational user interface interacts with the users to solve a query, defined as the set of questions selected and answered by the user during the conversation. The real way to get individualized interaction between a user and ReasInd is to present the user with a variety of options and to let the user choose what is of interest at that specific time. In our system, the user interacts with the system to fill in the gaps to retrieve the right cases (Figure 7).

A transformation algorithm was implemented in the research prototype as the combined capability of the query transformation agent and the ontology agent of the intelligent multi-agent information retrieval mediator. The system has different users profiles to help to user to build a particular environment, which contains his interest search areas in the industry repositories domain: Plan Managers, Assistants, Operators, and Engineers. In this intelligence profile setting, people are surrounded by intelligent interfaces merged, thus creating a computing-capable environment with intelligent communication and processing available to the user by means of a simple, natural, and effortless human-system interaction. If the information space is designed well, then this choice is easy, and the user achieves optimal information through the use of natural intelligence that is, the choices are easy to understand so that users know what they will see if they click a link, and what they annul by not following other links.

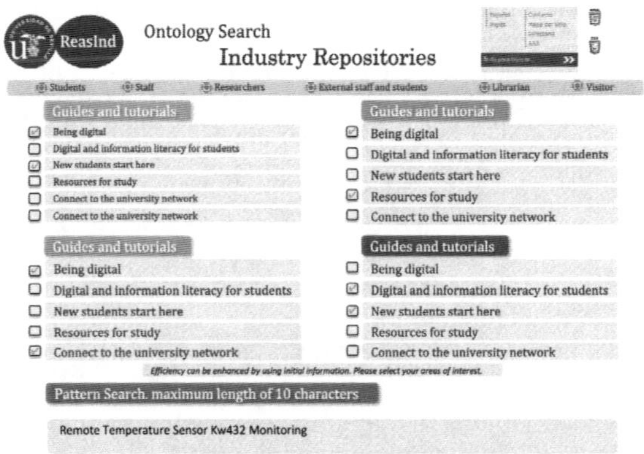

Figure 7. Graphical User interface

Profile agents assist the technicians with the search, according to the specifications they made. The search parameters in a profile, the start of a search, or the access to the list of retrieved knowledge can be controlled by invoking appropriate search operations, which extract metadata from plants resources. Ideally, profile agents learn from their experiments, communicate and cooperate with other agents, around in DIRs.

VII. Experimental Evaluation

As the private networks have grown from small networks into a large global infrastructure, the need to manage the huge number of hardware and software components within these networks more systematically has grown more important as well. In order to validate our approach, we have developed an intelligent control architecture in an industrial domain, specifically in an electric power system.

This system integrates the management knowledge into the network resources specifications. We study an example of alarm detection and intelligent troubleshooting. We have used a network that belongs to a company in the electrical sector Sevillana-Endesa's (SE) a Spanish power utility. ReasInd is used to optimize the operation of hundreds of connected sensors currently installed. The Spanish power grid company has a network using wireless on the regional high-tension power grid. These low-cost wireless sensors and accompanying analytics can dramatically improve plant performance, increase safety, and pay for themselves within months. The use of integrating knowledge in agents can help the system administrator in using the maximum capabilities of the intelligent network management platform without having to use another specification language to customize the application. To most companies, communications spending is an obscure recurring cost composed of complex bills, vendors, and services that can represent as much as 4% of their total revenue [28]. If we add to this an environment of ever-changing technology and typical business requirements such as mergers, multiple sites, and different geographic locations, the end result is a highly technical function with financial impacts that can easily be misunderstood and over-invested. It is necessary to analyze the entire telecommunications environment for an efficient management of the network resources.

We have used the Supervisory Control And Data Acquisition (SCADA) system due to the management limitations of network communication equipment (Figure 8).

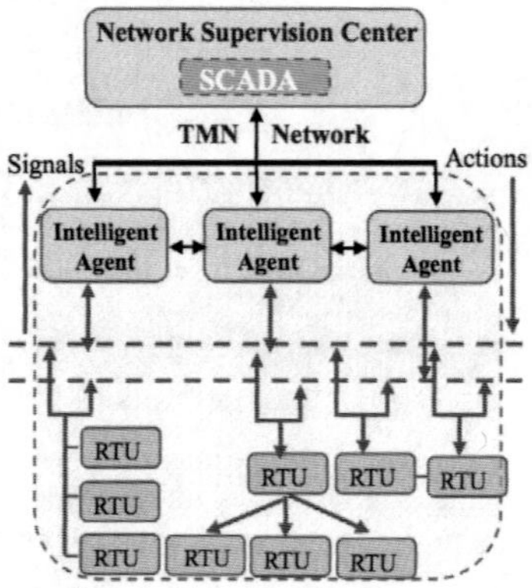

Figure 8. Elements of the prototype

SCADA consists of the following subsystems:

- Remote Terminal Units (RTUs) connecting to sensors in the process, converting sensor signals to digital data and sending digital data to the supervisory system.
- Communication infrastructure connecting the supervisory system to the RTUs.
- A supervisory computer system, acquiring data on the process and sending commands control to the process.

ReasInd monitors in real time, the network's main parameters, making use of the information supplied by the SCADA, placed on the main company building, and the RTUs that are installed at different stations. SCADA systems are configured around standard base functions like data acquisition, monitoring and event processing, data storage archiving, and analysis. The fundamental role of an RTU is the acquisition of various types of data from the power process, the accumulation, packaging, and conversion of data in a form that can be communicated back to the master, the interpretation and outputting of commands received from the master, and the performance of local filtering, calculation and processes to allow specific functions to be performed locally. The supervision below and RTU include all network devices and substation and feeder levels like circuit breakers, reclosers, autosectionalizers, the local automation distributed at these devices, and the communications infrastructure.

ReasInd allows the operator to search information, alarms, or digital and analogical parameters of measure, registered on each RTU. Starting from the supplied information, the operator is able to undertake actions in order to solve the failures that could appear or to send a technician to repair the equipment of the station. The system has the capability of selecting an agent, which is best suited for satisfying the client's requirement, without the client being aware of the details about the agent. Collaborative agents are useful, especially when a task involves several systems on the network.

VIII. EVALUATION AND CORROBORATIONS

Experiments have been carried out in order to evaluate the effectiveness of run-time ontology mapping. The main goal has been to check if the mechanism of query formulation, assisted by an agent, gives a suitable tool for augmenting the number of significant cases, extracted from DIRs, to be stored in the CBR. For our experiments, we considered 100 users with different profiles. So that we could establish a context for the users, they were asked to at least start their essay before issuing any queries to the system. They were also asked to look through all the results returned by the system before clicking on any result. In each experiment, we report the average rank of the user-clicked result for our baseline system, another search engine, and for our system ReasInd [29]. Then we calculated the rank for each retrieval document by combining the various values and comparing the total number of extracted documents and documents consulted by the user (Figure 9).

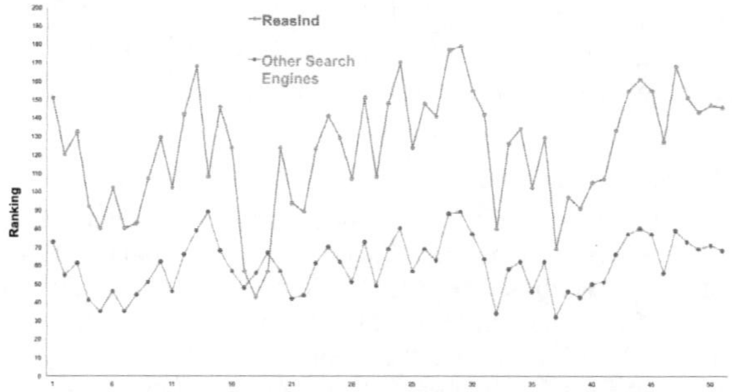

Figure 9. Performance ReasInd & traditional ES

In our study domain, we can observe that the best final ranking was obtained for our prototype and an interesting improvement over the performance of others search engines. Our system performs satisfactorily with about a 98.5 % rate of success in real cases.

During the experimentation, heuristics and measures that are commonly adopted in information retrieval have been used. Statistical analysis has been done to determine the important values in the results. While the users were performing these searches, an application was continuing to run in the background on the server, and capturing the content of queries typed and the results of the searches. We will discuss the issue of response time for five agents associated with transceiver resources. We can establish that our prototype improves the answer time and the average of the traditional search engine. The results for ReasInd are

25.4 % better than the time to execute searches in the traditional search engines.

IX. CONCLUSION AND FUTURE WORKS

Semantic models based on industry standards take that one step further, especially in intelligent techniques application. Semantic models play a key role in the evolving solution architectures that support the business goal of obtaining a complete view of "what is happening" within operations and then deriving business insights from that view. In this paper, we provide different possibilities, which semantic web opens for industry. One important objective is to study appropriate industrial cases, collect arguments, launch industrial projects and develop prototypes for the industrial companies that believe in the benefits of the Semantic Web.

We investigated how the semantic technologies can be used to provide additional semantics from existing resources in industrial repositories. This study addresses the main aspects of a semantic and intelligent information retrieval system architecture trying to answer the requirements of the next-generation semantic search engine. For this purpose, we presented ReasInd, a system based on ontology and AI architecture for knowledge management in industrial repositories. This scheme is based on the principle of the knowledge items that are abstracted to a characterization by metadata description, which is used for further processing. We have proposed to use ontology together with CBR in the acquisition of an expert knowledge in the specific industry domain. The study analyses the implementation results and evaluates the viability of our approaches in enabling search in intelligent-based digital repositories.

We conclude by pointing out an important aspect of the obtained integration: improving representation by incorporating more metadata from within the information and intelligent techniques into the retrieval process enhances the effectiveness of the knowledge retrieval.

Industrie 4.0 will play a crucial role in shaping the future in the next five to ten years in the world. Various strategy and working groups are working on the Industrie 4.0 extension of existing norms and standards. Future work will be concerned with the design of distributed and self-managed industry services, which are able to automatically discover, compose, and integrate heterogeneous components, able to manage heterogeneous knowledge and intelligence sources, able to create, deploy and exploit linked data, and able to browse and filter information based on semantic similarity and closeness.

REFERENCES

[1] A. Martín, M. Burbano, I. Monedero, J. Luque, and C. León. "Semantic Reasoning Method to Troubleshoot in the Industrial Domain," The Fifth International Conference on Intelligent Systems and Applications, INTELLI, InfoWare, November 2016, pp. 89-94.

[2] G. M. West, S. D. J. McArthur, and D. Towle, "Industrial implementation of intelligent system techniques for nuclear power plant condition monitoring," Expert Systems with Applications, Volume 39, Issue 8, pp. 7432-7440, 15 June 2012.

[3] S. Guo, C. Lee, and C. Hsu, "An intelligent image agent based on soft-computing techniques for color image processing," Expert Systems with Applications, Volume 28, Issue 3, pp. 483-494, April 2005.

[4] Y. Huang, J. Chen, Y. Kuo, and Y. Jeng, "An intelligent human-expert forum system based on fuzzy information retrieval technique," Expert Systems with Applications, Volume 34, Issue 1, pp. 446-458, January 2008.

[5] S. Yang and Y. Chang, "An active and intelligent network management system with ontology-based and multi-agent techniques," Expert Systems with Applications, Volume 38, Issue 8, pp. 10320-10342, August 2011.

[6] A. Gladun, J. Rogushina, F. Garcia-Sanchez, R. Martínez-Béjar, and J. Fernández-Breis, "An application of intelligent techniques and semantic web technologies in e-learning environments," Expert Systems with Applications, Volume 36, Issue 2, Part 1, 1922-1931, March 2009.

[7] S. Zhang, F. Boukamp, and J. Teizer, "Ontology-based semantic modeling of construction safety knowledge: Towards automated safety planning for job hazard analysis (JHA)," Automation in Construction, Volume 52, pp. 29-41, April 2015.

[8] F. Bertola and V. Patti, "Ontology-based affective models to organize artworks in the social semantic web, Information Processing & Management," Volume 52, Issue 1, Pp. 139-162, January 2016.

[9] H. Liu, M. Lu, and M. Al-Hussein, "Ontology-based semantic approach for construction-oriented quantity take-off from BIM models in the light-frame building industry," Advanced Engineering Informatics, Volume 30, Issue 2, pp. 190-207, April 2016.

[10] S. Zhang and J. Lai, "Exploring information from the topology beneath the Gene Ontology terms to improve semantic similarity measures," Gene, Volume 586, Issue 1, pp. 148-157, 15 July 2016.

[11] W. Lu et al., "Selecting a semantic similarity measure for concepts in two different CAD model data ontologies," Advanced Engineering Informatics, Volume 30, Issue 3, pp. 449-466, August 2016.

[12] C. Lucas, M. A. Zia, M. R. A. Shirazi and A. Alishahi, "Development of a multi-agent information management system for Iran power industry. A case study," 2001 IEEE Porto Power Tech Proceedings (Cat. No.01EX502), Porto, 2001, pp. 6.

[13] M. Mehrpoor, A. Gjærde, and O. I. Sivertsen, "Intelligent services: A semantic recommender system for knowledge representation in industry," 2014 International Conference on Engineering, Technology and Innovation (ICE), Bergamo.

[14] H. Chen, B. Liu, and W. He, "PISGrid: A Semantic Grid Infrastructure of Establishing Dynamic Virtual Organizations According to Requirement for Press Industry," 2006 IEEE/WIC/ACM International Conference on Web Intelligence and Intelligent Agent Technology Workshops, Hong Kong, 2006, pp. 287-290.

[15] H. Cheng, P. Zeng, L. Xue, Z. Shi, P. Wang, and H. Yu, "Manufacturing Ontology Development Based on Industrie 4.0 Demonstration Production Line," 2016 Third International Conference on Trustworthy Systems and their Applications (TSA), Wuhan, China, 2016, pp. 42-47.

[16] A. Badii, C. Lallah, M. Zhu, and M. Crouch., "Semi-automatic knowledge extraction, representation and context-sensitive intelligent retrieval of video content using collateral context modelling with scalable ontological networks," Signal Processing: Image Communication, Volume 24, Issue 9, pp. 759-773, 2009.

[17] M. Fernandez. et. Al., [online]. "Semantically enhanced Information Retrieval: An ontology-based approach, Web Semantics: Science, Services and Agents on the World Wide Web," In Press, Corrected Proof, Available online 01 July 2014.

[18] EIF. European Interoperability Framework Version 2. Retrieved from http://ec.europa.eu/isa/strategy/doc/annex_ii_eif_en.pdf, February, 2017.

[19] MAP. Aplicaciones utilizadas para el ejercicio de potestades. Criterios de Seguridad, Normalización y Conservación. Ministerio de

Administraciones Públicas. Retrieved from http://www.csi.map.es/csi/criterios/index.html, March 2017.

[20] SEC. Commission Staff Workking Paper: linking up Europe, the importance of interoperability for egovernment services, [Online]. Available from: http://europa.eu.int/ISPO/ida/export/files/en/1523.pdf, July 2017.

[21] T. Segaran, "Programming Collective Intelligence: Building Smart Web 2.0 Applications," Published by O'Reilly Media, August 23rd 2007.

[22] PROTÉGÉ. "The Protégé Ontology Editor and Knowledge Acquisition System," [Online], Available from: http://protege.stanford.edu/, July 2017.

[23] W3C. "RDF Vocabulary Description Language 1.0: RDF Schema," [Online]. Available from: http://www.w3.org/TR/rdf-schema/, July 2017.

[24] J. Toussaint and Cheng, K., "Web-based CBR (case-based reasoning) as a tool with the application to tooling selection," International Journal of Advanced Manufacturing Technology, Volume 29, Issue 1, pp 24–34, 2006.

[25] GAIA - Group for Artificial Intelligence Applications. jCOLIBRI project, "Distribution of the development environment," [Online]. Available from: http://gaia.fdi.ucm.es/research/colibri/jcolibri/, July 2017.

[26] H. Stuckenschmidt and F. V. Harmelen, "Ontology-based metadata generation from semi-structured information," K-CAP, pp. 163–170, ACM, 2011.

[27] G. Finnie and Z. Sun. "Similarity and metrics in case-based reasoning,". Int J Intelligent Systems 17 (3), pp. 273-287. 2002

[28] Global Communications Report - USC Annenberg, 2017.

[29] D. Amerland, "Google Semantic Search: Search Engine Optimization (SEO) Techniques That Get Your Company More Traffic, Increase Brand Impact and Amplify Your Online Presence," Que Publishing Kindle Edition, July, 2013. pp. 2013 – 229.

Object Sensing and Shape Detection Using Vibrissa Hair-like Sensors with Intrinsic Curvature

Carsten Behn*, Christoph Will*, Anton Sauter*, Tobias Preiß* and Joachim Steigenberger†

*Department of Mechanical Engineering
†Institute of Mathematics
Technische Universität Ilmenau, Ilmenau, Germany, 98693
Email: {carsten.behn, christoph.will, anton.sauter, tobias.preiss, j.steigenberger}@tu-ilmenau.de

Abstract—**Numerous mammals possess in addition to normal body hairs tactile hairs, also known as vibrissae or whiskers, to explore their environment. Biological observations have shown that rodents use their tactile hairs in the snout region (mystacial vibrissae) to estimate obstacle contact and obstacle shape within a few contacts of the tactile hair. Despite different morphology of animal vibrissae (e.g., cylindrically or conically shaped, pre-curved, multi-layer structure), these biological tactile hairs are modeled in a mechanical way to develop and analyze models concerning their bending behavior with a glance to get hints for a technical implementation as a technical sensor. We focus on an analytical description, numerical simulations and experimental verifications of an object scanning process to to achieve a better understanding of this sense. We investigate the bending behavior of cylindrically shaped rods with an intrinsic curvature, which are one-sided clamped and interact with a rigid obstacle in the plane. Hence, the sensing element vibrissa is under the load of an external contact force during object scanning and is frequently modeled as an Euler-Bernoulli bending rod allowing for large deflections. Most of the literature is limited to the research on cylindrical & straight, or tapered & straight rods. The (natural) intrinsic curved shape is rarely analyzed. Hence, the aim is to determine the obstacles contour by one quasi-static sweep along the obstacle and to figure out the dependence on the intrinsic curvature of the rod. The consideration of an intrinsic curvature makes the analytical treatment a bit harder and results in numerical solutions of the process. Nevertheless, at first, we focus on a constant intrinsic curvature and, then, present simulations and experiments using a variable one.**

Keywords–Vibrissa; intrinsic curvature; sensing; object scanning; contour reconstruction.

I. Introduction

In recent years, the design and development of vibrissae-inspired tactile sensors gain center stage in the focus of research. This paper contributes to these investigations of intelligent tactile sensors and extends the results of [1]. There is a great interest in tactile sensors, especially in the field of (autonomous) robotics, see e.g., [2]–[8], since these tactile sensors complement to and/or replace senses like vision, because they provide reliable information in a dark and noisy environment (e.g., seals detect freshet and turbulence of fish in muddy water [9]–[11]), and are cheaper in fabrication.

A. Motivation from Biology

In many technical developments, engineers often use biological systems as an inspiration. A tactile sensor system, which attracted attention in recent years, is the so-called *sinus hair*. This tactile sensory organ with incomparable abilities can be found on the body of mammals. Despite existing differences regarding musculature and localization, they are synonymously also known as *vibrissae* or *whiskers* [12]. Depending on their localization on the body they are used for several tasks like

- object recognition [13],
- object discrimination [10] [14], and
- perception of flow [10] [15], as well as
- for social behavior [16].

Sinus hairs differ from typical body hairs:

- they are thicker, longer and stiffer than body hairs [17],
- each sinus hair is supported/embedded in its own follicle-sinus complex (FSC), that is characterized by its exceptional arrangement of blood vessels, neural connections and muscles [18],
- they are made of dead material, i.e., the hair shaft itself has no receptors along its length [19], hence they are mainly used for the transmission for all tactile stimuli arising along the shaft, and
- they feature an intrinsic curvature, a conical shape, cylindrical cross-section and are made of different material with hollow parts (like a multi-layer system) [17] [20] [21].

As mentioned, rodents use their sinus hairs to acquire information about their surroundings. The movement and deformation of the vibrissa due to contacts to several objects can only be detected by mechanoreceptors in the FSC [2] [22]. Hence, the animal draws its conclusions about the environment only from these (measured) quantities at the base of the hair – the support reactions. We do not want to explain the transmission of mechanical stimuli during object contact to the mechanoreceptors in the follicle, rather we want to analyze the influence of the geometrical properties of a sinus hairs on these support reactions, which are used for object recognition and contour reconstruction.

B. Goal

In this paper, the investigations focus the influence of the *intrinsic curvature* to the bending behavior of a vibrissa due to an obstacle contact during object sensing. This intrinsic curvature is due to a kind of protection role: purely axial forces are prevented and, including the conical shape, the area of the tip of the vibrissa is limp. This results in a tangential contact to an object [20] [23]. We describe a quasi-static scanning process of obstacles: 1. analytical/numerical generation the observables in the support, which an animal solely relies on, 2. reconstruction of the scanned profile contour using only these observables, and 3. verification of the working principle by means of experiments. These steps were done in [8], [24] and [25] for cylindrical vibrissae. In [1], the influence of a *constant* intrinsic curvature was investigated, here, we extend these results to rods with a *variable* intrinsic curvature in this paper.

C. Arrangement

The paper is arranged as follows: We give a short overview on the related literature in Section II, which is quite rare and often starts up with some approximations of the problem. Section III is devoted to the governing equations describing an Euler-Bernoulli rod with intrinsic curvature under large deflections – nonlinear theory. In Section IV, we present the scanning process, which has to be divided into two phases: tip contact of the rod with the object, or tangential contact within the rod's length. For this, we set up two mechanical models to describe these scenarios – ordinary differential equations with boundary- or initial- condition. These equations are exemplarily solved in Section V – considering firstly a constant intrinsic curvature radius of the bending rod, and then a variable one. The results are performed to test the reconstruction algorithm to detect the obstacle's boundary. The effectiveness of the algorithm is then verified by experiments in Section VI using three different artificial vibrissae. Then, the paper closes in Section VII with a conclusion and an outlook on future work.

II. Some State of Art of Modeling Vibrissae with Intrinsic Curvature

From the biological point of view, there are a lot of works focussing on the determination of vibrissae parameters. Towal et al. [21] pointed out an important fact that the mostly vibrissae are curved in a plane. The deviation of the vibrissa from this plane (referred to the length) is less than 0.1%. In [21], [23] and [26]–[30], a vibrissa is described using a polynomial approximation of 2nd-, 3rd- and 5th-order, which is rather low. In contrast to this references, we present numerical results using one of order 10. In [23], it is stated that approximately 90% of rat vibrissae exhibit an intrinsic curvature $\kappa_0 \in (0.0065/mm, 0.074/mm)$, and in [28] that extremely curved vibrissa provide $\kappa_0 > 0.25/mm$. The authors of [17], [23], [28] publish the following dimensionless parameters

$$\frac{L}{d} \approx 30\,, \quad \frac{r_0}{d} \approx 90\,,$$

whereas L is the length, d is the base diameter, and r_0 is the intrinsic curvature radius of the vibrissa.

From the technical point of view, pre-curved vibrissae are rarely used in applications. In [23], [29], [30], experimental and theoretical investigations concerning the distance detection to a pole are presented, using a pre-curved artificial vibrissa, also incorporating the conical shape. The pros and cons of a positive (curvature forward, CF) and negative (CB) curved vibrissae are stated in [23] whereas the vibrissa is used for tactile sensing of a pole. The CF-scanning results in low axial forces, but higher sheer ones; CB the inverse results. Summarized, the pre-curvature influences mainly the support forces instead of the support moment.

III. Modeling

The deflection of a largely deformed rod with intrinsic curvature is described in using the so-called *Winkler-Bach-Theory*. A detailed derivation of the equations can be found in [32].

At first, we derive the equations of stress and deformation of the rod – using an infinitesimal small element of a rod with intrinsic curvature, presented in Figures 1–3, whereas we have the following relation between curvature κ and curvature radius r:

$$\kappa_0(s) = \frac{1}{r_0(s)} \tag{1}$$

$$\kappa(s) = \frac{1}{r(s)} \tag{2}$$

whereas the index "0" means undeformed state.

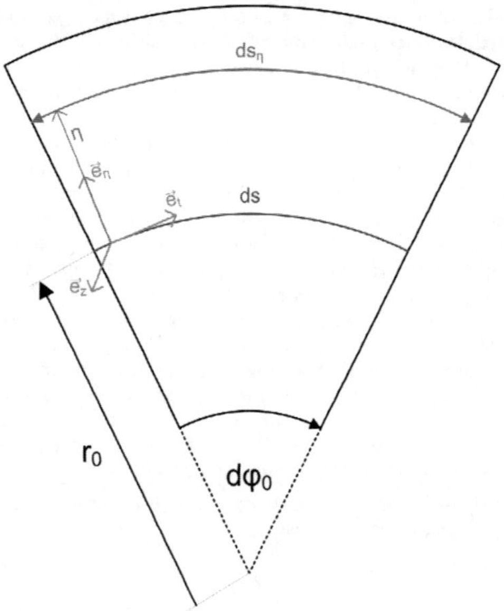

Figure 1. Initial state of no load.

$$d\varphi = d\varphi_0 + d\psi$$

The strain of the rod axis is

$$\varepsilon(s, \eta = 0) = \frac{du(s, \eta = 0)}{ds} \tag{3}$$

The length of a fiber in distance η to the rod axis is

$$ds_\eta(s, \eta) = (r_0(s) - \eta) \cdot d\varphi_0\,. \tag{4}$$

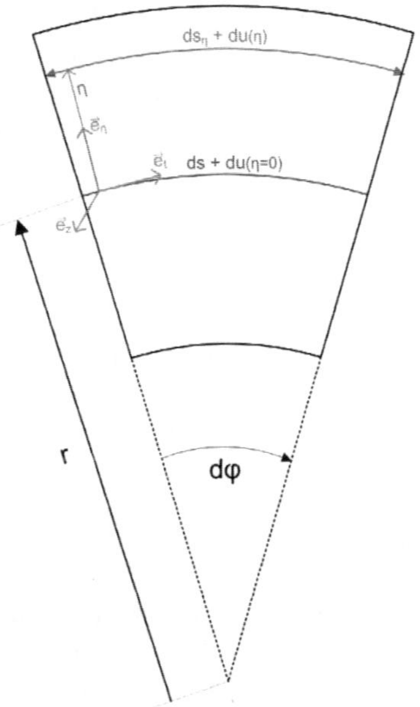

Figure 2. Deformed state of an infinitesimal rod element.

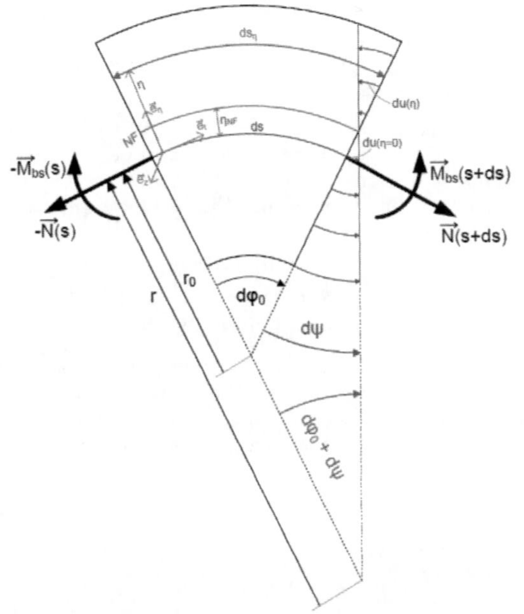

Figure 3. Rod element with stress resultants.

Hence, we get

$$\varepsilon(s,\eta) = \frac{du(s,\eta)}{ds_\eta(s,\eta)} = \frac{du(s,\eta=0) - \eta \cdot d\psi}{(r_0(s) - \eta) \cdot d\varphi_0} \tag{5}$$

$$= \frac{\varepsilon(s,\eta=0) \cdot r_0(s) \cdot d\varphi_0 - \eta \cdot d\psi}{(r_0(s) - \eta) \cdot d\varphi_0} \tag{6}$$

$$\rightarrow \varepsilon(s,\eta) = \varepsilon(s,\eta=0) + \left(\varepsilon(s,\eta=0) - \frac{d\psi}{d\varphi_0}\right)\frac{\eta}{r_0 - \eta} \tag{7}$$

To determine $\varepsilon(s,\eta=0)$ and $\dfrac{d\psi}{d\varphi_0}$ we introduce the stress resultants bending moment $\vec{M}_{bs}(s)$ and normal force $\vec{N}(s)$. Applying Hooke's law of elasticity (8)

$$\sigma(s,\eta) = E \cdot \varepsilon(s,\eta) \tag{8}$$

we get

$$N(s) = \int_A \sigma(s,\eta)\, dA = E \cdot \Bigg(\varepsilon(s,\eta=0) \cdot A + \left(\varepsilon(s,\eta=0) - \frac{d\psi}{d\varphi_0}\right) \cdot \int_A \frac{\eta}{r_0(s) - \eta}\, dA\Bigg) \tag{9}$$

$$M_{bs}(s) = -\int_A \sigma(s,\eta) \cdot \eta\, dA = -E \cdot \Bigg(\varepsilon(s,\eta=0) \cdot \underbrace{\int_A \eta\, dA}_{0} + \left(\varepsilon(s,\eta=0) - \frac{d\psi}{d\varphi_0}\right) \cdot \int_A \frac{\eta^2}{r_0(s) - \eta}\, dA\Bigg) \tag{10}$$

Introducing the following parameter, see [32],

$$\lambda(s) := \frac{1}{A} \int_A \frac{\eta}{r_0(s) - \eta}\, dA \tag{11}$$

yields:

$$\varepsilon(s,\eta=0) - \frac{d\psi}{d\varphi_0} = \frac{-M_{bs}(s)}{\lambda(s) \cdot r_0(s) \cdot E \cdot A} \tag{12}$$

$$\varepsilon(s,\eta=0) = \frac{1}{E \cdot A} \cdot \left(N(s) + \frac{M_{bs}(s)}{r_0(s)}\right) \tag{13}$$

Substituting (13) and (12) in (7) yields the equation of the stress:

$$\boxed{\sigma(s,\eta) = \frac{N(s)}{A} + \frac{M_{bs}(s)}{A\, r_0(s)} \cdot \left(1 - \frac{1}{\lambda(s)} \cdot \frac{\eta}{r_0(s) - \eta}\right)} \tag{14}$$

The determination of the equation of deformation is based on the consideration of the deformation of the rod axis ($\eta = 0$), having a glance to Figure 3:

$$ds + du(s,\eta=0) = r(s) \cdot (d\varphi_0 + d\psi) \tag{15}$$

Using

$$du(s,\eta=0) = ds \cdot \varepsilon(s,\eta=0) \quad \text{and} \quad ds = r_0(s) \cdot d\varphi_0$$

we get:

$$r_0(s) \cdot \Big(1 + \varepsilon(s,\eta=0)\Big) = r(s) \cdot \left(1 + \frac{d\psi}{d\varphi_0}\right) \tag{16}$$

Replacing $\frac{d\psi}{d\varphi_0}$ by (12) yields:

$$r_0(s) \cdot \Big(1 + \varepsilon(s,\eta=0)\Big) = r(s) \cdot \left(1 + \frac{M_{bs}(s)}{\lambda(s) \cdot r_0(s) \cdot E \cdot A} + \varepsilon(s,\eta=0)\right) \tag{17}$$

The arising formula for the curvature κ is:

$$\kappa(s) = \frac{1}{r(s)} = \frac{1}{r_0(s)} \cdot \left(1 + \frac{M_{bs}(s)}{\lambda(s) \cdot r_0(s) \cdot E \cdot A} \cdot \frac{1}{1 + \varepsilon(s, \eta = 0)}\right) \tag{18}$$

Now, replacing $\varepsilon(s, \eta = 0)$ by (13), there arises a formula for the curvature $\kappa(s)$ (after deformation) or the curvature radius $r(s)$, respectively:

$$\kappa(s) = \frac{1}{r(s)} = \frac{1}{r_0(s)} + \frac{M_{bs}(s)}{\lambda(s) r_0(s)^2 EA} \cdot \frac{1}{1 + \frac{1}{EA} \cdot \left(N(s) + \frac{M_{bs}(s)}{r_0(s)}\right)} \tag{19}$$

Having a glance to Figure 2 it is obvious:

$$ds\left(1 + \epsilon(s, \eta = 0)\right) = r \cdot d\varphi \tag{20}$$

$$\frac{d\varphi}{ds} = \frac{1}{r(s)}\left(1 + \epsilon(s, \eta = 0)\right) \tag{21}$$

Applying (18) we get:

$$\frac{d\varphi(s)}{ds} = \frac{1}{r_0(s)} \cdot \left(1 + \varepsilon(s, \eta = 0) + \frac{M_{bs}(s)}{\lambda(s) \cdot r_0(s) \cdot E \cdot A}\right)$$

Finally, using (13) there is the equation of deformation:

$$\boxed{\frac{d\varphi(s)}{ds} = \frac{1}{r_0(s)} \cdot \left(1 + \frac{N(s)}{EA} + \frac{M_{bs}(s)}{EAr_0(s)} \cdot \left(1 + \frac{1}{\lambda(s)}\right)\right)} \tag{22}$$

Considering the special case, that the radius of intrinsic curvature is much greater than the dimensions of the cross-section, then the influence of the normal force can be neglected [33]. Hence, the describing equations can be simplified to

$$\frac{d\varphi(s)}{ds} = \frac{1}{r_0(s)} + \frac{M_{bs}(s)}{E\, I_z}, \tag{23}$$

with second moment of area

$$I_z := \int_{(A)} \eta^2 dA,$$

and Young's modulus E, cross-section A, bending moment M_{bs}, and radius of pre-curvature r_0.

IV. Scanning Procedure

Here, we describe the scanning procedure of *strictly convex profile contours* using pre-curved technical vibrissae *in a plane*. This is done in two steps:

1. Because of analytical interest, we firstly generate the observables (support reactions) during the scanning process. Since our intension is from bionics, we simply model the support as a clamping (being aware that this does not match the reality). Hence, the support reactions are the clamping forces and moment $\vec{M}_{Az}$, $\vec{F}_{Ax}$, $\vec{F}_{Ay}$, which an animal solely relies on.
2. Then, we use these observables in an algorithm to reconstruct the profile contour.

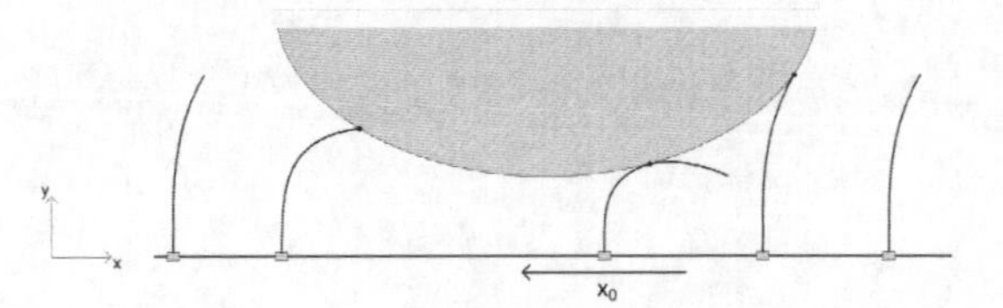

Figure 4. Scanning procedure using an artificial vibrissa; adapted from [8].

Figure 4 sketches the scanning process of a plane, strictly profile. For this scanning process, several assumptions are made:

- The technical vibrissa is moved from *right to the left* (negative x-direction), i.e., the base point is moved.
- The problem is handled *quasi-statically*, i.e., the vibrissa is moved incrementally (and presented in changes of the boundary conditions). Then, the elastically deformed vibrissa is determined.
- Since we do not want to deal with friction at the beginning, we assume an *ideal contact*, i.e., the contact force is *perpendicular* to the contact point tangent of the profile.

The scanned profile is given by a function $g : x \mapsto g(x)$, where $g \in C^1(\mathbb{R};\mathbb{R})$. Since the graph of g is convex by assumption, the graph can be parameterized by means of the slope angle α in the xy-plane. Then we have, [8]:

$$\begin{aligned} \frac{dg(x)}{dx} &= g'(x) = \tan(\alpha) \\ \longrightarrow x &= \xi(\alpha) := g'^{-1}(\tan(\alpha)) \\ y &= \eta(\alpha) := g(\xi(\alpha)) \end{aligned}$$

Therefore, each point of the profile contour is given by $(\xi(\alpha), \eta(\alpha))$, $\alpha \in (-\frac{\pi}{2}, \frac{\pi}{2})$. For generality, we introduce dimensionless variables, starting with the arc length s with $s = Ls^*$, $s^* \in [0, 1]$. Then, the basic units are:

$$[length] = \mathbf{L}, \quad [moment] = \frac{\mathbf{EI_z}}{\mathbf{L}}, \quad [force] = \frac{\mathbf{EI_z}}{\mathbf{L^2}}$$

Remark IV.1. *For the sake of brevity, we omit the asterisk "∗" from now on.*

A. Boundary-value Problem in Step 1

The system of differential equations (ODEs) describing the deformed pre-curved, technical vibrissa in a plane in dimensionless quantities is:

$$\left.\begin{aligned} \frac{dx(s)}{ds} &= \cos(\varphi(s)) \\ \frac{dy(s)}{ds} &= \sin(\varphi(s)) \\ \frac{d\varphi(s)}{ds} &= \frac{1}{r_{0L}(s)} + f\Big(\big(y(s) - \eta(\alpha)\big)\sin(\alpha) \\ &\qquad + \big(x(s) - \eta(\alpha)\big)\cos(\alpha)\Big) \end{aligned}\right\} \tag{24}$$

Observing Figures 4 and 5 gives the hint to distinguish two phases of contact between the vibrissa and the obstacle:

- *Phase A – tip contact:* We have still ODE-system (24) with the boundary conditions (BCs)

$$\begin{aligned} y(0) = 0\,, \quad \varphi(0) = \frac{\pi}{2}\,, \\ x(1) = \xi(\alpha)\,, \quad y(1) = \eta(\alpha) \end{aligned} \tag{25}$$

- *Phase B – tangential contact:* Only the BCs change:

$$\begin{aligned} & y(0) = 0\,, \quad \varphi(0) = \frac{\pi}{2}\,, \\ & x(s_1) = \xi(\alpha)\,, \quad y(s_1) = \eta(\alpha)\,, \quad \varphi(s_1) = \alpha \end{aligned} \tag{26}$$

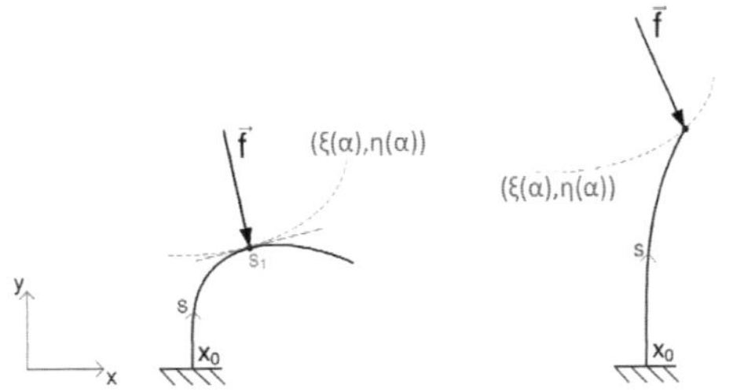

Figure 5. Contact of vibrissa and obstacle in *Phase A* (left) and in *Phase B* (right) during scanning process.

A direct inspection of the occurring problems (24)&(25) and (24)&(26) yield the choice of a shooting method to determine the parameters f and s_1, and finally with f the clamping reactions $\vec{M}_{Az}$, $\vec{F}_{Ax}$, $\vec{F}_{Ay}$.

B. Initial-value Problem in Step 2

Here, we use only the generated observables (measured in experiments) $\vec{M}_{Az}$, $\vec{F}_{Ax}$, $\vec{F}_{Ay}$ and known base of the vibrissa x_0 to reconstruct the scanned profile. Due to [31], we determine the bending moment, see Figure 6, to formulate the initial-value problem (IVP) in this step:

$$\left.\begin{aligned} \frac{dx(s)}{ds} &= \cos(\varphi(s)) \\ \frac{dy(s)}{ds} &= \sin(\varphi(s)) \\ \frac{d\varphi(s)}{ds} &= \frac{1}{r_{0L}(s)} - M_{Az} - F_{Ax}y(s) + F_{Ay}\big(x(s) - x_0\big) \end{aligned}\right\} \tag{27}$$

with initial conditions (ICs)

$$x(0) = x_0\,, \quad y(0) = 0\,, \quad \varphi(0) = \frac{\pi}{2} \tag{28}$$

Now, it is necessary – for each input $\{M_{Az}, F_{Ax}, F_{Ay}, x_0\}$ – to determine the contact point $(x(s_1), y(s_1))$ (note, that s_1 is known in step 1, but is not an observable). But, it is still unknown, in which phase we are. We only have

$$M_{bz}(s_1) = 0$$

In accordance to [8], we determine a decision criterion to distinguish both phase. The vibrissa is in Phase B, if and only

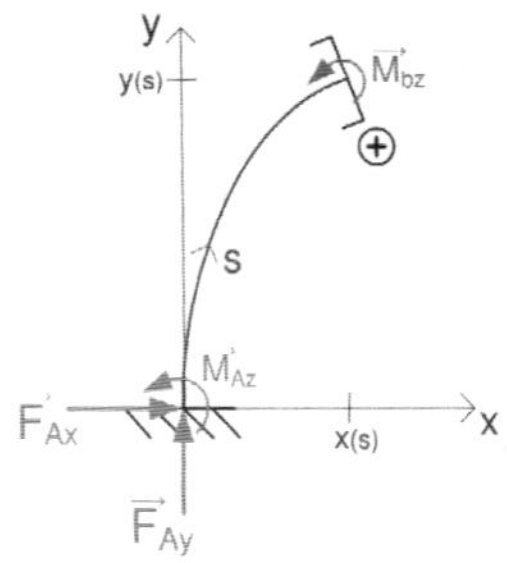

Figure 6. Applying method of sections to the vibrissa.

if it holds:

$$\boxed{M_{Az}^2 + \frac{2M_{Az}}{r_{0L}} - 2F_{Ay} = 0} \tag{29}$$

In comparison to the condition in [8], we get one new term $\frac{2M_{Az}}{r_{0L}}$. And, in a limiting case for $r_{0L} \longrightarrow \pm\infty$, condition (29) forms the condition in [8], which serves as a validation.

V. Simulations of Profile Scanning

Referring to [8], we consider a profile described by

$$g_1 \,:\, x \mapsto \frac{1}{2}x^2 + 0.3\,. \tag{30}$$

A. Scanning Using a Constant Intrinsic Curvature Radius

Here, we present numerical simulations of the described profile scanning algorithm (based of two steps). At first, we focus on a *constant* pre-curvature radius $r_{0L} \neq r_{0L}(s)$.

Exemplarily, the scanning process is performed for several values of r_{0L} and the results are presented in Figures 7–10.

Remark V.1. *Note, that the vibrissae in Phase B are only plotted to the contact point, just for clarity.*

One can clearly see, that the smaller the pre-curvature radius is no Phase A occurs, i.e., no tip contact, which might explain the protective role of the pre-curvature of vibrissae.

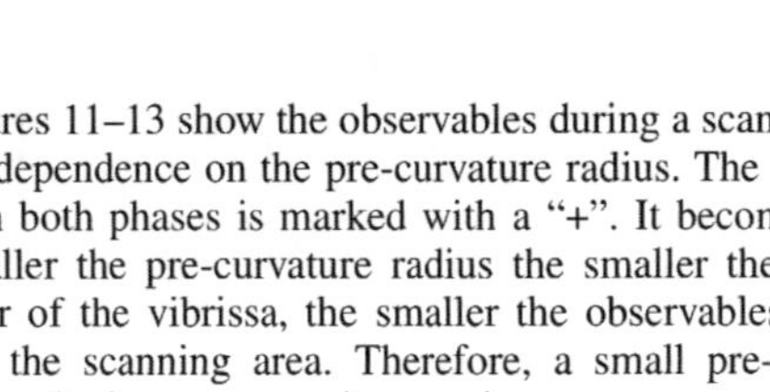

Figure 7. Profile scanning using a pre-curved vibrissa with $r_{0L} = -1000$: in blue *Phase A*, in red *Phase B*.

Figures 11–13 show the observables during a scanning process in dependence on the pre-curvature radius. The transition between both phases is marked with a "+". It becomes clear: the smaller the pre-curvature radius the smaller the bending behavior of the vibrissa, the smaller the observables, but the smaller the scanning area. Therefore, a small pre-curvature radius results in poor scanning results.

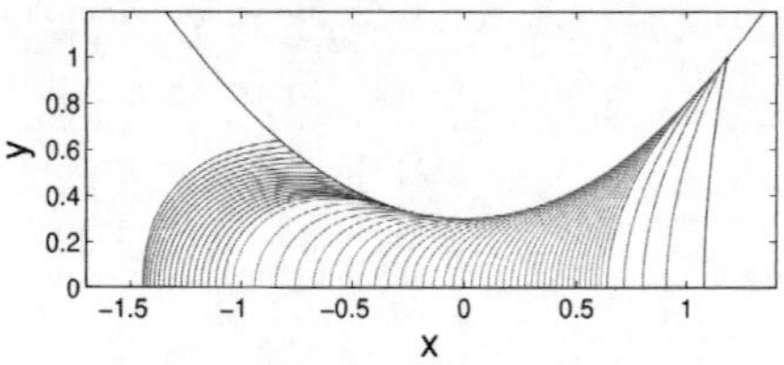

Figure 8. Profile scanning using a pre-curved vibrissa with $r_{0L} = -5$: in blue *Phase A*, in red *Phase B*.

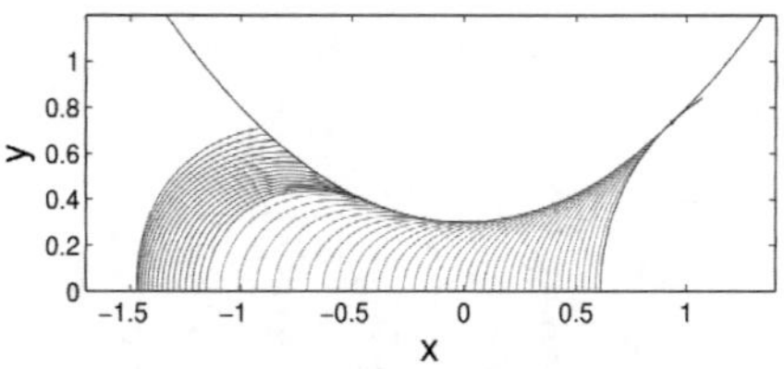

Figure 9. Profile scanning using a pre-curved vibrissa with $r_{0L} = -1$: in blue *Phase A*, in red *Phase B*.

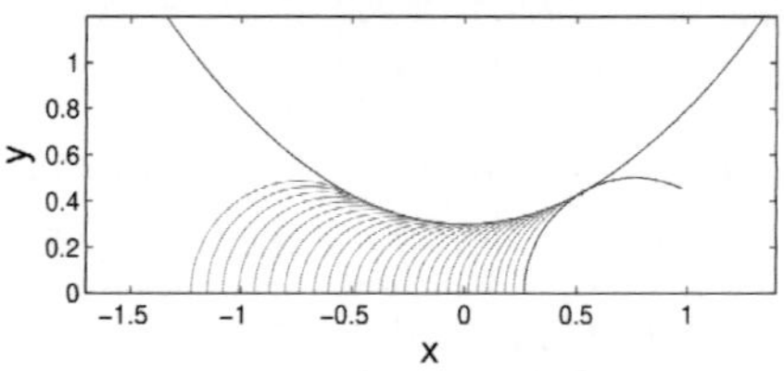

Figure 10. Profile scanning using a pre-curved vibrissa with $r_{0L} = -0.5$: in red *Phase B*, no Phase A.

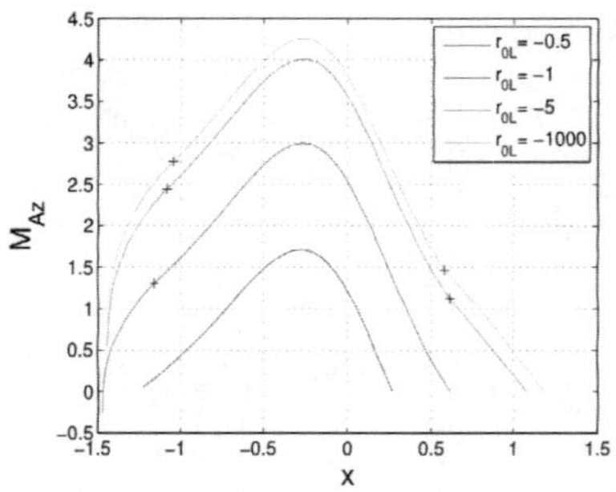

Figure 11. Clamping moment M_{Az} for varying pre-curvature radius r_{0L}.

The error of the reconstruction between the given and reconstructed profile is defined for single points according to [8]:

$$error = \sqrt{\left(x_k(s_{1k}) - \xi(\alpha_k)\right)^2 + \left(y_k(s_{1k}) - \eta(\alpha_k)\right)^2}, \tag{31}$$

whereby $(\xi(\alpha_k), \eta(\alpha_k))$ represent a point of the given profile and $(x_k(s_{1k}), y_k(s_{1k}))$ is the corresponding one of the reconstructed profile. Figures 14–17 present the reconstruction errors of the simulations. The magnitude of the error is from 10^{-7} to 10^{-6}, which is quite good.

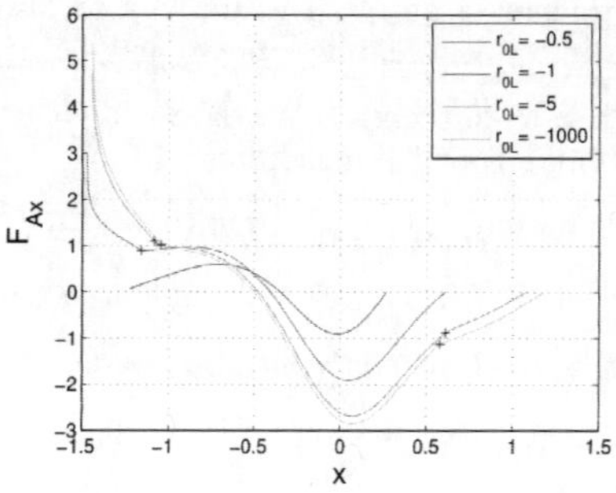

Figure 12. Clamping force F_{Ax} for varying pre-curvature radius r_{0L}.

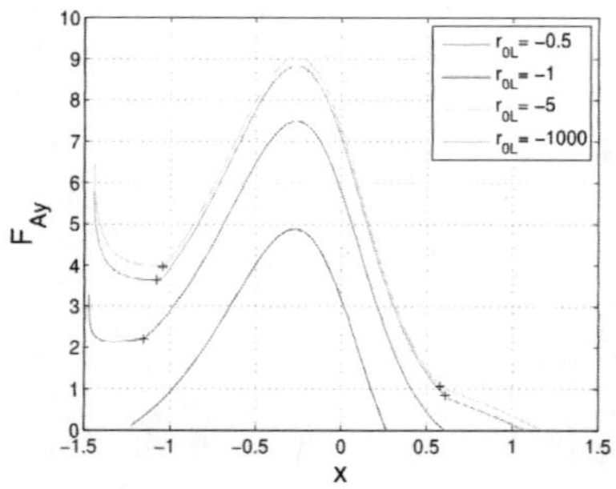

Figure 13. Clamping force F_{Ay} for varying pre-curvature radius r_{0L}.

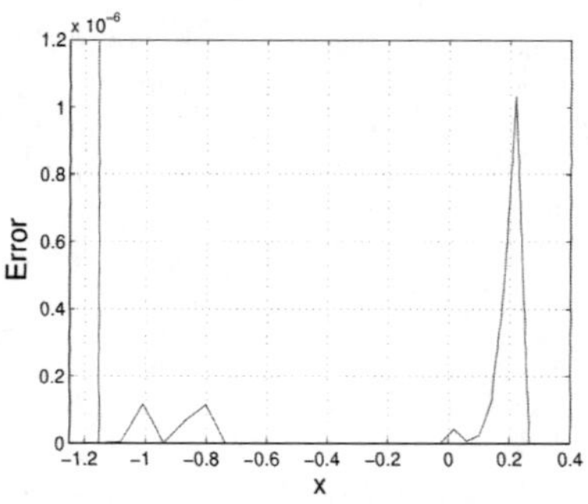

Figure 14. Error of given and reconstructed profile for $r_{0L} = -0.5$.

B. Scanning Using a Variable Intrinsic Curvature Radius

In this subsection, the parabola profile from (30) is scanned and reconstructed in using an artificial tactile rod with a variable intrinsic curvature of the form:

$$r_{0L}(s) = -5 + 4.2 \cdot s^{\frac{1}{3}}, \quad s \in [0, 1] \tag{32}$$

The scanning process is presented in Figure 18, the clamping reactions are displayed in Figure 19, and the reconstruction error is shown in Figure 20.

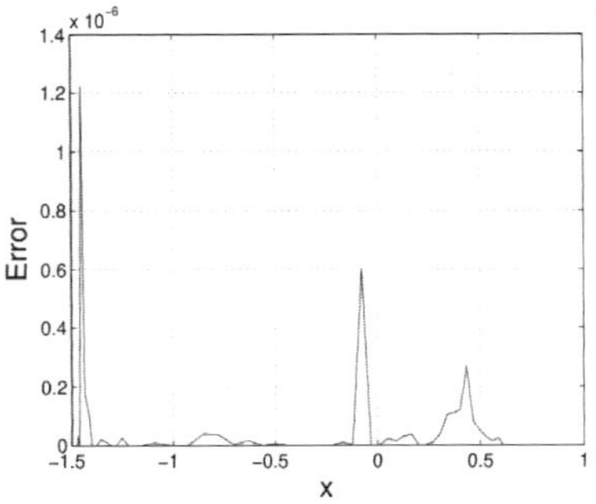

Figure 15. Error of given and reconstructed profile for $r_{0L} = -1$.

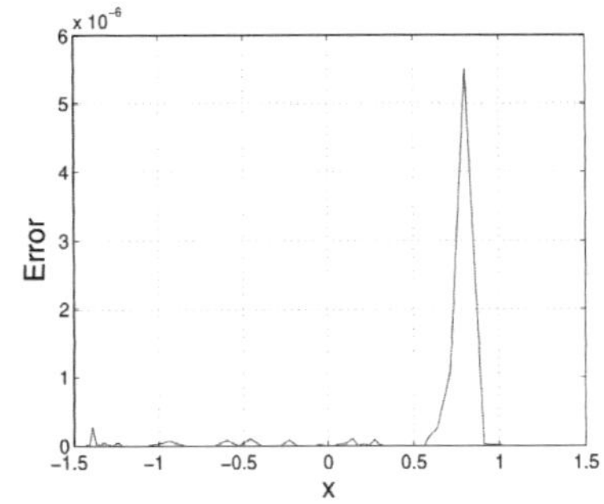

Figure 16. Error of given and reconstructed profile for $r_{0L} = -5$.

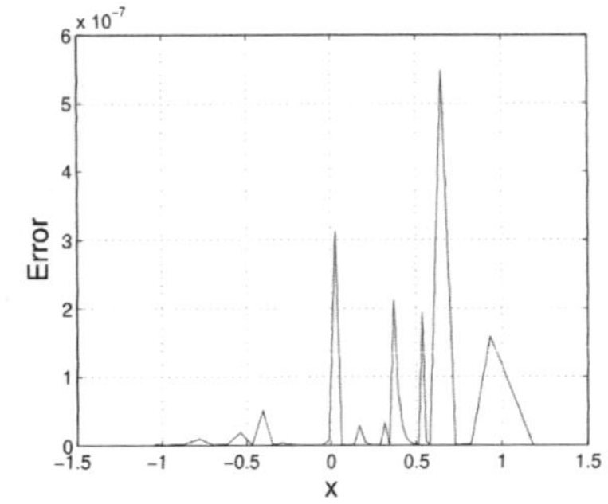

Figure 17. Error of given and reconstructed profile for $r_{0L} = -1000$.

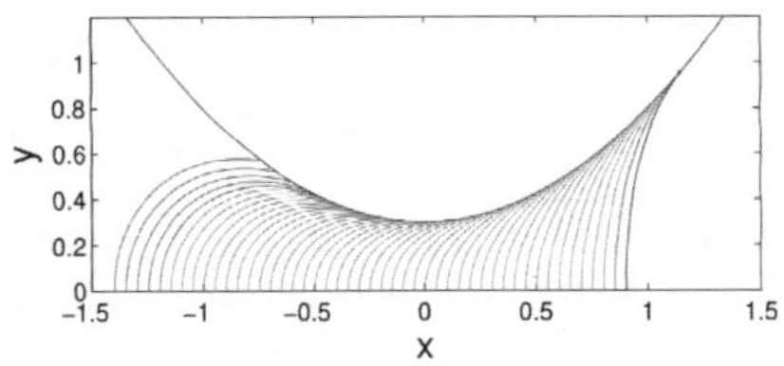

Figure 18. Profile scanning using a pre-curved vibrissa with $r_{0L}(s)$ of (32): in red *Phase B*, no Phase A.

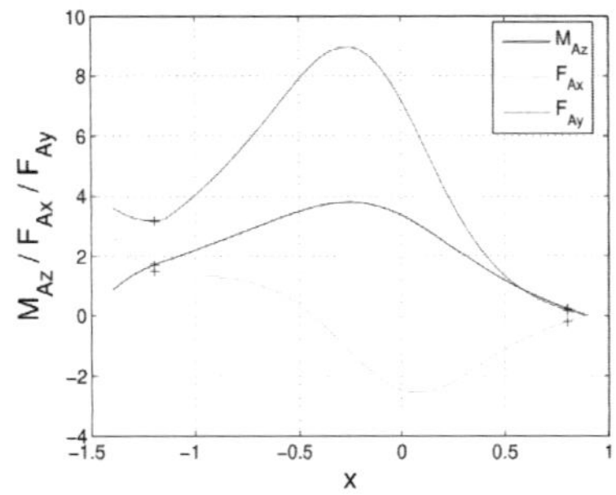

Figure 19. Clamping reactions varying pre-curvature radius $r_{0L}(s)$ of (32).

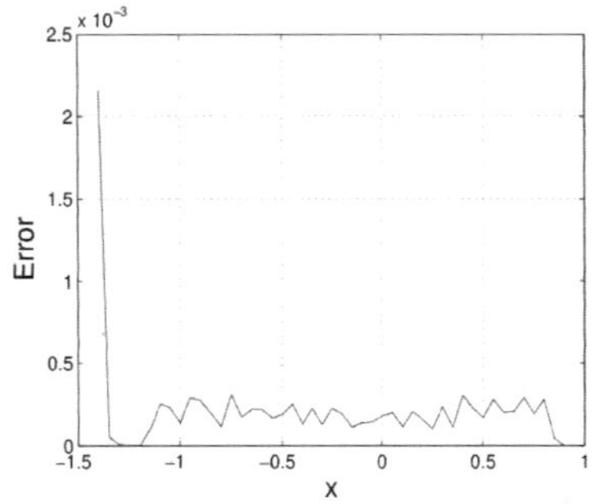

Figure 20. Error of given and reconstructed profile for $r_{0L}(s)$ of (32).

Comparing these results in using a rod with variable intrinsic curvature with the results using a straight cylindrical rod, i.e., r_{0L} is very high like $r_{0L} = 1000$ (see Figures 7, 11–13), than we can increase the scanned area of the profile whereas the clamping reactions still stay at their values. It is not really desirable to diminish the values of the clamping reaction because of possible measurement problems.

The numerical simulation of scanning object contours using artificial sinus hair-like tactile sensors of both constant and variable intrinsic curvature work very well. Therefore, we go on to the next step: experimental verification in the next section.

VI. EXPERIMENTS

To verify the algorithms, we present numerical investigations of scanning vibrissae with variable intrinsic curvature and experimental results, using the parabola profile

$$x \mapsto g_1(x) = 2x^2 + 0.55\,.$$

Three different technical vibrissae with different pre-curvature are used in an experiment. Figure 21 shows that the first vibrissa is a straight one, the second and the third one have a variable intrinsic curvature radius.

With the help of a computer-aided evaluation of the graphic representation of the vibrissae in Figure 21, their intrinsic curvature radius $r_{0L}(s)$ is determined in dependence on the arc length s as polynomials of order 10. This is rather new in literature, because a lot of works from literature restrict to a representation of the pre-curvature only to s^2-terms.

The simulated scanning processes are shown in Figures 23 and 24 for vibrissa 1 and 3.

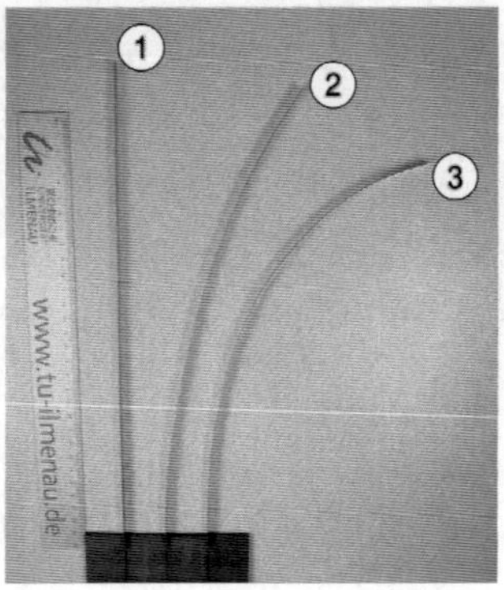

Figure 21. Three different pre-curved vibrissae for the experiment.

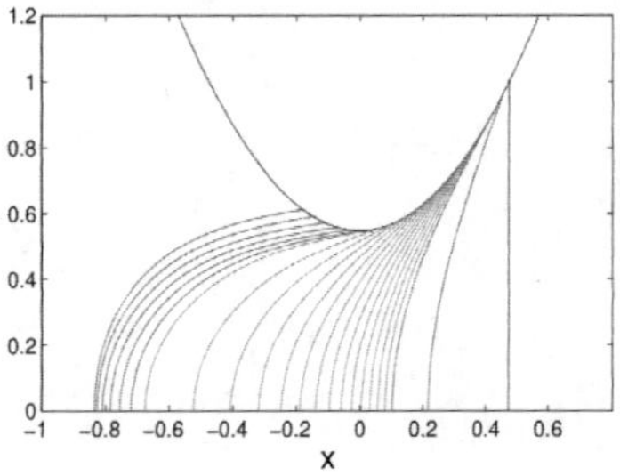

Figure 22. Scanning process using vibrissa 1 – in blue *Phase A*; in red *Phase B*.

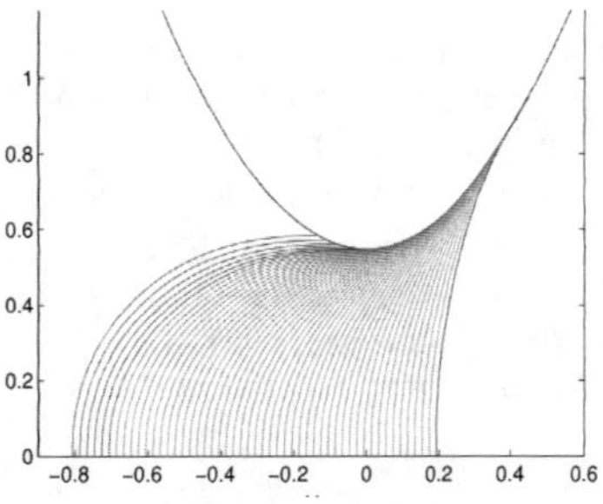

Figure 23. Scanning process using vibrissa 2 – in blue *Phase A*; in red *Phase B*.

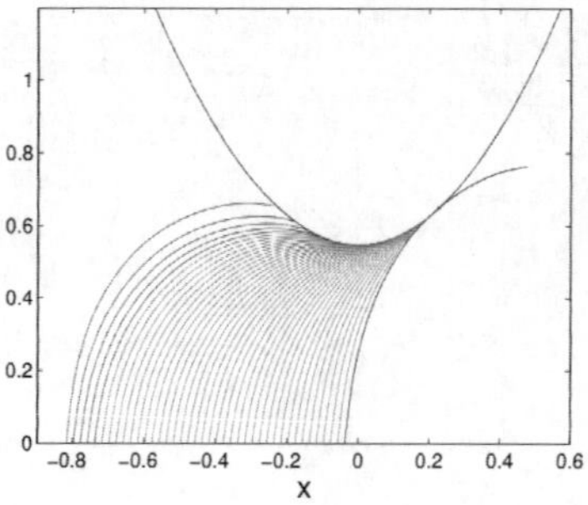

Figure 24. Scanning process using vibrissa 3 – in blue *Phase A*; in red *Phase B*.

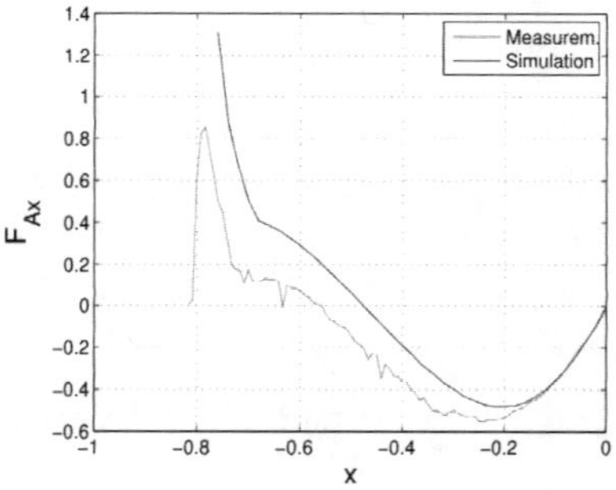

Figure 25. Experiment using vibrissa 3: clamping force F_{Ax} of a simulation and the experiment.

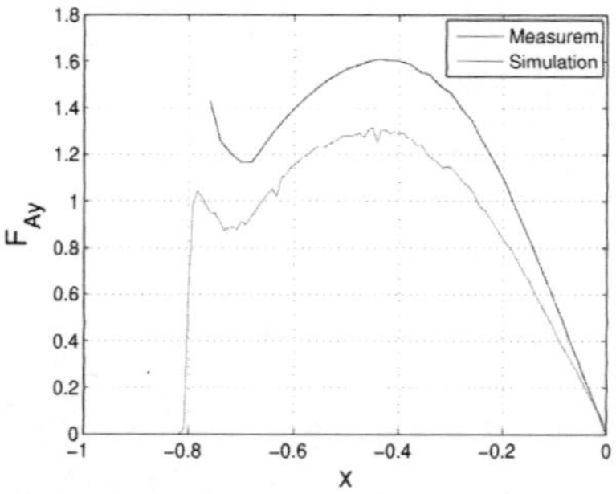

Figure 26. Experiment using vibrissa 3: clamping force F_{Ay} of a simulation and the experiment.

Figures 25–27 show exemplarily the observables (simulation vs. experiment) of the experiment using vibrissa 3. An easy inspection confirms prior results, that the maximal values of M_{Az}, F_{Ax} and F_{Ay} decrease the bigger the intrinsic curvature and the smaller the intrinsic curvature radius are. These figures show a good coincidence of the simulated and measured curves of the observables.

Summarizing, the following Figures 28–30 present the reconstruction of the profile. Compared to further simulations, we point out that the smaller the intrinsic curvature radius is the smaller is the reconstruction error. Finally, we conclude that it is promising to use pre-curved vibrissae for object contour scanning and reconstruction. The simulated and measured curves of the observables show up a good coincidence. The presented algorithms work effectively.

VII. Conclusion

Due to the functionality of animals vibrissae, the goal was to set up a model for an object scanning and shape reconstruction algorithm. For this, the only available information are the observables (support reaction, which an animal solely relies on) governed by one single sweep along the profile. Based on these observables, the object boundary has to be reconstructed.

It was possible to illustrate the characteristics and influences of pre-curved technical vibrissae in view of profile scanning. Based on the Winkler-Bach-Theory for pre-curved beams we set up the equations for a deformed vibrissa during a scanning process. We presented an algorithm to reconstruct the scanned profile in using the generated observables (which an

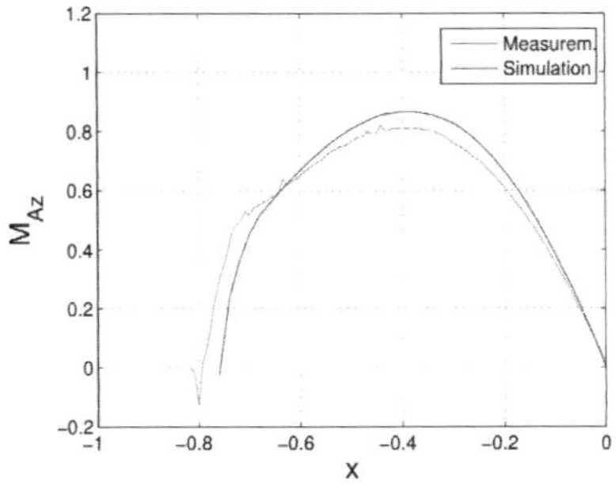

Figure 27. Experiment using vibrissa 3: clamping moment M_{Az} of a simulation and the experiment.

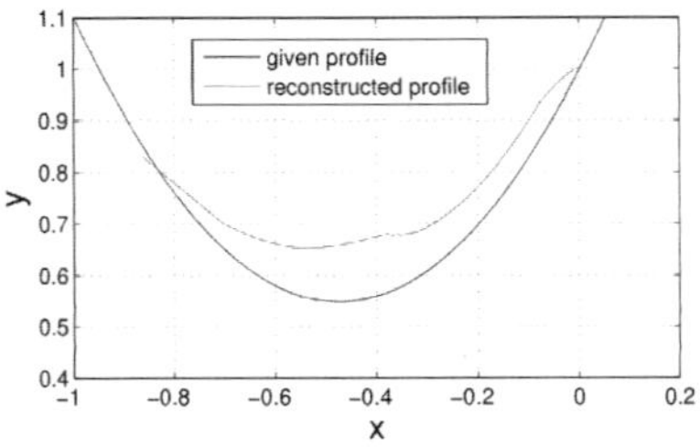

Figure 28. Given and reconstructed profile using vibrissa 1.

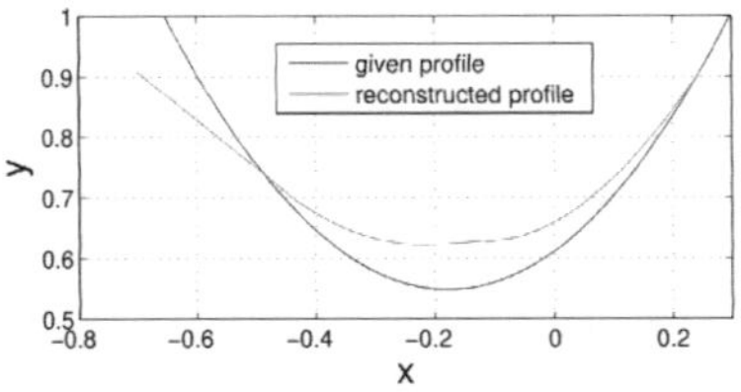

Figure 29. Given and reconstructed profile using vibrissa 2.

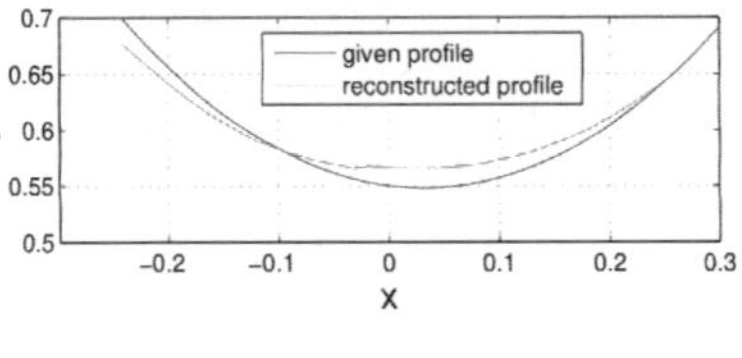

Figure 30. Given and reconstructed profile using vibrissa 3.

animal is supposed to solely rely on) via shooting methods. The reconstruction then was based on solving initial-value problems on contrast to the generation procedure where we solved boundary-value problems. The investigations respective the scanning of a strictly convex profile with a pre-curved vibrissae showed noticeable differences to the profile scanning with a straight vibrissa. The extrema of the bending reactions and the size of the scanned profile area depends on the pre-curvature radius of the vibrissa. Using a smaller radius, the tangential contact *phase B* in the scanning process could be enlarged. Experiments confirmed the numerical results and algorithms in this paper. Moreover, the investigation showed that the profile reconstruction works better with a pre-curved vibrissa.

REFERENCES

[1] C. Behn, J. Steigenberger, A. Sauter, and C. Will, "Pre-curved Beams as Technical Tactile Sensors for Object Shape Recognition," in *Proceedings INTELLI 2016: The Fifth International Conference on Intelligent Systems and Applications*, Barcelona (Spain), November 2016, IARIA, ISBN: 978-1-61208-518-0, pp. 7–12, 2016.

[2] R. Berg and D. Kleinfeld, "Rhythmic Whisking by Rat: Retraction as Well as Protraction of the Vibrissae Is Under Active Muscular Control," *Journal of Neurophysiology*, vol. 89, no. 1, pp. 104-117, 2002.

[3] G.R. Scholz and C.D. Rahn, "Profile Sensing With an Actuated Whisker," *IEEE Transactions on Robotics and Automation*, vol. 20, no. 1, pp. 124–127, 2004.

[4] M.J. Pearson et al., "A Biologically Inspired Haptic Sensor Array for use in Mobile Robotic Vehicles," in *Proceedings of Towards Autonomous Robotic Systems (TAROS)*, pp. 189-196, 2005.

[5] M.J. Pearson et al., "Whiskerbot: A Robotic Active Touch System Modeled on the Rat Whisker Sensory System," *Adaptive Behavior*, vol. 15, no. 3, pp. 223-240, 2007.

[6] D. Kim and R. Möller, "Biomimetic whiskers for shape recognition," *Robotics and Autonomous Systems*, vol. 55, no. 3, pp. 229-243, 2007.

[7] C. Tuna, J. H. Solomon, D. L. Jones, and M. J. Hartmann, "Object shape recognition with artificial whiskers using tomographic reconstruction," in *IEEE International Conference on Acoustics, Speech and Signal Processing (ICASSP)*, pp. 2537-2540, 2012.

[8] C. Will, J. Steigenberger, and C. Behn, "Object Contour Reconstruction using Bio-inspired Sensors," in *Proceedings 11th International Conference on Informatics in Control, Automation and Robotics (ICINCO 2014)*, September 2014, Vienna (Austria), IEEE, pp. 459-467, ISBN: 978-989-758-039-0, 2014.

[9] G. Dehnhardt, "Tactile size discrimination by a California sea lion (Zalophus californianus) using its mystacial vibrissae," *Journal of Comparative Physiology A*, vol. 175, no. 6, pp. 791-800, 1994.

[10] G. Dehnhardt and A. Kaminski, "Sensitivity of the mystacial vibrissae of harbour seals for size differences of actively touched objects," *The Journal of Experimental Biology*, vol. 198, pp. 2317-2323, 1995.

[11] G. Dehnhardt, B. Mauck, and H. Bleckman, "Seal whiskers detect water movements," *Nature*, vol. 394, pp. 235-236, 1998.

[12] M. Schmidt et al., "Technical, non-visual characterization of substrate contact using carpal vibrissae as a biological model: an overview," in *Proceedings of 58th International Scientific Colloquium – Shaping the future by engineering*, September 2014, Ilmenau (Germany).

[13] M. Brecht, B. Preilowski, and M.M. Merzenich, "Functional architecture of the mystacial vibrissae," *Behavioural Brain Research*, vol. 84, pp. 81-97, 1997.

[14] G.E. Carvell and D.J. Simons, "Biometric analyses of vibrissal tactile discrimination in the rat," *The Journal of Neuroscience*, vol. 10, no. 8, pp. 2638-2648, 1990.

[15] Y.S.W. Yu et al., "Whiskers aid anemotaxis in rats," *Science Advances*, vol. 2, no. 8, e1600716, 2016.

[16] S.Y. Long, "Hair-nibbling and whisker-trimming as indicators of social hierarchy in mice," *Animal Behaviour*, vol. 20, no. 1, pp. 10-12, 1972.

[17] D. Voges et al., "Structural characterisation of the whisker system of the rat," *IEEE Sensors Journal*, vol. 12, no. 2, pp. 332–339, 2012.

[18] J. Dörfl, "The musculature of the mystacial vobrissae of the white mouse," *Journal of Anatomy*, vol. 135, no. 1, pp. 147-154, 1982.

[19] S. Ebara et al., "Similarities and differences in the innervation of mystacial vibrissal follicle-sinus complexes in the rat and cat: A confocal microscopic study," *The Journal of Comparative Neurology,* vol. 449, no. 2, pp. 103-119, 2002.

[20] K. Carl et al., "Characterization of Statical Properties of Rats Whisker System," *IEEE Sensors Journals,* vol. 12, no. 2, pp. 340-349, 2012.

[21] R.B. Towal et al., "The Morphology of the Rat Vibrissal Array: A Model for Quantifying Spatiotemporal Patterns of Whisker-Object Contact," *PLoS Computational Biology,* vol. 7, no. 4, pp. 1–17, e1001120, 2011.

[22] A. Ahl, "The role of vibrissae in behavior: A status review," *Veterinary Reserarch Communications,* vol. 10, pp. 245-268, 1986.

[23] B.W. Quist and M.J.Z. Hartmann, "Mechanical signals at the base of a rat vibrissa: the effect of intrinsic vibrissa curvature and implications for tactile exploration," *Journal of Neuophysiology,* vol. 107, pp. 2298-2312, 2012.

[24] C. Will, J. Steigenberger, and C. Behn, "Quasi-static object scanning using technical vibrissae," in: Proceedings 58. International Colloquium Ilmenau (IWK), September 0812, 2014, Ilmenau, Germany. ilmedia, URL: http://nbn-resolving.org/urn:nbn:de:gbv:ilm1-2014iwk:3 [accessed: 2016-06-10], 2014.

[25] C. Will, J. Steigenberger, and C. Behn, "Bio-inspired Technical Vibrissae for Quasi-static Profile Scanning," Springer International Publishing Switzerland, J. Filipe et al. (eds.), ISBN: 978-3-319-26453-0, pp. 277-295, 2016.

[26] M. Knutsen, D. Derdikman, and E. Ahissar, "Tracking Whisker and Head Movements in Unrestrained Behaving Rodents," *Journal of Neurophysiology,* vol. 93, pp. 2294-2301, 2004.

[27] M. Knutsen, A. Biess, and E. Ahissar, "Vibrissal Kinematics in 3D: Tight Coupling of Azimuth, Elevation, and Torsion across Different Whisking Modes," *Neuron,* vol. 59, pp. 35-42, 2008.

[28] N.G. Clack et al., "Automated Tracking of Whiskers in Videos of Head Fixed Rodents," *PLoS Computational Biology,* vol. 8, no. 7, e1002591, pp. 1–8, 2012.

[29] S.A. Hires, L. Pammer, K. Svoboda, and D. Golomb, "Tapered whiskers are required for active tactile sensation," *eLife,* 2013, e01350, pp. 1–19, 2013.

[30] L. Pammer et al., "The mechanical variables underlying object localisation along the axis of the whisker," *The Journal of Neuroscience,* vol. 33, no. 16, pp. 6726-6741, 2013.

[31] G. Scholz and C. Rahn, "Profile Sensing With an Actuated Whisker," *IEEE Transactions on Robotics and Automation,* vol. 20, pp. 124–127, 2004.

[32] P. Gummert and K.-A. Reckling, "Mechanik (Mechanics)," 3rd edition, Vieweg, Braunschweig, Germany, 1994.

[33] A. Öchsner and M. Merkel, "One-Dimensional Finite Elements – An Introduction to the FE Method," Springer, Berlin, 2013.

Patterns to Inform a Study Setup for Biometric Image Data Capturing

Artur Lupp*, Alexander G. Mirnig*, Thomas Grah*, Andreas Uhl† and Manfred Tscheligi*

*Center for Human-Computer Interaction, University of Salzburg, Austria
Email: name.surname@sbg.ac.at
†Department of Computer Sciences, University of Salzburg, Austria
Email: uhl@cosy.sbg.ac.at

Abstract—**This paper presents an application of the contextual user experience (cUX) pattern approach for refining a study concept involving biometric image data. The study was concerned with the acquisition, inspection, and quality evaluation of Near Infrared (NIR) iris biometry images. After creating the initial draft of the study setup and during the design of the detailed study procedure, a number of questions arose, e.g., how to deal with the environmental light during image acquisition, which material to use for 3D printing, how to solve the problem of picking the right questionnaire, how to record high quality videos with mobile phones or even the differences between certain image formats. In order to capture and make these solutions more easily accessible, we used an adapted cUX pattern approach to provide the found solutions in the form of seven study design patterns.**

Keywords–design patterns; pattern reuse; study setup optimization.

I. Introduction

This paper is an extension of a full paper presented at PATTERNS 2017 [1]. Patterns, in general, are a well acknowledged method in Human-Computer Interaction (HCI), providing reliable and reproducible solutions for specific problems. They can be advantageously used to ease the communication between experts with different levels of expertise or even alternate disciplines. This is particularly useful in interdisciplinary areas and academic settings, where often a wide variety of levels of expertise are represented. During the design of an academic study with image recognition, we encountered a number of problems, which we found nontrivial and difficult to solve via standard literature, due to their specific nature. Since knowledge on pattern use and writing was available, we decided to capture the found solutions as patterns, in order to share them in an easy to access format.

The aim of this paper is to provide a more detailed description of the pattern writing process, a greater number of patterns than the original publication and finally an extended discussion. The already provided patterns, "Choosing the Right Light Sources to Examine NIR-Images Differences", "Lens Holder Construction for a Mobile Phone" and "Finding and Adjusting the Right Usability Questionnaire" covered the first steps of the study routine, whereas the more complex image acquisition and processing part had not been covered via patterns at that point. We took the opportunity to provide more solution patterns covering image acquisition and processing topics. Patterns (i.e., local binary patterns) in image application are commonly used to improve face detection and recognition. However, this type of patterns is not comparable to the solution patterns provided in this work. The solution patterns presented in this paper, aim to provide aid and helpful solutions for problems that may occur in the image application domain. With the addition of five new generated patterns covering the image application domain, this work now presents seven patterns in total.

Section II will give some insight into patterns and certain areas in the image application domain. A detailed explanation of the cUX pattern approach is presented in Section III. This section will describe the pattern generation process, starting from the context analysis and problem definition, whilst explaining all in-between steps until the finalization of a pattern. After the explanation of the pattern generation process, Section IV will provide an insight into the to be improved study setup. Section V will illustrate the seven solution patterns with the following *Titles*:

1) Choosing the Right Light Sources to Examine NIR-Images Differences
2) Lens Holder Construction for a Mobile Phone
3) High Quality Video Acquisition with the Nexus 5
4) Extract Media Information from Videofiles
5) Still Image Extraction from h264 Videos
6) Comparison Between Bitmap, Portable Network Graphic, and JPEG Images
7) Extraction of the Eye Area from Frontal Face Images

We will discuss our new findings, especially how to handle the new problems and the associated solutions in Section VI and conclude the paper in Section VII.

II. Related Work

This section will first provide a brief overview of patterns, their history, and pattern approaches. After that, a summary of relevant information and literature on image detection is provided.

A. Patterns

Patterns were first introduced by Christopher Alexander [2][3] as a means to capture working solutions for reoccurring problems in the field of architecture. His initial idea was to consider the act of constructing a building as the sum of a number of many individual problem solutions. These solutions, when described individually, can then be "rearranged" when constructing new or different buildings and not requiring the same problems be solved anew every time a new building is constructed. His ideas and methodology was adopted by Gamma et al. [4] for Software Engineering and related disciplines, and has been used as a tool in these domains since.

Patterns are nowadays considered less as an alternative to guidelines and other general means of guidance, and more as a supplement. This is because general documentation approaches are often either simplistic or high level [5][6]. Pattern solutions, on the other hand, are firmly embedded in the context their problems occur in. This makes a specific pattern less generally applicable – only when the problem contexts match to a sufficient degree. But it also makes the solutions they describe more specific, as well as practice relevant, and lends them to be used by novices and experts alike [7]. Patterns have been adopted by other domains as well, such as Web Design and HCI [8][9][10] and have also been suggested as a general, discipline-independent knowledge transfer tool [11].

B. Image Application

The mobile phone domain made huge advancements in terms of hardware technology over the last decade. Software, however, does not keep up this trend, especially when looking into image acquisition with mobile phones. The commonly used format for images is JPEG [12], which offers a decent image quality while maintaining a small file size. Videos are saved within a MPEG4 [13] container format housing a H.264/MPEG-4 AVC [14] video stream. H.264/MPEG-4 AVC is typically used for compressed (i.e., lossy) recording to save bandwidth, it is possible to create lossless-coded regions by choosing a special profile. However, there is currently no mobile phone available that is capable of using this special profile, thus all videos recorded with a mobile phone are lossy. Fortunately, object detection in the compressed domain is commonly applied [15][16][17][18][19], thus, face detection on compressed images or videos should not prove too challenging.

Object detection is the basis for face detection, which is picked as the central theme in one pattern, and can also be applied on compressed images and videos [20]. Viola and Jones [21][22] described a method for rapid object detection by using simple distinctive features called Haar-like features and a cascade of classifiers. This method distinguishes the area where the face is detected from the background, thus providing the area of interest. However, as the set of classifiers is pretty simple, the general error rate is high. To improve the detection rates, it is possible to use an extension [23] of the before mentioned Haar-like features in form of an improved cascade set, specially trained to decrease the general error rate. OpenCV [24] offers a good library to utilize this feature set for face and eye detection.

III. Approach

Generating patterns is a process over multiple stages that involves individuals (in this case researchers) working together in collaboration to create high quality patterns. This section will describe our approach, as well as the overall pattern creation process. The first step is the context analysis, followed by the problem definition. During the context analysis, we looked at the underlying study setup we wanted to improve, identifying possible problems that may occur and how the overall process could be refined. In a following discussion session, we collected the results from the context analysis by defining the overall issues and problems. After collecting all problems and ideas, the identified items were rated on a priority scale and compiled into list at the end of the discussion round. Thereafter, the compiled items were arranged in the sequence of the study setup routine to allow a fluid workflow.

1) Initial Pattern Mining & First Iteration: The compiled list serves as a basis for the initial pattern mining and is completed by the previously mentioned researchers. Each researcher is assigned several problems. The number of assigned problems or items per researcher varies and depends on the number of participating researchers, time constraints (if any) and the priority of the problem. Commonly, three to five problems per researcher was the aim, as a problem statement might result in more than one pattern. Therefore, it is advisable to not exceed the recommended number of problems, to ensure that the researchers have a manageable level of workload. Apart from that, the researchers should be competent and well-versed regarding the academic side of the problems they work on. In the case of optimizing a study setup that mostly focuses on video acquisition, image extraction and image processing, this meant that all of the participating researchers should be at least familiar with video recording and processing with image data, with added benefit if they had specialization in face detection and feature extraction.

The next step during pattern mining is the decision whether the problem statement is a high or a low level problem and if its level of granularity is such that it requires a single pattern or needs to be split into several patterns. Each researcher is then instructed to mine publications, presentations, demos, prototypes, books and other useful and available sources for solutions to the problem in question. The next step is the combination of the partial solutions and references into one full solution for the draft pattern. A draft pattern is written, beginning with a self explanatory *Title*. Then, each pattern is divided into six sections.

1) The *Intent* provides a short description and is followed by the
2) *Problem* statement, which is, in this case, a question.
3) After stating the problem, a *Scenario* is presented that is used as an example,
4) for which a *Solution* is provided.
5) The solution is backed up by *Examples*, usually illustrated with images.
6) The pattern ends by providing *Keywords*, matching the subject of the pattern.

The draft is then handed to another researcher for a first internal iteration, completing the initial pattern.

2) First Iteration Workshop: The first iteration workshop ideally consists of some or all participants that took part in the context analysis, as well as participants not previously involved, with the aim of introducing new viewpoints. The initial patterns are then read thoroughly by each participant. Each subcategory of a pattern (Title, Intent, Problem, etc.) is rated individually on a 5-point scale via a rating system provided by Wurhofer et al. [25]. If a pattern is rated 3 or lower in any subcategory, it is marked for iteration. After rating each pattern, the participants participate in a discussion session and conclude the workshop. The main goal in this round is to discuss the general pattern quality, as well as the overall impression of the collection, to identity problematic patterns.

3) Second Iteration & Workshop: The feedback and ratings gained from the first iteration workshop are worked into the patterns during the second iteration. This time, each pattern is iterated by at least two researchers, who are versed in the specific topic address by the pattern(s). The focus is on

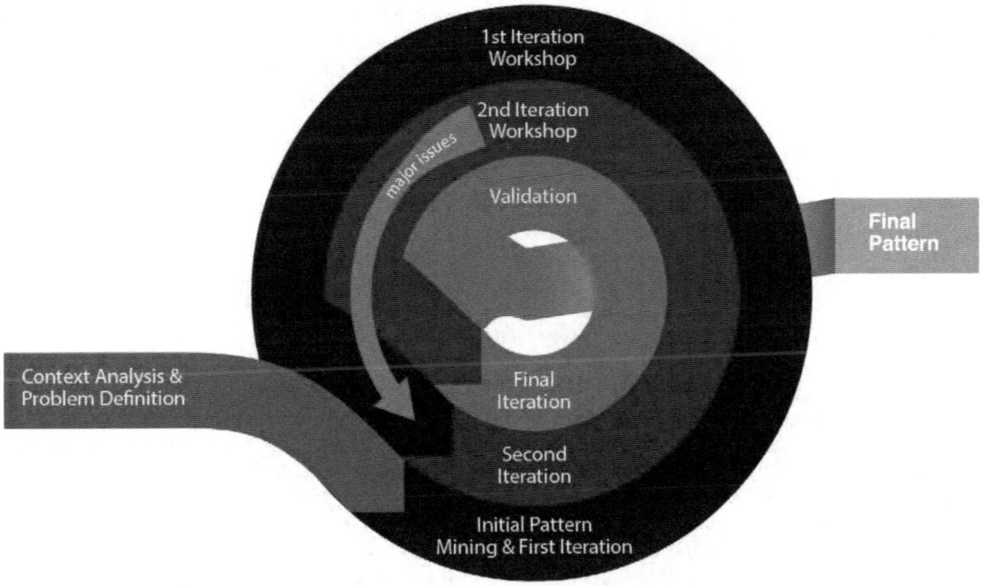

Figure 1. Graphical representation of the Pattern Generation Process adapted from [26].

improving and ensuring the practical relevance of the pattern by providing, e.g., additional implementation examples and best practices. As in the initial pattern creation, each pattern is cross-iterated again by a different researcher for typos, errors, etc., in order to provide a full and complete solution after this iteration. All additional iterations should only be targeting structure improvement, readability, and comprehensibility. Upon completion of this iteration, a second workshop following the same routine as the first one is conducted. It is advised to include new participants who were not part of the first workshop to provide an unbiased view in order to help to identify issues that might have been missed in the first workshop.

4) Final Iteration and Validation: Each pattern is again reworked with respect to the feedback and ratings gained in the second workshop. At this point, most minor issues should have been identified; however, it is still possible to encounter major issues. When a major issue is found in a pattern, it reenters the the reworking loop for another iteration workshop. Usually patterns that reenter the loop are put aside temporarily to ensure a fluid workflow. These patterns are taken up again, if either a new batch of patterns is created, the appropriate iteration phase is reached, or the rest of the patterns are finished.

Patterns with minor issues are corrected accordingly and enter the final validation stage of the pattern creation process. During this stage, each pattern is again rated using the same rating system as before, but without the workshop setting. If a pattern receives a rating of 3 or below in this stage, it reenters the same reworking loop as the patterns with major issues mentioned before. This happens rarely, if ever, as problematic patterns are usually identified before reaching this stage. All ratings above 3 validate the pattern, marking it as finished.

IV. Study Setup

We wanted to improve and optimize an existing study setup, dealing with biometric images. These biometric images had to be analyzed afterwards, with respect to image quality. The setup was divided into several steps. During the first step, study subjects have to capture videos with a customized LG Nexus 5 mobile phone. The IR-blocking filter was removed from the rear camera image sensor, to enable NIR image capturing. The built-in rear camera image sensor is a Sony Exmor R IMX 179. The sensor offers a Red-Green-Blue (RGB) sub pixel layout with $3264x2448$ (8 MegaPixel) pixels and a sensor size of $5.68mm$ ($1/3.2$"), leading to an effective pixel size of $1.4\mu m$. The pixel size is decent for a mobile phone released in 2013. Therefore, taking images or videos in twilight conditions is possible. However, a brighter environment is preferred due to less image noise. Each test subject had to record three frontal face videos using the stock camera lens and two different filters / lenses, which were mounted on the mobile phone. Afterwards, the test subjects had to fill in a questionnaire. Due to the time consuming video capturing process, the questionnaire needed to be short, while still maintaining a decent reliability.

The Nexus 5 was chosen because it was easily available at the time and it allows removing the IR-blocking filter, which is often permanently integrated (i.e., nondetachable) in other models on the market. Removing the filter is necessary for enabling NIR image capturing via the described method. The built-in rear camera image sensor is also integrated in, e.g., the Google PIXEL smartphone as a front facing camera and the approach described here is not limited to only this particular smartphone. While technology changes and advances, in the case of smartphone technology quite rapidly sometimes, the method for capturing images via the described method is likely to stay the same, barring differences in pixel size, pixel matrix on the image sensor, pre- or post processing. None of these impact the image making process in any significant way. Thus, the described process should be relatively robust to future technology advances, provided the models used allow removal of the IR-blocking filter.

We proposed patterns to refine the study concept using an approach similar to the pattern generation process for car user experience patterns described in detail by Mirnig et al. [27], with some minor changes. The first mandatory step in our approach was to analyze the study concept and the associated setup to extract the problem statements. This was done by organizing a workshop with the person responsible for the study concept and a group of HCI researchers accustomed with the pattern generation process. During the workshop, the study setup was explained as follows. Study participants have to capture three frontal face videos, one for NIR and visible light images without any lens, one with the IR-blocking filter / lens, and one with the NIR-only lens. As it is possible to extract high quality images from high resolution videos, it was decided to capture only videos instead of pure frontal face images. The two different lenses forced the researcher responsible, to change them after every recording, due to the current lens mounting method. To ensure a variety of captured videos, the test subjects had to record the videos in different light environments, which where not yet defined. The final step was the acquisition of data, relating to the usability of the video recording process. As the video capturing procedure was time consuming, the data acquisition had to be fast and reliable. The first workshop brought up the following main problems:

1) Which light sources and ambient environments need to be considered, to ensure a diversity of captured image or video data usually acquired during real life usage?
2) How can the lens / filter changing process be improved?
3) Is it possible to record higher quality videos with a LG Nexus 5?
4) Which tool can be used to extract media information from video files?
5) How can still images be extracted from videos recorded by a mobile phone?
6) Which file format should be used for an image when its extracted from a mobile phone video?
7) How can the eye area can be extracted from a frontal face image?

For each problem, a draft pattern was created. The draft pattern initially did not provide any final solutions. Thus, it was iterated and reworked until a working solution was found. After that, the pattern was rated and reworked again until it was finally validated. In the next section, we will present the solution patterns we generated. Each pattern provides a solution for a certain problem statement, previously mentioned in this section.

V. Solution Patterns

A. Choosing the Right Light Sources to Examine NIR-Images Differences

Intent: There are several variables one needs to take into account when taking pictures or videos with a mobile phone. Due to the usually small built-in image sensor in mobile phones, sufficient environmental light is a crucial point. Insufficient light leads to higher image noise, which is generally not preferred. However, to analyze a wide area of possible real life conditions, selecting different environments for image capturing is important. This pattern presents three possible scenarios covering the most important lighting conditions. The scenarios were selected to provide images with a quality sufficient for subsequent analysis in mind.

Problem: Which scenarios are needed in order to acquire analyzable data, covering indoor and outdoor lighting conditions that enable NIR image acquisition?

Scenario: The study needed special image acquisition scenarios to reflect actual real life scenarios as closely as possible. Additionally, the ambient light in at least one of the scenarios had to cover the NIR wavelength ($>= 700nm$) spectrum to enable NIR imaging.

Solution: To cover most real life scenarios of possible image capturing conditions, we proposed three scenarios: one outdoor scenario using indirect sunlight (e.g., via a glass reflection in the background) to enable NIR imaging and two indoor scenarios using different light environments to challenge the imaging sensor of the mobile phone.

- **Outdoor (variable ambient light conditions)** - The outdoor scenario is and should be variable. In this condition, the sun is providing the ambient light. Therefore, the image quality is depending on time, weather, and location. To ensure the best possible conditions for NIR image acquisition, daylight is necessary. Therefore, image acquisition in this scenario should be done during the daytime. An example of the outside condition is shown in Figure 3.
- **Indoor (dim light)** - The indoor scenario using a dim light source is intended to challenge the image sensor. The indirect artificial light provides sufficient luminosity for images to be taken, as pictured in Figure 4. Nevertheless, the provided light is dark enough to force the image sensor to use a higher sensitivity setting (this is also referred to as "ISO"), thus, resulting in more image noise. Note that image noise is not desirable in general, but, if the main concept of the study is to analyze the whole range of possible image qualities, it is mandatory to include this unfavorable condition.
- **Indoor (bright light)** - In contrast to the dim light indoor scenario, the bright light indoor scenario uses a very bright artificial white light source to illuminate the frontal face area. This scenario complements the previously mentioned scenarios. The bright artificial light, covers the spectrum visible to the human eye (from about 390 to $700nm$) and provides a decent environment needed to capture regular frontal face images and can be observed in Figure 5. However, conventional light sources are usually not suitable for NIR imaging, as they do not cover the spectrum above $700nm$ (see Figure 2).

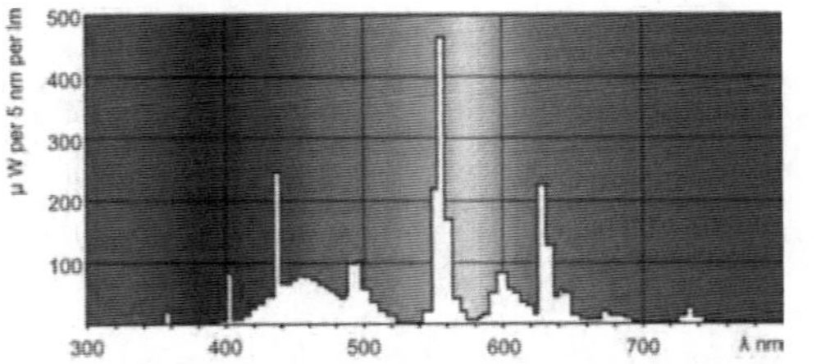

Figure 2. Philips TL5 HO 49W 865 Lamp [28] - Photometric Data.

Examples: This section shows nine sample images. They are grouped by the three proposed scenarios. Each group consists of three images: NIR only, NIR & visible light, and visible light only.

Figure 3. Outdoor - NIR only, NIR & visible light, visible light only (from left to right).

As mentioned in the solution section, the outdoor scenario provides sufficient light. This scenario provides the best NIR image quality, as the sunlight covers a wider spectrum compared to conventional light sources.

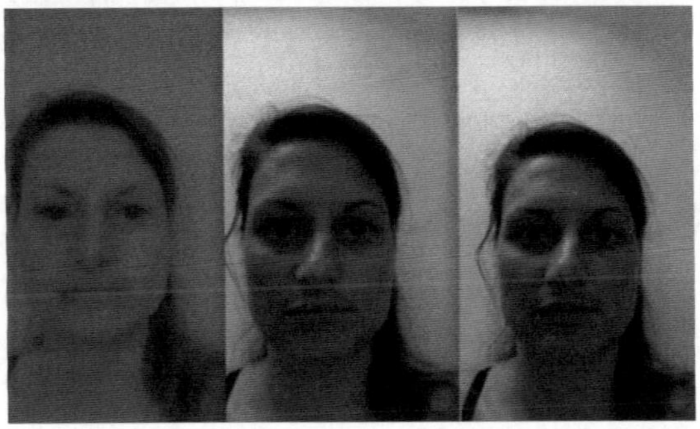

Figure 4. Indoor (dim light) - NIR only, NIR & visible light, visible light only (from left to right).

The indoor scenario with a dim indirect light source tends to induce image noise and is not optimal for NIR imaging.

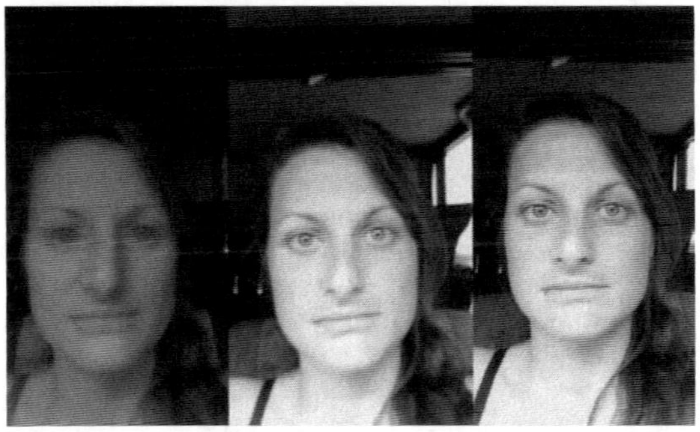

Figure 5. Indoor (bright light) - NIR only, NIR & visible light, visible light only (from left to right).

The last scenario provides a direct illumination of the facial area. It is very favorable for images captured in the visible spectrum, e.g., due to reduced image noise.

Keywords: NIR, visible light, wavelength, spectrum, image acquisition, illumination

B. Lens Holder Construction for a Mobile Phone

Intent: This pattern describes steps-by-step the construction of a lens holder for the Nexus 5 mobile phone.

Problem: Is it possible to create a method or item to reduced the lens change time and make the whole process more comfortable?

Scenario: Two different filters / lenses are each to be mounted on the mobile phone using a clip. This is very time consuming and elaborate. To ease the transition from one lens to another, they had to be mounted on a movable holder with the possibility to be mounted on the mobile phone.

Solution: A custom made movable lens holder mounted on a hard shell mobile phone case. The following points are describing a step-by-step guide to construct a lens holder for a mobile phone case:

- First, get a hard shell mobile phone case to work with. The case should be made of a robust material, e.g., polycarbonate. The easiest way to obtain a good mobile phone case is either by buying it or by printing one using a 3D printer. Note that the camera lens of the mobile phone should not stick out of the case, when it is mounted on the phone, as it will be tough or impossible to rotate the custom made lens changer afterwards.
- Measure the phone case and the lens width, length, and depth. Measurements should be taken as precisely as possible.
- Sketch the available items (i.e., lenses and phone case) with the measurements from the previous step.
- The sketch is then used to figure out, how to arrange the lenses in a way that allows them to cover the camera lens of the phone when the lens changer is being rotated.
- With the lenses arranged, pick a focus point between them. This is the pivot point of the lens changer. In our case, this point is the small circle in between the two bigger ones, illustrated in Figure 7.

- Craft a paper prototype of the lens holder. Sketch the lens changer with the exact measurements and cut it out. This prototype can be used to simulate the finished product. Try it out, and see if it fits your expectations, as depicted in Figure 6.
- Digitize the sketch and construct a 3D model. Note that it may be beneficial to add some room to move, especially if using a 3D printer that is not 100% accurate. An example of the digitized model is pictured in Figures 7 and 8 (left).
- Print the 3D model with a material that allows editing with tools (i.e., a file or a multifunction rotary tool) later on. In this case, PVC was used.
- Deburr the edges whilst occasionally trying to fit in the lenses. When everything fits accordingly, proceed with the next step. If anything is odd or needs refinement, redo the 3D modeling and print the item again.
- Drill the pivot point holes into the 3D printed item, as well as in the phone case, to combine them later on.
- Temporarily mount the printed lens holder to the phone with a screw, as shown in Figure 8 (right).
- Double check if everything is according to your needs.
- Finally, install the lenses into the lens holder and mount it to the phone case. See Figure 9 for the final result.

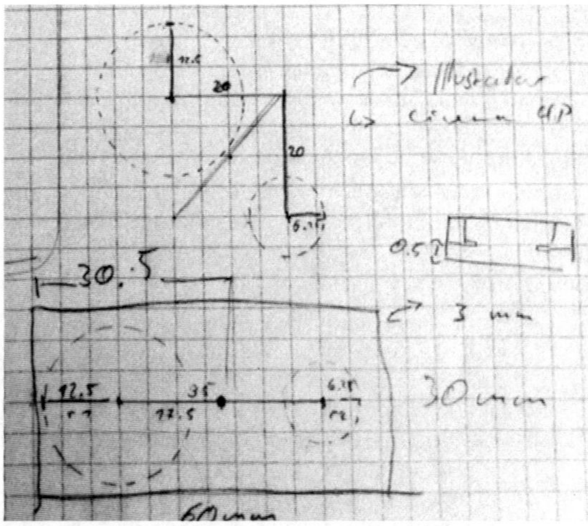

Figure 6. Sketch of the lens holder with exact measurements and radius.

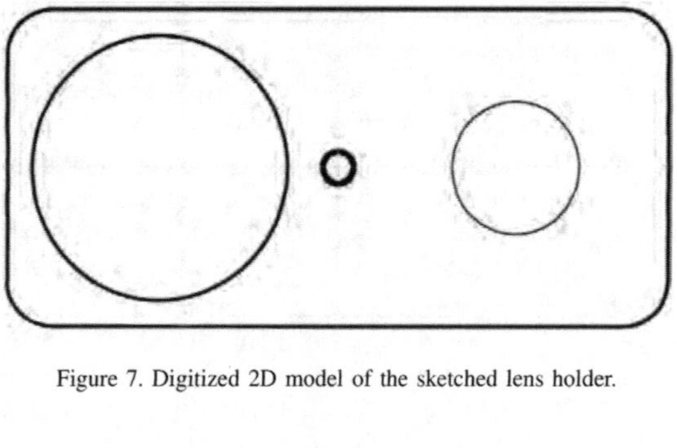

Figure 7. Digitized 2D model of the sketched lens holder.

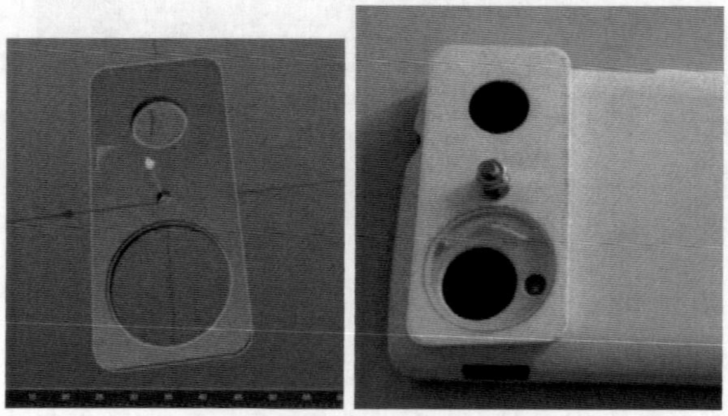

Figure 8. Lens holder 3D model (left). Printed lens holder with installed lenses/filters (right).

Figure 9. Final lens holder mounted on the phone case.

Examples: Figure 10 holds a QR Code that is linked to a video showing the lens holder in action. Figure 11 is picturing the effect of the different lenses on image acquisition.

Figure 10. YouTube Video - Nexus 5 Lens Holder Case [29].

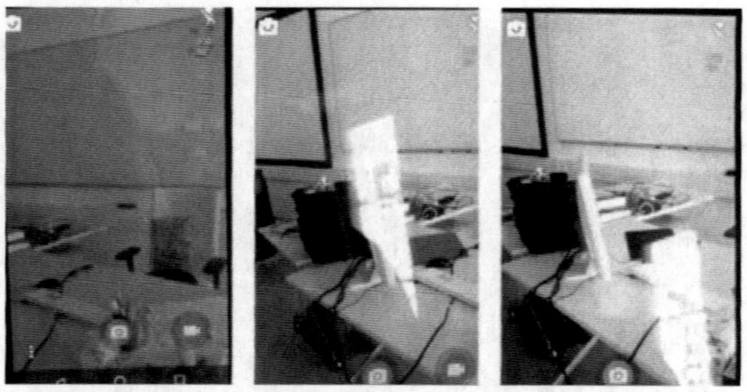

Figure 11. NIR, NIR and visible light, visible light only by using IR-blocking lens (from left to right).

Keywords: NIR, lens holder, phone case, PVC, polycarbonate, 3D modeling, 3D printing

C. High Quality Video Acquisition with the Nexus 5

Intent: This pattern describes the best way to record high quality videos on a Nexus 5 mobile phone.

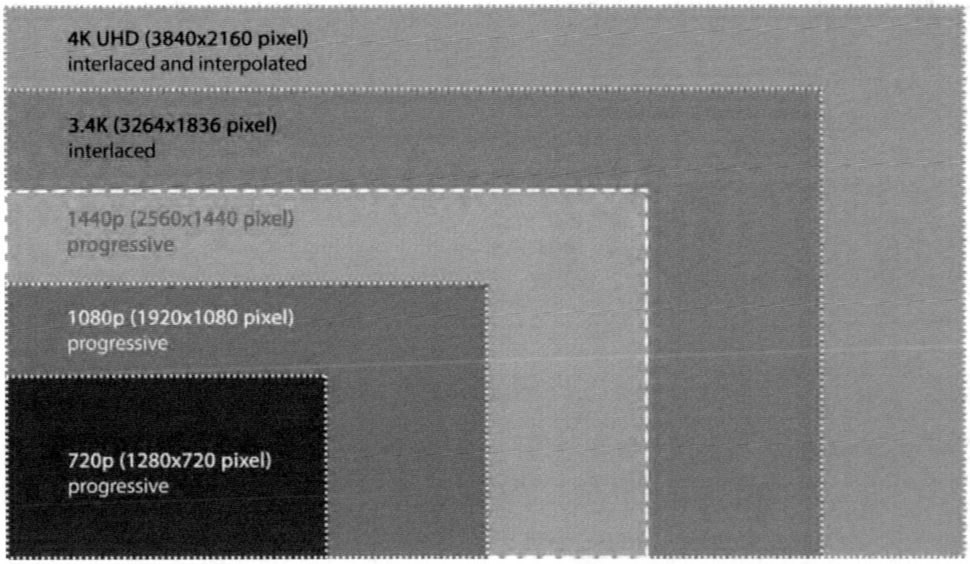

Figure 12. Comparison of available video resolution options for the LG Nexus 5 using SnapCam.

Problem: Out of the box video recording with mobile phones using the pre-installed video recording applications have certain limitations. Usually, the applications offer only a handful of pre defined resolution options to record videos in certain qualities, e.g., $1080p$ ($1920x1080$ pixel) for FullHD or $720p$ ($1280x720$ pixel) for HDReady. However, these options are usually not the highest technically possible video quality options the phones built-in image sensor might provide.

Scenario: For post-processing reasons, high quality still images have to be extracted from recorded video. Thus, the videos have to be recorded in the highest quality possible.

Solution: To enable the best possible video capturing quality on the Nexus 5, it is necessary to use a special application that is capable of exploiting the phones image sensor. Currently, the only app capable to do this using the Nexus 5 mobile phone is Snap Camera [30]. Snap Camera has a feature [31] that enables the recording of higher resolution videos with the built-in Nexus 5 image sensor (Sony Exmor R IMX 179).

The highest resolution with progressive video recording (i.e., each recorded frame is a full picture) provided by the application is $1440p$ ($1440x2560$ pixel).

Choosing the $1440p$ option has certain advantages:

- Higher resolution (compared to $1080p$ or $720p$).
- No interpolation (compared to $4K$).
- Progressive video recording (compared to $3.4K$ or $4K$).

However, there are some points to take into consideration:

- Using a higher resolution during video recording increases energy consumption. The battery will discharge faster.
- Snap Camera is not free; the app needs to be purchased for full use.

Examples: As you can see in Figure 12, the native resolution of the Nexus 5 image sensor is $3264x2448$ pixel. By choosing the available recording options provided by the google stock camera application $1080p$ or $720p$, the video would only use a fraction of the available resolution. The best choice for motion videos is $1440p$. This option records full pictures for each video frame. Thus, it is possible to extract single frames yielding the best possible image quality.

To enable the higher resolution video recording options in Snap Camera, it is necessary to toggle the Google Camera2 API and OpenGLES 2.0 settings in the "Other" menu from the application, as shown in Figure 13. Thereafter, it is possible to select $1140p$, $3.4K$, and $4K$ UHD as recording options (see Figure 14).

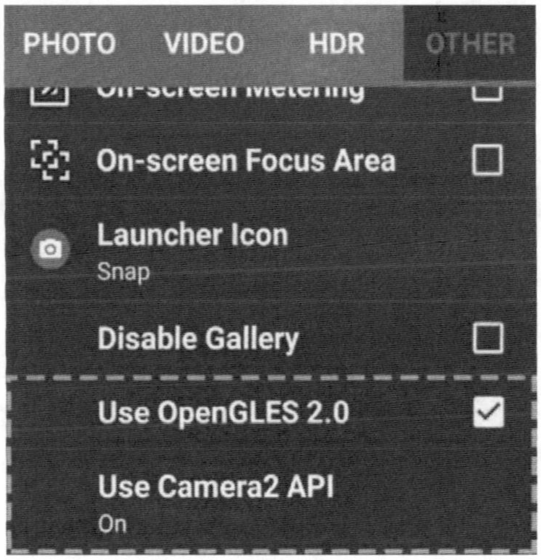

Figure 13. This Figure shows the adjustments that have to be made in SnapCam to enable video recording with higher resolutions on the Nexus 5.

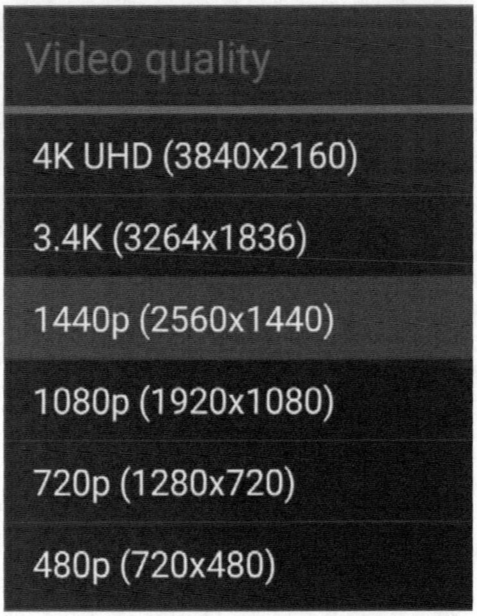

Figure 14. Listing of the available video recording options SnapCam is offering after unlocking higher resolutions.

Keywords: video recording, video acquisition, resolution, Nexus 5

D. Extract Media Information from Videofiles

Intent: This pattern describes the extraction of media information from video files with the help of FFmpeg or FFprobe.

Problem: Working with video files may prove as challenging, particularly if there is only limited knowledge on the settings (i.e., frame rate, codec, interlaced or progressive recording) used. However, this knowledge is vital for post processing video files and should, therefore, be brought to knowledge as soon as possible.

Scenario: In order to work efficiently with video files, the video specifications have to be acquired before even starting the post processing.

Solution: The first step is the installation of the FFmpeg [32] multimedia framework. The framework offers a variety of functions apart from scanning media files or extracting frames from video files and, therefore, is recommended for this task.

To scan a video file recorded with a common device, such as mobile phones or video cameras with FFprobe or FFmpeg, type in the following in a command window:

```
ffprobe <video_filename>
```

or

```
ffmpeg -i <video_filename>
```

Note that using FFmpeg / FFprobe to scan a file may take some time, depending on the input file duration and decoding complexity.

Examples: An example output for scanning the file “video.mp4” with FFmpeg / FFprobe:

```
ffmpeg -i video.mp4

Input #0, mov,mp4,m4a,3gp,3g2,mj2, from
   'video.mp4':

 Metadata:
   major_brand : mp42
   minor_version : 0
   compatible_brands: isommp42
   creation_time : 2016-04-15T12:42:54.000000Z
   com.android.version: 6.0.1
 Duration: 00:00:06.64, start: 0.000000,
      bitrate: 23292 kb/s
   Stream #0:0(eng): Video: h264 (Baseline)
      (avc1 / 0x31637661), yuv420p,
      2560x1440, 23857 kb/s, SAR 1:1 DAR
      16:9, 30.72 fps, 90k tbr, 90k tbn, 180k
      tbc (default)

   Metadata:
     rotate       : 90
     creation_time :
        2016-04-15T12:42:54.000000Z
     handler_name : VideoHandle
   Side data:
     displaymatrix: rotation of -90.00 degrees
   Stream #0:1(eng): Audio: aac (LC) (mp4a /
      0x6134706D), 48000 Hz, mono, fltp, 96
      kb/s (default)
   Metadata:
     creation_time :
        2016-04-15T12:42:54.000000Z
     handler_name : SoundHandle
```

The second line mentions the video file (i.e., video.mp4) used to generate the output. The relevant video information is found in the Stream section of the video Metadata part.

This Stream holds the following important information:

- Stream Number: The first video stream here is declared as #0.0, whereas the audio stream is declared as # 0:1 and followed by the language flag.
- Video Codec: In this case, the video was coded with “h264” using the “baseline” profile. Baseline is commonly applied for lower cost applications with limited hardware resources, e.g., for video conferences or mobile applications. Regarding the information within the parentheses, “avc1” is a different name for the H.264 codec, whereas “0x31637661” is a four character code (Hex to ASCII) equivalent: 0x61 = “a”, 0x76 = “v”, 0x63 = “c”, 0x31 = “1”.
- Colorspace: YUV420P is used for storing raw image data at a ratio of 4:2:0, meaning there is one color sample for every 4 luma samples. Thus, the color information is quartered (i.e., saving video bandwidth).
- Resolution: The file was recorded with the resolution of 2560x1440 pixel.
- Storage Aspect Ratio: The SAR defines the ratio of pixel dimensions. Square pixels are 1:1, whereas 1:2 for example would describe a rectangular pixels.

- Display Aspect Ratio: DAR defines the ratio of the width to height of a video file. The ration 16:9 is commonly known as Widescreen.
- Frame Rate: The Frame rate, expressed as frames per second or fps, is the rate at which consecutive frames (i.e., images) are displayed during video playback. In this example, the video has 30.72 frames that are displayed every second.
- tbr, tbn and tbc: These three values are three different timestamps FFmpeg / FFprobe provides.

Keywords: H.264, metadata, FFmpeg, FFprobe

E. Still Image Extraction from H.264 Videos

Intent: This pattern describes one of the best ways to extract high quality still images from H.264 videos.

Problem: There are several ways to extracting still images from a video e.g., with the highest quality possible. One option is taking screenshots by using common video player software (e.g., VLC [33][34]). However, this solution yields a low image quality.

Scenario: For post-processing reasons, high quality still images needed to be extracted from pre-recorded videos. After assuring that the recorded videos had the best possible quality, still images have to be extracted with the least loss of quality.

Solution: The first step is to extract the media information, as explained in Pattern *Extract Media Information from Videofiles*. It is vital to know the video codec and the frame rate, which was used to record the video, in order to extract the images. Finally, FFmpeg is used with the acquired information to extract the still images with the code provided in the example section.

Examples: In this example, the video was recorded on a LG Nexus 5 using the Snap Camera application with the 1440*p* option:

```
Input #0, mov,mp4,m4a,3gp,3g2,mj2, from
    ''video.mp4'':

  Metadata:
    major_brand : mp42
    minor_version : 0
    compatible_brands: isommp42
    creation_time : 2016-04-15T12:42:54.000000Z
    com.android.version: 6.0.1
  Duration: 00:00:06.64, start: 0.000000,
      bitrate: 23292 kb/s
    Stream #0:0(eng): Video: h264 (Baseline)
        (avc1 / 0x31637661), yuv420p,
        2560x1440, 23857 kb/s, SAR 1:1 DAR
        16:9, 30.72 fps, 90k tbr, 90k tbn, 180k
        tbc (default)

    Metadata:
      rotate      : 90
      creation_time :
          2016-04-15T12:42:54.000000Z
      handler_name : VideoHandle
    Side data:
      displaymatrix: rotation of -90.00 degrees
```

The important variables are:

- Filename: video.mp4
- Duration: 00:00:06.64
- Video Coced: h264

The following code shows how to extract still images from a "video.mp4" file using FFmpeg in a terminal (in this example, the command is executed in the same folder as the video file):

```
ffmpeg -ss 00:00:04 -t 00:00:00.04 -i
    video.mp4 -qscale:v 2 -r 30.72
    frontal\%4d.jpg
```

- [-ss 00:00:04]
  - This part of the command defines the start time of the image extraction. Ideally, this should be done during a frontal face scene with open eyes. In this case, the starting time is 00:00:04.
- [-t 00:00:00.04]
  - This part of the command defines the length of the timeframe in which images will be extracted. Here, the extraction will stop after 0.04 seconds.
- [-i video.mp4]
  - This command defines which input file should be used. It is possible to point the full path. In this case, the video is in the same folder and named "video.mp4".
- [-qscale:v 2]
  - -qscale:v is responsible for the quality of the extracted image. For .jpeg images, it is possible to use values between 2 and 31. The higher the number, the higher the .jpeg compression and, therefore, worse image quality. For best results, values between 2 and 5 should be used.
- [-r 25.0]
  - This part defines the frame rate. In our case, we are using 25.0 frames per second, i.e., one frame every 1/25 seconds.
- [frontal%4d.jpg]
  - This part can be divided in thee parts. "Frontal" is the name of the image, whereas the "%4d" part is a 4-digit automatically incremented number with leading zeros. In the case that multiple images are extracted from a video, this may come in handy. The final part is the file format ".jpg". In this example, ".jpg" image format is used to encode the extracted images.

Keywords: H.264, image extraction, FFmpeg

F. Comparison between Bitmap, Portable Network Graphic, and JPEG Images

Intent: This pattern shortly describes the differences, pros, and cons of .bmp, .png and .jpeg images.

Problem: As described in Pattern *Still Image Extraction from H.264 Videos*, still images can be extracted as .bmp, .png, and .jpeg files from video files. Which format to use, however, depends on certain characteristics the images have to meet, e.g., for post processing.

Scenario: Still images have to be extracted from a video file recoded with an android mobile phone. Now, it is a question of which file format to use for the image extraction.

Solution: Taking three variables into consideration - speed of extraction, image quality and file size, it is possible to quickly decide on a specific file format for the image extraction.

Speed of Extraction: If the speed of extraction is the crucial variable, .bmp is the best choice. Extracting frames as uncompressed .bmp files is the fastest way, due to the minimal processing power needed to extract the images from a vide file. In terms of extraction speed, .jpeg files come after .bmp. The .jpeg extraction is performance intensive, though, still faster than .png. Concluding in terms of extraction speed: $.bmp > .jpeg > .png$.

Image Quality: When image quality (e.g., no or less artifacts) is the main factor for the decision which file format to use, .bmp or .png files are the best choice. Both file formats allow lossless saving of image data. During the extraction process, .jpeg images always produce blocking artifacts, depending on the quality parameter used for .jpeg encoding as pictured in Figure 16. Concluding: $.bmp = .png > .jpg$ in terms of image quality.

File Size If a small image file size is targeted, then .jpeg should be preferred. In general, images using the .jpeg file format offer a small file size due the compression with the tradeoff in terms of image quality. While .png files are compressed as well, the compression is lossless and, therefore, resulting in a bigger file size compared to .jpeg. .bmp files are lossless as well, however, they are not compressed and yield a higher file size. As a rule of thumb in terms of file size: $.jpeg < .png < .bmp$.

Examples: This section shows a comparison of the different file formats .bmp, .png, and .jpeg with respect to extraction time, image quality, and file size. The **extraction time** (user + sys = cpu time used), in seconds, was acquired by inserting the "time" command before the FFmpeg extraction routine, which is a variation if the command presented in Pattern *Still Image Extraction from H.264 Videos* that extracts **n** frames per second from a $7.57s$ long video. The results can be seen in Table I for **n = 1**, Table II for **n = 2** and Table III for **n = 4** respectively.

```
time ffmpeg -i extract.mp4 -vf fps= n
    -qscale:v 2 frontal\%4d.jpeg
```

TABLE I. Extraction time for **n = 1**

	Extraction time **t** in seconds for 8 extracted images
.bmp	$22.216s + 0.478s = 22.694s$
.jpeg	$22.515s + 0.327s = 22.842s$
.png	$27.560s + 0.414s = 27.974s$

TABLE II. Extraction time for **n = 2**

	Extraction time **t** in seconds for 15 extracted images
.bmp	$22.445s + 0.677s = 23.122s$
.jpeg	$22.802s + 0.392s = 23.194s$
.png	$32.100s + 0.486s = 32.586s$

TABLE III. Extraction time for **n = 4**

	Extraction time **t** in seconds for 29 extracted images
.bmp	$22.489s + 0.985s = 23.474s$
.jpeg	$23.525s + 0.395s = 23.92s$
.png	$41.358s + 0.591s = 41.949s$

During encoding, .jpeg images produce blocking artifacts. Depending on the quality settings, the artifacts can be quite present as shown in Figure 16. To visualize the difference in terms of **image quality**, a comparison was done by calculating peak signal-to-noise ratio. Figure 15 shows the difference between two extracted frames, one using .bmp and the other .jpeg file format. The mostly red parts in the middle indicate the variance between the images ,whereas the white dots point out the identical parts. Typical PSNR values for compressed images range between $30dB$ and $50dB$, where higher is better; this comparison has a PSNR of $42.7731dB$ for all color channels.

Figure 15. Representation of image differences (middle) between an extracted .jpeg (left) and .bmp (right) frontal face image.

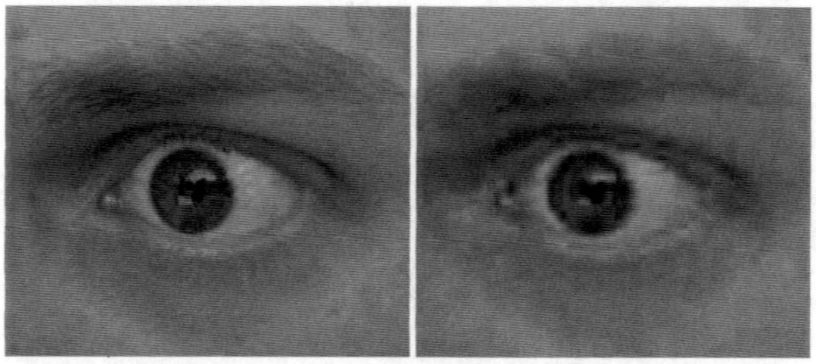

Figure 16. .jpeg image saved with highest quality settings (left) and with the lowest possible quality settings (right).

These are the **file size** differences of an extracted frame. The image used is the same as in Figure15, from a H.264 coded video with a resolution of $3840x2160pixel$.

- **.bmp**: 24.9MB
- **.png**: 6.2MB
- **.jpeg**: 448kB

Note that the size itself heavily depends on the resolution. Therefore, this example shows the variance in file size between the tree image formats.

Keywords: H.264, still image extraction, extraction time, image quality, file size, FFmpeg

G. Extraction of the Eye Area from Frontal Face Images

Intent: This pattern describes the detection of the eye area in frontal face images with the help of the OpenCV library.

Problem: Detecting eyes in an image is not as simple as it may seem at first. Object detection algorithms with the aim of finding eyes, for example, can not distinguish whether the detected area is a real eye or just something that the algorithm interprets as an eye. Therefore, it is necessary to enhance the detection rate by defining a certain region of interest by detecting the face first, in which the eyes can be found, before starting the eye detection routine.

Scenario: The eye area has to be detected and extracted from frontal face images for post processing.

Solution: Before programming the eye detection and extraction function, it is mandatory to prepare the following things:

- Frontal face image(s) that will be used for eye detection and extraction.
- A working installation of the OpenCV library [24] (installation guides for Windows [35], macOS [36], Linux [37])
- Haarcascade files for Frontal Face and Eye detection [38].

If needed, further information on Haar-like features can be found in Viola and Jones [21][22]. If all the aforementioned things are prepared, implement the eye detection, and extraction routine based on the following code example (C-Code translated from Python with added comments; adapted from [39]):

```
# Pseudocode example for the extraction of
    the eye area
program eye_extraction
# Load a frontal face image and haarcascades
    for face and eye detection
LoadFiles()
  image =
      cv.LoadImage('frontal_face_image.png')
  faceHaarCascade =
      cv.Load('haarcascade_frontalface_alt.xml')
  eyeHaarCascade =
      cv.Load('haarcascade_eye.xml')
# Face and Eye Detection
DetectFaceAndEyes(image, faceHaarCascade,
    eyeHaarCascade)
  # Convert the color image to grayscale for
      post processing
  grey = cv.CvtColor(image, gray)
  # Detect face
face = cv.HaarDetectObjects(image,
    faceHaarCascade)
# If faces is found
if face:
for ((x_pos, y_pos, width, heigh), n) in
    face:
# Create a bounding box around the face area
point1 = (int x_pos, int y_pos)
point2 = (int (x_pos + width), int (y_pos +
    heigh))
cv.Rectangle(image, point1, point2)
# Estimate the eyes position by setting the
    region of interest and remove the lower
    part of the face image to reduce the
    probability for false recognition
# The removal of the lower part can be seen
    in the last devision 'int((point2[1] -
    point1[1]) * 0.6))'.
# The '0.6' in the last devision indicates
    that approximately 1/3 of the lower
    part of the face is cut out
cv.SetImageROI(image, (point1[0],
            point1[1],
            point2[0] - point1[0],
        int((point2[1] - point1[1]) * 0.6)))
# Detect the eyes
eyes = cv.HaarDetectObjects(image,
    eyeHaarCascade)
# If eyes were found
if eyes:
# For each eye found
for eye1 and eye2 in eyes:
# Draw a rectangle around the eyes (code
    applies if eyes are horizontally
    aligned)
point1 = eye1_x_pos, eye1_y_pos)
point2 = (eye2_x_pos + eye2_width,
    eye2_y_pos+ eye2_heigh)
cv.Rectangle(image, point1, point2)
# Reset the image region of interest for
    the image to be drawn correctly
cv.ResetImageROI(image)
# Extract the eye area and save it
eye_area = cut.Out(image, point1, point2)
save.Image(eye_area, 'eye_area.png')
```

Examples: A frontal face image like the one depicted in Figure 17 should be loaded into the the program described by the code example.

Figure 17. Frontal Face Image used for face and eye detection and feature extraction.

Figure 18 shows a) a blue rectangle for the detected face area, b) two orange rectangles for each detected eye, and c) the final rectangle around both eyes covering the to be extracted eye area. The final output after extraction should look like the example image pictured in Figure 19.

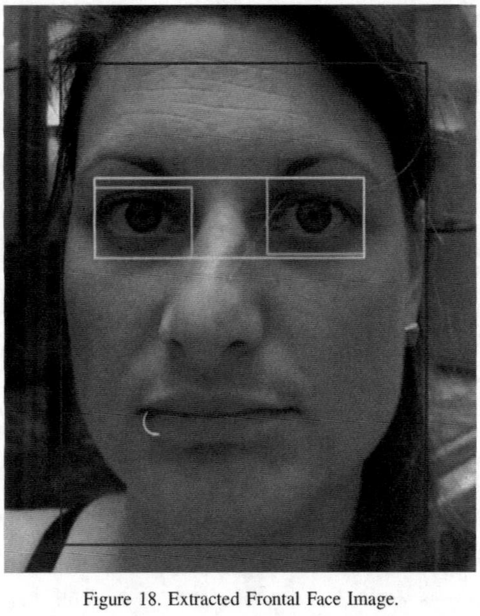

Figure 18. Extracted Frontal Face Image.

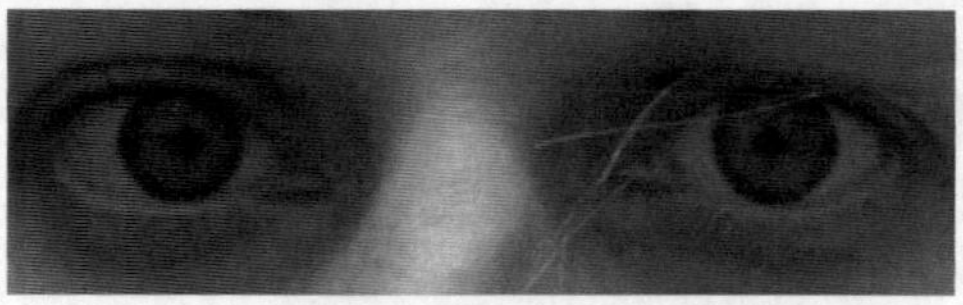

Figure 19. Extracted Frontal Face Image.

Keywords: H.264, image extraction, FFmpeg

VI. Discussion

Using the cUX pattern approach to create easy-to-use solutions allowed us to adjust and improve the overall study concept and setup in several ways. Apart from that, we also acquired a deeper insight into the pattern creation process overall. This gave us a chance to notice certain weak points in the creation process, which, when improved, would help to generate better patterns.

A. Pattern Generation Process

As mentioned at the end of Section III, each iteration and the following rework phase refines the pattern. The pattern is increasing in quality, with every feedback received during the iteration process. Bottom line, the more iterations processes a pattern runs through, the better it gets. In our case, we had a constant collaboration during the creation process of the patterns, which enabled us to get on demand feedback when necessary. Due to active collaboration, we had the possibility of continuous iterations, allowing us to interplay between problem statements and solutions. Usually, problem statements are defined in the beginning and changes can only be made during workshops. Solutions, however, are provided during the fist iteration, at the very earliest. Therefore, modifications can be made only after receiving feedback. Until then, the work on the pattern is on hold.

The interplay showed us a huge advantage, due to the possibility to refine the problem statement while simultaneously adjusting the solution. This induced the improvement of both the problem statement and the related solution leading to a higher quality pattern. The problem, however, was the recurring chance to rephrase the problem statement at any time. Thus, it was tempting to rephrase the problem statement to fit a certain solution, even when it was only covering a part of the statement. This behavior is not desired at all. Patterns are supposed to provide proven solutions. In the beginning, after describing the problem statements, we did not know if we could cover these criteria with our suggested solutions. However, we evaluated our patterns regarding that point through trial and error. Each and every solution we provide in our patterns was tested before it was adopted into the patterns. This was only possible due to the interplay and instant feedback and, therefore, can not be generally applied. However, we found that this way of verification improved the provided solutions to a high degree.

B. Pattern Sections

The next discussion point is the use of a *Topics* section proposed by the cUX pattern approach. Topics, in this case, are predefined keywords used to show the scope of the problem and, additionally, address one or more user experience factors.

We willingly omitted that section, as we saw no need for them in our created patterns. Topics may be beneficial to organize a collection of patterns, providing a variety of solutions for a large main field. Each pattern can be assigned to at least one of the topics. However, in our case, we only had a limited amount of problem statements that we wanted to address. Thus, creating a system in which we want to organize our patterns seemed unnecessary. Therefore, it was sufficient enough to provide keywords only at the end of the patterns. The keywords provide research topics and fields that may be related to the pattern and may be used to get more insight into certain areas covered or not sufficiently covered in the patterns.

C. More than one Solution

Patterns are by no means always the one and only possible solution for a certain problem. This is especially noticeable in problems concerning programming questions. The two main issues regarding programming questions in patterns are, for one, the programming language and, second, the implementation. Taking the pattern "Extraction of the Eye Area from Frontal Face Images" as an example, there were several ways to solve this problem. It is be possible to extract the eye area from the frontal face images by hand, image by image. This is very time consuming and inefficient, but it is a working solution. Thus, to optimize the procedure, the detection of the region of interest and the extraction needed to be automated, ideally by a program. One of the more versatile tools to accomplish that is the OpenCV library, which is supporting the most operating systems, but only a handful of programming language interfaces(i.e., C++, C, Python, and Java).

The problem is either to choose a certain language, preferably the most popular one, to provide a low-level solution or to provide a high-level description of the solution using pseudocode. Naturally, a low-level solution would be predestined to provide a copy and paste implementation that could be used right away. However, this would limit the usage of the pattern. To broaden the usage of the pattern, the decision was made to use a high-level description utilizing pseudocode without going far into the exact implementation. This is only one example from many that shows that a) there are many ways to solve a problem and b) the solution chosen heavily relies on the pattern creation team.

D. Aid & Explanation instead of direct Solutions

Apart from having difficulties to chose the best way to solve a problem, there are problems that can only be solved by providing a couple of possible ways to handle certain difficulties. "Comparison between Bitmap, Portable Network Graphic, and JPEG Images", for example, offers a solution in the way of providing the reader with vital information as a basis for deciding how to handle the problem of choosing a certain file format for image extraction. Each image format has its advantages and disadvantages. When compared to .png and .bmp files, .jpeg files are smaller, but offer the worst quality, as .jpeg files are automatically compressed. The extraction speed is decent, but by far not as fast as .bmp extraction; .png and .bmp files are lossless and offer the best image quality with the tradeoff of file size and, in case of .png files, extraction speed as well. Thus, there is no optimal solution without knowing the actual terms of use. The pattern can provide a solution in the form of aid and explanation to ease the decision of which file format to utilize for extraction; however, there is no one way solution for that kind of problems.

VII. Conclusion and Future Work

In this paper, we presented seven patterns to help design and refine a study setup for biometric image data acquisition analysis. By adapting an existing cUX design patterns approach, we were able to successfully document the study setup and its optimization in question and document these for future applications. The pattern structure and modular nature allows for further expansion and setup variations in the future. The presented patterns cover the most immediate problems for the specific setup but should not be considered a full pattern collection for biometric image data analysis. Nevertheless, the goal of creating additional solution patterns to improve the study setup, focusing on the image application domain, was fulfilled. We provided four additional patterns answering common problems in the image application domain.

Future work will have to focus on, not only reapplying these patterns and refine them further, but also expand towards related problems that could only be touched in the patterns above (e.g., further details on compression formats and artifacts, a wider range of file formats, more phone types or image acquisition devices in general, etc.). The existing patterns can already be used to inform future study setups with solutions regarding (a) choice of the right lighting conditions, (b) construction of a custom lens holder, (c) high quality video acquisition with a mobile phone, (d) the extraction of media information from video files, (e) extract still images from H.264 videos, and (f) the extraction of the eye area with the help of Haar-like features.

Further expansion will focus on providing more thorough solutions and suitability for more instances and broader contexts, towards a more profound knowledge base on biometric image analysis, suitable for an even wider range of users.

References

[1] A. Lupp, A. G. Mirnig, A. Uhl, and M. Tscheligi, "A Study Setup Optimization – Providing Solutions with Patterns," in PATTERNS 2017, The Ninth International Conferences on Pervasive Patterns and Applications, 2017, pp. 11-16.

[2] C. Alexander, "A Pattern Language: Towns, Buildings, Construction," Oxford University Press, New York, USA, 1997.

[3] C. Alexander, "The Timeless Way of Building," Oxford University Press, New York, USA, 1979.

[4] E. Gamma, R. Helm, R. Johnson, and J. Vlissides, "Design Patterns: Elements of Reusable Object-Oriented Software." Pearson, 1994.

[5] M. J. Mahemoff and L. J. Johnston, "Principles for a Usability-Oriented Pattern Language," In Proc. Australian Computer Human Interaction Conference OZCHI '98, IEEE Computer Society, 1998, pp. 132-139.

[6] A. Dix, G. Abowd, R. Beale, and J. Finlay, "Human-Computer Interaction," Prentice Hall, Europe, 1998.

[7] D. May and P. Taylor, "Knowledge management with patterns," Commun. ACM 46, 7, July 2003, pp. 94-99.

[8] J. Borchers, "A Pattern Approach to Interaction Design," AI & Society, 12, Springer, 2001, pp. 359-376.

[9] A. F. Blackwell and S. Fincher, "PUX: Patterns of User Experience," Interactions, vol. 17, no. 2., NY, USA: ACM, 2010, pp. 27-31.

[10] M. Obrist, D. Wurhofer, E. Beck, A. Karahasanovic, and M. Tscheligi, "User experience (ux) patterns for audio-visual networked applications: Inspirations for design," in Proceedings of the 6th Nordic Conference on Human-Computer Interaction: Extending Boundaries, ser. NordiCHI10. New York, NY, USA: ACM, 2010, pp. 343-352.

[11] A. G. Mirnig and M. Tscheligi, "Introducing a General Multi-Purpose Pattern Framework: Towards a Universal Pattern Approach," International Journal On Advances in Intelligent Systems, vol. 8, 2015, pp. 40-56.

[12] G. K. Wallace, "The JPEG still picture compression standard," IEEE transactions on consumer electronics, 1992, 38. Jg., Nr. 1, S. xviii-xxxiv.

[13] DRAFT, I. T. U. T. recommendation and final draft international standard of joint video specification (ITU-T Rec. H. 264— ISO/IEC 14496-10 AVC). Joint Video Team (JVT) of ISO/IEC MPEG and ITU-T VCEG, JVTG050, 2003, 33. Jg.

[14] H264, I. ISO/IEC 14496-10 AVC. Draft ITU-T Recommendation and Final Draft International Standard of Joint Video Specification.

[15] S. Rakshit, D.M. Monro, "An Evaluation of Image Sampling and Compression for Human Iris Recognition," IEEE Transactions on Information Forensics and Security 2(3), 2007, 605-612.

[16] M.A. Figueroa-Villanueva, N.K. Ratha, R.M. Bolle, "A comparative performance analysis of JPEG2000 vs. WSQ for fingerprint compression," In: Kittler, J., Nixon, M.S. (eds.) AVBPA 2003. LNCS, Springer, Heidelberg 2003, vol. 2688, pp. 385-392.

[17] R.C. Kidd, "Comparison of wavelet scalar quantization and JPEG for fingerprint image compression," Journal of Electronic Imaging 4(1), 1995, pp. 31-39.

[18] L. Granai, J.R. Tena, M. Hamouz, J. Kittler, "Influence of compression on 3D face recognition," Pattern Recognition Letters, 30(8), pp. 745-750.

[19] K. Delac, S. Grgic, M. Grgic, "Image compression in face recognition - a literature survey," In: Recent Advances in Face Recognition, I-Tech, 2008, pp. 236-250.

[20] P. Elmer, A. Lupp, S. Sprenger, R. Thaler, and A. Uhl, "Exploring compression impact on face detection using haar-like features," in Scandinavian Conference on Image Analysis. Springer, 2015, pp. 53-64.

[21] P. Viola, M.J. Jones, "Rapid object detection using a boosted cascade of simple features," In: Proceedings of the 2001 IEEE Computer Society Conference on Computer Vision and Pattern Recognition, CVPR 2001, vol. 1, pp. I-511-I-518.

[22] P. Viola, M.J. Jones, "Robust Real-Time Face Detection," International Journal of Computer Vision, 57(2), 2004, pp. 137-154.

[23] R. Lienhart, J. Maydt, "An extended set of Haar-like features for rapid object detection," In: Proceedings of the 2002 International Conference on Image Processing, vol. 1, 2002, pp. I-900-I-903.

[24] OpenCV. Available: http://opencv.org [Accessed: 20 - Aug - 2017]

[25] D. Wurhofer, M. Obrist, E. Beck, and M. Tscheligi, "A quality criteria framework for pattern validation," International Journal On Advances in Software, vol. 3, no. 1 and 2. IARIA, 2010, pp. 252-264.

[26] A. Mirnig, T. Kaiser, A. Lupp, N. Perterer, A. Meschtscherjakov, T. Grah, and M. Tscheligi, "Automotive User Experience Design Patterns: An Approach and Pattern Examples," International Journal On Advances in Intelligent Systems, vol. 9, 2016, pp. 275-286.

[27] A. G. Mirnig et al., "User Experience Patterns from Scientific and Industry Knowledge: An Inclusive Pattern Approach," in PATTERNS 2015, Seventh International Conference on Pervasive Patterns and Applications. IARIA, 2015, pp. 38-44.

[28] Philips MASTER TL5 HO 49W/865 UNP/40 - Product Page. Available: http://bit.ly/2kDgmOV [Accessed: 11 - Jan - 2017]

[29] YouTube Video - Nexus 5 Lens Holder Case. Available: https://youtu.be/J3dParRRQJg [Accessed: 11 - Jan - 2017]

[30] [App][2.3+]Snap Camera. Available: http://bit.ly/2iCujgO [Accessed: 31 - Jul - 2017]

[31] [App][2.3+]Snap Camera - 4k Video on Nexus 5 Feature. Available: http://bit.ly/2tQQW47 [Accessed: 31 - Jul - 2017]

[32] Download FFmpeg. Available: http://bit.ly/2v6qkNm [Accessed: 21 - Aug - 2017]

[33] VideoLAN. Available: http://www.videolan.org [Accessed: 20 - Aug - 2017]http://www.videolan.org

[34] VLC HowTo/Take a snapshot. Available: http://bit.ly/2wJ6AU5 [Accessed: 20 - Aug - 2017]

[35] OpenCV Installation - Windows. Available: http://bit.ly/2wmqx0f [Accessed: 20 - Aug - 2017]

[36] OpenCV Installation - macOS. Available: http://bit.ly/2ukmjoE [Accessed: 20 - Aug - 2017]

[37] OpenCV Installation - Linux. Available: http://bit.ly/2xvIzNE [Accessed: 20 - Aug - 2017]

[38] OpenCV Haarcascade Files. Available: https://github.com/opencv/opencv/tree/master/data/haarcascades [Accessed: 20 - Aug - 2017]

[39] DETECTING EYES WITH PYTHON & OPENCV. Available: http://bit.ly/2vHNjhc [Accessed: 20 - Aug - 2017]

Automotive Software Product Line Architecture Evolution: Extracting, Designing and Managing Architectural Concepts

Axel Grewe, Christoph Knieke, Marco Körner, Andreas Rausch,
Mirco Schindler, Arthur Strasser, and Martin Vogel
TU Clausthal, Department of Computer Science, Software Systems Engineering
Clausthal-Zellerfeld, Germany
Email: {axel.grewe|christoph.knieke|marco.koerner|andreas.rausch|
mirco.schindler|arthur.strasser|m.vogel}@tu-clausthal.de

Abstract—**The amount of software in cars has been growing exponentially since the early 1970s, and one can expect this trend to continue. To keep the software development for vehicles cost efficient, modular components with a high reuse rate cross different types of vehicles are used. Often, a product line approach is used to handle variability. As the underlying software product line architecture and its evolution are generally not explicitly documented and controlled, architecture erosion and complexity within the software product line architecture are growing steadily. In the long-term, this leads to reduced reusability and extensibility of the software artifacts, and thus, to a deterioration of evolvability. First, we propose methods used to extract initial product line architectures by recovery/discovery methods and describe our experiences gained from a real world example. Furthermore, we integrate this approach into an evolutionary incremental development process and show how a knowledge based process for architecture evolution and maintenance for architectural concepts can be implemented. The approach includes methods and concepts to create adequate architectures with the help of abstract design principles, patterns, and description techniques. Our approach helps software engineers to manage system complexity by suitable architectural concepts, by techniques for architecture quality measurements and by processes to iteratively evolve automotive software systems. We demonstrate our approach on a real world example, the longitudinal dynamics torque coordination from automotive software engineering.**

Keywords–Architecture Evolution; Software Product Lines; Architecture Quality Measures; Automotive Software Engineering.

I. Introduction

This paper is a substantial extension of the work presented at the ADAPTIVE 2017 conference [1]. Usually many variants of a vehicle exist – different configurations of comfort functions, driver assistance systems, connected car services, or powertrains can be variably combined, creating an individual and unique product. To keep the vehicles cost efficient, modular components with a high reuse rate cross different types of vehicles are required. With respect to innovative and sophisticated functions, coming with the connected car and automated resp. autonomous driving the functional complexity, the technical complexity, and the networked-caused complexity is continuously and dramatically increasing. It is, and will be in future, a great challenge to further manage the resulting complexity.

As the number of functions grows steadily in the evolutionary development of automotive software systems, the "essential" complexity of the product line architecture increases continuously. However, the "accidental" complexity of the

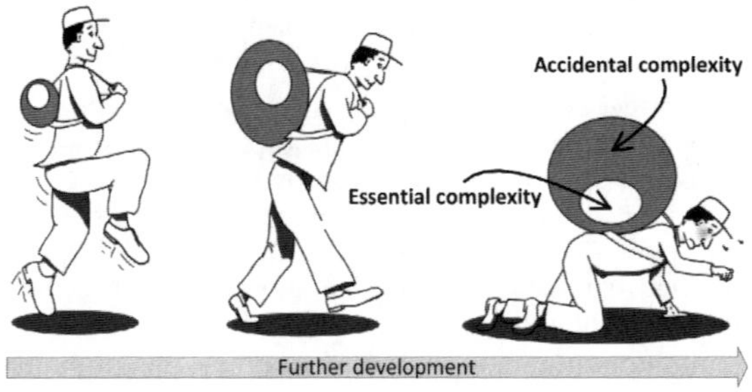

Figure 1. "Essential" vs. "Accidental" complexity

architecture of automotive software systems grows disproportionately to the essential complexity as illustrated in Figure 1 [2]. The growth of accidental complexity results from a "bad" architecture (product line architecture and product architecture) with strong coupling and a low cohesion, which have evolved over the time. "Bad" architectures increase accidental complexity and costs, hinder reusability and maintainability, and decrease performance and understandability.

A software system architecture defines the basic organization of a system by structuring different architectural elements and relationships between them. The reduction of accidental complexity of the software system architecture is crucial for the success of the system to be developed and its evolvability. By our definition, a "good" architecture is a modular and evolvable architecture, which should be built according to the following design principles:

1) Design principles for high cohesion
2) Design principles for abstraction and information hiding
3) Design principles for loose coupling

In this paper, we propose a sophisticated approach for extracting, designing and managing architectural concepts and thus enabling long-term evolution of automotive software product line architectures. By the term "architectural concepts" we subsume design patterns, architectural patterns or styles (see Section V). Our approach helps engineers to manage functional software systems complexity based on adequate architectures with the help of abstract principles, patterns, and description techniques. As an approach to manage automotive software product line architecture evolution, we propose the following steps:

(1) We often have to deal with an initially eroded software architecture which first has to be repaired. Thus, we propose methods used to extract initial product line architectures by recovery/discovery methods and describe our experiences gained from a real world example. The recovery/discovery approach is supported by an approach to extract architectural concepts from system realizations. (Sections IV and V)

(2) For designing automotive software product line architectures, we present architectural concepts developed within different industrial projects in the automotive domain involving different software architects and project members. Here, we aim to build the architecture according to the three design principles for a "good" architecture design mentioned above. In addition, we propose metrics to measure complexity of the design. Finally, a systematic approach for planning of development iterations and prototyping is introduced. (Section VI)

(3) Furthermore, we integrate this approach into an evolutionary incremental development process and show how a knowledge-based process for architecture evolution and maintenance for architectural concepts can be implemented. The term "knowledge-based" in this context means, that knowledge-based techniques like knowledge management are applied in the process. (Section VIII)

Step (1) of our approach is optional and only required in the case of an eroded software architecture, i.e., it is not intended for software product lines that are newly developed.

The paper is structured as follows: Section II gives an overview on the related work. Our overall development cycle for managed evolution of automotive software product line architectures is proposed in Section III. The first process activity to extract the initial architecture is proposed in Section IV. Section V introduces a new approach to extract concepts from source models. In Section VI we propose our methodology for designing and planning automotive product line architectures including long-term evolution. Section VII introduces a real world example, a longitudinal dynamics torque coordination software, from automotive software engineering. We apply our methodology for planning and evolving automotive product line architectures on this example and present the results of a corresponding case study. Section VIII extends the proposed methodology by an approach for knowledge-based architecture evolution and maintenance. Section IX concludes.

II. Overview on the Related Work

To the best of our knowledge no continuous overall development cycle for automotive software product line architectures exists. Next, we give an overview on the related work. Mostly, we focus on approaches that are related to automotive and embedded software systems.

A. Software Erosion

Van Gurp and Bosch [3] illustrate how design erosion works by presenting the evolution of the design of a small software system. The paper concludes that even an optimal design strategy for the design phase does not lead to an optimal design. The reason for this are unforeseen requirement changes in later evolution cycles. These changes may cause design decisions taken earlier to be less optimal.

In [4], a method is described to keep the erosion of the software to a minimum: Consistency constraints expressed by architectural aspects called architectural rules are specified as formulas on a common ontology, and models are mapped to instances of that ontology. Those rules can, e.g., contain structural information about the software like allowed communications. In [4], the rules are expressed as logical formulas, which can be evaluated automatically to the compliance to the product line architecture (PLA). These rules are extracted via Architecture Checker (ArCh) framework [5].

In order to enable the evolution of software product line architectures, architecture erosion has to be avoided. In [6], de Silva and Balasubramaniam provide a survey of technologies and techniques either to prevent architecture erosion or to detect and restore architectures that have been eroded. The approaches discussed in [6] are primarily classified into three generic categories that attempt to minimize, prevent and repair architecture erosion. The categories are refined by a set of strategies to tackle erosion: process-oriented architecture conformance, architecture evolution management, architecture design enforcement, architecture to implementation linkage, self-adaptation and architecture restoration techniques consisting of recovery, discovery and reconciliation. However, each approach discussed in [6] refers to architecture erosion for a single product architecture, whereas architecture erosion in software product lines is out of the scope of the paper. Furthermore, as discussed in [6], none of the available methods singly provides an effective and comprehensive solution for controlling architecture erosion.

B. Software Product Line Architecture Extraction

The aim of software product line extraction is to identify all the valid points of variation and the associated functional requirements of component diagrams. The work in [7] shows an approach to extract a product line from a user documentation. The Product Line UML-based Software Engineering (PLUS) approach permits variability analysis based on use case scenarios and the specification of variable properties in a feature model [8]. In [9] variability of a system characteristic is described in a feature model as variable features that can be mapped to use cases. In contrast to our approach, these approaches are based on functional requirements whereas our approach is focused on products.

C. Software Product Line Architecture Evolution and Life-Cycle Management

The work in [10] elaborates on the foundations of software product line engineering and provides experience-based knowledge about the two key processes, domain engineering and application engineering, and the definition and management of variability.

Holdschick [11] addresses the challenges in the evolution of model-based software product lines in the automotive domain. The author argues that a variant model created initially quickly becomes obsolete because of the permanent evolution of software functionalities in the automotive area. Thus, Holdschick proposes a concept how to handle evolution in variant-rich model-based software systems. The approach provides an overview of which changes relevant to variability could occur in the functional model and where the challenges are when reproducing them in the variant model.

D. Reference Architectures

In [12], reference architectures are assumed to be the basis for the instantiation of PLAs (so-called family architectures). The purpose of the reference architecture is to provide guidance for future developments. In addition, the reference architecture incorporates the vision and strategy for the future. The work in [12] examines current reference architectures and the driving forces behind development of them to come to a collective conclusion on what a reference architecture should truly be.

Nakagawa et. al. discuss the differences between reference architectures and PLAs by highlighting basic questions like definitions, benefits, and motivation for using each one, when and how they should be used, built, and evolved, as well as stakeholders involved and benefited by each one [13]. Furthermore, they define a reference model of reference architectures [14], and propose a methodology to design PLAs based on reference architectures [15], [16].

E. Software Product Line Architecture Design

Patterns and styles are an important means for software systems architecture specification and are widely covered in literature, see, e.g., [17], [18]. However, architecture patterns are not explicitly applied for the development of automotive software systems yet. For automotive industry, we propose the use of architecture patterns as a crucial means to overcome the complexity.

The work in [19] proposes a method that brings together two aspects of software architecture: the design of software architecture and software product lines. Deelstra et al. [20] provide a framework of terminology and concepts regarding product derivation. They have identified that companies employ widely different approaches for software product line based development and that these approaches evolve over time.

Thiel and Hein [21] propose product lines as an approach to automotive system development because product lines facilitate the reuse of core assets. The approach of Thiel and Hein enables the modeling of product line variability and describes how to manage variability throughout core asset development. Furthermore, they sketch the interaction between the feature and architecture models to utilize variability.

Flores et. al. [22] explain the application of 2GPLE (Second Generation Product Line Engineering) - an advanced set of explicitly defined product line engineering solutions - at General Motors.

F. Measurement of Software Product Line Architecture Quality

Siegmund et al. [23] present an approach for measuring non-functional properties in software product lines. The results are used to compute optimized software product line (SPL) configurations according to user-defined non-functional requirements. The method uses different metrics to measure three non-functional properties: *Maintainability*, *Binary Size*, and *Performance*. Siegmund et al. also discuss and classify the presented techniques to measure non-functional properties of software modules.

Passos et al. [24] show how automatic traceability, analyses, and recommendations support the evolution of SPL in a feature-oriented manner. They propose among other things a change-impact analysis to assess or estimate the impact and effort of a change. Furthermore, they regard metrics for architectural analysis. As a result, erosion and problems can be recognized at an early stage, and counter-measures can be taken. The ideas are illustrated by an automotive example.

In [25], product lines are measured with the metric *maintainability index* (MI). The "Feature Oriented Programming" is used to map an SPL to a graph. The values are transformed into several matrices. Next, singular value decomposition is applied to the matrices. The metric MI is then applied at different levels (product, feature, product line). The results show that by using the metric, features could be identified that had to be revised. The number of possible refactorings could be restricted.

In [26], several metrics are presented, which are specifically used for measuring PLAs. The metrics are applied to "vADL", a product line architecture description language, to determine the similarity, reusability, variability, and complexity of a PLA. The measured values can be used as a basis for further evolutionary steps.

G. Approaches on Multi Product Lines

The work in [27] gives a systematic survey and analysis of existing approaches supporting multi product lines and a general discussion of capabilities supporting multi product lines in various domains and organizations. They define a multi product line (MPL) as a set of several self-contained but still interdependent product lines that together represent a large-scale or ultra-large-scale system. The different product lines in an MPL can exist independently but typically use shared resources to meet the overall system requirements. According to this definition, a vehicle system is also an MPL assuming that each product line is responsible for a particular subsystem. However, in the following, we only regard classic product lines, since the dependencies between the individual product lines in vehicle systems are very low, unlike MPL.

H. Reuse of Software Artifacts in the Automotive Domain

To counteract erosion it is necessary to keep software components modular. But modularity is also a necessary attribute for reuse. Several approaches deal with the topic reuse of software components in the development of automotive products [28], [29]. In [28], a framework is proposed, which focuses on modularization and management of a function repository. Another practical experience describes the introduction of a product line for a gasoline system from scratch [29]. However, in both approaches a long-term minimization of erosion as well as a long-term evolution is not considered.

III. Basics

In this section we introduce our overall development cycle for managed evolution of automotive software product line architectures.

A. Overall Development Cycle

Our methodology for managed evolution of automotive software product line architectures is depicted in Figure 2. The left part of Figure 2 depicts the recovery and discovery activity for repairing an eroded software (see Section IV). This activity is performed once before the long term evolution cycle (right side of Figure 2) can start. The latter consists of two levels of development: The cycle on the top of Figure 2 constitutes the

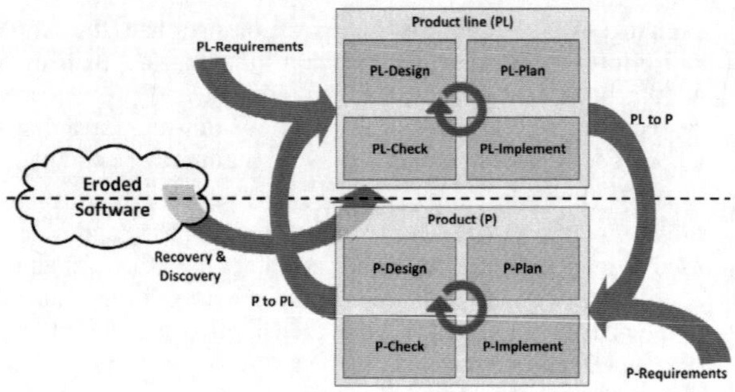

Figure 2. Overall development cycle

development activities for product line development, whereas the second cycle is required for product specific development. Not only both levels of development are executed in parallel but even the activities within a cycle may be performed concurrently. The circular arrow within the two cycles indicates the dependencies of an activity regarding the artifacts of the previous activity. Nevertheless, individual activities may be performed in parallel, e.g., the planned implementations can be realized from activity `PL-Plan`, while a new product line architecture is developed in parallel (activity `PL-Design`). The large arrows between the two development levels indicate transitions requiring an external decision-making process: The decision to start a new product development or prototyping (activity `PL to P`), and the inclusion and generalization of lessons learned during product development in the evolution of the SPL (activity `P to PL`), respectively.

We distinguish between the terms 'project' and 'product' in the following: A project includes a set of versioned software components, so-called modules. These modules contain variability so that a project can be used for different vehicles. A product on the other hand is a fully runnable software status for a certain vehicle that can be flashed and executed on an ECU and is based on a project in conjunction with vehicle related parameter settings.

In the following subsections, we will explain the basic activities of our approach in detail by referring to the terms depicted in Figure 2. Table I gives a brief overview on the objectives of each of the 13 activities, including inputs and outputs.

Software system and software component requirements from requirements engineering (`PL-Requirements`) and artifacts of the developed product from the product cycle in Figure 2 (`P to PL`) serve as input to the management cycle of the PLA. Activities `PL-Design` and `PL-Plan` aim at designing, planning and evolving product line architectures and are explained in detail in this paper (see Section VI).

The planned implementation artifacts are implemented in `PL-Implement` on product line level whereas in `P-Implement` product specific implementation artifacts are implemented. For the building of a fully executable software status for a certain vehicle project, the project plan is transferred (`PL to P`) containing module descriptions and descriptions of the logical product architecture integration plan with associated module versions. In addition, special requirements for a specific project are regarded (`P-Requirements`). The creation of a new product starts with a basic planned product architecture commonly derived from the product line (`P-Design`). The product planning in `P-Plan` defines the iterations to be performed. An iteration consists of selected product architecture elements and planned implementations. An iteration is part of a sequence of iterations.

Each planned project refers to a set of implementation artifacts, called modules. These modules constitute the product architecture. The aim of `PL-Check` and `P-Check` is the minimization of product architecture erosion by architecture conformance checking for automotive software product line development. Furthermore, we apply architecture conformance checking to check conformance between the planned product architecture and the PLA in `P-Design`.

B. General Structure and Definitions

The relation between PLA, products, and modules is illustrated in Figure 3. We indicate the development points $t \in \mathbb{N}$ by the timeline at the bottom. Next, we give brief definitions of the terms PLA, product, and module.

PLA: On the top of Figure 3 the different versions of the PLA are illustrated. A PLA consists of logical architecture elements $l \in \mathrm{LAE}$ (cf. `A`, `B`, `C` in Figure 3) and directed connections $c \in C$ between these elements. At each development point t exactly one version of the PLA exists. A certain PLA version is denoted by $\mathrm{pla}_x \in PLA$, with $x \in \mathbb{N}$ to distinguish between PLA versions. The sequence of PLA versions is indicated by the arrows between the PLAs in Figure 3.

Product: A product $\mathrm{p}_{i\_j} \in P$ has a product identifier i and a version index j, with $i, j \in \mathbb{N}$. The sequence of versions is indicated by the flow relation between products in Figure 3. We assume a distinct mapping of p_{i_j} to a certain $\mathrm{pla}_x \in PLA$. A product p_{i_j} contains a product architecture $\mathrm{pa}_{i\_j} \in PA$, where pa_{i_j} is a subgraph of the corresponding pla_x. The set of corresponding modules of a product is indicated by the dashed arrows in Figure 3.

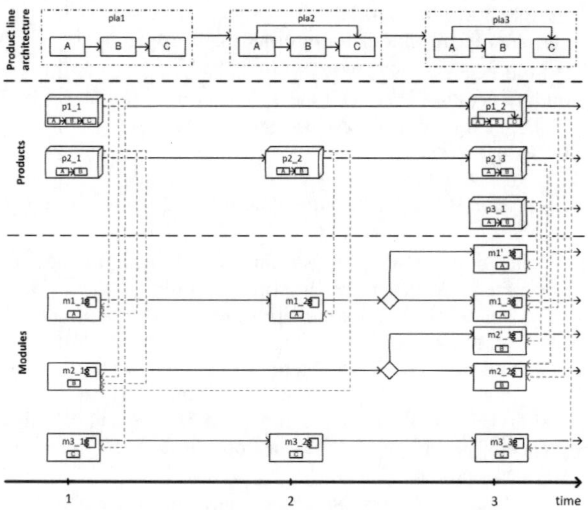

Figure 3. Relation between products, modules and PLA

TABLE I. EXPLANATION OF THE ACTIVITIES IN FIGURE 2.

Activity	*Input*	*Objective*	*Output*
PL-Design	Software system / component requirements and documentation from product development.	Further development of PLA with consideration of design principles. Application of measuring techniques to assess quality of PLA.	New PLA (called "PLA vision").
PL-Plan	PLA vision.	Planning of a set of iterations of further development toward the PLA vision taking all affected projects into account.	Development plan including the planned order of module implementations and the planned related projects.
PL-Implement	Development plan for product line.	Implementation including testing as specified by the development plan for product line development.	Implemented module versions.
PL-Check	Architecture rules and set of implemented modules to be checked.	Minimization of product architecture erosion by architecture conformance checking based on architecture rules.	Check results.
P-Design	Project plan and product specific requirements.	Designing product architecture and performing architecture adaptations taking product specific requirements into account. Compliance checking with PLA to minimize erosion.	Planned product architecture.
P-Plan	Product architecture.	Definition of iterations to be performed on product level toward the planned product architecture.	Development plan for product development.
P-Implement	Development plan for product development.	Product specific implementations including testing as specified by the development plan for product development.	Implemented module versions.
P-Check	Architecture rules and set of implemented modules to be checked.	Architecture conformance checking between PLA and PA.	Check results.
PL to P	Development plan for product line.	Defining a project plan by selecting a project from the the product line.	Project plan.
P to PL	Developed product.	Providing product related information of developed product for integration into product line development.	Product documentation and implementation artifacts of developed products.
PL-Requirements	Requirements.	Specification and validation of software system and software component requirements by requirements engineering.	Software system and software component requirements.
P-Requirements	Requirements in particular from calibration engineers.	Specification of special requirements for a certain vehicle product including vehicle related parameter settings.	Vehicle related requirements.
Recovery & Discovery	Source artifacts (developed products).	Recovery of the implemented PLA from the source artifacts (developed products) and discovery of the intended PLA.	Implemented and intended PLA.

Module: A module $m_{k\_l} \in M$ has a module identifier k and a version index l, with $k, l \in \mathbb{N}$. The sequence of versions is indicated by the flow relation between modules in Figure 3. We assume a distinct mapping of m_{k_l} to a certain $l \in \text{LAE} \cup \{\perp\}$. By $\perp$ we allow m_{k_l} not to be assigned to a logical architecture element, called unbound m_{k_l}. A logical architecture element can be assigned to several modules, but a module can only be assigned to exactly one or no logical architecture element. A module $m_{k\_l} \in M$ can belong to several products $p_{i\_j} \in P$.

As illustrated in Figure 3, we assume a high degree of reuse: The same module version may be included in different products. Branches of the development path are depicted by the diamond symbol. Module $m_{1'\_1}$ indicates a branch of the development path concerning module m_{1_3}.

IV. MAKING THE ARCHITECTURE EXPLICIT

With a high degree of erosion, a further development of the software is only possible at great effort. Before approaches to minimize erosion can be applied, the architecture must first be repaired. In this section, we investigate how approaches for architecture extraction can be adapted to be applied to automotive software product line architectures. First, we propose methods used to extract initial architectures. Next, in the second subsection, we give results and our experiences gained from a real world example.

A. Methods Used to Extract Initial Architectures and their Application

In this section we propose an approach for repairing an eroded software consisting of a set of product architectures (PAs) by applying strategies for recovery and discovery of the PLA (see left part of Figure 2). *Recovery* uses reverse engineering techniques to extract the implemented architecture from source artifacts, and *discovery* hypothesizes its intended architecture [6]. The proposed approach constitutes a substantial extension of the work presented in [30], where only a brief idea of the approach is introduced without any experimental results.

An explicit PLA definition constituting the top level architecture is important to coordinate the shared development between the OEM and the suppliers. Each product that is developed has a PA whose structure should be mapped onto the top level architecture. This top level architecture describes the structure of all realizable PAs. However, because of software sharing an overall assignment of top level groups to modules, and their interface, is missing. The knowledge of the overall, product independent structure is not explicitly documented, and therefore exists only implicitly in the minds of the participants. Further development of existing products and the development of new products lead to eroded PAs as an initially demanded structure is not available.

As a major challenge, we have to deal with product line development where a set of software components - so called *modules* - constitutes the basis for deriving a huge number of products. Therefore it is necessary to know about the derivable PAs from a given PLA. Two PLAs are distinguished: Current derivable PAs are captured by the *actual PLA* (APLA). All planned PAs for future development are captured by the *target PLA* (TPLA). In the Recovery & Discovery activity we recover the APLA and discover a TPLA candidate.

In the *Recovery & Discovery* activity we are using domain specific expertise and architecture related data from a repository to create the two PLAs. Figure 4 shows how the TPLA (*step d)*) and APLA (*step e)*) are created. For this purpose the APLA relevant elements are described by the recovered structure from data mining (*step b)*) and from functional analysis (*step c)*) using a set of PAs. The PAs are provided by *step a)*. Due to the ease of handling in the first iteration of *step a)* only some products are selected from the data dictionary. The following iterations extend the scope to more products. In the following all steps are summarized.

a) Select products from data dictionary: The aim of this step is to derive a small set of PAs to create common PLAs. Due to the huge number of products and their variants in the data dictionary, a selection is crucial for the creation of the initial APLA. A product is based on a software project. A software project defines the scope of modules, groups of modules, groups of groups (hierarchy) and interfaces reused for integration. The interface is described by modules and contains references to globally available variables. The required type and the provided type of references are distinguished. To realize a communication between two modules, it is necessary that one of the two modules provides the variable and the other consuming module requires the variable. We call this a dependency. Variables themselves store valuable data for the communication. A provided variable must also be declared (ANSI C like) and is therefore owned by the declaring module. PAs consist of modules, groups, and associated dependencies. All those elements have a set of data dictionary related attributes with a special meaning, which are considered to determine the initial selection of PAs. A problem arises when the exploration of extracted information is not manageable because of the big data set. Therefore we define selection criteria to extract a smaller set of PAs from the data dictionary. The following items describe examples for selection criteria in details:

- Projects and modules that have the release status. A project in release means that it is already integrated by TIER 1. A module in release means that it is already realized and positive tested by OEM.
- Modules that are referenced by selected projects.
- Projects that are related to one of the required engine control unit (ECU) generations.
- The most recent created modules and projects.

b) Recover PLA candidates using data mining: A very common approach to recover patterns and structures in large data sets is to use data mining methods and techniques. Many various techniques exist and are used in practice with different advantages and disadvantages for recovering an APLA. In this methodology we chose an approved approach, which provides good results in the field of recovery structures in information systems. The approach is called Spectral Analysis of Software Architecture (SPAA) [31], [32], [33] and is a generic approach to cluster software elements by their dependencies.

The SPAA approach is divided into three steps as visualized in Figure 5. First, all dependencies between all elements within the scope have to be identified. The type of dependency varies and depends on the kind of system, e.g., for object orientated information systems dependencies like classical call, extends, or implements relations are useful [32]. In the next step the constructed directed graph has to be weighted - the higher the edge weight value the lower the probability of cutting this edge in the clustering step. The weighted graph is clustered with a Spectral Clustering algorithm considering that this is a good heuristic to solve this NP-hard graph cut problem as described in [31] and [32].

As input data for the SPAA approach we choose all modules, which are contained in the selected products. Between these modules we determine dependencies depending on the provided and declared variables (see *step a)*). In this case the edge weight is defined as the sum of shared variables of the corresponding modules.

Often a heuristic is used to suggest the number of clusters. The preferred heuristic for Spectral Clustering is the eigengap heuristic, due to the fact that Spectral Clustering determines the eigenvalues of the normalized Laplacian, which are also used for this heuristic - described in detail in [31] and [32]. The application of Spectral Clustering results in a cluster separation of the weighted graph, as presented in [32] the modules can be clustered in a hierarchical way. Therefore the clusters have to be used as input data for the Spectral Clustering algorithm again. These procedure can be repeated with each generated cluster until the level of partitioning is satisfying. Summarizing, the elected data mining technique creates a PLA candidate of the selected products including a hierarchical grouping of modules and indicating the inter group dependencies.

c) Recover PLA candidates using functional analysis: The aim of this step is to recover a PLA candidate using a technique considering the functionality aspects. In the ECU software development most of them are open/closed control loop related functions [34], [35]. At first we create a number of processing function related groups, which are determined by expert knowledge. For each group a set of modules is referenced using the product scope. The references enable the tracing between PA elements and data dictionary modules. In the next step, the dependencies between the groups are created. Thereby only variables are considered that need to be shared between groups. The scope of other variables remains restricted. Some of the created groups may have a similar but more coarse grained function scope. Those can be again aggregated together, which leads to a hierarchical structure. Applying the above technique results in another PLA candidate, which consists of several hierarchical groups and group dependencies.

d) Integrate APLA from PLA candidates: The *steps b), c)* produce PLA candidates by different recovery techniques. Instead of *steps b)* and *c)*, other techniques from the field of architecture recovery could be used. But exactly one APLA is required for the following managing activities (see Section III). Therefore the integration of all available PLA candidates is necessary. We propose two essential steps for integration: At first groups are created, which represent the leafs of the APLA. Therefore the appropriate groups of the PLA candidates are compared and evaluated for reuse. Next the dependencies between groups in the APLA are determined. In the second step the aggregation of the leaf groups is created reusing groups of the appropriate level from the PLA candidates. The resulting groups are determined again by a comparison in an evaluation step. The second step is applied iteratively for each available PLA candidate level.

e) Discover TPLA candidate from automotive domain knowledge: As an initial starting point for the following managing activities (see Section III-A) a TPLA is needed. A TPLA contains at least the planned structure compared to

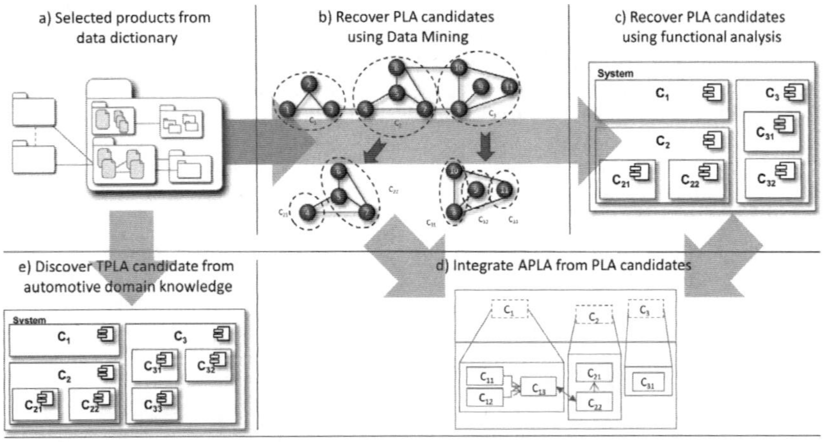

Figure 4. Overview of activity Recovery & Discovery

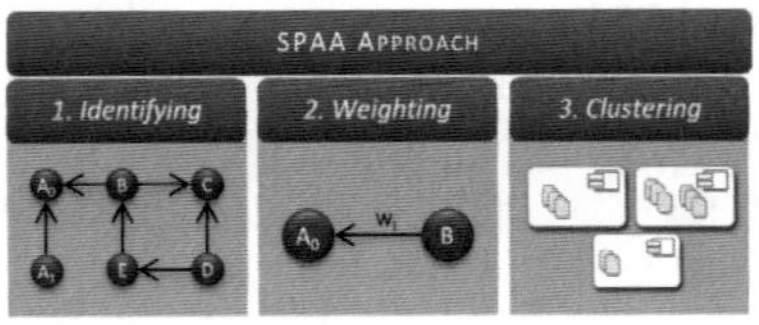

Figure 5. Overview: SPAA approach

the APLA. This knowledge has to be identified from product experts. As the architecture documentation is only available for individual projects, the knowledge for planned changes considering a PLA must be imposed using domain knowledge. To create the structure of a desired TPLA, group candidates and dependency candidates are identified from standardized automotive specific reference architectures [36], [37]. The TPLA is created iteratively considering the knowledge of experts.

B. Results from Real World Example

We have applied the methodology for extracting initial architectures on a real world example, the engine control unit software at Volkswagen. Next we show how we applied *step a)* to *step e)* to the example. We need to introduce the concept of the *function package* for further consideration. A function package references a set of modules or further function packages and serves for functional grouping.

a) Select products from data dictionary: As a starting point, we use the software repository of the engine control unit software at Volkswagen. The analysis was carried out in July 2015. At the time, the repository contained 21,734 versions of modules. First, the projects to be considered were selected. We wanted to consider a wide range of different projects. Thus, we have selected projects from two different suppliers and for different types of engines: From the first supplier a diesel and otto variant, respectively, and from the second supplier a diesel, otto, and otto-hybid variant. The following selection criteria were used to reduce the number of module versions: Only modules and function packages are selected

- that are not contained in a further function package,
- that are referenced by the selected projects,
- that have the release status, and
- that are the most recent created versions.

After applying the selection criteria, 162 modules and 43 function packages were selected.

b) Recover PLA candidates using data mining: We applied Spectral Clustering resulting in a cluster separation of the weighted graph. The procedure was repeated with each generated cluster until the level of partitioning was satisfying. A number of clusters with 16 or 18 clusters has turned out to be satisfying for all selected projects. Although the degree of cross-linking between the given modules is very small, the coupling between the clusters is relatively high. The cause of the high coupling may have various reasons, e.g., unsuitable parameterization or poor modularity.

c) Recover PLA candidates using functional analysis: From the study of the selected 43 function packages, abstract groups were identified by expert knowledge. Non-grouped elements are too complex for a manual, professional investigation. However, the generated groups have a high degree of interpretation (structural and technical).

d) Integrate APLA from PLA candidates: In this step, we first looked at the similarities and differences between the two PLA candidates from *step b)* and *step c)*. The aim was to derive a common APLA from the two PLA candidates. We built an integrated APLA for selected parts of the given PLA candidates. Here a lot of manual work is necessary. For the scope of the engine control software, the approach of *step d)* has ultimately not scaled. We could not provide the necessary manual work for building the integrated APLA for the entire engine control unit software with the two doctoral students working in the project.

e) Discover TPLA candidate from automotive domain knowledge: We analyzed several standardized automotive specific reference architectures [36], [37] to create a TPLA. There are recurring structures for combustion engines, for example: air system, fuel system, combustion model, etc.

Furthermore, there is a systematic structure of the hierarchies and dependencies, for example: driver's request, propulsion request on the power train, and power train units. We used this information to create a first draft of a TPLA for the engine control unit software. The TPLA is not specialized to a certain kind of engine like otto, diesel or hybrid. This draft TPLA was then discussed with experts from Volkswagen. Some minor adjustments were necessary until we had a final version of the TPLA.

Summary: By applying the proposed methodology, we could recover an APLA and discover a TPLA candidate. As shown in step d), however, difficulties have arisen in building an integrated APLA due to the size of the selected system. To handle such huge systems an automated process must be developed by further research. Even without performing the integration step, the two PLA candidates created are a useful basis for analyzing the current eroded system architecture. The essential structures could be made explicit by our approach.

The TPLA candidate and the APLA are then used in activity `PL-Design` and the subsequent activities (see Figure 2): The alignment of both PLAs is planned and implemented in order to repair the eroded architecture. Finally, the repaired architecture is further developed by the long term evolution cycle as described in Section III-A.

V. An Approach to Extract Concepts from System Realizations

For the specification of software architectures design patterns, architectural patterns or styles are an important and suitable means, also in other engineering disciplines [17]. We subsume these under the term of architectural concepts. An **architectural concept** is defined as: "*a characterization and description of a common, abstract and realized implementation-, design-, or architecture solution within a given context represented by a set of examples and/or rules.*"

At the architectural level, these are often associated with terms as a client-server system, a pipes and filters design, or a layered architecture. An architectural style defines a vocabulary of components, connector types, and a set of constraints on how they can be combined [17]. To get a better understanding of the wide spectrum of architectural concepts typical samples of concepts are listed in the following:

- *Conventions:* naming, package/folder structure, vocabulary, domain model ...
- *Design Patterns:* observer, factory, ...
- *Architectural Patterns:* client-server system, layered architecture, ...
- *Communication:* service-oriented, message based, bus, ...
- *Structures:* tiers, pipes, filters, ...
- *Security:* encryption, SSO, ...

Based on this and our experiences made during the application of our approach described in the previous Section IV, the development of a new approach focusing the architectural concepts was part of the ongoing research activities.

In this section we will introduce this new approach with the aim to support the Recovery & Discovery activity. In Section VIII we will give an outlook on how this approach can be integrated into an evolutionary incremental development process and how a knowledge based process for architecture evolution and maintenance for architectural concepts can be implemented.

A. Introduction of the Approach

Based on the experience made during the practical project work, it became apparent in the Recovery & Discovery activity that an important issue to get a substantiated comprehending of a product architecture is to make not only the architecture explicit, but also the architectural concepts. Looking at different products and their architectures, the concepts are very helpful to create a common product line architecture. For this reason, the following research question (RQ) was focused in the ongoing research process: *"How can developers' best practice be identified and reflected to the architecture level?"* - From this general research question the following three research questions were derived:

RQ 1: How can a concept be represented with regard to

(a) composition to higher and usually unknown abstract concepts and

(b) the transferability of knowledge to or from other systems?

RQ 2: How can architectural concepts be algorithmically extracted and identified with regard to

(a) the large number of different concepts and

(b) their variations on different abstraction levels and contexts?

RQ 3: How can a tool support be realized with regard to

(a) false positive results respectively concept candidates and

(b) the huge amount of source code (scalability) ?

The outcome of this research activity is the approach shown in Figure 6. In this and the following section the research questions will be answered in detail.

We start with some general definitions. A **Concept** C is described by a set of **Properties** P. For an **Element** E a so called **Detector** D is defined as the binary function $d_{p_j} \in D$ for a concrete property $p_j \in P$ and a concrete element $e_i \in E$:

$$d_{p_j}(e_i) = \begin{cases} 1 & \text{, iff the Element } e_i \text{ fullfills the Property } p_j \\ 0 & \text{, otherwise} \end{cases} \quad (1)$$

An element can be a system artifact like a class, a function or a dependency between two elements as well as a subset of artifacts and their dependencies of the realized systems.

As shown in Figure 6 the input for the extraction cycle is the realization of the systems. The system artifacts respectively the source code elements are transferred to the so called **System Snapshot** $\mathfrak{S}$. It represents the realization of a software system as a language independent model representation, but including the links to the original source code elements. The used meta-model is a further development of the model used in [5], [38] and [39].

Another data pool is the **Factbase** $\mathfrak{F}$, which represents the fulfillment of concepts for the concrete elements. It is divided

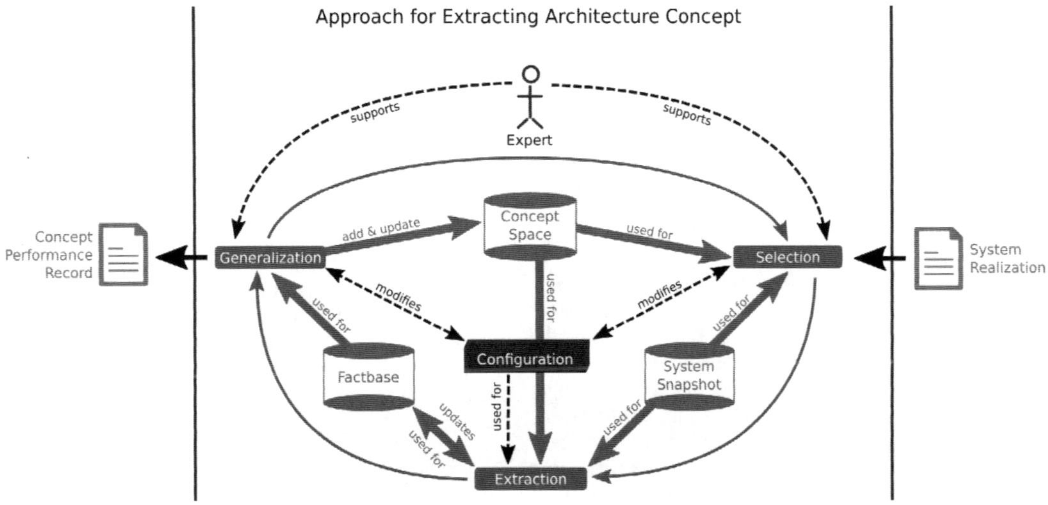

Figure 6. Approach to extract architectural concepts from system realizations

into three parts, two data-structures, which are organized in a table-structure, listing facts referring to elements respectively to dependencies and one data-structure describing facts about elements and the dependencies between them. These facts are organized in a graph-data-structure.

The last of the three data pools is the **Concept Space** Ω. It stores all known concepts, whereby a concept is represented as a named element and linked to its detector and examples, which fulfill this concept.

Altogether the defined process for extracting architectural concepts consists of three activities (blue boxes in Figure 6), which are performed iteratively and is called Extraction-Cycle. The connecting element between these activities is the **Configuration** Σ. Per iteration one configuration $\sigma_i \in \Sigma$ is created and used for the information exchange between the activities. Therefore, it includes all decisions that are made in an activity.

As shown during our studies it is not that difficult for an expert to decide, which system parts are relevant for a concrete analysis, as well as to validate if a concept is a "real" concept or not. Because of this finding we integrate an expert to support two activities.

The output of the approach is the so called **Concept Performance Record**. This record informs about the concepts that are found in the analyzed system realization.

In the following the three activities are introduced in detail.

1) The Selection Activity: In this step an expert decides, which parts from the system should be analyzed and what is the initial set of concepts, which should be used for it. The expert will be supported by typical tools presented in Section IV like SPAA, to get a system decomposition, which is performed on the System Snapshot for example. On the other hand it is possible to reduce the number of concepts from the Concept Space, because of some basic knowledge of the system, like if it is object orientated or not.

The selected sub set of the system and the selected set of concepts, which are represented by its detectors, are stored in the Configuration and used as input for the next step.

2) The Extraction Activity: This step is fully automated and generates first the Factbase based for the selected elements by executing each detector for each element. Next different algorithms from the field of machine learning and neural computation are used, which are named in detail in the following Section V-B, to extract potential new facts and/or combinations of them. These so called **Concept Candidates** $\hat{C}$ are added as non-valid concepts to the Factbase. This includes also the **Representatives** R of this concept candidate thus elements, which fulfill this new extracted concept.

If this extension step is completed, the transition to the generalization step takes place.

3) The Generalization Activity: After the Factbase has been enriched with new facts receptively potential new concepts, a validation of these facts is carried out in this activity by an expert. The expert decides on the basis of the representatives of this concept candidate, whether the concept is a real concept or not. These decisions are stored also in the configuration. Thus the configuration includes the information about selected detectors and system artifacts and the concepts newly extracted and validated on this basis.

Based on this decision making process new detectors are generated. This can be done manually or automated by training a so called neural-network detector with the representatives in order to detect these concepts in the future. Finally, this new knowledge has to be integrated into the Concept Space, thereby it will be checked whether the new extracted concepts are already contained in the Concept Space and have not been selected in this iteration. In this case, the expert has to decide if it is the same or a different concept, i.e., whether it should be added as new or the already existing detector is re-trained with the new representatives.

Furthermore, the expert has to decide whether the Extraction Cylce should be terminated or a further iteration should be executed. In the next iteration new concepts can be extracted, which are based on concepts learned in the previous iteration, or by selecting other system artifacts.

B. Implementation of the Approach

In this subsection a concrete implementation of the proposed approach will be described. The chosen algorithms are not fixed for the individual steps and can be replaced by algorithms, which perform better. In the following the algorithms are listed, which are used to fulfill and support the individual actions.

Within the Selection activity the SPAA approach, illustrated in Figure 5, is used to create different views of the system decomposition to support the expert by selecting relevant elements and detectors.

For the extracting of new concept candidates within the Extraction activity different clustering algorithms and a statistical analysis were implemented and benchmarked. The input for all algorithms is the generated Factbase. Statistical analysis based on the frequency analysis of occurring patterns gave first indication for potential concept candidates but was not practicable for a good automation of the extraction process.

Therefore, different clustering algorithms were used to group similar elements and to derive concept candidates from this clusters: Neural Gas [40], Growing Neural Gas [41], and a Self-Organizing-Map (SOM) [42] orientated on the work of Matthias Reuter [43], [44]. These algorithms are used to find concepts on the system element level to detect special data-objects like TransferObjects [45], for example. In addition, they are used to extract similar properties for the dependencies between elements to define different types of dependencies like special communication channels or different kinds of relations like an inheritance relation between two elements, which is typical for an object orientated realization, for example.

To extract new facts from the facts represented in a graph-structure, we use the following algorithms to find similarities and anomalies within the graph:

1) Graph Kernels [46],
2) Graph Clustering approaches like SPAA [31], [32], [33], and
3) t-SNE [47].

For the creation of new detectors by training them with the representatives, a SOM is used. The selection, parametrization and evaluation of suitable algorithms are an ongoing process and will be focused in future work.

C. Supporting Recovery & Discovery

In the introduction of this section three research questions were derived, which can be answered by the presented solution. The answers can be summarized as follows:

RQ 1: (a) Concepts can be represented by their characteristic properties, whereby they can be organized in a hierarchical way, so it is possible to define higher respectively even more complex concepts. Because of detector mechanism and the possibility to create new detectors by training them with the representatives of this concept, it is possible to abstract from concrete instances. (b) So it is possible to check any element, also from other systems, if it is fulfilling a concrete concept or not.

RQ 2: (a) It is possible to define for each well known concept a detector, but it is the goal of this approach to find new concepts by clustering elements and extracting structures, which may represent a concept. So it is easier for the expert to decide if this is a kind of concept and what is the objective of it. (b) Because of the Concept Space it is possible to find similar concepts and also to merge them or to define explicit new variants of an existing concept maybe for different contexts, for example.

RQ 3: (a) Because of the validation step within the Generalization activity recommended concepts, which are false positive results, are marked as anti-concepts and they are also stored in the Concept Space, so in the next iteration they can be filtered. (b) To handle a huge amount of source code files a tool supported decomposition process of the system was integrated into the Selection activity. Furthermore, the extraction cycle was designed as an iterative process, to focus step by step on different aspects or parts of the system but take the so far extracted knowledge into account.

With the help of this approach it is possible to integrate the aspect of architectural concepts into the Recovery & Discovery activity. For example, the Coordinator concept, which will be introduced in detail in the following Section VI-A and illustrated in Figure 8, can be determined with the presented approach.

In Figure 7 an excerpt of the Factbase is visualized representing elements and their dependencies. The different properties for elements and edges can be mapped to colors, and the edge weights are summing up the number of dependencies of the same type. As a result of the Extraction step the blue-green nodes (see Figure 7) are recommended as concept candidates. During validation of this candidate the expert looked to the representatives of this candidate and determined that this element is only connected to green nodes, which are Filters, by only one instance of a communication dependency to each node, which allows only the transmission of state and mode information. We call an element with such characteristic properties a coordinator. So the extracted candidate is a valid concept and can be integrated into the Concept Space including the creation of a detector to have the possibility to check any element if it is fulfilling the coordinator concept or not in the future.

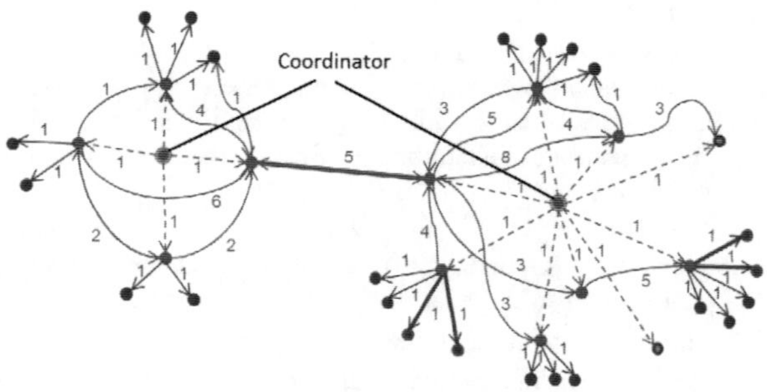

Figure 7. Excerpt of the Factbase

VI. Planning and Evolving Automotive Product Line Architectures

A. Concepts for Designing Automotive Product Line Architectures

Architectural concepts can be described in the form of classical patterns, by describing a particular recurring design problem that arises in specific design contexts and presents a well-proven generic scheme for its solution. The solution scheme specifies all constituent components, their responsibilities and relationships, and the way, in which they will collaborate [18].

In the same way, we will illustrate some examples that we worked out in our automotive domain projects. Generally, the central issue is the increasing complexity of software systems with their technical and functional dependencies. A mapping of these dependencies to point-to-point connections will result in a huge, complex and difficult to maintain communication network. This leads to a likewise huge effort in the field of maintenance and further development for these software systems - small changes result in high costs.

This problem of a not manageable number of connections emerged in many industrial projects we explored for our field study. In the following we will present architectural concepts, which are addressing this problem in particular. Figures 8 and 9 show different components, whereby the components `Coordinator` and `Support` are atomic components and the components labeled as `Filter` are not atomic components, i.e., they can be decomposable.

1) Architecture Design Principle "Coordinator - PipesAndFilters - Support": The complexity of a component increases artificially with every new product, without integrating new functions. The reason for this phenomenon is due to the fact that each component has to calculate the system state for itself and this for each existing environment and product the component will be used in. In general, components are analyzing system data like sensor values, for example, and process them to realize their functionality. Thereby, it happens very often that a processing function is implemented several times. Besides, data from other components is used, but this data can change over time, which can result in error states.

The design principle introduces a classification of data. If it is possible to classify the data, than it is possible to establish the typing of channels, as shown in Figure 8.

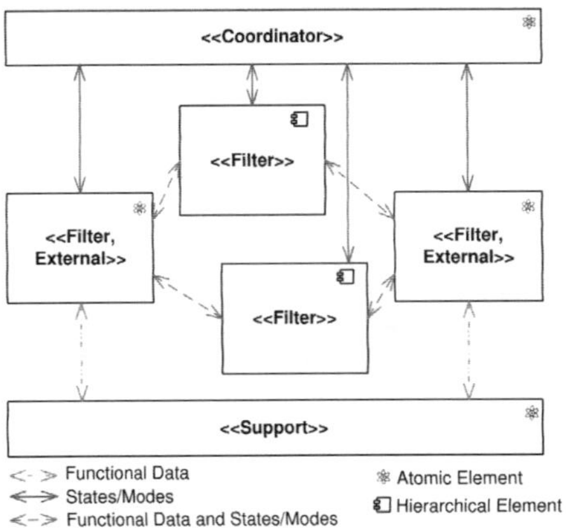

Figure 8. Architecture design principle: External elements

Each component has to declare a port for states and modes to uncouple the calculation of the system state from the component. The mode in which a component is currently located indicates the mode of execution of a certain function, like "kickdown", "emergency brake", "active", or"inactive", in the case of driving functions. A `Coordinator` component determines the global state for a set of components and uses the new defined port to coordinate the other components. The coordinator provides only states/modes and no functional data. A component in Figure 8 named as `Filter`, referring to the classical Pipes-and-Filters architecture pattern, can react to a state change automatically. Parameters are manipulated directly with the states/modes without an additional calculation. Components can be directly activated or stopped. The scheduling of the coordinator is independent from the scheduling of the other components, as each `Filter` checks the state/mode first. The functionality of the system is realized by the `Filter` components. For them it is allowed to exchange functional data as well as state and modes. Values required for the calculation within different components are provided by a so called `Support` component.

2) Architecture Design Principle "External Elements": Today it is customary that not all components are developed inhouse, some functions are implemented by external suppliers. But OEM components have requirements resulting in changes of interfaces, behavior or functionalities of theses externally developed functions and components. It is not that easy to identify these external components on architectural level, but this information is essential for an economic development process because changes of external components are very effort and cost intensive.

Figure 8 shows a simple solution to handle external elements: `Filter` components developed externally are annotated with `Filter, External`. By using this annotation, one can identify with little effort, which component is external, and which connections are affected.

so it is effortless to identify, which component is external, and which connections are affected.

3) Architecture Design Principle "Hierarchical Communication": Over the time more and more components and functionality are added to a product. Different developers with different programming styles are working on the same product. Components without any reference to each other are organized in the same package or other organizational and structural units. Due to this accidental complexity it is not possible for a developer, system integrator or architect to get a well-founded knowledge of the whole system.

As presented in Figure 9, a `Filter` component can be decomposable, a so called non-atomic component contains a structure, which follows the design principle visualized in Figure 8. It includes a `Coordinator` and `Support` component and an arbitrary number of `Filter` components. Whereby the inner `Filter` components have explicit defined responsibilities.

By this design principle a repetitive structure on each abstraction level is established, which enables an easy and technical independent orientation in the whole system.

4) Architecture Design Principle "Anvil-like Component Model": Components require knowledge about the behavior or the state/mode of the connected components. This results in a high coupling of components and the processing time increases, too.

As presented in Figure 10, a component consists of two parts with different responsibilities - `Execution control` and `Function algorithms`. Each part has a defined set

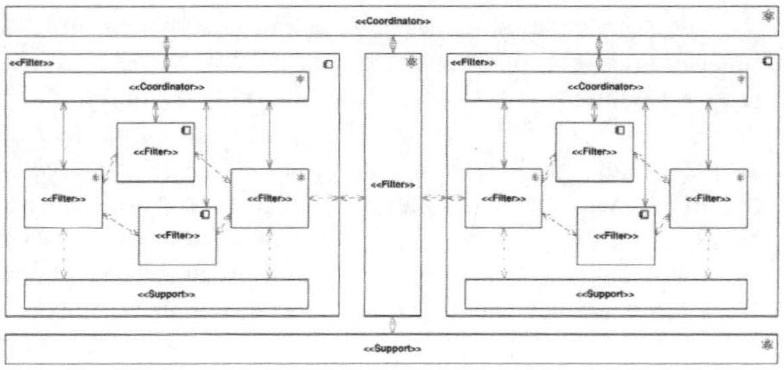

Figure 9. Architecture design principle: Hierarchical communication

of interfaces, types of communication channels, and exchange data. Due to the separation into two distinct areas, components are visualized as anvils (see Figure 10).

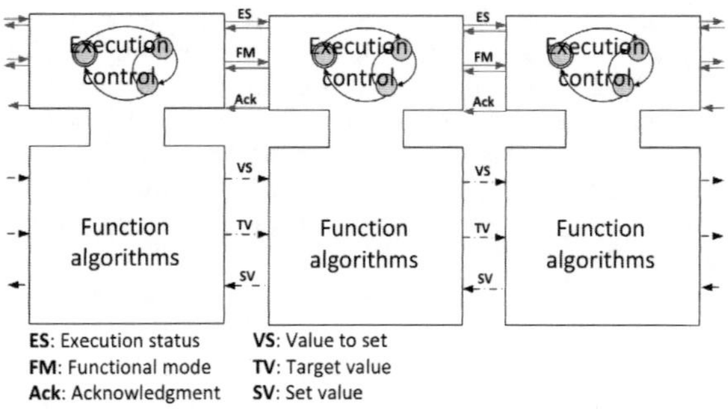

Figure 10. Architecture design principle: Anvil-like component model

The communication scheme is divided into two areas: the execution control and the functional algorithms. The execution control includes, on the one hand, the activation of the component, which is represented by the execution status. In addition, in the execution control, the functional mode (components' internal mode) of the component is determined. The execution control sends an acknowledgment to the predecessor component when this component is active. The execution control communicates only by states/modes.

The function algorithms are processed when the execution status is set. Component specific values are calculated in the function algorithms. As output, they supply a value to set (VS) and a target value (TV). VS is the value to be set by the actuator in the next computing cycle, e.g., the new torque value for the next cycle. TV is the value, which is to be achieved in the future, e.g., the torque value requested by driver. To achieve TV a set of computing cycles is required. The set value (SV) of the function algorithms is the value that is currently set by the actuator and is transferred in the opposite direction compared to VS and TV. The aim of SV is to inform the components about the value currently set by the actuator. The functional algorithms exchange only functional data with one another.

5) Architecture Design Principle "Feedback Channel": The complexity of component-based control systems is increasing continuously, since there are more and more functional dependencies between the individual components. A mapping of these dependencies on point-to-point connections between the components results in a complex, hard-to-maintain communication network.

In component-based control engineering systems, control cascades are generated by connecting several components consecutively. The main data flow in this system is called the effect chain. In more complex systems, there are several effect chains that can partly overlap. In an effect chain, there are functional dependencies between components that are not directly connected one behind the other. To resolve these functional dependencies, additional point-to-point connections are added, which we call "technical dependencies" between the components in the following. The additional direct point-to-point connections between the components increase the coupling between the components and lead to a deterioration in the fulfillment of non-functional requirements, such as maintainability, understandability and extensibility. For example, the technical dependencies have to be taken into account in a further development. The worst case is a complete graph with cross-links between all components.

As a solution to this problem we introduce *feedback channels* (patent pending): The introduction of feedback channels enables the dissolution of functional dependencies without the introduction of technical point-to-point connections (see Figure 11). The feedback channel is parallel to the effect chain. Thereby, the necessary functional information is passed through the components of the effect chain. The feedback is directed against the effect direction. Components of an effect chain must provide feedback. This creates a technical communication network, with which the functional information can be exchanged. Thus, there are only technical dependencies to neighboring components in the effect chain. The maintainability is improved as only technical dependencies on neighboring components in the effect chain have to be considered. Figure 11 shows the architecture design principle *feedback channel*.

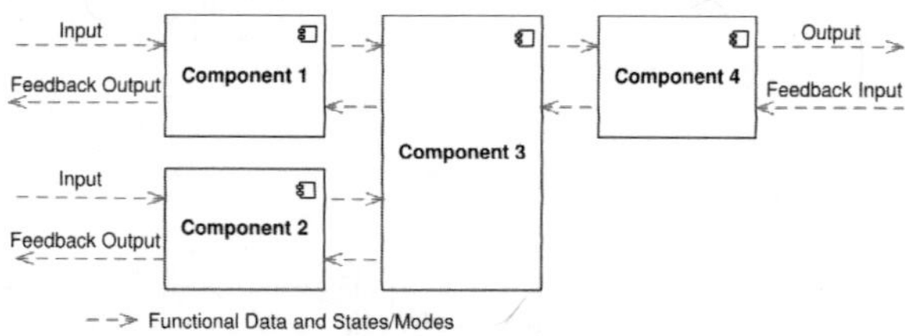

Figure 11. Architecture design principle: Feedback channel

All information / data from the end of the effect chain to the beginning of the effect chain are provided via the feedback. Thus, a component can adapt itself to the current situation in the effect chain without the necessity to create an explicit connection to all components in the effect chain. Furthermore, only the dependency of a component to the adjacent components of an effect chain exists. If the processing order of the components is selected s.t. all inputs are processed first and then the feedback, all components of the effect chain have the information on the current system state available in the next computing cycle. The effect chain to Figure 11 then looks as follows: The four components process their inputs in the effect direction. The components are then processed in the reverse order and the feedback is processed, i.e., from `Component 4` to `Component 1`. Here, components 1 and 2 can be interchanged in their processing.

In summary, the overall system is more maintainable and easier to expand by this architecture design principle. The individual components do not have to be connected to all components in order to know the system state. Through the feedback channel there is an information exchange between all components in the same computing cycle. Controllers can adapt themselves directly to the current system state without the necessity to have an explicit connection to the corresponding actuator.

Summary

The presented architectural concepts in this section were developed within different industrial projects in the automotive domain involving different software architects and project members. Nevertheless, there are similarities between the presented concepts, which become explicit by generalization and the representation by a uniform description language. Thereby, the projects focused the same as well as varying problem issues and requirements. With this representation technique it was possible to reuse the concepts in other projects to increase the quality in an early phase of development and to economize effort, because the projects start discussing about architectural concepts.

The architectural concepts presented in this paper are developed iteratively and in some cases the development time took over one year. As a result from our field study we can outline that there are similarities between the architectural evolution of product lines and the abstract and generic development process of concepts, which is not surprising. The evolution of an architectural concept looks like the same - reuse and adaptation in other projects, which sometimes results in a new concept. Besides we can observe that the different levels of abstraction we have for architecture descriptions, we can find for concepts, as well. For example, the architecture design principle VI-A4 (Anvil-like Component Model, Figure 10), describes coordinating functionality, status and mode information and functional data connections. All these aspects we can find in the design principle VI-A2 (Coordinator, PipesAndFilters, Support, Figure 8), too. With the difference that the `Anvil-like Component Model` concept is for low level control functions, whereas the other concept deals with components on another abstraction level - to clarify the `Anvil-like Component Model` principle can be applied for a `Filter`, for example.

Architectural concepts like the ones presented before and all other aspects mentioned in the introduction of this section, especially the specification of wording and naming conventions help to build a collective experience of skilled software engineers. They capture existing, well-proven experience in software development and help to promote good design practice [18].

The result of making these concepts explicit on this abstraction level leads to discussions about architectural problems and generic solution schemes. In particular at the product line architecture level the focus is shifted from the more technical driven problems upon the more abstract and software architecture oriented issues. Over time this leads to new architectural concepts, which are documented, evaluated, maybe extracted from existing products, but making them explicit and integrating them at the right places in the further development process.

Another very important aspect dealing with architectural concepts is the monitoring of the concrete realizations of them. In our approach the `Check` activity takes care of it. All the presented concepts can be represented by a logical rule set, as described in [5]. Related to the fact that all elements of the software are subjects to the evolution process, architectural concepts can change or had to be adapted over time. This means that the violation of an architectural rule indicates not always a bad or defective implementation, it can additionally give the impulse to review the associated concept and the context. In our approach the assessment of the rule violation is included in the `Check` activity and if there is an indication for a rule adaptation this will be analyzed and worked out in detail in the next `Design` activity. Overall it leads to a managed evolution.

B. Understanding of Architecture and Measuring of Architecture Quality

Software development is an evolutionary and not a linear process. The costs caused by errors in software in the last years, especially in the automotive industry, are very high (15-20% of earnings before interest and taxes [48]). Thus, it is necessary to understand and evaluate the architecture to support further development. In a vehicle, software will occupy a larger and larger part and the costs caused by errors will be rising. Therefore, it is important to control the quality of the software continuously. Problems/Errors can be detected early so that the quality of the software increases. The quality of the software depends in particular on the quality of the corresponding software architecture. In our approach, we use PLAs for automotive software product line development. PLAs are special types of software architectures. They do not only describe one system, but many products, which can be derived from this architecture. Variability of the architecture, reuse of products, and the complexity are important values to assess the quality of this architecture.

Today, metrics mainly focus on code level. The most common metrics are *Lines of Code*, *Halstead*, and *McCabe*. In object-oriented programming (OOP), *MOOD metrics* and *CK metrics* are used. However, these metrics are not suitable for measuring PLAs. For assessing a PLA, the most important value is variability, as the degree of variability increases complexity in PLAs. Further important values are complexity and maintainability of the possible products and the PLA. As modules of products shall be reused for other products, a high reuse-rate on the product level is an important objective of the PLA. A high reuse-rate also implies a high focus on maintainability of the products.

In our approach, we assess the *modification effort*, *reuse rate* and *cohesion* of a PLA, since we can thus evaluate the properties discussed above. In the following, we give formulas for the calculation of modification effort, reuse rate and cohesion. Here, we refer to the definitions of Section III-B, and the system structure depicted in Figure 3.

1) Modification effort: The modification effort measures the effort caused by the planned changes in the PLA: How many logical architecture elements (LAE), and products are affected by the change? The calculated result value is between 0 (no elements have to be changed) and 1 (all elements have to be changed). Simple changes can have a high impact to products and modules. The value supports the architect to improve understanding the architecture. Maybe there is a better solution to design the new PLA with less modification effort. The modification effort $\mathcal{E}$ to develop a new PLA version pla_{x+1} for a given PLA pla_x is calculated as follows on the level of PLA and products:

$$\mathcal{E}^{PLA} = \frac{number\ of\ concerned\ LAE}{number\ of\ all\ LAE} \tag{2}$$

$$\mathcal{E}^{P} = \frac{number\ of\ concerned\ products}{number\ of\ all\ products} \tag{3}$$

where *concerned LAE/products* denote the logical architecture elements/products that have to be modified or added/deleted when introducing the new PLA version. In Table II we apply $\mathcal{E}$ on the example in Figure 3.

TABLE II. MODIFICATION EFFORT FOR THE EXAMPLE OF FIGURE 3.

$\mathcal{E}$	$pla_1 \rightarrow pla_2$	$pla_2 \rightarrow pla_3$
$\mathcal{E}^{PLA}$	$\frac{\lvert\{A,C\}\rvert}{\lvert\{A,B,C\}\rvert} = \frac{2}{3}$	$\frac{\lvert\{B,C\}\rvert}{\lvert\{A,B,C\}\rvert} = \frac{2}{3}$
$\mathcal{E}^{P}$	$\frac{\lvert\{p_1,p_2\}\rvert}{\lvert\{p_1,p_2\}\rvert} = \frac{2}{2} = 1$	$\frac{\lvert\{p_1,p_2,p_3\}\rvert}{\lvert\{p_1,p_2,p_3\}\rvert} = \frac{3}{3} = 1$

Consider, e.g., step $pla_1 \rightarrow pla_2$ in Table II: Note that each module is assigned to only one LAE in this example. Hence, modules are not considered in this example. In practice an LAE can be assigned to several modules to realize functionality. In this step the architect adds a connection between the LAE A and LAE C on the PLA. The modification effort for the PLA is $\frac{2}{3}$, because two of three LAE are affected by this change. On product level the modification effort $\mathcal{E}^P$ is 1: p_{1_1} and p_{2_1} contain LAE A and are thus affected. Note that for $\mathcal{E}^P$ we do not specify the version index in the calculation in Table II.

In this example, all products are affected by the modification in both development steps. There is no other way to reduce the modification effort. However, new product versions are not released at each point in time even if the product is concerned by the PLA modification (see product p_1 at $time = 2$ in Figure 3).

2) Reuse rate: To keep the vehicles cost efficient, modular products with a high reuse rate cross different types of vehicles are desired. The aim is to reuse modules in different products. The reuse rate $\mathcal{R}^m$ of a module m in a certain PLA version pla_x is calculated as follows:

$$\mathcal{R}^{m} = \frac{number\ of\ usage\ of\ m\ in\ all\ products\ of\ pla_x}{number\ of\ all\ products\ of\ pla_x} \tag{4}$$

Average reuse rate $\mathcal{R}^M$:

$$\mathcal{R}^{M} = \frac{\sum \mathcal{R}^m}{number\ of\ all\ modules} \tag{5}$$

In Table III we apply $\mathcal{R}$ on the example in Figure 3.

Consider, e.g., pla_1 and $\mathcal{R}^{m1}$ in Table III: Modules m_{1_1} and m_{2_1} are both used in products p_{1_1} and p_{2_1}. Thus, the reuse rate is $\frac{2}{2} = 1$ (100%). In the example the average reuse rate for pla_1 is 0.84 (84%). This value constitutes a high degree of reuse. For pla_3 and $\mathcal{R}^{m1}$ the reuse rate has to take the new product p_{3_1} into account. As m_{1_3} is used in two products and the number of products is three, $\mathcal{R}^{m1} = \frac{2}{3}$ ($\approx$ 67%).

TABLE III. REUSE RATE FOR THE EXAMPLE OF FIGURE 3.

$\mathcal{R}$	pla_1	pla_2	pla_3
$\mathcal{R}^{m1}$	$\frac{2}{2}$	$\frac{1}{1}$	$\frac{2}{3}$
$\mathcal{R}^{m2}$	$\frac{2}{2}$	$\frac{1}{1}$	$\frac{2}{3}$
$\mathcal{R}^{m3}$	$\frac{1}{2}$	$\frac{0}{1}$	$\frac{1}{3}$
$\mathcal{R}^{m_1'}$	-	-	$\frac{1}{3}$
$\mathcal{R}^{m_2'}$	-	-	$\frac{1}{3}$
$\mathcal{R}^{M}$	$\frac{5}{2}/3 \approx 0.84$	$\frac{2}{1}/3 \approx 0.67$	$\frac{7}{3}/5 \approx 0.47$

In the example the average reuse rate in pla_3 is 0.47. The comparison between pla_1 and pla_3 shows that the reuse rate has deteriorated. This is to be expected since new products and modules are added. In the next planning activity of a new PLA these new modules should be used in more products to increase the reuse rate.

3) Cohesion: A high cohesion is preferable. The value for cohesion denotes the rate, how many export values of the modules are used inside a product. The higher the value, the better the cohesion of the product. We call export and import values of modules *exports* and *imports* in the following. The cohesion $\mathcal{A}^p$ of a product p is calculated as follows:

$$\mathcal{A}^{p} = \frac{number\ of\ all\ exports\ of\ all\ modules\ used\ in\ p}{number\ of\ all\ exports\ of\ all\ modules\ in\ p} \tag{6}$$

The average cohesion $\mathcal{A}^P$ of products of a PLA version is calculated as follows:

$$\mathcal{A}^{P} = \frac{\sum \mathcal{A}^p}{number\ of\ all\ products} \tag{7}$$

The cohesion of the PLA $\mathcal{A}^{PLA}$ is calculated as follows:

$$\mathcal{A}^{PLA} = \frac{number\ of\ all\ exports\ of\ modules\ used\ in\ all\ products}{number\ of\ all\ exports\ of\ all\ modules\ of\ all\ products} \tag{8}$$

In the following Table IV, we set randomly chosen values for exports and imports at $time = 1$ for the modules. We assume that the architect has access to the whole information of LAE, all products, and all modules at this time.

TABLE IV. EXPORTS AND IMPORTS AT TIME=1 IN FIGURE 3.

Module	*Number of export values*	*Number of import values*
m_{1_1}	3	1
m_{2_1}	4	3
m_{3_1}	2	3

TABLE V. COHESION FOR THE EXAMPLE OF FIGURE 3.

$\mathcal{A}$	pla_1	pla_2	pla_3
$\mathcal{A}^{p1}$	$\frac{1+1+0}{3+4+2} \approx 0.22$	-	$\frac{2+0+0}{3+4+2} \approx 0.22$
$\mathcal{A}^{p2}$	$\frac{1+0}{3+4} \approx 0.14$	$\frac{1+0}{3+4} \approx 0.14$	$\frac{1+0}{3+4} \approx 0.14$
$\mathcal{A}^{p3}$	-	-	$\frac{1+0}{3+4} \approx 0.14$
$\mathcal{A}^{P}$	≈ 0.18	≈ 0.14	≈ 0.17
$\mathcal{A}^{PLA}$	$\frac{1+1+0+1+0}{3+4+2+3+4} \approx 0.19$	$\frac{1+0}{3+4} \approx 0.14$	$\frac{2+0+0+1+0+1+0}{3+4+2+3+4+3+4} \approx 0.17$

Consider, e.g., pla_1 and $\mathcal{A}^{p_1}$ in Table V: Product p_{1_1} has three modules (m_{1_1}, m_{2_1}, m_{3_1}). In product p_{1_1} LAE A has a connection (export) to B and B has a connection (export) to C. In Table IV all export values are listed. The cohesion is calculated as follows:

$$\frac{\sum used\ exports\ of\ m_{1\_1}, m_{2\_1}, m_{3\_1}}{\sum all\ exports\ of\ m1\_1, m2\_1, m3\_1} = \frac{1+1+0}{3+4+2} \approx 0.22$$

For a whole PLA all used export values of modules in all products are aggregated. The result for pla_2 shows that the change operation concerns all products and a part of the LAE and modules. The expected cohesion in pla_3 is worse compared to pla_1. The quality of the PLA has slightly deteriorated. Modules realize more than one functionality because they are used in more than one project. Therefore, cohesion is competing to the reuse rate. It is planned to evaluate these metrics and determine the intervals of the values for "good" and "bad" with the help of experts in one of our industrial projects.

4) Applying change operations on a PLA: A software architect changes the PLA to fulfill new requirements. The aim is to implement the new requirements with the least possible adaptation on the product/module level.

Figure 12 exemplarily describes the procedure of applying change operations on a PLA. The procedure starts with the current PLA and all products and modules at $time = 1$. To make change operations, the software architect performs the following steps:

1) The architect adds a new change operation to the PLA.
2) The above metrics are performed on the intermediate PLA b. The results are considered as bad by the architect and the changes are rejected.
3) The architect adds a new change operation to the PLA. The above metrics are performed on the intermediate PLA. The results are evaluated as good and the PLA c serves as the basis for the next step.
4) The architect adds a new change operation to the PLA c.
5) The above metrics are performed on the intermediate PLA d. The results are considered as bad by the architect and the changes are rejected.
6) The architect adds a new change operation on the PLA c resulting in PLA e. Again, the metrics are applied. The results are rated as good. As all requirements have been implemented, PLA e is the new PLA vision and serves as input for the planning.

C. Planning of Development Iterations and Prototyping

In our case the planning of the further development involves several activities, e.g., performing planning of each modification of PLA and PA. The problem arises when `PL-Requirements` or `P-Requirements` needs to be realized within certain development time and within certain development costs. Planning solves the problem by defining timed activities considering the effort limitations.

Planning consists of a sequence of iterations. Iterations are defined as a number of architecture elements that must be realized in a time period bounded by t_{start} and t_{end} with $t_{start}, t_{end} \in \mathbb{N}, t_{start} < t_{end}$. Within each time period the activities `Design`, `Plan`, `Implement` and `Check` are ordered. The iteration is completed when all modifications are realized by `Design`, `Implement`, and checked to be conform to architecture rules by `Check`. An example of a sequence of three iterations is shown in Figure 3. In Figure 3, the expected result of modifications on PLA at several time points is defined, which corresponds to `PL-Plan`. Moreover, the expected result of modifications on PA are defined where products, modules and their mapping for three time points is shown in Figure 3.

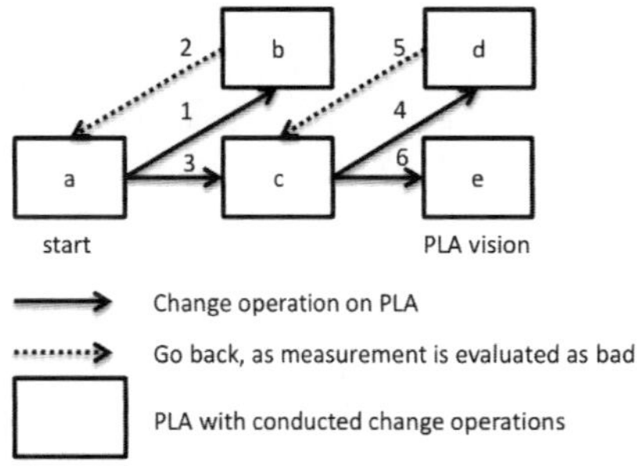

Figure 12. Example: Applying change operations on a PLA

The effort caused to realize the planned number of architecture elements is estimated by the activities `Design` and `Implement`, to achieve the PLA and PA development within given effort limitations. In case of a deviation between planned and actual estimations the initial plan is modified. Therefore, effort estimations are made by considering the necessary effort of PLA or PA modifications from `Design` and from `Implement`. In the following, details about effort estimations according to PLA and PA modifications are presented to achieve estimation based planning.

The first estimation concept is based on metrics to evaluate the modification effort. For example, modification effort according to connection structure and component structure is estimated by rating cohesion of components. Another estimation concept is to evaluate the effort based on modification realizing a new pattern in the appropriate PLA or PA. Hence, simple connection or component related modifications are lightweight, pattern based structure modifications are heavyweight. Modifications rated as heavyweight often involve a huge number of architecture components and products. Therefore, in such a case our methodology suggests to outsource such heavyweight modifications into a prototype projects. This special case is enclosed by the activity `PL to P` of our methodology.

VII. CASE STUDY

In this section we introduce a real world example, a longitudinal dynamics torque coordination software, from automotive software engineering. We apply our methodology for planning and evolving automotive product line architectures on this example and present the results of a corresponding case study.

A. Real World Example: Longitudinal Dynamics Torque Coordination

Our approach for designing the logical architecture described in the previous sections is based on our experience in the automotive environment. In numerous projects with the focus on software development for engine control units, we have developed architectural principles and concepts for architectural design and tested them on real sample projects. The following example shows frequent problems that arise as a result of strongly increasing accidental complexity.

In our example, we consider the control of the acceleration and braking process, which is controlled by the driver via the accelerator and brake pedal, respectively. The implementation of these controls was originally carried out on completely separate developments. In the course of time, however, additional functions have been added: Not only the driver can act here by actuating the throttle or brake pedal. There are a number of additional functions, such as the electronic stability control (ESP) or the adaptive cruise control (ACC), which can act as accelerator and decelerator. In the case of longitudinal dynamics torque coordination (see Figure 13), both acceleration and braking processes must be coordinated with one another since there are mutual interdependencies. A drive train coordinator (DTC) was introduced for the coordination of the acceleration path.

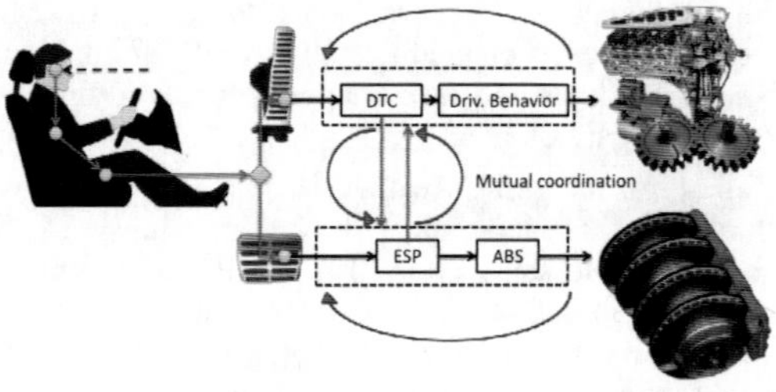

Figure 13. Automotive powertrain example: Mutual coordination

As a solution to the coordination problems, point-to-point connections between the software components were introduced, which however led to a strong increase in the accidental complexity: The realization of the reciprocal coordination of the requesters was implemented in the example by the addition of a new explicit communication for the solution of coordination problems (see Figure 13, "mutual coordination"). In addition, existing functions had to be replicated in another context for the realization of the explicit communication. As a result, redundancies were created in the software components. Furthermore, accidental complexity has increased disproportionately because of the wide interfaces and strong coupling within the architecture of the system.

Next, we describe how we applied the approaches introduced in the previous sections to manage the complexity of the example system. This paves the way for long-term maintenance and extensible architectures.

B. Origin of the Growing Accidental Complexity

In the following, the problems outlined above are explained in more detail using the real example. Later, we will show how by using different architectural principles, a significantly improved product line architecture with low accidental complexity can be build. This example is based on real industrial projects, but these have been simplified in this paper in order not to disclose business secrets.

The example consists of two systems that existed separately from each other in the past. The systems are, on the one hand, the acceleration path to the engine, where the driver generates a positive torque request to the engine by actuating the accelerator pedal. The other system is the braking path, on which the driver transmits a negative torque request, the so-called deceleration request, to the brake by actuating the brake. In both systems, the pedals were connected directly to the engine or the brake by a bowden cable.

With the development of increasingly better and more cost-effective electrotechnical systems, both systems have been further and further electrified. In the braking path, assistance systems were introduced to increase safety, such as the anti-lock braking system (ABS) and later an ESP. A control unit, the engine control unit, was introduced into the acceleration path, which led to the electric accelerator pedal in the 90s. This resulted in the elimination of the direct bowden cable to the engine. Furthermore, assistance systems have been developed, which optimally transfer the driver's request torque. By introducing electric motors, it is now also possible to set negative torques on the drive path. Thus, it was necessary that both systems exchange information with each other. As a result, all systems had to be connected to each other in order to be able to match the desired values with the real values of the motor and brake, respectively.

Architecture recovery: As outlined above, further developments have led to an erosion of the originally planned architecture. The implementations in the individual products have increasingly deviated from the planned product line architecture. Finally, the existing system was very difficult to handle in further developments. For this reason, the system had to be revised and, in particular, the architecture had to be repaired. Thus, we applied architecture recovery as described in Section IV. Recovery uses reverse engineering techniques to extract the implemented architecture from source artifacts. Figure 14 illustrates the recovered architecture. The black arrows show the data flow along the two paths. In addition to the physical set values, this data also contains information about the state of the assistance system as well as the information about the mode (kickdown, emergency brake, active, inactive, etc.), in which it is currently located. The blue arrows convey the changes of the values for the torque requests. These connections are required, since there are controllers in all systems, which are integrated over time if the behavior of their control loop is not known.

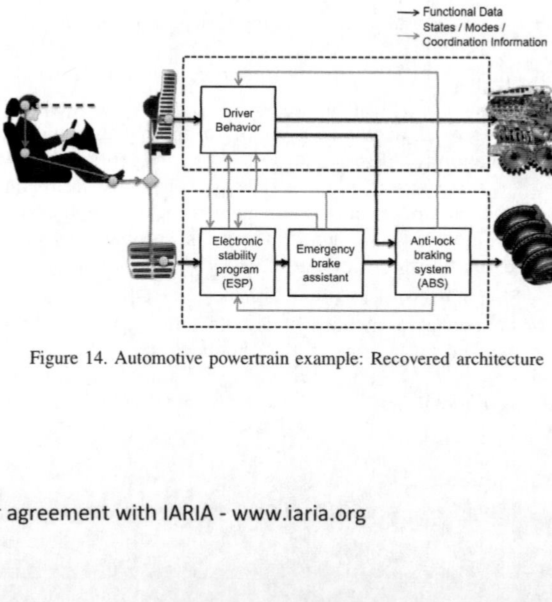

Figure 14. Automotive powertrain example: Recovered architecture

C. Applying our Approach on the Example

Design of the new PLA - Iteration 1: After the analysis of the system, it became clear that the coordination information had to be reduced. The first step was the introduction of a coordinator component with the architecture design principle *Coordinator-PipesAndFilters-Support*, which enabled the coordination of both torque paths (acceleration/brake). The result of this change is depicted in Figure 15.

Measuring of architecture quality - Iteration 1: The data flow was not changed by the introduction of the coordinator, s.t. the functional behavior of the assistance systems remained unchanged. However, many interfaces necessary for the coordination information could be removed. This has reduced the complexity of many assistance systems. The complexity of the ESP, e.g., could be reduced to the level of the essential complexity. However, the ABS assistance system has risen in complexity since a further interface for the coordination had to be added here. The coordinator is also a very complex system since the coordinator now contains the entire coordination effort, which was previously distributed to the individual assistance systems.

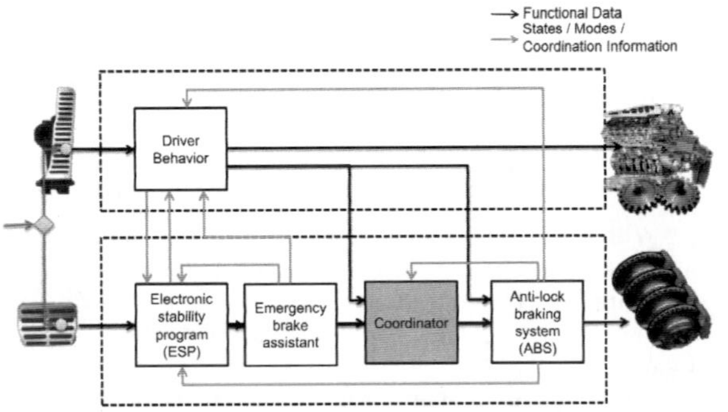

Figure 15. Reducing complexity by architecture design principle *coordinator*

Design of the new PLA - Iteration 2: In order to ensure that no additional coordination information interfaces are generated, the architecture design principle *feedback channel* (see Section VI-A5) is introduced for all components in the system. This ensures that all controllers are informed of the current situation in the system, without the need for additional interfaces to all components. The feedback interface has only to be added to the ESP assistance system. To optimize the information processing in the individual components, the architecture design principle *anvil-like component model* was introduced. Due to the division into the execution control and functional algorithms, the components became much more structured and readable. In the part functional algorithms, only all the technical complexities, which concern the function itself are contained. The part of the execution control contains all relevant system-dependent contents. This facilitates the development of each individual component, since adaptations, which have to be carried out solely because of a system change, only take place in the execution control. All tests regarding the functionality of the component can usually be adopted unchanged, since the functionality is implemented exclusively in the functional algorithms. The resulting product line architecture is shown in Figure 16.

Measuring of architecture quality - Iteration 2: By the new design the *modification effort* of a PLA could be improved significantly with regard to further development. If, e.g., a new assistance function is to be introduced, only few adaptations to the existing architecture are necessary. The evaluation of *cohesion* and *reuse rate* according to Section VI-B can not be carried out at this point because currently only a prototypical product version exists. It is, however, to be expected that the reduction of mutual interdependencies will lead to a significant increase in cohesion. In addition, the current implementation of the modules includes a high degree of variability, which increases the reusability in different products. Furthermore, the improved modification effort also contributes to an increased reusability over several subsequent product versions since adjustments are only necessary in a few places when new functions are introduced.

Planning of development iterations and prototyping: As shown in the example, the development was carried out in two iterations. Both iterations resulted in an executable prototype, which was tested extensively. The functionality was tested by means of the tool Time Partition Testing (TPT). TPT suits particularly well due to the ability to describe continuous behavior [49]. As a starting point for the tests, a simple environment model was created. The module and composite tests were carried out taking into account previously defined scenarios. The signals were then evaluated and compared with the scenarios.

As a result of the tests, neither errors were found in the module tests nor in the composite tests. The case study has demonstrated that the migration of the existing functionality into an improved architecture is possible by means of our approach.

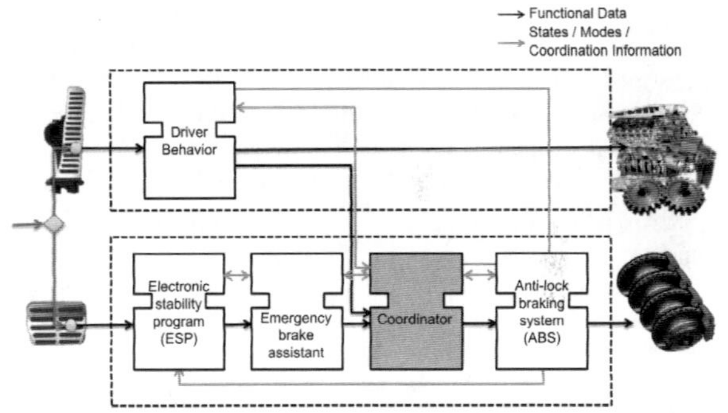

Figure 16. Reducing complexity by architecture design principle *feedback channel* and *anvil-like component model*

VIII. Knowledge-Based Architecture Evolution and Maintenance

In this section we will outline how the approach introduced in Section V can be extended to a holistic solution for managing architectural concepts during the evolution of the system life-cycle. As visualized in Figure 17 the approach can be embedded into an evolutionary incremental development process. After each implementation step the realization can be analyzed.

Thereby the generated Concept Performance Record can support the system architect to get a comprehension of the

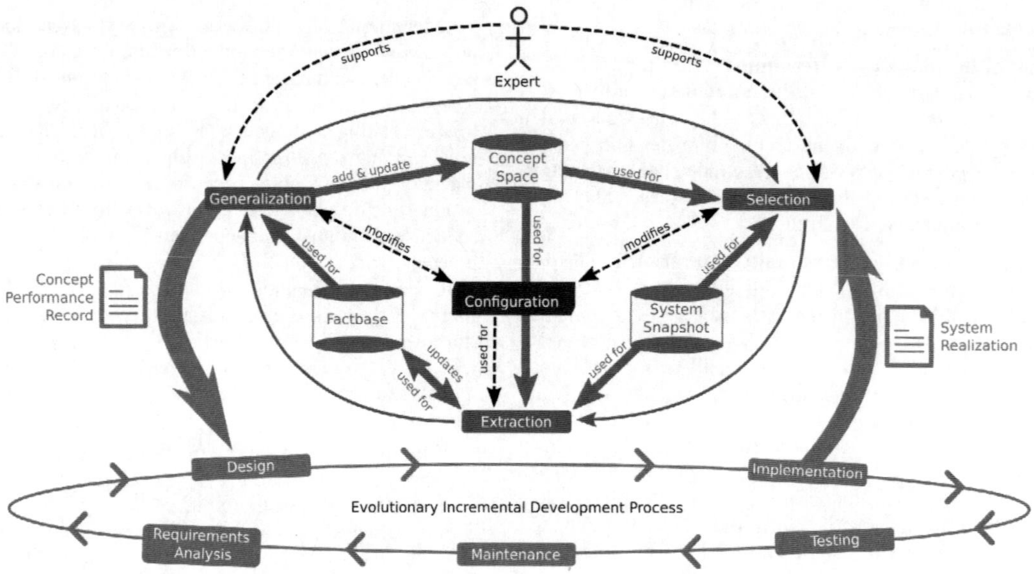

Figure 17. Overview of the approach to extract architectural concepts embedded into an evolutionary incremental development process

realized concepts. This information can be combined with the results from the `PL-Check` and `P-Check` activity (see Section III). As described the aim of the checking activities is to reduce the erosion of a product architecture by architecture conformance checking. The output of these activities are a list of violations. If the developer was not familiar with the architecture, for example, and this is the reason for the violation, it can still be fixed during the next implementation step by the developer, so that no erosion occurs. On the other hand it can be decided that the reason for the violation is reasoned by a not suitable architecture. In this case the Concept Performance Record can support by planning the architectural changes by making the aspects the developer has in mind explicit on the architectural abstraction level.

An additional issue is the improvement of the evolution and maintenance process by the monitoring of concepts. We can assume that the configuration and all data pools are stored in a repository and will be versioned. So we can answer the question: "What might happen with architectural concepts over time?" - they can be adapted to new requirements or in consequence of new technologies, frameworks or programming paradigms, for example. This can also lead to new concepts, which maybe replace old concepts, so it might be possible that extracted concepts will disappear over time. But these changes can be detected with the help of the detector mechanism, too, or in other words comparing two Concept Performance Records from different versions of a product will lead to indications of mutations and/or displacement of concepts. What on the other hand can help to detect product architecture erosion at an early stage.

IX. Conclusion

We introduced a sophisticated approach for extracting, designing and managing architectural concepts and thus enabling long-term evolution of automotive software systems. The approach aims to close the gap between product architectures and the product line architecture in the automotive domain. Thus, we used adapted concepts like architecture design principles, architecture compliance checking, and further development scheduling with specific adaptations to the automotive domain.

With a high degree of erosion, a further development of the software is only possible at great effort. Before approaches to minimize erosion can be applied, the architecture must first be repaired. Thus, we investigated how approaches for architecture extraction can be adapted to be applied to automotive software product line architectures. First, we proposed methods used to extract initial architectures. Next, we explained our experiences gained from a real world case study. In the case study, we could recover a PLA for the engine control unit software. However, difficulties have arisen in building an integrated PLA due to the size of the selected system. To handle such huge systems an automated process must be developed by further research.

Furthermore, we integrated this recovery/discovery approach into an evolutionary incremental development process. We focused on how the developers best practice can be identified and reflected to the architecture level. In addition, we showed how a knowledge based process for architecture evolution and maintenance for architectural concepts can be implemented.

Next, we proposed methods and concepts to create adequate architectures with the help of abstract principles, patterns, and description techniques. Such techniques allow making complexity manageable. We presented architectural concepts developed within different industrial projects in the automotive domain involving different software architects and project members. For example, we introduced feedback channels enabling the dissolution of functional dependencies without the introduction of technical point-to-point connection.

We suggested techniques for understanding of architecture and measuring of architecture quality. With the help of numerical results of these measurements, we can make a statement about complexity, as well as conclusions about a system.

Finally, we demonstrated our concepts by an industrial case study from the automotive domain. We described how we applied the approaches introduced in the previous sections to manage the complexity of the example system. We have shown that the application of the approach paves the way for long-term maintenance and extensible architectures.

REFERENCES

[1] A. Grewe, C. Knieke, M. Körner, A. Rausch, M. Schindler, A. Strasser, and M. Vogel, "Automotive Software Systems Evolution: Planning and Evolving Product Line Architectures," in Special Track: Managed Adaptive Automotive Product Line Development (MAAPL), along with ADAPTIVE 2017. IARIA XPS Press, 2017, pp. 53–62.

[2] F. P. Brooks, Jr., "No silver bullet essence and accidents of software engineering," Computer, vol. 20, no. 4, Apr. 1987, pp. 10–19.

[3] J. van Gurp and J. Bosch, "Design Erosion: Problems & Causes," Journal of Systems and Software, vol. Volume 61, 2002, pp. 105–119.

[4] S. Herold and A. Rausch, "Complementing Model-Driven Development for the Detection of Software Architecture Erosion," in 5th Modelling in Software Engineering (MiSE 2013) Workshop at Intern. Conf. on Softw. Eng. (ICSE 2013), 2013.

[5] S. Herold, "Architectural Compliance in Component-Based Systems. Foundations, Specification, and Checking of Architectural Rules." Ph.D. dissertation, Technische Universität Clausthal, 2011.

[6] L. de Silva and D. Balasubramaniam, "Controlling Software Architecture Erosion: A Survey," Journal of Systems and Software, vol. 85, no. 1, Jan. 2012, pp. 132–151.

[7] I. John and J. Dörr, "Elicitation of Requirements from User Documentation," in Ninth International Workshop on Requirements Engineering: Foundation for Software Quality. REFSQ '03, 2003.

[8] H. Gomaa, Designing Software Product Lines with UML: From Use Cases to Pattern-Based Software Architectures. Addison-Wesley Professional, 2004.

[9] P. Clements and L. Northrop, Software Product Lines: Practices and Patterns. Addison Wesley, 2001.

[10] K. Pohl, G. Böckle, and F. J. v. d. Linden, Software Product Line Engineering: Foundations, Principles and Techniques. Springer-Verlag, 2005.

[11] H. Holdschick, "Challenges in the Evolution of Model-based Software Product Lines in the Automotive Domain," in Proceedings of the 4th International Workshop on Feature-Oriented Software Development, ser. FOSD '12. ACM, 2012, pp. 70–73.

[12] R. Cloutier, G. Muller, D. Verma, R. Nilchiani, E. Hole, and M. Bone, "The Concept of Reference Architectures," Systems Engineering, vol. 13, no. 1, Feb. 2010, pp. 14–27.

[13] E. Y. Nakagawa, P. O. Antonino, and M. Becker, "Reference Architecture and Product Line Architecture: A Subtle but Critical Difference," in Proceedings of the 5th European Conference on Software Architecture, ser. ECSA'11. Berlin, Heidelberg: Springer-Verlag, 2011, pp. 207–211.

[14] E. Y. Nakagawa, F. Oquendo, and M. Becker, "RAModel: A Reference Model for Reference Architectures," in Proceedings of the 2012 Joint Working IEEE/IFIP Conference on Software Architecture and European Conference on Software Architecture, ser. WICSA-ECSA '12. Washington, DC, USA: IEEE Computer Society, 2012, pp. 297–301.

[15] E. Y. Nakagawa, M. Becker, and J. C. Maldonado, "Towards a Process to Design Product Line Architectures Based on Reference Architectures," in Proceedings of the 17th International Software Product Line Conference, ser. SPLC '13. New York, NY, USA: ACM, 2013, pp. 157–161.

[16] E. Y. Nakagawa, M. Guessi, J. C. Maldonado, D. Feitosa, and F. Oquendo, "Consolidating a Process for the Design, Representation, and Evaluation of Reference Architectures," in Proceedings of the 2014 IEEE/IFIP Conference on Software Architecture, ser. WICSA '14. Washington, DC, USA: IEEE Computer Society, 2014, pp. 143–152.

[17] M. Shaw and D. Garlan, Software Architecture: Perspectives on an Emerging Discipline. Upper Saddle River, NJ, USA: Prentice-Hall, Inc., 1996.

[18] F. Buschmann, R. Meunier, H. Rohnert, P. Sommerlad, and M. Stal, Pattern-Oriented Software Architecture - Volume 1: A System of Patterns. Wiley Publishing, 1996.

[19] J. Bosch, Design and use of software architectures: Adopting and evolving a product-line approach. Pearson Education, 2000.

[20] S. Deelstra, M. Sinnema, and J. Bosch, "Product derivation in software product families: a case study," Journal of Systems and Software, vol. 74, no. 2, 2005, pp. 173–194.

[21] S. Thiel and A. Hein, "Modeling and Using Product Line Variability in Automotive Systems," IEEE Softw., vol. 19, no. 4, Jul. 2002, pp. 66–72.

[22] R. Flores, C. Krueger, and P. Clements, "Mega-scale Product Line Engineering at General Motors," in Proceedings of the 16th International Software Product Line Conference - Volume 1, ser. SPLC '12. New York, NY, USA: ACM, 2012, pp. 259–268.

[23] N. Siegmund, M. Rosenmüller, M. Kuhlemann, C. Kästner, and G. Saake, "Measuring Non-Functional Properties in Software Product Line for Product Derivation," in Proceedings of the 2008 15th Asia-Pacific Software Engineering Conference, ser. APSEC '08. Washington, DC, USA: IEEE Computer Society, 2008, pp. 187–194.

[24] L. Passos, K. Czarnecki, S. Apel, A. Wasowski, C. Kästner, and J. Guo, "Feature-oriented Software Evolution," in Proceedings of the Seventh International Workshop on Variability Modelling of Software-intensive Systems, ser. VaMoS '13. New York, NY, USA: ACM, 2013, pp. 17:1–17:8.

[25] Gentzane Aldekoa and Salvador Trujillo and Goiuria Sagardui Mendieta and Oscar Daz, "Quantifying Maintainability in Feature Oriented Product Lines," in Proceedings of the 12th European Conference on Software Maintenance and Reengineering. IEEE, 2008, pp. 243–247.

[26] Zhang, T. and Deng, L. and Wu, J. and Zhou, Q. and Ma, C., "Some Metrics for Accessing Quality of Product Line Architecture," in 2008 International Conference on Computer Science and Software Engineering, vol. 2, 2008, pp. 500–503.

[27] G. Holl, P. Grünbacher, and R. Rabiser, "A Systematic Review and an Expert Survey on Capabilities Supporting Multi Product Lines," Inf. Softw. Technol., vol. 54, no. 8, Aug. 2012, pp. 828–852.

[28] B. Hardung, T. Kölzow, and A. Krüger, "Reuse of Software in Distributed Embedded Automotive Systems," in Proceedings of the 4th ACM international conference on Embedded software. ACM, 2004, pp. 203–210.

[29] M. Steger, C. Tischer, B. Boss, A. Müller, O. Pertler, W. Stolz, and S. Ferber, "Introducing PLA at Bosch Gasoline Systems: Experiences and Practices," in Software Product Lines. Springer, 2004, pp. 34–50.

[30] B. Cool, C. Knieke, A. Rausch, M. Schindler, A. Strasser, M. Vogel, O. Brox, and S. Jauns-Seyfried, "From Product Architectures to a Managed Automotive Software Product Line Architecture," in Proceedings of the 31st Annual ACM Symposium on Applied Computing, ser. SAC'16. New York, NY, USA: ACM, 2016, pp. 1350–1353.

[31] M. Schindler, "Automatische Identifikation und Optimierung von Komponentenstrukturen in Softwaresystemen," Master's thesis, TU Clausthal, 2010.

[32] M. Schindler, C. Deiters, and A. Rausch, "Using Spectral Clustering to Automate Identification and Optimization of Component Structures," in Proceedings of 2nd International Workshop on Realizing Artificial Intelligence Synergies in Software Engineering (RAISE), 2013, pp. 14–20.

[33] M. Schindler, A. Rausch, and O. Fox, "Clustering Source Code Elements by Semantic Similarity Using Wikipedia," in Proceedings of 4th Intern. Workshop on Realizing Artificial Intelligence Synergies in Softw. Eng. (RAISE), 2015, pp. 13–18.

[34] M. Körner, S. Herold, and A. Rausch, "Composition of Applications Based on Software Product Lines Using Architecture Fragments and Component Sets," in Proceedings of the WICSA 2014 Companion Volume, ser. WICSA '14 Companion. New York, NY, USA: ACM, 2014, pp. 13:1–13:4.

[35] D. Claraz, S. Kuntz, U. Margull, M. Niemetz, and G. Wirrer, "Deterministic Execution Sequence in Component Based Multi-Contributor Powertrain Control Systems," in Embedded Real Time Software and Systems Conference, 2012, pp. 1–7.

[36] K. Reif, Automobilelektronik - Eine Einführung für Ingenieure, 4th ed. Vieweg + Teubner, 2012.

[37] R. Isermann, Ed., Elektronisches Management motorischer Fahrzeugantriebe, 4th ed. Vieweg + Teubner, 2010.

[38] C. Deiters, Beschreibung und konsistente Komposition von Bausteinen für den Architekturentwurf von Softwaresystemen, 1st ed., ser. SSE-Dissertation. München: Dr. Hut, 2015, vol. 11.

[39] M. Mues, "Taint Analysis - Language Independent Security Analysis for Injection Attacks," Master's Thesis, TU Clausthal, Institute for Applied Software Systems Engineering, 2016.

[40] M. Cottrell, B. Hammer, A. Hasenfuß, and T. Villmann, "Batch and median neural gas," Neural Networks, vol. 19, no. 6, 2006, pp. 762–771.

[41] B. Fritzke, "A Growing Neural Gas Network Learns Topologies," in Proceedings of the 7th International Conference on Neural Information Processing Systems, ser. NIPS'94. Cambridge, MA, USA: MIT Press, 1994, pp. 625–632.

[42] T. Kohonen, "The self-organizing map," Neurocomputing, vol. 21, no. 1, 1998, pp. 1–6.

[43] M. Reuter and H. H. Tadijne, "Computing with Activities III: Chunking and Aspect Integration of Complex Situations by a New Kind of Kohonen Map with WHU-Structures (WHU-SOMs)," in Proceedings of IFSA2005, Y. Liu, G. Chen, and M. Ying, Eds. Springer, 2005, pp. 1410–1413.

[44] M. Reuter, "Computing with Activities V. Experimental Proof of the Stability of Closed Self Organizing Maps (gSOMs) and the Potential Formulation of Neural Nets," in Proceedings World Automation Congress (ISSCI 2008). TSI, 2008.

[45] A. Rausch, R. Reussner, R. Mirandola, and F. Plášil, Eds., The Common Component Modeling Example: Comparing Software Component Models. Springer, 2008, vol. 5153.

[46] A. Gisbrecht, W. Lueks, B. Mokbel, and B. Hammer, "Out-of-Sample Kernel Extensions for Nonparametric Dimensionality Reduction," in Proceedings of the European Symposium on Artificial Neural Networks, Computational Intelligence and Machine Learning (ESANN), vol. 2012, 2012, pp. 531–536.

[47] L. van der Maaten and G. Hinton, "Visualizing Data using t-SNE," Journal of Machine Learning Research, vol. 9, no. Nov, 2008, pp. 2579–2605.

[48] M. Bernard, C. Buckl, V. Döricht, F. M., L. Fiege, H. von Grolman, N. Ivandic, C. Janello, C. Klein, K.-J. Kuhn, C. Patzlaff, B. C. Riedl, B. Schätz, and C. Stanek, Mehr Software (im) Wagen: Informations- und Kommunikationstechnik (IKT) als Motor der Elektromobilität der Zukunft. fortiss GmbH, 2011.

[49] E. Lehmann, "Time Partition Testing – Systematischer Test des kontinuierlichen Verhaltens von eingebetteten Systemen," Ph.D. dissertation, Fakultät IV – Elektrotechnik und Informatik, TU Berlin, 2004.

Conversational Homes: A Uniform Natural Language Approach for Collaboration Among Humans and Devices

Dave Braines, Nick O'Leary, Anna Thomas
Emerging Technology,
IBM United Kingdom Ltd,
Hursley Park, Winchester, UK
Email: {dave_braines, nick_oleary, annaet}@uk.ibm.com

Daniel Harborne, Alun Preece, Will Webberley
Crime and Security Research Institute /
School of Computer Science and Informatics,
Cardiff University, Cardiff, UK
Email: {HarborneD, PreeceAD, WebberleyWM}@cardiff.ac.uk

***Abstract*—As devices proliferate, the ability for us to interact with them in an intuitive and meaningful way becomes increasingly challenging. In this paper we take the typical home as an experimental environment to investigate the challenges and potential solutions arising from ever-increasing device proliferation and complexity. We describe and evaluate a potential solution based on conversational interactions between "things" in the environment where those things can be either machine devices or human users. Our key innovation is the use of a Controlled Natural Language (CNL) technology as the underpinning information representation language for both machine and human agents, enabling humans and machines to trivially "read" the information being exchanged. The core CNL is augmented with a conversational protocol enabling different speech acts to be exchanged within the system. This conversational layer enables key contextual information to be conveyed, as well as providing a mechanism for translation from the core CNL to other forms, such as device specific API (Application Programming Interface) requests, or more easily consumable human representations. Our goal is to show that a single, uniform language can support machine-machine, machine-human, human-machine and human-human interaction in a dynamic environment that is able to rapidly evolve to accommodate new devices and capabilities as they are encountered. We also report results from our first formal evaluation of a Conversational Homes prototype and demonstrate users with no previous experience of this environment are able to rapidly and effectively interact with simulated devices in a number of simple scenarios.**

Keywords–IoT; Controlled Natural Language; Conversational Interaction.

I. Introduction

From an individual agent's perspective, the Internet of Things (IoT) can be seen as an increasingly large and diverse world of other agents to communicate with. Humans are agents too in this world, so we can observe four kinds of communication: (i) human-machine, (ii) machine-human, (iii) machine-machine, and (iv) human-human. There is a tendency to consider human-oriented (i, iv) and machine-oriented (ii, iii) interactions as naturally requiring different kinds of communication language; humans prefer natural languages, while machines operate most readily on formal languages. In this paper, however, we consider what the IoT world might look like where humans and machines largely use a common, uniform language to communicate. Our design goal is to support communication activities such as: the discovery of other agents and their capabilities, querying other agents and receiving understandable information from them, and obtaining rationale for an agent's actions. The proposed approach must be able to cope with rapid evolution of an IoT environment that needs to accommodate new devices, capabilities, and agent types. In Section II, we consider why human users might find such an environment more appealing when machines communicate using an accessible and human-friendly language, than when machines use a traditional machine-to-machine formalism. Section III substantiates our proposed approach using a series of vignettes, while Section IV presents evidence that human-machine and machine-machine interactions can be facilitated via a CNL communication mechanism as well as a full description and analysis of the recent initial Conversational Homes evaluation study. Section V concludes the paper.

This paper extends ideas first proposed in [1], specifically by reporting on the first formal evaluation of the conversational protocol described in that work. Sections I–III in this paper are largely unchanged from [1], with Section IV being substantially expanded to describe the evaluation setup and results. Section V is also updated to reflect these latest developments and our plans for future work.

II. Background and Related Work

A key part of our approach is to consider how humans "want" to interact with machines in the world. To help us gain insights into these latent human requirements we look towards existing trends and events occurring in the world and use these as inspiration to help us form our hypotheses about what a conversational environment for human-machine agents might entail. For example, in this work we consider recent interest in conversational technologies such as chatbots [2], conversational computing [3], and conversational agents [4]. The remainder of this section covers this human-motivated perspective and develops ideas first presented in [5].

A. Social Things

The advent of Twitter as a means of social communication has enabled a large number of otherwise inanimate objects to have an easily-accessible online presence. For example, Andy Stanford-Clark created an account for the Red Funnel ferries that service the Isle of Wight in the UK. The account [6] relays real-time information about the ferry arrivals and departures allowing a subscriber of the account to see if they are running on time.

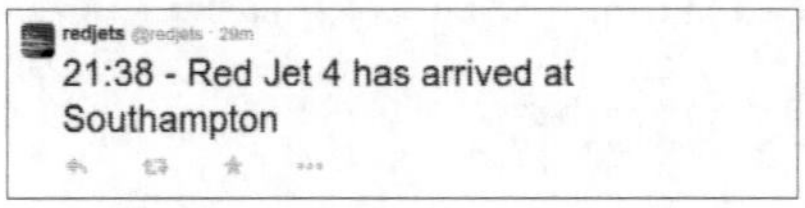

Figure 1: Redjet tweet example.

Another similar example is an unofficial account for London's Tower Bridge [7]. Its creator, Tom Armitage, created a system that took the published scheduled of bridge opening and closing times and produced a Twitter account that relayed that information.

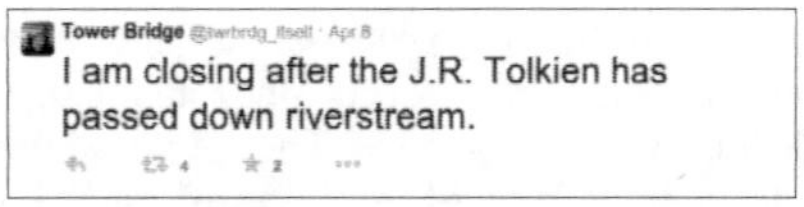

Figure 2: Tower Bridge tweet example.

A key difference between the ferries and the bridge accounts is that the ferries are just relaying information, a timestamp and a position, whereas the bridge is speaking to us in the first-person. This small difference immediately begins to bring a more human nature to the account. But, they are ultimately simple accounts that relay their state to whomever is following them, providing an easily consumable feed of information on an existing platform.

This sort of thing seems to have caught on particularly with the various space agencies. We no longer appear able to send a robot to Mars, or land a probe on a comet without an accompanying Twitter account bringing character to the events. The Mars Curiosity Rover has had an account [8] since July 2008 and regularly shares images it has captured. There's always a sense of excitement when these inanimate objects start to have a conversation with one another. The conversations between the European Space Agency Philae lander [9] and its Rosetta orbiter [10], as the former began to lose power and had to shutdown, generated a large emotional response on social media. The lander, which was launched into space years before social media existed, chose to use its last few milliamps of power to send a final goodbye.

The reality, of course, is that the devices did not create these tweets. Communication with them remains the preserve of highly specialized engineers, and their personalities are a creation of their public relations agencies on this planet. There are however, examples of machine participation on social media provided by social bots [11]. On occasion, these entities can masquerade as human agents and alter the dynamics of social sense-making and social influence.

B. Seamlessness vs Seamfulness

The IoT makes possible a future where our homes and workplaces are full of connected devices, sharing their data, making decisions, collaborating to make our lives better [12]. Whilst there are people who celebrate this invisible ubiquity and utility of computing, the reality is going to be much more complicated.

Mark Weiser, Chief Scientist at Xerox PARC, coined the term "ubiquitous computing" in 1988 as recognition of the changing nature of our interaction with computers [13]. Rather than the overt interaction of a user sitting in front of a computer, ubiquitous computing envisages technology receding into the background of our lives.

Discussion of ubiquitous computing often celebrates the idea of seamless experiences between the various devices occupying our lives. Mark Weiser advocated for the opposite; that seamlessness was undesirable and a self-defeating attribute of such a system. He preferred a vision of "Seamfulness, with beautiful seams" [14].

The desire to present a single view of a system, with no joins, is an unrealistic aspiration in the face of the cold realities of Wi-Fi connectivity, battery life, system reliability and the status of cloud services. Presenting a user with a completely monolithic system gives them no opportunity to connect with, and begin to understand, the constituent parts. That is not to say all users need this information all of the time, but there is clearly utility to some users some of the time: when you come home from work and the house is cold, what went wrong? Did the thermostat in the living room break and decide it was the right temperature already? Did the message from the working thermostat fail to get to the boiler? Is the boiler broken? Did you forget to cancel the entry in your calendar saying you'd be late home that day? Without some appreciation of the moving parts in a system, a user cannot feel any ownership or empowerment when something goes wrong with it. Or worse yet, how can they avoid feeling anything other than intimidated by this monolithic system that responds in a manner akin to, "I'm Sorry Dave, I'm afraid I can't do that".

This is the justification for beautiful seams: they help you understand the edges of a device's sphere of interaction, but should not be so big as to trip you up. For example, such issues exist with the various IP connected light bulbs that are available today. When a user needs to remember what application to launch on their phone depending on what room they are walking into and what manufacturer's bulbs happen to be in there, the seams have gotten too big and too visible.

Designer Tom Coates has written on these topics [15]. He suggests the idea of having a chat-room for the home:

"Much like a conference might have a chat-room so might a home. And it might be a space that you could duck into as you pleased to see what was going on. By turning the responses into human language you could make the actions of the objects less inscrutable and difficult to understand..."

This relates back to the world of Twitter accounts for Things, but with a key evolution. Rather than one-sided conversations presenting raw data in a more consumable form, or Wizard-of-Oz style man-behind-the-curtain accounts, a chat-room is a space where the conversation can flow both ways; both between the owner and their devices, and also between the devices themselves.

C. Getting Things Communicating

For devices to be able to communicate they need to share a common language. Simply being able to send a piece of data across the network is not sufficient. As with spoken language, the context of an interaction is important too.

This model of interaction applies to both the data a device produces, as well as the commands it can consume. There are a number of technologies available for producing such a shared model. For example: HyperCat [16], a consortium of companies funded by the UK Government's innovation agency in 2014. It provides a central catalog of resources that are described using RDF-like triple statements. Each resource is identified by a URI allowing for ease of reference. URIs are a key component in building the World Wide Web and are well understood, but they are a technology used primarily by computers. They do not provide a human-accessible view of the model.

Furthermore, to enable a dynamic conversation, any such model needs to be adaptable to the devices that are participating, especially when one of those participants is a human being.

D. Talking to Computers

The most natural form of communication for most humans is that of their own spoken language, not some JSON or XML encoded format that was created with the devices as the primary recipient. Technical specialists can be trained to understand and use technical machine languages, but this overhead is not acceptable to more casual everyday users who may wish to interact with the devices in their home. In addition to this, we are living in an age where talking to computers is becoming less the preserve of science fiction: Apple's Siri, OK Google, Microsoft Cortana all exist as ways to interact with the devices in your pocket. Amazon Echo exists as a device for the home that allows basic interaction through voice commands. This means that there is now a plausible expectation that an everyday person could interact with complex devices in their home in a natural conversational manner.

Natural Language Processing (NLP) is one of the key challenges in Computer Science [17]. In terms of speech understanding, correctly identifying the words being spoken is relatively a well-solved problem, but understanding what those words mean, what intent they try to convey, is still a hard thing to do.

To answer the question "Which bat is your favorite?" without any context is hard to do. Are we talking to a sportsperson with their proud collection of cricket bats? Is it the zookeeper with their colony of winged mammals? Or perhaps a comic book fan is being asked to choose between incarnations of their favorite super hero.

Context is also vital when you want to hold a conversation. Natural language (NL) is riddled with ambiguity. Our brains are constantly filling in gaps, making theories and assumptions over what the other person is saying. For humans and machines to communicate effectively in any such conversational home setting, it is important that contextual information can be communicated in a simple, but effective, manner. This must be achieved in a manner that is accessible to both the human and machine agents in this environment.

E. Broader considerations

The focus of our research and the evaluation described later in this paper are exploring whether the use of a CNL technology can ease and/or speed the development of conversational systems, such as for an IoT enabled home. With this in mind we have not specifically attempted to build a system which has a rich or complex grammar or dialogue system, nor have we tried to create extensive, rich models or ontologies of the domain. There is no dialogue management required in our solution for this evaluation, and the required ontologies can be incredibly simple for the basic initial evalution activities.

Instead we have shown an approach where simple models can be quickly created by less technical users, to become the basis for systems such as the one evaluated in this paper. Our contribution to the literature is in showing an approach where the complexity and development time of the underlying models can be substantially reduced, ideally to a rate where real-time extensions can be made as new devices and capabilities are released. Such capabilities will be essential in any multi-organisation complex environment such as the IoT devices that could be used in a home environment.

We do acknowledge a rich body of research in the domain of multi-model interfaces [18] [19], dialogue systems and dialogue management [20] [21] [22] which would relate to the subsequent development of a complete system (regardless of whether it was underpinned by a CNL technology), but have not attempted to position our work against these for this particular evaluation.

There is also extensive literature on ontology engineering and the use of such systems in the context of dialogue [23] [24] [25] but again these are acknowledged but not specifically relevant to this simple evaluation against rapidly development CNL ontologies in a languaged aimed at less technical users.

III. Controlled Natural Language

To avoid a lot of the hard challenges of NLP, a CNL can be used. A CNL is a subset of a NL that uses a restricted set of grammar rules and a restricted vocabulary [26]. It is constructed to be readable by a native speaker and represents information in a structured and unambiguous form. This also enables it to be read and properly interpreted by a machine agent via a trivial parsing mechanism without any need for complex processing or resolution of ambiguity. CNLs range in strength from weaker examples such as simple style guides, to the strongest forms that are full formal languages with well-defined semantics. In our work, to identify a unifying language for both human and machine communication, we are focused on languages at the strong end of the scale, but we additionally wish to retain the requirement for maximal human consumability.

Ambiguity is a key issue for machine agents: whilst human readers can tolerate a degree of uncertainty and are often able to resolve ambiguity for themselves, it can be very difficult for a computer to do the same. CNLs typically specify that words be unambiguous and often specify the meaning that is allowed for all or a subset of the vocabulary. Another source of ambiguity is the phrase or sentence structure. A simple example is concerned with noun clusters. In English, one noun is commonly used to modify another noun. A noun phrase with several nouns is usually ambiguous as to how the nouns should be grouped. To avoid potential ambiguity, many CNLs do not allow the use of more than three nouns in a noun phrase.

There are two different philosophies in designing a CNL. As mentioned previously a weaker CNL can be treated as a simplified form of NL with a stronger CNL as an English version of a formal language [27]. In the case of a simplified form of NL, it can allow certain degrees of ambiguity in order to increase human accessibility. It relies on standard NLP techniques, lexical-semantic resources and a domain model to optimize its interpretation.

The alternative is to treat a CNL as an entirely deterministic language, where each word has a single meaning and no ambiguity can exist. Whilst computationally very efficient, it can be hard for a human user unfamiliar with the particular lexicon and grammar to write it effectively. This is because it competes with the user's own intuition of the language. The closer a CNL is to corresponding NL, the more natural and easy it is to use by humans, but it becomes less predictable and its computational complexity increases. The converse is also true. The more deterministic the CNL is, the more predictable it is, but the more difficult it is for humans to use.

In summary, in the operational setting described in this paper a CNL is designed to support both human usage and machine processing. It provides:

1) A user-friendly language in a form of English, instead of, for example, a standard formal query language (such as SPARQL or SQL). Enabling the user to construct queries to information systems in an intuitive way.
2) A precise language that enables clear, unambiguous representation of extracted information to serve as a semantic representation of the free text data that is amenable to creating rule-based inferences.
3) A common form of expression used to build, extend and refine domain models by adding or modifying entities, relations, or event types, and specifying mapping relations between data models and terminology or language variants.
4) An intuitive means of configuring system processing, such as specifying entity types, rules, and lexical patterns.

A good balance between the naturalness and predictability of the CNL is fundamentally important, especially to the human users as the strength and formality of the language increases.

A. An Introduction to ITA Controlled English

In previous research, we have proposed a specific CNL that is a variant of "Controlled English" known as ITA Controlled English, or just "CE" in shorthand [28]. This has been researched and developed under the International Technology Alliance (ITA) in Network and Information Science [29]. CE is consistent with First Order Predicate Logic and provides an unambiguous representation of information for machine processing. It aspires to provide a human-friendly representation format that is directly targeted at non-technical domain-specialist users (such as military planners, intelligence analysts or business managers) to enable a richer set of reasoning capabilities [30], [31].

We assert that CE can be used as a standard language for representation of many aspects of the information representation and reasoning space [32]. In addition to more traditional areas such as knowledge or domain model representation and corresponding information, CE also encompasses the representation of logical inference rules, rationale (reasoning steps), assumptions, statements of truth (and certainty) and has been used in other areas such as provenance [33] and argumentation [34].

In the remainder of this section we give a number of examples of the CE language. These are shown as embedded sentences in **this style**. All of these sentences are valid CE and therefore directly machine processable as well as being human readable.

The domain model used within CE is created through the definition of concepts, relationships and properties. These definitions are themselves written as CE conceptualise statements:

```
conceptualise a ~ device ~ D.
conceptualise an
   ~ environment variable ~ E.
```

These statements establish the concepts within the CE domain model enabling subsequent instances to be created using the same CE language:

```
there is an environment variable named
'temperature'.
```

A slightly more advanced example would be:

```
conceptualise a
   ~ controlling thing ~ C that
   is a device and
   ~ can control ~
     the environment variable E.
```

This defines "controlling thing" as a sub-concept of "device" and that it can have a "can control" relationship with an "environment variable". This therefore allows statements such as:

```
there is a controlling thing named
'thermostat' that
   can control the environment variable
   'temperature'.
```

In the latter conceptualise statement, "can control" is an example of a CE verb singular relationship. Functional noun relationships can also be asserted:

```
conceptualise a ~ device ~ D that
   has the value E as ~ enabled ~.
```

These two types of relationship construct allow a concept and its properties to be richly defined in CE whilst maintaining a strict subset of grammar. The use of verb singular and functional noun forms of properties provides a simple, but effective, mechanism to enable the conceptual model designer to use a language that is more natural and appealing to the human agents in the system.

The "is a" relationship used within conceptualise sentences defines inheritance of concepts, with multiple inheritance from any number of parents being a key requirement. It also allows any instance to be asserted as any number of concurrent concepts; an essential tool when attempting to capture and convey different contexts for the same information.

Whilst the examples given above are deliberately simplistic the same simple language constructs can be used to develop rich models and associated knowledge bases. The CE language has been successfully used in a wide range of example applications [35]. CE has been shown working with a reasonable number of concepts, relationships, queries and rules and has been used to model and interact with complex real-world environments with a high level of coverage and practical expressivity being achieved.

In our previous research into the application of the CE language we have observed that by gradually building up an operational model of a given environment, it is possible to iteratively define rich and complex semantic models in an "almost-NL" form that appeals to non-specialist domain users. For example, if the concept "device" was extended to include location information, the following query could be used to identify all devices of a particular type within a particular location:

```
for which D is it true that
   (the device D
     is located in the room V) and
   (the device D can measure
     the environment variable
        'temperature') and
   (the value V = 'kitchen').
```

Note that we do not expect casual users to write CE queries of this complexity; the later conversational interaction section will show how users can do this in a more natural form.

The model can be extended with rules that can be used to automatically infer new facts within the domain. Whenever such facts are inferred the CE language is able to capture rationale for why a particular fact is held to be true:

```
the room 'kitchen'
   is able to measure
      the environment variable
         'temperature' and
   is able to control
      the environment variable
      'temperature'
because
   the thermometer 't1'
      is located in the room 'kitchen' and
      can measure
         the environment variable
            'temperature' and
   the radiator valve 'v1'
      is located in the room 'kitchen' and
      can control
         the environment variable
            'temperature'.
```

From these basic examples you can see how the CE language can be used to model the basic concepts and properties within a given domain (such as an operating environment for IoT devices). Through assertion of corresponding instance data and the use of queries and rules it is possible to define the specific details of any given environment. It should also be clear to the reader that whilst human-readable the core CE language is quite technical and does not yet meet the aspiration of a language that would appeal to everyday casual users. The language itself can be improved, and as reported in earlier research there is the ability to build incrementally usable layers of language on top of the CE core language [36]. However, in addition to all of these potential advances in the core language there is also a key innovation that has been recently developed, which is to build a rich conversational protocol on top of the CE language [37]. This provides a mechanism whereby casual users can engage in conversation with a CE knowledge base using their own NL in a manner similar to human-human conversation.

B. *Conversational Interaction*

To enable a conversational form of CE, earlier research [38] has identified a requirement for a number of core interaction types based on speech-act theory:

1) A confirm interaction allows a NL message, typically from a human user, to be provided, which is then refined through interaction to an acceptable CE representation. This is useful for a human user who is perhaps not fully trained on the CE grammar. Through multiple such interactions, their experience builds and such interactions become shorter.
2) An ask/tell interaction allows a query to be made of the domain model and a well-formulated CE response given.
3) A gist/expand interaction enables the CE agent to provide a summary form ("gist") of a piece of CE, possibly adapted to a more digestible NL form. Such a gist can be expanded to give the underlying CE representation.
4) A why interaction allows an agent in receipt of CE statements to obtain rationale for the information provided.

This "conversational layer" is built within the core CE environment and is defined using the CE language. Within the CE model, these interactions are modeled as sub-types of the card concept.

```
conceptualise a ~ card ~ C that
   is an entity and
   has the timestamp T as ~ timestamp ~ and
   has the value V as ~ content ~ and
   ~ is to ~ the agent A and
   ~ is from ~ the agent B and
   ~ is in reply to ~ the card C.
```

The concept of an agent is introduced to represent the different parties in a conversation. This model provides a framework for such agents to interact by CE statements. By developing a conversational protocol using the CE language it enables the same language to be used for the domain in question (e.g., IoT devices in the home), as well as the act of communication. This means that agents with different operational domains can still communicate using a standard conversational model, so even if they cannot decode the items being discussed they are at least able to participate in the conversation. This idea is central to the proposed approach for conversationally enabled human and machine agents in an IoT context described in this paper.

C. Agent and ce-store interaction

In our ongoing experiments using the CE language we are able to define models, build knowledge bases, build machine agents and enable conversational interaction between them using some key components, which we will refer to here as ce-store. The Java-based implementation of the full ce-store [39] is publically available from github and an additional javascript-based version [40] is also available, specifically engineered to enable operation at the edge of the network, i.e., in a mobile browser environment.

For example, the domain model shown earlier in this paper is created through CE, (including the concepts, relationships and instances) and held within an instance of the ce-store, also referred to as a CE knowledge base. This store can either be maintained at a central point in the architecture, or distributed across systems through a federated set of separate ce-store instances. A centralized store provides a more straightforward system to maintain and ensures a single, shared model. Distributing the store allows for more localized processing to be done by the agents without having to interact with the system as a whole. Distributing the store also enables different agents to have different models, and for models to be rapidly extended "in the field" for only those agents that require those changes.

The choice of agent architecture influences how the store should be structured. When considering the types of conversation a chat-room for the home may need to support, there are two possible approaches.

1) The human user interacts with a single agent in the role of a concierge for the home. This concierge agent uses the CE knowledge base to maintain a complete situational awareness of the devices in the home and is able to communicate with them directly (see Figure 3). Interactions between concierge and devices do not use CE; only the concierge has a CE knowledge base.
2) The human user interacts with each device, or set of devices, individually. There may still be an agent in a concierge style role, but conversations can be directed at individual devices of interest as required (see Figure 4). Here, the concierge and all devices can communicate using CE and all have their own CE knowledge bases.

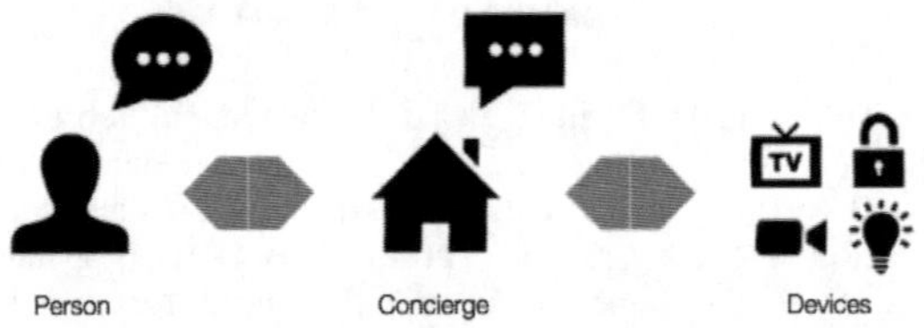

Figure 3: The human user interacts (via CE) only with the concierge.

Whilst the former would be sufficient to enable purely human-machine interaction, one of the goals of this work is to enable the human to passively observe the interaction of the devices in the home in order to help the human gain awareness of how the system is behaving. This will better enable the human user to see normal behavior over time and therefore prepare them for understanding anomalous situations when they arise.

Figure 4: The human user can interact (via CE) directly with all devices and with devices via the concierge.

As such, the latter approach is more suited for these purposes, perhaps with a concierge agent who is additionally maintaining the overall situation awareness from a machine-processing perspective.

D. Modelling the Conversation

In our proposed Conversational Homes setting there are a number of styles of interaction a human may wish to have with the devices in their home. This section considers four such styles and how they can be handled within a CE environment.

1) Direct question/answer exchanges: This is where a user makes a direct query as to the current state of the environment or one of the devices therein. For example: "What is the temperature in the kitchen?"

Through the existing conversational protocol and embedded simple contextual NL processing a machine agent is able to break down such a statement to recognize its intent. By parsing each word in turn and finding matching terms within the ce-store it can establish:

- it is a question regarding a current state ("What is ...")
- it is regarding the temperature environment variable instance
- it is regarding the kitchen room instance

At this point, the machine agent has sufficient information to query the ce-store to identify what devices in the model are in the right location and capable of measuring the required variable. If such a device exists, it can be queried for the value and reported back to the user. Otherwise, a suitable message can be returned to indicate the question cannot be answered, ideally conveying some indication of why not.

If the question is ambiguous, for example by omitting a location, the agent can prompt the user for the missing information. The concept of ambiguity for this kind of question is also captured in CE, for example by stating that for such an environment variable a location must be specified, perhaps even with a default location that can be assumed. With this knowledge available in CE the agent is able to determine that extra information is still required and can request this from the user as part of the conversation. The agent maintains information regarding the state of the conversation such that prompts can be made without requiring the user to repeat their entire question with the additional information included. By using the conversational protocol on top of the core CE language the human user and the device are able to converse in NL, for example:

User: *What is the temperature?*
Agent: *Where? I can tell you about the kitchen, the hall and the master bedroom.*
User: *The kitchen.*
Agent: *The temperature in the kitchen is 22C*

Other simple question types can be handled in this way, such as "where is...".

2) Questions that require a rationale as response: This is where a user requires an explanation for a current state of the system "Why is the kitchen cold?"

As with a direct question, an agent can parse the question to identify:

- it is a question asking for a rationale ("Why is ...")
- it has a subject of kitchen
- it has a state of cold that, through the CE model, is understood to be an expression of the temperature environment variable.

To be able to provide a response, the model supports the ability to identify what can affect the given environment variable. With that information it can examine the current state of the system to see what can account for the described state. For example, "the window is open" or "the thermostat is set to 16C".

3) An explicit request to change a particular state: This is where a user, or a machine agent, makes an explicit request for a device to take an action "Turn up the thermostat in the kitchen"

To identify this type of statement, the model maintains a set of actions that can be taken and to what devices they can be applied. By incrementally matching the words of the statement against the list of known actions, a match, if it exists, can be identified. Further parsing of the statement can identify a target for the action.

```
conceptualise an ~ action ~ A that
   ~ is reversed by ~ the action B and
   ~ can affect ~ the controlling thing M.

if (the action A
   is reversed by the action B)
then (the action B
   is reversed by the action A).
```

The CE above demonstrates the ability to define a rule. These are logic constructs with premises and conclusions that get evaluated by the ce-store against each new fact added. Where a match in the premises is found, new facts are generated using the conclusions (with corresponding rationale). In this simple case it allows two-way relationships to be established without having to explicitly define the relationship in both directions.

```
there is an action named 'turn on'.
there is an action named 'turn off'.
the action 'turn on'
   is reversed by the action 'turn off'.
```

When a device receives an action, the trigger concept can be used to chain further sequences of actions that should occur. For example, when applied to a thermostat, the action "turn up" should trigger the action "turn on" to be applied to the boiler.

```
there is a trigger named ' tr1' that
   has 'turn up' as action and
   has 'boiler' as target device and
   has 'turn on' as target action.

the thermostat 'ts1'
   will respond to the trigger 'tr1'.
```

There is a natural point of contact here, with the popular 'If This Then That' framework (IFTTT) [41], specifically in that the use of conversational interactions could provide a nice way to implement IFTTT functionality. In future work we may consider the extent CE could be applied in IFTTT scenarios, and used to support a user-friendly form of programming for real-world objects, devices and situations.

4) An implicit desire to change a state: The styles considered so far have been explicit in their intent. There is another form whereby a statement is made that states a fact, but also implies a desire for an action to be taken.

This relies on Grice's Maxim of Relevance [42]. In the context of a conversation with the devices in a house, a statement such as "I am cold" should be taken as a desire for it to be warmer. The underlying information that can allow this Gricean inference to be implemented by machine agents using a simple algorithm is shown below:

```
there is a physical state
    named 'cold' that
  is an expression of
    the environment variable
      'temperature' and
  has 'warmer' as desired state.

there is a desired state
    named 'warmer' that
  has 'temperature' as target and
  has 'increase' as effect.
```

Once the intention of the statement has been identified, the store can be queried to find any actions that satisfy the requirement. These actions can then be offered as possible responses to the statement, or possibly automatically enacted.

Through these four simple dialogue examples we have demonstrated that through the use of a CE knowledge base and a set of machine agents using the conversational protocol a human user could carry out basic interactions with the devices in their home (human-machine). We have also shown how those devices convey key information back to the user, or ask follow on questions to elicit additional information (machine-human). These same interactions using the same CE language can be used to enable direct communications between machine agents regardless of human involvement (machine-machine). Whilst we have not explicitly demonstrated human-human communication it is clear that this can easily be supported within a system such as this, for example, by enabling different human users within the home to use the same chat environment to converse with each other directly and then easily direct their questions or actions to machine agents when needed.

It is the use of this common human-readable CE language that enables the passive observation of system state and agent communications at any time without development of special tooling to convert from machine specific representation formats to something that human users can directly read. The CE language enables machine or human users to change or extend the conceptual models the system is operating on, as well as allowing them to define new knowledge, queries or rules.

Whilst it would be possible to demonstrate the same capabilities using more traditional Semantic Web languages they would be aimed at machine processability rather than human consumability and would therefore require additional components to be developed to allow conversational interaction and the inclusion of the human users in the conversation.

IV. Evaluation

As set out in the introduction, our hypothesis is that CNL can enable machine-machine, machine-human, human-machine and human-human interaction in a dynamic environment. The previous section has given illustrative examples of how we envisage the approach working in a range of use cases.

A. *Earlier work*

Through a series of experiments, we are building an evidence base to show the feasibility and effectiveness of the approach, in two respects: (i) that humans without any significant degree of training are able to engage in dialogues using a combination of NL and CNL; and (ii) that the approach supports environments that can rapidly evolve to accommodate new devices and capabilities as they are encountered.

In earlier work we have sought evidence for (i), specifically: we have to date run a series of trials in controlled conditions, focusing on the proposition that users with little or no training in the use of CE can productively interact with CE-enabled agents. We reported the results of the first of these studies in [38]. Twenty participants (undergraduate students) were assigned a task of describing scenes depicted in photographs using NL, and given feedback in the form of CE statements generated via NLP by a software agent. The agent had been constructed rapidly to perform simple bag-of-words NLP with a lexicon provided by having four independent people provide scene descriptions in advance of the study. The results were promising; from 137 NL inputs submitted by the 20 subjects, with a median of one sentence for each input, a median of two CE elements was obtained by NLP for each input. In other words, with no prior training in the use of CE or prior knowledge of the domain model constructed for the scenes, users were able to communicate two usable CE elements (typically an identified instance and a relationship) per single-sentence NL input.

The ability of the CE agent to extract meaningful elements from the user's input and confirm these in CE form was constrained by the rapid construction of the background domain knowledge base. In effect, the agent's limited knowledge about the world led to results that were characterized by high precision, but relatively low recall, since the agent was engineered only to be "interested" in a narrow range of things. In this respect, however, we see these results as applicable to our Conversational Homes scenarios, where the concerns of home-based devices and the affordances users expect them to provide will be similarly narrow. Further studies are planned in settings more closely aligned with the examples in the previous section, and the remaining sections of this paper talk in more detail about the first specific Conversational Homes evaluation in this series.

In our second trial, 39 participants (undergraduate students) assigned to three groups conducted a crowdsourcing task using a conversational agent deployed on mobile devices, entering observations via NL and confirming machine-generated CE that was then added to a collective knowledge base in real time [43]. Usability of the conversational agent was operationalised as task performance [44]: the number of user-inputted NL messages that were both machine interpretable (i.e., could be mapped to CE) and confirmed by the user. Overall, despite close to no training, 74% of the participants inputted NL that was machine interpretable and addressed the assigned crowdsourcing task. Participants reported positive satisfaction based on scores from the System Usability Scale (SUS) [45], with means in the high 60s being consistent with good usability.

In terms of our requirement (ii), that the approach supports environments that can rapidly evolve to accommodate new devices and capabilities as they are encountered, we have constructed and demonstrated experimental prototypes for sensing asset selection for users' tasks, as described in [46]. Again, while these prototypes are not exactly aligned with the scenario of home automation (instead being more concerned with sensing systems such as autonomous aerial vehicles and ground systems) these experiments have shown that the CE-based approach supports the rapid addition of new knowledge. This includes not only of types of asset, but also of asset capabilities (that can be used to match assets to tasks). In many ways, the home setting is simpler than, say, an emergency response or search-and-rescue scenario, so we believe that the positive outcomes of these experiments are translatable into the domestic context.

An arguable difference between the home versus emergency response or search-and-rescue settings is the degree of training that a user can reasonably be expected to have obtained in the use of the available devices. In the home setting, this must always be minimal. In the other setting, however, minimal training is still desirable, since users should not necessarily be experts in the operation of sensing systems [47]. In any case, we argue that this usability point is addressed under (i) above. Also, in many cases, the addition of knowledge about new devices and their capabilities will typically be provided by the originators of the devices rather than end-users, though our approach does not preclude a "power" user from providing additional knowledge to their local environment.

B. User Evaluation

Based on the results summarised above that provided evidence that untrained users can quickly learn to interact with complex systems using our CNL and conversational technology, our most recent work aims to validate the Conversational Homes concept by means of a study with 12 participants. The primary goal of this research is to determine whether it is possible to build such an environment using a CNL basis as described earlier in this paper and, if so, whether the time and effort taken to do so is an improvement over traditional programming approaches. During the build phase factors such as time and complexity were not explicitly measured, although it should be noted that the entire model and fact-base for the evaluation were able to be successfully built entirely in the Controlled English language using the ce-store runtime environment without the need for any additional code or modifications to that environment. The entire end-to-end development time of the application was 2 days for 1 person, the majority being spent on developing the custom JavaScript code to render the live schematic view and the conversation. Within this 2 days development time only a couple of hours were spent on model and fact-base development, using just a plain text editor to write the CE languagestatements.

Since we are not trying to measure the comparative cost and benefit of the development time of environments such as these, the evaluation itself is therefore aimed at the untrained participants using the resulting environment. For this, we followed the same model as for our second trial summarised above, operationalising usabilty as task performance [43], specifically: whether participants can use the Conversational Homes chat interface to successfully interact with the environment to achieve simple goals or get simple information from the system as to the state of different components. The study was designed as a series of 5 simple tasks that were given to the participants in a group setting with each participant interacting with a separate local environment. The total available time for the study was 20 minutes, with each task taking 2-3 minutes. The tasks were communicated to the group via a shared projected screen with simple instructions; the instructions for each task (see subsections below) were shown to all users, with the text remaining on the screen for the duration shown. No additional information or guidance was given and the participants were free to use the conversational interface and/or the schematic to interact with the system as needed. Each task attempted to serve a different purpose, with the tasks, descriptions and planned purposes listed in the subsections below:

1) Task 1 – Simple query:

- Instructions: "Find out which lights are switched on..."
- Duration: 3 minutes
- Purpose: To establish whether the participants were able to use the conversational interface to determine the state of the lights. The live schematic view could also be used for this purpose since it shows the states of all lights, however we were expecting to see evidence of the participants asking this question via conversation.
- Success: The participant asks a question where the answer contains the state of all lights that are switched on.

2) Task 2 – Simple state change:

- Instructions: "Shut the front door"
- Duration: 2 minutes
- Purpose: State changes for items within the Conversational Homes can only be achieved via conversational interaction. To prevent the participants simply typing in the exact guidance text we deliberately did not specify the word "shut" in our model (e.g., as a synonym for "close"). This meant that participants must at least experiment with trivial restatements of the guidance in order to discover the correct term used to model the "close" action.
- Success: A statement from the participant that results in the "Front Door" state becoming "Closed".

3) Task 3 – Group state change:

- Instructions: "Turn on all the lights in the bedroom"
- Duration: 2 minutes
- Purpose: Achieve a state change for a group of devices. We deliberately designed this task so that the users could type the exact guidance text into the system in order to achieve the desired result. This was to contrast with Task 2 where we deliberately left out the obvious form in order to force the user to seek alternatives.
- Success: One or more statements from the participant that results in all of the lights in the bedroom state becoming "On".

4) Task 4 – Multiple state changes:

- Instructions: "It's bedtime... Get the house in the right state for bed (It's a hot night)"
- Duration: 3 minutes
- Purpose: The description for this task is deliberately ambiguous and more descriptive. This was intentional and designed to see whether the participants could successfully translate a generic and high-level desired state into specific actionable requests. We anticipated that this would be interpreted as switching off lights and opening the bedroom window.
- Success: Statements that result in (at least) the turning off of the bedroom lights and the opening or closing of the bedroom window. The suggestion that "It's a hot night" was intended to elicit an opening of the window, however we realise that cultural differences could yield different responses, for example closing the window to ensure that air conditioning works efficiently. Even the turning off the bedroom lights may not meet every participants definition of the "...right state for bed..." but we needed to see some evidence of state change towards the target goal and therefore chose these two conditions as valid indicators of task completion.

5) Task 5 – Open ended:

- Instructions: "Freestyle: Talk to the house using phrases you'd actually want to use in real life. We have temperature sensors and door cameras plus we can add any other devices of capabilities into the system. They won't work but will be a great source of ideas :)"
- Duration: 5 mins
- Purpose: The purpose of this task was simply to elicit a wider range of interactions from the participants to inform the design of future evaluation studies and enable them to express themselves in ways that would be desirable to them in such a system.

The system was instrumented to record all conversational interactions (human and system generated) as well as all state changes that occurred. These interactions and state changes were subsequently analysed post-study for all users and are the basis for the results section (Section IV-E) later in this paper.

Note that the Conversational Homes environment is entirely simulated for this study: there is no linkage to actual sensors or devices in the physical world. It should be noted however that integrating this simulated environment into physical devices is extremely easy, assuming that the devices have APIs and are able to be queried and have their states changed programmatically. From an implementation perspective it is simply a case of recording the relevant information to locate and interact with each device (e.g., IP address, port and any required credentials) within the CE language. Having done so it is then trivial to write (in CE) a trigger that will be called each time a state change instance is generated by the system. The state change instance contains all details required to modify the device and the target state so the trigger in question can simply call some very generic code or invoke a generic web service that will simply invoke the target device API with the required credentials and parameters to make the desired change occur.

C. Participants

The participants for this study were drawn from a sample of convenience: they were all members of the IBM UK Emerging Technology team excluding authors of this paper and those familiar with the underlying research context and technologies being developed. The study was run once over a 30 minute period with the participants volunteering to participate in the study over their lunch break. There were a total of 12 participants, each of whom brought their own device (laptop or tablet) to enable them to participate in the study. All participants were "untrained users" with no prior experience of the technologies used in the study and had not previously seen or heard about the Conversational Homes user interface. Each participant was asked to login to the browser-based system and provide a unique userid (name) to be identified by. To ensure no capture of personal information, each of the usernames was substituted for a single letter in the range A-L post-study. In this paper users are thus referred to in this style (i.e., "User A") with this indicating a single anonymised human participant within the study. The entire cohort were located in a single large room with a projected screen displaying the guidance for each task. Participants were allowed to talk to each other if needed but we observed that generally the participants worked alone and with relatively little chatter or verbal discussion between them.

D. Design and Hypothesis

For this evalution, our hypothesis was that the Conversational Homes agent would have good usability, operationalised as performance of the five simulated household tasks.This builds upon our earlier general hypothesis that CNL can enable machine-machine, machine-human, human-machine and human-human interaction in a dynamic environment such as this, and accounts for the development of the specific conversational home agent and user interface.

The CE resources for this evaluation are publically available online [48] as is the custom browser-based user interface that was developed specifically for this evaluation [49]. Figure 5 shows this user interface and each participant within the study interacted solely via this environment. Each participant was operating entirely alone, with each conversational home being a separate instance purely for the use of that single participant and no ability for messages from one participant to access the contents or state of any other participants environment.

The user interface is broken into two fundamental components: The left-hand schematic view, and the right-hand chat interface.

The left-hand schematic view is a "live" representation of the conversational home that is built around a single level apartment unit. It is described as live since the state of all the sensors and actuators are rendered dynamically. This means that as lights are switched on or off, or as doors/windows are opened/closed, the visual state of the conversational home schematic is updated accordingly. These state changes happen regardless of the source of the change, i.e., if someone used some other interface to change the state then the schematic would update even if the change had not originated in the right-hand conversation pane.

The right-hand chat interface is built to mimic commonplace messaging applications that all users will already be familiar with on iOS and Android platforms. Messages from the human user are displayed in right-aligned green boxes and messages from the conversational home are displayed left-aligned in white boxes. There are no restrictions on the format, style or content of the messages that the human user can type, although the ability for the system to correctly interpret the messages from the human users is affected by brevity, precision and whether the text is "on-topic" for the conversational home environment.

There are a number of sensors, actuators and spaces that comprise the conversational homes environment and each of these are shown in the schematic in Figure 5. From bottom-left to top-right, the rooms and their contents are:

- Building Hallway
  - Front Door
- Front Room
  - Front-to-Hallway Door
  - Front Left Window
  - Front Right Window
  - Front Room Temp Sensor
  - Front Room Window Camera
  - Front Room Door Camera
  - Back Overhead (light)
  - Front Overhead (light)

Figure 5: Conversational Homes User Interface.

   - Side lamp (light)
- Hallway
   - Hallway Overhead (light)
- Bathroom
   - Bathroom-to-Hallway Door
   - Bathroom Window
   - Bathroom Overhead (light)
- Cupboard
   - Cupboard-to-Bedroom Door
- Bedroom
   - Bedroom-to-Hallway Door
   - Bedroom Window
   - Bedroom Temp Sensor
   - Bedroom Door Camera
   - Bedroom Window Camera
   - Bedroom Overhead (light)
   - Bedroom Lap (light)

In Figure 5 The different states can be seen visually. For example: The Bathroom-to-Hallway Door is closed whereas the other Hallway doors are open, the Bathroom light is off whereas the Bedroom lights are on, and one of the Front room windows is open whereas the other windows are closed.

E. Results

The study was carried out on 19th August 2017 from approximately 12:30 to 12:50 British Summer Time. There were 12 participants, drawn from the IBM UK Emerging Technology team who sent a total of 367 messages across the 5 simulated household tasks.

The full set of results and corresponding guidance for each of the 5 tasks can be found online in the Open Science Framework [50]. The headline results were that our set of untrained users were able to quickly learn how to interact with the Conversational Homes system in order to find the state of various sensors and to interact with the environment to affect the correct state changes for the tasks. Of the 4 tasks undertaken with measurable success criteria: all users were able to successfully complete 3 out of 4 of the tasks and the fourth (more complex) task was successfully completed by 10 out of 12 of the users. On average each user was able to complete the 3 simple tasks in around 30 seconds, with the fourth (more complex) task taking around 1 minute 30 seconds on average to complete. The primary result, therefore was that the Conversational Homes agent had good usability in user performance of the simulated household tasks, consistent with our earlier experimental work reported previously.

Figure 6 shows the individual participants cumulative assertion counts during the study, with each of the time periods for the 5 tasks shown. We observe a steady upwards progressions for each user, even when taking into account only the valid assertions made during the study, i.e. those assertions deemed to have been correctly interpreted by the system. These results suggest that the proposed conversational approach mediated by the CNL technology can be effectively used with little or no training: a sizeable majority of users were able to make successful use of the interface and query or assert information in a relatively short period. They were largely able to complete their tasks in a short time period even when multiple attempts were required due to interpretation of their NL input was not initially successful.

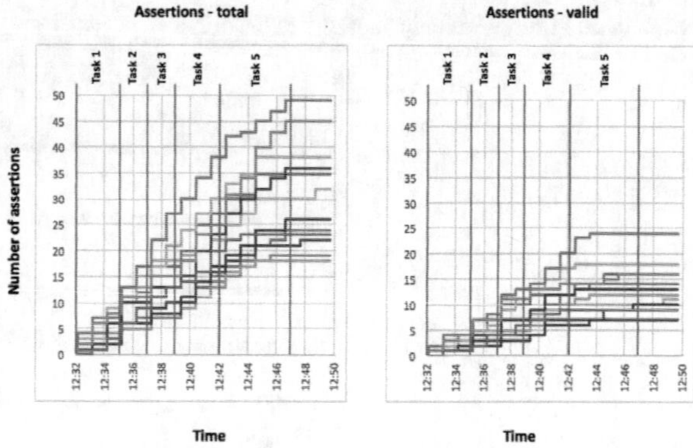

Figure 6: Individual Participants Cumulative Assertions over time.

TABLE I: Overall user statistics

User	Msgs sent	Msgs rcvd	State changes	Duration	Msg freq
A	19	91	39	13:11	42 secs
B	27	80	35	13:18	30 secs
C	34	74	49	16:51	30 secs
D	35	139	72	11:35	20 secs
E	19	91	41	11:59	38 secs
F	28	115	58	12:39	20 secs
G	22	50	8	15:01	41 secs
H	36	44	28	14:13	24 secs
I	51	128	72	18:20	22 secs
J	28	125	85	14:29	31 secs
K	24	131	31	11:04	28 secs
L	45	169	67	14:18	19 secs

Table I shows the overall user statistics for the study, showing the overall number of messages sent, received and the frequency of message sends for each user. The number of state changes are also shown; these are created each time a light is switched on or off, or a door/window is opened or closed. It is interesting to note that the message frequency is relatively low (in the range 20-41 seconds), suggesting that the participants were carefully considering their inputs rather than simply firing many messages in to the interface.

Table II shows the average number of NL messages and average time taken to complete each of the tasks. Note that Task 5 is not shown since it was a freestyle task with no completion criteria. The number of messages is low and the time to completion is fast for each of the tasks with the exception of task 4. Task 4 required multiple separate messages in order to complete and was deliberately ambiguous in order to better test the participants and this can be seen in the resulting time-to-completion statistics.

These results show that the Conversational Homes chat interface could be plausibly useful to untrained novice users even with the relatively immature level of NL processing currently available within our CNL-based solution. Even with a relatively high level of failed interpretations the participants were generally able to achieve the stated task goals in a short period of time and with relatively few messages. We believe that this is an encouraging result and justifies the pursuit of further evidence in the future to determine whether other factors like the richness of the model contribute to observable outcomes such as the ability to complete tasks or the number of misinterpretations of the NL messages.

TABLE II: Task level statistics

Task	Msgs to complete	Time to complete	Completion
Task 1	1.3	00:33	12
Task 2	1.9	00:35	12
Task 3	1.3	00:26	12
Task 4	4.2	01:31	10

As in our earlier usability study, subjective usability assessment was performed by asking the participants to complete the SUS [45] questionnaire. Participants reported positive satisfaction with a mean of 69 indicating a good degree of perceived usability across the group, consistent with the previous results in [43] and providing converging evidence for the usability of the conversational agent.

F. *Observations and Discussion*

In order to process the results we manually reviewed each of the sent messages to determine whether the system had correctly interpreted the text, and in cases of misinterpretation what category of misinterpretation it was.

1) Text interpretation analysis: Each of the text messages has been analysed and classified as "successfully interpreted" or not, however there are a number of common reasons for incorrect interpretation as well as some potential improvements to even the successfully interpreted messages.

In all of the cases of misinterpretation, or interpretation improvements, there are simple remedial actions that can be taken in the CE model and fact-base to catch each of these cases and handle them correctly. This is often through the addition of synonyms or through extension of the model to support additional capabilities not envisaged in the original modelling exercise (e.g., the addition of new device types, or new actions for existing device types). In all of these cases the effort required to extend the model is small, and the level of technical skill is low. The tooling (such as ce-store) that has been developed for studies in environments such as these mean that the changes can be deployed extremely quickly, potentially in real-time as issues are identified and resolved. However this entire approach is based on the assumption that all possible phrases and terminology could be identified in advance and therefore designed into the model and fact-base. This leads to a system with a high degree of accuracy and a low false-positive rate but one that is very brittle and must be focused on a particular domain to achieve that accuracy. Better hybrid approaches may be possible, for example using Machine Learning techniques to classify messages into a form that can be handled by the underlying CE models. This would be a small change but may enable a much wider set of phrases to be correctly handled with the existing system and without needing to continually update the CE model as new language is encountered. This approach could also help to handle evolving terminology and slang as it is adopted by the user community.

The remaining sub-sections deal with each of the types of misinterpretation encountered during this study.

2) Successful interpretations with room for improvement: These messages are classified as correctly interpreted since they do give enough information to provide the answer requested, or perform the action requested. However, from a human interpretation perspective they would be perceived to be "not quite right", usually due to some violation of a Gricean maxim [42] such as quantity:

- Too much information
  e.g., *"Which lights are on?"*
  Currently lists the states of all lights, including those that are off. This should really only list lights in the state specified.
- Ignoring unknown qualifiers
  e.g., *"Turn all the lights off downstairs"*
  The action was performed globally, e.g., turning off all the lights, and the unknown qualifier (e.g., downstairs) was quietly ignored. A more human-like reaction would be to either question the unknown qualifier or at least confirm that it was ignored.
- Ignoring current state
  e.g., *"Turn on bedroom lights"*
  The action was correctly interpreted and carried out regardless of the current state of the lights. A more human response would be to feedback that the lights were already on rather than saying they were switched on in cases where they were already on.
- Common sense defaults
  e.g., *"Close the bedroom door"*
  This would result in the Bedroom-to-Hallway door being closed and the Cupboard-to-Bedroom door being closed. This is arguably the incorrect behavior as the user probably meant the "main" bedroom door (Bedroom-to-Hallway door) rather than all bedroom doors.

3) Misinterpretations: In many cases the messages sent by the human users were not able to be interpreted at all. The reasons for these misinterpretations fall into a number of categories described below:

- Spelling mistakes
  e.g., *"turn on th elights"*
  Using our CNL and defined vocabulary based approach it is simply impossible to handle all possible misspellings and typos. As mentioned previously, this is an area where the use of additional lexical analytics or machine learning capabilities could be useful to augment the basic CNL solution to better handle issues such as typos.
- Unmapped synonyms
  e.g., *"shut"*
  We deliberately left out "shut" as a synonym for "close" to see whether participants would attempt obvious alternatives. Other less obvious synonyms were simply missed due to the speed of implementation and lack of testing.
- Split phrases
  e.g., *"Turn all the lights on"*
  Since "Turn on" is the trigger phrase this common practice of splitting the phrase "turn on" with the subject ("all the lights"), i.e., "Turn something on", causes the trigger phrase to be ignored. This is easily addressed through a simple additional lexical extension to the natural language processing capability within ce-store to handle split phrases such as these.
- Ignoring key filter words
  e.g., *"Only list the lights that are on"*
  Since all lights are listed regardless of state this means the message was not interpreted correctly as the intent was clearly to filter using "only" to list those of a specified state.
- Ignoring key action words
  e.g., *"How many lights are on"*
  This should return a number rather than a list of all lights and their individual states.
  e.g., *"What is x?"* or *"Where is x?"*
  This should return a description (or location) of the item in question.
- Conditionals
  e.g., *"if something then do something"*
  Some users indicated these kinds of rules, which were often interpreted by performing the action and ignoring the conditional.
- Out of scope
  e.g., *"Turn on all the cameras"*, or *"lock the doors"*, or *"What is the temperature in the bedroom"*, or *"Turn up the temperature"*
  A number of sensors were modeled and shown on the schematic but unavailable for interaction. Some users wrote messages to attempt to interact with these items.
- Off topic
  e.g., *"Import velociraptors"*, or *"activate discoball"*
  Messages relating to things that were not defined in the model. These mainly came in Task 5, which was the open-ended "Freestyle" task designed to elicit open-ended and off topic messages.
- Complex sentences
  e.g., *"Which rooms are the lights switched on in?"*
  The response should give a list of rooms, not a list of lights.

G. Limitations

In Section III we describe the extent of our research into CNL technology and the full conversational protocol that can be supported based on our earlier work to model speech act theory. Evaluation of this full protocol is not possible within this initial study and the conversations that are possible between human users and machine agents are limit to simple single-turn "tell" and "ask/tell" interactions with responses coming back to the human user in gist forms. By single-turn we mean that there is no possibility for reference back to previous statements within the current study. This rules out styles of interaction such as anaphoric reference (e.g., "Are the lights in the bedroom on?", followed by "Ok, turn them on please" where "them" is an anaphoric reference to "the lights in the bedroom" from the previous dialogue phrase). Again, the research basis for this work does explicitly support multi-turn dialogue and features such as anaphoric reference but these were not enabled for this study.

Another key design decision was that within this particular study the human users are never exposed to the raw CNL of the underlying system. Specifically, in Section III-B we discuss two possible modes of interaction between the human users and the system components: "Concierge only" interactions, and "Direct communication to any device" interactions (including an optional concierge agent if needed). We also note that the latter is the most powerful of the two interaction patterns and that in the latter cases all devices and human users would be able to interact via CNL. For this initial study we have implemented the "concierge only" mode as the is the initial exercise in a planned series of experiments intended to further develop the capabilities of the system and the devices within the simulated environment. Communication between the human users and the system is always via a single concierge agent, and in cases where state changes are needed (e.g., switching on a light) the human user "tells" the concierge in NL the desired state change, the concierge agent attempts to interpret the NL into CNL and passes the CNL into the ce-store to reflect the state change requested by the user. Within our conversational protocol it is possible for the concierge to show the CNL to the human user to seek their confirmation (in the form of a "confirm" card) and only pass confirmed CNL into ce-store, but for this study we felt that this confirm stage was not needed due to the simplicity of the tasks being undertaken. In the results analysis we do identify cases (especially "Ignoring unknown qualifiers") where a confirm step back to the human user would help in some cases to prevent unexpected outcomes.

Finally, we note that of the 4 interaction styles listed in Section III-D we only support two in this study. Support for the other two (rationale and implicit desire to change state) are more subtle and advanced cases and may be considered for future studies. The two supported interaction styles are "Direct question/answer exchange" and "An explicit request to change a particular state".

V. Conclusion and Future Work

In this paper we have explored the use of conversations between humans and machines, motivated by a desire for "beautiful seams". We assert that this approach could enable better understanding of complex system such as a set of IoT devices in a home. In this paper, we have shown how semantic representations can be used in a human-friendly format through the use of a CNL technology known as ITA CE. Through the use of a conversational protocol built on top of the core CE language we show how human and machine agents are able to communicate using this single language. Examples of the CE language are provided throughout the paper showing how different concepts can be constructed and the subsequent data for the knowledge base can be provided in the same CE language. Through a set of four typical types of interaction we show how human users can interact with the devices in such an environment, and we note that whilst we have focused these four examples on a human-machine interaction, the exact same approach applies to machine-machine as well. Some additional discussion around what machine-human and human-human forms would look like is mentioned. Building on the initial success with the study reported in Section IV future work may include designing and conducting more advanced experiments in the conversational home setting, specifically to address some of the limitations described in Section IV-G and advance our experimental capability to better reflect the full potential identified in the CNL and conversational research work.

Our work also continues into the wider investigation into the potential for human-machine conversational capabilities, specifically with the JavaScript-based CENode component [40], which is designed specifically for CNL processing at the very edge of the network (directly in the end users mobile phone or tablet browser environment). Some of this latest work is informally reported for IoT interactions [51] and integration with the popular Alexa platform [52]. In our desire to investigate the potential for integration of machine learning capabilities into the core CNL approach we also plan to investigate easy to use online services such as IBM Watson Conversation [53] as a potential front-end and dialogue orchestration component, which would process all incoming NL from the human users and convert into a simplified form before presenting to our CNL implementation. If successful this could provide a significant improvement in handling a wider set of synonyms, spelling mistakes and other forms of evolving language without needing to predefine them in the CNL environment.

Acknowledgment

This research was sponsored by the U.S. Army Research Laboratory and the U.K. Ministry of Defence under Agreement Numbers W911NF-06-3-0001 and W911NF-16-3-0001. The views and conclusions contained in this document are those of the authors and should not be interpreted as representing the official policies, either expressed or implied, of the U.S. Army Research Laboratory, the U.S. Government, the U.K. Ministry of Defence or the U.K. Government. The U.S. and U.K. Governments are authorized to reproduce and distribute reprints for Government purposes notwithstanding any copyright notation hereon.

References

[1] N. OLeary, D. Braines, A. Preece, and W. Webberley, "Conversational homes," in *9th International Conference on Advanced Cognitive Technologies and Applications (COGNITIVE17)*, 2017, pp. 82–89.

[2] R. Dale, "The return of the chatbots," *Natural Language Engineering*, vol. 22, no. 5, pp. 811–817, 2016.

[3] M. Witbrock and L. Bradeško, "Conversational computation," in *Handbook of Human Computation*. Springer, 2013, pp. 531–543.

[4] J. Lester, K. Branting, and B. Mott, "Conversational agents," *The Practical Handbook of Internet Computing*, pp. 220–240, 2004.

[5] N. O'Leary. (2014) Conversational iot. [Online]. Available: http://knolleary.net/2014/12/04/a-conversational-internet-of-things-thingmonk-talk/ (Visited on 27-Nov-2017)

[6] A. Stanford-Clark. (2008) Redjets on twitter. [Online]. Available: https://twitter.com/redjets (Visited on 27-Nov-2017)

[7] T. Armitage. (2008) Tower bridge on twitter. [Online]. Available: https://twitter.com/twrbrdg_itself (Visited on 27-Nov-2017)

[8] (2008) Mars curiosity on twitter. [Online]. Available: https://twitter.com/MarsCuriosity (Visited on 27-Nov-2017)

[9] (2010) Philae lander on twitter. [Online]. Available: https://twitter.com/Philae2014 (Visited on 27-Nov-2017)

[10] (2011) Rosetta probe on twitter. [Online]. Available: https://twitter.com/ESA_Rosetta (Visited on 27-Nov-2017)

[11] E. Ferrara, O. Varol, C. Davis, F. Menczer, and A. Flammini, "The rise of social bots," *Communications of the ACM*, vol. 59, no. 7, pp. 96–104, 2016.

[12] L. Atzori, A. Iera, and G. Morabito, "The internet of things: A survey," *Computer networks*, vol. 54, no. 15, pp. 2787–2805, 2010.

[13] M. Weisser, "The computer for the twenty-first century," *Scientific American*, vol. 265, no. 3, pp. 94–104, 1991.

[14] M. Chalmers, "Seamful design and ubicomp infrastructure," in *Proceedings of Ubicomp 2003 Workshop at the Crossroads: The Interaction of HCI and Systems Issues in Ubicomp*. Citeseer, 2003.

[15] T. Coates. (2014) Interacting with a world of connected objects. [Online]. Available: https://medium.com/product-club/interacting-with-a-world-of-connected-objects-875b4a099099#.nd00bbs5n (Visited on 27-Nov-2017)

[16] Hypercat. [Online]. Available: http://hypercat.io (Visited on 27-Nov-2017)

[17] M. Bates and R. M. Weischedel, *Challenges in natural language processing*. Cambridge University Press, 2006.

[18] R. L. C. Delgado and M. Araki, *Spoken, multilingual and multimodal dialogue systems: development and assessment*. John Wiley & Sons, 2007.

[19] B. Dumas, D. Lalanne, and S. Oviatt, "Multimodal interfaces: A survey of principles, models and frameworks," *Human machine interaction*, pp. 3–26, 2009.

[20] G. Churcher, E. S. Atwell, and C. Souter, *Dialogue management systems: a survey and overview*. University of Leeds, School of Computing Research Report 1997.06. 1997., 1997.

[21] P.-H. Su, M. Gasic, N. Mrksic, L. Rojas-Barahona, S. Ultes, D. Vandyke, T.-H. Wen, and S. Young, "Continuously learning neural dialogue management," *arXiv preprint arXiv:1606.02689*, 2016.

[22] D. R. Traum and S. Larsson, "The information state approach to dialogue management," in *Current and new directions in discourse and dialogue*. Springer, 2003, pp. 325–353.

[23] D. Mouromtsev, L. Kovriguina, Y. Emelyanov, D. Pavlov, and A. Shipilo, "From spoken language to ontology-driven dialogue management," in *International Conference on Text, Speech, and Dialogue*. Springer, 2015, pp. 542–550.

[24] M. S. Yakoub, S.-A. Selouani, and R. Nkambou, "Mobile spoken dialogue system using parser dependencies and ontology," *International Journal of Speech Technology*, vol. 18, no. 3, pp. 449–457, 2015.

[25] G. Meditskos, E. Kontopoulos, S. Vrochidis, and I. Kompatsiaris, "Ontology-driven context interpretation and conflict resolution for dialogue-based home care assistance," in *Paschke A, Burger Al, Splendiani A, Marshall MS, Romano P. Proceedings of the 9th International Conference Semantic Web Applications and Tools for Life Sciences (SWAT4LS); 2016 Dec 5-8; Amsterdam, The Netherlands.[Place unknown]:[CEUR]; 2016.[5 p.]*. CEUR Workshop Proceedings (CEUR-WS. org), 2016.

[26] T. Kuhn, "A survey and classification of controlled natural languages," *Computational Linguistics*, vol. 40, no. 1, pp. 121–170, 2014.

[27] R. Schwitter, "Controlled natural languages for knowledge representation," in *Proceedings of the 23rd International Conference on Computational Linguistics: Posters*. Association for Computational Linguistics, 2010, pp. 1113–1121.

[28] D. Mott, "Summary of ita controlled english," *ITA Technical Paper, http://nis-ita.org/science-library/paper/doc-1411a (Visited on 27-Nov-2017)*, 2010.

[29] A. Preece and W. R. Sieck, "The international technology alliance in network and information sciences," *IEEE Intelligent Systems*, vol. 22, no. 5, 2007.

[30] D. Mott, C. Giammanco, M. C. Dorneich, J. Patel, and D. Braines, "Hybrid rationale and controlled natural language for shared understanding," *Proc. 6th Knowledge Systems for Coalition Operations*, 2010.

[31] T. Klapiscak, J. Ibbotson, D. Mott, D. Braines, and J. Patel, "An interoperable framework for distributed coalition planning: The collaborative planning model," *Proc. 7th Knowledge Systems for Coalition Operations*, 2012.

[32] D. Braines, D. Mott, S. Laws, G. de Mel, and T. Pham, "Controlled english to facilitate human/machine analytical processing," *SPIE Defense, Security, and Sensing*, pp. 875 808–875 808, 2013.

[33] J. Ibbotson, D. Braines, D. Mott, S. Arunkumar, and M. Srivatsa, "Documenting provenance with a controlled natural language," in *Annual Conference of the International Technology Alliance (ACITA)*, 2012.

[34] F. Cerutti, D. Mott, D. Braines, T. J. Norman, N. Oren, and S. Pipes, "Reasoning under uncertainty in controlled english: an argumentation-based perspective," *AFM*, 2014.

[35] D. Braines, J. Ibbotson, D. Shaw, and A. Preece, "Building a living database for human-machine intelligence analysis," in *Information Fusion (Fusion), 2015 18th International Conference on*. IEEE, 2015, pp. 1977–1984.

[36] D. Mott and J. Hendler, "Layered controlled natural languages," in *3rd Annual Conference of the International Technology Alliance (ACITA)*, 2009.

[37] A. Preece, D. Braines, D. Pizzocaro, and C. Parizas, "Human-machine conversations to support multi-agency missions," *ACM SIGMOBILE Mobile Computing and Communications Review*, vol. 18, no. 1, pp. 75–84, 2014.

[38] A. Preece, C. Gwilliams, C. Parizas, D. Pizzocaro, J. Z. Bakdash, and D. Braines, "Conversational sensing," in *SPIE Sensing Technology+ Applications*. International Society for Optics and Photonics, 2014, pp. 91 220I–91 220I.

[39] D. Braines. (2015) Ita controlled english store (ce-store). [Online]. Available: https://github.com/ce-store (Visited on 27-Nov-2017)

[40] W. Webberley. (2016) Cenode.js. [Online]. Available: http://cenode.io/ (Visited on 27-Nov-2017)

[41] If this then that. [Online]. Available: https://ifttt.com/ (Visited on 27-Nov-2017)

[42] H. P. Grice, "Logic and conversation," *1975*, pp. 41–58, 1975.

[43] A. Preece, W. Webberley, D. Braines, E. G. Zaroukian, and J. Z. Bakdash, "SHERLOCK: Experimental evaluation of a conversational agent for mobile information tasks," *IEEE Transactions on Human-Machine Systems*, vol. in press, 2017.

[44] J. Nielsen, *Usability engineering*. AP Professional, 1994.

[45] J. Brooke *et al.*, "Sus-a quick and dirty usability scale," *Usability evaluation in industry*, vol. 189, no. 194, pp. 4–7, 1996.

[46] A. Preece, D. Pizzocaro, D. Braines, and D. Mott, "Tasking and sharing sensing assets using controlled natural language," in *SPIE Defense, Security, and Sensing*. International Society for Optics and Photonics, 2012, pp. 838 905–838 905.

[47] A. Preece, T. Norman, G. de Mel, D. Pizzocaro, M. Sensoy, and T. Pham, "Agilely assigning sensing assets to mission tasks in a coalition context," *IEEE Intelligent Systems*, vol. 28, no. 1, pp. 57–63, 2013.

[48] Github - conversational homes controlled english. [Online]. Available: https://github.com/ce-store/conv-homes (Visited on 27-Nov-2017)

[49] Github - conversational homes user interface. [Online]. Available: https://github.com/annaet/conversational-homes-viz (Visited on 27-Nov-2017)

[50] Conversational homes - experimental results. [Online]. Available: https://osf.io/pfskx/ (Visited on 27-Nov-2017)

[51] Cenode in iot. [Online]. Available: https://flyingsparx.net/2017/06/26/cenode-iot/index.html (Visited on 27-Nov-2017)

[52] Alexa, ask sherlock. [Online]. Available: https://flyingsparx.net/2017/07/19/cenode-alexa/index.html (Visited on 27-Nov-2017)

[53] Ibm watson conversation service. [Online]. Available: https://www.ibm.com/watson/services/conversation/ (Visited on 27-Nov-2017)

Resources and their Description for Additive Manufacturing

Felix W. Baumann*†, Julian R. Eichhoff*, Dieter Roller*
*Institute of Computer-aided Product Development Systems
University of Stuttgart
Email:

baumann, eichhoff, roller

@informatik.uni-stuttgart.de
†TWT GmbH Science & Innovation
Ernsthaldenstr. 17, Stuttgart
Email: felix.baumann@twt-gmbh.de

Abstract—**For an enhanced automated usage of 3D-printers in case of multiple available 3D-printers, such as in Cloud Manufacturing or Cloud Printing services, the requirement arises to select and provision suitable resources for user provided model files. As Additive Manufacturing (AM) consists of a number of different technologies, ranging from fabrication using thermoplastic extrusion to electron beam based curing of metal powder, the necessity is evident to enable users to describe limitations, capabilities, interfaces and requirements for a these resources in a machine readable and processable format. This resource description enables the discovery and provisioning of appropriate resources within a service composition, where 3D-printing resources are regarded as manufacturing services themselves. In order to compose a service from these hardware resources, the comprehensive description of such resources must be provided. With this work, we provide an abstract and universal capability description framework of such 3D-printing resources. The framework consists of an ontology for the resources of the AM Domain, a flexible Extensible Markup Language (XML) schema and the implementation in a cloud-based 3D-printing system. With this resource description both hard- and software resources are universally defined. Applied to systems with multiple 3D-printers, a scheduling component is capable of resource discovery. This selection is based on the matching of described capabilities, status information and derived requirements from specific 3D-printing job definitions. This work provides a framework for the description of resources in the AM domain with an ontology, based on a collection of identified resource descriptors extracted from literature.**

Keywords—***3D Printing; Additive Manufacturing; Resource Description; Capability Description; Service Selection; Service Discovery***

I. Introduction

This work is an extension to Baumann et al. [1], presented at the ADASERC conference 2017.

For the efficient usage of 3D-printing resources in Cloud Manufacturing (CM) scenarios, it is necessary to identify and schedule the existing resources. This scheduling is in accordance with the requirements of the user and the relevant 3D-printing application or request. 3D-printing resources are mainly 3D-printers of various types, makes and models. These 3D-printers are characterised and differentiable by their capabilities, specifics and constraints for their usage. Similar usage of an abstracted description of resources is described in Grangel-González et al. [2], where industrial machinery is equipped with an “Administrative Shell”, which is used to interface with various devices. In a cloud printing environment, where these resources are considered part of a service, it is possible to compose them into new services to achieve tasks such the efficient execution of 3D-printing requests. This work offers a practical service composition framework and tool for the description required to establish service compositions within a 3D-printing service in the domain of Additive Manufacturing (AM). For this work, the applicability of the proposed resource description is analysed.

As 3D-printing is comprised of a number of different technologies, ranging from thermoplastic extrusion fabrication, over photopolymerisation to other methods, it is a prerequisite to understand these technologies and their specific parameters and differences. One thermoplastic extrusion based method is called Fused Deposition Modeling (FDM) (also Fused Filament Fabrication or Free Form Fabrication (FFF)). Fabrication on the basis of curing of photopolymers in a vat is called Stereolithography (SLA). Laser-based fabrication methods are either Selective Laser Melting (SLM) or Direct Metal Laser Sintering (DMLS). Other methods exist to create physical objects directly from digital models, such as Laminated Object Manufacturing (LOM). Besides the understanding of these technologies and methods, it is important to be able to describe them in a comprehensive and machine-understandable way. Furthermore, it is important to express the inherent and derived capabilities and restrictions of these technologies and machines. The different technologies do not only differ in the materials they are able to process but also in the quality that is achievable. They further differ in the geometric and structural features they can reproduce, in the cost they effect, and the means they are controlled by or programmed with. For the automated usage in a distributed service scenario, with a number of different 3D-printing resources involved, the service must be able to select an appropriate device or devices for any given user submitted task.

For the hardware providers, it is beneficial if their equipment is utilized to a high degree. This is required in order to amortise their assets on time and also to be ecologically sound [3]. For the users, such an automated and swift resource allocation is pertinent. This equates to a reduced turnaround time and also the promise of higher product quality due to optimum capability and requirements matching. For service operators, the automated resource allocation is an intrinsically motivated requirement for the operation of such a service.

With this work, a solution for the description of differing capabilities, restraints and requirements of various 3D-printing resources is provided. This solution provides an extensible, flexible, comprehensive and usable description format for the use in AM scenarios. The solution combines existing approaches for the description of resource capabilities and extends these for the usage in 3D-printing. The proposed solution is currently implemented in a prototype service to facilitate scheduling and selection of AM resources.

This work is motivated by the following five use cases:

3D-printer selection: The resource description, applied to a database of commercially available 3D-printers can serve as a purchasing guide for end-users/consumers or other potential buyers of 3D-printers [4], [5]. This will especially be the case if the information is readily available as a Web-service and supports pro-active user-questioning, e.g., a wizard.

Automated facility planning: In future modular factory designs, the dynamic reconfiguration of the shop floor [6] is becoming relevant. With a machine readable resource description, layouting and planning software can place the manufacturing resources at an appropriate location.

Scheduling in 3D-printing services: In this use case the resource description is the foundation for the scheduling algorithm that selects the most appropriate available 3D-printing resource for any given processing request, based on the constraints and preferences provided by the user and derived from the model data [7], [8].

Recommender systems for CAD development: Based on the resource description, a software system can support Computer Aided Design (CAD) designers with information and recommendations for geometrical and topological features within models that are manufacturable with 3D-printing resources available to a company.

Technological improvement: Through an extended understanding of the specific resources for different technologies, commonalities can be identified and improvements on specific technologies and implementations can be enabled.

This work is an extended version of [1] and structured as follows: Starting with related work in Section II, a review of existing publications is performed. In Section III, the approach for the resource description is described, its underlying concepts and sources as well as the implementation and evaluation. In Section IV, the implementation and its results are discussed and analysed. Lastly, Section V provides a summary of this work.

II. Related Work

In the work by Pryor [9], the implementation of a 3D-printing service within an academic library is described. The system consists of two low-cost hobbyist 3D-printers and a 3D scanner. Of relevance to this work is the description of the workflow for the user handling. Pryor describes the processing workflow as purely manual with the data being deployed by the users either via a web form or email. The library staff performs sanity checking, pre-processing (i.e., positioning, slicing, machine code generation) and manual scheduling of the 3D-printer resource. The text does not provide an analysis of the time required for the staff to perform these tasks.

In the article by Vichare et al. [10], the authors propose a Unified Manufacturing Resource Model (UMRM) for the resource description of machines within the manufacturing domain. Specifically, the authors aim to describe Computer Numeric Control (CNC) machines and their associated tools in a unified way to represent the capabilities of these systems in their entirety. Their work provides a method to describe a CNC machine in an abstract sense for use in software, e.g., for simulations. As part of the collaborative peer-robot control system described in the work by Yao et al. [11], an ontology for a resource description is partially described, on which we build our work. This ontology distinguishes between hardware and software resources, as well as capability and status description. The authors provide an exemplary Extensible Markup Language (XML) schema definition for such a resource description, on which we extend upon. The *3D Printer Description File Format Specification* (3PP) by Adobe [12] is very relevant to this work, as it describes the 3D-printer's capabilities in XML format as deemed necessary by Adobe, presumably for the application within their software. This work contains an extensive listing of possible attributes relevant to a resource description, on which we base our work. The 3PP format is limited to FDM 3D-printers. The definition includes hardware and material description but only partially caters for software support. In the publication by Chen et al. [13], the authors provide another approach to the problem of model-fabrication resource mismatch by the introduction on an abstract intermediary specification format. The authors propose this reducer-tuner model to abstract design implementations for the application to a variety of 3D-printers whereas our work proposes a 3D-printer resource description that enables the matching of suitable machines to specific model files. In the work by Dong et al. [14], the problem of scheduling in AM is handled by a rule-based management of autonomous nodes, i.e., 3D-printers. This system is based on an ontology for 3D-printing of which some excerpts are presented in this work. From this example, our work is influenced and extends on missing attributes. Yadekar et al. [15] propose a taxonomy for CM systems that are closely related to AM. This taxonomy is focused on the concept of uncertainty and only briefly discusses the taxonomical components that define the manufacturing resources. The main distinction for the authors is the division into soft and hard resource groups. In the work by Mortara et al. [16], a classification scheme for direct writing technologies, i.e., AM, is proposed. The authors define the scheme for three dimensions, namely technology, application, and materials. The properties of specific materials are discussed exemplary in brief. A listing of potential properties for the varying technologies and materials is missing.

III. Materials and Methods

From existing literature, software and expertise, we construct an ontology that is described in the following Section. This ontology is the basis for the extension of the properties proposed, that are relevant to the domain of AM. In this work, we exclude concepts like business process related capabilities, and knowledge and abstract ability related mapping, i.e., it is not possible to express certain abilities of people, teams or companies, e.g., the level of knowledge for the design of objects for AM. The properties are derived from literature, software and 3D-printer documentations. The following requirements are expressed to guide the generation of the ontology and properties list:

RQ1 The ontology and properties list must be flexible and extensible. Flexibility means that for specific application scenarios where only subsets of properties and relations are of interest, these must be expressible within the proposed ontology or resource description. Extensibility denotes the property to be able to incorporate future, currently unforeseen, properties of technology and materials.

RQ2 The resource description must be able to reflect temporal, local and other ranges of validity and restrictions. Conditional validity is to be reflected. With this requirement we reflect the necessity that certain properties, e.g., material strength, are only valid and guaranteed for a certain period.

RQ3 The resource description must be able to distinguish between general concepts of things, e.g., 3D-printers and materials, that form a class and its individual instantiation that might have differing properties and attributes.

In this work, the following separation of information description is performed for the resource description:

Materials: Encompasses all physical materials that are processed, or used during the digital fabrication. Also includes physical materials that are required for the digital fabrication process as indirect or auxiliary material.

Software: Encompasses all software and Information technology (IT) components that are involved in the model creation phase, the object fabrication phase or that are used for the control and management of digital fabrication equipment.

Processes: Encompasses all intangible processes, data and information that is generated, consumed, transformed or influenced by in any phase of the digital fabrication process. Business processes are part of this grouping.

Technology: Encompasses all hardware and machine equipment that is used for the object fabrication, as well as pre- and post-processing.

We exclude status information and status dependent properties from our resource description and ontology.

The resource description must be able to reflect required properties and information of all currently available 3D-printing technologies, regardless of the technology classification following any schema, such as the classification by Gibson et al. [17], the classification by Williams et al. [18] or the ISO/ASTM Standard 52900:2015 [19] classification. This work identifies common attributes between technologies and enables technology specific properties. As a guideline for the creation of the ontology and the resource description itself a distinction between object classes and their actual instances is followed. Given the example of a 3D-printer, the class is formed of all 3D-printers from a certain manufacturer and are of a certain make share a number of attributes like physical volume and number of printheads. Those general attributes might be extended by attributes pertaining to a certain 3D-printer that belongs to a user and is situated at a physical location. The general attributes might also be altered for a specific 3D-printer, as it might weight more than the original 3D-printer due to added extensions or modifications, or its build envelope is smaller than the original's due to a hardware defect.

A. Sources

Properties are extracted from datasheets from the following manufacturers and models:

3D Systems, Inc.: ProJet 7000 SD & HD, ProX 950, sPro 140, ProX DMP 200, ProX 800, ProX SLS 500, ProJet CJP 360, ProJet 1200, CubePro
Arcam AB: Arcam Q10 Plus, Arcam Q20 Plus, Arcam A2X
B9Creations LLC: B9Creator V1.2
CEL: CELRobox
Deltaprintr: Delta Go
EnvisionTEC GmbH: 3D-Bioplotter Starter Series, SLCOM1
EOS GmbH: EOS M 100, EOS M 290, FORMIGA P 110, EOS P 396, EOSINT P 800
ExOne GmbH: S-Max, S-Print, M-Flex Prototype 3D Printer
FlashForge Corp.: Creator Pro 3D
Formlabs Inc.: Form 2
LulzBot/Aleph Objects, Inc.: TAZ 6
Makerbot Industries, LLC: Replicator+, Replicator Z18
Mcor Technologies Ltd.: ARKe, IRIS HD
Optomec Inc.: LENS 450, Aerosol Jet 200
Renishaw plc.: RenAM 500M
RepRap: Prusa i3
SeeMeCNC: ROSTOCK MAX V3
SLM Solutions Group AG: SLM 125, SLM 280 2.0
Stratasys Ltd.: uPrint SE, Objet24, Dimension Elite, Fortus 380mc, Objet1000 Plus
Ultimaker B.V.: Ultimaker 3, Ultimaker 2+
UP3D/Beijing Tiertime Technology Co., Ltd.: UPBOX+
voxeljet AG: VX 200, VX 2000
WASP c/o CSP s.r.l.: DeltaWASP 20 40 Turbo

Furthermore, properties and capability attributes are extracted from publicly available slicing software (e.g., *Slic3r* [20], *Cura* [21], and *Netfabb* [22]) and acquired through experimentation. On the ontological concept itself, we refer to the work by Gruber [23] and the book by Fensel [24]. Following the distinction of ontologies by Ameri and Dutta [25], we classify our ontology as lightweight. For the construction of the ontology a list of key terms is compiled from existing glossaries and literature. The sources for the following list of key terms include:

- http://3dprintingforbeginners.com/glossary
- http://3dprinthq.com/3d-printing-glossary
- https://www.sculpteo.com/en/glossary
- https://ultimaker.com/en/resources/11720-terminology
- https://www.gov.uk/government/uploads/system/uploads/attachment_data/file/445232/3D_Printing_Report.pdf

The key terms are the following:

1) Synonyms
   a) 3D Printer
   b) 3D Printing
   c) Additive Manufacturing
   d) Rapid Manufacturing
   e) Generative Manufacturing
   f) Digital Fabrication
   g) Additive Layer Manufacturing
2) Object
3) Model
4) File
5) File formats
   a) GCode
   b) STL
   c) AMF
   d) 3MF
   e) VRML
6) File types
   a) Log files
   b) Model files
   c) Configuration files
7) Software (types)
   a) Slicer
   b) CAD
   c) Modeller
   d) Control software
8) Technology
   a) FFF/FDM
   b) SLS
   c) SLM
   d) SLA
   e) EBM
   f) LOM
   g) Bioprinting
   h) Binder Jetting
   i) 3D Printing
   j) DMLS
   k) LENS
   l) MJS
9) Machine components
   a) Firmware
   b) Extruder
   c) Heat bed
   d) VAT
   e) Resin tank
   f) Nozzle
   g) Gantry
   h) Hot end
   i) Motor
      i) Nema 17
      ii) Stepper motor
   j) Belt
   k) Lens
   l) Electron source
   m) Vacuum chamber
   n) Build chamber
10) Material
   a) Support material
   b) Extrudate
   c) Binder
   d) acrylonitrile butadiene styrene (ABS)
   e) PLA
   f) PVA
11) Process related actions
   a) Post-processing
   b) Pre-processing
   c) Slicing
   d) Positioning
   e) File transformation
12) 3D Print
   a) Raft
   b) Object
   c) Shell
   d) Infill
      i) Infill percentage
      ii) Infill strategy
      iii) Infill geometry
   e) Overhang
13) Object features
   a) Wall
   b) Hole
   c) Surface
   d) Solid
14) Properties
   a) Machine properties
      i) Build volume
      ii) Build/Print speed
      iii) Extrusion speed
      iv) Travel speed
      v) Layer resolution
      vi) Positioning precision
   b) Material Properties
      i) Price per unit
      ii) Material form

A) Pellets
B) Filament
C) Resin
D) Powder

B. Properties

The following properties are identified from literature and technology documentation. These properties are listed in the appendix in order to avoid a disruption of the text flow. The provided listing is sufficient to describe relevant properties of AM machinery, i.e., 3D-printers, and the associated materials.

The properties can be further classified as either static, e.g., the serial number of a 3D-printer or its coordinate system, or dynamic, e.g., the owner or location of a 3D-printer. Dynamic properties are often dependent properties, which is a further classification applied to the properties. Dependent properties are influenced and depend upon a 3D-printer component, e.g., the nozzle and its diameter, the material, e.g., surface roughness achievable differs for materials processable or parameters selected during the 3D-printing process. This classification is not provided with this work due to brevity. The properties in the listing (see I) are for the hardware resources, i.e., the 3D-printer as well as its components and the material associated with the 3D-printer.

In the following table I, we list the an excerpt of the attributes, the category they belong to, the list of dependent factors, the unit the attribute is represented in, the source where the attribute is referenced from, possible restrictions based on printing mechanism, examples where appropriate and the respective classifications. The complete listing is presented in the appendix. In the listing the abbreviation **EXP** indicates attributes that are not referenced from literature but are either derivatives from literature referenced attributes, common knowledge or are derived from experiments. The unit **[String]** is an array of strings, meaning that the attribute is described by distinct texts. Furthermore, square brackets denote other types of arrays as indicated. The unit **Int** denotes an integer, **Bool** a boolean variable.

C. Implementation

In this Section, the implementation of both the ontology and the relevant core classes are described. Furthermore, information on a possible scheduling metric based on a cost estimation method and the resulting information flow in the implemented service is described.

The ontology is constructed using the protégé software version 5.1.0, see http://protege.stanford.edu/. The ontology is generated based on the properties brought forward in Section III-B. The guiding principle for the ontology is the flexibility of the properties that are applicable to 3D-printers, material and inherent constraints. The ontology is created based on the identified properties and derived concepts from literature and documentation.

The implementation in software to manage the specific properties of the resource description and to evaluate the applicability of the description is performed in the proposed 3D-printing cloud service by the authors [26], [27].

The implementation in the service is performed to enable provisional scheduling for 3D-printing resources based on availability, build volume and processable material type. In scheduling, some form of ordering metric must be provided. In this work, this metric is based on a proposed cost metric as described further in the text.

The cost metric is defined in [28] and serves as a prototypical implementation of cost estimation within AM.

The cost is calculated as (see Equation (1)) follows:

$$\begin{aligned} \text{Cost} = {} & (\text{Discount}(T, P, U) + \text{Profit}(U)) \\ & \times (\text{Machine} + \text{Material}(O, P, S, SO) \times \text{Factor B} \\ & + \text{Duration}(O, S, SO) \times \text{Factor U} + \text{Factor A} \\ & + \text{Factor C}(O, P)) \end{aligned} \tag{1}$$

With the following abbreviations used in the equation: 1) T for team 2) P for 3D-printer 3) U for user 4) O for object 5) S for slicer and, 6) SO for slicing options The cost for a 3D-print is dependent upon the 3D-printer selected (base cost), the material that is consumed and the time required for 3D-printing. Within the service, these attributes are user selectable for each materialtype and 3D-printer that is under the control of the user.

The scheduling of resources is implemented to adhere to a user selected criterion, e.g., lowest cost possible or fastest execution available. These criteria are calculated based on the proposed resource description that finds suitable and available manufacturing resources first and then calculates the expected cost. The user and resource operator are queried for confirmation before the actual commitment to ensure legal agreement on the execution. The operator is able to forfeit the manual confirmation to enable automated operation.

From Baumann et al. [28] we use this explanation for the parts of the cost formula (see Equation (1)).

Material is a factor that adjusts the cost to the material chosen.

Factor A is a factor that compensates for required time associated with pre-heating of the AM resource and other preparatory tasks not dependent upon the build volume.

Factor B is a factor that compensates for required material used for raft and support structures.

Factor C is a factor that compensates for the required cooling time and the parts removal.

Factor U is an uncertainty factor associated with the 3D-printing time estimation that is generally unreliable to a certain extend for which this factor compensates.

Discount is a factor to address requirement of discounting for certain teams, members or machines.

Machine is a factor representing the base cost of usage of a certain 3D-printer.

Profit is a factor to address commercial interests of 3D-printer owners to offset the net-costs of a 3D-print for a profitable endeavor

Based on the cost metric, scheduling is implemented in the service as described below.

In Figure 1, the processing flow for the registration of a hardware resource with the 3D-printing service is depicted.

TABLE I: Properties in Additive Manufacturing – Excerpt

Name	Category	Unit	Source	Meaning	Only Applicable for	Example	Static	Dynamic	Independent	Dependent
Operating Temperature Min	Printer	°C	Delta Go	The lowest ambient temperature the 3D printer is specified for operation		15 °C	x		x	
Operating Temperature Max	Printer	°C	Delta Go	The highest ambient temperature the 3D printer is specified for operation		30 °C	x		x	
Operating Humidity Min	Printer	%	Delta Go	The lowest ambient humidity the 3D printer is specified for operation		10% RH	x		x	
Operating Humidity Max	Printer	%	Delta Go	The highest ambient humidity the 3D printer is specified for operation		90% RH	x		x	
Machine Weight	Printer	kg	TAZ 6	The gross weight of the 3D printer		10.6 kg	x		x	
Machine Length	Printer	mm	ProX DMP 200	The machine dimension (Length)		342 mm	x		x	
Machine Height	Printer	mm	ProX DMP 200	The machine dimension (Height)		380 mm	x		x	
Machine Depth	Printer	mm	ProX DMP 200	The machine dimension (Depth)		389 mm	x		x	

In this figure, the user dispatches a 3D-printing requirement (Job) with the service, for which a number of implicit and explicit requirements and restrictions are also deposited. A hardware resource registers its capabilities with the service, that is then stored with the resource registry. The service queries the resource registry for a suitable hardware resource for a job and issues the appropriate commands for a 3D-printing execution on this resource. On completion or failure, the user issuing the job is notified.

1) Core Classes: The core classes in the ontology are described in this Section. A visual representation of the ontology is depicted in Figure 2. In this figure, the classes are depicted as circles, with the relationships between them depicted as arrows with the relationship name as labels. This graph is created using the *WebVOWL* service [29].

MaterialGroup and **Material**, these classes denote the materials that are relevant for the description of the capabilities of the 3D-printing resource. The materials have an influence on a number of quality properties, e.g., the surface roughness. The materials a 3D-printing resource can process are relevant for the selection of the appropriate 3D-printing resource.

PrintingTechnology, **PrinterType**, and **Printer**, are classes to represent the underlying technology of a 3D-printing resource, e.g., a FDM based technology or a

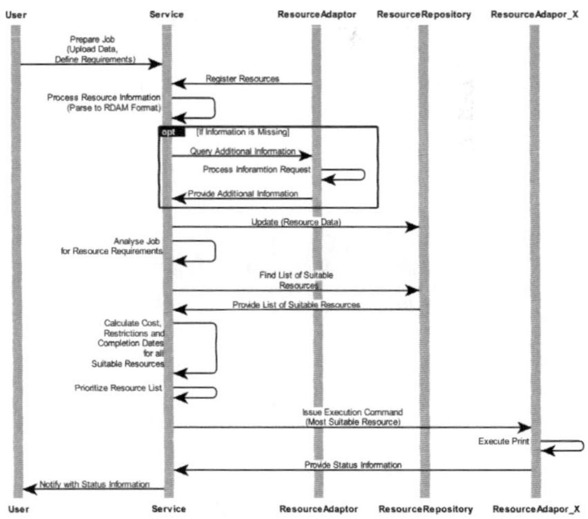

Fig. 1: Processing Flow for the Registration and Selection of a Hardware Resource

Electron Beam Melting (EBM) technology as well as the

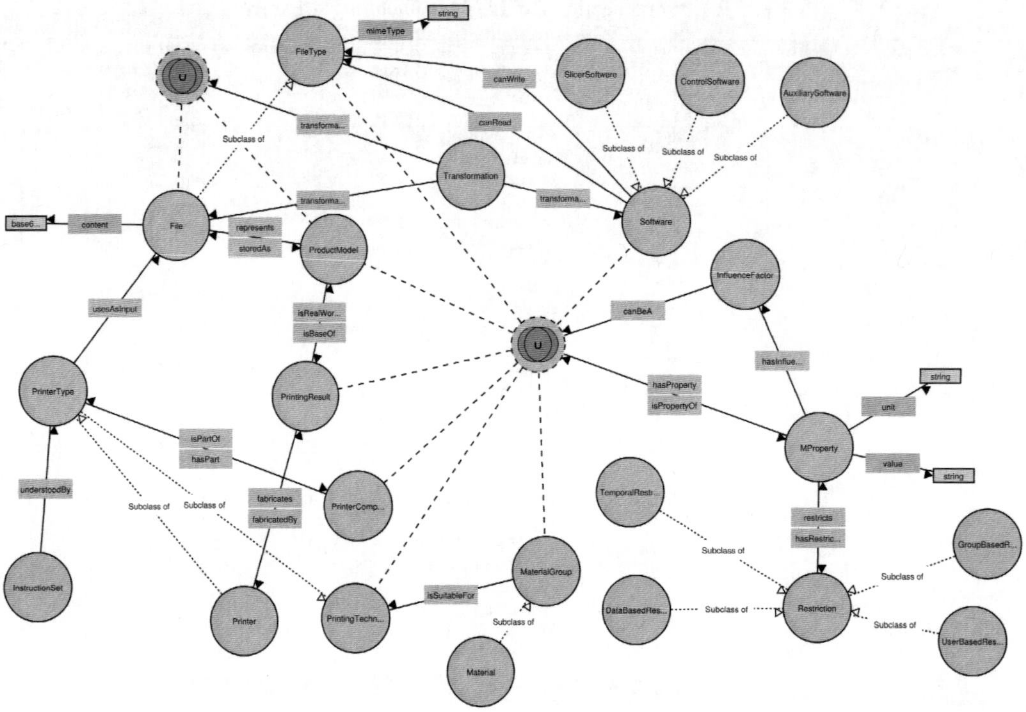

Fig. 2: 3D-printing Ontology

3D-printer class, which can be understood for example as a specific model line from a hardware manufacturer (e.g., the Replicator Series from Makerbot Industries). Hardware resources of a PrinterType have a number of common attributes that extend the PrintingTechnology. The Printer denotes the make of a specific PrinterType, e.g., the *MakerBot Replicator 2X* from Makerbot Industries. Instances of this Printer class have further common attributes extending the attributes of the PrinterType. Instances of the Printer class are actual 3D-printers that have further attributes like owner and a physical location.

PrinterComponent, is the class for the physical and immaterial components that are part of the specific 3D-printer. Every component can have a unbounded number of properties as described below. For example the printhead and its nozzles are components of a 3D-printer in the case of FDM technology and an electron source is a component of a EBM type 3D-printer.

Software, denotes all software that is used in the 3D-Printing Process (3D-PP). Software is used to control the 3D-printing resource, to convert files from one format into another, to prepare and process the files required for the control of the 3D-printer and to evaluate and monitor the 3D-print itself.

MProperty, this class is the generalisation of properties that are applicable to either the Material, Materialgroup, PrintingTechnology, PrinterType, Printer, PrinterComponent, Software, ProductModel or File. The guiding principle for the creation of this ontology is to enable flexibility and expandability, so this generalised property can hold all properties listed above (see Section III-B) and future properties.

Restriction, is a class that reflects the ability to enable restrictions on MProperties as the properties can be applicable only for a specified period of time or for a certain group of people. For example the property of filament quality might be linked to a certain expiration date.

InfluenceFactor, is a class that reflects the multi-dimensional influences on properties by a defined number of factors. For example the nozzle diameter can influence the extrusion rate in case of a FDM 3D-printer.

D. Resource Description Schema

From the ontological concept, an XML schema definition is constructed, which follows the principle of flexibility by encapsulation of properties in a flexible element. The property element is applicable to all relevant types of the schema, namely the PrintingTechnology, PrinterType, Printer, Printercomponent, Materialtype, and Material.

All properties are extended to allow for restrictions based on user, group or temporal conditions. The properties can be influenced by any other class of the schema to reflect interdependent relations between components. The following example justifies this construction: In the 3D-printer, the property of the material deposition rate is dependent upon the technology in use, the material processed and, in case of the FDM technology, the nozzle diameter of the extruder installed in the 3D-printer. See the following excerpt from the schema definition on the components properties and the implementation on the influencing factors:

```
<xs:complexType name="influence">
<xs:sequence minOccurs="1" maxOccurs="1">
<xs:element name="id" type="xs:ID"
  minOccurs="1" maxOccurs="1" />

<xs:choice>
<xs:element ref="tdp:MaterialType" />
<xs:element ref="tdp:Material" />
<xs:element ref="tdp:PrinterType" />
<xs:element ref="tdp:Printer" />
<xs:element ref="tdp:PrinterComponent" />
<xs:element ref="tdp:PrintingTechnology" />
</xs:choice>

<xs:element name="influenceMethod"
  type="xs:string" />
</xs:sequence>
</xs:complexType>

<xs:complexType name="validity">
<xs:sequence>
<xs:element name="id" type="xs:ID"
  minOccurs="1" maxOccurs="1" />
<xs:element name="validityCondition"
  type="xs:string"
  minOccurs="1" maxOccurs="unbounded" />
</xs:sequence>
</xs:complexType>

<xs:complexType name="mproperty">
<xs:sequence>
<xs:element name="unit"
  type="xs:normalizedString"
  minOccurs="1" maxOccurs="1"/>
<xs:element name="description"
  type="xs:normalizedString"
  minOccurs="1" maxOccurs="1"/>
<xs:element name="value"
  type="xs:normalizedString"
  minOccurs="1" maxOccurs="1"/>
<xs:element name="name"
  type="xs:normalizedString"
  minOccurs="1" maxOccurs="1" />
<xs:element name="added"
  type="xs:dateTime"
  minOccurs="1" maxOccurs="1" />
<xs:element ref="tdp:influence"
  maxOccurs="unbounded" />
<xs:element ref="tdp:validity"
  maxOccurs="unbounded" />
</xs:sequence>
</xs:complexType>
```

IV. Discussion

The proposed resource description offers the ability to the user to select the appropriate 3D-printing resource in a scenario where restrictions for the suitable 3D-printing resources can be derived, from either the users input or from the provided data files. Within a 3D-printing service, the user is enabled to state preferences and restrictions, such as the desired quality of the 3D-printed object or cost restrictions, based on which the service itself can query appropriate hardware resources for their availability and suggest them to the user. Furthermore, based on the provided models the service can exclude certain hardware resources if they are not fitting for the task to be executed. For example, if the model file is analysed and found to contain features under a certain threshold, the hardware that is not capable of manufacturing features of this dimension are to be excluded.

A perceived problem with the flexibility of the ontology and resource description is the requirement for contextual property checking within the service itself. As opposed to strict formalities possible with the XML Schema Definition (XSD) definition, this flexibility hinders such formality checking. The 3D-printing service must be equipped with a component that is capable of evaluating the provided properties and check them for completeness, applicability and correctness. The resource description also allows for the encapsulation of third-party 3D-printing services within the 3D-printing service itself, where the capabilities of these services are regarded as a resource and described as such.

V. Conclusion

This work provides an ontology of the AM domain with extensible and flexible constructs. The derived XSD provides flexibility for extensions, based on future developments of 3D-printing hardware. The flexibility also allows for user-centric extensions and use-cases. The use case for this work is the deployment in a 3D-printing service but other use cases are also provided, such as the use within a recommender system for the design and modelling phase, or purchase recommendation systems. The list of properties (Table II) can form a basis for further research and individual extension. The examples provided are intended to ease understanding of the list's compilation.

In future work, it is recommended to extend the ontology to include concepts that enable the expression of immaterial capabilities and abilities, such as the expertise in certain domains, e.g., Aerospace engineering, medical engineering or bioprinting, in AM. Furthermore, it is recommended to enable the expression of proficiency in areas related to the 3D-printing lifecycle or process itself, e.g., proficiency with the design process, with the software / IT components or with legal and business concepts for AM.

This schema will be fully implemented and evaluated in an upcoming project. In this project, the evaluation will be on the usefulness and usability of the ontology. This evaluation will utilise both expert and user surveys. Furthermore, the evaluation will compare this proposed method in respect of expressiveness and suitability.

Acknowledgment

The authors would like to thank Julia Holzschuh for her contributions to this work.

Appendix

TABLE II: Properties in Additive Manufacturing

Name	Category	Dependent Upon	Unit	Source	Meaning	Only Applicable for	Example	Static	Dynamic	Independent	Dependent
Operating Temperature Min	Printer		°C	Delta Go	The lowest ambient temperature the 3D printer is specified for operation		15 °C	x		x	
Operating Temperature Max	Printer		°C	Delta Go	The highest ambient temperature the 3D printer is specified for operation		30 °C	x		x	
Operating Humidity Min	Printer		%	Delta Go	The lowest ambient humidity the 3D printer is specified for operation		10% RH	x		x	
Operating Humidity Max	Printer		%	Delta Go	The highest ambient humidity the 3D printer is specified for operation		90% RH	x		x	
Machine Weight	Printer		kg	TAZ 6	The gross weight of the 3D printer		10.6 kg	x		x	
Machine Length	Printer		mm	ProX DMP 200	The machine dimension (Length)		342 mm	x		x	
Machine Height	Printer		mm	ProX DMP 200	The machine dimension (Height)		380 mm	x		x	
Machine Depth	Printer		mm	ProX DMP 200	The machine dimension (Depth)		389 mm	x		x	
Install Size Length	Printer		mm	SLM 125	The length required for the installation/-placement of the 3D printer		1200 mm	x		x	
Install Size Height	Printer		mm	SLM 125	The height required for the installation/-placement of the 3D printer		770 mm	x		x	
Install Size Depth	Printer		mm	SLM 125	The depth required for the installation/-placement of the 3D printer		1950 mm	x		x	
Build Envelope Height	Printer	No. Extruders	mm	SLM 125	The height of the build envelope		100 mm		x		x
Build Envelope Width	Printer	No. Extruders	mm	SLM 125	The width of the build envelope		100 mm		x		x
Build Envelope Depth	Printer	No. Extruders	mm	SLM 125	The depth of the build envelope		100 mm		x		x
Build Envelope Radius	Printer	No. Extruders	mm	Delta Go	The radius of the build envelope; for polar coordinate based systems		250 mm		x		x

TABLE II: Properties in Additive Manufacturing – continued

Name	**Category**	**Dependent Upon**	**Unit**	**Source**	**Meaning**	**Only Applicable for**	**Example**	**Static**	**Dynamic**	**Independent**	**Dependent**
Machine Data Connection	Printer		[String]	ProX DMP 200	The connection from the 3D printer to a workstation or network		USB 2.0, SD-Card, TCP/IP	x		x	
Electrical Input Rating	Printer		V	ProX DMP 200	Description of the required electrical connection for the 3D printer		400 V	x		x	
Mimimum Possible Hole Diameter	Printer	Print Technology + Material	mm	Shapeways	Description of the minimum hole diameter possible to print		1 mm		x		x
Positioning Accuracy X	Printer		μm	Ultimaker 3	Description of the accuracy achievable by the machine in positioning in the X axis		50 μm	x		x	
Positioning Accuracy Y	Printer		μm	Ultimaker 3	Description of the accuracy achievable by the machine in positioning in the Y axis		50 μm	x		x	
Positioning Accuracy Z	Printer		μm	Ultimaker 3	Description of the accuracy achievable by the machine in positioning in the Z axis		50 μm	x		x	
Repeatability X	Printer		μm	ProX DMP 200	Capability of the 3D printer to produce repeatable results within a given margin, along the X axis		20 μm	x		x	
Repeatability Y	Printer		μm	ProX DMP 200	Capability of the 3D printer to produce repeatable results within a given margin, along the Y axis		20 μm	x		x	
Repeatability Z	Printer		μm	ProX DMP 200	Capability of the 3D printer to produce repeatable results within a given margin, along the Z axis		20 μm	x		x	
Print Accuracy X	Printer	Material	μm	Orion Delta	Description of the accuracy achievable by the machine in printing in the X axis		100 μm		x		x
Print Accuracy Y	Printer	Material	μm	Orion Delta	Description of the accuracy achievable by the machine in printing in the Y axis		100 μm		x		x

TABLE II: Properties in Additive Manufacturing – continued

Name	Category	Dependent Upon	Unit	Source	Meaning	Only Applicable for	Example	Static	Dynamic	Independent	Dependent
Print Accuracy Z	Printer	Material	μm	Orion Delta	Description of the accuracy achievable by the machine in printing in the Z axis		150 μm		x		x
Number of Extruders	Printer	No. Extruders	Int	Replicator	The number of extruders installed in a 3D printer	FDM	2		x		x
Nozzle Diameter	PrinterComponent	Per Extruder	[mm]	Replicator+	The diameter of each extruder installed in a 3D printer	FDM	0.4 mm, 0.3 mm	x			x
Temperature Extruder Min	PrinterComponent	Per Extruder	[° C]	3D-Bioplotter	The minimum temperature a extruder can work with	FDM	30 °C, 70 °C		x		x
Temperature Extruder Max	PrinterComponent	Per Extruder	[°C]	TAZ 6	The maximum temperature a extruder can achieve	FDM	260 °C, 290 °C		x		x
Layer Thickness Min	Printer	Nozzle + Material	μm	Uitimaker 2+	The lowest layer size that the 3D printer is capable of printing		100 μm		x		x
Layer Thickness Max	Printer	Nozzle + Material	μm	Ultimaker 2+	The highest layer size that the 3D printer is capable of printing		400 μm		x		x
Movement Speed Min	Printer	Print Head	$\frac{mm}{s}$	Ultimaker 3	The minimum speed that the print head can be moved without any extrusion	FDM	200 $\frac{mm}{s}$		x		x
Movement Speed Max	Printer	Print Head	$\frac{mm}{s}$	DeltaWASP 20 40 Turbo	The maximum speed that the print head can be moved without any extrusion	FDM	900 $\frac{mm}{s}$		x		x
Extrusion (Movement) Speed Min	Printer-Component	Print Head + Nozzle	$\frac{mm}{s}$	EXP	The minimum speed that the print head can be moved while extruding	FDM	100 $\frac{mm}{s}$		x		x
Extrusion (Movement) Speed Max	Printer-Component	Print Head + Nozzle	$\frac{mm}{s}$	TAZ 6	The maximum speed that the print head can be moved while extruding	FDM	600 $\frac{mm}{s}$		x		x
Print Head Acceleration Max	Printer	Print Head	$\frac{mm}{s^2}$	Slic3r	The maximum acceleration that the print head is capable of	FDM	150 $\frac{mm}{s^2}$		x		x
Print Bed Speed X Min	Printer		$\frac{mm}{s}$	EXP	In case of a moveable print bed this denotes the minimum speed that the print bed can be moved in the X axis		10 $\frac{mm}{s}$	x		x	

TABLE II: Properties in Additive Manufacturing – continued

Name	Category	Dependent Upon	Unit	Source	Meaning	Only Applicable for	Example	Static	Dynamic	Independent	Dependent
Print Bed Speed X Max	Printer		$\frac{mm}{s}$	EXP	In case of a moveable print bed this denotes the maximum speed that the print bed can be moved in the X axis		100 $\frac{mm}{s}$	x		x	
Print Bed Speed Y Min	Printer		$\frac{mm}{s}$	EXP	In case of a moveable print bed this denotes the minimum speed that the print bed can be moved in the Y axis		10 $\frac{mm}{s}$	x		x	
Print Bed Speed Y Max	Printer		$\frac{mm}{s}$	EXP	In case of a moveable print bed this denotes the maximum speed that the print bed can be moved in the Y axis		100 $\frac{mm}{s}$	x		x	
Print Bed Speed Z Min	Printer		$\frac{mm}{s}$	EXP	In case of a moveable print bed this denotes the minimum speed that the print bed can be moved in the Z axis		10 $\frac{mm}{s}$	x		x	
Print Bed Speed Z Max	Printer		$\frac{mm}{s}$	EXP	In case of a moveable print bed this denotes the maximum speed that the print bed can be moved in the Z axis		100 $\frac{mm}{s}$	x		x	
Print Bed Acceleration X Min	Printer		$\frac{mm}{s^2}$	EXP	In case of moveable print bed this denotes the minimum acceleration of the print bed in the X axis		5 $\frac{mm}{s^2}$	x		x	
Print Bed Acceleration X Max	Printer		$\frac{mm}{s^2}$	Slic3r	In case of moveable print bed this denotes the maximum acceleration of the print bed in the X axis		50 $\frac{mm}{s^2}$	x		x	
Print Bed Acceleration Y Min	Printer		$\frac{mm}{s^2}$	EXP	In case of moveable print bed this denotes the minimum acceleration of the print bed in the Y axis		5 $\frac{mm}{s^2}$	x		x	
Print Bed Acceleration Y Max	Printer		$\frac{mm}{s^2}$	Slic3r	In case of moveable print bed this denotes the maximum acceleration of the print bed in the Y axis		50 $\frac{mm}{s^2}$	x		x	

TABLE II: Properties in Additive Manufacturing – continued

Name	Category	Dependent Upon	Unit	Source	Meaning	Only Applicable for	Example	Static	Dynamic	Independent	Dependent
Print Bed Acceleration Z Min	Printer		$\frac{mm}{s^2}$	EXP	In case of moveable print bed this denotes the minimum acceleration of the print bed in the Z axis		5 $\frac{mm}{s^2}$	x		x	
Print Bed Acceleration Z Max	Printer		$\frac{mm}{s^2}$	Slic3r	In case of moveable print bed this denotes the maximum acceleration of the print bed in the Z axis		50 $\frac{mm}{s^2}$	x		x	
Print Bed Temperature Max	Printer	Heating Cartridge	°C	TAZ 6	The maximum temperature the print bed can be set to		150 °C	x			x
Print Bed Temperature Min	Printer	Print Bed Cooling	°C	3D-Bioplotter	The minimum temperature the print bed can be set to; active cooling of print bed is uncommon		-30 °C		x		x
Binder Material	Material	Print Technology + Material	[String]	S-Print Furan	A list of materials that can be used as a binder for a 3D printer	Powder Based Technology	Furan		x		x
Processable Material	Printer	Extruder	[String]	TAZ 6	A list of materials that are processable by the 3D printer		ABS, PLA, Nylon		x		x
Processable Material Grain Size Min	Printer	Per Processable Material	μm	S-Print Furan	The minimum size of powder grains that the 3D printer can process	Powder Based Technology	2 μm	x		x	
Processable Material Grain Size Max	Printer	Per Processable Material	μm	S-Print Furan	The maximum size of powder grains that the 3D printer can process	Powder Based Technology	30 μm	x		x	
Max Object Weight	Printer		kg	ProJet 7000 SD & HD	Denotes the maximum weight, All objects of a build can have without skewing or damaging the build plate		9.6 kg	x		x	
Lead Time Influencing Factors	Printer		[String]	EXP	A list of factors influencing the lead time		Cleaning, Model Preparation		x		x
Lead Time Formula	Printer		String	EXP	A formula that can be used to estimate/calculate the lead time required for a print				x		x
Requires Personal Attendance During Print	Printer		Bool	EXP	Indicator that states if personal attendance during the printing process is required or not		Yes	x		x	

TABLE II: Properties in Additive Manufacturing – continued

Name	Category	Dependent Upon	Unit	Source	Meaning	Only Applicable for	Example	Static	Dynamic	Independent	Dependent
Requires Manual Interaction for Start	Printer		Bool	Fortus 380mc	Indicator that states if personal attendance during the preparatory process is required or not		No	x		x	
Requires Manual Interaction for End	Printer		Bool	Fortus 380mc	Indicator that states if personal attendance during the stopping process is required or not		Yes	x		x	
Resolution X Min	Printer	Material	mm	Ultimaker 3	Synonym to Print Accuracy X		600 dpi		x		x
Resolution Y Min	Printer	Material	mm	Ultimaker 3	Synonym to Print Accuracy Y		600 dpi		x		x
Resolution Z Min	Printer	Material	mm	Ultimaker 3	Synonym to Print Accuracy Z		800 dpi		x		x
Operation Allowed for User	Printer	Business Process	[String]	EXP	A list of all users allowed to work on or with the 3D printer		PrinterAdmin, JorgeS, PaulK		x		x
Operation Allowed for Group	Printer	Business Process	[String]	EXP	A list of all user-groups allowed to work on or with the 3D printer		ShopfloorC2, Shopfloor C3		x		x
Maximum Achievable Surface Roughness	Material	Printing Technology + Material	μm	ProX DMP 200	The maximum average achievable surface roughness for a 3D printer		4 μm		x		x
Systematic Shrinkage during Build	Material	Printing Technology + Material	Bool	EXP	Indicator that states if there is systematic shrinkage of the object during the printing process		Yes		x		x
Atmosphere Pressure	Printer		Bar	SLM 125	The required atmospheric pressure for the 3D printer build envelop		6 Bar	x		x	
Atmosphere Connection	Printer		String	SLM 125	The connection of the 3D printer for externally connected atmospheric supply systems		Self-storing connection	x		x	
Atmosphere Content	Printer		[String]	SLM 125	The required atmospheric makeup for the 3D printers build envelope		Argon, Nitrogen	x		x	
Consumables	Printer		[String]	SLM 125, Arcam Q10plus	A list of consumables required for the printing process		1 $\frac{l}{h}$ He	x		x	

TABLE II: Properties in Additive Manufacturing – continued

Name	Category	Dependent Upon	Unit	Source	Meaning	Only Applicable for	Example	Static	Dynamic	Independent	Dependent
Compressed Air Supply	Printer		String	Formiga P 110	Specification of the required compressed air connection to the 3D printer		min. 6 000 hPa (87 psi); 10 $\frac{m^3}{h}$ (13.08 m^3)	x		x	
Atmosphere Consumed	Printer		$\frac{l}{min}$	SLM 125	Specification of the amount of externally supplied atmosphere the 3D printer is consuming during a printing process		70 $\frac{l}{min}$	x		x	
Beam Focus Diameter	Printer-Component	Laser lens	μm	SLM 125	The diameter of the laser beam	Laser Based Systems	70 μm		x		x
Laser Energy	Printer-Component		W	SLM 125	The energy that is put out by the laser	Laser Based Systems	400 W	x		x	
Scanning Speed Min	Printer		$\frac{mm}{s}$	[30]	The lowest speed that the laser beam can scan across the build surface	Laser Based Systems	80 $\frac{mm}{s}$	x		x	
Scanning Speed Max	Printer		$\frac{mm}{s}$	[30]	The highest speed that the laser beam can scan across the build surface	Laser Based Systems	90 $\frac{mm}{s}$	x		x	
Laser Type	Printer		String	ProX DMP 200	A specification of the laser type		CO2	x		x	
Power Supply	Printer		A	FORMIGA P 110	The amperage of the power supply to the 3D printer		32 A	x		x	
Power Consumption	Printer		KW	FORMIGA P 110	The wattage of the power supply to the 3D printer		3 KW	x		x	
Power Phase Requirement	Printer		Int	ProX DMP 200	The phase requirement of the power supply to the 3D printer		1 Phase, 3 Phase	x		x	
Precision Optics	Printer-Component		String	EOS M 400	The specification of the laser optics in the 3D printer	Laser Based Systems	F-theta-lenses	x		x	
Legal Conformity Certificates	Printer		[String]	ZPrinter 150	A list of legal conformity certificates for the 3D printer		CE, NFPA	x		x	
Workstation Requirement Ram Min	Printer		MiB	ZPrinter 150	The minimum amount of RAM required for the workstation controlling the 3D printer		8192 MiB	x		x	
Workstation Requirement OS	Printer		[String]	ZPrinter 150	A list of possible operating systems required for the workstation controlling the 3D printer		current Windows operating system	x		x	

TABLE II: Properties in Additive Manufacturing – continued

Name	Category	Dependent Upon	Unit	Source	Meaning	Only Applicable for	Example	Static	Dynamic	Independent	Dependent
Workstation Requirement CPU Min	Printer		String	ZPrinter 150	The minimum CPU speed required for the workstation controlling the 3D printer		Intel I5 2.3 GhZ	x		x	
Workstation Requirement Net	Printer		String	ZPrinter 150	The specification for the network connection required for the workstation controlling the 3D printer		Ethernet 1 Gbps, RJ-45 Plug	x		x	
Resolution X	Printer	Material	dpi	ZPrinter 150	Synonym to Print Accuracy X		4000 dpi		x		x
Resolution Y	Printer	Material	dpi	ZPrinter 150	Synonym to Print Accuracy Y		4000 dpi		x		x
Resolution Z	Printer	Material	dpi	ZPrinter 150	Synonym to Print Accuracy Z		4000 dpi		x		x
Number of Jets	Printer		Int	ZPrinter 150	The number of jets in a 3D printer	MJM	304	x		x	
Accepted File Formats	Printer	Firmware	[String]	ZPrinter 850	A list of file formats that the 3D printer is capable of processing		STL, VRML, PLY, FBX, 3DS, ZPR		x		x
Number of Colors	Printer	Print Head	Int	ZPrinter 850	The number of colors that are printable by the 3D printer		390000		x		x
Color Model	Printer	Firmware	String	ProJet CJP 360	The color model used by the 3D printer		CMY, CMYK, Monochrome		x		x
Manufacturer	Printer		String	EOS M 400	The manufacturer of the 3D printer		Zcorp	x		x	
Model	Printer		String	EOS M 400	The model of the 3D printer		Zprinter 850	x		x	
Serial Numbers	Printer		[String]	EXP	To be distinguished between the manufacturer assigned serial number, And possibly a serial number within the institution that utilizes the 3D printer		Mfg: 83892-2883-233, Int: 3838-B	x		x	
Object Bounding Box X Min	Printer	Printing Technology + Material	mm	Shapeways	The minimum size (along the X axis) of any object to be printed		1 mm		x		x
Object Bounding Box X Max	Printer	Printing Technology + Material	mm	Shapeways	The maximum size (along the X axis) of any object to be printed		100 mm		x		x
Object Bounding Box Y Min	Printer	Printing Technology + Material	mm	Shapeways	The minimum size (along the Y axis) of any object to be printed		1 mm		x		x

TABLE II: Properties in Additive Manufacturing – continued

Name	Category	Dependent Upon	Unit	Source	Meaning	Only Applicable for	Example	Static	Dynamic	Independent	Dependent
Object Bounding Box Y Max	Printer	Printing Technology + Material	mm	Shapeways	The maximum size (along the Y axis) of any object to be printed		200 mm		x		x
Object Bounding Box Z Min	Printer	Printing Technology + Material	mm	Shapeways	The minimum size (along the Z axis) of any object to be printed		1.5 mm		x		x
Object Bounding Box Z Max	Printer	Printing Technology + Material	mm	Shapeways	The maximum size (along the Z axis) of any object to be printed		80 mm		x		x
Min Supported Wall Thickness	Material	Printing Technology + Material	mm	Shapeways	Minimum thickness of any wall (that is supported) of an object that is to be printed		0.8 mm		x		x
Min Unsupported Wall Thickness	Material	Printing Technology + Material	mm	Shapeways	Minimum thickness of any wall (that is not supported) of an object that is to be printed		0.9 mm		x		x
Min Supported Wire	Material	Printing Technology + Material	mm	Shapeways	Minimum thickness of any wire (that is supported) of an object that is to be printed		1 mm		x		x
Min Unsupported Wire	Material	Printing Technology + Material	mm	Shapeways	Minimum thickness of any wire (that is not supported) of an object that is to be printed		1 mm		x		x
Min Emboss Detail Width	Material	Printing Technology + Material	mm	Shapeways	Minimum width of embossed detail on an object to be printed		0.45 mm		x		x
Min Emboss Detail Height	Material	Printing Technology + Material	mm	Shapeways	Minimum height of embossed detail on an object to be printed		0.45 mm		x		x
Min Engraved Detail Width	Material	Printing Technology + Material	mm	Shapeways	Minimum width of engraved detail on an object to be printed		0.5 mm		x		x
Min Engraved Detail Height	Material	Printing Technology + Material	mm	Shapeways	Minimum height of engraved detail on an object to be printed		0.5 mm		x		x

TABLE II: Properties in Additive Manufacturing – continued

Name	Category	Dependent Upon	Unit	Source	Meaning	Only Applicable for	Example	Static	Dynamic	Independent	Dependent
Min Escape Holes	Material	Printing Technology + Material	String	Shapeways	Description of the type, placement and number of escape holes in an object		More than one hole at the objects lowest points and the top side		x		x
Clearance	Material	Printing Technology + Material	mm	Shapeways	Distance required between any parts of the object or between objects to avoid fusing		2 mm		x		x
Enable Interlocking Parts	Material	Printing Technology + Material	Bool	Shapeways	Indicator if the printing of interlocking parts is feasible		Yes		x		x
Maximum Angle for Unsupported Overhang	Material	Printing Technology + Material	°	EXP	The angle up to which slopes can be constructed without the requirement of supporting structures		45°		x		x
Available Infill Patterns	Software	Version	[String]	Slic3r	A list of available infill patterns for non solid printing		ZigZag, Honeycomb, Random		x		x
Active Cooling Extrudate	Printer-Component	Active Cooling Component	Bool	EXP	Indicator if the extrudate is actively cooled using a fan or not	FDM	Yes		x		x
Hot Pause Ability	Printer	Firmware	Bool	EXP	Ability to pause a print without cooling the extruders		Yes		x		x
Cold Pause Ability	Printer	Firmware	Bool	CELRobox	Ability to halt and resume a print for a longer period of time		Yes		x		x
Requires Support Structure	Printer	Printing Technology + Material	Bool	EOSINT P 800	Describes if the object to be printed requires a support structure or if it can be printed without		No		x		x
Cathode Type	Printer		String	Arcam Q10plus	Describes the cathode, i.e., the electron source, of the 3D printer	EBM	Single crystaline	x		x	
Vacuum Pressure	Printer		mbar	Arcam Q10plus	The pressure of the vacuum required for operation of the 3D printer	EBM	5×10^{-4} mbar	x		x	
Material Supply Format/-Packaging	Printer		String	ProJet 7000 HD & SD	Describes the format in which the material is provided to the 3D printer		Cartridge, Powder, Filament, Pellets	x		x	

TABLE II: Properties in Additive Manufacturing – continued

Name	Category	Dependent Upon	Unit	Source	Meaning	Only Applicable for	Example	Static	Dynamic	Independent	Dependent
Noise (Operation)	Printer		dBa	ProJet 7000 HD & SD	The amount of noise emitted by the 3D printer during operation		65 dBa	x		x	
Noise (Preparation)	Printer		dBa	EXP	The amount of noise emitted by the 3D printer during the preparation phase		55 dBa	x		x	
Noise (Idle)	Printer		dBa	EXP	The amount of noise emitted by the 3D printer while idle		40 dBa	x		x	
Laser Wave Length	Printer		nm	ProX DMP 200	Wavelength of the laser unit in the 3D printer	Laser Based Systems	1070 nm	x		x	
Material Deposition Mechanism	PrinterType		String	ProX DMP 200	Similar to the peel mechanism, describes the method with which the powder is spread for the next layer		Roller, Scraper	x		x	
Number of Print Heads	Printer		Int	ProJet CJP 360	The number of individual print heads in the 3D printer		4	x		x	
Filament Diameter	Material	Nozzle + Material	mm	Replicator+	Diameter of the filament usable with the 3D printer	FDM	1.75 mm		x		x
Stepper Motors	Printer-Component		[String]	Prusa i3	Description of Stepper Motors		Nema 17	x		x	
Build Plate Material	Printer-Component		String	Ultimaker 3	Description of the material of which the build plate/print bed is made of		Bor-Silicat glass	x		x	
Nozzle Heat Up Time	Printer	Heating Cartridge	s	Ultimaker 3	Time required for the extruder to heat up to operating temperature, most commonly about 240 °C		300 s		x		x
Build Plate Heat Up Time	Printer	Build Plate	s	Ultimaker 3	Time required for the build plate/print bed to heat up to operating temperature, most commonly about 120 °C		120 s		x		x
Build Speed	Printer	Nozzle + Material	$\frac{mm^3}{s}$	Ultimaker 2+	Indicates the maximum amount of material per second that is deposited during the print		16 $\frac{mm^3}{s}$		x		x

TABLE II: Properties in Additive Manufacturing – continued

Name	Category	Dependent Upon	Unit	Source	Meaning	Only Applicable for	Example	Static	Dynamic	Independent	Dependent
Platform Leveling Mode	Printer		String	UPBOX+	Describes the mechanism that is used to level the build plate/print bed		Full automatic leveling with integrated leveling probe	x		x	
Laser Class	Printer		Int	Form 2	Classification for the laser system of the 3D printer	Laser Based Systems	Class 1	x		x	
Laser Certification	Printer		String	Form 2	Describes the certification for the laser unit in the 3D printer	Laser Based Systems	EN 60825-1:2007 certified	x		x	
Peel Mechanism	Printer		String	Form 2	Describes the mechanism that is used to peel, i.e., wet the top surface, of an object	SLA		x		x	
Resin Fill Mechanism	Printer		String	Form 2	Describes the mechanism that is used to fill the vat with resin	SLA	Automatic fill mechanism	x		x	
Extruder Heater Cartridge Wattage	Printer	Per Extruder	[W]	ROSTOCK MAX V3	Watts that the heating cartridge of the extruder consumes		40 W		x		x
Extruder Heater Cartridge Voltage	Printer	Per Extruder	[V]	EXP	Voltage with which the heating cartridge for the extruder is driven		24 V		x		x
Firmware Name	Printer		String	Creator Pro 3D	Describes the firmware that is installed on the 3D printer		Sailfish, Marlin		x	x	
Firmware Version	Printer		String	EXP	Firmware version indicator		5.0.1		x	x	
Deposition Rate	Printer	Material	$\frac{kg}{h}$	LENS 450	Rate of which material is deposited, i.e. At which rate an object is printed		0.5 $\frac{kg}{h}$		x		x
Special Facility Requirements	Printer		String	Objet24	Description of special requirements for installation of the 3D printer		None	x		x	
Network Connectivity	Printer		String	Dimension Elite	Describes the kind and speed of the network connectivity of the 3D printer		Ethernet TCP/IP 10/100Base-T	x		x	
Automatic Material Recognition	Printer		Bool	CELRobox	Indicator for the presence of any kind of automatic material recognition system in the 3D printer		Yes	x		x	

TABLE II: Properties in Additive Manufacturing – continued

Name	**Category**	**Dependent Upon**	**Unit**	**Source**	**Meaning**	**Only Applicable for**	**Example**	**Static**	**Dynamic**	**Independent**	**Dependent**
Internal Lighting	Printer	Lighting Component	String	CELRobox	Describes if and what kind of internal lighting is present in the 3D printer		Full RGB		x		x
Enclosed Build Envelope	Printer		Bool	CELRobox	Indictor for presence of an enclosed build envelope		No	x		x	
3rd Party Material Compatible	Printer		Bool	CELRobox	Indicator for the (allowed) use of compatible third party material		Yes	x		x	
Nozzle Offset X	Printer-Component	Nozzle	mm	EXP	For multi-nozzle systems the offset of each nozzle to the middle of the print head (X axis)		5 mm		x		x
Nozzle Offset Y	Printer-Component	Nozzle	mm	EXP	For multi-nozzle systems the offset of each nozzle to the middle of the print head (Y axis)		0 mm		x		x
Nozzle Offset Z	Printer-Component	Nozzle	mm	EXP	For multi-nozzle systems the offset of each nozzle to the middle of the print head (Z axis)		0 mm		x		x
Coordinate System	Printer		String	EXP	Cartesian, Polar, Spherical or other coordinate system that is used by the printer for movement and positioning		Cartesian coordinate system	x		x	
Printer Geometry	Printer		String	EXP	Cartesian, Polar or Spherical geometry of the printer. Also possible to denote robot based geometry		Polar geometry	x		x	
Coordinate System Origin	Printer		String	EXP	Denotes the origin of the 3D printer that is used for referencing		Origin is at top right corner of 3D build envelope				
Absolute Density	Material		$\frac{g}{cm^3}$	ProX DMP 200	Material property		4.51 $\frac{g}{cm^3}$	x		x	
Relative Density	Material		%	ProX DMP 200	Material property		100.00%	x		x	
Cytotoxicity (ISO 10993-5)	Material		Int	ProX DMP 200	Material property		Grade 0	x		x	
Melting Point	Material		°C	ProX DMP 200	Material property		1668 °C	x		x	
Magnetic Permeability	Material		$\frac{H}{m}$	ProX DMP 200	Material property		1.0008 $\frac{H}{m}$	x		x	

TABLE II: Properties in Additive Manufacturing – continued

Name	Category	Dependent Upon	Unit	Source	Meaning	Only Applicable for	Example	Static	Dynamic	Independent	Dependent
Electrical Resitivity	Material		$n\Omega\times m$	ProX DMP 200	Material property		740 $n\Omega\times m$	x		x	
Specific Heat Capacity	Material	Temperature-Range	$[\frac{J}{kg\times K}]$	ProX DMP 200	Material property		0–100 °C: 500 $\frac{J}{kg\times K}$		x		x
α/β Transus Temperature	Material		°C	ProX DMP 200	Material property		882 °C	x		x	
Micro Vickers Hardness	Material		Hv	ProX DMP 200	Material property		210 Hv	x		x	
Coefficient of Thermal Expansion	Material	Temperature-Range	$[\frac{1}{°C}]$	ProX DMP 200	Material property		20–100 °C: 7.71 $\times 10^{-6}$ / °C, 20–300 °C: 9.4 $\times 10^{-6}$ / °C		x		x
Macro Rockwell C Hardness	Material		HRC	ProX DMP 200	Material property		30 HRC	x		x	
Thermal Conductivity	Material	Temperature	$[\frac{W}{m\times K}]$	ProX DMP 200	Material property		50 °C: 16 $\frac{W}{m\times K}$		x		x
Flexural Modulus	Material		MPa	ProX 800	Material property		1660 MPa	x		x	
Flexural Strength	Material		MPa	ProX 800	Material property		55 MPa	x		x	
Tensile Modulus	Material		MPa	ProX 800	Material property		1590 MPa	x		x	
Tensile Strength	Material		MPa	ProX 800	Material property		38 MPa	x		x	
Elongation at Break	Material		%	ProX 800	Material property		13.00%	x		x	
Impact Strength	Material		$\frac{J}{m}$	ProX 800	Material property		19 $\frac{J}{m}$	x		x	
Heat Deflection Temp	Material	Pressure	[°C]	ProX 800	Material property		60 psi: 58 °C, 264 psi: 51 °C		x		x
Viscosity	Material	Temperature	[cps]	ProX 800	Material property		30 °C:25, 50 °C:20		x		x
Shore Hardness	Material		D	ProX SLS 500	Material property		73 D	x		x	
Dielectric Constant	Material	Frequency	[Int]	ProX SLS 500	Material property		3.31		x		x
Dielectric Strength	Material		$\frac{kV}{mm}$	ProX SLS 500	Material property		18.1 $\frac{kV}{mm}$	x		x	
Volume Resistivity	Material		$\Omega\times cm$	ProX SLS 500	Material property		7.2 $\times 10^{1}4\Omega\times cm$	x		x	
Flammability	Material	Length	[String]	ProX SLS 500	Material property		HB		x		x
Young's Modulus	Material		GPa	ProX DMP 200	Material property		105 GPa	x		x	
Yield Strength	Material		MPa	ProX DMP 200	Material property		320 MPa	x		x	
Ultimate Tensile Strength	Material		MPa	ProX DMP 200	Material property		450 MPa	x		x	

REFERENCES

[1] Felix W. Baumann and Dieter Roller. Resource Description for Additive Manufacturing – Supporting Scheduling and Provisioning. In *Proceedings of The Ninth International Conferences on Advanced Service Computing (ADASERC)*, pages 41–47. IARIA, 2017.

[2] Irlán Grangel-González, Lavdim Halilaj, Gökhan Coskun, Sören Auer, Diego Collarana, and Michael Hoffmeister. Towards a semantic administrative shell for industry 4.0 components. In *2016 IEEE Tenth International Conference on Semantic Computing (ICSC)*, pages 230–237, 2 2016.

[3] Vincent A. Balogun, Neil Kirkwood, and Paul T. Mativenga. Energy consumption and carbon footprint analysis of Fused Deposition Modelling: A case study of RP Stratasys Dimension SST FDM. *International Journal of Scientific & Engineering Research*, 6(8):442–447, August 2015.

[4] D. A. Roberson, D. Espalin, and R. B. Wicker. 3d printer selection: A decision-making evaluation and ranking model. *Virtual and Physical Prototyping*, 8(3):201–212, 2013.

[5] Matthew Fumo and Rafiq Noorani. Development of an Expert System for the Selection of Rapid Prototyping and 3D Printing Systems. In *Proceedings of the 6th International Conference on Computer Science Education: Innovation & Technology*, pages 14–18, 2015.

[6] Octavian Morariu, Cristina Morariu, and Theodor Borangiu. Shop-floor resource virtualization layer with private cloud support. *Journal of Intelligent Manufacturing*, 27(2):447–462, 2016.

[7] Mitsuo Gen and Lin Lin. Multiobjective evolutionary algorithm for manufacturing scheduling problems: state-of-the-art survey. *Journal of Intelligent Manufacturing*, 25(5):849–866, 2014.

[8] Manuel Dios and Jose M. Framinan. A review and classification of computer-based manufacturing scheduling tools. *Computers & Industrial Engineering*, 99:229–249, 2016.

[9] Steven Pryor. Implementing a 3d printing service in an academic library. *Journal of Library Administration*, 54(1):1–10, 2014.

[10] Parag Vichare, Aydin Nassehi, Sanjeev Kumar, and Stephen T. Newman. A Unified Manufacturing Resource Model for representing CNC machining systems. *Robotics and Computer-Integrated Manufacturing*, 25(6):999–1007, 2009. 18th International Conference on Flexible Automation and Intelligent Manufacturing.

[11] Yuan Yao, Dong Chen, Lei Wang, and Xiaoming Yang. Additive Manufacturing Cloud via Peer-Robot Collaboration. *International Journal of Advanced Robotic Systems*, 13(3):1–12, 2016.

[12] Adobe Systems Incorporated. 3D Printer Description File Format Specification, 2014. Version 1.0 draft 3.

[13] Desai Chen, David I. W. Levin, Piotr Didyk, Pitchaya Sitthi-Amorn, and Wojciech Matusik. Spec2Fab: A Reducer-tuner Model for Translating Specifications to 3D Prints. *ACM Transactions on Graphics*, 32(4):1–10, July 2013.

[14] Chen Dong, Yao Yuan, and Wang Lei. Additive manufacturing cloud based on multi agent systems and rule inference. In *2016 IEEE Information Technology, Networking, Electronic and Automation Control Conference*, pages 45–50, May 2016.

[15] Yaser Yadekar, Essam Shehab, and Jörn Mehnen. Taxonomy and uncertainties of cloud manufacturing. *International Journal of Agile Systems and Management*, 9(1):48–66, 2016.

[16] Letizia Mortara, Jonathan Hughes, Pallant S. Ramsundar, Finbarr Livesey, and David R. Probert. Proposed classification scheme for direct writing technologies. *Rapid Prototyping Journal*, 15(4):299–309, 2009.

[17] Ian Gibson, David Rosen, and Brent Stucker. *Additive Manufacturing Technologies - 3D Printing, Rapid Prototyping, and Direct Digital Manufacturing*. Springer New York, 2 edition, 2015.

[18] Christopher B. Williams, Farrokh Mistree, and David W. Rosen. A Functional Classification Framework for the Conceptual Design of Additive Manufacturing Technologies. *Journal of Mechanical Design*, 133(12):1–11, December 2011.

[19] ISO/ASTM 52900:2015 Additive manufacturing — General principles — Terminology, 2016.

[20] Alessandro Ranellucci, Henrik Brix Andersen, Nicolas Dandrimont, Mark Hindness, Petr Ledvina, Y. Sapir, Mike Sheldrake, and Gary Hodgson. Slic3r – g-code generator for 3d printers. http://slic3r.org, 2011. Accessed: 2016-11-28.

[21] Ultimaker B.V. Cura 3d printing slicing software. https://ultimaker.com/en/products/cura-software, 2015. Accessed: 2016-10-21.

[22] Inc Autodesk. Why netfabb? https://www.netfabb.com, 2011. Accessed: 2016-10-20.

[23] Thomas R. Gruber. Toward principles for the design of ontologies used for knowledge sharing? *International Journal of Human-Computer Studies*, 43(5):907–928, 1995.

[24] Dieter Fensel. *Ontologies: A Silver Bullet for Knowledge Management and Electronic Commerce*. Springer-Verlag Berlin Heidelberg, 2 edition, 2004.

[25] Farhad Ameri and Debasish Dutta. An Upper Ontology for Manufacturing Service Description. In *ASME 2006 International Design Engineering Technical Conferences and Computers and Information in Engineering Conference*, volume 3, pages 651–661, September 2016.

[26] Felix Baumann, Oliver Kopp, and Dieter Roller. Universal API for 3D Printers. In Heinrich C. Mayr and Martin Pinzger, editors, *INFORMATIK 2016. Lecture Notes in Informatics (LNI)*, volume P-259, pages 1611–1622. Gesellschaft für Informatik, 2016.

[27] Felix Baumann, Julian Eichhoff, and Dieter Roller. *Collaborative Cloud Printing Service*, pages 77–85. Springer International Publishing, 2016.

[28] Felix W. Baumann, Oliver Kopp, and Dieter Roller. Abstract api for 3d printing hardware and software resources. *International Journal of Advanced Manufacturing Technology*, 2016. Submitted - Under Review.

[29] Steffen Lohmann and Stefan Negru. Vowl: Visual notation for owl ontologies. http://vowl.visualdataweb.org, 2016. Accessed: 2016-10-20.

[30] Pavel Hanzl, Miroslav Zetek, Tomáš Bakša, and Tomáš Kroupa. The Influence of Processing Parameters on the Mechanical Properties of SLM Parts. *Procedia Engineering*, 100:1405–1413, 2015.

All URLs are last checked on November 20, 2017.

The Social Scaffolding of Machine Intelligence

Paul R. Smart
Electronics & Computer Science
University of Southampton
Southampton, UK
Email: ps02v@ecs.soton.ac.uk

Aastha Madaan
Electronics & Computer Science
University of Southampton
Southampton, UK
Email: madaan.aastha@gmail.com

Abstract—**The Internet provides access to a global space of information assets and computational services. It also, however, serves as a platform for social interaction (e.g., Facebook) and participatory involvement in all manner of online tasks and activities (e.g., Wikipedia). There is a sense, therefore, that the Internet yields an unprecedented form of access to the human social environment: it provides insight into the dynamics of human behavior (both individual and collective), and it additionally provides access to the digital products of human cognitive labor (again, both individual and collective). Such access is interesting from the standpoint of research into machine intelligence, for the human social environment looks to be of crucial importance when it comes to the evolutionary and developmental origins of the human mind. In the present paper, we develop a theoretical account that sees the Internet as providing opportunities for online systems to function as socially-situated agents. The result is a vision of machine intelligence in which advanced forms of cognitive competence are seen to arise from the creation of a new kind of digital socio-ecological niche. The present paper attempts to detail this vision with respect to the notion of socially-scaffolded cognition. It also describes some of the forms of machine learning that may be required to enable online systems to press maximal cognitive benefit from their new-found informational contact with the human social world.**

Keywords*–*internet; social intelligence; language; machine intelligence; machine learning.

I. INTRODUCTION

There can be little doubt that the Internet represents a milestone in human technical achievement. As a technical accomplishment, the Internet stands testament to our species' capacity for invention, innovation and complex problem-solving. But in this respect, it seems that our species is unique. No other form of terrestrial life is able to build a global communication system, observe the distant reaches of the cosmos, or plumb the murky depths of mathematical mysteria. (Neither, for that matter, are they able to contemplate their species-specific cognitive character and serialize their thoughts in the form of an academic paper!) In a cognitive sense, therefore, we humans are clearly special, for it is only the anatomically modern human mind that has managed to scale the lofty heights of the cognitive mountain. But in being special, we are also very much alone. Cetaceans, chimps and cephalopods are all capable cognizers; but none are in a position to challenge the cognitive supremacy of our own species. The cognitive world, it seems, is bit around a wall that separates two ostensibly distinct cognitive kinds. On one side of that wall we find ourselves; on the other, we find the rest of terrestrial life.

The extent to which we will always be alone (or, indeed, special) is, of course, a moot point. From our vantage point in the cognitive eyrie, we are currently seeking to understand the forces and factors that make our human minds materially possible. And in the light of such understanding, we are striving to build machines in our own cognitive image. It is this undertaking—the traditional focus of Artificial Intelligence (AI) and machine intelligence research—that is perhaps the most difficult of our technical undertakings. Despite some notable successes, the attempt to engineer advanced forms of machine intelligence—machines that emulate our own distinctive forms of cognitive competence—remains, for the most part, a work in progress. The route to human-level intelligence, it seems, is not straightforward. And perhaps this is why we humans find ourselves alone atop the cognitive mountain—the solitary surveyors of the low-lying cognitive terrain.

In the present paper, we wish to consider a particular path up the cognitive mountain. It is a path that focuses attention on the role of the Internet in supporting the emergence of machines with human-like cognitive capabilities. The general aim is perhaps best captured in the form of a question: What impact (if any) does the Internet have on the attempt to engineer machines with human-level intelligence?

There are, to be sure, a number of ways that we might respond to such a question. We might, for example, point to the way in which the Internet has yielded a superabundant supply of widely available digital data, such as image, text and video resources. Such resources have arguably shaped the course of AI research, stimulating research into new forms of machine learning (such as those being explored by Google DeepMind). There is also a sense in which the Internet has played something of an indirect role in advancing the cause of AI. We might, for example, point to the way in which the Internet has yielded a superabundant supply of money for major technology vendors, leading to eye-watering levels of investment in AI-related research.

A different kind of response to the question of how the Internet relates to machine intelligence is to be found in one of our earlier papers [1]. In the context of that paper, we suggested that the Internet, or at least a specific component of the Internet—namely, the Social Web—is poised to yield state-of-the-art advances in machine intelligence. The basis for such optimism was to be found in the (perhaps rather inchoate) claim that the Internet provides a form of informational contact with the *human social environment*, where the notion of the human social environment was cast as the realm in which human behavior (both individual and collective) occurs. As a result of such contact, we suggested that the Internet provides opportunities for machines to observe and interact with humanity, as well as exploit the products of human cognitive and epistemic labor. Thus construed, the Internet was seen to support the emergence of a new kind of cognitively-potent informational ecology: a socio-ecological niche, pregnant with cognitive opportunity.

The present paper introduces a number of extensions to our earlier paper based on the comments and feedback we received from the academic community. These extensions reflect both a broadening and a narrowing of scope. The scope is broadened in the sense that we focus on the Internet rather than just the Social Web. This particular shift in focus is probably of little consequence, for the term "Internet" in the present paper is intended as a catch-all term that encompasses a multiplicity of Internet-related technologies. This includes the World Wide Web, as well as the Web's more specific instantiations, such as the Social Web.

The other shift of focus—the one involving a narrowing of scope—is perhaps more significant. In the present paper, we restrict our attention to a particular kind of cognition, one that goes by the name of *socially-scaffolded cognition*. The meaning of this term will become clearer throughout the course of the paper (see Section II). For present purposes, however, socially-scaffolded cognition can be viewed as a form of cognition whose origins depend on the properties of a social environment (or aspects thereof). This conception is broadly consistent with the flavor of existing work, which links the notion of scaffolded cognition to the acquisition of particular forms of cognitive competence [2]. As we shall see, however, the precise meaning of the term "scaffolded cognition," and its status as an independent cognitive kind, distinct from, say, the likes of extended or embedded cognition, is still a matter that is open to philosophical debate (and disagreement). In this respect, the account of scaffolded cognition offered in Section II represents an attempt to more clearly delineate the notion of scaffolded cognition and distinguish it from other, ostensibly similar, cognitive kinds. This reflects one of the ways the present paper contributes to the philosophical and cognitive scientific literature.

In addition to changes in scope—manifested as the loosening of technological constraints and the tightening of cognitive bonds—the present paper offers a more detailed exposition of some of the mechanisms that may allow certain kinds of intelligent system to press maximal cognitive benefit from Internet-mediated forms of informational contact with the human social world. Relative to the original paper, this particular extension corresponds to neither a constriction nor a dilation of scope. It is, instead, an attempt to highlight the relevance of existing research to socially-scaffolded forms of machine intelligence. Such a move could be seen as marking the first tentative steps towards a concrete empirical research agenda, with perhaps potentially profound implications for the development of (e.g.) cognitive computing systems. For the most part, however, our aim in the present paper is to establish the theoretical basis for research in this area. We thus focus our attention on the following issues:

1) Why is the notion of socially-scaffolded cognition relevant to AI research?
2) How is the Internet apt to function as a cognitively-potent informational ecology—one that supports the emergence of advanced forms of machine intelligence?

In addressing these issues, we attempt to draw on ideas, insights and empirical findings that are strewn across a rich array of academic disciplines. This is, of course, a high-risk strategy: In taking the transdisciplinary path, one often embarks on a treacherous journey into the intellectual wilderness—an interdisciplinary no man's land where the intellectual payoff is, at best, uncertain and the reputational rewards (relative to one's academic career) are probably zero. So be it. Inasmuch as the following is deemed to yield little in the way of a genuine advance in our understanding of how to build an intelligent machine, we will at least take comfort in the fact that we have saved someone else the journey.

The structure of the paper is as follows: Section II focuses on the notion of scaffolded cognition and develops a developmentally-oriented conceptual account that distinguishes scaffolded cognition from ostensibly similar cognitive kinds, such as extended cognition and embedded cognition. Section III seeks to highlight the relevance of social forces and factors to human intelligence. It does this by describing the way in which the human mind is shaped by the human social environment, in both an evolutionary and an ontogenetic sense. Such insights provide the basis for Section IV, which discusses the way in which the Internet allows certain kinds of AI systems—dubbed *social machines*—to function as socially-situated or socially-embedded agents. Section V surveys a number of different forms of machine learning, namely, social, active, language, predictive and incremental learning. The aim here is to identify some of the cognitive prerequisites for a social machine—the capabilities that enable a social machine to press cognitive benefit from its informational contact with the human social environment. Finally, in Section VI, we summarize some of the core ideas discussed throughout the paper and mention some areas for future theoretical and empirical work.

II. Scaffolded Cognition

One way of understanding the significance of the human social environment to the development of human cognitive capabilities (in both a phylogenetic and an ontogenetic sense) is via the notion of *scaffolded cognition* [2][3]. The term "scaffolded cognition" is typically (although not always) used to refer to a cognitive ability that emerges as the result of an agent's exposure to scaffolding resources, where the resources in question form part of the environment of a cognitive agent and play an active role in shaping the agent's cognitive development. In the case of socially-scaffolded cognition, such resources are most obviously thought of as other human individuals, as well as perhaps the products of human cultural innovation (i.e., artifacts, knowledge, norms, language, tools, practices, and so on). It is these resources—the material elements of what we call the human social environment—that help to shape the course of human cognitive development and the trajectory of human cognitive evolution. In an important sense, it is our exposure (and response) to such resources that makes us what we are—a species able to negotiate cognitive terrains that lie beyond the ken of other earthly critters.

Our aim in the present paper is to apply the notion of socially-scaffolded cognition to the realm of AI systems. In particular, we suggest that the path to state-of-the-art advances in machine intelligence may be revealed by a consideration of the ways in which various forms of social scaffolding shape the course of human cognitive development and (over longer timescales) the course of human cognitive evolution. Before we begin to unpack this claim, however, it will help to have a clearer understanding of what is meant by the notion of scaffolded cognition. This is important, because the term "scaffolded cognition" is one that is used in different ways within the cognitive scientific literature. The term is perhaps most often encountered in the context of educational or developmental psychology, but this is not always the case. In addition, scaffolded cognition is only one among a number of cognitively-oriented concepts that have been the focus of cognitive scientific attention, and the relationships between these concepts are, it has to said, not fully understood. It is easy, for example, to think of scaffolded cognition as denoting a particular kind of cognition, i.e., a *cognitive kind*. But much the same could be said about other elements of the cognitive scientific lexicon, including the notions of extended [4]–[6], embedded [7], situated [8], distributed [9] and embodied cognition [10]. Distinguishing between these concepts and identifying their relationships to one another is a major theoretical undertaking, and it is not one that we can hope to achieve in the present paper. That said, there is a particular need to understand the distinction between scaffolded cognition and at least some other cognitive kinds, most notably extended cognition and embedded cognition. This is important, because the relevance of the Internet to issues of machine intelligence has been the focus of previous work. In particular, Smart [11] has suggested that the Internet provides opportunities for both extended and embedded forms of machine intelligence, and the human social environment is deemed to be relevant in both cases. At a minimum, therefore, we need to understand how (and to what degree) the appeal to scaffolded cognition provides us with a novel view of the Internet and its contributions to machine intelligence.

Perhaps the most significant obstacle to a successful discrimination between scaffolded cognition and other cognitive kinds lies in the fact that appeals to scaffolded cognition are sometimes encountered outside of a developmental context. Clark [12], for example, discusses the way in which a variety of external scaffolds, including public language and culture, help to "mold and orchestrate behavior" in adaptive or strategic ways [12, pp. 32–33]. Relative to Clark's vision of the human mind as an extended cognitive organization—one in which cognitive processing routines rely on a multiplicity of resources drawn from the biological, social and technological realms—it is perhaps easy to see scaffolded cognition as related to the notion of extended cognition. This is especially so if scaffolding resources are deemed to play a role that goes beyond the mere causal dependence of cognitive processing routines on aspects of the external environment. In fact, something along these lines is suggested by Arnau et al. [13], as part of their attempt to define scaffolded cognition:

> Scaffolded cognition is the idea that (at least some of) our cognitive capacities both depend on and have been transformed by our manipulation of environmental resources. The claim here is not about mere causal dependence, but about integrative coupling between internal and external elements. [13, p. 56]

What is crucial here is the claim that scaffolded cognition involves something more than "mere causal dependence." One way of making sense of this claim is via an appeal to the distinction between causal and constitutive relevance [14][15], where the notion of constitutive relevance implies that some resource is an intrinsic element of the physical fabric that realizes or constitutes some phenomenon of interest. (This contrasts with the more familiar notion of causal relevance, where some resource is seen to cause the occurrence of some phenomenon.) In the case of extended cognition, the claim is that some extra-organismic resource is of constitutive relevance to some cognitive phenomenon (e.g., a given cognitive process), and it therefore forms part of the physical machinery that realizes the cognitive phenomenon in question. One way of thinking about scaffolded cognition, therefore, is to see it as a form of cognition in which some form of extra-organismic scaffolding resource is constitutively relevant to cognition.

The problem with this proposal is immediately obvious: By appealing to issues of constitutive relevance, the distinction between extended and scaffolded cognition is obscured, perhaps to the point where the two concepts are indistinguishable. In this sense, the appeal to "integrative coupling" in the aforementioned quote by Arnau et al. is problematic because it resembles similar appeals to integrative coupling made in respect of extended cognition (see [16]).

In the interests of distinguishing scaffolded cognition from extended cognition, we may opt to drop our allegiance to constitutive relevance and recast the relevance relation as one of causal relevance. In other words, when we reflect on the relation between some scaffolding resource and a particular cognitive capacity, it may make sense to view the relation in purely causal terms. The problem, in this case, is that by embracing the notion of causal relevance we are in danger of confusing scaffolded cognition with another kind of cognition, namely, embedded cognition [7]. Like extended cognition, embedded cognition recognizes the dependence of cognitive properties on elements that lie external to the cognitive system. In this case, however, the dependence relation is best understood with respect to the notion of causal relevance rather than constitutive relevance.

The upshot of all this is a dilemma that turns on the relationship between the properties of a cognitive system and the role played by some extra-systemic resource. If we conceive of this relationship in such a way that the resource is constitutively relevant to the properties of a cognitive system, then scaffolded cognition emerges as nothing more than extended cognition. On the other hand, if we drop the appeal to constitutive relevance and instead conceive of the relationship from the standpoint of causal relevance, then what we are left with is nothing other than embedded cognition. Either way, the notion of scaffolded cognition looks to be conceptually redundant.

Our approach to the resolution of this dilemma is rooted in an appeal to the notion of *mechanistic explanation*, which is a form of explanation that focuses on the mechanisms that are deemed to be responsible for some phenomenon of interest (e.g., [17]). Two kinds of mechanistic explanation look to be of particular importance when it comes to extended and embedded cognition. These are *causal mechanistic explanation*, which is tied to claims of causal relevance, and *constitutive mechanistic explanation*, which is tied to claims of constitutive relevance (see [15]). One way to think about the distinction between embedded and extended cognition is thus to see embedded and extended cognitive systems as the targets of different kinds of mechanistically-oriented explanatory account: causal mechanistic explanations are thus best suited for embedded cognition, while constitutive mechanistic explanations are best suited for extended cognition (see [18]).

So much for embedded and extended cognition. But what about scaffolded cognition? Is there a particular kind of mechanistic explanation that is apt for scaffolded cognition, and is this form of explanation sufficiently distinct from mechanistic explanations of the causal or constitutive stripe?

In fact, we suggest that scaffolded cognition is best approached from the perspective of what are called *developmental explanations* [15][19]. Such explanations seek to trace the historical lineage of a phenomenon, helping us understand how the phenomenon relates to an interacting nexus of causally-active historical forces and factors. Developmental explanations are, in essence, an attempt to detail the causal history of phenomena, and, in this sense, they bear much in common with the sorts of explanations encountered in the historical sciences [20]. (Indeed, we regard historical explanation as a particular form of developmental explanation.) As with causal and constitutive mechanistic explanations, developmental explanations are typically cast as a particular form of mechanistic explanation. In other words, developmental explanations resemble other forms of mechanistic explanation in that their explanatory heft inheres in the attempt to provide a complete description of the mechanisms that are responsible for some target phenomenon. It is perhaps tempting to refer to such mechanisms as *developmental mechanisms*, although the previous use of this term is mostly confined to the realms of developmental biology [21]. For present purposes, we will use the terms "developmental explanation" and "developmental mechanism" in a generic sense to refer to explanations and mechanisms that are encountered in a variety of disciplinary contexts. These include developmental biology (ontogenetic explanations), history (historical explanations), and evolutionary biology (evolutionary explanations).

We have already seen how issues of constitutive/causal explanation and constitutive/causal relevance can be used to discriminate between extended and embedded cognition. The same approach, we suggest, can be used to inform our theoretical understanding of scaffolded cognition. Scaffolded cognition can thus be thought of as a particular form of cognition (i.e., a cognitive kind) that is the apt target of a particular kind of explanatory approach. Just as constitutive explanations are appropriate to extended cognition, and causal explanations are appropriate to embedded cognition, so developmental explanations, we suggest, are appropriate to scaffolded cognition. As with extended and embedded cognition, scaffolded cognition involves resources that are located external to the boundaries of a cognitive system. In the case of scaffolded cognition, however, these resources are deemed to be of *developmental relevance* with regard to whatever cognitive phenomenon is the target (i.e., the explananda) of mechanistic explanation. In fact, these resources are nothing other than what we have been calling scaffolding resources. In essence, scaffolding resources are the material elements of developmental mechanisms that are described by developmental explanations. Thus construed, developmental relevance can be regarded as a particular kind of explanatory relevance. Just like causal and constitutive relevance (which are also forms of explanatory relevance), developmental relevance highlights the relevance of some extra-systemic resource for the purposes of (developmentally-oriented) mechanistic explanations.

There is, of course, a sense in which developmental explanations are similar to causal explanations, and this might be seen to serve as a source of confusion when it comes to the distinction between scaffolded cognition and embedded cognition. Just like causal explanations, developmental explanations reveal the ways in which a set of causally-active antecedent forces and factors conspire to yield some sort of outcome. There is, however, no reason why this should lead to confusion between the notions of scaffolded and embedded cognition. Embedded cognition seeks to explain cognitive phenomena with respect to causal influences that operate in the here-and-now, and, as a result, the resources picked out by the notion of causal relevance are always ones that are present in the local environment of a cognitive system. Such need not be the case with scaffolded cognition. In the case of scaffolded cognition, the relevant resources (scaffolding resources) need not be present in the local environment of a cognitive system. Indeed, in some cases, such resources may no longer exist. Issues of spatial and temporal proximity are thus of crucial importance for embedded cognition, but they are of relatively little importance for scaffolded cognition.

This is also, as it happens, the reason why developmental explanation/relevance cannot be equated with constitutive explanation/relevance. The resources that are relevant to constitutive explanations are always deemed to be physically present because they form part of the mechanism that realizes occurrent cognitive phenomena. Such is not the case with scaffolding resources, and it is for this reason that the concept of scaffolded cognition cannot be equated with extended cognition.

Having said all this, it should be noted that the relationship between the notions of causal, constitutive and developmental relevance is still something that is up for grabs. Ylikoski [15], for example, suggests that developmental explanations are at times complex amalgams of constitutively and causally relevant factors. Developmental explanations, he suggests, sometimes involve complex forms of reciprocal causation and mutual influence that are difficult to track with simple causal accounts. The result, it seems, is that developmental explanations are not purely constitutive explanations, but neither are they purely causal explanations. Perhaps it is this inextricable entanglement between constitutive and causal relevance, spread out over (sometimes significant) periods of time, that best accommodates the intuition that scaffolded cognition relies on something more than "mere causal dependence" and involves some degree of "integrative coupling" [13].

The result of all this is a conception of scaffolded cognition that appeals to the notions of developmental explanation and developmental relevance. Scaffolded cognition is, in essence, a developmentally-oriented concept. One virtue of this developmentally-oriented conception is that it is nicely aligned with the bulk of research into scaffolded cognition, most of which has been undertaken in an educational or developmental context. The conception also, however, provides a means of discriminating scaffolded cognition from extended and embedded cognition, and it does so in such a way as to (perhaps) reveal why these concepts have proved so hard to disentangle.

III. The Social Origins of Human Intelligence

The form of scaffolded cognition that concerns in the present paper is referred to as *socially-scaffolded cognition*.

This is a form of scaffolded cognition that is distinguished with respect to the nature of the resource that does the scaffolding (see [2]). In the case of socially-scaffolded cognition, we are interested in situations where the social environment (or some aspect thereof) plays a role in the developmental emergence of cognitive capabilities.

Why should socially-scaffolded cognition be of any interest or relevance to those interested in machine intelligence? To answer this question, it will help to introduce two substantive strands of empirical and theoretical research: one focused on the evolution of the human cognitive system; the other, on the ontogenetic development of human cognitive capabilities.

Let us first direct our attention to issues of human cognitive evolution. There is clearly something special about human cognition—something that makes our own species cognitively unique. But what is it about the evolutionary history of our species that accounts for this remarkable divergence in cognitive power and sophistication?

One response to this question focuses on the selection pressures arising from the physical environment—the need to find food, ward off predators, deal with climatic changes, and so on. The inadequacy of this account is immediately obvious: it fails to explain what it is that gives human cognition its rather distinctive flavor. Why is it that humans—and only humans—are in possession of advanced cognitive capabilities? Presumably, we humans are not alone in having to deal with a range of ecological challenges, so why has evolution not driven other forms of terrestrial life to evolve a similar cognitive profile?

A different (albeit related) response focuses on the challenges thrown up by a particular kind of ecological niche: the human (or, perhaps better, hominin) social environment. According to approaches of this ilk, the forces and factors that account for the evolutionary emergence of the modern human mind are not to be found in the physical environment of our hominin ancestors. Instead, it is suggested that the well-spring of human cognitive success is to be found in the socio-ecological realm. The idea, in essence, is that the human mind evolved to deal with the vagaries of an environment that was itself constituted by other humans (and their minds). In other words, we humans 'created' the specific socio-ecological niche from which the modern human mind emerged. The human mind, according to this view, corresponds to something of a socially-created artifact—a device that was forged in a crucible of our own creation.

This idea actually comes in a variety of flavors. It surfaces, in somewhat different forms, in a number of recent evolutionary hypotheses, including the social brain hypothesis [22], the Machiavellian intelligence hypothesis [23], the cultural intelligence hypothesis [24], the social intelligence hypothesis [25], the sexual selection hypothesis [26], and the ecological dominance-social competition hypothesis [27]. What unites these hypotheses is a claim about the evolutionary significance of intra-specific social competition. Flinn [28], for example, suggests that:

> ...the human psyche was designed primarily to contend with social relationships, whereas the physical environment was relatively less important. Most natural selection in regard to brain evolution was a consequence of interactions with conspecifics, not with food and climate...To a degree that far surpasses that of any other species, human mental processes must contend with a constantly changing information environment of their own creation. (pp.73–74)

There are two aspects to this socially-oriented account of human cognitive evolution that are worth highlighting. The first is the emergence of a form of runaway directional selection in which the emergence of cognitively, socially, and behaviorally sophisticated individuals merely serves to exacerbate existing social selection pressures, increasing the complexity of the social environment that evolution must contend with. We thus encounter something of a positive feedback loop, in which individual cognitive sophistication leads to greater social complexity, which in turn leads to ever-greater demands for cognitive sophistication. The result is something of a red queen situation (see [29]): cognitive sophistication begets social complexity, which in turn intensifies the drive toward cognitive sophistication. For the sake of convenience, let us dub this *the red queen of socio-ecological complexity*.

The mechanism that lies at the heart of this particular red queen is well-documented. Its lineage can be traced to Humphrey [30] who cast the feedback loop as a form of ratchet, a "self-winding watch to increase the general intellectual standing of the species" (p. 311). This is a useful metaphor, in the sense that it helps us see human cognitive evolution as something of an autocatalytic process—one in which a particular form of cognitive-evolutionary progress lays the foundation for yet further increments in cognitive power and sophistication [27]. The metaphor is also useful in that it draws attention to the dynamic nature of the human social environment. In contrast to the physical environment, whose features are, for the most part, relatively enduring (or at least predictable from one generation to the next), the topography of the social terrain is riven by the tectonic forces of cognitive-evolutionary change.

There is, however, another aspect to this theoretical account that highlights the rather unique nature of the human social environment. In addition to being a dynamically changing environment—one whose complexity tracks progressive increases in human cognitive sophistication—the human social environment is also one that is shaped by the forces of cultural evolution. This obviously adds to the unpredictability of social environments across inter-generational timeframes; but it also (and perhaps more importantly) lays the foundation for the diversification of social environments *within* any given generation. The upshot is that, from the standpoint of evolution, the human socio-ecological niche is one whose features are, at best, difficult to predict. Faced with such a situation, there is perhaps little that evolution can do except yield organisms that are equipped with a combination of powerful learning mechanisms and extraordinary levels of (cognitive) phenotypic plasticity:

> Once human cultural evolution began to accelerate and languages began to change rapidly, there would have been strong selection for general and language-specific increases in brain plasticity. Since the one thing that is consistently stable in a rapidly changing culture is the culture's context-dependent flexibility (which the cultural evolutionary process itself creates), there is persistent selection for increasingly flexible and sophisticated ways of learning, including language-learning. [31, p. 2154]

It is this particular form of phenotypic plasticity that is the source of a second red queen, one that we will dub *the red queen of socio-ecological variability*. To help us understand this particular red queen, note that phenotypic plasticity, when situated within the specific context of cultural innovation and learning, is the source of a second ratchet-like mechanism that drives the evolution of ever-greater levels of plasticity. The reason for this is that phenotypic plasticity goes hand-in-hand with phenotypic variability, and phenotypic variability contributes to precisely the sorts of socio-cultural differentiation that make the human socio-ecological niche so hard for evolutionary processes to predict. The result is a positive feedback loop, in which socio-ecological variability drives the evolution of cognitive plasticity, which in turn gives rise to ever-more opportunities for socio-ecological diversification.

It is at this point that our attention begins to switch from phylogeny to ontogeny. For the complex and capricious nature of the human social environment may be useful in helping us understand some of the characteristic features of human ontogeny. The first of these concerns the plasticity and structural lability of the human brain, which looks to be particularly pronounced in human infants and young adults (e.g., [32]). The second is the protracted nature of human maturational processes (i.e., the period of extended development known as childhood). Both these features can be regarded as adaptations to a complex and inconstant human social environment. The developmental profile of the human brain, for example, may provide the basis for extreme forms of neural plasticity, in which the structural and functional architecture of the biological brain adapts to the demands thrown up by a complex and unpredictable environment [33][34]. Similarly, the functional significance of extended development (or childhood) is typically cashed out in terms of the opportunities for learning. In particular, it has been suggested that an extended period of development is required to enable human individuals to learn the skills required in later life [35]. Interestingly, human infants are born helpless, and they remain immature for longer than might be expected [36]. It is easy to regard this period of neonatal altriciality as something of a costly encumbrance that is imposed on infants (and parents), and which hampers the opportunities for subsequent social learning. Note, however, that in being helpless, the human infant is totally dependent on her human care-givers, and this establishes the basis for particularly intimate forms of social interaction—the very stuff that drives socially-scaffolded development. In this sense, the altricial status of young human infants, while easily glossed as something maladaptive and costly, can also be seen to lay the foundation for future forms of socially-directed or socially-inflected learning. As noted by Nelson [37], this period of "enforced dependent sociality is both the foundation for the social mind of humans and for the particular course of social-cognitive development found in the human child" (p. 367).

The social environment plays an important role in shaping human cognitive development throughout childhood, and often well into adulthood. And it is here that we find the bulk of research into scaffolded cognition. One of the foremost proponents of socially-scaffolded development is the Soviet psychologist, Lev Vygotsky. Vygotsky argued that the nature of our interaction with socially-significant others holds the key to understanding human cognition (see [38]). Human intelligence is, according to Vygotsky, something that emerges as a result of social interactions with other human beings.

The upshot of all this is a vision of the human mind that is thoroughly social, both in origin and in orientation. We have seen how the ever-changing topography of the social terrain plays a crucial role in shaping the trajectory of human cognitive evolution, and we have also seen how social interactions are poised to play a crucial role in cognitive development. Being social, it seems, is what *makes* us human. Irrespective of whether our attention is focused on issues of phylogeny or ontogeny, the human social environment emerges as of crucial importance in our attempts to understand the developmental mechanisms that give rise to that most marvelous, and yet most mysterious, of cognitive devices: the modern human mind.

IV. Social Machines

Inasmuch as we see the human mind as a socially-created artifact—or a socially-engineered cognitive machine—then perhaps a consideration of social forces and factors is relevant to our ongoing effort to develop AI systems. Perhaps, in other words, a consideration of the social realm enables us to trace a path to the top of the cognitive mountain—a path that was followed (and in some sense forged) by our own species. It is, no doubt, a precarious and ill-defined path, one whose course is punctuated by soaring cliffs and gaping chasms. But it is, nevertheless, a path. And, given our solitary status at the top of the cognitive hierarchy, it may very well turn out to be the only path available.

There is, of course, nothing new in the idea that a consideration of the social environment is relevant to the effort to build intelligent machines. The idea is, in fact, the mainstay of the field of social and (to a lesser extent) developmental robotics [38]–[41], both of which emphasize the role of social interaction and engagement in the development of advanced cognitive capabilities. Consider, for example, the following quotes from Kerstin Dautenhahn and colleagues, both of which appeal to ideas rehearsed in the previous section (see Section III):

> If social intelligence, in evolutionary terms, 'came first' in the development of primate intelligence, and then later was applied to other domains, then one may extrapolate and apply this 'evolutionary history' to machines, too. Accordingly, from an evolutionary perspective, then intelligent robots need to be socially intelligent robots. [41, p. 295]

> Our research is based on the assumption that in order to study the cognitive development of robots we have to consider the 'robot in society', i.e., using Vygotsky's approach to see social interactions as fundamental, and as a context which can scaffold the development of cognitively richer functionalities. [42, p. 6]

The theoretical position proposed in the present paper is based on precisely these sorts of assumptions. The only significant difference is the nature of the system that is seen to be the beneficiary of socially-scaffolded development. In the case of social robotics, of course, the relevant system is typically some form of robot, typically one that is implemented as a physical entity, equipped with a real 'body' that serves as the basis for robot–human and sometimes robot–robot interactions. The systems of interest in the present paper are somewhat different. We are interested in a class of systems that operate in the online realm of the Internet and which typically exist in the form of computer programs. In this sense, the kinds of intelligent system that we are interested in would no doubt be regarded as 'disembodied' and thus incapable of functioning as socially-situated agents. While we do not wish to contest the claim that some sort of distinction should be made between a purely online system and a real-world robot, it is not clear that the notion of embodiment is best placed to motivate this distinction. A fuller discussion of this issue would take us too far afield; however, it is worth noting that some kinds of online system might be regarded as embodied by virtue of the forms of real-world sensory/motor contact provided by (e.g.) the Internet of Things (IoT) [11]. It is also worth noting that some have questioned the extent to which issues of embodiment apply *only* to the realm of real-world, physical systems, as opposed to their purely virtual counterparts [43][44].

In any case, our primary interest in the present paper is the extent to which the Internet enables AI systems to be embedded or situated within the human social environment. Central to this idea is the claim that the Internet provides a form of informational contact with the human social environment. This particular claim will probably require little in the way of a detailed defense, for the Internet has undoubtedly provided a rich array of opportunities for conventional computational systems to engage with human agents and observe their behavior at both an individual and collective level. The Social Web is just one example of this. With the advent of social networking sites, microblogging services, and media sharing systems, the online environment affords ever-deeper insights into the dynamics of human social behavior [45]. Additional forms of contact are arguably provided by an ever-expanding array of mobile and portable computing devices, Internet-enabled sensors, and IoT devices.

It is, of course, easy to think that this notion of the Internet providing contact with (or access to) the human social environment should be interpreted solely in observational terms, i.e., as the Internet enabling machines to monitor human behavior at both the individual and collective levels. In fact, a somewhat broader notion is in play here. We see the Internet as providing access to an online ecology of human-generated digital assets, some of which indirectly contribute to the (social) shaping of machine-based capabilities. Consider, for example, the way in which the addition of descriptive tags and annotations to a set of image resources assists with the development of machine vision systems [46]. Here, human contributions yield a body of training data that is apt to support a particular kind of machine learning. Such possibilities are explicitly recognized by those who seek to engage human subjects in computationally-difficult tasks. With respect to citizen science systems, for example, Lintott and Reed [47] note that one of the limiting factors in the development of automated processing solutions is the availability of sufficiently well-structured training data sets, and that one of the key advantages of citizen science projects is the provision of such data sets. Similarly, when it comes to a class of systems known as Games With A Purpose (GWAPs), von Ahn and Dabbish [48] are keen to stress the role of human contributions in giving rise to ever-more intelligent (and human-like) forms of machine-based processing:

> By leveraging the human time spent playing games online, GWAP game developers are able to capture large sets of training data that express uniquely human perceptual capabilities. This data can contribute to the goal of developing computer programs and automated systems with advanced perceptual or intelligence skills. [48, p. 67]

The key point, here, is that by virtue of human contributions, a set of digital resources that were previously too ill-structured to support machine learning are transformed into something that is much better aligned with the requirements of machine learning algorithms. Something along these lines also applies to systems such as IBM Watson [49], which benefit from the online availability of socially-generated and socially-structured resources (e.g., Wikipedia). In these cases, advances in machine intelligence derive from the access the Internet provides to the human social environment, but it is not a form of access that can be characterized solely in observational terms.

The basic vision, then, is one of the Internet providing a form of informational access to the human social environment. Relative to this vision, we suggest that the Internet provides opportunities for AI systems to be embedded or situated within the human social environment, enabling them to benefit from various forms of socially-scaffolded development. For the purposes of this paper, we will refer to these socially-situated systems as *social machines*. A social machine is thus a particular kind of intelligent system that benefits (in a cognitive sense) from Internet-mediated forms of informational contact with the human social environment. It is, in essence, a machine whose cognitive capabilities are tied to its status as a socially-situated agent.

V. Socially-Scaffolded Cognition and Machine Learning

Clearly, not every kind of intelligent system is likely to qualify as a social machine. The status of social machines as socially-situated or socially-embedded (see [38][50]) systems perhaps goes some way to limning the relevant class of systems. But even the notion of social situatedness seems somewhat insufficient. Mere exposure to the human social environment will not cause a socially-oriented cognitive critter to develop human-level cognitive abilities. If it did, then we would recognize dogs and budgies as kindred cognitive spirits.

As it stands, therefore, the notion of a social machine remains somewhat vague. It is, in particular, unclear what kinds of intelligent system should be counted as social machines. What are the peculiar features of a social machine that enable it to function as a socially-situated agent? What are the details of its cognitive architecture? What are the ways in which a social machine is poised to benefit from socially-scaffolded development? What is it that enables a social machine to press maximal cognitive benefit from its immersion in a socio-ecological niche? And why should the human social environment (as opposed to any other kind of environment) be of particular relevance to the emergence of advanced cognitive capabilities?

In the present section, we attempt to provide some initial answers to these questions. For the most part, we restrict our attention to the realm of learning. Obviously, there is more to being a social machine than just learning. It may be, for example, that only certain kinds of computational organization are able to fully benefit from the forms of learning detailed below. It is, in addition, at least plausible that only certain kinds of system (e.g., neural networks) are able to exhibit the kinds of fluid, context-sensitive response that are typically associated with intelligent behavior—something that is nicely captured by Clark's [5, p. 107] notion of *intrinsic suitability*. Perhaps, to extend Clark's claims about intrinsic suitability, there is only one kind of computational substructure (a connectionist-style deep learning system, perhaps) that is able to grapple with the complexity of the human social environment and yield something vaguely reminiscent of human-level intelligence. In the interests of space (and, to be honest, the limits of our own intellectual horizons), we will avoid a detailed discussion of these sorts of architectural issues (although see Section V-D for some initial thoughts in this area).

A selective focus on learning seems particularly apt given the developmentally-oriented conception of scaffolded cognition that was proposed in Section II. It is also one that accommodates the discussion in Section III concerning the role of the human social environment in scaffolding the ontogenetic and phylogenetic emergence of the human cognitive system. There is clearly a sense in which learning is perhaps somewhat better suited to accommodate ontogenetic forms of social scaffolding—the forms of scaffolding that occur during the lifetime of a single individual. But perhaps the appeal to learning can also be extended to the domain of evolutionary mechanisms. As is noted by Chalup [51], "[d]uring the time phase of evolution the structure of the genome undergoes a process of phylogenetic learning which is based on evolutionary concepts such as selection and mutation" (p. 448).

In what follows we direct our attention to the following forms of learning: social learning, active learning, language learning, predictive learning and incremental learning. The discussion of these forms of learning reveals what we take to be some of the essential features of a social machine. These include:

- **Phenotypic Plasticity:** Plasticity is clearly the *sine qua non* of a learning system. As such, this feature is relevant to all forms of learning. Issues of plasticity are particularly relevant when it comes to changes in the computational organization of a system as a result of maturational processes. These issues are discussed in the context of incremental learning (see Section V-E).
- **Active Engagement:** A recent focus of cognitive science research is the way in which learners self-structure their learning experiences and thus influence their own learning experiences. These issues are tackled in the context of research into active learning (see Section V-B).

The ensuing discussion is also intended to highlight some of the features of the human social environment that make it of particular interest as both the target of learning and as a context in which learning occurs. These features are perhaps most clearly resolved with regard to the following forms of learning:

- **Social Learning:** The human social environment serves as a source of knowledge that, at least in some cases, can be used to bypass other forms of learning. Such a vision bears a close resemblance to the apprenticeship model of human cognitive evolution, as discussed by Sterelny [52].
- **Predictive Learning:** One of the features of the human social environment is its complexity, which is determined, at least in part, by the cognitive sophistication of its human inhabitants. In negotiating the social environment, a machine learning system must learn to navigate a terrain whose topography is both complex and unstable. The attempt to gain a predictive toehold in this terrain may lead to the emergence of a representational and computational economy that profoundly alters the cognitive repertoire of a social machine.
- **Language Learning:** Finally, we suggest that in dealing with the human social environment, social machines are gifted a particularly potent cognitive tool in the form of language. Such a tool can be seen to magnify other forms of scaffolded development, open up new learning opportunities, and, perhaps most importantly, lay the foundation for profound shifts in cognitive functionality.

A. Social Learning

By virtue of the access it affords to the human social environment, the Internet provides a number of opportunities to observe and monitor different aspects of human behavior. This is important, for we humans are the locus of particular kinds of skill and expertise that reflect our experience with particular domains. Such forms of skill and expertise are typically driven by bodies of knowledge that we have acquired through extensive training and experience, much of which is itself scaffolded by the human social environment. This presents a challenge for the machine-based emulation of human cognitive competence. If human competence develops as a result of the scaffolding provided by a surrounding nexus of social and cultural resources—if, in other words, human capabilities are the products of socially-scaffolded learning experiences—then perhaps it should come as no surprise that human cognitive tasks pose something of a challenge for machine-based systems.

It is here, we suggest, that the Internet provides us with an opportunity to extend the reach of machine-based capabilities. The basic idea is that the Internet can be used as a form of *social observatory*—one that enables machines to observe the human social environment and acquire information about various forms of human competence. From this perspective, the Internet can be seen to support a particular form of *social learning*: it enables us to treat the human social environment as a source of information and knowledge that can be mined and monitored as a means of extending the cognitive and epistemic reach of machine-based systems.

All of this no doubt sounds uncomfortably vague, so let us consider a specific example—one that is admittedly hypothetical yet not so remote as to lie beyond our current technological horizons. The example concerns the effort to develop Autonomous Road Vehicles (ARVs), such as self-driving trucks and cars. ARVs obviously have a range of capabilities, and not all these capabilities are ones that need rely on social learning (at least of the sort we are discussing here). When it comes to an ability to respond to a multitude of driving-relevant situations, however, it looks likely that ARVs will need to possess some of the 'commonsense' knowledge that human drivers have acquired as a result of their experience behind the wheel. Such experience underlies our ability to anticipate the likely behavior of other road users, our ability to behave appropriately at an intersection, our ability to adjust our driving behavior given specific meteorological conditions, and so on. An experienced human driver thus embodies a wealth of knowledge and experience, at least some of which looks to be relevant to the design of autonomous vehicles.

How do we go about building vehicles that possess the behavioral competence and road-related *savoir faire* exhibited by the typical human driver? One option is to enlist the use of conventional knowledge elicitation techniques [53] in order to create formal models of the relevant body of human knowledge. The problem with this approach is that it is likely to require substantial time and effort, especially when one considers the complexity of the target domain, not to mention the diversity of driving practices exhibited by both individuals and cultural groups.

Here is another approach: track the behavior of human-driven vehicles as they move around the road network and then attempt to extract and formalize interesting regularities from the resultant body of 'experiential data'. Such data sets are likely to be particularly valuable in cases where it is possible to track the precise behavior of vehicles at particular locations, such as at an intersection, a roundabout, or a notorious black spot. Additional value comes from the ability to track other kinds of information, such as the use of driver signaling mechanisms (e.g., the use of indicators and headlights) and information about prevailing meteorological conditions (e.g., the presence of fog).

It might, of course, be suggested that human drivers are not the most suitable role models for ARVs, especially if one reflects on the popularity of *The Fast and the Furious* movie franchise. However, even if human behavior should fail to provide a suitable template for machine behavior, it may still be important to learn about such behavior as the basis for anticipating (and responding to) certain situations. This seems particularly relevant to the ARV case, where, in all likelihood, we will encounter a transitional era in which autonomous vehicles are required to share the road with human drivers. There is, in addition, no reason why we should regard the end-product of social learning as being solely about the acquisition of some form of purely behavioral competence. Social learning may thus support the acquisition of knowledge about the unwritten rules of social conduct—the culturally-specific norms, conventions, and practices that shape the dynamics of human social behavior. Social learning thus provides us with a socially- and empirically-grounded approach to what is commonly referred to as machine ethics (also known as machine morality, artificial morality, or computational ethics) [54]. In essence, the idea is to rely on the human social environment to provide insight about the unwritten 'rules' that govern behavior in different social situations. Such knowledge seems particularly important in situations where machines are required to participate in social processes or interact with human agents. Autonomous vehicles are, of course, a case in point. When it comes to the effort to develop ARVs, therefore, social learning may provide a solution to Walport's [55] worry about the need to codify "tacitly accepted 'rules of the road' norms" (p. 24).

The main point of the ARV example is that it helps us see how a particular form of (observational) access to the human social environment can provide insight into bodies of experientially-grounded knowledge, some of which may be relevant to the attempt to engineer a particular kind of intelligent system. The vision is thus one in which advanced forms of machine intelligence come about as the result of a deliberate attempt to learn from the human social environment. According to this vision, machine intelligence is, in a sense, parasitic on human experience: it relies on the experience that humans have in order to short-circuit the acquisition of particular forms of cognitive and behavioral competence, many of which may be hard to acquire via other means.

There is, of course, no reason to think that social learning is restricted to the realm of ARVs. With the advent of the IoT, an increasing number of everyday objects are poised to shed light on the nature of our embodied interactions with a plethora of everyday artifacts, perhaps providing insight into the structure of epistemic actions (see [56]) and culturally-nuanced forms of cognitive practice (see [57]). Needless to say, when it comes to considering the significance of such devices, the emphasis is typically on the way in which issues of network-enablement help or hinder *human* action. But in light of the present discussion, we can perhaps begin to ask ourselves whether there is any reason why such devices should not be used in roughly the same manner as a network-enabled automobile, i.e., as a source of information about the kinds of skill and expertise that might be required to exhibit competence in some otherwise intractable task domain. This is surely a laudable target for machine intelligence research, irrespective of whatever technical challenges confront the effort; for why assume that *a priori* methods can always yield the level of behavioral and cognitive complexity required to deal with domains where human forms of competence only seem to emerge as the result of extensive training and experience?

Based on the foregoing examples, it might be thought that the notion of social learning only applies to situations involving the real-time monitoring of human behavior, as provided, perhaps, by IoT devices. Real-time monitoring, however, is not an essential feature of social learning. What is crucial to social learning is merely the idea of the Internet providing access to information about the strategies, knowledge and experiences of human agents. There is no requirement here for real-time monitoring. Indeed, for the most part, we suspect that social learning will be undertaken with respect to previously acquired data sets, as opposed to real-time data streams. Such data sets include those that are already available. As is noted by Myaeng et al. [58], blog posts, online community services, and social media sites track the experiences and knowledge that humans have managed to distil from the environment and encode in digital form. Such resources provide the basis for what a Myaeng et al. [58] refer to as *experiential knowledge mining*, which is defined as "the process of acquiring experiential knowledge, as opposed to a priori knowledge, from a variety of multimedia sources that describe human experiences of various sorts" [58, p. 33].

From the standpoint of social learning, therefore, the human social environment serves as the target of a particular kind of knowledge acquisition. The main virtue of this vision is that it helps to expand the horizons of efforts that seek to emulate human-level competence in some domain of interest. In particular, it provides us with an alternative means of acquiring knowledge that might be difficult, costly or (perhaps) impossible to acquire via other means. Although this is clearly not the place to undertake a detailed analysis of the situations in which social learning is appropriate, we suspect that it is the nature of the target knowledge that determines the suitability of social learning approaches. In particular, we suggest that Internet-mediated social learning is perhaps best suited to the acquisition of knowledge that is tacit (i.e., difficult to verbalize), experiential (i.e., derived from experience and training), and socially-entrenched (i.e., socially-acquired and socially-manifested). The knowledge associated with the aforementioned ARV case possesses all these features. Such knowledge is, for the most part, tacit and therefore hard to express (at least in linguistic form). It is also knowledge that is acquired as a result of extensive experience and training and therefore qualifies as a form of experiential knowledge. Finally, it is a form of knowledge that is socially entrenched. This particular feature is difficult to describe in summary form, but it is perhaps most easily thought of as a form of knowledge that depends on the social environment for its acquisition or expression. When it comes to driving-related knowledge, for example, what we confront is a body of knowledge that is often tied to the interactions between individual drivers. Such knowledge is not the sort of knowledge that can be (easily) expressed independently of other social agents, and it is thus not the sort of knowledge that can be acquired (in a knowledge engineering sense, at least) without the support of a suitably rich social environment. It is this 'social' aspect that is perhaps most important when it comes to social learning. Tacit and experiential knowledge obviously present specific challenges to knowledge engineers; however, they are not beyond the reach of contemporary knowledge elicitation techniques (see [53]). Socially-entrenched knowledge is somewhat different, however, often requiring the observation and analysis of large-scale social interactions. It is in this sense, perhaps, that we can begin to understand the significance of the Internet from a knowledge engineering perspective [59]. By affording access to the human social environment, the Internet functions as a form of social observatory, enabling machines to prospect for epistemic gold in terrains that were previously beyond their reach.

B. *Active Learning*

We have seen how the Internet provides an unprecedented form of contact with the human social environment, opening up an array of opportunities for AI systems to observe and monitor human behavior. And we have seen how such forms of contact provide the basis for at least one form of machine learning. There is, however, a risk associated with this idea of the Internet functioning as a form of social observatory. The risk is that we lose sight of the way in which AI systems are able to play an active role in shaping the course of their own (socially-scaffolded) cognitive development. When we view the Internet as a form of observatory, there is a danger that we see machines as merely passive observers of the human social realm. This is, we suggest, a highly impoverished view of the learning opportunities made available by the Internet.

There is, however, no reason why we should restrict ourselves to this purely passive view of machine learning. There are a number of ways in which AI systems can play a more active role in socially-mediated learning processes. One example of this comes from studies into so-called citizen science systems [47]. One of the challenges confronting such systems is the need to ensure the continued engagement of the human community in the face of the human proclivity for boredom and distraction. A number of studies have attempted to address this problem by developing statistical models that predict the likelihood of user disengagement [60], and such models can be used to implement an array of intervention strategies that seek to sustain human interest [61][62]. As noted by Mao et al. [60]:

> The ability to predict forthcoming disengagement of individual workers would allow systems to make targeted interventions, such as providing especially interesting tasks to workers at risk of becoming bored, directing support to struggling new workers, helping with the timing of special auxiliary materials or rewards, and encouraging workers to return in the long run. (p. 1)

Needless to say, the ability to maintain user interest in a task is a relatively weak example of a machine playing an active role in socially-mediated learning. A better example comes from research into what is called *active learning* [63][64]. Active learning is a form of machine learning in which a machine learning system exerts some control over the learning process, actively structuring its training experiences in a manner that yields the best learning outcome. Such forms of control have been shown to yield a number of benefits. For example, active learning has been shown to improve the efficiency of the learning process by reducing the number of training examples that are required to reach near-optimal levels of performance on an image processing task [65].

For the most part, active learning involves the adaptive selection and sequencing of specific training experiences. In the context of an image processing task, for example, an active learning system may decide what images will be the focus of learning efforts, as well as the order in which the images will be processed. Such decisions are typically informed by routines that estimate the optimality of different response options relative to the system's current state, previous learning experiences, and overall learning objectives. In this sense, active learning systems can be seen to implement something akin to a 'metacognitive' ability, with one form of 'cognitive' processing (i.e., that associated with optimality assessments) influencing the behavior of other parts of the cognitive economy (e.g., the shape of specific learning routines).

A good example of active learning in an Internet context is provided by Barrington et al. [66]. Barrington et al. describe the use of an online game, called Herd It, in which groups of human individuals are required to annotate a musical resource with descriptive tags. These annotations are used to train a supervised machine learning system that ultimately aims to perform the annotation task independently of the human agents. All of this is broadly in line with the general shape of machine learning; but what makes Barrington et al.'s system of particular interest is the way in which the machine shapes the course of its own learning by actively selecting the resources to be annotated by human players. This is important, because it gives the machine an opportunity to select those forms of feedback that are likely to be of greatest value relative to its subsequent 'cognitive' development. In the words of Barrington et al. [66], "the machine learning system actively directs the annotation games to collect new data that will most benefit future model iterations" (p. 6411).

A consideration of active learning thus expands our understanding of the forms of contact that the Internet provides with the human social environment. Rather than seeing the Internet solely as a form of social observatory—one that permits a largely passive form of observational contact with humanity—we can now entertain a more active (and interactive) view of the Internet. On this view, the Internet provides machines with an opportunity to influence human behavior, altering the nature of the information flows that underpin the emergence of specific forms of cognitive proficiency.

C. Language Learning

The advent of the Internet (and especially the Web) has led to a burgeoning of research interest into all things linguistic. Such interest is evidenced by research into Natural Language Processing (NLP) (e.g., [67]), information extraction [68], and sentiment analysis [69]. Other research efforts aim to develop various forms of language-enabled agents, i.e., computational agents that are able to exhibit proficiency in the use of natural language expressions. Work in this area includes research into so-called social bots [70], chatbots [71] and conversational agents [72].

The reason for this renewed interest in language-related technologies is, at least in part, due to the wealth of linguistic content that is available in the online realm. Such content provides us with a substantive body of linguistic data that can be used to inform large-scale analytic efforts. It should also be clear that the Internet has transformed the incentives that drive research and development in this area—consider, for example, the use of Twitter feeds as a means of predicting (and perhaps influencing!) the outcome of political elections [73]. The upshot is that language learning has become an important focus of attention for the machine learning community.

How does this renewed interest in linguistic analysis impact the present discussion on machine intelligence? The most obvious answer to this question is that machines will become increasingly proficient in understanding human language, and as a result of this understanding, they will be better placed to exploit our linguaform contributions to the online realm (e.g., they will have an improved ability to distil information and knowledge from resources such as Wikipedia, Twitter, Facebook and so on). It should also be clear that enhancements in linguistic proficiency often go hand-in-hand with improvements in communicative ability. There can be little doubt that such communicative abilities play an important role in extending the cognitive reach of an agent community. Indeed, we might be inclined to view communication as a form of networking capability that enables agents to 'connect' with an array of cognitively-potent resources. This applies as much to human agents as it does to their synthetic counterparts. As noted by Merlin Donald [74], when it comes to human language, "[i]ndividuals in possession of reading, writing, and other visuographic skills...become somewhat like computers with networking capabilities; they are equipped to interface, to plug into whatever network becomes available" (p. 311). Linguistic competence can therefore be seen to work in concert with other forms of scaffolded development, enabling machines to distil knowledge from online textual sources and providing the basis for communicative exchanges with human agents. Such capacities are likely to be of crucial importance when it comes to the social scaffolding of machine intelligence.

Communication is no doubt important when it comes to the ability of machines to press maximal cognitive benefit from the human social environment. But there are other ways to think about the cognitive significance of language. Of particular interest is what is sometimes called the supracommunicative view of language function [75][76]. The general idea, in this case, is that language plays a role in enhancing, transforming, or otherwise altering the cognitive capabilities of the language-wielding agent. There are a number of ways of unpacking this claim; for present purposes, however, we will limit our attention to three (not altogether distinct) manifestations of the supracommunicative view. These are the transformative, the augmentative and the configurative/programmatic views.

The transformative view derives from the work of the philosopher, Daniel Dennett [77]. Dennett suggests that our ontogenetic immersion in a linguistic environment contributes to an effective reorganization of the human cognitive economy, yielding a shift from parallel processing into something that more closely resembles the information processing profile of a conventional (symbol-manipulating) computational machine. Interestingly, Dennett proposes that some of the most distinctive features of human cognition (including human consciousness) emerge as a result of our attempts to get to grips with the linguistic domain. Inasmuch as we accept these claims, it should be clear that a simple communicative view of language is unlikely to do justice to the potential impact of the Internet on future forms of machine intelligence: By immersing intelligent systems in a linguistically-rich environment, and by forcing such systems to assimilate linguaform representations deep into their cognitive processing routines, we potentially endow machines with the sorts of abilities and insights that only us language-wielding human agents are able to grasp.

Another take on the cognitive role of language comes in the form of the augmentative view. The most vocal proponent of this view is Andy Clark [75][76][78]. Clark see language as a particularly potent form of socially-derived cognitive scaffolding that performs a variety of cognition-enhancing roles:

> Embodied agents encounter language first and foremost as new layers of material structure in an already complex world. They also come to produce such structures for themselves, not just for communicative effect but as parts of self-stimulating cycles that scaffold their own behaviour. These layers of structure play a variety of cognition-enhancing roles. They act as new, perceptually simple targets that augment the learning environment, they mediate recall and help distribute attention, they provide a key resource for freezing and inspecting complex thoughts and ideas, and they seem fit to participate in truly hybrid representational ensembles. All these benefits are available both 'online' (in the presence of written words on a page, or sounds in the air) and then 'offline' (thanks to covert self-stimulating cycles that engage much of the same machinery used in the ecologically primary case). [79, p. 373]

Empirical support for the augmentative view comes from a variety of quarters [39][80][81]. In studies with human subjects, language has been shown to play a productive role in category learning [39][81], and such effects have also been observed in computer simulations, with linguistic labels supporting category learning in artificial neural networks [82][83]. Exposure to a linguistic environment also appears to bolster the cognitive performance of certain non-human animal species, such as chimpanzees [84] and parrots [85]. Although these studies are often seen as failures from a language learning perspective (no one doubts, for instance, that the animals in these studies failed to acquire human-level language abilities), the studies are nevertheless remarkable in demonstrating that even minimal forms of linguistic competence are able to augment the cognitive profile of such animals, and they do so in ways that are reminiscent of human-level cognitive achievements [84].

A final way to unpack the supracommuncative view of language is to emphasize the way in which language can be used to configure and control a set of cognitively-relevant resources. This is what we will call the configurative/programmatic view of language. Perhaps the most explicit expression of the idea behind this view is provided by Lupyan and Bergen [81]. They see language as a tool or control system that can be used to 'program' the mind. In the case of human minds, for example, Lupyan and Bergen [81] highlight the ways in which linguistic stimuli can be used to shape aspects of the human cognitive economy, presumably by altering the dynamics of neural processing. Exposure to linguistic stimuli has thus been shown to alter certain forms of perceptual processing, boosting the extent to which previously unseen objects enter visual awareness [86]. Linguistic cues can also be used to activate and reactivate certain forms of mental content. The activation of visual images, for example, typically depends on visual input. With language, however, we are able to exert control over our imaginative faculties. A mental image of the Colosseum, for example, can be evoked simply by exposing our minds to the word "Colosseum" (see [39]).

To some extent the configurative/programmatic view bears much in common with the transformative and augmentative views of language. Clark, for example, has often appealed to the idea of language as a tool that helps to tame the restive information processing dynamics of the biological brain. "Encounters with words and with structured linguistic encodings," he suggests, "act so as to anchor and discipline intrinsically fluid and context-sensitive modes of thought and reason" [87, p. 263]. A key difference between the augmentative and configurative/programmatic views emerges in respect of the nature of the resources that are controlled by linguistic stimuli. In the case of the configurative/programmatic view, it is not just our own minds that are controlled via language, it is also the minds of others. And in shaping the minds of others, we are able to exert some degree of control over the social environment:

> We can sculpt the minds of others into arbitrary configurations through a set of instructions, without having to go through laborious trial-and-error learning. We can cause someone to imagine something, to recall a memory, to do (or not do) something. [81, p. 409]

The result is a view of language as a form of generic control system, one that can be used to configure (and thereby shape the behavior of) a variety of disparate resources. When applied to the social domain, the configurative/programmatic view helps us see language as on a par with physical action, in that it can be used to intervene in the social environment (just as physical actions can be used to alter the structure of the physical environment). This is an image that dovetails with the earlier discussion of active learning (see Section V-B). For in using language to manipulate the minds of others, there can be little doubt that we are in possession of a tool for structuring the nature of our contact with the human social world. In this sense, language affords a degree of control over socially-scaffolded forms of development.

The communicative, transformative, augmentative and configurative/programmatic views thus provide us with a complex picture of the cognitive impact of language. In directing their learning efforts to the linguistic realm, machines are potentially poised to exploit some of the cognitive virtues of language. Such virtues are perhaps most easily understood with respect to the augmentative and transformative views; however, in developing linguistic competence, we should not forget that language also influences the nature of the cognitive contact that machines have with the human social environment, opening up new arenas for scaffolded development (the communicative view) and providing new opportunities for machines to shape the structure of their learning experiences. Inasmuch as we aspire to build machines that emulate the performance profile of the human cognitive system, language learning thus looks to be of crucial importance. It may indeed be the case that human-level cognizing is inextricably linked to language, and that an ability to emulate human cognition is predicated on an ability to negotiate the linguistic domain. Something along these lines is, in fact, suggested by Mirolli and Parisi [39]. Commenting on the role of language in the development of robotic systems, they suggest that it "may be impossible to develop a human-like cognitive robotics without endowing robots with the capacity of using language for themselves as humans do" (p. 301).

D. Predictive Learning

According to an increasingly popular theory in theoretical neuroscience, the biological brain is a hierarchically-organized system in which higher-level neural regions are engaged in a continuous effort to the predict the activity of lower-level neural regions [88][89]. This model—which we will dub the predictive processing model—has proved attractive for a variety of reasons. For example, it provides an explanation for reciprocal connectivity between anatomical brain regions, and it also promises a unified account of perception, action and cognition [89][90]. The model has also proved attractive with respect to the recent efflorescence of research into deep learning [91]. Deep learning systems thus incorporate some of the features of the predictive processing model, and this may account for their superior performance in a number of task domains.

The kind of learning implemented by the predictive processing model of brain function is perhaps best characterized as *predictive learning*. It is a form of learning in which higher-levels of the predictive processing hierarchy seek to predict the activity of lower levels. In the brain, this learning is assumed to be driven by prediction error, reflecting the mismatch between predicted and actual patterns of brain activity. In essence, the goal of predictive learning is to minimize the global prediction error that is generated by the biological brain as part of its attempt to predict what is in effect its own activity. Given that such activity is ultimately tied to the external environment (via the receipt of sensory information), predictive learning leads to structural changes that reflect the brain's attempt to secure a predictive grasp of the environment in which it is embedded. This is important, for it is believed that one of the outcomes of predictive learning is the establishment of a generative model that reflects the causal structure of the local learning environment. "A generative model," Clark [89] suggests, "...aims to capture the statistical structure of some set of observed inputs by inferring a causal matrix able to give rise to that very structure" (p. 41). It is in this sense that predictive learning is sometimes seen to yield models that embody the causal structure of mechanisms that give rise to bodies of sensory information:

> In brief, biological systems can distil structural regularities from environmental fluctuations (like changing concentrations of chemical attractants or sensory signals) and embody them in their form and internal dynamics. In essence, they become models of causal structure in their local environment, enabling them to predict what will happen next and counter surprising violations of those predictions. [92, p. 2101]

It is here that we begin to creep up on a novel, albeit contentious, proposal regarding the role of the Internet in supporting the emergence of advanced forms of machine intelligence. In short, the idea is that in the attempt to form a generative model of data that derives from the human social environment, a hierarchically-organized predictive processing system may come to acquire a 'deep understanding' of human behavior at both the individual and collective (social) levels. This 'deep understanding' is reflected in the way in which a predictive processing system comes to embody the causal structure of the social domain. A generative model of the human social environment can thus be seen to lead to a deep understanding of the causal processes that govern the shape of human behavior, just as the operation of brain-based predictive processing regimes are deemed to yield a deep understanding of the causal processes that govern the structure of incoming sensory information [90]. A good probabilistic generative model for individual human behavior (or larger-scale patterns of social flux) would therefore seek to capture the ways that patterns of human behavior are generated by an inferred nexus of interacting distal causes.

This idea is suggestive, for it may help to shed light on the mechanisms that underlie various forms of social intelligence. When it comes to the realms of individual human behavior, for example, the notion of acquired generative models may help us understand the basis for folk psychological characterizations of the behavior of both ourselves and others. Our conventional approach to explaining human behavior in terms of beliefs, hopes, fears, desires and dreams may thus reflect nothing more than our attempt to gain a predictively- and explanatory-potent toehold on the social realm, with human psychological states being ascribed to individual agents as part of the brain's attempt to make sense of complex bodies of social data. Such a view may provide insight into some of the most mysterious elements of our mental lives, including that ever-elusive phenomenon we call conscious experience. Perhaps, for example, we are aware of ourselves as psychological agents precisely because we model our own behavior in the way we model others. If true, the result is a view of human consciousness that appeals to the way in which the shape of our own mental lives owes much to the structure of the social environment in which we are embedded. In essence, the idea is that we should understand human consciousness as a form of socially-scaffolded cognition.

Echoes of this sort of view can, in fact, be found in the works of Lev Vygotsky, one of the pioneers of scaffolded cognition research:

> The mechanism of social behavior and the mechanism of consciousness are the same. We are aware of ourselves in that we are aware of others; and in an analogous manner, we are aware of others because in our relationship to ourselves we are the same as others in their relationship to us. [93, p. 29]

The view is also evident in work of a more recent nature. Graziano and Kastner [94], for example, describe a theoretical account of self-awareness that is rooted in an appeal to socially-oriented predictive processes:

> In the present hypothesis, the human brain evolved mechanisms for social perception, a type of perception that allows for predictive modeling of the behavior of complex, brain-controlled agents. There is no assumption here about whether perception of others or perception of oneself emerged first. Presumably they evolved at the same time. Whether social perception is applied to oneself or to someone else, it serves the adaptive function of a prediction engine for human behavior. [94, p. 109]

Inasmuch as such accounts provide insight into the forces and factors that give rise to human conscious experience, they may help to reveal the significance of socially-oriented predictive learning to the creation of conscious machines.

This is, to be sure, a grand claim, and no doubt many issues need to be resolved before the idea can be taken seriously. One of these relates to the nature of the informational contact that machines have with the human social environment. Do the digital traces provided by the online realm provide us with a sufficiently rich and detailed representation of the dynamical profile of human behavior, one that is apt to yield (via predictive learning) a generative model that traces the causal contours of human behavior at both the individual and collective levels? The answer to this question is unclear at the present time, although it should be noted that the Internet plays an increasingly important role in a variety of human activities, and it is thus poised to provide ever-more detailed insights into the shape of human behavior. Crucially, the success of some predictive analytics platforms already attests to the predictive potential of at least some forms of online data. New predictive apps, such as Google Now, for example, are able to make predictions based on the analysis of various data sources, and they do so in a way that is sometimes seen to belie an uncanny knowledge of their user base.

This is not to say that the view of the human social environment as provided by the Internet will be exactly the same as that enjoyed by a human individual. There are clearly important differences in the kind of information that is accessible to an online machine learner as opposed to the information that is made available to a human observer of the social realm. It is not clear, however, that such differences should always be seen as placing machine-based systems at a disadvantage. Consider, for instance, the way in which the Internet affords a panoptic view of social processes that operate at a variety of social scales (e.g., at the level of teams, groups, organizations, communities and societies). The application of predictive learning to such bodies of social data may give rise to generative models that embody the causal structure of social mechanisms (i.e., the mechanisms that govern the behavior of social systems). In essence, we suggest that in the attempt to secure a predictive grasp on bodies of social data, a machine learning system could be forced to approach a social system in much the same way that it approaches an individual human agent, yielding a generative model that captures some of the hidden causal forces that operate (perhaps) exclusively at the social or societal level. The result is a rather unique vision of machine intelligence. It is a vision in which social systems are themselves perceived as psychologically-rich and complex entities. And it is a vision in which the goal of learning is to make sense of the social world—to develop a deep understanding of the various forces and factors that govern the flux of social data. A social machine, it seems, is not just a machine that is situated or embedded within society (although that is indeed the case). Neither is it simply a machine whose 'mind' is, in some sense, a product of society (although that it is also true). A social machine is a machine that is, we suggest, poised to develop a novel kind of mind, a mind that is specifically oriented to the social realm—a mind of society.

Some insight into the potential value of socially-oriented predictive learning is provided by recent studies using deep learning techniques. One such study is described by Phan et al. [95]. They used a combination of computational ontologies and deep learning techniques to yield a system that generated predictions of individual human behavior in the health domain. What is interesting about this study is that by incorporating structured representations of domain-specific knowledge (in the form of ontologies) into the learning regime, the resultant system was able to not only predict human behavior, but also generate explanations for such behavior. Such results, Phan et al. [95] suggest, indicate a "deep understanding of...human behavior determinants" (p. 311).

Another interesting application of deep learning techniques concerns the attempt by Vondrick et al. [96] to predict human action sequences from video images. This study is of particular interest because the training corpus for the deep learning system consisted of 600 hours of unlabeled video downloaded from the YouTube website. Vondrick et al.'s study thus exemplifies one of the ways in which the Internet/Web provides a form of informational access to the human social environment in a manner that can be used to support the development of predictive capabilities. YouTube videos are, of course, uploaded by human users, and they do not always afford an unfiltered insight into what we might call ecologically-normal patterns of human behavior. The step from YouTube to more direct and real-time observational data streams is, however, a short one. There is no reason, for example, why the approach of Vondrick et al. [96] could not be applied to the data provided by Internet-enabled video recording devices, such as webcams and CCTV devices.

Finally, consider a study by Lv et al. [97] involving the use of deep learning methods for the purposes of traffic flow prediction. This study is interesting for a variety of reasons. Firstly, Lv et al. remind us of the wealth and diversity of information that can be used for predictive purposes. This includes information from "inductive loops, radars, cameras, mobile Global Positioning System, crowd sourcing, social media, etc." (p. 865). A second point of interest concerns the focus of Lv et al.'s study, which is nicely aligned with the earlier discussion of social learning (recall the discussion of the ARV case in Section V-A). This is a useful reminder that one form of learning (e.g., predictive learning) can be used to support other forms of learning (e.g., social learning). Finally, note that the target of Lv et al.'s [97] study is a 'collective system' comprised of multiple elements (i.e., vehicles), each of which is controlled by a human agent. This is, as such, a nice example of the attempt to model the behavioral profile of a particular form of 'social system'. In this respect, Lv et al.'s study provides some insight into the sorts of approaches that might be relevant to the acquisition of socially-oriented generative models.

E. Incremental Learning

The notion of socially-scaffolded cognition encourages us to take a developmental perspective with respect to machine intelligence. In particular, we are encouraged to see machine-based cognitive capabilities as emerging from a developmental matrix that includes (among other things) the human social environment. In considering the opportunities for socially-scaffolded development, however, it is easy to overlook the fact that the cognitive wherewithal of human infants is not the same as their adult counterparts. It is here that we encounter a productive point of contact with work that shows how maturational shifts in cognitive, sensory and motor capabilities may be of crucial relevance to the emergence of advanced forms of cognitive competence [98]–[103].

The idea that 'immaturity' may be of adaptive value with regard to the ontogenetic emergence of certain capabilities was first discussed by Turkewitz and Kenny [104]. According to their hypothesis, immaturity alters the kind of information a learning system can process, thereby altering what is sometimes called the 'effective' structure of the learning environment. During the initial stages of development, the complexity of the learning environment is reduced as a result of the relative immaturity of sensorimotor systems. As development proceeds, however, maturational processes lead to the progressive attenuation of initial processing constraints, limitations, and biases, and this, in turn, leads to an increase in the complexity of the training data. When all of this is applied to the cognitive domain, the result is a proposal regarding the role of maturational parameters in the acquisition of advanced forms of cognitive competence. According to this proposal, various forms of 'immaturity' may be of crucial significance when it comes to a cognitive system's ability to achieve the sorts of cognitive success that mark the end of the developmental process.

What are the implications of this proposal for socially-scaffolded forms of machine intelligence? Perhaps the best answer to this question comes from research into a specific form of machine learning, known as *incremental learning* [51]. Incremental learning, as defined by Kirby and Hurford [105], is:

> ...the idea of some learning-related resource starting at a low value, which then gradually increases while (but not necessarily because) the organism matures. Also essential to incremental learning is the proposition that the initial low (immature) value of the resource actually facilitates, or even enables, the early stages

> of learning. Later stages of learning are in turn facilitated, or enabled, by higher-valued settings of the resource concerned. [105, p. 4]

Some insight into the potential importance of incremental learning is revealed by a classic study by Jeffrey Elman [99]. Elman sought to determine whether a particular kind of artificial neural network, called a recurrent neural network, could acquire a form of grammatical competence characterized by an ability to learn about verb agreement and clause embedding in sentences such as: "The girls who the teacher has picked for the play which will be produced next month practice every afternoon" [99, p. 4]. As part of the training regime, the sentences were presented to the network one word at a time, and the main objective of the network was to predict the next word in the sentence. As Elman [99] notes, this task "forces the network to develop internal representations which encode the relevant grammatical information" (p.5).

Unfortunately, Elman's initial attempts to get the network to learn about grammatical structure were in vain. Not only did the network fail to develop a fully generalizable performance profile, it also failed to adequately master the data on which it was trained. As part of the effort to account for these results, Elman deployed an alternative training regime, one in which the network was initially presented with examples of very simple sentences and then progressively exposed to the more complex ones. The aim was to isolate the precise point at which the network's performance broke down—at what level of sentential complexity would the network prove to be incapable of making further progress?

The results of this alternative training regime were surprising. Elman discovered that when presented with staged training inputs (each increasing in complexity) the network was able to realize its original training objectives. Indeed, what seemed to be important to the network's ultimate ability to learn about grammatically complex sentences was that its training regime was structured in such a way that it was able to learn about the simple cases first. Once the network was proficient in handling these simple cases, it was then able to deal with the more complex cases. It was almost as if the network's success with the simple cases laid the foundation for subsequent success in dealing with the more complex cases.

Moving on from this result, Elman explored the effect of a further manipulation. In this case, rather than impose restrictions on the sequential complexity of the training inputs, Elman used an incremental memory solution in which the recurrent feedback (provided by a layer of context units) was gradually increased as training progressed. The effect of this manipulation was to limit the temporal window in which linguistic inputs could be processed, thereby forcing the network to focus (at least initially) on the simplest training cases. Then, as the memory provided by the recurrent units was increased over the course of training, the network was able to deal with progressively more complex inputs. The effect of the incremental memory solution was thus the same as that achieved by the staged input training case: it promoted an initial under-sampling of the training data in such a way that the network's long-term ability to learn about complex grammatical regularities was enhanced.

As Elman notes, this is an important discovery, because it may help to shed light on the functional significance of a developmental progression in neurocognitive resources. Thus, rather than see the working memory limitations of young children as a computational shortcoming that needs to be overcome in order to reveal the functional profile of adult cognition, Elman's findings suggest that immature cognitive capabilities may play an important (and perhaps indispensable) role in enabling young infant minds to acquire adult forms of linguistic competence. Commenting on the role of memory limitations in language learning, Elman states that:

> ...the early limitations on memory capacity assume a more positive character. One might have predicted that the more powerful the network, the greater its ability to learn a complex domain. However, this appears not always to be the case. If the domain is of sufficient complexity, and if there are abundant false solutions, then the opportunities for failure are great. What is required is some way to artificially constrain the solution space to just that region which contains the true solution. The initial memory limitations fulfil this role; they act as a filter on the input, and focus learning on just that subset of facts which lay the foundation for future success. [99, p. 9–10]

Here, then, is one example where a form of limited or restricted processing may help an agent achieve success in what could otherwise prove to be an intractable problem domain. By imposing a set of constraints on the kinds of information structures that can be processed, maturational processes can be seen to support the progressive reshaping of the effective structure of the linguistic environment, or at least the nature of the language learning task that confronts the learning system. Perhaps this insight goes some way toward understanding the problems that adult humans often experience in learning a second language [106][107]. In learning a new language, it might be thought that adults are in a much better position than young infants. And, at least during the early stages of language learning, adults do indeed appear to make more progress [100]. Their early successes, however, appear to come at a substantial cost: as time passes, the young infants quickly overtake the adult learners and rapidly become proficient in the target language. In this case, the early constraints in cognitive processing seem to be playing a productive role in enabling the human infant to approach the language learning task in the most effective manner.

Language is not the only domain where developmentally-significant alterations in maturational parameters have been studied in a machine learning context. An important source of information regarding the functional role of early limitations in the development of advanced cognitive and behavioral capabilities comes from recent work in developmental and evolutionary robotics [98][102]. Gómez et al. [98], for example, describe an intriguing set of results pertaining to the development of sensorimotor capabilities in a real-world robotic system. They report that a developmental profile characterized by progressive increments in the complexity of sensory, motor and neurocomputational subsystems results in a profile of task performance that is superior to that of a robot in which the relevant maturational processes are disabled. Commenting on this developmentally-grounded dissociation in 'adult' performance profiles, they suggest that:

> ...rather than being a problem, early morphological and cognitive limitations effectively decrease the

> amount of information that infants have to deal with, and may lead to an increase in the overall adaptivity of the organism. [98, p. 119]

More recent studies, again using real-world robots, have extended these results to the domain of social cognition. Nagai et al. [108] thus demonstrate that gradual increments in the spatiotemporal resolution of a robot's visual system enables it to discriminate between actions that are generated by itself and other agents. Immature vision, Nagai et al. [108] suggest, helps to shape the early perceptual environment of a system in such a way as to support the subsequent emergence of socially-relevant capabilities, such as the ability to discriminate the 'self' from others and engage in imitative behavior.

The general lesson to emerge from research on incremental learning is that early limitations in one or more parameters of a cognitive system (human or machine) may play a productive role in enabling that system to deal with the challenges of a complex (and perhaps otherwise intractable) problem domain. This seems to be of particular importance when it comes to the sorts of challenges faced by socially-situated machines. For such systems must learn to negotiate a highly complex domain, characterized by linguistic expressions and digital traces of human behavior. In tackling such domains, it may be necessary to recapitulate some of the maturational processes that operate in the case of human cognitive development. We have already seen how this sort of idea might be applied to the realm of language learning—recall the work by Elman [99]—and extensions of this work may be relevant to the attempt to furnish machines with more advanced natural language processing abilities (see Section V-C). Incremental learning may also be important when it comes to the attempt to develop predictive models of human behavior (see Section V-D) or the attempt to press maximal cognitive benefit from various forms of social learning (see Section V-A). In all these cases, the target domain concerns some aspect of human behavior, and the objective of the learner is to achieve the sort of competence that enables them to navigate, explore and negotiate the complexities of the human social world. In the human case, it looks likely that issues of development and maturation play a potentially crucial role in enabling infant minds to develop into fully-fledged adult cognizers. Inasmuch as this is true, is there any reason to think that AI systems will be able to bypass a stage of relative cognitive immaturity? One of the goals of AI is to implement systems that exhibit the capabilities characteristic of human *adults*. But inasmuch as human cognitive capabilities emerge as the result of maturation and socially-scaffolded development, is there any reason to think that AI systems can forgo the equivalent of a larval stage and proceed directly to the end-stage of the cognitive developmental process? Such an assumption looks to be particularly precarious if we accept that the human social environment forms part of a complex developmental system that drives human forms of mental metamorphosis.

VI. Conclusion and Future Work

There are good reasons to think that our status as social animals and our embedding within a social environment are of crucial importance when it comes to understanding the distinctive features of the human cognitive system. This is the case, irrespective of whether our attention is focused on issues of phylogeny or ontogeny. From a phylogenetic perspective, the human mind may have evolved to deal with the challenges and demands of a social environment whose complexity and variability increased across the course of human evolution. Similarly, from an ontogenetic perspective, it seems that the human social environment may have played a crucial role in shaping the course of cognitive development, enabling a cognitively altricial human infant to emerge as one of Planet Earth's most precocious cognizers. This is, to be sure, a compelling image. It is an image in which the human mind is viewed as a product of the human social environment, a device of our own creation, a socially-manufactured cognitive machine.

But it is not just our view of human intelligence that stands to be transformed by this image; it is also our view of machine intelligence. For inasmuch as we strive to build AI systems in our own cognitive image—as machines that emulate our own, species-specific form of intelligence—then it is surely worth considering the extent to which the human social environment is poised to play a productive role in yielding the next generation of intelligent machines.

This is the idea that we have attempted to develop in the present paper. Our claim is that the Internet provides an unprecedented form of informational contact with the human social environment, and that this contact occurs at multiple levels of social organization, from individual human agents through to teams, groups, communities, and societies. By virtue of this contact, the Internet enables AI systems to be the beneficiaries of various forms of socially-scaffolded cognitive development. In short, we suggest that the Internet provides opportunities for the implementation of what we called social machines, i.e., machines that are able to benefit (in a cognitive sense) from their contact with humanity. Thus construed, a social machine is similar to a socially-situated robot [38][41]. The main difference is that a social machine operates in the online realm, and the limits of its social ecology are thus co-extensive with the social reach of the Internet.

Needless to say, there are various ways in which the present work could be extended (an no doubt improved). One area for future work concerns the kinds of systems that are able to benefit from their contact with the human social environment. In particular, it is unclear whether a particular kind of computational substructure—such as a hierarchically-organized predictive processing economy—is a prerequisite for human-like forms of cognitive competence. In addition to research into machine learning, therefore, future work should aim to consider the kinds of cognitive architecture that may be required to support socially-scaffolded development.

Another area of interest concerns the relevance of additional forms of learning. In addition to the forms of learning discussed in the present paper (i.e., social, active, language, predictive, and incremental learning), it may be important to consider learning mechanisms that bias, direct or promote interest in the social environment. It seems likely that an ability to benefit from social-scaffolding, and indeed the status of a system as a socially-situated agent, may depend on the sensitization of reward mechanisms to social feedback, or the implementation of motivational mechanisms that encourage or enable socially-oriented forms of learning. In this respect, it may be useful to consider work relating to reinforcement learning, intrinsic motivation and curiosity-driven learning [109]–[111]. There is, of course, no reason why these forms of learning (as well as those discussed in the present paper) should be studied independently, and there is likely to be considerable merit in combining different forms of learning within a single system.

A further area of work relates to the application of the present approach to other kinds of cognition. For the most part, we have limited our attention to scaffolded cognition. In future work, it may be useful to extend this analysis to other cognitive kinds, such as extended, embedded, and embodied cognition. (See Smart [11][112] for some initial steps in this direction.)

The cognitive significance of the Internet is typically judged relative to its impacts on human cognition [113][114]. This is, of course, understandable. It is natural for us to wonder (and sometimes worry) about the implications of the Internet for our species, especially when it comes to its effects on our cognitive capabilities. For such capabilities are the hallmark of humanity: it is our cognitive profile that sets us apart from other forms of terrestrial life, and it is such capabilities that enable us (and only us) to actively shape the course of our cognitive destiny—to engineer something like the Internet and then worry about its cognitive consequences. But the cognitive implications of the Internet do not end at the borders of the human mind. In creating the Internet, our species has established a new kind of informational ecology, one that opens up new opportunities for research into machine intelligence. In the present paper, we have focused on one particular opportunity. We have suggested that the Internet provides an unprecedented form of informational contact with the human social environment, enabling machines to exploit opportunities for socially scaffolded cognitive development. It is through such forms of contact, perhaps, that we will witness the emergence of a new kind of cognitive machine, a machine whose mind is as much a product of society as are the human minds it seeks to emulate.

ACKNOWLEDGMENT

This work is supported under SOCIAM: The Theory and Practice of Social Machines. The SOCIAM Project is funded by the UK Engineering and Physical Sciences Research Council (EPSRC) under grant number EP/J017728/1 and comprises the Universities of Southampton, Oxford and Edinburgh.

REFERENCES

[1] P. R. Smart, "Machine intelligence and the social web: How to get a cognitive upgrade," in *9th International Conference on Advanced Cognitive Technologies and Applications (COGNITIVE'17)*, V. Gripon, O. Chernavskaya, P. R. Smart, and T. T. Primo, Eds. Athens, Greece: International Academy, Research, and Industry Association (IARIA), 2017, pp. 96–103.

[2] J. Sutton, "Scaffolding memory: Themes, taxonomies, puzzles," in *Contextualizing Human Memory*, C. Stone and L. Bietti, Eds. New York, New York, USA: Routledge, 2016.

[3] K. Sterelny, "Minds: Extended or scaffolded?" *Phenomenology and the Cognitive Sciences*, vol. 9, no. 4, pp. 465–481, 2010.

[4] A. Clark and D. Chalmers, "The extended mind," *Analysis*, vol. 58, no. 1, pp. 7–19, 1998.

[5] A. Clark, *Supersizing the Mind: Embodiment, Action, and Cognitive Extension*. New York, New York, USA: Oxford University Press, 2008.

[6] R. Menary, Ed., *The Extended Mind*. Cambridge, Massachusetts, USA: MIT Press, 2010.

[7] R. D. Rupert, "Challenges to the hypothesis of extended cognition," *Journal of Philosophy*, vol. 101, no. 8, pp. 389–428, 2004.

[8] P. Robbins and M. Aydede, Eds., *The Cambridge Handbook of Situated Cognition*. New York, New York, USA: Cambridge University Press, 2009.

[9] E. Hutchins, *Cognition in the Wild*. Cambridge, Massachusetts, USA: MIT Press, 1995.

[10] L. A. Shapiro, Ed., *The Routledge Handbook of Embodied Cognition*. New York, New York, USA: Routledge, 2014.

[11] P. R. Smart, "Situating machine intelligence within the cognitive ecology of the Internet," *Minds and Machines*, vol. 27, no. 2, pp. 357–380, 2017.

[12] A. Clark, *Being There: Putting Brain, Body and World Together Again*. Cambridge, Massachusetts, USA: MIT Press, 1997.

[13] E. Arnau, S. Ayala, and T. Sturm, "Cognitive externalism meets bounded rationality," *Philosophical Psychology*, vol. 27, no. 1, pp. 50–64, 2014.

[14] C. Craver, "Constitutive explanatory relevance," *Journal of Philosophical Research*, vol. 32, pp. 3–20, 2007.

[15] P. Ylikoski, "Causal and constitutive explanation compared," *Erkenntnis*, vol. 78, no. 2, pp. 277–297, 2013.

[16] S. O. Palermos, "Loops, constitution, and cognitive extension," *Cognitive Systems Research*, vol. 27, pp. 25–41, 2014.

[17] C. F. Craver and L. Darden, *In Search of Mechanisms: Discoveries Across the Life Sciences*. Chicago, Illinois, USA: The University of Chicago Press, 2013.

[18] D. M. Kaplan, "How to demarcate the boundaries of cognition," *Biology & Philosophy*, vol. 27, no. 4, pp. 545–570, 2012.

[19] V.-P. Parkkinen, "Developmental explanation," in *New Directions in the Philosophy of Science*, M. C. Galavotti, D. Dieks, W. J. Gonzalez, S. Hartmann, T. Uebel, and M. Weber, Eds. London, UK: Springer, 2014.

[20] D. Little, "Disaggregating historical explanation: The move to social mechanisms," in *The Routledge Handbook of Mechanisms and Mechanical Philosophy*, S. Glennan and P. M. Illari, Eds. New York, New York, USA: Routledge, 2018.

[21] A. C. Love, "Developmental mechanisms," in *The Routledge Handbook of Mechanisms and Mechanical Philosophy*, S. Glennan and P. M. Illari, Eds. New York, New York, USA: Routledge, 2018.

[22] R. I. M. Dunbar, "The social brain hypothesis," *Evolutionary Anthropology*, vol. 6, no. 5, pp. 178–190, 1998.

[23] R. W. Byrne and A. Whiten, *Machiavellian Intelligence: Social Expertise and the Evolution of Intellect in Monkeys, Apes, and Humans*. Oxford, UK: Oxford University Press, 1988.

[24] E. Herrmann, J. Call, M. V. Hernández-Lloreda, B. Hare, and M. Tomasello, "Humans have evolved specialized skills of social cognition: The cultural intelligence hypothesis," *Science*, vol. 317, no. 5843, pp. 1360–1366, 2007.

[25] H. Kummer, L. Daston, G. Gigerenzer, and J. B. Silk, "The social intelligence hypothesis," in *Human By Nature: Between Biology and the Social Sciences*, P. Weingart, S. D. Mitchell, P. J. Richerson, and S. Maasen, Eds. Mahwah, New Jersey, USA: Lawrence Erlbaum Associates, 1997.

[26] G. Miller, *The Mating Mind: How Sexual Choice Shaped the Evolution of Human Nature*. London, UK: Vintage, 2000.

[27] M. V. Flinn, D. C. Geary, and C. V. Ward, "Ecological dominance, social competition, and coalitionary arms races: Why humans evolved extraordinary intelligence," *Evolution and Human Behavior*, vol. 26, no. 1, pp. 10–46, 2005.

[28] M. V. Flinn, "Culture and developmental plasticity: Evolution of the social brain," in *Evolutionary Perspectives on Human Development*, 2nd ed., R. L. Burgess and K. MacDonald, Eds. Thousand Oaks, California, USA: Sage Publications, 2005.

[29] M. Ridley, *The Red Queen: Sex and the Evolution of Human Nature*. New York, New York, USA: Perennial, 2003.

[30] N. K. Humphrey, "The social function of intellect," in *Growing Points in Ethology*, P. P. G. Bateson and R. A. Hinde, Eds. Cambridge, UK: Cambridge University Press, 1976.

[31] E. Jablonka, S. Ginsburg, and D. Dor, "The co-evolution of language and emotions," *Philosophical Transactions of the Royal Society B: Biological Sciences*, vol. 367, no. 1599, pp. 2152–2159, 2012.

[32] Z. Petanjek *et al.*, "Extraordinary neoteny of synaptic spines in the human prefrontal cortex," *Proceedings of the National Academy of Sciences*, vol. 108, no. 32, pp. 13 281–13 286, 2011.

[33] K. Sterelny, "An alternative evolutionary psychology?" in *The Evolution of Mind: Fundamental Questions and Controversies*, S. W. Gangestad and J. A. Simpson, Eds. New York, New York, USA: The Guilford Press, 2007.

[34] L. Malafouris, *How Things Shape the Mind: A Theory of Material Engagement*. Cambridge, Massachusetts, USA: MIT Press, 2013.

[35] M. V. Flinn and K. Coe, "The linked red queens of human cognition, coalitions, and culture," in *The Evolution of Mind: Fundamental Questions and Controversies*, S. W. Gangestad and J. A. Simpson, Eds. New York, New York, USA: The Guilford Press, 2007.

[36] A. Montagu, "Neonatal and infant immaturity in man," *Journal of the American Medical Association*, vol. 178, no. 1, pp. 56–57, 1961.

[37] K. Nelson, "Evolution and development of human memory systems," in *Origins of the Social Mind: Evolutionary Psychology and Child Development*, B. J. Ellis and D. F. Bjorklund, Eds. London, UK: The Guilford Press, 2005.

[38] J. Lindblom and T. Ziemke, "Social situatedness of natural and artificial intelligence: Vygotsky and beyond," *Adaptive Behavior*, vol. 11, no. 2, pp. 79–96, 2003.

[39] M. Mirolli and D. Parisi, "Towards a Vygotskyan cognitive robotics: The role of language as a cognitive tool," *New Ideas in Psychology*, vol. 29, no. 3, pp. 298–311, 2011.

[40] M. Lungarella, G. Metta, R. Pfeifer, and G. Sandini, "Developmental robotics: A survey," *Connection Science*, vol. 15, no. 4, pp. 151–190, 2003.

[41] K. Dautenhahn, "A paradigm shift in artificial intelligence: Why social intelligence matters in the design and development of robots with human-like intelligence," in *50 Years of Artificial Intelligence: Essays Dedicated to the 50th Anniversary of Artificial Intelligence*, M. Lungarella, F. Iida, J. Bongard, and R. Pfeifer, Eds. Berlin, Germany: Springer, 2007.

[42] K. Dautenhahn and A. Billard, "Studying robot social cognition within a developmental psychology framework," in *Third European Workshop on Advanced Mobile Robots*, Zürich, Switzerland, 1999.

[43] M. Wheeler, "What matters: Real bodies and virtual worlds," in *SmartData: Privacy Meets Evolutionary Robotics*, I. Harvey, A. Cavoukian, G. Tomko, D. Borrett, H. Kwan, and D. Hatzinakos, Eds. New York, New York, USA: Springer, 2013.

[44] P. R. Smart and K. Sycara, "Situating cognition in the virtual world," in *6th International Conference on Applied Human Factors and Ergonomics*, Las Vegas, Nevada, USA, 2015.

[45] M. Strohmaier and C. Wagner, "Computational social science for the World Wide Web," *IEEE Intelligent Systems*, vol. 29, no. 5, pp. 84–88, 2014.

[46] S. Dieleman, K. W. Willett, and J. Dambre, "Rotation-invariant convolutional neural networks for galaxy morphology prediction," *Monthly Notices of the Royal Astronomical Society*, vol. 450, no. 2, pp. 1441–1459, 2015.

[47] C. J. Lintott and J. Reed, "Human computation in citizen science," in *Handbook of Human Computation*, P. Michelucci, Ed. New York, New York, USA: Springer, 2013.

[48] L. von Ahn and L. Dabbish, "Designing games with a purpose," *Communications of the ACM*, vol. 51, no. 8, pp. 58–67, 2008.

[49] D. Ferrucci *et al.*, "Building Watson: An overview of the DeepQA project," *AI Magazine*, vol. 31, no. 3, pp. 59–79, 2010.

[50] K. Dautenhahn, B. Ogden, and T. Quick, "From embodied to socially embedded agents—implications for interaction-aware robots," *Cognitive Systems Research*, vol. 3, no. 3, pp. 397–428, 2002.

[51] S. K. Chalup, "Incremental learning in biological and machine learning systems," *International Journal of Neural Systems*, vol. 12, no. 6, pp. 447–465, 2002.

[52] K. Sterelny, *The Evolved Apprentice: How Evolution Made Humans Unique*. Cambridge, Massachusetts, USA: MIT Press, 2012.

[53] N. R. Shadbolt and P. R. Smart, "Knowledge elicitation: Methods, tools and techniques," in *Evaluation of Human Work*, 4th ed., J. R. Wilson and S. Sharples, Eds. Boca Raton, Florida, USA: CRC Press, 2015.

[54] C. Allen, W. Wallach, and I. Smit, "Why machine ethics?" *IEEE Intelligent Systems*, vol. 21, no. 4, pp. 12–17, 2006.

[55] M. Walport, "The Internet of Things: Making the most of the Second Digital Revolution," UK Government Office for Science, London, UK, Tech. Rep., 2014.

[56] D. Kirsh and P. Maglio, "On distinguishing epistemic from pragmatic action," *Cognitive Science*, vol. 18, pp. 513–549, 1994.

[57] R. Menary, "Cognitive practices and cognitive character," *Philosophical Explorations*, vol. 15, no. 2, pp. 147–164, 2012.

[58] S.-H. Myaeng, Y. Jeong, and Y. Jung, "Experiential knowledge mining," *Foundations and Trends in Web Science*, vol. 4, no. 1, pp. 1–102, 2012.

[59] N. R. Shadbolt, "Knowledge acquisition and the rise of social machines," *International Journal of Human–Computer Studies*, vol. 71, no. 2, pp. 200–205, 2013.

[60] A. Mao, E. Kamar, and E. Horvitz, "Why stop now? Predicting worker engagement in online crowdsourcing," in *Conference on Human Computation and Crowdsourcing (HCOMP-2013)*, Palm Springs, California, USA, 2013.

[61] A. Segal *et al.*, "Improving productivity in citizen science through controlled intervention," in *24th International World Wide Web Conference*, Florence, Italy, 2015.

[62] A. Segal, Y. Gal, E. Kamar, E. Horvitz, A. Bowyer, and G. Miller, "Intervention strategies for increasing engagement in crowdsourcing: Platform, predictions, and experiments," in *25th International Joint Conference on Artificial Intelligence*, New York, New York, USA, 2016.

[63] B. Settles, "Active learning," *Synthesis Lectures on Artificial Intelligence and Machine Learning*, vol. 6, no. 1, pp. 1–114, 2012.

[64] D. Cohn, "Active learning," in *Encyclopedia of Machine and Data Mining*, C. Sammut and G. I. Webb, Eds. New York, New York, USA: Springer, 2017.

[65] A. Holub, P. Perona, and M. C. Burl, "Entropy-based active learning for object recognition," in *IEEE Online Learning for Classification Workshop*, Anchorage, Alaska, USA, 2008.

[66] L. Barrington, D. Turnbull, and G. Lanckriet, "Game-powered machine learning," *Proceedings of the National Academy of Sciences*, vol. 109, no. 17, pp. 6411–6416, 2012.

[67] F. Ciravegna, S. Chapman, A. Dingli, and Y. Wilks, "Learning to harvest information for the Semantic Web," in *First European Semantic Web Symposium*, Heraklion, Crete, Greece, 2004.

[68] S. Sarawagi, "Information extraction," *Foundations and Trends in Databases*, vol. 1, no. 3, pp. 261–377, 2008.

[69] B. Pang and L. Lee, "Opinion mining and sentiment analysis," *Foundations and Trends in Information Retrieval*, vol. 2, no. 1–2, pp. 1–135, 2008.

[70] E. Ferrara, O. Varol, C. Davis, F. Menczer, and A. Flammini, "The rise of social bots," *Communications of the ACM*, vol. 59, no. 7, pp. 96–104, 2016.

[71] R. Dale, "The return of the chatbots," *Natural Language Engineering*, vol. 22, no. 5, pp. 811–817, 2016.

[72] J. Lester, K. Branting, and B. Mott, "Conversational agents," in *The Practical Handbook of Internet Computing*, M. P. Singh, Ed. Boca Raton, Florida, USA: Chapman & Hall/CRC, 2004.

[73] A. Tumasjan, T. O. Sprenger, P. G. Sandner, and I. M. Welpe, "Predicting elections with Twitter: What 140 characters reveal about political sentiment," in *Fourth International AAAI Conference on Weblogs and Social Media*, Washington D.C., USA, 2010.

[74] M. Donald, *Origins of the Modern Mind: Three Stages in the Evolution of Culture and Cognition*. Cambridge, Massachusetts, USA: Harvard University Press, 1991.

[75] A. Clark, "Magic words: How language augments human computation," in *Language and Thought: Interdisciplinary Themes*, P. Carruthers and J. Boucher, Eds. Cambridge, UK: Cambridge University Press, 1998.

[76] ——, "How to qualify for a cognitive upgrade: Executive control, glass ceilings and the limits of simian success," in *The Complex Mind: An Interdisciplinary Approach*, D. McFarland, K. Stenning, and M. McGonigle-Chalmers, Eds. Basingstoke, England, UK: Palgrave Macmillan, 2012.

[77] D. Dennett, *Consciousness Explained*. Boston, Massachusetts, USA: Little, Brown & Company, 1991.

[78] A. Clark, "Material symbols," *Philosophical Psychology*, vol. 19, no. 3, pp. 291–307, 2006.

[79] ——, "Language, embodiment, and the cognitive niche," *Trends in Cognitive Sciences*, vol. 10, no. 8, pp. 370–374, 2006.

[80] G. Lupyan, "The centrality of language in human cognition," *Language Learning*, vol. 66, no. 3, pp. 516–553, 2016.

[81] G. Lupyan and B. Bergen, "How language programs the mind," *Topics in Cognitive Science*, vol. 8, no. 2, pp. 408–424, 2016.

[82] G. Lupyan, "Carving nature at its joints and carving joints into nature: How labels augment category representations," in *Modelling Language, Cognition and Action*, A. Cangelosi, G. Bugmann, and R. Borisyuk, Eds. Singapore: World Scientific, 2005.

[83] P. G. Schyns, "A modular neural network model of concept acquisition," *Cognitive Science*, vol. 15, no. 4, pp. 461–508, 1991.

[84] R. K. Thompson, D. L. Oden, and S. T. Boysen, "Language-naive chimpanzees (*Pan troglodytes*) judge relations between relations in a conceptual matching-to-sample task," *Journal of Experimental Psychology: Animal Behavior Processes*, vol. 23, no. 1, pp. 31–43, 1997.

[85] I. M. Pepperberg and S. Carey, "Grey parrot number acquisition: The inference of cardinal value from ordinal position on the numeral list," *Cognition*, vol. 125, no. 2, pp. 219–232, 2012.

[86] G. Lupyan and E. J. Ward, "Language can boost otherwise unseen objects into visual awareness," *Proceedings of the National Academy of Sciences*, vol. 110, no. 35, pp. 14 196–14 201, 2013.

[87] A. Clark, "Word, niche and super-niche: How language makes minds matter more," *THEORIA: An International Journal for Theory, History and Foundations of Science*, vol. 71, no. 3, pp. 255–268, 2005.

[88] K. Friston, "The free-energy principle: A unified brain theory?" *Nature Reviews Neuroscience*, vol. 11, no. 2, pp. 127–138, 2010.

[89] A. Clark, *Surfing Uncertainty: Prediction, Action and the Embodied Mind*. New York, New York, USA: Oxford University Press, 2016.

[90] ——, "Whatever next? Predictive brains, situated agents, and the future of cognitive science," *Behavioral and Brain Sciences*, vol. 36, no. 3, pp. 181–253, 2013.

[91] G. E. Hinton, S. Osindero, and Y.-W. Teh, "A fast learning algorithm for deep belief nets," *Neural Computation*, vol. 18, no. 7, pp. 1527–1554, 2006.

[92] K. Friston, "A free energy principle for biological systems," *Entropy*, vol. 14, no. 11, pp. 2100–2121, 2012.

[93] L. S. Vygotsky, "Consciousness as a problem in the psychology of behavior," *Soviet Psychology*, vol. 17, no. 4, pp. 3–35, 1925/1979, original work published 1925.

[94] M. S. A. Graziano and S. Kastner, "Human consciousness and its relationship to social neuroscience: A novel hypothesis," *Cognitive Neuroscience*, vol. 2, no. 2, pp. 98–113, 2011.

[95] N. Phan, D. Dou, H. Wang, D. Kil, and B. Piniewski, "Ontology-based deep learning for human behavior prediction in health social networks," *Information Sciences*, vol. 384, pp. 298–313, 2017.

[96] C. Vondrick, H. Pirsiavash, and A. Torralba, "Anticipating visual representations from unlabeled video," in *IEEE Conference on Computer Vision and Pattern Recognition*, Las Vegas, Nevada, USA, 2016.

[97] Y. Lv, Y. Duan, W. Kang, Z. Li, and F.-Y. Wang, "Traffic flow prediction with big data: A deep learning approach," *IEEE Transactions on Intelligent Transportation Systems*, vol. 16, no. 2, pp. 865–873, 2015.

[98] G. Gómez, M. Lungarella, P. Eggenberger Hotz, K. Matsushita, and R. Pfeifer, "Simulating development in a real robot: On the concurrent increase of sensory, motor, and neural complexity," in *Fourth International Workshop on Epigenetic Robotics*, Genoa, Italy, 2004.

[99] J. L. Elman, "Learning and development in neural networks: The importance of starting small," *Cognition*, vol. 48, no. 1, pp. 71–99, 1993.

[100] D. F. Bjorklund, "The role of immaturity in human development," *Psychological Bulletin*, vol. 122, no. 2, pp. 153–169, 1997.

[101] D. F. Bjorklund and B. L. Green, "The adaptive nature of cognitive immaturity," *American Psychologist*, vol. 47, no. 1, pp. 46–54, 1992.

[102] M. Lungarella and L. Berthouze, "Adaptivity through physical immaturity," in *2nd International Workshop on Epigenetic Robotics: Modeling Cognitive Development in Robotic Systems*, Edinburgh, Scotland, 2002.

[103] E. L. Newport, "Maturational constraints on language learning," *Cognitive Science*, vol. 14, no. 1, pp. 11–28, 1990.

[104] G. Turkewitz and P. A. Kenny, "Limitations on input as a basis for neural organization and perceptual development: A preliminary theoretical statement," *Developmental Psychobiology*, vol. 15, no. 4, pp. 357–368, 1982.

[105] S. Kirby and J. R. Hurford, "The evolution of incremental learning: Language, development and critical periods," Department of Linguistics, University of Edinburgh, Edinburgh, UK, Tech. Rep. Occasional Paper EOPL-97-2, 1997.

[106] A. W. Kersten and J. L. Earles, "Less really is more for adults learning a miniature artificial language," *Journal of Memory and Language*, vol. 44, no. 2, pp. 250–273, 2001.

[107] B. P. Cochran, J. L. McDonald, and S. J. Parault, "Too smart for their own good: The disadvantage of a superior processing capacity for adult language learners," *Journal of Memory and Language*, vol. 41, no. 1, pp. 30–58, 1999.

[108] Y. Nagai, Y. Kawai, and M. Asada, "Emergence of mirror neuron system: Immature vision leads to self-other correspondence," in *IEEE International Conference on Development and Learning*, Frankfurt, Germany, 2011.

[109] P.-Y. Oudeyer and L. B. Smith, "How evolution may work through curiosity-driven developmental process," *Topics in Cognitive Science*, vol. 8, no. 2, pp. 492–502, 2016.

[110] A. G. Barto, "Intrinsic motivation and reinforcement learning," in *Intrinsically Motivated Learning in Natural and Artificial Systems*, G. Baldassarre and M. Mirolli, Eds. Berlin, Germany: Springer, 2013.

[111] J. Gottlieb, P.-Y. Oudeyer, M. Lopes, and A. Baranes, "Information-seeking, curiosity, and attention: Computational and neural mechanisms," *Trends in Cognitive Sciences*, vol. 17, no. 11, pp. 585–593, 2013.

[112] P. R. Smart, "Human-extended machine cognition," *Cognitive Systems Research*, in press.

[113] P. R. Smart, R. Heersmink, and R. W. Clowes, "The cognitive ecology of the Internet," in *Cognition Beyond the Brain: Computation, Interactivity and Human Artifice*, 2nd ed., S. J. Cowley and F. Vallée-Tourangeau, Eds. Cham, Switzerland: Springer International Publishing, 2017.

[114] P. R. Smart, R. Clowes, and R. Heersmink, "Minds online: The interface between web science, cognitive science and the philosophy of mind," *Foundations and Trends in Web Science*, vol. 6, no. 1–2, pp. 1–232, 2017.

The Modular Structure of Housing Utilities: Analyzing Architectural Integration Patterns

Peter De Bruyn and Herwig Mannaert

Normalized Systems Institute
Faculty of Applied Economics
University of Antwerp, Belgium
Email:{peter.debruyn, herwig.mannaert}@uantwerp.be

Jeroen Faes, Tom Vermeire and Jasper Bosmans

Department of Management Information Systems
Faculty of Applied Economics
University of Antwerp, Belgium
Email:{jeroen.faes,tom.vermeire,jasper.bosmans}@student.uantwerp.be

***Abstract*—Modularity is considered a powerful concept within many domains. While modular artifacts are believed to have the potential to exhibit several beneficial characteristics such as evolvability, the actual realization of this evolvability or flexibility remains challenging. This paper considers houses as modular structures and employs the combinatorics underlying Normalized Systems Theory, as well as the integration patterns it proposes, to analyze design alternatives for the incorporation of electricity, heating, air conditioning and Internet access utilities within houses. The paper demonstrates that the integration patterns can be applied at several modular granularity levels. An analysis is presented regarding the currently most frequently used integration patterns (as well as their level of application), and those patterns that should deserve additional exploration. The adopted approach to analyze the modular design alternatives for housing utilities is believed to be applicable within other domains as well.**

Keywords*–*Modularity; Housing; Evolvability; Normalized Systems; Architectural Patterns.

I. INTRODUCTION

Modularity is a powerful concept used in many application domains (including computer science, product engineering, organizational sciences, and so on) and is generally assumed to provide benefits including evolvability. Nevertheless, obtaining such adaptability or evolvability in practice can be challenging. The different modules in a system might be dependent on one another, so that a change in one module might lead to (few or many) changes in other modules. Some of these ripple effects may be due to so-called cross-cutting concerns in the sense that they are required across the whole modular structure (e.g., security in a software application). As a cross-cutting concern is, by definition, present in many modules of a system, it is clear that changes in that regard can easily impact several places within a modular structure (e.g., every data entity should be adapted so that it can securely stored in order to create a more secure overall software application).

Also houses can be considered as modular structures. They exhibit several abstraction levels (e.g., houses consisting of rooms and built by bricks) and could benefit from evolvability (e.g., connecting an additional room to an existing house). Moreover, houses seem to contain several cross-cutting concerns (e.g., water and electricity supply) and subject to ripple effects when undergoing change (e.g., the need to drill into existing walls or even tear down walls in order to be able to provide an additional room with water because the connecting old walls did not provide any connection), hampering their evolvability. This paper extends a previous paper [1] by investigating and illustrating the applicability of modularity reasoning (and in particular the concept of cross-cutting concerns) within the design of housing utilities. We argue that, in general, the utilities within houses can be considered as cross-cutting concerns. Whereas our earlier work focused on the electricity and heating utilities, this paper also analyzes airconditioning and Internet access utilities in a housing context, thereby further supporting our claim of the applicability of our reasoning. We propose design alternatives for housing utilities based on the modular integration patterns for cross-cutting concerns as suggested by the combinatorics underlying Normalized Systems Theory (NST) [2]. The theory is suitable for this purpose as it aims to provide prescriptive guidance on how to design evolvable modular systems.

It is important to mention upfront that none of the authors of this paper are experts within the domain of housing architecture. Therefore, the intention of the paper is not the prescribe in detail how housing architectures should be improved in the future. Rather, we intend to show that it makes sense to apply the modularity reasoning presented within NST (which originated at the software level) to other domains in which modularity plays a prominent role. We will structure this paper as follows. In Section II, we provide a brief overview of related work regarding modularity, NST and evolvable housing. Next, in Section III, we present the set of considered integration patterns for modular structures. We then apply these patterns for the concerns electricity (Section IV), heating (Section V), air conditioning (Section VI) and Internet access (Section VII). Finally, we offer our reflections and conclusions in Sections VIII and IX, respectively.

II. RELATED WORK

In this section, we discuss some areas of related research. We briefly discuss, consecutively, modularity, NST and some earlier work on the evolvable design of houses.

The modularity concept generally refers to the fact that a system is subdivided into a set of subsystems. Modular artifacts are deemed interesting due to several potential benefits that are attributed to it. For instance, designing a system in a modular way is expected to lower the complexity as the design can be decomposed into a set of smaller (less complex) problems [3]. Also, once a module has been well designed and tested, it can be reused in other systems without significant additional costs. Another major benefit expected from modularity is increased flexibility or evolvability. In a modular artifact, one particular part (module) of the system can be substituted for another version of it, without the need to build up the artifact again from scratch. This type of plug-and-play behavior allows for variation (using the same set of available module versions, different aggregations or variants can be realized) and evolvability (over time, an artifact can evolve from one variant to another) and has been considered as the "power" of modularity [4].

The realization of a good modular design in practice, enabling the mentioned advantages like evolvability, is very challenging. It is generally accepted that the coupling (dependencies and interactions) between the modules in a system should be studied and minimized [3][5][4]. However, how this should be attained is unclear and few theoretically underpinned and generally accepted practical implications are available in literature. One approach which aims to provide a theoretically founded framework with practical implications, is NST. The origins of NST are situated in the formulation of a set of design theorems for the creation of evolvable software systems. Here, evolvability is operationalized by demanding Bounded Input Bound Output (BIBO) stability on ever growing systems. The theory proves that the isolation of all change drivers in separate constructs (Separation of Concerns), the stateful calling of processing functions (Separation of States) and the ability to update data structures or processing functions without impacting other data structures or processing functions (Version Transparency) are necessary conditions in order to obtain stability [6]. It has been shown that these theorems can actually be formulated in more general terms for modular systems [7] and seem to appeal to the basic combinatorics regarding modularity [2]. More specifically, the promise of modularity is that maintaining a particular amount of versions of modular building blocks will result in an exponential amount of available system variants. However, in case a modular system is not well designed (e.g., by not adhering to the theorems), a change in one particular version of one particular module may have an impact (ripple effects) on other (versions of) modules. This number of impacts will typically grow (in an exponential way) with the size of the system and its dependencies.

Adhering to the NST design theorems is difficult as they demand a very strict and fine-grained design of a system, and every violation will result in a limitation of the evolvability of the system. Experience with respect to the realization of such systems has shown that such design becomes much more realistic in case a set of design patterns (so-called "elements") are employed [2]. Each individual element is a generic modular structure for a basic functionality for the type of system at hand and can be parametrized (and if necessary, customized) over and over again when an actual system is built. For instance, in the case of software systems, a general structure for data, task, flow, connector and trigger elements was provided [2]. Stated otherwise, the set of modules constituting an element becomes a reusable module at a higher abstraction (or granularity) level. In essence, each element provides a core functionality (e.g., representing data) as well as an incorporated integration with the relevant cross-cutting concerns in the domain (e.g., security and persistency for data). In order to maximize the envisioned evolvability, it is important that these cross-cutting concerns are integrated at the most fine-grained level possible (such as these elements) and that the parts in the elements connecting or dealing with the cross-cutting concerns are properly separated in distinct modules that are version transparent.

As we stated above that houses can be considered as modular systems and contain cross-cutting concerns, NST seems to be applicable in this domain. To the best of our knowledge, little previous work exists on the evolvable modular design of houses. Some interesting exceptions do however exist. In terms of academic research for instance, Keymer [8] lists and discusses a set of design strategies for increasing the possibilities of buildings to accommodate change, some of them pointing to relevant cross-cutting concerns in this respect (i.e., several ways of distributing services such as heating, ventilation, electrical wiring, plumbing, etcetera). Or, when considering real-life projects, the Hivehaus "modular living space" project [9] can be considered as an interesting effort in dealing with the design of houses in a modular way while taking care of the proper integration of cross-cutting concerns (see Section VIII). Therefore, the use of underlying theory such as NST (and the integration patterns following from this, as discussed in Section III) to analyze the modular design of houses in a more systematic way is in our view an interesting extension of existing work. Whereas our earlier publication [1] focused on the electricity and heating utilities, we now also conduct a similar analysis to airconditioning and Internet access utilities.

III. Patterns for Cross-Cutting Concern Integration

Based on NST and the implications of its theorems [2], we differentiate between the following integration patterns of cross-cutting concerns. As a first category of integration patterns, we consider cross-cutting concern modules added to the main modules wherein each of the cross-cutting concern modules handles the full functionality of that cross-cutting concern itself. We call this the *embedded integration pattern* and refer to it as *configuration 1*. This embedded module can be dedicated (in case the module was customly designed for the system at hand) or standardized (in case a standardized module is employed to handle the concern). We refer to the first variant as *configuration 1A* and the second one as *configuration 1B*. For modules in the context of a software system, think of a separate module added to a data entity taking care of the persistency of that data entity in a custom designed way (1A) or by using a standard module (1B) for this purpose.

As a second category of integration patterns, we consider cross-cutting concern modules added to the main modules wherein the cross-cutting concern modules are merely connections ("relay modules") to a more elaborate (external) implementation framework of the cross-cutting concern that is actually performing the needed functionality. We call this the *relay integration pattern* and refer to it as *configuration 2*. Such relay modules can connect to a dedicated framework (in case the framework was customly designed for the system at hand) or standardized framework (in case the framework is standardized and, for instance, publicly available). We refer to the first variant as *configuration 2A* and the second one as *configuration 2B*. For modules in the context of a software system, think of a separate module added to a data entity serving as a proxy to a persistency framework, which was specifically designed for its own system (2A), or to an available standard solution such as JPA (2B). Finally, we mention the option to let the relay modules connect to another module (i.e., a *framework gateway*) and in which only this framework gateway directly connects to the external implementation framework. We refer to this third variant as *configuration 2C*. For modules in the context of a software system, think of a dedicated gateway module connecting to the JPA framework but allowing all relay modules to be technologically independent of this framework by calling the gateway in a JPA agnostic way.

IV. Electricity Patterns

In this section, we consider the electricity utility within houses as a cross-cutting concern. We consider the integration architectures as proposed in Section II at the modular granularity level of a city or community, house, room and device. Afterwards, we consider some advanced issues and reflections.

A. City or community level

Most cities and communities of developed countries need electricity, so it can be considered as a cross-cutting concern. Here, we consider how a city or community can power its electrical grid as a whole (the distribution of electricity to individual buildings is discussed later on).

A first option could be to have all cities/communities have there own electricity generation (configuration 1). In primitive communities, custom built solutions might be considered (1A), but typically the use of standard solutions (1B) would be more realistic (e.g., the reproduction of a typical power plant by means of nuclear reactions, coal, etc.). However, this often lacks economies of scale (it is more efficient to have large power plants producing energy for more than 1 city or community) so typically a city's electricity grid is connected to a national electricity grid with one or more electricity plants dividing the electricity over a large set of cities and communities (configuration 2). Each country might create its own specifically designed grid connecting with the multiple cities and communities (2A) or make use of a standardized electrical power distribution network between cities (2B).

While this latter solution is most frequently opted for, it also has some drawbacks in terms of dependencies. For instance, if the central grid goes down, all connected cities and communities are lacking electricity. Therefore, in reality, most electrical grids are divided into several isolated areas avoiding that a problem in a particular part of the grid to get escalated into the complete (national) electricity grid. Moreover, changes in the standardized network still have their impact on the relay modules (which should nevertheless be encapsulated within the cross-cutting concern handling relay module and not be incorporated within the core module itself). Consider for instance a change in the voltage of the network or from alternating current (AC) to direct current (DC). In fact, the limitations (at that time) for distributing DC over long distances (in order to be able to adopt integration pattern 2B), was one of the main reasons for the general prevalence of AC in the so-called "War of the Currents". One could even imagine the situation in which all cities plug their individual grids into a centralized relay module (power supply) tapping into the global electricity grid (2C) and shielding the individual cities and communities from changes in the standardized framework used.

B. House level

Within every city, community or electricity grid area, electricity typically has to be available within every house. Therefore, it constitutes a cross-cutting concern at this level as well. Sometimes, individual houses have the possibility to generate their own electricity by using, for instance, a fuel based electricity generator, solar panels, heat pumps, etc. Furthermore, new technological developments have allowed the creation of home based batteries with large storage capacities, even allowing to store electrical power for a whole house for a considerable amount of time. As this provides a significant amount of independence and sometimes offers budget friendly solutions, this integration pattern can be interesting in certain situations. Moreover, a certain amount of flexibility is enabled as each individual house can choose for the most suitable type of energy in their situation (e.g., those areas with a high exposure to sun light might opt for solar panels instead of a wind mill). In that case (except when they want to transmit the overcapacity to the central electricity distribution network), no distribution framework (see previous subsection) is required and the generators and batteries support the modules for the adoption of integration pattern 1 (typically configuration 1B).

Most people, however, do not opt for the duplication of power generators and batteries in each and every individual house and choose for the option of a connection module plugging into the publicly available electrical power distribution network (typically standardized, so configuration 2B). Similar as stated above, dependencies regarding the availability of the distribution network as well as changes in the power distribution network affecting all connection modules of houses, remain possible disadvantages of this integration pattern.

C. Room level

Within every house or building, most if not all rooms require electricity in terms of a set of available sockets where individual devices (cfr. infra) can be plugged in. Therefore, it constitutes a cross-cutting concern at this level as well. Based on the integration patterns we summarized in Section III and similar to our reasoning expressed above, it would be theoretically possible for each room in a house to generate the electricity required (configuration 1A if custom designed, configuration 1B if a standard solution is opted for). Nevertheless, individual heat pumps, electricity generators, etc. for individual rooms are —to the best of our knowledge— typically not applied. Therefore, configuration 2 (typically 2B) is applied by having sockets plugging into the grid network of the house. In certain situations, configuration 2C might be relevant as well. For instance, houses employing a combination of electrical sources (tapping from the publicly available grid, as well as producing a portion of energy themselves by solar panels) could benefit from having the possibility of shifting between them (e.g., using the solar energy when electricity is being generated or available on the local battery and the public grid in all other cases). By having the relay modules (sockets) connecting to a gateway switching module (connecting to the solar panels and public grid), only one electricity grid for such house should be created.

D. Device level

Ultimately, electrical power should be made available to individual devices for which it is required in order to work properly. One possibility to obtain this power is by having a built-in generator or battery in a device. While the generator variant hardly exists in practice, batteries within devices are common practice. Such batteries exist in both custom built variants (integration pattern 1A) or by the use of general purpose variants (integration pattern 1B). A configuration like this obviously provides the device a certain degree of autonomy (i.e., the device can operate on its own) and absence of specific dependencies in this respect. For instance, such configuration might be of great importance for devices to be used witin an Internet of Things (IoT) context. However, incorporating batteries in every device might be a significant engineering challenge (sometimes even simply impossible) and requires the duplication of a battery in each device. Therefore, in many cases a centralized configuration will be adopted in which the device is connected to a custom developed (configuration 2A) or, typically, a standardized electrical grid (configuration 2B).

Recall that we noted in Section IV-A that historically, AC was chosen above DC at the level of cities and communities due to (among other things) its possibility to transport electrical current along larger distances. The consequences of this choice ripple down to the lower modularity granularity levels, such as the level of the devices, which then have to deal with electricity delivered at AC. However, most electrical devices need DC to function properly. As stated above, it is the relay module that should encapsulate these kind of dependencies regarding the external framework and ensure conversions for mutual compatibility if required. Therefore, an adapter (typically with a device specific connection) is often included at the level of the cross-cutting connecting module (i.e., between the device and the electrical grid) in order to convert AC (coming in from the plug) to DC at the right voltage (typically also resulting in a certain degree of loss of electrical power, which is converted into heat, depending on the efficiency of the adapter). *This clearly shows the duplication of the AC to DC conversion functionality present within all relay modules (here: adapters).* Moreover, in terms of flexibility and adaptability, this situation nicely illustrates that changes in the external framework (e.g., a conversion of AC to DC within the public electrical grid) would impact all relay modules. In case the AC/DC conversion would not be separated in a distinct module (e.g., the conversion would be performed in the devices themselves instead of via a separately in/unpluggable adapter), the impact would be even more profound as the devices themselves should be adapted. Based on our analysis of the different modular granularity levels, one could argue for the need to investigate the option to have AC/DC conversion happening at the house level instead of the device level. This way, the duplication of adapters for each separate device could be eliminated and the dependence on DC would be avoided. More specifically, such situation would correspond to the cross-cutting concern integration pattern 2C where the main modules are the devices, the sockets are the relay modules (no need for adapters anymore) and the centralized AC/DC converter would fulfill the role of the gateway module. In fact, recent initiatives regarding new possible electricity (micro)grid configurations seem to suggest these type of integration patterns [10].

E. Overview and advanced issues

Table I provides an overview of the granularity-integration pattern combinations for the electricity provisioning of houses. We can observe that, at most modularity levels, a standardized integration pattern (i.e., 1B and 2B) is opted for. This tends to indicate a certain maturity within the respective domain, which is in accordance with our expectations. While dependence on the external framework is an important limitation regarding integration pattern 2B, we remark that an interesting research avenue regarding integration pattern 2C at the device level can be identified. Further, the table illustrates that, when aiming for maximum flexibility, the integration of concerns tends to be solved at more fine-grained levels (going downwards in Table I) and in a more standardized externally enabled way (going to the right in Table I) in the long run.

TABLE I. OVERVIEW OF THE DIFFERENT GRANULARITY-INTEGRATION PATTERN COMBINATIONS REGARDING ELECTRICITY.

	1A	*1B*	*2A*	*2B*	*2C*
city/community				•	
house		•		•	
room				•	•
device	•	•		•	○

•: currently employed, ○: to be explored

Further, the electricity cross-cutting concern might be enriched with additional features for which our proposed granularity levels and integration patterns might prove useful during the analysis of their realization options. Consider for instance on/off switching. Many devices (such as light bulbs) using electricity to function need to be able to switched on (i.e., emit light) and off (i.e., dim the light). Typical approaches consist of a switch attached to the lamp itself (required in case of configuration 1) or a separate switch integrated into the electrical grid of the house itself (the integration structure of the external framework in case of configuration 2). While this approach has worked well for many years it still requires manual intervention at the location of the switch and, in the latter case, requires the reconfiguration and integration of the switches when a lamp would be relocated within the house. During the last decade, attention has grown for more advanced home domotics in which switches can be managed by software (e.g., allowing to automatically switch devices on at a predefined time slot) and in a remote way. Again, this could be done by placing individual sensors/programmable controllers with individual remote controllers (configuration 1B, if standardized equipment is used). Alternatively, a network of sensors/programmable controllers could be used having one central management and remote control (configuration 2B, if standardized equipment is used), which manages all connected switches. This would also allow the use of aggregated actions, such as switching on or off all light bulbs at once at a predefined time slot, and enable parameter reconfiguration in a centralized way. Integration configuration 2C could even be opted for when, for instance, all sensors/programmable controllers connect to one central connection module allowing to be manipulated by means of multiple remote controllers and protocols (e.g., a traditional remote, smartphone, etc.).

V. HEATING PATTERNS

In this section, we consider the heating utility within houses as a cross-cutting concern. We consider the integration architectures as proposed in Section II at the modular granularity level of a city or community, house, room and brick. Afterwards, we consider some advanced issues and reflections.

A. City or community level

As all households need heating, a source of heat should be transported to or be generated within every house. Therefore, it represents a genuine cross-cutting concern within a housing context. In contrast with the electricity concern we discussed in Section IV, it is rather rare and exceptional that heating is generated and provided at the city or community level, which implies that heating is provided at more fine-grained modular levels (cf. infra). Some initiatives at the higher level of the city or community can however be noted. For instance, an initiative in Rotterdam was recently reported [11] in which residual heat from petrochemical companies around its port is recuperated. While it concerns warmed water being generally too cold to be useful for industrial purposes, it might still suffice to provide the heating for (a large amount of) houses. Referring to the case of Rotterdam, it is claimed that heating can be provided for up to 500.000 households in its surrounding area via a so-called heat network by means of pipelines. In terms of the NST integration patterns, this would correspond to integration pattern 1 at the level of Rotterdam's area (and more specifically 1A as it is a first and, by definition, non-standardized implementation of the concern). Clearly, this initiative was inspired by the fact that this allows for efficiency gains as the considered household do not have to produce their own heat in one way or the other: as the heat would otherwise be "lost", it is now recuperated at a very low cost. Therefore, the heat at the level of each house can be tapped from an external network (i.e., integration pattern 2 can be adopted at this level, cf. infra).

B. House level

As stated before, most houses take care of their own heat generation: a house typically has a central heating system meaning that a central heating boiler uses electricity (cfr. supra) or petroleum to generate heat and convert cold into warm water. Another option could be to use heat pumps. This water will then be distributed along the different rooms in the house later on (cfr. infra). Considering the granularity level of a house, this therefore means that typically integration pattern 1 is opted for (and more specifically 1B, as most households use a standardized heat generator for this purpose). This way of working clearly implies certain benefits such as independence from external heat generation providers. However, one might wonder whether this is always the most efficient or environment friendly way of working. As we mentioned in Section V-A, it is interesting to see that certain initiatives are being taken into the exploration of other integration patterns, such as the so-called heat distribution networks. Here, heated water is produced in a central location for multiple houses and then distributed among them. Therefore, integration architecture 2A (as the solution is typically not yet highly standardized) is opted for in this case.

C. Room level

While a garage or cellar might not be in need of explicit heating, most other rooms within a house (such as the living room or bathroom) are. As a consequence, it can be considered as a relevant cross-cutting concern at this level as well. As mentioned before, most houses today employ a central heating system in which heated water is produced at one centralized place in the house and then transported via water pipes to the required rooms in which a heating element/radiator is present. The warm water causes the element to warm up and release its heat into the room, after which the water (which partly cooled down) returns to the central heating system. As these systems and their pipe networks are highly standardized and commonplace, integration architecture 2B is typically applied. This allows an efficient generation of heat but also clearly entails a dependency of all rooms on this central heating system: in case it would fail or be replaced in such way that the old pipe network no long suffices, all rooms would be heavily affected. Using a framework gateway that decouples the pipe network from the boiler might prevent this and would even allow to switch between different sources of heat (electrically generated, via a heat pump or via the external heat distribution network), which would correspond to integration architecture 2C. In case of absence of a central heating system, integration architecture 1 might still be used. For instance, some houses (although a minority) still use systems in which radiators are placed within rooms. These radiations use the plug to tap electricity and generate heat at their own spot (representing configuration 1B). The use of a fireplace corresponds to the same architecture as well (or configuration 1A in case it concerns a custom designed fireplace). And theoretically speaking, one might also think of situations in which each room is equipped with things such as its own heat pump, although such solutions —at this point in time— are very expensive and inefficient.

D. Brick level

Finally, in order to have more homogeneous heat dispersion in rooms, heating elements incorporated in the floor are sometimes adopted. In such design, the heating pipes are traditionally also connected with a central heating boiler, representing integration architecture 2. Nevertheless, such design is typically not really scalable or flexible as changes (for example, extensions of the heating system to other or larger rooms) might require to break up the floor as a whole. In addition, designing standardized solutions might be more difficult as many rooms take on different shapes and sizes. As a purely speculative and thought provoking alternative, we therefore envision the integration of the heating cross-cutting concern at the level of an individual brick as represented in Figure 1 [2]. In every such element, standardized transport pipes would be embedded for the transportation of hot water, nicely fitting onto the pipes of every similar adjoining brick. This would provide a remarkable degree of scalability when compared to traditional floor heating: as different rooms are built or expanded throughout time, additional bricks (with integrated pipes) could be used, enlarging the area that can be heated. Clearly, just as it was the case for the device level for the electricity concern, the brick level seems to represent the most fine-grained modularity level where the heating cross-cutting concern can be meaningfully integrated.

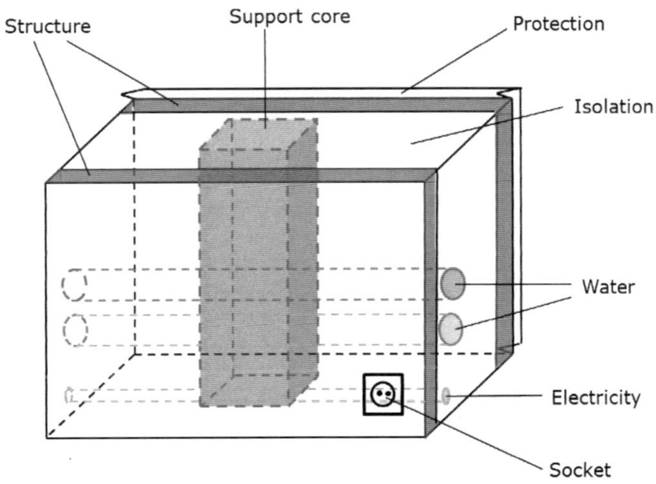

Figure 1. A construction element integration cross-cutting concerns [2].

E. Overview and advanced issues

Table II provides an overview of the granularity-integration pattern combinations for the heating of houses. We can observe that, at most modularity levels, a standardized integration pattern (i.e., 1B and 2B) is opted for. An exception is the integration of heat at the city or community level, which still resides a non-standardized variant (1A), but could easily evolvable towards configuration 1B as it gains maturity. Again, this tends to indicate a certain maturity within the respective domain, which is in accordance with our expectations. As the dependency on the external framework is an important limitation regarding the use of integration pattern 2B, we can identify an interesting research avenue regarding integration pattern 2C at the room level. Additionally, we propose to consider the integration of the cross-cutting concern at an even more fine-grained level (i.e., a brick) in the future. Further, the table illustrates that, when aiming for maximum flexibility, the integration of concerns tends to be solved at more fine-grained levels in a more standardized externally enabled way (stated otherwise: evolving towards the right lower corner in Table II).

TABLE II. OVERVIEW OF THE DIFFERENT GRANULARITY-INTEGRATION PATTERN COMBINATIONS REGARDING HEATING.

	1A	*1B*	*2A*	*2B*	*2C*
city/community	•				
house		•	•		
room		•		•	○
brick				○	

•: currently employed, ○: to be explored

Further, it should be clear that the heating cross-cutting concern is highly related to the preservation of heat by, for example, insulation. Also here, the same modular aggregation levels might be relevant: the house (e.g., an isolating roof), the room (e.g., a well-closing door or insulation being put behind a wall) and the brick (e.g., insulation incorporated in every individual brick). And similar to the on/off switching of electricity consuming devices, heat distribution throughout a house might benefit from more specific, remote and/or automated management (of its subparts). For instance, in order to allow certain rooms in the house (e.g., the living rooms) to be heated and others (e.g., the garage) not for a certain period of time, an operating panel may be provided for every radiator turning it on and off or even measuring the current temperature and matching it with a predefined temperature goal. In more advanced settings, a central management unit at the level of the house could be provided in which a goal temperature for multiple zones could be specified. Based on this information, heat can be released by those radiators standing in zones in which the temperature is lower than specified.

VI. Air Conditioning Patterns

In this section, we consider the air conditioning utility within houses as a cross-cutting concern. Whereas heating as discussed in Section V aims to increase the room temperature within houses in case the temperature is lower than desired, air conditionning aims to decrease the room temperature in case the temperature is higher than desired. We consider the integration architectures for air conditioning as proposed in Section II at the modular granularity level of a house, room and brick. Afterwards, we consider some advanced issues and reflections.

A. House level

In case houses are equipped with an air conditioning system, some houses have a centralized, electricity driven, cool air producing unit. This cold air is then distributed along the different rooms in the house later on (cfr. infra). Considering the granularity level of a house, this therefore means that typically integration pattern 1 is opted for (and more specifically 1B, as most households use a standardized cool air generator for this purpose). We are not aware of any air conditioning generation/distribution at a higher granularity than a house, such as a city or community as was the case for electricity and heating, which would allow houses to tap cooled air from an external network. This would constitute a configuration 2A or 2B at the level of a house, and 1A or 1B at the city or community level. As we can imagine several very challenging issues of such configuration and given the fact that the market base for air conditioning is currently still rather limited, we leave this aggregation level out of scope. The current way of working clearly implies certain benefits such as independence from external cool air generation providers.

B. Room level

In contrast with the electricity and heating concern, not all rooms (or even the majority of them) within a house are always equipped with air conditioning if a house has provisionings in this regard (e.g., only the bedroom and living room). We mentioned above that some houses employ a central cooling system in which cooled air is produced at one centralized place in the house. This heat is then transported via tubes to the required rooms in which an air fan is present. Therefore, such situations correspond to configuration 2 at the level of the rooms. For the authors, not being experts in air conditioning as well as the other cross-cutting concerns, there is no full clarity regarding the fact whether this constitutes a 2A (custom built) or 2B configuration. However, this issue is not due to a shortcoming of our modularity or integration pattern reasoning, but solely due to our lack of expertise in the specific area of, in this case, air conditioning. It is obvious that this configuration allows an efficient generation of cool air but also clearly entails a dependency of all rooms on this central cooling system: in case it would fail or be replaced in such way that the old tube network no long suffices, all rooms would be heavily affected. Using a framework gateway, which decouples the pipe network from the cooling system, might prevent this and would even allow to switch between different sources of cool air production. This would correspond to integration architecture 2C. In many houses having air conditioning, no central cooling mechanism is present. Instead separate (mobile) air conditioning devices are put into each room to be cooled (with a hose to be connected to the outside environment to expel hot air). Therefore, this corresponds to integration architecture 1 (and more specifically 1B as it generally concerns highly standardized devices). As we know from our discussion above, this configuration implies the duplication of these air conditioning devices in each room for which cooling is preferred.

C. Brick level

Just as we discussed for the case of the electricity and heating cross-cutting concerns, we might envision the integration of the air conditioning cross-cutting concern at the level of an individual brick as a purely thought provoking possibility, as represented in Figure 1 [2]. In every such element, standardized transport pipes would be embedded for the transportation of cooled water or air, nicely fitting onto the pipes of every similar adjoining brick. This would provide a remarkable degree of scalability when compared to the traditional integration alternatives: as different rooms are built or expanded throughout time, additional bricks (with integrated pipes) could be used, enlarging the area that can be cooled. Clearly, just as it was the case for the device level for the electricity and heating concern, the brick level seems to represent the most fine-grained modularity level at which the heating cross-cutting concern can be meaningfully integrated.

D. Overview and advanced issues

Table III provides an overview of the granularity-integration pattern combinations for the air conditioning within houses. While at first sight, the air conditioning might seem completely analogous to the heating concern discussed before (i.e., cooling instead of heating), some important differences and nuances can be observed. First, airconditioning is not a mandatory or strictly necessary cross-cutting concern within houses. Indeed, many houses or buildings exist in which no airconditioning is present (which may in fact even represent the majority of the houses). Secondly, somewhat related or being a consequence of the previous point, is that the way how the air conditioning concern is integrated within the modular structure of houses is less mature when compared to heating. No concern provisioning is, to the best of our knowledge, present at the level of a city or community. And while the concern provisioning at the level of the house and room is standardized in case of configuration 1, this is not the case (or at least not completely clear) when configuration 2 is opted for. Therefore, we anticipate that these 2A configurations will or can tend towards a configuration 2B (and later on 2C) in the future, as the domain further gains maturity. Next to the exploration of possible air conditioning management at the level of cities and communities, these transitions might constitute interesting avenues for research. Also here, we might propose to consider the integration of the cross-cutting concern at an even more fine-grained level (i.e., a brick) in the future. Moreover, these findings correspond with our intuition that a concern with a somewhat lower adoption rate exhibits a somewhat lower degree of maturity.

TABLE III. OVERVIEW OF THE DIFFERENT GRANULARITY-INTEGRATION PATTERN COMBINATIONS REGARDING AIR CONDITIONING.

	1A	*1B*	*2A*	*2B*	*2C*
city/community	○				
house		•	○		
room		•	•		
brick				○	

•: currently employed, ○: to be explored

Further, it should be clear that also the air conditioning cross-cutting concern is highly related to the way how insulation is managed and that the same modular aggregation levels might be relevant: the house (e.g., an isolating roof), the room (e.g., a well-closing door or insulation being put behind a wall) and the brick (e.g., insulation incorporated in every individual brick).

VII. INTERNET ACCESS PATTERNS

In this section, we consider the need to provide Internet access within houses as a cross-cutting concern. We consider the integration architectures as proposed in Section II at the modular granularity level of a house, room and device. Afterwards, we consider some advanced issues and reflections.

A. House level

Within most cities and communities in developed countries, access to Internet access is considered as a crucial resource for all inhabitants. As it is typically required to distribute such

Internet access across all houses within such community, it can be considered as a genuine cross-cutting concern. The main connections for Internet, being considered as a network of networks, are formed by backbones constructed by government and Internet provider companies (the so-called Tier 1, Tier 2 and Tier 3 networks). When we discuss Internet access as a cross-cutting concern in this paper, we mean the way how an artifact connects to an internet connection provided by an Internet provider in its area.

In order to obtain such connection, most houses have an individual subscription to an Internet provider (e.g., through a connection achieved by fibre). This provider will make sure that the subscriber gets an IP address, can access the Internet by downloading and uploading information, etc. So while the Internet itself is clearly to be considered as an external framework, the access point is provided at the level of an individual house. Therefore, when studying the way how the connection to the Internet is made, this can be considered as the usage of integration pattern 1B (as typically, standardized routers —sometimes even provided by the Internet providers— will be used for this purpose). Such integration provides certain appealing characteristics. This configuration allows each household to make independent choices (e.g., to subscribe or not subscribe to an Internet connection) and flexibility in terms of the Internet provider of their own preference.

B. Room level

Within every house or building, most if not all rooms require Internet access these days in order to use TVs, radios, computers and other devices in a meaningful way. Therefore, it constitutes a cross-cutting concern at this level as well. In most contemporary designs of houses, rooms connect to the Internet connection as obtained at the level of the house (configuration 2), instead of subscribing and making a separate connection on their own. This can be due to the fact that separate Internet subscriptions are considered overkill for each room (given the large download and upload limits for each single subscription) as well as the fact that the internal network within the house (connecting the devices within one house) is typically distributed via the same medium and technology.

The distribution of the Internet connection to rooms can be done via different media. For instance, UTP cables having a RJ45 connector can be drawn within the walls or on the ground to which many digital devices can connect. Another option is to opt for the wireless distribution of Internet access via Wifi. While it could be that the router making the initial connection with the Internet provider (see Section VII-A) already provides a Wifi signal that can reach one or multiple rooms, Wifi repeaters (capturing and repeating the Wifi signal in order to extend the network) are generally required in (some) rooms. Alternatively, the network and Internet access can be distributed via so-called powerlines, in which the signals are distributed over the electricity network (see Section IV) and captured via plugs in the electricity sockets, which expose the signals via Wifi or a connection for UTP cables.

Typically, the above mentioned connection points for the provisioning of Wifi within the rooms of a house are standardized. In some cases, the repeaters or plugs might be specific for the Internet provider chosen. This means that, in case another Internet provider would be chosen later on, different repeaters or plugs might be required and configuration 2B is adopted. In some cases, such as with the use of UTP cables and RJ45 connectors, no Internet provider specificity is present within the access point at the level of the room and therefore configuration 2C is present: one could easily change the chosen Internet provider without an arising need to change the connectors.

C. Device level

While Internet access is distributed among the different households and their rooms, the Internet access should ultimately be disclosed to individual devices for which it is required in order to work properly and provide access to Internet services. The most straightforward solution would probably be to use the provisioned UTP or Wifi connection at the room level (see above) for connecting the devices. This would correspond to configuration 2. More specifically, as most devices use a highly standardized network card as a relay to the house level Internet connection, this generally corresponds to a 2C configuration as changing the Internet provider would not impact these connections. In some cases, one might argue that configuration 2B is still applicable as sometimes, a change in Internet provider might require the adaptation of certificates, username and/or password.

As another possibility, devices can perform their connection to an Internet provider themselves in a dedicated way. This means that they do not use the room or house level provided Internet access but instead will access the Internet via a separate subscription. One might think of smartphones having a mobile subscription with a data package and accessing the Internet via a 3G or 4G connection. Or of all kinds of other devices connecting to LoRa or Sigfox services in order to access the Internet. In the context of the ever increasing popularity of the IoT, it is interesting to see that our modularity and integration pattern reasoning as set out in Section III clearly indicates that such configuration is highly suitable for such purposes due to its associated independence and flexibility in terms of the choice of a provider. However, this implies that the configuration and connection capability to the mentioned IoT services should be duplicated in each of the devices. Recall that we also made a brief referral to the IoT context during the discussion of the same integration pattern of another cross-cutting concern as well (see Section IV-D).

D. Overview and advanced issues

Table IV provides an overview of the granularity-integration pattern combinations for the electricity provisioning of houses. We can observe that, at all modularity levels, a standardized integration pattern (i.e., 1B and 2B) is opted for, with in some cases even a 2C configuration (indicating the presence of a framework gateway). This tends to indicate a rather high maturity within the respective domain, which could be argued to be rather congruent with our experiences in everyday life: indeed, in most cases today it is rather easy to equip an increasing amount of devices in a household with Internet access. While the table does not explicitly indicate integration patterns to be explored and researched for this cross-cutting concern, the next section (see Section VIII) will suggest some general possibilities for exploration that are also applicable for this Internet access cross-cutting concern (especially in case one is opting for the distribution of Internet access by the use of UTP cables). Further, the table once again illustrates that, when aiming for maximum flexibility, the integration of concerns tends to be solved at more fine-grained levels (going downwards in Table IV) and in a more standardized externally enabled way (going to the right in Table IV) in the long run.

TABLE IV. OVERVIEW OF THE DIFFERENT GRANULARITY-INTEGRATION PATTERN COMBINATIONS REGARDING INTERNET ACCESS.

	1A	1B	2A	2B	2C
house		•			
room				•	•
device		•		•	•

•: currently employed, ○: to be explored

VIII. Reflections

Sections IV till VII showed that the integration of cross-cutting concerns such as electricity, heating, air conditioning and Internet access can and have to be dealt with at several modular granularity levels and can be solved in multiple ways. During the drawing of a building plan, an experienced architect will take into account these cross-cutting concerns in advance: the wires for the electricity and water pipes for the water distribution will be provided, space for central heating boiler will be assured, and so on. And although some heuristics and best practices exist, this still means that the integration problem of these concerns has to be dealt with by every architect again, every time a house is constructed. As mentioned in Section II, NST was inspired by the need for adaptability and flexibility. In the context of a house, this would for instance correspond to the possibility of incorporating an additional room, or choosing another provider for a particular cross-cutting concern (e.g., switching from tapping electricity from the public distribution network to self-generated solar energy). However, it is generally known that the distribution of housing cross-cutting concerns —such as the ones we considered in this paper— may cause significant problems during such house extensions or adaptations. Many times, this leads to unforeseen ripple effects, including the drilling into walls and floors, and even tearing down (parts of) walls. As we explained in Section II, NST therefore proposes to use a set of predefined design patterns (called "elements") that already solve this integration problem for a particular functionality of a modular system and can then be used over and over again.

In the context of housing and their cross-cutting concerns, we would envision an elementary construction element as such fine-grained element [2] as is represented in Figure 1. We already suggested such a brick for heating and airconditioning, but it is clear that a construction element might provide the integration of more than one cross-cutting concern (e.g., water supply, electricity, physical support, wired Internet access provisioning, etc.). Different types of such building blocks might exist, such as for inner or outer walls, for floors and ceilings, with and without certain utilities, etc. The adaptation problems and their associated ripple-effects would be less frequent by the use of such building blocks as it is often the set of cross-cutting concerns that causes these invasive drilling and tearing down activities and these would then already be integrated in the most elementary building block of a house. As they are used, the construction elements would provide the cross-cutting concerns and integrate fluently with the other previously installed building blocks. Moreover, an architect designing a new house would have to spend less effort into the integration issues regarding the cross-cutting concerns as the elements already deal with it. As we are no domain experts, we are not in a position to elaborate in detail how these building blocks should actually look like in practice. However, we do think that it would be worthwhile for such building blocks to be subject to intensive research and development, which might for instance result in connections and isolations of fluid conduits and electrical conductors that are superior with respect to handcrafted plumbing. As these building blocks would be rather general and used over and over again, the resources invested would have a significant pay off due to the high-quality re-used solution.

So while in most cases, architects take the house as the main level of modular granularity, it is interesting to see that some initiatives have been initiated to adopt the individual rooms of a house as a modular unit. It even seems that some kind of elements have been proposed in this context, such as in the Hivehaus "modular living space" initiative [9]. Here, houses are assembled as aggregations of prefabricated (e.g., hexagonal) modular parts, wherein the distribution of auxiliary facilities has been integrated upfront. Clearly, the design freedom concerning the house is then limited to an aggregation of these modular building blocks. This is due to the phenomenon we mentioned in Section II: the cross-cutting concerns should be integrated at the most fine-grained modular level as possible, as this determines the flexibility of the resulting artifacts. It is for this reason that we encourage the exploration of a construction element, integrating several cross-cutting concerns as discussed above.

Finally, we wish to remark that very similar conclusions or analyses can be made for other utility concerns within houses such as water distribution or media (audio, video) as well. We anticipate that the bottom line of such analysis will be highly similar: first, the distribution of the cross-cutting concern should be considered at different modular aggregation levels. At each level, centralized (integration pattern 1) or non-centralized (integration pattern 2) integration patterns can be chosen, each in a non-standarized (A) or standardized (B) way. Whereas the decentralized version offers benefits in terms of freedom of choice, the centralized alternative might typically generate other benefits such as economies of scale. A centralized version then has to deal with the fact that all modules plugging in are dependent on the framework unless a gateway module assuring version transparency (2C) is used.

IX. Conclusions

This paper presented an overview of the different possible integration patterns (with their associated benefits and drawbacks) for the heat, electricity, air conditioning and Internet access distribution utilities in a housing context, which we consider as cross-cutting concerns within a modularity perspective. It is important to stress that none of the authors claim to be experts in any of the specific cross-cutting concerns discussed (e.g., electricity, heating, etc.). Instead, the analysis was based on general knowledge within this domain. Also, with regard to general modularity reasoning, no significant new principles or knowledge was presented. Our actual contributions are situated elsewhere and are twofold. First, our goal was to show that the cross-cutting integration patterns for modular structures as proposed in [2] (and illustrated within the domain of software systems) are, at first sight, indeed relevant and applicable in a domain outside software as well. Given our non-expert status in the housing industry, we encourage actual domain experts to scrutinize and validate or refine our initial analyses. Second, we proposed and illustrated an approach to analyze and report on the different modular integration patterns for cross-cutting concerns within a domain. That is, is seems valuable to start with describing certain specificities and challenges in the domain at hand. Next, the different (hierarchical) granularity levels in the domain as well as the relevant cross-cutting concerns could be listed. For each cross-cutting concern, all possible combinations of granularity levels and cross-cutting concern integration patterns can be considered and analyzed in terms of their respective benefits and drawbacks. Some of these configurations might already exist, others might prove to be interesting avenues for future developments and still others might be purely theoretical considerations. We find it encouraging that we recently succeeded in applying the same thought experiment (i.e., applying modularity reasoning in terms of the possible integration architectures for cross-cutting concerns) within another domain (being artifacts and concepts related to logistics) [12]. Therefore, we hope that this paper might incite researchers and experts within other domains (e.g., all kinds of manufacturing and product designs) to perform similar analyses within their respective areas of expertise.

REFERENCES

[1] P. De Bruyn, J. Faes, T. Vermeire, and J. Bosmans, "On the modular structure and evolvability of architectural patterns for housing utilities," in Proceedings of the Ninth International Conference on Pervasive Patterns and Applications (PATTERNS), 2017, pp. 40–45.

[2] H. Mannaert, J. Verelst, and P. De Bruyn, Normalized Systems Theory: From Foundations for Evolvable Software Toward a General Theory for Evolvable Design. Koppa, 2016.

[3] H. Simon, The Sciences of the Artificial. MIT Press, 1996.

[4] C. Y. Baldwin and K. B. Clark, Design Rules: The Power of Modularity. Cambridge, MA, USA: MIT Press, 2000.

[5] D. Parnas, "On the criteria to be used in decomposing systems into modules," Communications of the ACM, vol. 15, no. 12, 1972, pp. 1053–1058.

[6] H. Mannaert, J. Verelst, and K. Ven, "The transformation of requirements into software primitives: Studying evolvability based on systems theoretic stability," Science of Computer Programming, vol. 76, no. 12, 2011, pp. 1210–1222, special Issue on Software Evolution, Adaptability and Variability.

[7] P. De Bruyn, "Generalizing normalized systems theory : towards a foundational theory for enterprise engineering," Ph.D. dissertation, University of Antwerp, 2014.

[8] M. Keymer, "Design strategies for new and renovation construction that increase the capacity of buildings to accommodate change," Master's thesis, Massachusetts Institute of Technology, 2000.

[9] Hivehaus, http://hivehaus.co.uk/, Last accessed on February 4th, 2017.

[10] Emerge Alliance, http://www.emergealliance.org/, Last accessed on February 4th, 2017.

[11] M. Duusma, "Restwarmte haven r'dam moet 500.000 huizen verwarmen," 2007, https://www.nrc.nl/nieuws/2017/03/23/energie-z-holland-uit-restwarmte-haven-rdam-a1551649, Last accessed on July 12th, 2017.

[12] P. De Bruyn, H. Mannaert, and P. Huysmans, "Exploring evolvable modular patterns for transportation vehicles and logistics architectures," in Proceedings of the Ninth International Conference on Pervasive Patterns and Applications (PATTERNS), 2017, pp. 46–51.

Exploring Evolvable Modular Patterns within Logistics

Peter De Bruyn and Herwig Mannaert
Normalized Systems Institute
Faculty of Applied Economics
University of Antwerp, Belgium
Email:{peter.debruyn, herwig.mannaert}@uantwerp.be

Philip Huysmans
Antwerp Management School
Belgium
Email:philip.huysmans@ams.ac.be

***Abstract*—Many domains employ the concept of modularity as a key aspect during their design. While the use of modularity characteristics is believed to enable several beneficial effects, such as evolvability, the actual realization of this evolvability or flexibility remains difficult. This paper analyzes a set of modular structures, which can be identified within transportation vehicles and logistic architectures. We employ Normalized Systems Theory (NST), a theory on how to create evolvable modular structures, as our theoretical basis to analyze these transportation and logistic structures in terms of the flexibility and adaptability they do (not) enable. For these structures, multiple design alternatives exist of which the theory can clearly highlight the respective benefits and drawbacks. This paper is an extended version of an earlier conference proceeding and demonstrates that NST is useful to analyze transport related modular structures at different levels of granularity. Additionally, we reflect upon the modularity characteristics of a recent logistics initiative called "The Physical Internet".**

Keywords*–*Modularity; Transportation; Logistics; Evolvability; Patterns; Physical Internet.

I. Introduction

This paper is an extended version of an earlier conference proceeding [1] in which the implications of applying Normalized Systems Theory (NST) to the modular architecture of transportation and logistics concepts is studied.

In many domains including computer science, product engineering, and organizational sciences, modularity has proven to be a powerful concept. A modular system is typically considered as a system, which is subdivided into a set of interacting subsystems. Several potential benefits are attributed to modular artifacts. Amongst other things, designing a product while using a set of modules is associated with a lower amount of complexity as the design is broken up into a set of smaller (less complex) problems [2]. Also, flexibility or evolvability are deemed to be improved in this way. Indeed, it allows one module of the system to be swapped for another version of it, without having to redesign the artifact from scratch. This allows some kind of plug-and-play behavior enabling variation (different aggregations based on the same set of modular building blocks can be formed) and evolvability (an artifact can evolve from one variant to another over time) and is deemed very powerful.

Achieving these benefits in reality is however quite challenging. Often, coupling (dependencies and interactions) between the modules in the system exist, which should be minimized [2][3][4]. However, specific ways on how this should precisely be done are often absent or ambiguous. For instance, some concerns in a modular system are cross-cutting (e.g., security in a software application) in the sense that their functionality is required throughout the entire system (e.g., every data entity should be securely stored). Adapting certain aspects of such cross-cutting concerns is often problematic as it typically creates profound ripple-effects throughout the system (i.e., a change in one module triggers a change in several other modules), which is clearly contradictory with the purpose of evolvability.

This paper focuses on the modular structures within the context of transportation vehicles and logistic architectures. It is clear that transportation vehicles (such as cars, trucks, boats, airplanes, trains) are modular structures at several abstraction levels (a car consisting out of a trunk, chassis, engine, etc. of which the engine consists out of several cylinders etc.) and could benefit from evolvability (e.g., replacing or upgrading particular parts or even extending the vehicle with additional seating places or engines). Also, the concept of cross-cutting concerns seems relevant within this context. That is, transportation artifacts need multiple auxiliary facilities in their design such as electricity and communication, which are needed in most of their components. More specifically, several of these auxiliary facilities within the modular design of physical artifacts (such as the different design options to distribute heating) were already discussed using an NST perspective in another publication [5] in a housing context. Analogous conclusions for these facilities can be drawn in the context of transportation artifacts. What differentiates transportation artifacts from other types of artifacts, is the presence of the additional and crucial concern of *propulsion*. Every transportation mechanism should, somehow, provide the ability for its cargo to be transported from one location to another. This propulsion can be realized by means of different driving mechanisms and different integration architectures, which will be the main focus of our exploratory analysis in this paper. However, most transportation vehicles are designed in such way that they lack true evolvability in several ways (e.g., extending the seating capacity of a car or adding additional cylinders in the engine is typically impossible). This paper studies the implications of different design alternatives for transportation vehicles and logistic architectures in terms of their evolvability. The considered design alternatives are based on the modular integration patterns as suggested by Normalized Systems Theory (NST) [6]. The theory is relevant in this context as it studies in-depth the necessary conditions in order to design evolvable modular systems.

It is important to mention upfront that none of the authors of this paper are experts within the domain of transportation or logistics. Therefore, the intention of this paper is not the prescribe in detail how architectures within this industry should be improved in the future. Rather, we intend to show that it makes sense to apply the modularity reasoning presented within NST (which originated at the software level) to this other domain in which we believe modularity is playing an important role.

The remainder of this paper is structured as follows. In Section II, we provide a brief overview of NST and the ways it describes to integrate the different modules within a system. We then apply these patterns to the analysis of transportation vehicles (e.g., cars, airplanes) in Section III. In Section IV, we analyze the modular architectures and integration of so-called cross-cutting concerns and ponder on some new initiatives and trends present within the logistics industry, which seem to exhibit certain similarities with NST's (more general) modularity approach. Finally, we offer our conclusions in Section V.

II. Modularity and NST Integration Patterns

A. NST and combinatorics

NST is a theory providing the formulation of design theorems, which are proven to be necessary conditions for obtaining an evolvable software system [6]. The authors operationalize evolvability by demanding Bounded Input Bound Output (BIBO) stability, even for systems growing in an unlimited way. The theorems prescribe that all change drivers should be separated in distinct constructs (Separation of Concerns), processing functions should be called statefully (Separation of States) and data structures or processing functions should be up-datable without impacting other data structures or processing functions (Version Transparency) [7]. Further, these theorems can actually be reformulated for modular systems in general [8] and related to basic combinatorics [6]. More specifically, it is illustrated that modularity suggests that maintaining a particular amount of versions of modular building blocks should allow for an exponential amount of available system variants. However, when modularity is applied arbitrarily (e.g., by not adhering to the theorems), changing one particular version of one particular module may result into ripple effects to other (versions of) modules. This number of impacts can exponentially grow with the size of the system, which is clearly harmful for the evolvability of a (software) system.

B. Patterns for cross-cutting concern integration

Adherence to the NST theorems results in a very fine-grained modular system. This fine-grained design should be established very meticulously as every violation of every design theorem is proven to result eventually into ripple effects due to change. This is very hard to achieve in practice and therefore, "elements" (i.e., modular design patterns) are proposed to enable the construction of such systems in a realistic setting [6]. Each of these elements provides a generic reusable modular structure for a basic functionality of the type of system one is creating. To fit the specific situation at hand, they can be parametrized and, if necessary, customized. A system is then created as being a set of parametrized instantiations of these generic modular elements. For software systems, data, task, flow, connector and trigger elements were defined as generic modular structures providing the basic functionalities of most information systems [6]. One can therefore conclude that the modules forming an element become (as a whole) a reusable module at a higher level of abstraction. Internally, every element takes care of a core functionality (e.g., the representation of data), and provides integration with some relevant cross-cutting concerns for that system (e.g., data security and persistency). To maximally enable evolvability, these cross-cutting concerns need to be integrated at the lowest modular granularity level possible (forming elements). The parts in the elements connecting or dealing with the cross-cutting concerns need to be properly isolated in separate modules being version transparent.

In general, different integration patterns for dealing with cross-cutting concerns can be distinguished. One possibility is to add cross-cutting concern modules directly to the main modules. Each cross-cutting concern module will then, by itself, handle the full functionality of that cross-cutting concern. We call integrations of this type the *embedded integration pattern* and will refer to it as *configuration 1*. More specifically, such embedded module can either be dedicated (i.e., the module was specifically designed for the considered system) or standardized (i.e., a standardized module for handling the cross-cutting concern is chosen). The first option is referred to as *configuration 1A*, while the latter one will be referenced as *configuration 1B*. In the context of software systems, imagine for instance a separate module added to a data entity to take care of data persistency in a custom designed way (1A) or by adopting a standard module (1B) for the same goal.

Another possibility is to add the cross-cutting concern modules to the main modules in such way that the cross-cutting concern modules only act as connections (or "relay modules") to an (external) framework, which implements the cross-cutting concern more elaborately and will therefore actually perform the needed functionality. We call integrations of this type the *relay integration pattern* and will refer to it as *configuration 2*. More specifically, a relay module can link to a dedicated framework (i.e., the framework was specifically designed for the considered system) or standardized (possibly even publicly available). The first option is referred to as *configuration 2A* while the latter one will be referenced as *configuration 2B*. In the context of a software system, imagine for instance a separate module added to a data entity acting as a proxy to a specifically designed persistency framework (2A) or to a widely used standard solution, such as Java Persistence API (2B). Finally, it is also possible to have a relay module connecting to a *framework gateway* module. Here, it is only the framework gateway that connects directly to the external framework. This third variant is referred to as *configuration 2C*. In the context of a software system, imagine for instance a dedicated gateway module that connects to the JPA framework allowing all cross-cutting concern relay modules to call the gateway without being dependent on JPA themselves.

As a modular field matures, it will create several levels of granularity among which it will need to integrate its relevant cross-cutting concerns. Also, the concern will typically be embedded at a deeper level (i.e., more fine-grained), and towards a more standardized (from A to B) and relayed (i.e., 2B and 2C) way.

III. Transportation Vehicle Patterns

The identification of modules within a system is often a recursive issue [2]: at different levels of granularity, parts and subparts can be discerned. Therefore, when studying modularity within the domain of transportation, we propose to focus on the modular structure and its integration patterns at different levels: the vehicle, cargo and vehicle component levels.

A. The vehicle level

Regarding transportation, it is clear that most types of vehicles (such as cars, trucks, airplanes) provide their own propulsion mechanism, both in terms of power storage (e.g., fuel) and energy generation (typically by means of an engine). Since in most cases, extensively tested and highly standardized modules are used for this purpose, this clearly aligns with integration pattern 1B as introduced in Section II. This has benefits in terms of flexibility: different types of vehicles might use different types of power source (e.g., diesel, gas, electricity) or have different power needs (e.g., related to the cargo capacity). It also provides a high amount of independence and autonomy. A downside of such an architecture is clearly that the propulsion mechanism needs to be, by definition, embedded within every individual transport vehicle and that for instance technological advancements are not automatically dispersed over all available vehicles unless each of their mechanisms (e.g., engines) are individually updated or replaced. Another drawback is the fact that this does not allow the realization of any possible economies of scale arising from producing energy on a larger scale (i.e., for many vehicles at once).

While the other integration architectures are used less frequently, they are not completely inconceivable for transportation vehicles. Consider for instance an electrical train. While the propulsion forces are generated internally using electrical engines, the electrical power used for this purpose is generated externally. This electrical power is tapped from an externally available framework or, in this case, the electrical distribution network available along the train tracks. Therefore, one could argue that —to a certain extent— this aligns already to some extent with integration pattern 2B. One could even go one step further. Consider for instance the case of the Transrapid magnetic levitation train, or the recently proposed Hyperloop. In these types of transportation, the vehicles are propelled by the propulsion forces generated in or around the vehicle tracks. This would even more narrowly fit into the mentioned integration pattern 2B. While such centralized architectures introduce a dependency on the external framework employed (e.g., if the energy distribution network is down, no vehicle will be able to advance), they have clear benefits as well. For instance, they would be able to benefit from economies of scale regarding efficiency, or flexibility with respect to the introduction of (for instance) more environmentally friendly techniques for power generation.

Returning to the design of cars, it is clear that such mechanisms (i.e., as described in integration pattern 2) would only be possible in case the roads contain propulsion mechanisms or conduct power. As this is currently not the case, the electrical power for electrical cars can only be stored internally in batteries (but generated externally) and the design of the distribution mechanism for propulsion remains tied to integration pattern 1B. Specifically focusing our attention on airplane vehicles, one can note that aircrafts require large amounts of propulsion power, which would make the use of an architecture in which the aircraft taps into an externally available standardized framework via a relay module (i.e., integration pattern 2B) extremely tempting. Nevertheless, the intertwining of propulsion and lift (which is specific for aircrafts) would make this design very difficult, and the notion seems to be completely incompatible with the current degrees of freedom airplanes enjoy to use the airspace. Indeed, such an architecture would entail the need for some kind of tubes encompassing the vehicles, which could in their turn remove the need for lifting forces. In other words, such an architecture would probably cease to be genuine air transport.

Nevertheless, as this configuration has been realized for certain transportation vehicles and offers potential for others (e.g., cars) in the future, we believe that the exploration of (the feasibility) of technologies enabling these kind of integration architectures would be very worthwhile.

B. The cargo level

It is interesting to note that the transportation industry has already, rather explicitly, adopted a high degree of modularity standardization at the level of their cargo. This can be found in the context of today's logistics landscape, in which it is important to be able to transport goods by means of cross-mode transportation. That means that, in order to go from point A to B, multiple vehicles of often different nature are employed. For instance, a laptop ordered in the USA to be delivered in Antwerp, might travel by a combination of airplane and/or boat, train, truck and car. In order to facilitate such logistic routes, the packaging of the cargoes (i.e., the goods to be transported) are packaged, is standardized to a large extent by means of *containerized freight*. That is, while for some type of goods customized transportation mechanisms still exist (e.g., for the transportation of steel coils, roll-on roll-off (RoRo) goods, bulk goods, etc.), the majority of non-bulk goods is transported by means of containers. Such containers can clearly be considered as standardized cargo modules in terms of several of their properties such as their dimensions (height, length, depth), securing mechanisms, maximum load, etc.

From a modularity point of view, one can see that in such case various sound design principles are applied, implying a set of accompanying important benefits. First, this existing containerized modular freight architecture enables the decoupling or encapsulation of the cargo from the transport vehicle (cf. infra). This decoupling allows to freely combine both decoupled parts (here: cargo and transport vehicle) without having to adapt one or the other for this purpose. Stated otherwise: substitution of the modular parts is made easy. Indeed, the standardization of freight containers in terms of dimensions and securing mechanisms allows the recombination of goods on different transportation modes at the level of the individual containers. As long as goods can be securely stowed within these standardized containers, thousands of them can be loaded by cranes on sea-going cargo ships, be switched to barges in batches of tens or maybe hundred containers, routed individually within a harbor, and further shipped towards customers via trains (in a set up to 20) and/or trucks (mostly individually). Similarly, as most transportation vehicles are designed in correspondence with the standardized dimensions of the freight containers, they can transport all types of goods and do not need to undergo specific changes when, for instance, a truck has to transport couches instead of laptops. Second, the modular architecture of the cargo makes it possible to upscale or downscale the total cargo on one vehicle within certain limits. For instance, as long as a ship is large enough, one can extend the overall cargo by simply increasing the number of containers. Or, as long the traction of a locomotive is powerful enough, additional containers can be added to a transportation train. We therefore conclude that already an important amount of flexibility is achieved in terms of the type of cargo as well as the transportation mode and scale.

Interpreting the situation sketched above in terms of our modular integration architectures as described in Section II, this means that integration architecture 2C is applied. That is, it is clear that no embedded architecture is present as the container itself has no propulsion mechanisms incorporated into it. Instead, the container has standardized connections to connect into different types of vehicles (see Section III-A) which, at their turn, have the capacity to provide the required propulsion for one or several containers. As these connections are version transparent in terms of a large set of different vehicles (truck, train and even boat), no dependency regarding a specific type of external network is present and therefore we would be inclined to categorize the propulsion provisioning in this situation as using architecture 2C.

Further, in terms of this containerized freight, it is important to mention that, conceptually speaking, the idea of containerization should not necessarily be limited to freight alone. For instance, one can easily imagine that similar cargo modules could be made for humans as well, although such containers would clearly have to be made more human-friendly, and the practicality and added value might —at this point in time— be questionable.

Finally, it is interesting to note that certain players in industry are still looking for additional ways to modularize freight in a more efficient way. For instance, Airbus was only recently —in late 2015— granted a patent for a modular removable aircraft cabin, in which the whole cabin (i.e., the space for all passengers) can be substituted by another cabin [9]. The fact that major industry players are working on these kinds of ideas, seems to support the fact that such ideas on modularization in (air) transportation should definitely not be considered ludicrous nor obvious.

C. The vehicle components level

In order to further explore the modular integration in the context of transportation vehicles, it is interesting to ponder on the decoupling or encapsulation of the various concerns at the level of the vehicle components, such as those of a car. Here, relevant concerns could be the passenger cabine (providing a comfortable place for passengers to sit), the trunk (providing storage space for luggage), the chassis (protecting the car from the outside world) or the engine (generating the propulsion force). It is remarkable to note that, in many cases, the compatibility of these modular components of transportation vehicles seems restricted to vehicles of one particular model or, in some cases, multiple models of one manufacturer. This means that, when again considering a car, most passenger cabines, trunks, chassis parts, etc. can only be replaced by their exact copies. Stated otherwise, a trunk that was designed for car model A is typically not able to be used for a car model B as it would simply not fit due to size limitations, aerodynamic constraints, weight, etc. This is due to a high degree of coupling between the individual components we consider and their model or manufacturer specifications. It would certainly provide some added value to customers if the modules implementing these major concerns would be decoupled, encapsulated, and standardized in accordance with integration architecture 1B as discussed in Section II, allowing plug-and-play behavior. In such case, consumers would for instance be able —for a certain car size category— to purchase the chassis, the engine, the passenger cabine, the trunk, etc. all independently from different vendors.

Moreover, each of these modules could then be replaced or upgraded independently as well. For example, the engine could be replaced when it breaks down, but could also be upgraded in order to have a more powerful, modern, or environmentally cleaner engine. One could even imagine to introduce an electrical engine in a car that was originally equipped with as gas or diesel engine. Of course, we mention once again that we are no experts in car manufacturing and do not elaborate on the specific manufacturing details of each aspect of the design. Moreover, we are aware of the fact that it would not be straightforward to keep the decoupling or encapsulation of the various modules intact throughout the course of significant technological evolutions in time. Nevertheless, the advantages of such design from a sustainability point of view would obviously be significant: cars could become more efficient and cleaner without ending up in a junkyard after a limited amount of years.

Some indications suggest that the amount of coupling between vehicle components or between the vehicle and its components is not equally large among different industries. For instance, the airplane industry seems to succeed in having a better decoupling and encapsulation of certain parts of an airplane. For example, manufacturers of jet engines and the aircraft are typically different firms. In order to remain viable as an industry, this implies (and necessitates) that the engine and the rest of the vehicle should, at least to some extent, be decoupled. However, though an engine can be replaced, aircrafts are clearly designed for a certain type and amount of engines.

Considering the components of transportation vehicles at a still more fine-grained modular level, one could imagine an even more fine-grained modular structure for, for instance, car engines where cylinders could be replaced, upgraded, or simply added in order to increase the engine power. Again, in order to enable these possibilities, the modules at this very fine-grained level should be designed in such a way that they are clearly decoupled, encapsulated and standardized, corresponding to integration architecture 1B.

D. Overview and advanced issues

Table I provides an overview of the granularity-integration pattern combinations for the case of transportation vehicles. We can observe that an interesting and advanced modular architecture already seems to be in place at the cargo level. This tends to indicate that the industry has reached a rather high maturity level regarding this issue. As far as the vehicle and vehicle component modularity levels are concerned, interesting avenues for a further exploration of the modular integration architecture can be remarked. This certainly holds for the case of vehicle components, where the design of fully decoupled and encapsulated modular parts still seems to be in-progress. The table further illustrates that, when aiming for maximum flexibility, the integration of concerns tends to be solved at more fine-grained levels (going downwards in Table I) and in a more standardized way enabled by an external framework (going to the right in Table I) in the long run.

Furthermore, it is interesting to make the mental exercise of applying NST reasoning in a more complete way and adopt the notion of NST elements, which we introduced in Section II. When employing such elements to build a system, a large set of very tightly integrated, small and fine-grained modules are used to form the aggregated system (instead of one monolithic and non-scalable building block). Translating this idea to the components of an engine, one could imagine an engine as an aggregation of smaller integrated engines (with all required subcomponents for a small engine) delivering propulsion forces. This would theoretically mean that the propulsion power could be increased by adding more engines, and that the various small engines could be replaced and upgraded independently, even combining combustion engines and electrical engines. Once again, this could have significant benefits from a sustainability point of view. Also, this would partly solve some of the scalability issues we mentioned in Section III-A, for instance in cases when carrying additional cargo within a particular vehicle would be restrained due to limitations in the capacity of the vehicle's engine.

TABLE I. OVERVIEW OF THE DIFFERENT GRANULARITY-INTEGRATION PATTERN COMBINATIONS REGARDING TRANSPORTATION VEHICLES

	1A	*1B*	*2A*	*2B*	*2C*
vehicle		•		◦	
cargo					•
vehicle components		◦			

•: currently employed, ◦: to be explored

Going one step further, elements might be conceivable at a higher granularity level as well. That is, elements might be designed that also provide the integration of these small engines with non-propulsion concerns. Suppose for instance one-person transport modules or vehicles that can be aggregated or combined at any time into more-person modules. Assume further that these one-person modules have their own propulsion mechanisms and storage spaces, which are automatically combined when several modules are aggregated. This would mean that the propulsion power and the storage room would be proportional to the size of the vehicle, which would be proportional to the number of passengers. And one could further imagine that each one of those units could be enabled to tap into external propulsion power if available (cf. integration architecture 2B or 2C), while producing its own propulsion power otherwise (cf. integration architecture 1B).

One could even explore what this could possibly mean for air transportation. When considering the design of airplane artifacts, one can note that they differentiate themselves from ground transportation artifacts by the fact that another concern next to propulsion becomes apparent: the need to obtain lift. Adding this concern to the design is obviously not trivial. Indeed, both concerns —propulsion and lift— are even tightly coupled in current airplanes: the lift force is based on the velocity and therefore on the propulsion of the vehicle. This actually represents an omnipresent risk in airplanes: without propulsion, there is no lift anymore. Nevertheless, we do think that a similar reasoning based on elements is valid for air transportation. For instance, one could imagine small integrated transport modules or vehicles for a few persons, that can be aggregated or combined at any time into larger airplane modules. From an energy or sustainability point of view, it would clearly be very appealing to be able to adapt the size and propulsion power of the airplanes to the number of registered passengers.

As we are no domain experts, we are clearly not entitled to discuss the outlook of modular structures for transport propulsion in depth or judge on their practical feasibility. We also do not have any intention to oversimplify the difficulties and complexities one would be confronted with during the design of such elements. For example, the design of such modular architectures obviously does not liberate the designer from the laws of physics that need to be obeyed at all times: when considering the elements for air transportation, the relationship between the weight of the vehicle and the wing surface creating the lift, should result in the required equilibrium at the cruising speed, both for the singular and aggregated vehicles. However, instead of making such architectures impossible, these physical constraints could serve as boundary conditions to solve the design equations. So, instead of elaborating in detail on the actual design of such modular building blocks (such as the elements), our main goal is to illustrate the relevance of our modularity approach for the design of transportation vehicles and to show what kind of possibilities normalized evolvable transport architectures could unleash. For instance, the scalability issue mentioned in Section III-A, would probably be largely solved if the industry would manage to realize such elements.

IV. LOGISTIC ARCHITECTURES

Whereas Section III focused on the modular architecture of (individual) vehicles, the viewpoint of modularization and its integration architectures can also be applied at a higher conceptual level such as logistics in general and its associated supply chain. That is, transportation can and is increasingly considered as a type of service, i.e., the service of something being transported from place X to Y in a timely and not too costly fashion. How the transportation is precisely executed (with which transportation means, at once or in several stages, etc.) is often of less or sometimes even no importance. Considering transportation as a service often also shifts the responsibility of collecting the remuneration or payment from the client to the scope of the service provider. For instance, one might think of situations where a client is prepared to pay a certain fee for the transportation of a particular good from location A to B by point in time P, and in which it is the service provider's responsibility to determine how this will be performed.

It is particularly interesting to see how recent initiatives in the business world are being taken in the context of this servitization. In this section, we will focus on two aspects of this servitization and their relation to the modularity aspects we discussed above. First, in Section IV-A, we focus on the (public) transport of people and the emergence of Mobility-as-a-Service (MaaS). Next, in Section IV-B, we focus on how the Physical Internet (PI) is aiming to revolutionize the transportation of goods.

A. Mobility-as-a-Service

The emergence of the concept of Mobility-as-a-Service is primarily driven by the idea that, given the increasing number of people living in major cities, it becomes unsustainable to have each individual person possessing his or her own car and use that for their private transportation needs. Some of the problems associated with such situation include the exploding amount of traffic leading to congested roads and associated traffic jams, increased pollution and the fact that it is inefficient in terms of capital spending (i.e., the high expenses of having a dedicated car including its insurance, maintenance, etc. for a device that is often more than 90% of the time unused). Therefore, the mission of MaaS and most of its providers is to enable consumers to make the switch from primarily using private cars for their transportation means towards (sustainable) shared mobility resources (such as taxi, car sharing, tram, bus, train, bike) or, stated otherwise, "to make it easier and more rewarding to use sustainable modes of transport in urban areas" [10, p. 4]. Attempts towards this direction could be, but should not necessarily be limited to [11]:

- *Simplified car ownership*: car manufacturers offering services that enable the usage of one physical vehicle with multiple owners. On top of financial services to handle purchasing and leasing, technological services (e.g., scheduling of vehicle use) and cost distribution calculation services are offered. The primary motivation behind these initiatives is presented as a reduction of the inefficiency of capital spending.
- *Peer transport services*: while initiatives in the simplified car ownership category focus on reducing the inefficiency of capital spending but remain within well-trusted boundaries of an individual's network, peer transport services seek to radically remove these inefficiencies by leveraging the excess capacity of all nearby means of transport. Available transport capacity is offered through a digital platform, where algorithms determine optimal matches between demand and supply. In this category, the service providers do not own the physical means of transport themsevles. Rather, they provide the technological platform and offer payment services.
- *Car sharing*: in car sharing initiatives, an organization commits itself to ownership of a fleet of transportation means. As a result, a more consistent and reliable service can be offered when compared to the previous categories.
- *Extended multi-modal planner*: a company offering advanced planning services by suggesting customers routes that may involve a combination of different transportation modals if those options appear to be the most efficient onces. Obviously, such planners might allow you to buy a ticket for the suggested route as well.
- *Combined mobility services*: a neutral third-party company that combines multiple mobility services as one offering (one subscription, unified invoicing, etc.) towards its customers (often complemented with an app for mobile devices, a website, etc.).
- *Integrated public transport*: focusing on the combined offering of public transport options, but optionally combined with other modes of transport as well.
- *Mobility broker*: similar mobility subscriptions as the options described above, but offered as part of a house rent. The mobility services are therefore required to be incorporated within the general planning process of urban areas.

As multiple sustainable transportation means are available for customers, customers could (in theory) choose from different alternatives (on a day-to-day basis) for the same transport or even combine several of them within one voyage. This often requires customers to manage a complex set of tickets or subscriptions that may turn the whole trajectory into something quite expensive and restricts the traveler's comfort. Therefore, the rationale behind MaaS additionally aims to enable customers to actually make use of this myriad of transportation means in the combination and timing they prefer or need (e.g., on day 1 using a combination of tram and a shared bike to go to work and on day 2 a shared car due to the rainy weather) in a comfortable way, i.e., by subscribing to only one provider or platform. Indeed, as Kamargianni et al. mention, "the complexity of using a variety of transport models (i.e. different payment methods, subscriptions, different mobile applications for each operator, lack of integrated information etc.) discourages many people from taking advantage of them" [12, p. 3295].

Therefore, an important characteristic of MaaS is its ability to provide *integration* for the customer in order to improve user friendliness and adoption. Some conceptualizations of MaaS would therefore only consider bullet points 4 till 8 as genuine implementations of MaaS as only these variatns include the combination (and therefore require the integration) of different types of transport. Conceptually, the goal is clearly to provide an integration of all the shared mobility resources for the customer. This issue has been formulated in a more specific way by Kamergianni et al. by splitting up the general concept of integration into three main elements [12, p. 3295]:

- *Ticket & Payment integration*: having one ("smart") card to be able to pay within different modes of transportation;
- *Mobility package*: a package for customers in which they (pre)pay for different modes of transportation;
- *ICT integration*: providing a digital integrated interface (often for smartphone) to give a single point of access regarding information for each of the different modes of transportation.

While the ICT integration between the different mobility providers is obviously challenging and crucial for a fluent user experience, we do not further focus on this issue in the remainder of this section. Rather, we will pay attention to the first two main elements listed as they both are related to payment issues and provide an interesting angle to look at a non-tangible part of each transportation service: the remuneration a mobility service provider should get for offering its services. Additionally, the integration of ticketing and payment are considered as stages necessarily preceding the ICT integration phase [13]. As all transportation services have to be remunerated in one way or the other, one could argue that this constitutes a genuine cross-cutting concern for mobility services: whether you take the tram, bus, taxi, shared car, etc., there will always be one or multiple mobility provider(s) that has/have to be compensated for the efforts performed. Therefore, our modularity approach and the adjoining reasoning regarding cross-cutting concern integration patterns is considered as a useful point of view in this regard. Specifically in a context where multiple mobility services are present and can be used during one voyage, interesting questions on how to integrate this concern in an efficient way, arise. First, we discuss how the payment concern is currently integrated in logistics (i.e., pre-MaaS). Next, we analyze how MaaS attempts to change this and reflect on the question whether we can still see some possible points for improvements based on our theoretical basis. For this end, similarly as we did in Section III, we will make use of tables representing different modular aggregation levels and how the cross-cutting concern is or can be integrated at each of these levels. It is important to be aware that in Tables II and III, we clearly consider another cross-cutting concern than in Table I. Whereas the latter focused on the integration of the propulsion concern for transportation vehicles, the former tables will focus on the integration of the payment concern for mobility services.

TABLE II. OVERVIEW OF THE DIFFERENT GRANULARITY-INTEGRATION PATTERN COMBINATIONS REGARDING THE REMUNERATION OF MOBILITY SERVICES IN A PRE-MAAS CONFIGURATION

	1A	*1B*	*2A*	*2B*	*2C*
mobility provider		•			
trip		•		•	

•: currently employed

In order to analyze the pre-MaaS phase, we consider Table II. Here, only two rows are included, i.e., trip and mobility provider. Typically, it is possible to pay directly for a single trip in cash when using a public service provider (e.g., at the cab or bus driver), which would correspond to the integration of the payment cross-cutting concern by means of configuration 1B (1 because it is embedded, B because generally standardized cashier systems are being used). However, many of these public transport providers also offer subscriptions or multi-ride tickets. A devaluation mechanism is then typically present in the vehicles, registering for instance an additional ride on the multi-ride ticket or verifying the validity of the subscription card. As a consequence, this corresponds to integration configuration 2B at the level of the trip (i.e., the payment is being performed but in a relay fashion as a connection is made to an external framework at a higher modularity aggregation level, here: mobility provider) and integration configuration 1B at the level of the mobility provider (e.g., bus or tram company) as the actual payment is made here in a dedicated way. Remark that at the level of the trip, integration architecture 2B still implies that the connection to the mobility provider is specific for the particular provider the customer is using (e.g., the bus company one is making use of). This also implies that a customer will be required to engage in multiple subscriptions or multi-ride tickets for each mobility provider of each transport mode one is making use of.

TABLE III. OVERVIEW OF THE DIFFERENT GRANULARITY-INTEGRATION PATTERN COMBINATIONS REGARDING THE REMUNERATION OF MOBILITY SERVICES IN A POST-MAAS CONFIGURATION

	1A	*1B*	*2A*	*2B*	*2C*
mobility platform		•			
mobility provider		•		•	○
trip		•		•	•

•: currently employed, ○: to be explored

As mentioned above, precisely this issue (which can be derived from Table II) was one of the driving forces behind the idea of MaaS: avoiding the need for consumers to buy separate (multi-ride) tickets or subscriptions for each of the mobility services one is using as this inefficiency is assumed to be an important obstacle for people to start using a (combination of) the available durable public transport means in a city. The offered alternative can be represented by means of Table III. Remark that an additional row is added to the table, i.e., the mobility provider platform. This level becomes relevant in situations such as MaaS where an aggregation of multiple service providers is envisioned. When further analyzing the table, one can find that 1B (standardized dedicated) payments at the level of a trip are typically still possible (as was the case in the pre-MaaS situation), which is therefore not a differentiating characteristic for MaaS service models. Also the traditional one-provider subscription mechanism remains available (a 1B configuration at the level of the mobility provider and 2B configuration at the level of the individual trip) but is equally not a differentiating characteristic for MaaS service models. However, as soon as one considers MaaS as a new concept, the payment can also be performed at a higher and additional modular aggregation level (i.e., a mobility platform) providing a customer the possibility to, for instance, sign up for one subscription and have access to several transportation means (e.g., tram, bus, bike and car sharing). Therefore, at the level of this mobility platform, this corresponds to integration architecture 1B. Regarding the trip level, the integration architecture can move from 2B to 2C. Indeed, as mentioned above, this was the very main reason why MaaS was initiated in the first way. Integration structure 2C at the level of the trip allows a customer who wants to pay his trip, to use one and the same card for different mobility providers. Stated otherwise, switching between different providers becomes easier. Another significant difference with the pre-MaaS situation is the fact that now, the integration architecture at the level of the mobility provider can be moved from 1B to 2B: when, for instance, a traveler will scan his or her "MaaS transport card", the devaluation mechanism will (most probably) register a trip and its properties at the level of the mobility provider, which at its turn makes use of another external framework to assure its remuneration, i.e., that of the mobility platform. Remark that at the level of the mobility provider, integration architecture 2B still implies that the connection to the mobility platform is specific for the particular platform one is making use of (e.g., the MaaS mobility provider active in a particular city).

Based on our description of the transition from the pre-MaaS to the post-MaaS era in terms of the different payment integration configurations and the adjoining tables, certain commercial issues currently relevant within the MaaS field can be deducted and put into a modularity integration context. First, as the integration configuration at the level of the trip moves from 2B to 2C, this implies that customers can easily switch from one provider to the other within their subscription. While this increases the comfort level of the passenger and was the intention of the MaaS concept, service providers consider this both as a benefit as well as a potential treat. The flexibility in service provider is generally considered beneficial due to the fact that the mobility platform brings in new customers who can experiment with their services (whereas they otherwise, without the MaaS subscription, might not choose to do so) and therefore increase their revenue. When dividing the competitive landscape between the providers "within" and "outside" the portfolio of the mobility platform, an advantage is typically attributed to the providers within the joint-venture. However, such flexibility may also increase the competition between the service providers within the portfolio. Indeed, as a customer can –within his or her subscription– freely choose between all alternatives (depending on the revenue distribution model adopted by the mobility provider), other providers within the portfolio might become indirect competitors (e.g., customers may switch their preferences towards the usage of shared bikes instead of buses). Currently, most MaaS providers have one mobility provider within their portfolio for each type of transport (i.e., one shared cars provider, one shared bikes provider, etc.). When a mobility platform would one day decide to include multiple providers of the same transport type into its portfolio, fellow portfolio members might even become each others direct competitors. Therefore, some mobility providers advocate the current situation in which their mobility platform only has one provider for each type of service. It is however unclear to which extent platform owners will follow this request as they have created integrations allowing the incorporation of multiple providers of the same service type in a fluent way. Similar competitive dynamics were equally portrayed by Sochor et al. [10]. Second, as the integration configuration at the level of the mobility provider is currently at 2B, this means that, for instance, the card used to register trips is still bound to one specific mobility platform. Using the same card for multiple mobility platforms would clearly further enhance the flexibility provided to the customer, but increase the competition in the platform's market in case multiple mobility mobility platforms would be active in the same region. However, switching this integration from 2B to 2C would provide a more mature modular cross-cutting integration situation, but would (similarly as was the case at the level of the individual mobility service providers), also imply a higher degree of competition for certain players in the market.

In summary we can state that the transition towards a MaaS configuration allows a more mature integration of the remuneration cross-cutting concern in person related logistics as the concern is integrated deep into the modular structure (i.e., until the level of the individual trip) and aggregated via 2B or 2C connections. The exploration of a 2C integration architecture at the level of the mobility provider could contribute to an even more mature modular cross-cutting integration.

As discussed in the beginning of this section, we elaborated mainly on the remuneration concern. However, integration issues in fine-grained service offerings become even more challenging when multiple concerns are considered at once. Consequently, the applicability of our analysis can be expected to increase as the amount of concerns relevant to MaaS increase and the resulting analysis might provide insights to decision takers when confronted with multiple MaaS vendors and parties. As we discussed above in the context of remuneration, platform providers can hold a significant amount of market power by controlling the management of such concerns and many other servitized markets have demonstrated how power over the platform guarantees strong economic returns. Therefore, it can be expected that various service providers will attempt to create initial platforms (as the ones mentioned in the beginning of this section) and continue to enlarge their scope (in terms of revenue and client base, but equally adding and dealing with additional concerns).

B. The Physical Internet

Modularization within the context of transportation is not necessarily limited to the analysis of the vehicles and their load or the service provisioning, but can also be applied at the level of the logistics supply chain. For instance, triggered by the current inefficiencies of most logistics networks (e.g., use of partly empty trucks, suboptimal routes, traffic jams, overusage of highly polluting transportation modes) the *Physical Internet (PI) Initiative* aims to design "an open global logistics system founded on physical, digital and operational interconnectivity through encapsulation, interfaces and protocols" [14, p. 152]. In order to achieve this goal, they propose to design a global logistics system based on the basic architectural principles adopted by the Internet for the distribution of digital information. This means that cargo is transported as a set of (smaller) packages, will reach its destination by traveling via a set of connecting nodes, may follow different routes (possibly upfront undetermined) and employs an open infrastructure (public stock facilities or transportation providers) to this end. Related to our focus, it is interesting to observe that the initiators of the project explicitly coin the importance of well-designed modular structures in logistics and the problems associated with the opposite situation: "Innovation is bottlenecked, notably by lack of generic standards and protocols, transparency, modularity and systemic open infrastructure" [15, p. 5].

Whereas the exhaustive analysis of all listed characteristics for this new logistics system is outside the scope and purpose of this paper, some of them can easily be related to our integration pattern analysis presented above. First, regarding the cargo level, it is remarkable that within the PI approach the current freight containers are considered useful, but still too coarse-grained. Instead, a set of unitary and composite π-containers acting as world-standard, smart, green and modular containers is called for. They would differ from the currently used containers by being smaller (causing less "empty space" in containers), (de)composable (allowing to attach or disconnect multiple containers to each other), having advanced securing and sealing possibilities, being equipped with smart sensors and controllers, have conditioning capabilities if required, etc. Stated otherwise, the authors of the initiative argue that one large cargo container is not sufficient and should be considered as a modular system on its own. Of course, the decoupling between cargo and vehicle should be maintained as it was the case for current containers. Therefore, at the vehicle level, vehicles should be manufactured adhering to this new π-container standard. Further, a global Physical Internet could spur the development of vehicles optimized (e.g., using the most adequate integration patterns) for the trajectory that they are required to serve (i.e., in some trajectories external propulsion mechanisms may be present, in others not).

Moreover, the vision of the Physical Internet refers to the logistics network as an additional aggregation level, which supersedes transportation vehicles (i.e., the aggregation level upon which we mainly elaborated in Section III) and needs to be redesigned adhering to modularity guidelines. For example, [15, p. 10] states that logistics networks need to "evolve from point-to-point hub-and-spoke transport to distributed multi-segment intermodal transport". The current logistics networks allow a certain level of intermodal transport, as discussed in Section III-B. For example, a container can be used on multiple modes of transport such as trains, ships, and trucks, without the freight itself being handled. However, the smaller granularity of the cargo as proposed by the Physical Internet will encourage smaller segments and more advanced optimization of these different segments. Once routing decisions can be optimized for a single package, as opposed to an aggregation of packages in a container, advanced algorithms based on the routing algorithms of the digital internet can be leveraged. This vision is in line with our observations based on modularity reasoning on other abstraction levels, but needs to cope with the same practical challenges as discussed earlier. For instance, this vision requires the development of nodes that are highly optimized for load breaking: disassembling aggregations of cargo into individual constituents, calculating the optimal route for each individual π-container, and reassembling new aggregations. As such, these nodes will need to be technologically more advanced than the current logistics hubs.

Many node-to-node segments will still be operated by traditional transportation vehicles, because of the economies of scale of these vehicles. However, because of the small granularity of a single segment and the load breaking capabilities of the nodes, the optimal transportation vehicle can be re-evaluated for each individual segment. Consider the final segment an individual package has to travel in order to reach an individual customer. In certain instances, individual air transport using a drone could be the fastest way to fulfill such a segment. Organizations such as Amazon are already experimenting with this technology, albeit within very strict limitations: the final delivery needs to be very close to an Amazon depot (a traditional hub), and strict weight limitations are enforced. This last limitation relates to the lift concern of air transportation vehicles discussed earlier in Section III-D. Current research demonstrates how this concern can be made scalable without introducing couplings with other concerns, such as drone control [16]. This research shows how cargo can be attached to multiple supporting drones, which, based on force sensing, follow the movement of one primary controlled drone. The primary drone can now be controlled as if it was the sole transport vehicle, albeit with a scalable propulsion concern. This can be considered as an illustration of how state-of-the-art research is able to make advancement towards NST integration patterns previously considered practically impossible. Indeed, NST prescribes that the integration of concerns needs to be solved at the most fine-grained levels, for which several practical obstacles have been identified in the past within the context of air transportation vehicles (cf. supra). The research of Tagliabue et al. [16] demonstrates the practical feasibility of adhering to this principle: a scalable integration of the lift concern at the level of an individual π-container. As such, we believe that further research elaborating on the use of NST as a theoretical underpinning for R&D in the logistics domain would be highly valuable.

V. CONCLUSION

This paper presented an overview of different modular structures that can be identified within the logistics industry. In particular, we studied the alternative integration options regarding the propulsion cross-cutting concern for transportation vehicles (with their associated benefits and drawbacks), using NST as the theoretical basis. We applied a similar reasoning at the level of logistic architectures. Here, we analyzed the integration architecture configurations regarding the remuneration cross-cutting concern within a logistics network. Regarding both the propulsion and the remuneration concern, we observed that the logistics industry already applies a rather mature implementation. However, some suggestions for future research and development could be made based on our theory and it was shown that some recent developments and trends such as the Internet of Things or the use drones seem to facilitate some of these avenues. It is important to stress that none of the authors claim to be transportation or logistics experts. Instead, generally available knowledge within the domain was used as the primary source for the analysis. The main contribution is situated in the fact that we show the applicability and relevance of NST in a context (i.e., transportation and logistics) outside the original application domain of the theory (i.e., software systems). Given our non-expert status in the transportation and logistics domain, we encourage actual experts to scrutinize and validate or refine our initial analyses provided. Additionally, future research could be directed towards the application of a similar analysis regarding the integration of cross-cutting concerns into (physical) artifacts within a particular domain outside the logistics industry.

REFERENCES

[1] P. De Bruyn, H. Mannaert, and P. Huysmans, "Exploring evolvable modular patterns for transportation vehicles and logistics architectures," in Proceedings of the Ninth International Conference on Pervasive Patterns and Applications (PATTERNS), 2017, pp. 46–51.

[2] H. Simon, The Sciences of the Artificial. MIT Press, 1996.

[3] D. Parnas, "On the criteria to be used in decomposing systems into modules," Communications of the ACM, vol. 15, no. 12, 1972, pp. 1053–1058.

[4] C. Y. Baldwin and K. B. Clark, Design Rules: The Power of Modularity. Cambridge, MA, USA: MIT Press, 2000.

[5] P. De Bruyn, J. Faes, T. Vermeire, and J. Bosmans, "On the modular structure and evolvability of architectural patterns for housing utilities," in Proceedings of the Ninth International Conference on Pervasive Patterns and Applications (PATTERNS), 2017, pp. 40–45.

[6] H. Mannaert, J. Verelst, and P. De Bruyn, Normalized Systems Theory: From Foundations for Evolvable Software Toward a General Theory for Evolvable Design. Koppa, 2016.

[7] H. Mannaert, J. Verelst, and K. Ven, "The transformation of requirements into software primitives: Studying evolvability based on systems theoretic stability," Science of Computer Programming, vol. 76, no. 12, 2011, pp. 1210–1222, special Issue on Software Evolution, Adaptability and Variability.

[8] P. De Bruyn, "Generalizing normalized systems theory : towards a foundational theory for enterprise engineering," Ph.D. dissertation, University of Antwerp, 2014.

[9] U.S. Patent US 9,193,460 B2, 2015.

[10] J. Sochor, H. Strömberg, and I. MariAnne Karlsson, "Implementing mobility as a service: Challenges in integrating user, commercial, and societal perspectives," Transportation Research Record: Journal of the Transportation Research Board, no. 2536, 2015, pp. 1–9.

[11] R. Quintero, H. Moons, M. Traverso, M. Caldas, I. Sknner, A. van Grinsven, M. 't Hoen, and H. van Essen, "Revision of the eu green public procurement criteria for transport – technical report and criteria proposal (2nd draft)," European Commission, Tech. Rep., 2017.

[12] M. Kamargianni, W. Li, M. Matyas, and A. Schfer, "A critical review of new mobility services for urban transport," Transportation Research Procedia, vol. 14, 2016, pp. 3294—3303, transport Research Arena TRA2016. [Online]. Available: http://www.sciencedirect.com/science/article/pii/S2352146516302836

[13] M. Kamargianni, M. Matyas, W. Li, and A. Sch´afer, "Feasibility study for "mobility as a service" concept in london," UCL Energy Institute — Department for Transport, May 2015.

[14] B. Montreuil, R. D. Meller, and E. Ballot, Physical Internet Foundations. Berlin, Heidelberg: Springer Berlin Heidelberg, 2013, pp. 151–166.

[15] B. Montreuil, "Toward a physical internet: meeting the global logistics sustainability grand challenge," Logistics Research, vol. 3, no. 2, 2011, pp. 71–87.

[16] A. Tagliabue, M. Kamel, S. Verling, R. Siegwart, and J. Nieto, "Collaborative Object Transportation Using MAVs via Passive Force Control," ArXiv e-prints, Dec. 2016.

Design Patterns for Gradual Composition of Adaptive Graphical User Interfaces

Samuel Longchamps, Ruben Gonzalez-Rubio

Université de Sherbrooke
Sherbrooke, Québec, Canada
Email: {samuel.longchamps, ruben.gonzalez-rubio}@usherbrooke.ca

***Abstract*—Graphical user interfaces (GUI) in modern software are increasingly required to adapt themselves to various situations and users, rendering their development more complex. To handle complexity, we present in this paper three design patterns, *Monitor*, *Proxy router* and *Adaptive component*, as solutions to the gradual implementation of adaptive behavior in GUI and general component-based software. Rather than proposing new adaptation mechanisms, we aim at formalizing a basic structure for progressive addition of different mechanisms throughout the development cycle. To do so, previous work on the subject of design patterns oriented toward adaptation is explored and concepts related to similar concerns are extracted and generalized in the new patterns. These patterns are implemented in a reference Python library called AdaptivePy, which is used to provide practical examples of their applications. Also, a GUI application case study is presented and compared to a functionally equivalent *ad hoc* implementation. We observe that separation of concerns is promoted by the patterns and testability potential is improved. Moreover, adaptation of widgets can be previewed within a graphical editor. This approach is closer to the standard workflow for GUI development, which is not possible with the *ad hoc* solution. Because the patterns suit any components-based software, they can be applied together or individually in different applications to solve specific adaptation challenges.**

Keywords–adaptive; design pattern; graphical user interface; context; library.

I. INTRODUCTION

Modern software application developers face many challenges, but one recurring challenge is to build their software in such a way that it can be used on different platforms, by different types of persons and in a variety of contexts. While an application has a some specific purpose, there are many ways to provide the service it offers such that all users are satisfied.

An example of this principle in our daily lives is a bank. While its core business is to keep their customers' money safe and make it grow, they offer a variety of packages to suit different types of customers. A bank also interacts with its customers differently depending on their knowledge regarding the financial market.

Implementing such adaptive behavior in software applications remains a challenge. As applications become increasingly complex and distributed, many implement adaptation in an *ad hoc* manner and recurrent solutions have rarely been formalized. One area of modern applications where adaptation requirements have flourished is graphical user interfaces (GUI). Because they are generally engineered using a descriptive language and oriented toward specific platforms, it is hard to produce a single GUI, which automatically adapts itself to its multiple usage contexts [1].

Many researchers have proposed models and frameworks to implement adaptive behavior in a generic manner for components-based software [2]–[5]. These solutions typically require significant effort to modify an existing software architecture and make specific technological choices and assumptions. They are limited both in terms of gradual integration to the software and in portability, for a framework usually targets a certain application domain (e.g., distributed client-server systems). As a more portable approach, we propose to use design patterns for formalizing structures of components that can be easily composed to produce specialized adaptive mechanisms. While some work has been done to propose design patterns for the implementation of common adaptive mechanisms [6]–[9], the present work aims at generalizing widespread concepts used in these patterns. In doing so, their integration in existing software is expected to be easier and more predictable.

As a proof-of-concept, a reference implementation of the design patterns has been done as a Python library called AdaptivePy. An application was built as a case study using the library to validate the gains provided by the patterns compared to an *ad hoc* solution. Special attention was paid to the compatibility to modern GUI design workflow. In fact, rather than create a specialized toolkit or create a custom designer tool that would include the design patterns' artifacts, the Qt cross-platform toolkit along with the Qt Designer graphical editor were used. The application workflow is presented and compared to original methods and advantages are highlighted. We expect that through the case study, the patterns' usage and advantages will be clearer and offer hints on how to structure an adaptive GUI.

This paper is an extended version of a conference paper published in the proceedings of Adaptive 2017 held in Athens, Greece [1]. We extend on the previous paper by providing a more in-depth description of the patterns and by providing additional examples as practical demonstrations of how to apply the patterns using AdaptivePy. Also, more specialized challenges related to the design of adaptive applications are identified and solved with minimal code examples

The remainder of this paper is organized as follows. Fundamental concepts of software adaptation extracted from previous work are described in Section II. The design patterns inspired from the concepts are presented in Section III. AdaptivePy is presented and followed by practical example usages in Section IV. The prototype application with adaptive GUI is presented in Section V and an analysis of the gains procured by the use of the proposed design patterns are presented in Section VI. The paper concludes with Section VII and some future work is discussed.

II. CONCEPTS OF SOFTWARE ADAPTATION

This section presents major concepts of adaptation from related work classified in three concerns: data monitoring, adaptation schemes and adaptation strategies.

A. Adaptation Data Monitoring

The context of a software refers to the environment in which it is executed. Example contextual data are the geographical position, light intensity, temperature, but also the computing platform on which an application is executed. A computing platform can be composed of many parts such as hardware components, operating system, computing capability and, in the case of GUI, user-interface toolkit [10].

Contextual data on which customization control rely, referred to as *adaptation data* in this paper, can come from various sources, both internal (for "self-aware" applications) and external (for "self-situated" or "context-aware" applications) [11]. Given these two types of adaptation data, we consider a system fully *adaptable* if it can both be customized based on internal and external adaptation data. If the system is autonomous in the control of both matter, then it is considered fully *adaptive*. The level of adaptivity and adaptability can provide more or less control over customization and flexibility of adaptation. Each application use case can benefit from a certain level of both [12]. A challenge is therefore to make it easy to implement and change the level of adaptivity and adaptability wanted for any application feature throughout the development process.

The acquisition of contextual data to be used as adaptation data is part of a primitive level, which is necessary for other more complex adaptation capabilities to be implemented [13]. Contextual data is usually acquired by a monitoring entity (sensors/probes/monitors) responsible for quantizing properties of the physical world or internal state of an application [8], [14]–[18]. Multiple simple sensors can be composed to form a complex sensor, which provides higher-level contextual data (Sensor Factory pattern [18]). Internal contextual data can be acquired simply by using a component's interface, but when the interface does not provide the necessary methods, introspection can be used (Reflective Monitoring [18]). When a variety of adaptation data is monitored, it provides a modeled view of the software context, which may be shared within a group of components. Some event-based mechanism with registry entities can be used to propagate adaptation data to interested components (Content-based Routing [18]). Quantization can be done on multiple abstraction levels and thresholds can be used to trigger adaptation events (Adaptation Detector [18]). This is then used to proactively alert some external adaptation mechanism to perform a selection of the most appropriate components and check if no system constraints are violated.

A system using external data for adaptation would be considered self-situated while one using internal data would be considered self-aware [11]. Self-situated systems are also referred to as context-aware, where context is the operational environment [19]. Context-aware will be used in this paper rather than self-situated to emphasize the distinction between self (internal) and context (external) as categories of adaptation data.

Self-awareness is a basic requirement for self-adaptivity since it is through a representation of itself that a system can deduce how it satisfies given constraints and modify itself to improve their satisfaction. Self-awareness can be achieved through self-monitoring of a system's components by software entities as it is the case for autonomic managers in the MAPE-K model [11].

A recurrent problem shared by any monitoring system is the need for agreement between components, which perceive different contexts, e.g., when there is no centralized coordination controller. To be tackled, this problem needs a form of structure for synchronization and sharing of data. Another major challenge is the inherent complexity of managing, requesting and using adaptation data. Testability of components requiring certain adaptation data is finally undermined since each different value potentially lead to a different behavior of the component and every other depending on it. There is a need to explicitly evaluate expected ranges of monitored adaptation data and prevent contextual view mismatch between interacting components.

B. Adaptation Schemes in Components

Four main types of adaptation concerns or objectives have been proposed by Hinchey and Sterritt [11]: self-configuration, self-healing, self-optimization and self-protection. Different qualities a system must have to enable these objectives are to be self-aware, self-situated, self-monitored and self-adjusted. While some concrete solutions have been proposed for self-optimization and self-healing [20], our main concern for the design of GUI is self-configuration. We synthesize two prominent types of adaptation schemes for self-configuration used in components-based software engineering: *component substitution* and *parametric adaptation*.

a) ***Component substitution:*** The underlying principle of component substitution is to replace a component by a functionally equivalent one with regard to a certain set of features. This can also be done by adding an indirection level to the dispatching of requests and forwarding them to the appropriate component. The first pattern applying this concept is probably the Virtual Component pattern by Corsaro, Schmidt, Klefstad, *et al.* [6]. It is similar to the adaptive component proposed by Chen, Hiltunen, and Schlichting [21], but adds the principle of dynamic (un)loading of substitution candidates. In both cases, an abstract proxy is used to dispatch requests to a concrete component, which is kept hidden from the client. This approach is also used by Menasce, Sousa, Malek, *et al.* [22], who proposed architectural patterns to improve quality of service on a by-request dispatch to one or many components. To maintain the software in a valid state before, during and after the substitution, many techniques have been proposed, such as transiting a component to a quiescent state [23], [24] and buffering requests [25]. State transfer between components can be used when possible, otherwise the computing job must be restarted [21], [24]. An application of this principle in GUI could be to replace a checkbox by a switch. This is seen in touch-enabled GUI where a mouse or a touch panel can be used as a pointing device.

b) ***Parametric adaptation:*** Rather than substituting a whole component by a more appropriate one, parametric adaptation relates to how a component can adapt itself to be more appropriate to a situation. This is usually done by tuning *knobs*, configurable units in a component (e.g., variables used in a computation). Knobs can be exposed in a *tunability* *interface* [2] for use by external control components, either included by design or automatically generated at the meta-programming level (e.g., with special language constructs, such as annotations [13]). An example of this adaptation pattern is how different implementations of an algorithm are chosen based on their respective tradeoffs between quality metrics (performance, precision, resources usage, etc.). The tunability domain of each knob is explicit and may vary over time. For example, if a new algorithm is discovered in the middle of a large computing job, an adaptation mechanism that is kept aware of the knob's possible values is able to switch to it if it judges that it will perform better overall [26]. The difference between parametrization and customization through an application's business logic is subtle and can be subjective to a certain point. Many applications apply customization on the basis of information we consider as adaptation data. One major difference that can be identified is that when a component is customized, the knowledge of what can be customized is not shared explicitly to other components as an adaptation space. This adaptation space is the domain of customization that can *safely* be applied.

A current problem is that these two types of adaptation, component substitution and parametrization, are rarely if at all used cooperatively. A software might be adaptive in that it reconfigures its architecture by swapping components, but the concrete components remain unchanged and the adaptation knowledge is centralized, often in the form of rule-based constraints, which are limited in reusability and reside at a higher abstraction level than the individual components. On the other hand, when a component uses data to adapt its behavior, this knowledge is hidden as implementation detail and the limits of its adaptation space are unknown to other parts of the system. The difficulty to acquire and interpret this knowledge is a limitation of both approaches that can be tackled by including it in a basic structure of adaptive component. Furthermore, the ability to reason about how adaptivity constrains and impacts components is a key information which can be used by adaptation mechanisms. Making this knowledge both explicit and accessible is therefore desirable.

C. Adaptation Strategies

No single adaptation strategy is universal for all software. Most past work has been done on applying component substitution using various strategies. For example, many researchers have explored rule-based constraints along with an optimization engine to devise architectural reconfiguration plans [2], [16]. This popular approach has tainted proposed frameworks that tend to be limited to this strategy only. An important principle is that strategies are separate from the component's implementation and can be easily changed. In fact, it is desirable to externalize adaptation strategies in order to be able to easily develop, modify and test them separately. Ramirez [8] calls this class of design patterns "decision-making", since they relate to when and how adaptation is performed. Because these design patterns are concrete adaptation strategies, their artifacts are mainly related to specific strategies (e.g., inference engines, rules, satisfaction evaluation functions). The approach of this class of patterns is typically related to rule-based constraints solving, but a more general goal is to select which plan or components from a set to reconfigure the system with.

III. Design Patterns

This section presents design patterns that realize the concepts presented in Section II with some improvements. When used together, we believe they provide the sought structure for adaptive software. Unified modeling language (UML) diagrams are used to show the structure of the patterns in a standardized way.

A. Monitor Pattern

Classification: Monitor and analyze.
Intent: A monitor provides a value for one type of adaptation data to interested entities.
Motivation: There is a need to quantize raw contextual data as parameters of adaptation data with explicitly defined domain and in specialized modules decoupled from the rest of the application. Adaptation data needs to be reasoned about in arbitrarily high abstraction level and be proactive in the adaptation detection process. Agreement for monitored data should be implied by design in order to allow for safe information sharing among interacting components.
Structure: Fig. 1 shows the structure of the monitor pattern as a UML diagram.

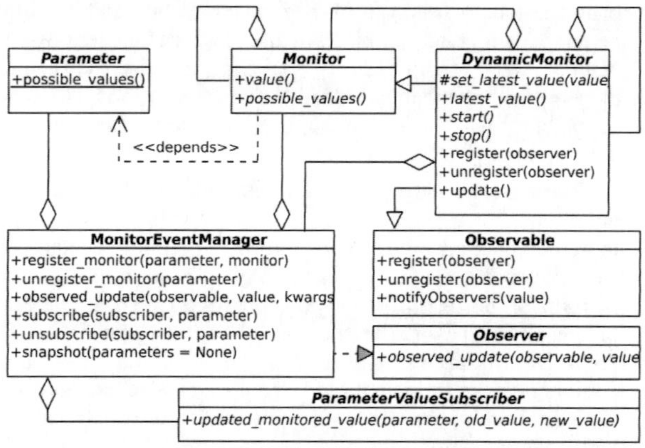

Figure 1. Monitor pattern UML diagram

Participants:

- **Parameter:** A parameter is one type of adaptation data as defined in Section II-A. Its possible values domain is explicitly defined and forms a state space. Many range types can be used to model a parameter's domain.
- **(Static) Monitor:** Provides a stateless (further referred to as "static") means of acquiring a value within a subset of a certain parameter's domain. Formally, $\Omega_M \subseteq \Omega_P$ for possible values Ω of monitor M and parameter P. A monitor can be an aggregation of other static monitors, but not of dynamic monitors.
- **Dynamic monitor:** Additionally to providing a value for a parameter, schedules the acquisition of the value and alerts an observer that a new value has been acquired. Some form of polling or interrupt-based thread awakening needs to be employed along with a previous value to know if the value has changed compared to the latest value, in which case an event

notification is triggered to interested entities. This makes it inherently stateful. Like a static monitor, it can be an aggregation of other monitors. The particularity is that it can aggregate both static and dynamic monitors.

- **Monitor event manager:** Registry entity that allows for a client component to subscribe to a parameter and be alerted when a new value is acquired. Similarly, a dynamic monitor can be registered within the manager and provide a value to any subscriber of the corresponding parameter. In such manager, monitors and parameters are related by a one-to-one relationship; a given parameter can only be monitored by a single monitor.
- **Observable/Observer:** See Gang of Four observer pattern [27]. Used for monitor registering mechanism.
- **Parameter value subscriber:** Provides a means to be notified when a new value of a parameter it has subscribed to has been acquired.

Behavior: An adaptation data type can be formalized as a parameter in terms of the quantized values the system expects to use. A static monitor provides a means to concretely quantize raw contextual data from a sensor or introspection to a value within a defined domain expected by the system. The quantization can be done using fixed or variable thresholds. A dynamic monitor adds scheduling behavior, which allows to provide a value based on accumulated data over time and apply filtering. The monitor event manager is alerted by monitors and dispatches the new value to related subscribers. The dependency regarding subscribers is with the parameters for which they requested to be notified, but actual monitoring is done separately.
Consequences: As monitors are hierarchically built, higher-level abstraction information can be provided. This pattern allows the analysis step of a MAPE-K loop [15] to be done through hierarchical construction of monitors: a parameter can define high-level domain values that are provided by a monitor composed from lower-level ones and components can use this to simplify their adaptation strategies. High-level adaptivity logic is reusable in that parameters are abstract and can easily be shared among projects. Monitors can be chained such that only the concrete data acquisition has to be redone between projects, keeping scheduling and filtering as reusable entities.
Constraints: To assure agreement between interacting components, it is necessary for adaptive components which depend on a common parameter to also subscribe to the same monitor event manager. These components are therefore part of the same *monitoring group*. This can be checked statically or be assumed by contract. The need for a one-to-one relationship between a monitor and a parameter within a monitoring group is based on this agreement requirement. A monitoring group can be thought of as a single entity that cannot have duplicate or contradicting attributes, e.g., it cannot be at two positions at once. In this example, an attribute is a parameter and a monitor is the entity providing the value for this attribute.
Related patterns: Sensor factory, reflective monitoring, content-based routing, adaptation detector [8], information sharing, observer [27].

B. Proxy Router Pattern

Classification: Plan and execute.
Intent: A proxy router allows to route calls of a proxy to a component chosen among a set of candidates using a designated strategy.
Motivation: When implementing component substitution, a way to clearly separate concerns relating to the adaptation logic (choice of substitution candidate) and the execution of substitution (replacing a component or forwarding calls to it) are difficult to implement in an extensible way. The proxy pattern [27] allows to forward calls to a designated instance, but does not specify how control of the routing process should be implemented. Candidate components need to be specified in a way that does not necessitate immediate loading or instantiation and that is mutable (to allow runtime discovery). To maximize reusability, strategies should be devised externally.
Structure: Fig. 2 shows the structure of the proxy router pattern as a UML diagram.

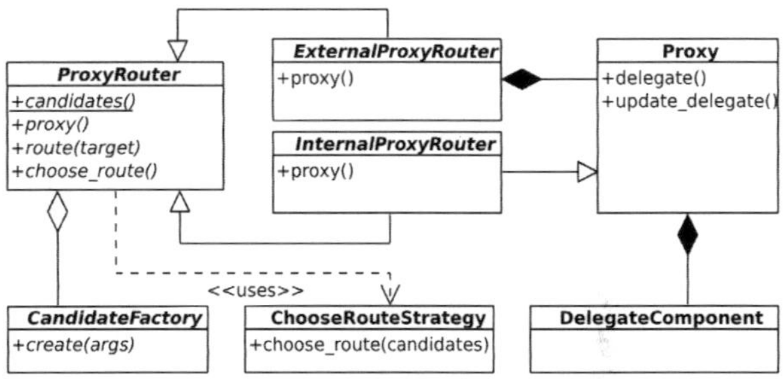

Figure 2. Proxy router pattern UML diagram

Participants:

- **Proxy:** Gang of Four [27] proxy pattern, with the exception that the interface is not necessarily specified (e.g., forwarding to introspected methods). It is responsible for making sure no calls are lost when a new delegate is set.
- **Delegate component:** Concrete component that is proxied. It must be specified as part of the proxy router's candidates set.
- **Proxy router:** Keeps a set of component candidates and allows to control the routing of the calls a proxy receives to the appropriate candidate chosen by some strategy. The proxy router is responsible for ensuring any state transfer and initialization of candidate instances.
- **Candidate factory:** Gang of Four [27] factory pattern for a candidate. Used as part of candidates definition. Can do local loading/unloading for external candidates.
- **Choose route strategy:** Concrete strategy to choose which candidate among a set to use, based on Gang of Four [27] strategy pattern. It uses accessible information from the application, candidates (e.g., adaptation space, descriptor, static methods) or any inference engine available to make a choice.
- **External/Internal proxy router:** Depending on the use, a proxy router can *use* an external proxy (as

a member) or internally *be* a proxy (through inheritance). To allow for both schemes, a means to acquire the proxy is provided and returns either the member object (external) or a reference to the proxy router itself (internal).

Behavior: A set of candidates is either statically specified or discovered at runtime (e.g., looking for libraries providing candidates). The proxy router is then initialized by choosing a candidate using the strategy and controls the proxy to set an instance of the chosen candidate as active delegate. At any time, a new candidate can be chosen and set as active delegate of the proxy.
Consequences: The proxy router pattern allows for flexible and extensible specification of component substitution. The strategies to choose a candidate to route to can be reused in any project with consistent information acquisition infrastructure, such as the one provided by the monitor pattern. Candidates need not be specified statically and control related to routing can be done both internally and externally.
Constraints: Strategies might rely on certain project specific information that is not portable. Separating specific from generally applicable strategies and composing them should help with this constraint.
Related patterns: Adaptive component [21], virtual component [6], master-slave [28], component insertion/removal, server reconfiguration [8], proxy [27].

C. Adaptive Component Pattern

Classification: Analyze and plan.
Intent: Use monitored adaptation data to control parametric adaptation and component substitution by making adaptation spaces explicit.
Motivation: A basic structure is needed to easily add adaptive behavior in the form of parametrization or substitution. Components need a way to explicitly provide means for adaptation strategies to reason about their adaptation space in order to formulate plans. This information should be external to a base component if the adaptation is to be added gradually. Most importantly, an adaptive component must behave like any non-adaptive component and be used among them without side effects on the rest of the system. Complementarily to monitors, which provide values within a domain explicitly defined by a parameter, components require a certain domain of values they support and are expected, by contract, to adapt themselves to (parametrically or by substitution). This domain is an *adaptation space* that can be reasoned about to devise efficient adaptation strategies.
Participants:

- **Adaptive:** An adaptive component that defines means for acquiring the adaptation space. It can be used as a subscriber to a parameter value provider. The adaptation space is a dictionary of parameters with a set of values it supports. To acquire monitored values, it has a reference to one and only parameter value provider. It can therefore subscribe to a parameter and receive updates when a new value is detected, triggering parametric adaptation when needed. If an unexpected value (outside its adaptation space) is received, an exception can be raised and some higher-level adaptation mechanism can be fired (e.g., substitute the component for another one).
- **Monitor event manager:** Parameter value provider realized with the monitor pattern (see Section III-A).
- **Parameter value subscriber:** Provides a means to be notified when a new value of a parameter it has subscribed to has been acquired (see Section III-A).
- **Proxy router:** Proxy router pattern (see Section III-B)
- **Adaptive proxy router:** Adaptive version of a proxy router allowing to drive the routing process (substitution) using monitored data.

Structure: Fig. 3 shows the structure of the adaptive component pattern as a UML diagram.

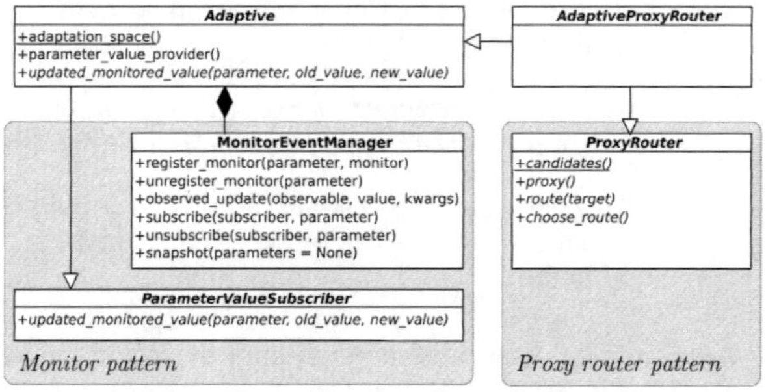

Figure 3. Adaptive component pattern UML diagram

Behavior: A component to be made adaptive can inherit the adaptive interface or a specific decorator can be created if the component's code should remain unchanged. The adaptive implementation defines what base adaptation space it will support. For example, in GUI implementations, this could be the availability of a toolkit or the type of input medium used (e.g., touch screen, mouse/keyboard, pen). Then, knobs can be defined within the component and used as variables to compute, for example, its size or lay outing specifications. Tuning can be done when an updated parameter value is received. For substitution, the process is the same, but uses the AdaptiveProxyRouter interface. Specific strategies can be created, using as many generic filters as possible (e.g., filter out candidates with adaptation space not overlapping with a snapshot of the current state).
Consequences: Because of the explicit declaration of adaptation space, strategies can be reasoned about how a component can behave in a situation. For example, a strategy can use the fact that a component's space is too specific or too wide. A significant advantage is that this can be previewed and tested by mocking the corresponding monitors (assuming that the designer's device has the adequate dependencies). Any component can be made adaptive and does not require modifications to other components. Even a parameter value provider can become gradually more complex. It could initially be based on a configuration file, which is essentially static during the application's execution, and be replaced by a more elaborate one when needed. Because of the support for both parametric adaptation and component substitution, the basic structure proposed in this pattern is suitable for virtually any adaptive mechanism based on monitored data and components adaptation spaces.
Constraints: Like stated in Section III-A, interacting adaptive components must subscribe to the same parameter value

provider to assure consistency in decision-making processes. While arbitrarily large hierarchies of adaptive components can be composed, there is an inherent overhead induced in the adaptation and routing process. Because a component subscribing to some parameter value provider such as the monitor event manager has no guarantee that this parameter is being actively monitored, adaptive components need to define a default behavior or immediately request a snapshot of the current state. If exceptions are used for non-monitored parameters (no value in the snapshot), their handling should be carefully done based on how monitors are registered (e.g., if monitors are concurrently registered as components are created). To minimize this effect, it is preferable to register monitors prior to creating any adaptive component.
Related patterns: Monitor (III-A), proxy router (III-B), adaptive component [21], virtual component [6].

IV. Patterns Realized

This section aims at providing a more practical foundation for the usage of the patterns presented in Section III. An overview of AdaptivePy, a library implementing the patterns, is first presented. Then, minimal use cases for the patterns are provided and implemented using AdaptivePy. These should demonstrate how the common problems identified are solved by the patterns and practically put in place. Finally, an introduction to the use of the patterns for GUI implementations with AdaptivePy and Qt is presented.

A. AdaptivePy

AdaptivePy implements artifacts from all three design patterns described in this paper. The library is freely available from the PyPi repository (`https://pypi.python.org`) under the name "adaptivepy" and is distributed under LiLiQ-P v1.1 license. The Python language was chosen because it is reflective, dynamically typed and many toolkit bindings are freely available. Beyond the patterns, AdaptivePy provides some useful implementations:

- Enumerated and discrete-value parameters
- Monitor event manager with a global instance as default provider for adaptive components
- Polling (pushed values) and pull dynamic monitor as decorators over static monitors
- Fixed (always provides the same value) and random static monitors
- Methods for operations on adaptation space (extension, union, filter)
- Strategy for choosing the most restricted component with narrowest adaptation space for a set of parameters
- Automatic computation of aggregated adaptation space for substitution candidates of a proxy router

While AdaptivePy is a fully working implementation of the patterns presented in this paper, it is possible to make different choices to realize the artifacts. For example, the MonitorEventManager artifact presented in the *Monitor* pattern could be realized as multiple managers, which coordinate the view on the environment and the propagation of the monitored values. Because the main objective in this paper is to demonstrate the technique for a single-host GUI, a centralized MonitorEventManager was deemed more appropriate.

One area in which special care must be taken when implementing the patterns is to minimize the work necessary to expand the amount of monitors and components. Since a complex system is expected to be composed from hundreds, if not thousands of components, the work necessary to add a new parameter, monitor or strategy must be kept minimal. This challenge is greatly mitigated by the use of a dynamic language like Python, where it is possible to compose classes at runtime.

It is necessary to mention that the aim of AdaptivePy is primarily demonstrative in the sense that it illustrates the applicability of the patterns presented in this paper. While crucial to the success of adaptation in any given application, the end-user's perception of increased usability due to adaptation is not the purpose of AdaptivePy. In fact, the effect of adaptation is expected to greatly vary from one application to the other, depending on what is adapted and when it is triggered. AdaptivePy, and consequently the patterns presented in this paper, aim at counteracting the complexity of implementing different adaptation strategies and structures in a gradual manner. Having each concern changeable and testable as separately as possible is then expected to provide the best end-user perceived usability with maximal predictability and minimal development effort through prototyping and A/B testing.

For each of the three patterns presented in this paper, a small example using AdaptivePy is given and explained.

B. Monitor Pattern

As presented in Section III-A, the *Monitor* pattern is concerned with acquisition and analysis of adaptation data. To express the environment in terms of contextual data, there is a need to model the environment into data of known range. This quantization is done on some raw data, which could be coming from an hardware sensor, network data provider or any process executing on the host machine (including the monitoring application itself).

An important aspect of the modeling of the environment is that raw data can be further refined into higher-level data through the cascading of monitors. For example, a hardware sensor could provide temperature data ranging from $-50°$ to $50°$C at $0.5°$ intervals. A higher-level modeling of this data could be to classify the values into an enumeration of three temperature levels: { Cold, Normal, Hot }. Table I shows a possible classification of the temperature levels as provided by the hardware sensor.

The artifact from the *Monitor* pattern that allows to provide a range of possible values is the parameter. The state space of the hardware sensor provided data is discrete, expressed as a range with step $[-50, 50[$: $0.5°$C. The state space of the temperature level is an enumeration with three unique values. These parameters can be monitored by static monitors since they are stateless, assuming the hardware sensor can be queried

TABLE I. Suggested Classification of Temperature Levels

Level	Range
Cold	$[-50, 18[$
Normal	$[-18, 30[$
Hot	$[30, 50[$

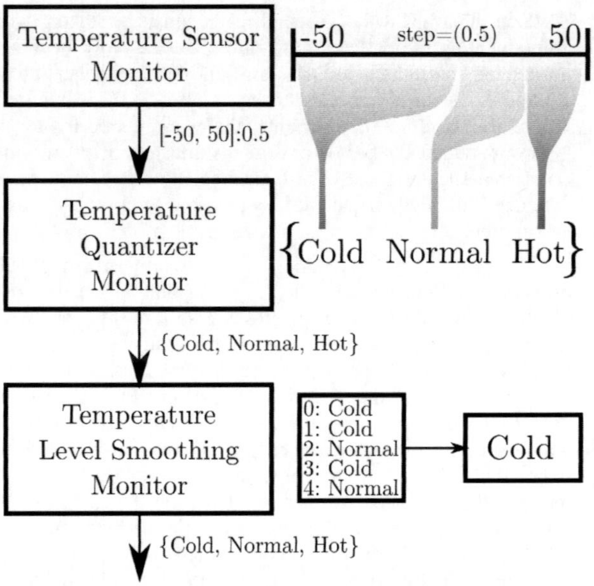

Figure 4. Realization of a temperature monitoring architecture

at any given time. By using this temperature sensor monitor, a second monitor could realize the classification algorithm based on the predefined thresholds presented in Table I. This monitor is considered *complex* because it relies on other monitors.

A refinement to this monitoring structure is to filter the monitored data. In fact, the hardware sensor's raw data might provide subsequent values oscillating between two quantized levels. A smoothing monitor could then be realize to address this issue. A simple moving average filter could be implemented and provide an average of the past M values. Another approach would be to provide the temperature level, which represents most of the past M samples. In all cases, because some state is necessary (previous values), the monitor is considered dynamic rather than static. An implication of being a dynamic monitor is that time affects its output value. At any time, a *latest value* can be queried and used in a snapshot of the system's current contextual state.

Fig. 4 provides a summarized view of the monitoring architecture as described previously. AdaptivePy allows to implement this architecture with minimal effort. Listing 1 shows how to declare the identified parameters using AdaptivePy. Similarly, Listing 2 shows how to declare the monitors using AdaptivePy and the threshold values from Table I.

We see from Listing 1 that parameters can be defined to represent adaptation data as state spaces in a trivial way. These parameters are then used in Listing 2 to define the possible values that can be provided by the monitors. We see that the monitors provide all the possible values of their corresponding parameter. This means that, at runtime, the application can encounter every state of the modeled environment. In this example, we see the cascading feature of the monitors to further refine contextual data into high level adaptation data. The *TempSensorMonitor* acquires raw sensor data, quantized into a discrete range. Then, the *TempQuantizerMonitor* turns this discrete state space into a higher level enumerated state space. Finally, the *TempLvlSmoothingMonitor* applies the `most_common` function to the last five values to smooth variations. A feature of this last monitor is that it is not stateless, which prevents it from being used by other static monitors. It is therefore turned into a DynamicMonitor using a default implementation that is pull-based. This default implementation is realized using the instance decorator *PullDynamicMonitorDecorator*. A pull-based dynamic monitor uses an external scheduling mechanism to perform updates during the lifetime of the application. It is omitted for simplicity in this example. However, it could trivially be implemented as a button the user has to push or as a polling mechanism using a timer which triggers an update at regular intervals.

```
RawTemperature = DiscreteParameter(-50.0, 50.0, 0.5)

class TemperatureLevel(EnumeratedParameter):
    low = 0
    medium = 1
    high = 2
```

Listing 1. Parameter declaration using AdaptivePy

```
class TempSensorMonitor(Monitor):
    def value(self):
        # Query the hardware sensor
    def possible_values(self):
        return RawTemperature.possible_values()

class TempQuantizerMonitor(Monitor):
    def value(self):
        value = TemperatureSensorMonitor().value()
        if -50 <= value < 18:
            return TemperatureLevel.Cold
        elif 18 <= value < 30:
            return TemperatureLevel.Normal
        else # 30 <= value < 50
            return TemperatureLevel.Hot
    def possible_values(self):
        return TemperatureLevel.possible_values()

class TempLvlSmoothingMonitor(Monitor):
    def __init__(self):
        self._last_five_values =
            [TemperatureLevel.Cold] * 5
        self._current_index = 0
    def value(self):
        value = TempQuantizerMonitor().value()
        self._last_five_values[self._current_index]
            = value
        self._current_index += 1
        self._set_latest_value(
            most_common(self._last_five_values))
    def possible_values(self):
        return TemperatureLevel.possible_values()

TempLvlSmoothingDynamicMonitor = \
    PullDynamicMonitorDecorator(
        TempLvlSmoothingMonitor())
```

Listing 2. Monitor definition using AdaptivePy

C. Proxy Router Pattern

A proxy router, as presented in Section III-B, is a component that acts as a proxy and can be controller to route to different delegates. The group corresponding to the possible delegates is called the *substitution candidates* of the proxy router. An important element to the maintainability of an applications is the possibility to change parts related to a concern without affecting others. The *Proxy Router* pattern favorises decoupling of the code related to choosing the appropriate substitution delegate at an appropriate time and how to realize the substitution itself. Because strategies are highly dependent on specific application domains, they are expected to vary from one application to the other. However, the way components substitution can be implemented is mostly independent from the application domain.

A major challenge which transcends application domains is how to determine when adaptation should take place. In GUI, frequent changes in the layout of controls might destabilize users who have learned the position of certain controls. However, a GUI can improve responsiveness and better accommodate various types of users by adapting to their needs. For each scenario, specific strategies for these choices might be implemented and tested. One example of such strategy is to prevent applying adaptation when the user is using the application or a specific feature. By modeling a "busy" state for the user, it is possible to create a strategy that is aware of this state and provides the same substitution candidate as before until the user is not busy anymore. Similarly to monitors, one could cascade various routing strategies to create a more complex strategy.

A benefit of cascading strategies is that it allows to create generic strategies that rely on domain agnostic adaptation data such as the busy state discussed previously. Also, it is possible to control the timing of adaptation and computational load through filtering. Using the *Proxy Router* pattern, it is possible to realize multiple strategies and apply them to a common structure which is reusable across applications.

Assuming a parameter "Busy" with an enumerated state space of {yes, no} and a monitor "BusyMonitor" that provides all of the parameter's possible values, one can implement the cascading of strategies with AdaptivePy as shown in Listing 3. The proxy router *MyProxyRouter* is a trivial proxy router with two substitution candidates: *Candidate1* and *Candidate2*. It uses the *InternalProxyRouter* scheme (see Section III-B), which implements the router through inheritance. In AdaptivePy, the implementation of the proxy redirects calls to the `__getattr__` method to the delegate object's `__getattr__`, which makes the object behave as if it truly is the delegate. *MyProxyRouter* uses an externally defined strategy for routing that is represented as *MyStrategy* and instantiated in *MyProxyRouter*'s constructor.

An interesting feature of *BusyFilterStrategy* is that it is an adaptive strategy. Being adaptive, it has access to the "Busy" state which is being monitored by "BusyMonitor", in this case registered to the global monitor event manager. It acquires the "Busy" state through a local snapshot, that is a structure regrouping all the states the component is aware of. It does so in the `choose` method and then decides whether the value of the chosen candidate should be updated by querying the cascaded strategy or not.

By breaking down strategies into reusable sub-strategies that can be cascaded, the maintenance and extensibility of an application can be improved. Because it is possible to modify strategies individually and to cascade them as high level blocks in the proxy router, the lack of reusability in strategies is mitigated. Also, the challenge of determining when to adapt can be solved in steps rather than all at once. By gradually adding strategic elements to the proxy router as a common structure, components of an application that were not adaptive can acquire adaptive behavior as substitution candidates and strategies are developed rather than by refactoring the structure each time.

```
class MyProxyRouter(AdaptiveInternalProxyRouter):
    @classmethod
    def candidates(cls, arguments_provider=None):
        return { Candidate1: lambda: Candidate1(),
                 Candidat2: lambda: Candidat2() }
    def __init__(self):
        super().__init__()
        self._busy_filter = BusyFilterStrategy()
        self._specific_strategy = MyStrategy()
    def choose_route(self):
       return self._busy_filter.choose(lambda:
           self._specific_strategy.choose_route(
               self.candidates()))

@AdaptationSpace({Busy: Busy.possible_values()})
class BusyFilterStrategy(Adaptive):
    def __init__(self):
        super().__init__()
        self._candidate = None
    def choose(self, cascade_strategy):
        busy_state = self.local_snapshot().get(Busy)
        adapt = self._value is None or \
            busy_state == Busy.no
        if adapt:
            self._candidate = cascade_strategy()
        return self._candidate
```

Listing 3. Proxy router with filter strategy definition using AdaptivePy

D. Adaptive Component Pattern

Section IV-C contained an example of an adaptive component in the form of an adaptive strategy. In fact, the requirements to become adaptive are minimal: define an adaptation space and join and monitoring group by subscribing to a single parameter value provider. From that point on, a component is alerted when state changes within its adaptation space are detected. Also, it can request a local snapshot of the states corresponding to the parameters in its adaptation space. Using these values, it can apply parametric adaptation and, if it is a proxy router, component substitution.

Using the *Adaptive Component* pattern, it is possible to transform a previously non-adaptive component into an adaptive one. AdaptivePy utilizes the Python class decorators semantic to inject an adaptation space to any class. Then, by inheriting from the *Adaptive* class, a component can join a specific a parameter value provider by specifying it in the *Adaptive* constructor. This parameter value provider is realized using the MonitorEventManager from the *Monitor* pattern. It can then subscribe to any of the parameters in its adaptation space.

The declaration of a simple adaptive component is presented in Listing 4. Reusing the monitors from Section IV-B, the adaptive component *TempAdaptiveComponent* uses the temperature to adapt parametrically in the `updated_monitored_value` method. We see that, contrarily to the other examples, the adaptation space does

```
from adaptivepy.state_space.enumerated_state_space
    import EnumeratedStateSpace as Ess

@AdaptationSpace({TemperatureLevel:
    Ess({TemperatureLevel.Low,
         TemperatureLevel.Normal})})
class TempAdaptiveComponent(Adaptive):
    def __init__(self,
          parameter_value_provider=None):
          super().__init__(parameter_value_provider)
          self._subscribe_to_all_parameters()
    def updated_monitored_value(self, parameter,
          old_value, new_value):
          # Implement parametric adaptation
          if new_value is TemperatureLevel.Low:
              ... # Do something
          else: # new_value is Temperature.Normal
              ... # Do something else
```

Listing 4. Adaptive component definition using AdaptivePy

not fully cover the parameter's possible values. Because it is not supported, the implications of reaching the `TemperatureLevel.Hot` state are undefined for this component. If an application uses this component and can reach this state, component substitution should be implemented to swap this component with another one which supports the missing states. An advantage of this design is that a developer can focus on an explicitly defined region of an application's adaptation space and ignore other states in their implementation. This is seen in the implementation of the `updated_monitored_value`, where only the states defined in the adaptation space are handled. In this way, if the `new_value` is not `TemperatureLevel.Low`, it can only be `TemperatureLevel.Normal`. This is the case because the component has no knowledge of `TemperatureLevel.Hot`.

By specializing adaptive components, the service they offer is expected to be better suited at the region of adaptation space they define. By adding specialized component and adaptive behavior to non-adaptive components, an application can be ported to an adaptive form gradually. Also, because the patterns presented in this paper serve specific concerns, the adaptive components are not expected to be affected by changes in the monitoring or their structural arrangement when used for an application. The latter is possible because of the basic structure provided by the proxy routers and by the self-contained nature of components-based software.

E. Patterns applied to GUI

The patterns presented in this paper can be applied to GUI to create adaptive components as custom widgets and layouts. The general-use toolkit Qt was chosen for the case study, therefore this section will focus on Qt implementations. Qt provides a graphical editor, Qt Designer, for designing the GUI in a language independent descriptive language. Since this is the *de facto* approach, it is also the favored workflow. Note that this is true for many other toolkits (e.g., Gtk with Glade, JavaFX with SceneBuilder).

An *ad hoc* solution would be to add a placeholder widget in the GUI and replace them at runtime with the adequate component. Setting the appropriate control needs to be done entirely programmatically, along with any customization necessary, in the window's class that owns the control. This leads to a lack of extensibility, a tangling of concerns between the adaptation concern and the components' own concern. Moreover, the approach is not compatible with normal GUI design workflow, which involves previewing the application in the graphical editor before adding logic.

By controlling monitors from the *Monitor* pattern, one can visualize any adaptation done by components for the given toolkit. If a different toolkit is to be used (e.g., when porting an application), the necessary work is to create a candidate component for a proxy router using the new toolkit and adding a toolkit parameter value as an adaptive space definition. A conversion from one description language to the other would also be needed. As for the structure provided by the *Proxy Router*, only the binding to the toolkit's widget replacing logic is to be ported. As for the *Adaptive component* pattern, the components simply need to support the adequate portion of the adaptation space, which includes a toolkit parameter if any adaptation logic is dependent on different toolkit.

In this paper, because Python is used rather than C++ (Qt's native language), an external plugin for Qt Designer is necessary to load custom widgets. This is provided by PyQt as "libpyqt5" for GNU/Linux. Custom widgets are created using the `QPyDesignerCustomWidgetPlugin` base class. Fields can also be added using `pyqtProperty` and use the underlying adaptive component's interface to customize the component. This is especially useful with proxy router components since any customization is automatically applied to any candidate and state transfer can be more easily handled. It is also possible to use properties to control adaptive behavior by means of exposed knobs.

V. PROTOTYPE

Adaptivity can help in improving usability in different ways. One usability principle of graphical user interfaces is to take into account the user's cognitive limitations into consideration for the presentation of controls. For example, the number of elements in a group one can remember from short-term memory is used to limit the number of grouped controls displayed to the user. This number is not confidently known, but some suggested that chunks of 4 ± 1 elements can be accurately remembered using short-term memory, while it was originally estimated to be averaging around 7 ± 2 [29]. We draw inspiration from this usability principle in our case-study prototype application.

The case study application is a special poll designed to favor polarization. Five yes/no questions are asked to a user and answered by selecting the most appropriate response among a list of options. The possible options provided include yes, no, mostly yes, mostly no and 50/50. To favor polarization, statistics from the previous answers are used to restrict the range of options provided to the user. If the polarization is judged insufficient because of mixed responses (low polarization), fewer options are provided. On the contrary, if virtually all users have answered yes (high polarization), more options in between will be given. The workflow of the application is to start the "quiz" using a Start button, choose appropriate options and send the form using a Submit button. If some options remain unselected, a prompt alerting the user is shown and the form can be submitted again once all options are selected.

The adaptation used is a form of *alternative elements* [30]. This provides a form of "plastic" GUI in that it adapts itself, but retains its usability [31]. The GUI is made plastic by replacing control widgets displaying the available options at runtime, conserving the option selection feature in any resulting interface. To minimize the visual overload, some widgets are more appropriate than others to display them, while some cannot display certain amounts of options. A checkbox can handle two options with a single control. Radio buttons could handle many options, but to follow the usability guideline of congnitive limitation, we could use it to display up to four options at a time. Finally, a combo box can handle many options, but it does not display all the options on the window unless it is clicked. For our usage, it is a better choice for five and more options. Of course, radio buttons can hold more options and the combo box less, but the amounts suggested represent the ranges they better suit the usability principle. Because many other variables need to be taken into account and affect the usability, the ranges can be chosen by a designer and further refined through user testing, which means they must be easy to edit.

Polarization levels act as adaptation data to drive adaptation. An appropriate solution would allow to design the GUI within Qt Designer and to preview of the adaptation directly, rather than having to add the business logic beforehand. It would also allow for gradual addition and modification of control widget types without necessitating changes in unaffected modules.

The toolkit used for this application is Qt 5 through the PyQt5 wrapper library. It is a cross-platform toolkit library, which provides implementations of widgets like checkboxes, combo boxes are radio buttons groups. The concrete work is therefore limited to implementing how these components can replace each other at the appropriate time and how they are included in a main user interface. We are therefore more interested in the underlying structure of adaptation within the application than specific adaptation strategies and their user-perceived effectiveness. Once an appropriate structure is in place, we expect these can be more easily devised, tested and improved.

VI. Comparing Ad hoc and AdaptivePy

The windows shown on Fig. 5 are the resulted GUI for the application in all three polarization states. Because this case study's focus is on GUI, the monitoring of past responses was simulated and a random monitor is used instead. This monitor updates its value by means of a polling dynamic monitor every second, allowing to easily observe adaptation.

To emphasize the differences between the *ad hoc* solution and the one using patterns, adapters for each three control widgets (checkbox, radiobox and combobox) were created and are used in both applications. They all implement a common interface `OptionsSelector`, which defines common operations on the controls such as `set_text` for the question labelling and `set_options` that takes pairs of text and corresponding value for averaging past answers. The goal is to compare the implementation of adaptation rather than adding new type of adaptation, thus the same control abstraction approach was used for controls in both cases.

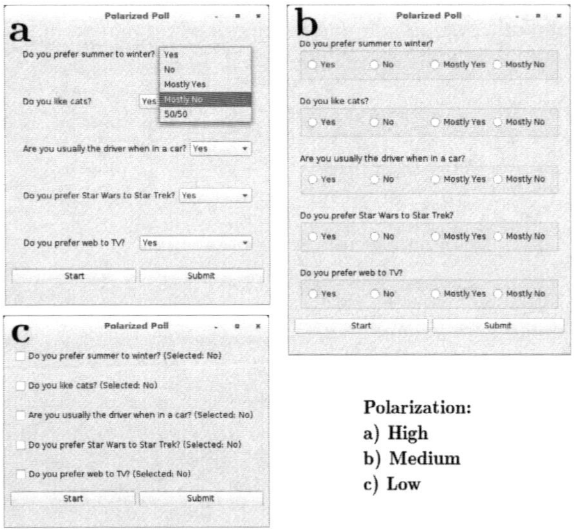

Figure 5. Adaptive case study application "Polarized Poll"

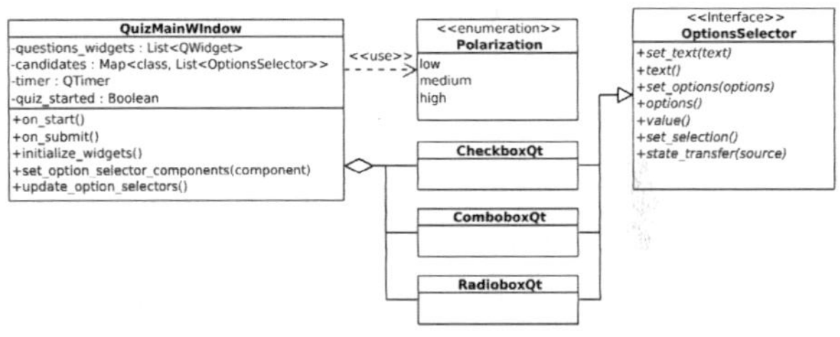

Figure 6. Simplified UML diagram of *ad hoc* implementation of case study application

A. Ad hoc *Application*

A simplified UML diagram of the *ad hoc* implementation is shown on Fig. 6. The chosen approach is to add placeholder widgets in QuizMainWindow which will be substituted by an appropriate component instance at runtime: CheckboxQt, ComboboxQt or RadioboxQt. A polarization level defined in the enum Polarization is bound to each of these types. A timer within QuizMainWindow polls the polarization value and calls `set_options_selector_components` with the appropriate type. Adaptation control, along with any customization necessary, is entirely done in QuizMainWindow.

Fig. 7 shows Qt Designer as the main window is created for the *ad hoc* implementation. Notice that because placeholder components are blank, no feedback is given to the designer. It is therefore not possible to test the controls or set the question label. This makes the approach incompatible with the usual GUI design workflow, which involves previewing the application in the graphical editor before adding business logic.

When analyzing the *ad hoc* code, it is obvious that separation of concerns is not respected since the option selection logic is tangled to its owner element, the main window. Concerns such as scheduling for recomputing polarization and component substitution are mixed with GUI setup and handling

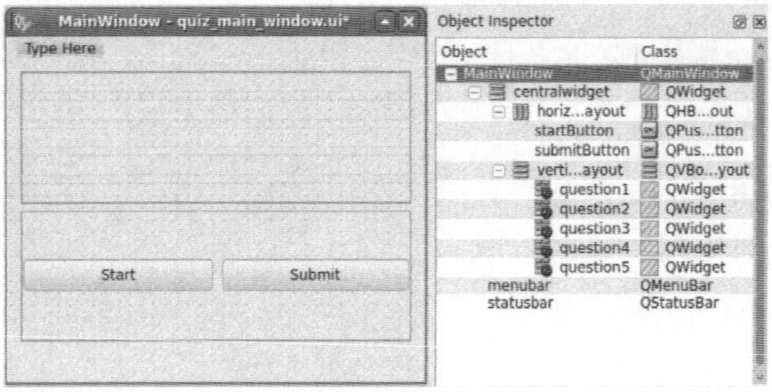

Figure 7. Qt Designer using plain widgets as placeholder for *ad hoc* implementation

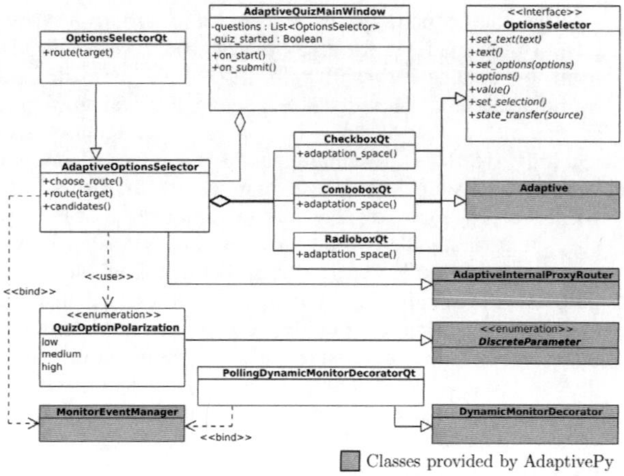

Figure 8. Simplified UML diagram of case study application implementation using AdaptivePy

of the business flow. This leads to a lack of extensibility, a tangling of concerns and limits unit testing of components. A method is used to select which control component to use based on the polarization, but this solution remains inflexible. The knowledge of adaptation is hidden and cannot be used to devise portable strategies.

One of our goals is to gradually add adaptation mechanisms to GUI implementations, but this is difficult since modification of important classes will add risk of introducing defects. Also, there is no easy way to work on adaptation mechanisms separately from the application. In fact, we cannot separately test the adaptation logic and integrate it after. Another limitation, in this case specific to GUI, is that all settings specific to the widgets (e.g., question labels) cannot be set from the graphical editor. This is a strong deviation from the usual GUI workflow. Generally, the lack of cohesion induced by the inadequate separation of concerns is a sign of low code quality. Because no adaptation mechanism can easily be introduced, modified and reused in other projects, the *ad hoc* implementation works for its specific application case, but is subject to major efforts in refactoring when requirements and features will be added throughout its development cycle.

B. Application Using AdaptivePy

A simplified UML diagram of the application is shown on Fig. 8. From it, we see that the polarization is a discrete parameter and is used by AdaptiveOptionsSelector, specifically to define its adaptation space based on the ones provided by its substitution candidates: CheckboxQt, ComboboxQt and RadioboxQt. Additionally to adaptation by substitution, RadioboxQt can parametrically adapt to changes of polarization levels {low, medium}, since they respectively correspond to 2 and 4 options. Its behavior is that the appropriate number of options is shown depending on the polarization level. AdaptiveQuizMainWindow is free of adaptation implementation details and simply uses the AdaptiveOptionsSelector instances as a normal OptionsSelector. OptionsSelectorQt is a subclass to AdaptiveOptionsSelector, which is used as a graphical proxy to candidate widgets. It also defines properties used in Qt's graphical editor Qt Designer, in this case the question label.

Every AdaptiveOptionsSelector instance is made a subscriber to the QuizOptionPolarization parameter at initialization. They are updated when a change in the monitored value is detected, i.e., when a monitor detects a value is different from the previous one. This is because identical subsequent parameter values are expected by default to lead to the same state, so they are filtered out. In the case of AdaptiveOptionsSelector, because it is a proxy router, `choose_route` is called to determine which substitution candidate to route to. Prior to using an adaptation strategy to select the most appropriate candidate, inappropriate ones can be filtered out using `filter_by_adaptation_space`. This function, provided by AdaptivePy, takes a list of candidates along with a snapshot of the current monitoring state and only returns those with adaptation space supporting the current context. Then, a strategy like `choose_most_restricted` is used to choose among valid components. If no component is valid, an exception is raised. With a candidate chosen, all that remains is configuring the proxy router by calling the `route` method with the chosen candidate. This method must also take care of state transfer between the previous and new proxied components. This feature is already defined in the common interface OptionsSelector as `state_transfer`. The `route` method takes care of the state transfer and updates the proxy (done by the library). Subscription to the polarization parameter is done at initialization.

Fig. 9 shows Qt Designer as the main window is created with the AdaptivePy-based implementation. When compared to Fig. 7, we notice that the designer has a full view of how the application will look. Moreover, the currently displayed adaptation can be controlled through the setup of the monitors. For example, it is possible to replace the random value by one acquired from a configuration file and trigger adaptation manually. Also, each question is simply a OptionsSelectorQt component rather than a placeholder component and the question is entered directly from the graphical editor using the label property (bottom-right). A major advantage is that adaptive components can be reused in other interfaces because they are provided as standalone components. The need for easy edition of adaptation spaces is also addressed by modifying or overriding the `adaptation_space` method of adaptive components.

The main difference compared to the *ad hoc* implementation is that no adaptation concern can be found in the owner

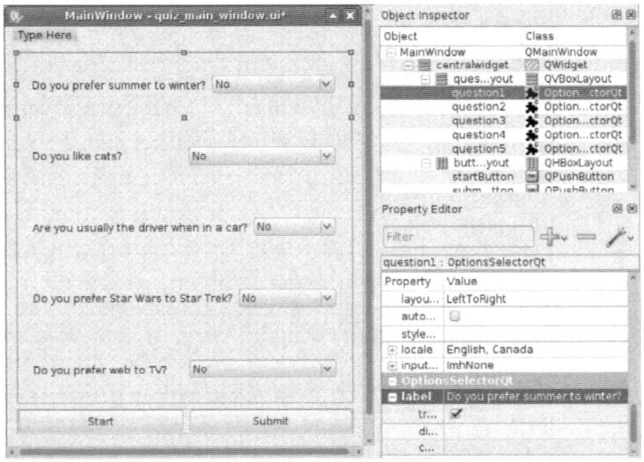

Figure 9. Qt Designer using adaptive components developed with AdaptivePy

class, the main window. An enumerated discrete parameter with three polarization values (low, medium and high) is monitored by a polling dynamic monitor decorator over a random static monitor. To create the adaptive component, an adaptive proxy router was used as a base with candidates being the three same control classes as the *ad hoc* implementation, but in adaptive form (each having an adaptation space related to different polarization levels).

To create the custom widget, two classes are necessary: a dedicated class, which inherits QWidget and its related factory with metadata used by Qt Designer such as its name, group and description. A template class was created to ease this step. The only logic specific to the options selector is related to additional properties. In this case, a string property for the question label along with binding to the options selector's interface method (getter and setter) is used. The option values are also set by this class to centralize the customization logic (this could also have been done using a property). Finally, the logic regarding the lay outing was implemented as a layout with a single element: the proxy delegate. When routing, the QWidget adapter removes the proxy delegate from the layout and adds the new one provided by the base option selector class (described previously). No additional modification other than removing the logic related to the old options selector implementation was necessary.

The adaptation logic is essentially located in the adaptive proxy router class: AdaptiveOptionsSelector. Because adaptation is separated from the rest of the business logic, the main window class can use the adaptive components without the knowledge of adaptation. The only logic remaining is with regard to buttons handling (Start and Submit buttons). It is clear in this implementation that the knowledge of adaptation space, which was hidden in the *ad hoc* implementation, is used to efficiently choose a substitution candidate. More so, the radiobox is suitable for two to four options and therefore covers low and medium polarization through parametric adaptation. It could then be used instead of the checkbox if a strategy for choosing the less restricted candidate had been used or if a malfunction is detected in the checkbox implementation rendering it inadequate as a candidate. This parametric adaptation behavior cannot easily be included in the *ad hoc* implementation since the knowledge of polarization is kept at the owner component level. The component would need to provide a mean through its interface to customize a component based on polarization, but this would affect all other components as well.

Self-healing action such as replacing a failing component can be realized by monitoring the components and including this logic as a strategy. This is not easily realizable in the *ad hoc* implementation. In the prototype, a radio box could safely replace a checkbox since it parametrically covers its full adaptation space, overlapping on {low} polarization. Also, from this case study, we can see that arbitrarily large hierarchies of adaptive and non-adaptive components can be built without tangling code or affecting other components when adding new adaptive behavior.

VII. Conclusion and Future Work

Design patterns presented in this paper can be used as a basic structure to accomplish various levels of adaptation in GUI. Adaptive components can be used with other modules such as recommendation engines to provide more or less automation and proactive adaptation. Monitors can also be extended and even implemented as adaptive components themselves, relying on other more primitive monitors. Proxy routers allow to simplify hierarchical development of arbitrarily large sequences of component substitutions. The patterns form together an effective approach for the integration of various adaptation mechanisms and, in the case of GUI, can be used to provide a more usual workflow than the *ad hoc* implementation.

AdaptivePy, as a reference library, is an example of the viability of the patterns when used in a concrete implementation. Although simple examples and a prototype application were used to observe gains, the solution is applicable to more complex scenarios where multiple parameters, monitoring groups and large hierarchies of adaptive components. The patterns are general enough that they can be used for adding adaptive behavior based on user, environment and platform variations.

Although an analysis of the prototype has been done using concepts of separation of concerns and quality principles in Section VI, there is a lack of quantitative metrics directly aimed at adaptive software. Example of metrics that would be interesting to automatically acquire are the quality in term of adaptation space coverage, adaptation complexity for a set of components sharing a common context and a measure of overhead in adaptation realization in a large hierarchy. Acquiring these metrics would allow to easily compare strategies used for component adaptation and provide guidelines to developers on which strategy is most appropriate in certain circumstances.

Future work will focus on exploring adaptation quality metrics such that verification and validation methods can be used as an objective evaluation of gains. New metrics using concepts of the design patterns presented in this paper will therefore be explored. The goal is to better quantify the quality level of prototypes with regards to adaptation.

References

[1] S. Longchamps and R. Gonzalez-Rubio, "Design patterns for addition of adaptive behavior in graphical user interfaces," in *Proceedings of the Ninth International Conference on Adaptive and Self-Adaptive Systems and Applications*, 2017, pp. 8–15.

[2] F. Chang and V. Karamcheti, "A framework for automatic adaptation of tunable distributed applications," *Cluster Computing*, vol. 4, no. 1, pp. 49–62, 2001, ISSN: 1573-7543.

[3] E. Bruneton, T. Coupaye, M. Leclercq, V. Quéma, and J.-B. Stefani, "The fractal component model and its support in java," *Software: Practice and Experience*, vol. 36, no. 11-12, pp. 1257–1284, 2006.

[4] Y. Maurel, A. Diaconescu, and P. Lalanda, "Ceylon: A service-oriented framework for building autonomic managers," in *2010 Seventh IEEE International Conference and Workshops on Engineering of Autonomic and Autonomous Systems*, Mar. 2010, pp. 3–11.

[5] M. Peissner, A. Schuller, and D. Spath, "A design patterns approach to adaptive user interfaces for users with special needs," in *Proceedings of the 14th International Conference on Human-computer Interaction: Design and Development Approaches - Volume Part I*, ser. HCII'11, Orlando, FL: Springer-Verlag, 2011, pp. 268–277.

[6] A. Corsaro, D. C. Schmidt, R. Klefstad, and C. O'Ryan, "Virtual component - a design pattern for memory-constrained embedded applications," in *In Proceedings of the Ninth Conference on Pattern Language of Programs (PLoP*, 2002.

[7] G. Rossi, S. Gordillo, and F. Lyardet, "Design patterns for context-aware adaptation," in *2005 Symposium on Applications and the Internet Workshops (SAINT 2005 Workshops)*, Jan. 2005, pp. 170–173.

[8] A. J. Ramirez, "Design patterns for developing dynamically adaptive systems," Master's thesis, Michigan State University, 2008.

[9] T. Holvoet, D. Weyns, and P. Valckenaers, "Patterns of delegate mas," in *2009 Third IEEE International Conference on Self-Adaptive and Self-Organizing Systems*, Sep. 2009, pp. 1–9.

[10] K. Majrashi, M. Hamilton, and A. Uitdenbogerd, "Multiple user interfaces and cross-platform user experience: Theoretical foundations," in *CCSEA 2015*, AIRCC Publishing Corporation, 2015, pp. 43–57.

[11] M. G. Hinchey and R. Sterritt, "Self-managing software," *Computer*, vol. 39, no. 2, pp. 107–109, 2006.

[12] M. Peissner, D. Häbe, D. Janssen, and T. Sellner, "Myui: Generating accessible user interfaces from multimodal design patterns," in *Proceedings of the 4th ACM SIGCHI Symposium on Engineering Interactive Computing Systems*, ser. EICS '12, Copenhagen, Denmark: ACM, 2012, pp. 81–90.

[13] M. Salehie and L. Tahvildari, "Self-adaptive software: Landscape and research challenges," *ACM Transactions on Autonomous and Adaptive Systems (TAAS)*, vol. 4, no. 2, p. 14, 2009.

[14] M. L. Berkane, L. Seinturier, and M. Boufaida, "Using variability modelling and design patterns for self-adaptive system engineering: Application to smart-home," *Int. J. Web Eng. Technol.*, vol. 10, no. 1, pp. 65–93, May 2015, ISSN: 1476-1289.

[15] IBM, "An architectural blueprint for autonomic computing," IBM Corporation, Tech. Rep., 2005.

[16] S. Malek, N. Beckman, M. Mikic-Rakic, and N. Medvidovic, "A framework for ensuring and improving dependability in highly distributed systems," in *Architecting Dependable Systems III*, R. de Lemos, C. Gacek, and A. Romanovsky, Eds. Berlin, Heidelberg: Springer Berlin Heidelberg, 2005, pp. 173–193.

[17] V. Mannava and T. Ramesh, "Multimodal pattern-oriented software architecture for self-optimization and self-configuration in autonomic computing system using multi objective evolutionary algorithms," in *Proceedings of the International Conference on Advances in Computing, Communications and Informatics*, ser. ICACCI '12, Chennai, India: ACM, 2012, pp. 1236–1243.

[18] A. J. Ramirez and B. H. Cheng, "Design patterns for developing dynamically adaptive systems," in *Proceedings of the 2010 ICSE Workshop on Software Engineering for Adaptive and Self-Managing Systems*, ACM, 2010, pp. 49–58.

[19] M. Parashar and S. Hariri, "Autonomic computing: An overview," in *Proceedings of the 2004 International Conference on Unconventional Programming Paradigms*, ser. UPP'04, Le Mont Saint Michel, France: Springer-Verlag, 2005, pp. 257–269.

[20] D. Weyns, S. Malek, and J. Andersson, "On decentralized self-adaptation: Lessons from the trenches and challenges for the future," in *Proceedings of the 2010 ICSE Workshop on Software Engineering for Adaptive and Self-Managing Systems*, ser. SEAMS '10, Cape Town, South Africa: ACM, 2010, pp. 84–93.

[21] W.-K. Chen, M. A. Hiltunen, and R. D. Schlichting, "Constructing adaptive software in distributed systems," in *Distributed Computing Systems, 2001. 21st International Conference on.*, Apr. 2001, pp. 635–643.

[22] D. A. Menasce, J. P. Sousa, S. Malek, and H. Gomaa, "Qos architectural patterns for self-architecting software systems," in *Proceedings of the 7th International Conference on Autonomic Computing*, ser. ICAC '10, Washington, DC, USA: ACM, 2010, pp. 195–204.

[23] H. Liu and M. Parashar, "Accord: A programming framework for autonomic applications," *IEEE Transactions on Systems, Man, and Cybernetics, Part C (Applications and Reviews)*, vol. 36, no. 3, pp. 341–352, May 2006, ISSN: 1094-6977.

[24] J. Zhang and B. H. C. Cheng, "Model-based development of dynamically adaptive software," in *Proceedings of the 28th International Conference on Software Engineering*, ser. ICSE '06, Shanghai, China: ACM, 2006, pp. 371–380.

[25] H. Gomaa, K. Hashimoto, M. Kim, S. Malek, and D. A. Menascé, "Software adaptation patterns for service-oriented architectures," in *Proceedings of the 2010 ACM Symposium on Applied Computing*, ser. SAC '10, Sierre, Switzerland: ACM, 2010, pp. 462–469.

[26] P. Kang, M. Heffner, J. Mukherjee, N. Ramakrishnan, S. Varadarajan, C. Ribbens, and D. K. Tafti, "The adaptive code kitchen: Flexible tools for dynamic application composition," in *2007 IEEE International Parallel and Distributed Processing Symposium*, Mar. 2007, pp. 1–8.

[27] E. Gamma, R. Helm, R. Johnson, and J. Vlissides, *Design Patterns: Elements of Reusable Object-oriented Software*. Boston, MA, USA: Addison-Wesley Longman Publishing Co., Inc., 1995.

[28] H. Gomaa and M. Hussein, "Software reconfiguration patterns for dynamic evolution of software architectures," in *Software Architecture, 2004. WICSA 2004.*

Proceedings. Fourth Working IEEE/IFIP Conference on, Jun. 2004, pp. 79–88.

[29] N. Cowan, "The magical number 4 in short-term memory: A reconsideration of mental storage capacity," *Behavioral and Brain Sciences*, vol. 24, no. 1, pp. 87–114, 2001.

[30] M. Bezold and W. Minker, *Adaptive multimodal interactive systems*. Springer Science & Business Media, 2011.

[31] J. Coutaz, "User interface plasticity: Model driven engineering to the limit!" In *Proceedings of the 2Nd ACM SIGCHI Symposium on Engineering Interactive Computing Systems*, ser. EICS '10, Berlin, Germany: ACM, 2010, pp. 1–8.

International Journal on Advances in Intelligent Systems, vol 10 no 3 & 4, year 2017, http://www.iariajournals.org/intelligent_systems/

Creating New Views and Insights by Computing Spatial Cogwheel Modules for Knowledge Integration

Claus-Peter Rückemann
Westfälische Wilhelms-Universität Münster (WWU),
Leibniz Universität Hannover,
North-German Supercomputing Alliance (HLRN), Germany
Email: ruckema@uni-muenster.de

Abstract—**This paper presents the research and implementation of applying the new methodology Cogwheel Modules for creating new views and insights from knowledge integration. The target is advanced knowledge mining, e.g., complex discovery, and decision making. The paper provides both results of the present research of the methodology and an implementation, including a case study on different views and possible insight from an application in the spatial domain. The implementation includes modules required for a complete workflow as well as generators for creating results, specifying spatial data and content. The case study utilises topics, techniques, and data from geosciences, archaeology and multi-disciplinary context. The methodology is using integrated knowledge resources for complex knowledge mining by creating workflows applying specialised tools. The resulting methodology can be applied with any disciplines and with combinations of general, as well as specialised tools. The results of the knowledge mining can be used for gaining insight and creating automated learning processes, especially with long-term knowledge resources, which are continuously in development. The method can be used for practical mining procedures to gain insight as well as further develop available multi-disciplinary knowledge resources. The goal of this research is to create new views and insights from the available knowledge resources.**

Keywords–Knowledge-based Views and Insights; Cogwheel Modules Methodology; Data-centric Knowledge Mining; Universal Decimal Classification; Advanced Computing.

I. INTRODUCTION

This research is focussed on creating new views and insights from content of knowledge resources. The methodology, which is deployed allows to compute "Cogwheel Modules" and peel information from knowledge resources. A workflow can use the process to iterate in an arbitrary number of turnarounds in order to create a possible knowledge integration.

The fundaments of the new method of Cogwheel Modules were presented at the DigitalWorld and GEOProcessing 2017 conference in Nice, France [1].

The work is based on the integration of knowledge resources referring to universal classification and application components for solving complex tasks, e.g., for knowledge mining. Target of this research on the methodology of 'Cogwheel Modules' is to create different views based on integrating knowledge resources and specialised application components for a gain in knowledge, cognition, and insight.

Creating views means the creation of exhaustive context for knowledge objects and their entities. The primary context can be a knowledge context, which allows further analysis and processing. Based on the primary context, a secondary context can be created, e.g., a result matrix, a listing, or a visualisation.

The integration of knowledge discovery and decision making processes can result in extremely challenging tasks. The quality of results from knowledge mining is primarily connected with content and algorithms. The language or method used for expressing a 'question' and automating its translation in general is not of concern for this research.

Data resources, whatever their size is, do not automatically deliver high quality results. In most cases, content and algorithms are limiting possibilities to answer complex and staggered questions in reasonable ways. Contributions to these deficiencies result from data, algorithms, and their implementations. Therefore, high quality knowledge resources, including factual, conceptual, procedural, and metacognitive knowledge, description, and documentation are increasingly important. In consequence, advancing methodologies for knowledge mining is a focus of comparable importance.

Different knowledge references and data require different tools. Several disciplines contribute and specialised approaches and solutions have to be used on context for coping with any slightly complex question. Built on such in-deficit foundation, there is no direct and common practice on how to integrate specialised algorithms and applications with each other without a methodology. Appropriate methodologies will allow to integrate advanced knowledge resources and to modularise several tasks within a knowledge mining workflow. In addition, this research presents more close insights from a case study and the knowledge, especially conceptual knowledge required and provides additional new context examples, factual knowledge, and further case study results.

This paper is organised as follows. Section II introduces the methodology for creating views with advanced knowledge mining. Section III describes the Cogwheel Modules Methodology. Section IV presents an implementation and case study and how to create a primary context. Section V discusses an excerpt of secondary new resulting context, especially different visualisation views leading to new insights. The discussion includes references and associations with the workflow implementation resulting from the implementation and application of the methodology, based on previous work and re-usable components. Section VI summarises the lessons learned, conclusions, and future work.

II. Motivation

The motivation for the research on a new methodology for creating new views from knowledge integration results from the unsatisfactory and non-knowledge centric instruments and state of integration available. For many knowledge mining challenges, e.g., seeking good answers to complex questions, there are no solutions available for integrating complex knowledge resources and arbitrary application components. A sample question is:

Which natural events associated with the creation of crater structures with a diameter larger than 100 m could have been directly notable by human population within the last thousands of years and are still observable on-land at the area of todays' continent of Europe and which knowledge is associated with such events?

The question is quite precise but present possibilities mostly cannot achieve appropriately precise results in order to answer such questions. If one is not satisfied with arbitrary lists of hundreds of snippets of information mostly not part of an answer instead of an on-topic result then we have to find better ways. A solution is to flexibly integrate high quality data with conceptual knowledge and suitable application components with appropriate features. Due to the complexity of integration, the state of the art resources together with supportive data and component resources will be presented and discussed when required in the following section.

III. Cogwheel Modules Methodology

With this research, a methodology is defined by a sequence of steps. The steps can be a set of procedures in order to create a result for a knowledge mining process, e.g., with a discovery process. The procedures can include data, knowledge, formal descriptions, and implementations, e.g., collecting data, retrieving information, and algorithmic specifications. The purpose can range from delivering to creating and answer to an open question, e.g., delivering knowledge for a learning or decision making process. The methodology uses a formal description of knowledge, data and information, as well as required research techniques. Content and context are represented by any knowledge objects and data available in time and space. Data may be structured and unstructured.

1a) Identification of a knowledge mining challenge.
1b) Phrasing of a problem or question.
1c) Identification of a solution or answering strategy.
1d) Context description and modeling.
1e) Mapping of sub-challenges to possible partial solutions.
1f) Interface creation for partial solutions.
2a) Creation and / or selection of Cogwheel Modules (modularisation into sub-challenges and partial solutions).
2b) Knowledge and information: Identification or creation and / or selection of nuclei and facets.
2c) Peeling of information-nuclei from existing evidence.
2d) Milling of nuclei.
2e) Information processing.
2f) Data selection including nuclei and facets.
2g) Information object turnaround.
3a) Workflow implementation (incl. Cogwheel Modules).
3b) Analysis of results.
3c) Learning process and persistent documentation.
3d) Improvement process.

We can identify three main groups within the methodology. 1a) to 1f) is a preparatory phase, 2a) to 2g) describes a gearbox of knowledge mining, and 3a) to 3d) is a consecutive phase.

The modules allow to assign specialised applications and specialised features to separate modules as will be shown in the following implementation. Options and features of specialised applications can be documented, including conceptual knowledge, with the learning process and to cope with reoccurring requirements. The methodology allows to create different approaches for a workflow.

IV. Implementation and Case Study

The methodology was applied to practical situations. The following case study presents a practical workflow implementation from 1 to 3 (challenge identifying question to workflow implementation) based on the above gearbox of knowledge, including the required Cogwheel Modules with their mapping to important components and steps, their implementation and results. The goal is to create primary context and –in a consecutive process– secondary context, which in the case means spatial visualisation.

The starting point is the above sample question. The required compositions of features and criteria can become quite complex and are commonly not implemented in any single application or component. Therefore, the integration of appropriate application components can be desirable or even required.

The plethora of information from the knowledge resources is narrowed by the conceptual knowledge, the references to classifications, e.g., to the mapping and data of:

- Craters (any, e.g., Earth and other planets),
  - volcanic features including craters,
  - impact craters including meteorites, ...
- confirmed (and non-confirmed) structures/craters,
- structures observable on-land,
- age less than (about) 9999 years old,
- larger than 100 m diameter.

The respective workflow requires a number of special calculations as well as criteria Cogwheel Modules for knowledge resources and spatial components.

Applying a universal classification can be used to classify the appropriate objects, the associated application components, and the respective required options for a Cogwheel Module, e.g., for the calculations and filters.

In this case, the two groups of components involved with creating a solution are a) advanced knowledge resources and b) knowledge mining including conceptual knowledge references, spatial data and applications.

The definition of data-centricity used is: "The term data-centric refers to a focus, in which data is most relevant in context with a purpose. Data structuring, data shaping, and long-term aspects are important concerns. Data-centricity concentrates on data-based content and is beneficial for information and knowledge and for emphasizing their value. Technical implementations need to consider distributed data, non-distributed data, and data locality and enable advanced data handling and analysis. Implementations should support separating data from technical implementations as far as possible." [2].

According to this, the implementation of the methodology is as far data-centric as possible and allows a systematic application.

The following sections describe the essentials of the preparatory phase up to the partial solutions and the Cogwheel Modules required, including the handling of the nuclei and information processing. The sub-challenges are presented with their mapping to applications. Relevant excerpts of data and information are discussed in anticipation of the final results. The concluding section shows the workflow implementation used for creating the final results.

A. *Multi-disciplinary knowledge resources identification*

The knowledge resources hold arbitrary multi-disciplinary knowledge (e.g., documentation of factual, conceptual, procedural, and metacognitive knowledge), in various structures as well as unstructured, objects, and references, including information on digital objects and realia objects, e.g., media objects and archived physical specimen. These resources provide the prerequisites in order to create efficient Cogwheel Modules and handle knowledge and information nuclei and facets for peeling and milling processes.

1) Factual knowledge: The knowledge resources also contain information on various types of crater features like volcanic craters and impact craters. Especially, the Earth's impact crater container in the knowledge resources container holds data and references for all known impact craters on Earth.

The knowledge resources provide factual and conceptual data, e.g., crater types, crater/impact ages, and confirmed impact events.

The impact features container holds the Kaali impact, represented by its major impact crater. The minor craters of this impact event are referenced from this object and from sub-objects, all of which contain their factual and referenced data.

Figure 1 shows a spatial presentation overview of terrestrial (meteorite) impact features resulting from the impact features container. The spatial presentation is using a Robinson projection in order to cover arbitrary locations with a continuous visualisation in a common way.

The multi-disciplinary knowledge resources were used to create various computational views of impact craters on Earth [3] with any more details. The multi-disciplinary views, including conceptual knowledge represented by classifications, enable an association of various characteristics common with different information in collections [4].

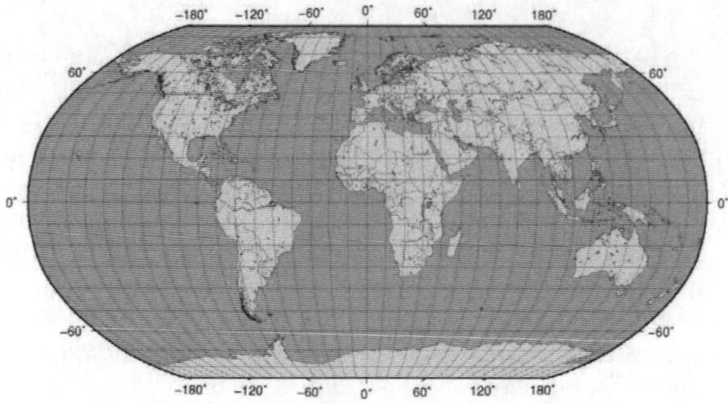

Figure 1. Impactmap – computed worldwide spatial distribution of classified terrestrial impact features (meteorite) from available object entries [3].

In this case, Earth surface information, georeferenced geophysical and geological factual data, have been associated.

Table I lists the factual container data used from the LX Foundation Scientific Resources [5] (not an acronym) referenced for the Kaali crater field object and relevant with the mining challenge.

TABLE I. RESULTING FACTUAL DATA REFERENCED FOR THE KAALI CRATER FIELD (EXCERPT, LX RESOURCES).

Crater Number	*Coordinates (lat/lon)*		*Diameter (m)*	*Elevation (m)*
1	58.371270	22.664737	39	24.10
2	58.367407	22.672298	25	25.90
3	58.366556	22.677637	76	21.99
4	58.371982	22.675092	33	24.91
5	58.370815	22.675611	20	21.90
6	58.370861	22.663155	13	29.90
7	58.370306	22.671848	26	22.90
8	58.367460	22.672577	15	25.99
9	58.372715	22.669419	110	34.14

The crater field consists of 9 known craters. Crater number 9 is the major crater. Craters 1 to 8 form sub-container objects, which deliver the data.

In order to illustrate general facilities with modified Cogwheel Modules, information peeling and milling, even for case studies with different knowledge resources, we can take a look into the context and quality of the data involved in this case.

The factual knowledge criteria for impact crater classification on basis of a physical view (criteria classification) are:

- Size of the impacting object,
- Speed of the impacting object,
- Material of the impacting object,
- Composition and structure of the target rock,
- Angle that the impacting object hits the target,
- Gravity of the target object respective planet,
- Physical attributes, e.g., porosity, of impacting object,
- Age of the impact,
- Size of the impact,
- Structure of the crater.

Further associated phenomena (indicator classification) are impact crater indicators on the other hand, which are:

- Planar fractures in quartz,
- Shocked quartz,
- Glass fragments.

For creating Cogwheel Modules and enabling views, factual knowledge not only contains facts like measurements and documentation. Factual knowledge supports analysis and visualisation, e.g., comparing knowledge objects and creating a spatial distribution and visualisation.

2) Conceptual knowledge: Advanced knowledge from integration of universal classification and spatial information can provide new insights when applied with knowledge mining [6]. The use of the Universal Decimal Classification (UDC) is widely popular, e.g., in library context, geosciences [7], and mapping [8] as provided by the Natural Environment Research Council (NERC) [9] via the NERC Open Research Archive (NORA) [10].

The small excerpts of the knowledge resources objects only refer to main UDC-based classes, which for this part of the publication are taken from the Multilingual Universal Decimal Classification Summary (UDCC Publication No. 088) [11] released by the UDC Consortium under the Creative Commons Attribution Share Alike 3.0 license [12] (first release 2009, subsequent update 2012).

Data in the knowledge resources carries references to classifications. Examples are references to UDC for any discipline and object, e.g., natural sciences and history.

Here, besides the central UDC:539.63 (impact effects) and UDC:539.8 (other physico-mechanical effects), referred top level groups for geodesy, cartography, and geography are UDC:528 [13], UDC:910 [14], and UDC:912 [15]. Tables II and III show excerpts of the conceptual data (UDC) used for geodetic / cartographic and geographic classification.

TABLE II. CLASSIFICATION WITH KNOWLEDGE RESOURCES: GEODETIC AND CARTOGRAPHIC CONCEPTUAL DATA (LX).

UDC Code	*Description (English, excerpt)*
UDC:5	MATHEMATICS. NATURAL SCIENCES
UDC:52	Astronomy. Astrophysics. Space research. Geodesy
UDC:528	Geodesy. Surveying. Photogrammetry. Remote sensing. Cartography
UDC:528.4	Field surveying. Land surveying. Cadastral survey. Topography. Engineering survey. Special fields of surveying
UDC:528.5	Geodetic instruments and equipment
UDC:528.7	Photogrammetry: aerial, terrestrial
UDC:528.8	Remote sensing
UDC:528.9	Cartography. Mapping (textual documents)

TABLE III. CLASSIFICATION WITH KNOWLEDGE RESOURCES: GEOGRAPHIC CONCEPTUAL DATA (LX).

UDC Code	*Description (English, excerpt)*
UDC:9	GEOGRAPHY. BIOGRAPHY. HISTORY
UDC:91	Geography. Exploration of the Earth and of individual countries. Travel. Regional geography
UDC:910	General questions. Geography as a science. Exploration. Travel
UDC:910.2	Kinds and techniques of geographical exploration
UDC:912	Nonliterary, nontextual representations of a region

Composite classification based on these top level classification references can refer to special items, e.g., cartographic bibliographies, historical atlases, and globes. Summarised, the classification can be used as glueing component classifying the knowledge object space and the implementation space, e.g., respective resources, objects, application components, and features of application components. This also provides the base for the creation of conceptual knowledge objects.

For creating views, conceptual knowledge not only provides a universal system of knowledge space, it contains classification and allows context references. Conceptual knowledge can provide a range of precise as well as fuzzy context for knowledge objects. Especially, conceptual knowledge allows the creation of conceptual knowledge objects. For example, impact features and meteorites can be classified in the following groups.

Table IV shows conceptual data (UDC) used for the basic classification of impact events and meteorites.

TABLE IV. CLASSIFICATION WITH KNOWLEDGE RESOURCES: IMPACT EVENTS KNOWLEDGE RESOURCES CLASSIFICATION (LX).

UDC Code	*Description (English, excerpt)*
UDC:500	Natural sciences
UDC:523	Solar system
UDC:523.68	Meteors. Meteoroids. Meteorites
UDC:530	Physics
UDC:539	Physical nature of matter
UDC:539.63	Impact effects
UDC:539.8	Other physico-mechanical effects

The excerpt also shows the context of meteorites and impact effects in `UDC:5`.

An object carousel generated for impact craters, shows the different types present in the knowledge resources groups and their crater categories (Figure 2). For the task of creating a carousel all categories are selected (red colour). The resulting categories are micro crater, multi-ring crater, elongate crater, complex crater, and simple crater.

Any objects in the categories can carry attributes like time and space as well as objects in other categories, which allows to have dimensions across disciplines. According conceptual knowledge "filters" have been applied to the other criteria like geological time types and sub-types.

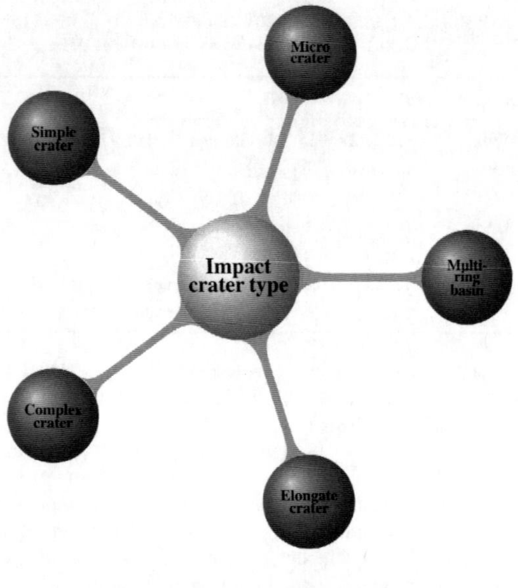

Figure 2. Object Carousel computed for impact crater categories, supporting the creation of new primary context.

Regarding the knowledge mining process all categories can be used. After finding results with a possibly high relevance the categories provide further information for context and analysis.

B. Supportive data and component resources

In this case, referring to spatial distribution and distance, supportive data and component resources are geoscientific data and mapping components.

Appropriate data was required for the criteria, which are related to topographic data. In the past, the georeferenced objects have been used with various data, e.g., with the Global Land One-kilometer Base Elevation Project (GLOBE) [16] and the 2-minute gridded global relief data (ETOPO2v2) [17].

For the required resolution of the results presented here, the knowledge resources had to be integrated with data based on the gridded ETOPO1 [18] 1 arc-minute global relief model data [19]. For special purposes data can be composed from various sources, e.g., adding Shuttle Radar Topography Mission (SRTM) data [20] from the Consultative Group on International Agricultural Research (CGIAR) [21].

The horizontal datum of ETOPO1 is World Geodetic System geographic, which was established in 1984 (WGS84) and later revised. The WGS84 specifications and references are provided by the National Geospatial-Intelligence Agency (NGA) [22] and as EPSG:4326 from the European Petroleum Survey Group Geodesy (EPSG) [23]. The vertical datum of ETOPO1 is "sea level". The source elevation data were not converted by the authors of ETOPO1 to a common vertical datum because of the large cell size of 1 arc-minute.

The Generic Mapping Tools (GMT) [24] suite application components are used for handling the spatial data, applying the related criteria, and for the visualisation.

Further, supportive components can be Google Earth or Google Maps presentation [25], Marble [26], and OpenStreetMap (OSM) [27]. [28].

For creating views, supportive data and component resources can provide data and features, which allow to refer to different context and add different kind of interactivity.

C. Peeling and milling of context references for views

Advanced analysis of research data is becoming increasingly important. For example, services supporting researchers especially for categorising texts with a special context are in development for many years [29]. Nevertheless, these services do not provide features beyond term context and text analysis.

The knowledge resources can fully support context and provide references to multi-disciplinary knowledge, e.g., photo media objects related to an object (Figure 3).

```
1 Photo-Object: Birgit Gersbeck-Schierholz, Hannover, Germany.
2 media: YES 20160629 {LXC:DETAIL--M-} {UDC:(0.034)(044)770} LXDATASTORAGE://...
   kaali2016_1.JPG ...
3 media: YES 20160629 {LXC:DETAIL--M-} {UDC:(0.034)(044)770} LXDATASTORAGE://...
   kaali2016_2.JPG ...
4 media: YES 20160629 {LXC:DETAIL--M-} {UDC:(0.034)(044)770} LXDATASTORAGE://...
   kaali2016_3.JPG ...
5 media: YES 20160629 {LXC:DETAIL--M-} {UDC:(0.034)(044)770} LXDATASTORAGE://...
   kaali2016_4.JPG ...
6 media: YES 20160629 {LXC:DETAIL--M-} {UDC:(0.034)(044)770} LXDATASTORAGE://...
   kaali2016_5.JPG ...
7 Object-Discoverer: Birgit Gersbeck-Schierholz, Hannover, Germany.
8 Photo-Object: Claus-Peter Rückemann, Minden, Germany.
9 media: YES 20160629 {LXC:DETAIL--M-} {UDC:(0.034)(044)770} LXDATASTORAGE://...
   img_0086.jpg
```

Figure 3. Information peeling: Media entries from knowledge resources objects (multi-disciplinary geosciences collection, LX, excerpt).

The examples objects are referred by conceptual knowledge and contextual knowledge references. The excerpt shows referenced media for "Kaali crater" after the peeling process from the object. The excerpt of an object associated with a knowledge object is shown in Figure 4.

```
1 Lilium ... [Biology, Botany]:
2            (lat.) Lilium martagon.
3            Earth mull vegetation.
4            Indicator: Eutrophic, leach enriched, clayey and loamy soils, shadow
              and penumbra location.
5            ...
6            Syn.: Türkenbundlilie
7            Syn.: martagon lily
8            Syn.: Turk's cap lily ...
```

Figure 4. Information peeling of Lilium martagon knowledge resources object (multi-disciplinary geosciences collection, LX, excerpt).

The excerpt shows an object "Lilium martagon" associated with the "Kaali crater" object after the information peeling process from this object. Figure 5 lists an excerpt of associated bibliographic references for an object.

```
1 cite: YES 20070000 {LXK:Kaali Kraater; Kaali crater; meteorite; impact} {UDC:
   ...} {PAGE:----..----} LXCITE://Tiirmaa:2007:Meteorite
2 cite: YES 20160000 {LXK:Kaali Kraater; Kaali crater; meteorite; impact} {UDC:
   ...} {PAGE:----..----} LXCITE://Tiirmaa:2016:Scars
3 cite: YES 20120000 {LXK:Kaali Kraater; Kaali crater; meteorite; impact;
   Excalibur; sword} {UDC:...} {PAGE:----..----} LXCITE://Faure:2012:Estonians
4 cite: YES 20160000 {LXK:Kaali Kraater; Kaali crater; meteorite; impact;
   Tutankhamun; dagger} {UDC:...} {PAGE:----..----} LXCITE://
   Comelli:2016:Tutankhamun
```

Figure 5. Information peeling: Citation entries from knowledge resources objects (multi-disciplinary geosciences collection, LX, excerpt).

The referenced citation entries are the result of the information peeling process from the Kaali crater object and refer to bibliographic references for meteorite craters on the island of Saaremaa [30] as well as to meteorite craters in Estonia [31].

Other references point to information for meteorite-material-usage, e.g., in context with archaeological and historical or mythical context.

One example is King Arthur's sword Excalibur ('Ex-Kali-bur') [32], which is directly associated with Kaali and the mother goddess Kali and its metal material. An association exists via metal object classification and "sword" synonyms (Figure 6).

```
Cutter
Dagger
Knife
Lance
Poniard
Saber
Sabre
Scimitar
Sword
```

Figure 6. Synonyms of 'cutter-sword' group from knowledge resources objects (LX, excerpt).

The association links to King Tutankhamun's 'dagger' in Egypt [33], which is made with meteorite iron from impact craters in the Libyan desert, as proved by available modern analysis.

This reference shows a remarkably comparable set of facts and references (king, sword, meteorite, iron, impact, ...) for which we still have the authentic realia object.

D. *Workflow implementation and phases*

For the case study, the required data and configuration is manually selected for the preparatory phase. The consequent modules act on basis of that data, especially conceptual knowledge and factual knowledge.

The central Cogwheel Module `cogwheel_criteria` in the knowledge mining gearbox utilises a sequence `lximpactsselect_crae_criteria` containing a number of components

1) `lximpactsselect_crae_date`
2) `lximpactsselect_crae_confirmed`
3) `lximpactsselect_crae_age_historic`
4) `lximpactsselect_crae_diameter`

for handling the criteria for the event date range, confirmed and not confirmed events, the date range, and the crater diameter. In this case the components can be considered as filter processes.

The spatial modules of the workflow (`cogwheel_world`, `cogwheel_region`) utilise the features latitude and longitude, wet / land criteria, criteria evaluation, spatial distance computation, map projection, and visualisation.

The respective components are provided by GMT suite applications, especially `pscoast` and `gmtselect`. The GMT applications have to care for longitude, latitude, elevation and contribute to the applying topographical data related criteria, for topography related decision making within the information object turnaround.

The later association of knowledge objects, referenced media objects, and citation objects is supported by conceptual knowledge and discovery processes. In the consecutive phase results are analysed and persistently documented in order to improve the knowledge resources and mining algorithms.

Please keep in mind that it is not the intention of the examples that others should repeat the case study and its modules but with realising the details required they can create modules for their own knowledge scenarios, based on the methodology using the named or their own, additional components.

V. Secondary Context and Resulting Views

Earths' impact crater objects from the classified LX factual knowledge resources are used as a factual and conceptual knowledge source for computing results, considering the respective context and selection criteria. Result can be a group of craters, fitting to all the criteria, after the mining algorithm is applied to the integrated knowledge resources and methods.

The following sections describe the creation of secondary views and possible new insights based on the Cogwheel Modules Methodology and provide a discussion of the above implementation case study with its resulting primary context.

A. *Result of implemented workflow*

Figure 7 shows the resulting output, including the necessary topography (longitude, latitude, elevation), data, and information used, after the result was visualised via GMT.

Criteria for decision making are the resulting target structures (meteorite craters) on land (topography and coverage), especially confirmed Earth crater groups (meteorite impact features, bullets, red, blue, and green colours), age and size of (on-land) structures, and a reasonable catchment area for Europe (blue),

A catchment center has been chosen, a circular area with a respective radius of 3000 km, automatically fitted with the map projection. The blue circle marks a reasonable area to cover the continent of Europe in this context. The blue and green bullets mark the craters inside that area. The data, items, and marks are automatically computed and visualised.

The final resulting object (bullet, green colour), which fits all criteria is the Kaali crater field, Saaremaa, Estonia. This result is based on a large amount of knowledge resources and application resources in the preparatory phase, an advanced gearbox with compute intensive Cogwheel Modules, and a workflow implementation using a range of large supportive data and component resources, as described. Further analysis can, e.g., select a relevant area containing the resulting object in order to create additional context with the object itself. Another strategy can be to find comparable objects and context, which were outside the range when having first phrased the question.

The region of positive final result of the applied knowledge mining is computed and presented via GMT, too. Figure 8 shows the region of the Kaali crater field on the island of Saaremaa, Estonia in its topographic context.

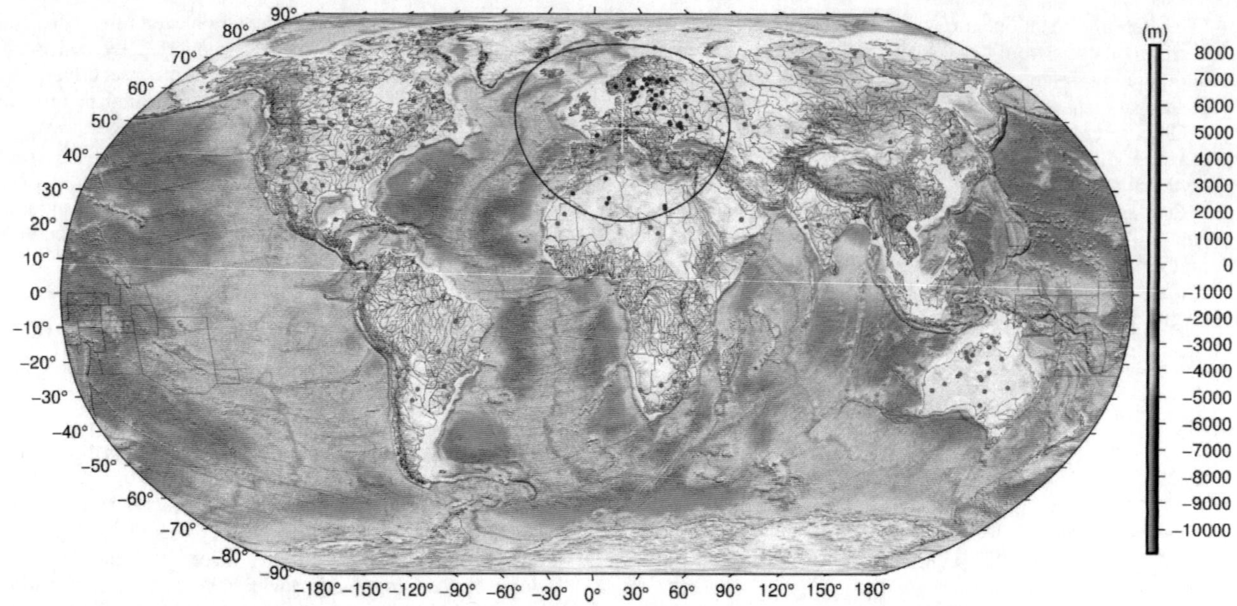

Figure 7. Knowledge mining methodology applied (LX factual and conceptual knowledge, factual data). Criteria are resulting crater groups (meteorite impacts, all coloured bullets), age and size of (on-land) structures, area, topography (all coloured bullets). Final result: Kaali crater field (green), Saaremaa, Estonia.

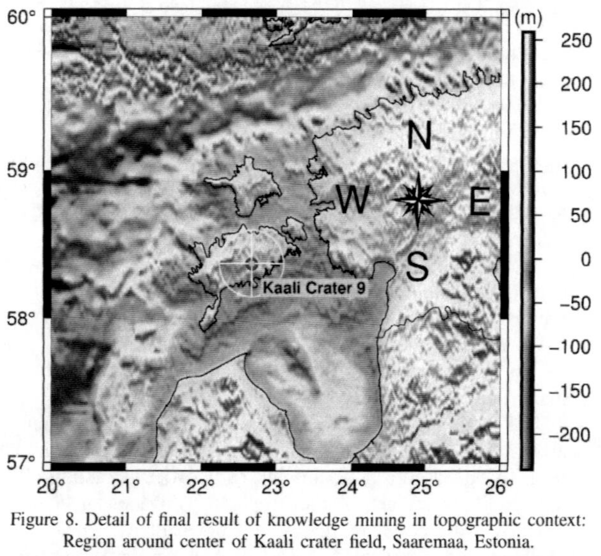

Figure 8. Detail of final result of knowledge mining in topographic context: Region around center of Kaali crater field, Saaremaa, Estonia.

The bullet and the cross mark the center of the crater field (labeled Kaali Crater 9). The yellow ring marks an area of 25 km around the major crater.

B. Resulting spatial description

Arbitrary different representations can be computed and generated from the result matrices. It is possible even to generate many different types spatial descriptions.

The Keyhole Markup Language (KML) is an Extensible Markup Language (XML) based format for specifying spatial data and content. It is considered an official standard of the Open Geospatial Consortium (OGC).

The KML description can be used with many spatial components and purposes, e.g., with a Google Earth or Google Maps presentation [25], with a Marble representation [26], using OpenStreetMap (OSM) [27] and national instances [28] in order to create arbitrary context.

Figures 9, 10, and 11 show the complementary excerpts from KML data generated for the results of the discovery with this case study.

The excerpts contain the objects of the Kaali crater field, Saaremaa, Estonia. In detail, the first excerpt holds the top part of the generated KML.

```
<?xml version="1.0" encoding="UTF-8"?>
<kml xmlns="http://www.opengis.net/kml/2.2" xmlns:gx="http://www.google.com/kml/
ext/2.2">
    <Document>
<!-- (c) CPR, LX-Project, 1992 to 2016 -->
        <name>Kaali Meteor Crater Field</name>
```

Figure 9. KML data top (excerpt) generated for results of the discovery from factual knowledge (LX): The Kaali crater field, Saaremaa, Estonia.

It contains the formal configuration, e.g., the XML version, the encoding, and the KML schemes to be used in addition with a general name for the generated spatial description. The middle part contains most of the factual data, which was compiled during the preparatory phase, the knowledge mining, and the consecutive phase.

It includes the major and minor crater groups with their coordinates and elevation and also includes balloon style label popup information.

```
    <Folder>
        <name>Minor Meteor Crater</name>
        <Style id="meteorcraterminor">
            <BalloonStyle>
            <text>$[description]</text>
            </BalloonStyle>
            <IconStyle>
            <Icon>
            <href>http://maps.google.com/mapfiles/kml/paddle/grn-blank.png</
             href>
            </Icon>
            </IconStyle>
        </Style>
        <Placemark>
            <name>Kaali Kraater 1</name>
            <description>Kaali Impact Crater Field</description>
            <styleUrl>#meteorcraterminor</styleUrl>
            <LookAt>
                <longitude>22.664737</longitude>
                <latitude>58.371270</latitude>
                <altitude>0.0000000000</altitude>
                <range>9352719.7459717896</range>
            </LookAt>
            <ExtendedData>
                <Data name="isBookmark">
                    <value>true</value>
                </Data>
            </ExtendedData>
            <Point>
                <coordinates>22.664737,58.371270,24.1</coordinates>
            </Point>
        </Placemark>
        ...
    </Folder>
    <Folder>
        <name>Major Meteor Crater</name>
        ...
    </Folder>
        ...
```

Figure 10. KML central data (ex.) generated for results of the discovery from factual knowledge (LX): The Kaali crater field, Saaremaa, Estonia.

The third excerpt holds the bottom part of the generated KML with the range markers. The ellipses mark the location of longer passages of data generated for the KML code, which repeat comparable entries and entities but which are not relevant for the demonstration here.

```
            ...
        <Folder>
            <name>Circle 1 km radius around major crater</name>
            <description><![CDATA[circle radius 1 km]]></description>
            ...
                <tessellate>1</tessellate>
                <coordinates> 22.686508001199286,58.37271385997719,0.0 ... </
                 coordinates>
            ...
        </Folder>
    </Document>
</kml>
```

Figure 11. KML data bottom (excerpt) generated for discovery results from factual knowledge (LX): The Kaali crater field, Saaremaa, Estonia.

The complement of both parts form the XML based document, which can be structured and documented to any required extent. It allows to separate structure and style for the required data representation and application.

There are many more features with the components and KML, which can be used in context with spatial mapping, computation, and visualisation, without describing details.

C. Resulting associated information: Spatial mapping

The resulting satellite view shows the area of the Kaali crater field, Saaremaa, Estonia (Figure 12). Besides the major crater, further features of the crater field are not immediately visible. The reason is that the features are small in relation and they can be hidden from the satellite view, e.g., under vegetation.

Figure 12. The resulting area of the Kaali crater field, Saaremaa, Estonia (Google Earth data, flat view). Major crater visible without mark.

The integrated knowledge from different context can deliver relevant information. For example, topography, elevation data, vegetation coverage, water bodies, infrastructure information are important information, which can be used in context with the knowledge mining.

The final result from the knowledge mining with the classified LX factual knowledge can be projected onto online satellite data of the area of the Kaali crater field. The result from object and sub-objects is shown in Figure 13.

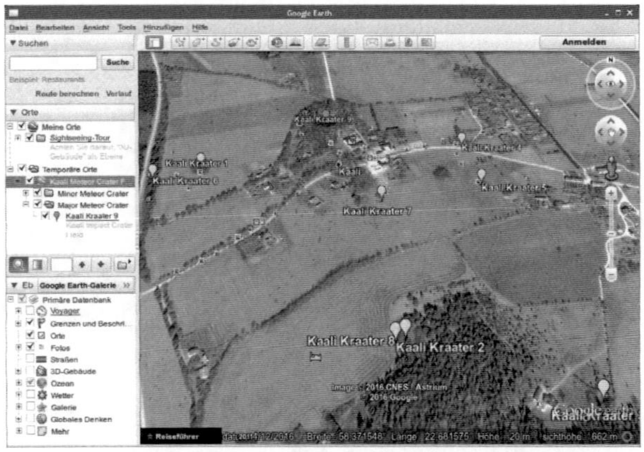

Figure 13. The resulting area of Kaali crater field, Saaremaa, Estonia, factual knowledge (craters red and green) (LX) projected onto Google Earth data.

The interactive map shows the nine craters known for the crater field. The major crater is marked in red colour, the minor craters are marked in green colour.

The final result from the knowledge mining with the classified LX factual knowledge can be projected onto online vector and navigation data (Figure 14).

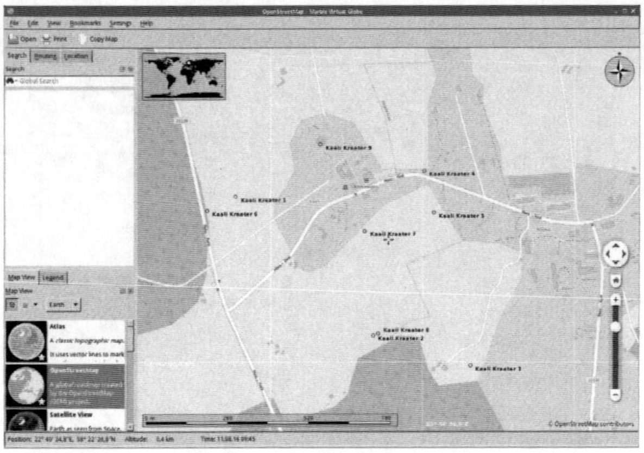

Figure 14. The resulting area of Kaali crater field, Saaremaa, Estonia, factual knowledge (craters 1 to 9) (LX) projected onto OSM data via Marble.

The integration shows craters 1 to 9 of the Kaali crater field area projected onto OSM data via Marble.

D. Resulting associated information: Media references

The integrated knowledge resources can contain references to any data, e.g., media objects. Media objects contain own references, e.g., classification, citations, documentation, and keywords and can therefore contribute in many ways to new insight – besides their intrinsic media content. The following photo data (Figure 15) from the media references for "Kaali crater" were delivered in association from the final result of the knowledge mining workflow.

Figure 15. Integrated media photo objects associated with the knowledge object "Kaali crater", Saaremaa, Estonia, referring to [34] (LX resources).

The references of these media photo objects (Figure 3) are part of objects in the knowledge resources. Media results (1–5) [34] and specimen (6) photos from the Natural Sciences Specimen Archive are dated June 29, 2016.

The photos and physical samples have been taken in 2016 by the Knowledge in Motion (KiM) natural sciences and archaeology sections at the Kaali meteorite crater field on the island of Saaremaa, Estonia, during the Geo Exploration and Information (GEXI) [35] Baltic research and studies campaign.

In detail, the resulting photo objects of the examined site (from left to right, from top to bottom) show in this sort order:

1: Major crater, view in northern direction.
2: Major crater, view in north-eastern direction.
3: Major crater, view in western direction.
4: Path towards major crater, view from southern direction.
5: Vegetation, Lilium martagon, at top of crater rim (referring to Figure 4).
6: Specimen crater pond material (quartz, melane particles, lacustrine deposits, biogenic material).

The references included in the knowledge mining workflow (Figure 5) provide the complementary information that fine particles from the Kaali crater include impactor remains (esp. significant Ni-Wüstite, Ni-Maghemite, Ni-Goethite, Hematite, Magnetite, Taenite, Kamacite), spherules and splash-forms.

The analysis of the referenced media content, e.g., Lilium martagon, delivers the information that this flower is an indicator plant [36], indicating natural resources, e.g., showing mining resources. This will also show context with the references, both with impactor remains and with activities in prehistorical and historical times and associated remains and mythical context.

The media references are part of the context created for the views. These references can also be used when creating a secondary context, e.g., a spatial and dynamical visualisation, based on the results.

E. Consecutive criteria and range markers

The above resulting media references are directly referenced with the Kaali crater, especially with the major crater of the crater field. If we use further criteria, e.g., available with the spatial context and projection, we can associate additional context, e.g., Points Of Interest (POI), in the range around the Kaali crater. The generated KML can be used to express such ranges (Figures 16 and 17). The spatial algorithms and features available with the respective applications can be used to create complementary insight from individual context.

For example, further context for a primary view can be created by calculation of context considering a range. Considering range means calculating distance in a spatial representation.

The resulting perspective satellite view shows the area of the Kaali crater field, Saaremaa, Estonia, including circular range markers (Figure 16). The range markers (visible 1 km and 2 km diameter) mark an area around the major impact in the crater field. The same data is used with Marble (in this zoom the 1 km diameter range marker is visible in the window) and OSM context data (Figure 17). Not only that all the known crater structures appear to be located inside the close range around the major impact: That way the results can be analysed in arbitrary different context with the integrated knowledge, information, algorithms, and methods available from the chosen target.

Consecutive associations and further consecutive references can be computed, making use of the new context and features [37].

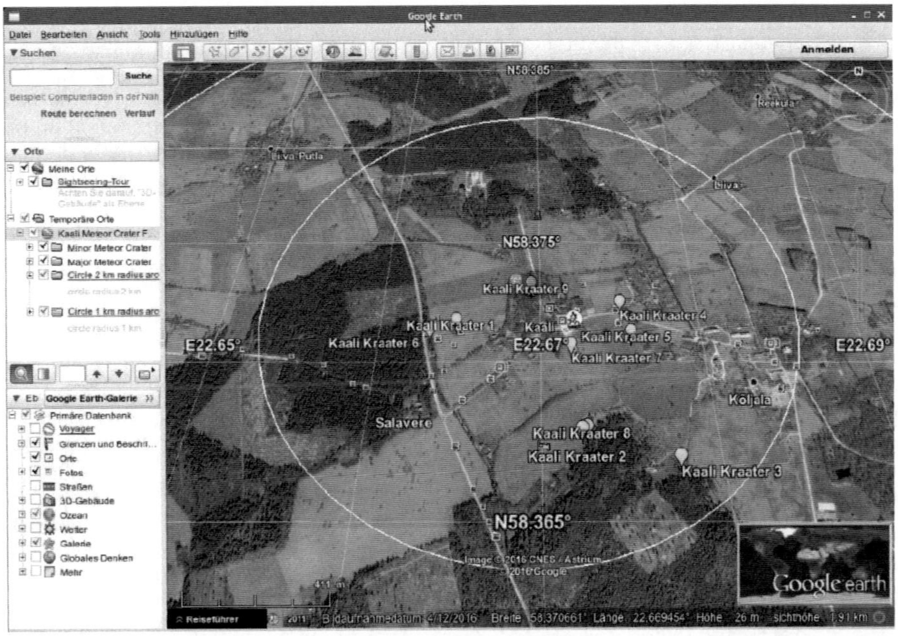

Figure 16. Secondary context with satellite data: Range markers at the area of the Kaali crater field, Saaremaa, Estonia (Google Earth), with range markers, major, and minor craters in a portable, interactive, and dynamical environment, presenting the resulting knowledge in context of a perspective satellite view.

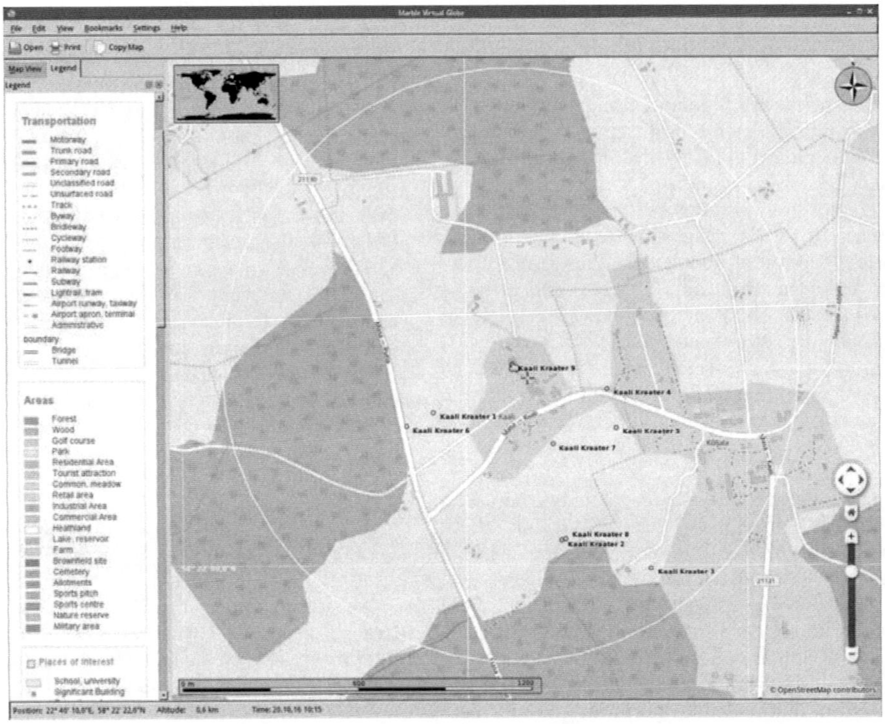

Figure 17. Secondary context with street data and legends: Resulting area of the Kaali crater field, Saaremaa, Estonia (Marble, OSM data), with range markers, major, and minor craters in a portable, interactive, and dynamical environment, presenting the resulting knowledge in context of land use and transportation.

Google Earth provides satellite data and POI, Marble with OSM provides vector street and feature data and different POI data. The secondary context examples using satellite and OSM data showed the range circles and the generated selection legend with the circles from the generated KML data as well as the legends on available transportation infrastructure context and on area context, e.g., forest areas, farm areas, residential areas, and lake reservoirs.

The spatial context provides an arbitrary number of thematic knowledge, which can be integrated with the results in order to compute new views and insight. The applied components allow to combine an arbitrary number of methods. For example, perspective visualisations can give additional information and enable to create references in that "spatial-range" context of integrated knowledge KML based animations can allow flight-over animations in the context of the associated thematic knowledge. These are just two of many examples for the spatial context only.

The region referenced fuzzy contextualisation for spatially expressed thematic context, e.g., weather and climate map data [38], can, e.g., also make the method beneficial for businesses like planning agencies and insurance companies.

These are the core items of the methodology implemented for this case study, from preparatory phase and knowledge mining to the consecutive phase with the analysis of results. There are no optional items, which should be described in detail, as the fine-tuning always depend on what the implementor wants to achieve for a certain task.

VI. Conclusion

Creating context and views for gaining insights from content of knowledge resources is a most challenging task. This research successfully deployed the Cogwheel Modules Methodology for advanced knowledge mining and generating data, especially for knowledge integration and the goal of creating new views, which lead to new insights and cognition.

The methodology case study implementation showed how primary context and secondary can be created and how the views can be visualised. The examples showed a series of newly generated spatial views, which open a wide new context of complementary dimensions, which can further be used to associate additional references. The case study also showed that this way the context can be extended very efficiently and that new insight can be the result, which was out of scope before.

The implementation proved that the methodology can be an excellent support for advanced knowledge mining. Generating views also means using general and specialised tools, which allow to add new knowledge from resources.

As soon as views proof to extend a context efficiently the process can be used for creating automated learning processes and saving the views with long-term knowledge resources for future use. Besides the practical benefits for knowledge mining the methodology also contributes to the further development of multi-disciplinary knowledge resources.

Creating spatial views is one of an arbitrary number of possible applications. The major phases of the methodology were applied for the implementation. Nevertheless, creating spatial Cogwheel Modules with spatial components and multi-disciplinary knowledge from knowledge resources demonstrated the methodology in a very instructive way.

The paper provides the results from the research and data-centric implementation of a case study of integrated knowledge and methods for answering knowledge mining challenges like complex questions and a number of instructive examples for creating primary and secondary context views.

The case study is focussing on knowledge mining challenges associated with geosciences and archaeology. Therefore, one category of the relevant generated context is spatial context, implemented in modules for spatial analysis and visualisation.

The base of the view creation is the identification and mapping of required resources – knowledge resources and partial solutions, mapping of complementary components in their context, and excerpts of associated knowledge used for information peeling generating a base for the information processing. The resources provide conceptual and factual knowledge in integration with appropriate context data and application components for computing and visualisation.

The mapped application components – tools and filters – were used complementary for handling the complex resources, systematically peeling of information nuclei and facets, milling, and consecutive information processing, including decision making integrating spatial and conceptual criteria. The results of the knowledge mining information object turnaround, can itself become part of the knowledge resources.

The methodology and the view creation can be applied to many application scenarios, especially where a solution can only be gained by integration of different data and approaches. Examples are multi-disciplinary knowledge mining scenarios integrating natural sciences and archaeology. Comparable reasonable results are not possible with any tested services, e.g., even large search engines accessing data in depth and width of the knowledge spectrum.

The various approaches also provide potential for optimisation for special priorities. In most cases, the optimisation can consider the individual challenges and the use of special algorithms and applications.

Future work concentrates on analysis of complementary context features, beyond spatial views, and further improving the long-term multi-disciplinary knowledge resources. On module side for knowledge mining the creation, utilisation, and documentation of advanced components with the Cogwheel Modules is in focus.

Acknowledgements

We are grateful to the Knowledge in Motion (KiM) long-term project, Unabhängiges Deutsches Institut für Multi-disziplinäre Forschung (DIMF), for partially funding this implementation, view modules case study, research and studies campaign, and publication under grants D2015F1P04604, D2017F1P04708, and to its senior scientific members, especially to Dipl.-Biol. Birgit Gersbeck-Schierholz, Leibniz Universität Hannover, Germany, to Dr. Friedrich Hülsmann,

Gottfried Wilhelm Leibniz Bibliothek (GWLB) Hannover, Germany, and to Dipl.-Ing. Martin Hofmeister, Hannover, Germany, for fruitful discussion, inspiration, practical multi-disciplinary case studies, and the analysis of advanced concepts. We are grateful to Dipl.-Ing. Hans-Günther Müller, Cray, Germany, for his work for providing flexible practical solutions to architectural challenges and excellent technical support. We are grateful to all national and international partners in the Geo Exploration and Information cooperations for their constructive and trans-disciplinary support. We are grateful to the postgraduate participants of the European Legal Informatics Study Programme (EULISP) for prolific discussion of scientific, legal, and technical aspects and for feedback, contributions, and reuse of results regarding High Performance Computing and Return of Investments projects and case studies over the last ten years. We thank the Science and High Performance Supercomputing Centre (SHPSC) for long-term support for the associated research cooperations.

REFERENCES

[1] C.-P. Rückemann, "Methodology and Integrated Knowledge for Complex Knowledge Mining: Natural Sciences and Archaeology Case Study Results," in Proceedings of The Ninth International Conference on Advanced Geographic Information Systems, Applications, and Services (GEOProcessing 2017), March 19 – 23, 2017, Nice, France. XPS Press, 2017, Rückemann, C.-P. and Doytsher, Y. and Xia, J. C. and Braz, F. J. (eds.), pages 103–109, ISSN: 2308-393X, ISBN-13: 978-1-61208-539-5, URL: http://www.thinkmind.org/index.php?view=article&articleid=geoprocessing_2017_7_10_30036 [accessed: 2017-06-05].

[2] C.-P. Rückemann, Z. Kovacheva, L. Schubert, I. Lishchuk, B. Gersbeck-Schierholz, and F. Hülsmann, Best Practice and Definitions of Data-centric and Big Data – Science, Society, Law, Industry, and Engineering. Post-Summit Results, Delegates' Summit, September 19, 2016, The Sixth Symposium on Advanced Computation and Information in Natural and Applied Sciences (SACINAS), The 14th International Conference of Numerical Analysis and Applied Mathematics (ICNAAM), September 19–25, 2016, Rhodes, Greece, 2016, URL: http://www.user.uni-hannover.de/cpr/x/publ/2016/delegatessummit2016/rueckemann_icnaam2016_summit_summary.pdf [accessed: 2017-06-05].

[3] C.-P. Rückemann, "From Multi-disciplinary Knowledge Objects to Universal Knowledge Dimensions: Creating Computational Views," International Journal On Advances in Intelligent Systems, vol. 7, no. 3&4, 2014, pages 385–401, ISSN: 1942-2679, LCCN: 2008212456 (Library of Congress), OCLC: 826628364, TMDL: intsys_v7_n34_2014_4, URL: http://www.iariajournals.org/intelligent_systems/intsys_v7_n34_2014_paged.pdf [accessed: 2017-06-05].

[4] C.-P. Rückemann, "Long-term Sustainable Knowledge Classification with Scientific Computing: The Multi-disciplinary View on Natural Sciences and Humanities," International Journal on Advances in Software, vol. 7, no. 1&2, 2014, pp. 302–317, ISSN: 1942-2628, URL: http://www.iariajournals.org/software/soft_v7_n12_2014_paged.pdf [accessed: 2017-06-05].

[5] "LX-Project," 2017, URL: http://www.user.uni-hannover.de/cpr/x/rprojs/en/#LX [accessed: 2017-06-05].

[6] F. Hülsmann and C.-P. Rückemann, "Advanced Knowledge from Universal Classification and Spatial Information," KiMrise, KiM Meeting, August 8, 2016, Knowledge in Motion, Hannover, Germany, 2016.

[7] T. V. Loudon, "Geoscience after IT: Part N, Cumulated References," Computers and Geosciences, vol. 26, no. 3, 2000, ISSN: 0098-3004, British Geological Survey, Natural Environment Research Council (NERC), UK, URL: http://nora.nerc.ac.uk/2410/1/Part_N.pdf [accessed: 2017-06-05].

[8] B. Stevenson, "Servicing Map Users at Aalborg University Library," LIBER Quarterly, vol. 10, 2000, pp. 454–464, ISSN: 1435-5205, DOI: 10.18352/lq.7616, URL: https://www.liberquarterly.eu/articles/10.18352/lq.7616/galley/7652/download/ [accessed: 2017-06-05].

[9] "Natural Environment Research Council (NERC)," 2017, UK, URL: http://www.nerc.ac.uk/ [accessed: 2017-06-05].

[10] "NERC Open Research Archive (NORA)," 2017, Natural Environment Research Council (NERC), UK, URL: http://nora.nerc.ac.uk [accessed: 2017-06-05].

[11] "Multilingual Universal Decimal Classification Summary," 2012, UDC Consortium, 2012, Web resource, v. 1.1. The Hague: UDC Consortium (UDCC Publication No. 088), URL: http://www.udcc.org/udcsummary/php/index.php [accessed: 2017-06-05].

[12] "Creative Commons Attribution Share Alike 3.0 license," 2012, URL: http://creativecommons.org/licenses/by-sa/3.0/ [accessed: 2017-06-05].

[13] "UDC 528: Geodesy. Surveying. Photogrammetry. Remote sensing. Cartography," 2017, Universal Decimal Classification (UDC), URL: http://udcdata.info/027504 [accessed: 2017-06-05].

[14] "UDC 910: General questions. Geography as a science. Exploration. Travel," 2017, Universal Decimal Classification (UDC), URL: http://udcdata.info/068129 [accessed: 2017-06-05].

[15] "UDC 912: Nonliterary, nontextual representations of a region," 2017, Universal Decimal Classification (UDC), URL: http://udcdata.info/068183 [accessed: 2017-06-05].

[16] "Global Land One-kilometer Base Elevation Project (GLOBE)," 2017, National Geophysical Data Center (NGDC), National Centers for Environmental Information (NCEI), National Oceanic and Atmospheric Administration (NOAA), NOAA Satellite and Information Service (NESDIS), U.S. Department of Commerce (DOC), URL: http://www.ngdc.noaa.gov/mgg/topo/globe.html [accessed: 2017-06-05].

[17] "2-Minute Gridded Global Relief Data (ETOPO2v2)," 2006, June, 2006, World Data Service for Geophysics, Boulder, USA, National Geophysical Data Center, National Centers for Environmental Information (NCEI), National Oceanic and Atmospheric Administration (NOAA), URL: http://www.ngdc.noaa.gov/mgg/fliers/06mgg01.html [accessed: 2017-06-05].

[18] "ETOPO1 1 Arc-Minute Global Relief Model," 2008, World Data Service for Geophysics, Boulder, USA, National Geophysical Data Center, National Centers for Environmental Information (NCEI), National Oceanic and Atmospheric Administration (NOAA), URL: http://www.ngdc.noaa.gov/mgg/global/relief/ETOPO1/data/ [accessed: 2017-06-05].

[19] C. Amante and B. W. Eakins, "ETOPO1 1 Arc-Minute Global Relief Model: Procedures, Data Sources and Analysis," 2009, NOAA Technical Memorandum NESDIS NGDC-24. National Geophysical Data Center, NOAA. DOI: 10.7289/V5C8276M, World Data Service for Geophysics, Boulder, USA, Nat. Geophysical Data Center, Nat. Centers for Env. Inf. (NCEI), Nat. Oceanic and Atmospheric Admin. (NOAA).

[20] "CGIAR Consortium for Spatial Information (CGIAR-CSI)," 2017, URL: http://www.cgiar-csi.org [accessed: 2017-06-05].

[21] "Consultative Group on International Agricultural Research (CGIAR)," 2017, URL: http://www.cgiar.org [accessed: 2017-06-05].

[22] "World Geodetic System (WGS)," 2012, National Geospatial-Intelligence Agency (NGA), URL: http://earth-info.nga.mil/GandG/wgs84/index.html [accessed: 2017-06-05].

[23] "Spatial reference for EPSG:4326," European Petroleum Survey Group Geodesy (EPSG), URL: https://epsg.io/4326 [accessed: 2017-06-05].

[24] "GMT - Generic Mapping Tools," 2017, URL: http://gmt.soest.hawaii.edu/ [accessed: 2017-06-05].

[25] "Google Maps," 2017, URL: http://www.google.com/maps [accessed: 2017-06-05].

[26] "Marble," 2017, URL: https://marble.kde.org/ [accessed: 2017-06-05].

[27] "OpenStreetMap (OSM)," 2017, URL: http://www.openstreetmap.org [accessed: 2017-06-05].

[28] "OpenStreetMap (OSM) - Deutschland," 2017, URL: http://www.openstreetmap.de [accessed: 2017-06-05].

[29] A. Wildschütz, "Named-Entity Recognition Framework – Qualitative Text Analysis in EGI-Engage (in German: Named-Entity Recognition Framework – Qualitative Textanalyse in EGI-Engage)," GWDG Nachrichten, Gesellschaft für wissenschaftliche Datenverarbeitung mbh Göttingen, vol. 10/16, 2016, pp. 15–17.

[30] R. Tiirmaa, Scars of Stars on the Island of Saaremaa. Commission of Meteoritics of Estonian Academy of Sciences, (post 2005), Booklet on Kaali Kraater, Saaremaa, Estland.

[31] R. Tiirmaa, V. Puura, A. Soesoo, and S. Suuroja, Estonian Meteorite Craters, 2007, MTÜ GEOGuide Baltoscandia. Tallinn (ed.), Inst. of Geology at Tallinn Univ. of Technology; University of Turku, Dept. of Geology; ISBN: 978-9985-9834-1-6, URL: http://www.gi.ee/geoturism/MetCraters_ENG_062011_100dpiS.pdf [accessed: 2017-06-06].

[32] G. Faure and T. M. Mensing, The Estonians; The long road to independence. Lulu.com, 2012, ISBN: 978-1-105-53003-6, URL: https://books.google.ru/books?id=hnq7AwAAQBAJ [accessed: 2017-06-05].

[33] D. Comelli, M. D'orazio, L. Folco, M. El-Halwagy, T. Frizzi, R. Alberti, V. Capogrosso, A. Elnaggar, H. Hassan, A. Nevin, F. Porcelli, M. G. Rashed, and G. Valentini, "The meteoritic origin of Tutankhamun's iron dagger blade," Meteoritics & Planetary Science, vol. 51, no. 7, Jul. 2016, pp. 1301–1309, the Meteoritical Society, DOI: 10.1111/maps.12664.

[34] B. Gersbeck-Schierholz, "Where the Sun has Taken a Rest: The Kaali Meteorite Crater," KiM On-site Summit, Knowledge in Motion, June 29, 2016, On-Site Summit Meeting, Knowledge in Motion Baltic Research and Studies Campaign 2016, "Unabhängiges Deutsches Institut für Multi-disziplinäre Forschung (DIMF)", Saaremaa, Estonia, 2016.

[35] "Geo Exploration and Information (GEXI)," 1996, 1999, 2010, 2017, URL: http://www.user.uni-hannover.de/cpr/x/rprojs/en/index.html#GEXI [accessed: 2017-06-05].

[36] B. Gersbeck-Schierholz and C.-P. Rückemann, "Decoding Manifests of Knowledge: The Lilium Martagon Case," KiM Sky Summit, Knowledge in Motion, November 14, 2016, Sky Summit Meeting, "Unabhängiges Deutsches Institut für Multi-disziplinäre Forschung (DIMF)", Barcelona, Spain, 2016.

[37] C. Hansel and C.-P. Rückemann, "Approaches Finding Context and Decisions," KiM Summit, June 14, 2017, Knowledge in Motion, Hannover, Germany, 2017.

[38] C.-P. Rückemann and O. Lau, "The Knowledge - Data Science Relation: Examples and Definitions," KiMrise, Knowledge in Motion Meeting, August 24, 2017, Knowledge in Motion, Hannover, Germany, 2017.

An SME Decision Support System Utilising Defined Scoring Methods

Daniel Pashley
Industrial Doctorate Centre in Systems
University of Bristol
Bristol, UK
dp13092@bristol.ac.uk

Theodore Tryfonas, Andrew Crossley
Department of Civil Engineering
University of Bristol
Bristol, UK
{theo.tryfonas, andrew.crossley}@bristol.ac.uk

Chris Setchell
Imetrum Limited
Bristol, UK
chris.setchell@imetrum.com

Abstract — **When companies engage in innovation, the appropriate selection of projects to invest resource in is paramount. In order to do this effectively, they need to research appropriate opportunities to create sufficient understanding. The various opportunities available need to be rationalised to match with the resource available. There are several rationalisation methods available, including Portfolio Management, Scoring Methods and Decision Support Systems. However, there are few that combine to be utilised by Small and Medium Sized Enterprises effectively. This work adds to the field of Small and Medium Sized Enterprise Decision Support by proposing an approach combining opportunity investigation, review and recommendation such that the most appropriate candidate innovation can be selected and taken forwards for development.**

Keywords - Portfolio Management; Scoring Methods; Decision Support Systems.

I. Introduction

Scoring methods, such as the Absolute method from [1] or the risk-reward matrix from [2], can be utilised to repeatedly review attributes of potential development projects. Selecting an innovative development approach indicates business intentions going forwards. In order to make a success of this approach, it has to be ingrained at a business wide strategic level. Businesses often form their strategy around the development of new products [3]. This can take several forms including incremental [3], radical [4],and disruptive [5]. These different strategies lead to a number of products making up the company's portfolio [6]. The difficulty for companies comes from selecting which of the next generation of potential developments should join the existing portfolio [7].

Currently there are a number of tools available to companies to aid this selection process including the Balanced Scorecard [8]. However, these methods introduce the potential for subjectivity, bias and an undue focus on particular attributes, when others may be of greater use to the company. This research and paper focuses on proposing three new methods to evaluate potential development projects that can be combined to form key elements of a Portfolio Management process.

During the process of identifying new development projects, capturing and understanding information is critical and makes a core part of this process. Utilising a process of capture, comparison and ranking, from a company's perspective, as to which are the most critical pieces of information can allow for directed capture and review. This forms a simple process, especially from the Small and Medium Sized Enterprise (SME) perspective of limited resource [9], which can result in clear understanding via prioritisation of the development options available.

There are many tools available to aid companies in making the necessary decisions, as to which development path they should select, these are a form of Decision Support Systems [10]. These use available information, of varying types per system, and a calculation method to recommend which option should be selected [10]. However, the calculation systems make decisions. They present recommendations on the decisions that should be made based on the available information; it is then up to the user to make the decision. Therefore, it is critical that Decision Support Systems are able to combine the most relevant information in a suitable way for a recommendation to be made. In some cases, utilising trends or previous data is not sufficient to deliver a recommendation. Instead the input of experts within the relevant field is required to ensure that the captured information is synthesised and understood correctly.

The aim of this work was to use the most relevant information attributes to help make recommendations on the development direction the SME should pursue. This process, while intended for a single SME, should also aim to be as universal as possible to other companies in a similar position. The underlying process used was taken from [11] and [1]. These pieces of work deliver a necessary level of understanding for company processes to reach the point at which such a method would be required. In addition, they deliver processes to capture and review relevant information on technological innovation which can be used as the basis for a Decision Support System, for this specific application.

An ethnographic stance was used to conduct this work. from a first-hand perspective [12], utilising experience of the problem space. It also requires observation of people's behaviour [13] and engagement with the problem [14] to deliver the required solution. This approach was selected in relation to an industrial problem experienced by a highly innovative SME, herein referred to as "the SME". The problem experienced was based upon the SMEs highly adaptable core intellectual property exploited in multiple technological applications. The SME has limited resource meaning that investment in innovative development projects had to be focused on those carrying the highest chance of success. Therefore, the purpose of the research project was to deliver a method to enable the appropriate selection between available possible innovative developments. This work was conducted in a cyclical manner within the SME to iteratively evolve the proposed *Decision Support System* to a point at which recommendations made could be utilised within conventional decision processes.

The paper has the following structure. Background literature is introduced to cover Portfolio Management, Strategy and Decision Making. Then the proposed *Decision Support System* is discussed and evaluated. Finally, conclusions are drawn based on the presented work.

II. Background Literature

Strategy is an instrument for keeping a high level of performance and to enable success [15]; this is focused company wide to achieve competitive advantage [16]. For a company, strategy is outlined such that it can aim to achieve set goals [17]. A company may select different types of strategy depending on what it is that they are aiming to achieve. Some strategies include first to market [16] and product differentiation [18]. In order to adopt a strategy there are three stages. The first is selection; in which a company should select a strategy which takes them towards their goals that will work across environments [19]. Once the strategy is selected, the finer details need to be formulated based on the company's knowledge [20]. Finally the strategy is implemented which requires buy in from all company levels [4] to ensure it is enacted as desired. Carefully designing and enacting strategy is critically important to differentiated activities such as innovation [4] as negative results can result from failing to be innovative in relation to the company's products or service.

The process of innovation can be seen as one whereby something new is done to bring benefit [21]. This benefit is in terms of the customer and the company performance [22]. The innovation process is so important, that it is one of the top priorities for 71% of companies [23]. However, it is an activity that pervades throughout a company including aspects such as culture, technology and resources [21]. There are several different forms of innovation. Two of the most common are process and product innovation. Process innovation is focused on the way in which firms carry out their activities [24]. Product innovation ensures the introduction of a new product to meet perceived market needs [25], based on the company's understanding. In addition to being focused on delivering something new, the innovation process is formed to be delivered in a certain way. A prime example of this is radical innovation; whereby the innovation of products or processes are driven by the technology being created, not the market [26]. This form of innovation can deliver significant returns [27] as it is reported as being responsible for 61% of profits even though it is only 38% of revenue [27]. Therefore, the innovation can be seen as a way to generate new revenue streams differentiated from the competition.

Many companies rely on innovation to achieve a competitive position within their market [7]. The challenge associated with this is assessing these opportunities [28] so the available resources can be distributed appropriately, to ensure the selected projects can be supported. With limited resources, which is always a concern, effectively managing an effective development pipeline is critical [29]. This helps to maximise returns by only allowing appropriate projects to begin. Within business, this distribution of resource is a managerial decision [30]. As such, the decision requires the necessary attention being placed on planning and understanding projects.

It is not uncommon for several options to present themselves at the same time or to be implemented together [30] alongside existing projects. However, the challenge is determining what new product has a chance of becoming a success [28]. So the question is " how to do the correct projects?" [7]. One approach is to use a conceptual funnel [31] which narrows down all potential projects into those with a higher chance of success. Activities such as investigation, evaluation and prioritising of potential projects are conducted within this conceptual funnel [29]. Prioritising potential projects, as part of the conceptual funnel, allows for an appropriate distribution of resources [7] to those projects that warrant them most. Approaches that are used to do this are either quantitative or qualitative, using techniques that range from rigorous tests to social-science methods [28].

A prominent approach to aid in the management of active and potential projects is Portfolio Management [6]. This has been developed to coordinate multiple projects towards the same strategic goals [32] and is commonly used to manage the composition of a company's product portfolio, including potential new product development [6]. This is commonly used in a planning capacity by managers or key players in an organisation [6] and ties into the management of the development pipeline [29]. As a part of this process, a primary filter can be used to draw attention to particular potential projects [2] based on attributes such as their market potential. This can aid in removing those potential projects that would not deliver on their promise or are only pitched due to internal political reasons [7].

There are several methods and frameworks discussed in literature for Portfolio Management. One method presented in [2] scores a potential project with respect to a number of criteria. However, when these same criteria are given to multiple people for review there is a strong possibility that different results are returned due to differing individual experience, making this approach highly subjective. The risk-reward matrix is also presented in [2] with the most desirable case being to have a project that is both low risk and high reward. Other methods include the organisation wide selection process in [33], the data envelopment analysis and Balanced Scorecard method in [34]. Additional methods are also presented in [7], [28], [35].

When using the presented methods, decision attributes that are commonly used are cost-benefit and cash-flow [35]. These are converted into a single determinant such as Net Present Value (NPV) or Internal Rate of Return (IRR) [7] so that they can be readily compared. However, there are several attributes that are unable to be converted into a financial measure. These include risk, route to market and engagement opportunities; all critical aspects to understand in relation to a potential technology development. Therefore, by using purely financial measures, only part of the picture is seen [36]; whereas by using other attributes a more holistic view is attained. Thus, an approach is desired that can deal with multiple types of attribute and still deliver comparable measures.

Any decision made affects the future [37]. For a company, this relates to potential project selection and ultimate offering. These decisions methods can therefore be thought of as anticipatory [38] in the way that they try to anticipate the future and make the best decision for it. An anticipated future could be caused by their introduction of a new product or service and is related to their Portfolio Management approach. Therefore, Portfolio Management is concerned with the future [39] and ensuring a company is set to be as prepared and positioned as best it can to cope with the identified futures. To aid in this, Decision Support Systems are used by decisions makers, via a set of computerised methods which capture multiple data points [10]. These are best adopted to cater for the inherent uncertainty in Portfolio Management [40] coming from the environment and the nature of the data collected. It is common for companies to collect vast amounts of data in relation to potential developments; however extracting something meaningful from it is the true challenge [41]. Decision Support Systems can help by utilising this collected data to deliver guidance on selecting a course of action. There are several forms of Decision Support Systems including data driven, model driven and knowledge driven [10]. Each form uses a variety of inputs to deliver a recommendation on how to approach the future that can then be enacted by the company.

A different slant needs to be taken when relating the previous concepts of business strategy, innovation, Portfolio Management and decision making to SMEs. SMEs are more flexible in terms of structure, meaning they can be more ambitious than their size would otherwise suggest [42]. However, their owners and managers fear loss often more than the gain [42], often hindering the attainment of success. Yet they can be highly innovative in achieving their objectives. For SMEs, innovating is a necessity for survival [43]. However, being innovative relies on a riskier business strategy [44]. Furthermore, SMEs can find it hard to obtain the required finance [44], skills and knowledge [45] to support their innovations. Therefore when managing their portfolios, extra care has to be taken to balance the risk of any innovative path [46]. This is because SMEs cannot afford to make decisions with inherent risk [47].

The existing literature as discussed here, presents how for SMEs, the ascertainment of their innovative strategy is fraught with difficulties. These include identifying appropriate innovations, researching and selecting between them. Conventional approaches are limited in their focus on understanding financial measures, yet this is only a segment of the overall picture. This drastically affects the Portfolio Management approach taken to focus on only those projects that present the least risk and financial impact; however, these will fail to yield the greatest return. Investigating these opportunities to encompass more attributes can deliver a deeper understanding beyond the financial, enabling the SME to reach its true potential via effective and suitable innovation.

III. A Decision Support System to Support Innovation Optioneering

Some companies have portfolios that are made up of multiple products and services. To keep operating they are required to innovate and improve the portfolio and fulfil the needs of their customers. This process of product and service improvement, whether that is incremental or radical, needs to be selected from the other available courses of action. For SMEs these decisions, as to which courses of action to back, become ever more critical due to their smaller portfolio of more specialist products and services. They are likely to have a small number of products offering them a marketable proposition. In addition, they are also limited by resources that can be committed to development. This means that they have to be extra vigilant in committing resources to developments that are more certain to deliver the next step in the company's evolution and revenue. To aid in this, there are many Decision Support Systems available. However, for an SME the focus comes down to being sure they are utilising suitable information to make their decisions as well as ensuring the collected information is used appropriately in the pursuit of the correct decisions. It is therefore proposed to deliver a *Decision Support System* designed to aid the decision process by utilising information of importance to SMEs and then by reviewing this to deliver a clear prioritisation of the development paths available. This would have the potential to improve their processes and indicate which path would bring them the highest levels of return and success.

A. *Underlying Structure*

In the process flow outlined by [11], there are several key phases for SMEs to progress through in order to move from the identification of an idea to its creation. These phases are Ideation, Research, Selection and Development. The process that was outlined in [11] details the relevant information to understand the innovation to be conducted, including prospective sources. In the Selection phase, core activities include the comparison of identified ideas using decision methods and prioritisation.

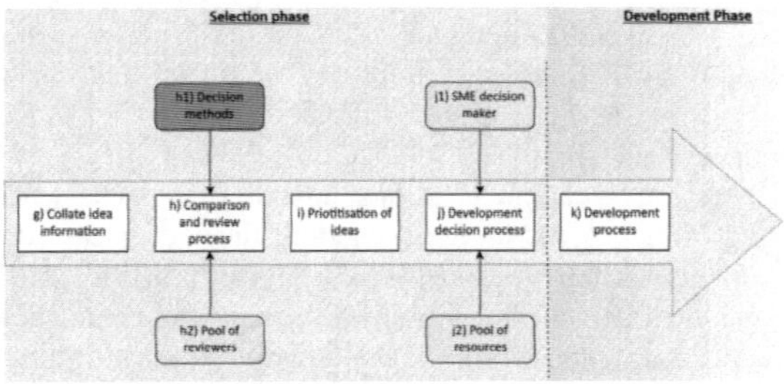

Figure 1. Selection and Development Phases from [11]

In Figure 1 it can be seen how with the collection of captured information precedes the Comparison and review process. This uses relevant Decision methods which form the basis of this paper's contribution to the body of knowledge.

The proposed *Decision Support System* uses the Weighted Sum Model at its heart. This is comprised of a weighted sum of related values [48]; which necessitates both values and their respective weights. The scores originate from the attributes identified in [11] but are aggregated together to create a description of four Scoring Factors. These were defined to be Development Potential, Resource Applicability, Commercial Viability and Payoff Expected. The Development Potential of an opportunity is defined as a metric for the likelihood for success in delivering the required technology. This can be based on the requirements of the final solution and the development process needed. The Resource Applicability describes the suitability of assigning resource to a particular project based on the amount needed and how it is to be spent. The Commercial Viability relates to how the potential development would succeed if it were entered into its respective market in the face of current competition. Finally, the Payoff Expected describes the likely returns based on the proposed technology for the relative customers/end users.

As introduced in [11], there are identified to be several critical attributes to understand in order to initiate technological innovation. These were utilised as a starting point and via the ethnographic nature of this work, those identified were modified and several others were added; these are shown in Table I.

Table I. Identified Information Attributes

Attribute	Definition
State of the art technology	What makes up the current state of the art offerings
Technological challenge	What is identified to be the limiting factor with these
Existing protection	Are there any patents protecting these offerings
Engagement opportunities	Who can be engaged with during this development
Requirements of solution	What would the requirements of the solution be
Versions of solution	What are the possible versions of the solution
Development process	What process would be required per solution
Need for innovation	What for each solution would need making from scratch
Required resource	What resources are required; money, people etc.
Availability of resource	Is the resource available or how can it be captured
Protection	What steps can be taken to protect any development
Target market	What is the target market and its characteristics
Value to customer	What of this solution is of value to the customer

Based on the utilisation of these attributes, a complete understanding can be created in relation to a technological innovation opportunity. In particular, this is designed to be utilised from the perspective of a company aiming to undergo this process themselves.

In order to describe each Scoring Factor, these information attributes need to be combined and aggregated together. This has been achieved by utilising the logic of the Hierarchy Process Model made up of distinctive layers [49]. To understand each Scoring Factor, a breakdown will be achieved via the question of "*How is y defined?*". Then when traversing up the hierarchy, the statement "*x* is used to define *y*" is used. Based on this, the breakdown shown in Table II is created.

Table II. Scoring Factor Breakdown

Scoring Factor	Attribute
Development Potential	State of the art technology
	Existing protection
	Requirements of solution
	Technological challenge
	Versions of solution
	Need for innovation
	Development process
	Engagement opportunities
Resource Applicability	Requirements of solution
	Required resource
	Availability of resource
	Need for innovation
	Development process
Commercial Viability	Existing protection
	Engagement opportunities
	Target market
	Value of solution
	Competitors
Payoff Expected	Technological challenge
	Required resource
	Availability of resource
	Protection
	Value of solution
	Engagement opportunities

Based on the breakdown shown in Table II, each Scoring Factor can be defined as a summation of the information collected for each appropriate attributes. This can therefore also be used as a way to combine reviews of individual attributes into larger sections.

In addition to the Scoring Factors for the Weighted Sum Model, there are associated weighting values used to give the final score and ranking. These Scoring Factors have associated weights called: Development Risk Aversion, Resource Spending Aversion, Commercial Risk Aversion and Payoff Expected. The Development Risk Aversion weight refers to the unwillingness of a company to enter a development project that displays anything less than a complete assurance of success. The Resource Spending Aversion describes how averse the company is to committing resources of any kind to a project. Commercial Risk Aversion relates to the level at which a company views a competitive market as being unfavourable. Finally, Payoff Expected weight describes the level at which the company expects there to be a return from any investment in a development project. These weights are assigned based upon the balance of these factors and therefore forms a basic description of the company.

In addition to weighting values to represent the company using this approach, the Reviewers who will evaluate the captured information are also weighted, such that those with different knowledge and perspective will have a respective impact. In total, three different Reviewers are involved in this process. As per [11], information is collected in relation to three main areas, State of the Art, Course of Actions and Business Case. To result in an appropriate and valid score, a Reviewer must be paired with the information that best reflects their expertise. For this, three Reviewers are defined; the Technology Expert, Developer and Manager. The Technology Expert is described as someone who understands the field in relation to a specific opportunity. The Developer, is either a hardware or software developer and therefore understands the process of creating an opportunity. Finally, the Manager understands the potential business implications of selecting an opportunity to pursue, such as the cost on the business and the target market. It is expected that a different person will occupy each Reviewer role, and therefore their related weight will be set based on the worth and validity of that person's review. However, it is also possible for the same person to occupy multiple reviewer posts; in this case the setting of their weighting value is even more critical. In this eventuality, the weighting values should be set with respect to the areas where their expertise lies.

The weights are defined and calculated for the company and Reviewer profiles at the start of the process, with the company profile set once for the use of the framework. Reviewer profile weights are changed on the start of a new project when new Reviewers are involved; as shown in (1).

$$\phi = s_{\phi} \cdot \sigma_{\phi} \tag{1}$$

$$\text{Where } \phi \in \{\alpha, \beta, \gamma, \delta, \varepsilon, \zeta, \eta\}$$

Where α is the Development Risk Aversion Weight, β is the Commercial Risk Aversion Weight, γ is the Resource Spending Aversion Weight, δ is the Payoff Expected Weight, s is the score given and σ is calculated in (2).

$$\sigma = 1 \div r \tag{2}$$

Where r is the normalisation factor for each of the utilised scoring methods; i.e., 5.

An example of this would be as shown in (3).

$$\alpha = s_{\alpha} \cdot \sigma_{\alpha}$$

$$\sigma = {}^{1}/_{5} \quad (3)$$

$$\alpha = 4 \cdot 0.2 = 0.8$$

This gives a weighted score relative to the Development Risk Aversion Weight, in this example. Furthermore, the Reviewer scores are weighted based on their respective importance (weighting value). The weighting value relevant to them is applied to every score they enter, this is calculated as follows where; ε is the Technology Expert Weight, ζ is the Developer Weight, η is the Manager Weight.

$$c = b \cdot \tau$$

$$\text{Where } \tau \in \{\varepsilon,\ \zeta,\ \eta\} \quad (4)$$

$$\text{This gives } \phi = c_{\phi} \cdot \sigma_{\phi}$$

In (4), *b* is the score entered by the Reviewer and c is the resulting score with their weighting applied. By doing this, the final score calculated is adjusted as to the relative importance of each Reviewer as defined during the setup of the Decision Support System.

The overall formula demonstrating the WSM is given in (5).

$$A_i^{WSM} = \sum_{j=1}^{n} w_j a_{ij} \quad (5)$$

$$\text{for } i = 1, 2, 3, \ldots, \text{m}$$

Where there are *n* criteria, *m* alternatives, w_j as the weight and a_{ij} is the performance criteria. An example of this over 4 criteria and weights would give (6).

$$WSM = (n_1 \cdot w_1) + (n_2 \cdot w_2) + (n_3 \cdot w_3) + (n_4 \cdot w_4) \quad (6)$$

B. Reviewing Information Attributes

The scores for each attribute are given by utilising one of three scoring methods. Scoring has been a project selection technique since its origin in the 1950's [28]. Scoring methods help to estimate how attractive a project is and, which path to take [2]. In addition, they introduce sufficient rigor in the selection process while not being overly complex to discourage use [28]. Furthermore, they can also accommodate non-quantitative or "fuzzy" and non-detailed data whilst also being customised for the organisation they are deployed in [28]. To construct the proposed scoring methods, three key properties were identified to differentiate between the types of attribute and therefore, which method can be used to apply a score. These properties are *Independent*, *Comparable* and *Bounded*. **Independent** refers to the ability of an attribute to be scored in isolation, with the score it receives being in no way related to those before or relying on those from another attribute. **Comparable** means that the only way to effectively score an attribute is through comparing it to several other instances. **Bounded** relates to the possible inputs that can be associated to that attribute, which can be of any value but will always be between two points, i.e., maximum and minimum.

Table III. Possible property combinations

Combination	Independent (I)	Comparable (C)	Bounded (B)
1	Y	Y	Y
2	Y	Y	N
3	Y	N	Y
4	Y	N	N
5	N	Y	Y
6	N	N	Y
7	N	Y	N
8	N	N	N

Not all the combinations described in Table III are possible to be applied together. Combination 1 cannot occur as attributes cannot be both Independent and Comparable due to these properties not aligning. Combinations 2 and 4 are not possible as an Independent parameter that is also non-Bounded, would effectively change each time it is used and would therefore require older versions to be changed, making it none Independent. Finally, combinations 6 and 8 are not possible as an attribute can be neither Independent nor Comparable, as they must be mutually exclusive. This leaves combinations 3, 5 and 7. Each of these combinations are derived to make a viable method of applying a score to attributes.

Table IV. Scoring methods based on property combinations

Method	Combination	I	C	B
Absolute	3	Y	N	Y
Balance	7	N	Y	N
Comparative	5	N	Y	Y

Each of the methods shown in Table IV will now be presented along with an example demonstrating their use.

The first method, *Absolute*, is based on combination 3 as shown in Table IV. In this, the attributes being reviewed can be dealt with in isolation and have no bearing on others of the same type, they do not require direct comparison to be evaluated and are bounded by the number of responses that can be taken. Therefore, this method can be thought of as a simple selection between the possible outcomes. For example, a question could be posed such as the number of geographical regions that a technology could enter; this would then be combined with six possible choices representing the number of regions. From this, the Reviewer would select that, which best fits the information they are presented with.

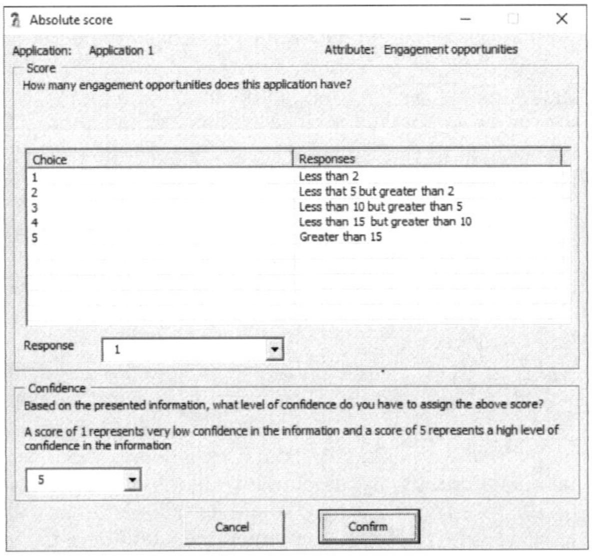

Figure 2. Absolute Scoring Method

As can be seen in Figure 2, the *Absolute* method has been coded in a Graphical User Interface (GUI) to facilitate ease of use for the Reviewer such that they can arrive at the most valid result for the question asked. In this example, they are asked about the possible number of engagement opportunities for a development opportunity. A selection is then made, based on the descriptions matching the information presented.

The second scoring method is the *Balance* method and is described by combination 7 in Table IV. The attributes being reviewed using this method cannot be treated independently; so, all previous values need updating for a new review. In addition, it is comparable and requires comparison to other values already reviewed and it is not bounded, so the values entered can be of any size. This method is used to evaluate financial attributes, due to their unbounded nature. The required process is more complex than the *Absolute* method due to several rules being followed to deliver a normalised final score per attribute. These are based on the concept of a normalised scale onto, which all attributes are scored. In principle, this can be thought of as a numbered scale ranging from a lower bound to a maximum with steps in between; one and five with incremental steps of one, for example. This would result in a normalised scale with five fixed positions (normalised scores). When a value is entered, from a calculation of cost for example, this new value is compared to all those already entered to deliver the normalised score. If this attribute is the first to be entered, it is assigned the middle position on the normalised scale, in the case of the one to five example given, this would result in a normalised score of three. When there are two attributes entered, these are assigned to the extremes of the normalised scale, resulting in one and five as normalised scores in the example given earlier. When additional values are entered, a calculation is required to achieve a certain normalised score. This value is called Step Change and is given by (7).

$$Step\ Change = (Largest\ Value\ - Smallest\ Value) \div Numberof\ Step \quad (7)$$

With this value for Step Change, it is added onto the lowest value on the scale accumulatively until the maximum value is reached. Utilising these at each point on the normalised scale, all remaining entries are evaluated. In effect, these values form barriers for, which those entered must be larger than to progress to the next normalised score.

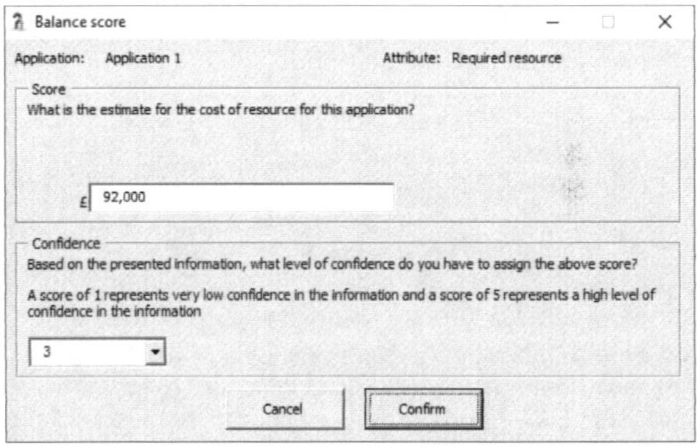

Figure 3. Balance Scoring Method

In Figure 3, the *Balance* methods GUI can be seen. This presents a question to the Reviewer along with a place to entered their calculation for cost of all resources for the application at hand.

The final method is named *Comparative*, due to its structure necessitating comparisons. This method is for use with complex attributes or those that can be defined as "fuzzy" and are difficult to assign an absolute value on, which to base multiple perceptions of the same problem. To enable this method, the pairwise comparison process and underlying calculations of the Analytic Hierarchy Process (AHP) are utilised. Using these comparisons, it is easier to define preference between sets of options than defining absolute values. This is presented to the Reviewer through a series of comparisons based on a range of values representing the whole normalised scale in use. As with the *Balance* method, the normalised scale is defined between two values with a defined step size between them. The normalised scale is used once the values from the AHP are calculated, following the completion of the pairwise comparisons. All values of the AHP calculations can always be summed to 1. The normalisation process occurs with these scores. For this process, a number of rules are followed to deliver the normalised score. If there is only one value to review, the middle score on the normalised scale is automatically assigned. From here, values are assigned to the fixed positions on the normalised scale around the centre until all are filled. Next, the largest and smallest values are placed at the extremes of the normalised scale, with the remaining being evenly distributed between them. With this distribution complete, the values are rounded down to the next normalised score available.

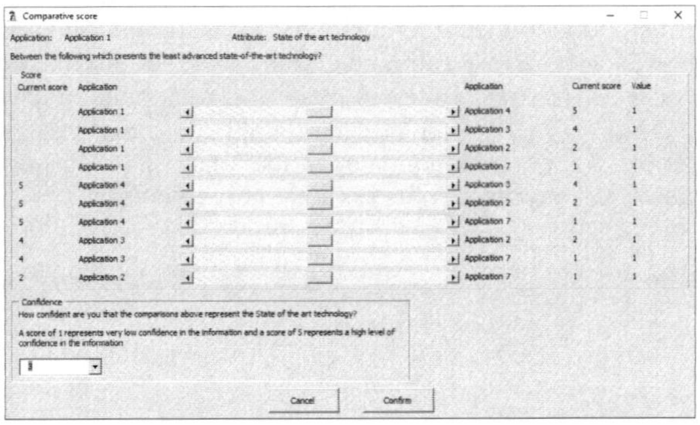

Figure 4. Comparative Scoring Method

In Figure 4, the pairwise comparison method between combinations of opportunities with respect to a single attribute can be seen. To conduct the comparison, the slider for each pair is moved to one of the possible nine positions to demonstrate a level of preference between the opportunities based on the presented information in each case.

Table V. Scoring Methods per Attribute

Attribute	Assigned method
State of the art technology	Comparative
Technological challenge	Comparative
Existing protection	Comparative
Engagement opportunities	Absolute
Requirements of solution	Comparative
Versions of solution	Absolute
Development process	Comparative
Need for innovation	Comparative
Required resource	Balance
Availability of resource	Comparative
Protection	Comparative
Target market	Comparative
Value to customer	Comparative

Using each of the three scoring methods, *Absolute*, *Balance* and *Comparative*, it is possible to review any attribute by appropriate selection, based on the three principles in Table IV. They can then result in reduced bias on the final scores calculated in each case, meaning a more repeatable and trustworthy outcome is reached.

As shown in Table V, each attribute has a Scoring Method assigned to enable the review of captured information. These were selected based on the definition of each method shown in Table IV.

Each of these reviews for the defined attributes is combined with a measure of uncertainty in relation to the conducted review. This measure of uncertainty allows for the review to consider the quality, amount and source of information. With this, a poor quality, inadequate or untrustworthy source can have its review score graded downwards so it does not have the same level of impact as that from an industry expert for example. This is based on work by [50]. In application, this is defined as "Certainty" in the review that has been conducted as shown in (8). The values entered by each Reviewer are utilised to weight down their respective scores.

$$b = d \cdot (c \div g) \tag{8}$$

Where d is the calculated Certainty score, c is the selected Certainty by the Reviewer, g is the range of possible Certainty scores, d is the entered score by the Reviewer and b is the adjusted review score for Certainty.

The level of certainty entered by the Reviewer can be seen in Figure 2, Figure 3 and Figure 4 at the bottom of each console. In each of these, the Reviewer selects from a five-point scale with five representing complete confidence in the review completed and one being very low confidence. This is driven by the information they are presented with and the understanding it delivers in relation to the opportunity in question.

C. Calculation and Use of Final Score and Ranking

With this calculation for Certainty, the overall calculation for the final score for an application is as follows. It is important to note how the calculated scores are not done so in any specified units, with larger scores showing a more suitable application. The scores for each factor are calculated upon the completion of the entry for the grading for a proposed technological innovation. This is a summation for all values entered in relation to each factor to be used in the later calculation of the final score; this is demonstrated in (9).

$$E = \{b \in R \mid 0 < b \leq r\}$$

$$\psi = \sum E_{\psi} \tag{9}$$

Where $\psi \in \{\theta, \iota, \kappa, \lambda\}$

Where θ is Development Risk Aversion Score, ι is the Commercial Risk Aversion Score, κ is the Resource Spending Aversion Score and λ is the Payoff Expected Score.

This is calculated based on the scores for each factor and its associated weight value using the WSM described earlier as shown in (10).

$$F = \theta \cdot \alpha + \iota \cdot \beta + \kappa \cdot \gamma + \lambda \cdot \delta \tag{10}$$

Where F is the final score for the application.

In addition, based on the certainty values entered earlier for each review, an overall certainty of the application is calculated. This demonstrates the potential variability of the final score based upon the values entered. The benefit is that when reviewing the results, the potential maximum and minimum score for an application can be seen; which can be used for deeper levels of comparison. This utilises the core method described in [50] and is demonstrated in (11) and (12).

$$\begin{gathered} Initial\ CF = w_1 \cdot x_1 \\ Current\ CF = Previous\ CF + (1 - Previous\ CF) \cdot (w_i \cdot x_i) \\ Uncertainty = 1 - Total\ CF \end{gathered} \tag{11}$$

Where w is the weight between 1 and 0 and x is the value. The second calculation in the process is repeated as required based on the available weights and values. To utilise this method, the entered confidence values by each of the three Reviewers are averaged and then utilised in (10).

$$\begin{gathered} h = \bar{t} \cdot \varepsilon \\ p = h + (1 - h) \cdot (\bar{y} \cdot \zeta) \\ q = p + (1 - p) \cdot (\bar{u} \cdot \eta) \\ v = F \cdot q \end{gathered} \tag{12}$$

Where $\bar{t}$ is the Technology Expert average confidence, $\bar{y}$ is the Developer average confidence, $\bar{u}$ is the Manager average confidence, h is the initial Certainty calculation, p is the second Certainty calculation, q is the third Certainty calculation and v is the relative uncertainty.

Based on these, results are calculated such as those in Figure 5. The examples shown are not from any particular commercial projects.

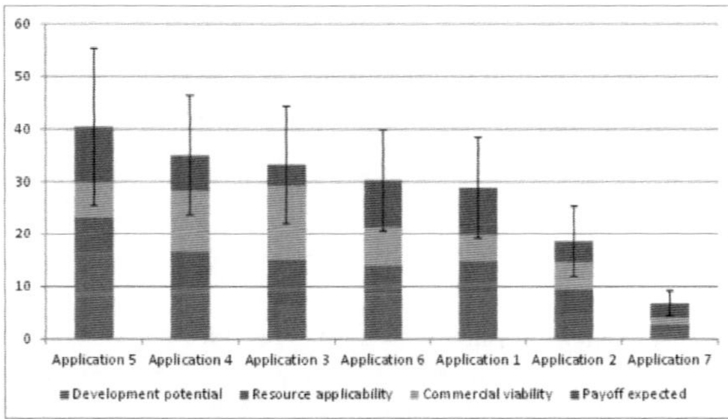

Figure 5. Example Results Export

The results from the calculations are shown in Figure 5. The overall score from the Weighted Sum Model are given by the overall score from each bar and the results for each segment coming from the Scoring Factors. Onto each of these, the calculated certainty is added in the form of an error bar. In the example shown, there are several conclusions that can be drawn based on the overall scores and the sizes of each segment of the bars. For example, it can be seen how Application 3 shows significantly greater Commercial Viability than the other applications; whereas Application 5 shows the greatest Development Potential. It is these aspects that aid in the selection process, not only the overall score; therefore, the additional visibility that is delivered by this approach can be seen, making it more than a pure ranking of opportunities.

A threshold is placed onto this, to demonstrate the potential development paths that carry the most worth and should therefore be considered by the company decision makers. This threshold is to be devised by the company using this approach such that the relevant number of opportunities are taken forwards for consideration. As with a greater number of suitable opportunities taken forwards, the chance for selecting the one that delivers the desired success increases. Considering the graph shown in Figure 5 with a threshold set at 30, only the top three applications would be deemed to be worthy of consideration for the distribution of resources. In addition, Application 6 would be sitting on the threshold with Application 1 being close behind, showing clear potential but not sufficient to pass outright. Therefore, in this case, additional research would be required to deliver a clear indication one way or another.

Attribute	Application 1	Application 2	Application 3	Application 4	Application 5	Application 6	Application 7
State of the art technology	1.8	0.6	2.4	3	3.2	1.2	0.8
Technology challenge	1.8	1.6	0	2	2.4	0.6	0.6
Existing protection	0.6	0.8	0.4	0.6	0	3	0
Engagement opportunities	0.8	0.8	5	5	0.8	3	0.8
Requirements of solution	1.8	0.8	3.2	3	1.6	0.6	0
Versions of solution	1	0	0	0	5	0	0
Development process	1.8	1.6	3.2	3	2.4	0.6	0.6
Need for innovation	0	1.2	2.4	0	1.8	0	0
Required resource	0.6	1.2	1.2	1.8	1.2	3	0.6
Availability of resource	1.8	0	1.6	0	0	1.2	0
Protection	2.4	0.6	0	1.2	3	1.8	0.8
Target market	1.8	0.8	0.6	1.2	4	3.2	0
Value of solution	2.4	0.6	1.2	1.8	4	2.4	0.8

Figure 6. Normalised Scores with applied Certainty

Finally, Applications 2 and 7 would demonstrate a score to be significantly below that of the threshold, meaning these options should not selected for additional research to potentially increase their scores to a point whereby they could be considered. Using such a threshold, a clear indication can be given as to the opportunities worthy of consideration, as only picking that with the largest score is an unsuitable technique.

In addition to the ability to present a ranking based around four scoring factors and the related certainty, further visibility of the cause of these scores is reached via a breakdown of the review and calculation stages.

As shown in Figure 6, the individual scores per application and attribute can be seen. This increases the utility of this approach by delivering visibility of the exact attributes where an opportunity achieves better or worse scores than those they are being compared to. By presenting this information, the decision-making process can be further aided by demonstrating not only, which opportunity presents the greatest scores with respect to the Scoring Factors, but also, which particular attributes are responsible. This can aid in deciding between two opportunities with very similar overall scores.

Overall, the proposed Decision Support System has been built into an application that provides a GUI to each identified role as to increase the ease of use. It has two user classes, Admin and Reviewer. The Admin class is responsible for setting profile weights, adding Reviewers and creating new opportunity investigations and assigning them to the appropriate Researcher and Reviewer. In a conventional implementation, the usage procedure would be as follows.

Firstly, the Amin class of user is required to set up the Decision Support System for use. This involves defining the company position via the use of the weighting values. The weighting values are also required to be set for the Reviewers based on who will carry out the review process. From here, the development opportunities to be investigated are added and the Reviewers assigned. Following this, the Researcher will use the defined information capture procedure based on [11] and the expansion of the required attributes shown in Table I, to capture an understanding of the development opportunity at hand. From here, the Reviewers will deliver their scores by utilising the defined Scoring Methods outlined. Once this is completed, the final score and ranking will be automatically produced for exporting by the Admin class user. It is important to note, how the user experience alters, based upon their classification. Throughout the appendices, various screenshots are shown of the interface for the devised Decision Support System.

IV. System Evaluation

To evaluate the proposed *Decision Support System*, several internal evaluations were conducted within the SME. These involved most staff and utilised several previous opportunity investigations analysed by the proposed system. Due to these still being commercially sensitive, they cannot be discussed in detail. In addition, due to this confidentiality and the limitations in staff numbers, it is acknowledged that the population size used for this evaluation was limited, yet it represented most of the company. Two separate areas of evaluation were conducted; the first analysed the performance of the described scoring methods and the second focused on the acceptance and validity of the recommendations made by the *Decision Support System*. The evaluation of the scoring methods is limited to the *Comparative* method alone due to this being the most complex. The *Absolute* and *Balance* methods required simple selections or calculations of values to result in the Normalised Score.

The first area of evaluation investigated the consistency of the *Comparative* method as this is the method used the most due to most attributes being complex and "fuzzy" in nature. To do this, a commonly used technique based on selecting a score from a set number of categories was compared to. For this, several opportunities were presented to several staff within the SME along with a defined set of categories to score them and the *Comparative* method. For both methods, scores were assigned to each of the five opportunities and also a position in a ranking. In the case of the category based method, the scores were assigned utilising a set of criteria and the ranking based upon each opportunity being placed in positions 1 – 5. For the *Comparative* method, the scores were extracted from the method before normalisation and the final ranking was obtained following normalisation. As the *Comparative* method calculates the scores of each opportunity in a way that always sums to one, the scores assigned utilising the category based method would require normalisation to allow for comparison. This normalisation is shown in (13).

$$A = \begin{pmatrix} A_{11} & \cdots & A_{1N} \\ \vdots & \ddots & \vdots \\ A_{N1} & \cdots & A_{NN} \end{pmatrix}$$

$$A_{11} + A_{12} + \cdots A_{1N} = \sum_{n=1}^{N} A_{1n} \qquad (13)$$

$$C_{ij} = \begin{cases} \frac{1}{\sum_{n=1}^{N} A_{ij}}, & i = j \\ 0, & i \neq j \end{cases}$$

$$B = C \cdot A$$

Where A is a matrix of entered score values, C is matrix for scaling each row and B is the normalised matrix.

In addition, in several cases it was required that outliers were removed for effective statistical analysis. This was due to participants delivering scores or ranking values that were significantly different from the others, meaning direction comparisons and averaging was disrupted. For this, the Median Absolute Deviation method was utilised as this demonstrates significant robustness to outliers. The equation for this is given in (14).

$$MAD(\{Y_i\}_{i=1 \cdots N}) = median(\{|Y_i - median(\{Y_i\}_{i=1 \cdots N})|\}_{i=1 \cdots N}) \qquad (14)$$

Where Y is a collection of numbers.

To compare the results from each aspect of this evaluation, the participant's scores and rankings were averaged; this allowed for direct method comparison between the two approaches. Averages were also conducted per method based on those from the previous step to show the overall similarities between methods. In addition, the participants were grouped together with respect to their roles within the SME. The scores and rankings entered were also averaged per role group to investigate if participants were like their colleagues from similar backgrounds and skillsets. In addition, following the completion of both aspects of this evaluation, several questions were asked of each participant in the form of a questionnaire to obtain their opinions about the process they just experienced. This will add further insight into the preference between the two methods and experience in use, even if the results from the comparisons prove inconclusive or unexpected in any way.

For the presentation of evaluation results, the Category method is abbreviated to CAM and the Comparative method is abbreviated to COM. In addition, "WO/O" will stand for "Without Outliers".

Table VI. Application Score Variances with and without Outliers

	Applications					
Method	**1**	**2**	**3**	**4**	**5**	**Average**
CAM	0.004	0.004	0.003	0.004	0.005	0.004
COM	0.017	0.006	0.020	0.015	0.023	0.016
CAM - WO/O	0.004	0.004	0.001	0.004	0.003	0.003
COM- WO/O	0.001	0.001	0.020	0.015	0.015	0.010

The results presented in Table VI lead to several conclusions about the two methods evaluated. Firstly, in the case where outliers were not removed, the category based method demonstrated consistently lower variance per application. This is due to the nature of the way the scores are selected for this approach being defined and can therefore only be of five possibilities in this case; whereas the *Comparative* method utilises a calculation approach based upon 90 possible positions of the sliders for the pairwise comparisons. This results in significantly more variability leading into the score calculations. In the second half of Table VI, several outliers are removed, resulting in more equality between the two methods. This demonstrates the sensitivity of the *Comparative* method in its calculations based upon the positions of the results of the pairwise comparisons.

Table VII. Application Ranking Position Variance

	Applications					
Method	**1**	**2**	**3**	**4**	**5**	**Average**
CAM	1.69	0.69	2.01	1.64	2.69	1.744
COM	1.76	1.56	1.01	1.01	3.09	1.686

In Table VII, the average ranking assigned to each application by both methods can be seen. The number demonstrated by each method to have the lowest variance is roughly equal. However, the two applications whereby the *Comparative* method demonstrated lower variability (application 3 and 4) was significantly more so that the others; which were much closer between each method. This illustrates how these two cases were positioned more favourably during the pairwise comparisons by most of the SME's participants. Again, the calculated ranking is shown to be sensitive to the increased number of positions in the pairwise comparison, yet the average across all applications is very similar. This points towards each method being equally capable of being used for delivering consistent rankings over a wide range of participant backgrounds and skills.

Table VIII. Participant Group Score Variance

	Participant Group				
Method	Software Developer	Sales	Office & Admin	Applications Support	Tech
CAM	0.003	0.001	0.0004	0.001	0.001
COM	0.016	0.010	0.001	0.009	0.010

The results presented in Table VIII present the variance per participant group; in each of the groups, there are two participants. These results show how the category based method delivers increased consistency within the same participant groups, showing how similarly people view information based on their background and skillset. Again, this demonstrates the sensitivity of the *Comparative* method between positions selected by the user as to the score calculated.

Table IX. Participant Group Ranking Positions

	Participant Group				
Method	Software Developer	Sales	Office & Admin	Applications Support	Tech
CAM	1.80	1.30	1.80	0.30	1.80
COM	0.60	0.80	0.10	0.85	1.40

In Table IX, the variance of the ranking positions calculated per participant group is shown; based upon the same groups as those used in Table VIII. Here, it can be seen how the *Comparative* method delivers repeatedly greater levels of consistency within participant groups than the category based method. This is due to the defined calculation process converting the scores entered by the participant into the normalised ranking. Whereas, using the category based approach, this is done manually, and therefore the difference in approaches becomes apparent. This therefore demonstrates the utility of this method in delivering consistent reviews over participants but the careful selection of those to deliver the review is important. Such a decision should be made by the company's management prior to the evaluation based on availability, skillset and experience. This may also highlight to those selecting the Reviewers that the SME lacks in certain skills or experiences, and should endeavour to fill these gaps.

This evaluation has resulted in understanding several aspects of the defined scoring method. Firstly, the delivery of scores is more sensitive than a category based approach, which is more commonly used, due to the increased number of possibilities the Reviewer can select. When viewing an entire population, containing those of several different backgrounds and skillsets, the resulting ranking is also less consistent. However, when comparing those of a similar background and skillset, the results become far more consistent. This case is far more likely in actual use, whereby those of a similar background and skillset are selected to review the same information for each opportunity, leading to increased consistency and comparability between cases.

Following the scoring aspect of the evaluations, the participants were asked several questions in relation to their perception on the two presented methods of delivering scores and rankings in the form of a questionnaire. This specifically related to their preference between them and any problems they could foresee. The general feedback illustrated a perception that using the category based method would lead to difficulty with larger datasets. In addition, this method was noted to be more difficult to deploy, as the definition of each scoring category was not a perfect description of the opportunities for evaluation. Furthermore, participants noted how their internal definition of categories would differ between multiple Reviewers, reducing comparability. In relation to the *Comparative* method, this was better received due to the ease of use and the reduced comprehension required for the application of scores. This was due to the configuration necessitating only a comparison to other opportunities. It was also perceived that this approach would lead to increase consistency due to the defined approach. However, during the evaluation it was noted to be more consistent, but only when compared to those of a similar background. Nonetheless, this would be more representative of an actual implementation, with those from similar backgrounds reviewing the same information attributes, leading to greater consistency and comparability.

The next stage of the evaluation focused on the acceptance of the resulting ranking and the success experienced by those opportunities selected to be taken forwards based upon the *Decision Support Systems* recommendations. To conduct this evaluation, a semi-formal interview process, driven via the use of a questionnaire, was conducted with the SME's decision maker, the Managing Director. For this, questions were asked in relation to the created ranking, the ease of understanding, successes of selected opportunities and changes that would be made in hindsight.

Based on presented results rankings from the proposed *Decision Support System*, clear understanding could be attained as to the position of opportunities within the ranking. This also included where each opportunity was positioned within the ranking and the aspects leading to this, based upon the four scoring factors. Furthermore, the uncertainty presented indicated to the Managing Director, which opportunities were the riskiest, due to the size of the error bar. It was also noted how succinct information on each opportunity would be required alongside the graphical information to make a decision. Furthermore, it would also be required to include aspects of day-to-day operations in comparison to these development opportunities to decide on how to proceed. These points illustrate trust in the presented information and a utility to the decision-making process, but the necessity for several additions in the future.

The second element of this evaluation was to gauge the success of the opportunities selected to be taken forwards because of the recommendations made. This would be utilised to evaluate whether they were the right decisions in retrospect. Over the course of the Decisions Support Systems development, two opportunities were selected to be taken forwards. One was a software add-on to the SME's existing product range, with the other becoming a project made up of several individual opportunities that were closely related. Since introduction, the software add-on has experienced significant industrial attention but with slow adoption, increasing from 2 sales in year 1 to 18 by the end of the second quarter of year 3. This means an accumulative value of approximately £130k, not including additional system costs. The Managing Director noted how this new product has received significant attention, which is promising, yet it has not converted into sufficient orders to generate the desired revenue. This was judged to be due to there being limited features as a part of this offering, resulting in aspects of the related tests being incompatible with the current offering. For it to be considered a complete success it was noted that this offering would be required to increase its capabilities to encompass the remaining features and to result in a step change in orders to match the industrial attention observed.

The second opportunity taken forwards, comprised of several related opportunities, was selected on the promise of creating a new business segment for the SME and offering significant returns due to displacing existing technologies noted to have several limitations. However, due to the resource constraints of the SME, funding was sought from an external source. This funding was not obtained due to the competition nature of the funding source; meaning this project has progress little past an extended evaluation of the technology and market. Yet the Managing Director still viewed this selection as the right course of action, given the information available and recommendations made. It was also viewed to be the path to take these applications forwards as a group rather than individually as these would present the greatest return in this way; while offering an increased number of avenues to investigate for taking this project forwards.

Finally, the main outcome was that both opportunities were selected, utilising the recommendations made, aligning with those making the company decisions. As yet neither has progressed to the point desired due to the ability of the SME to fund and advance these products to the desired stage. Therefore, the potential success of the selected business opportunities is a constraint of the SME rather than of the *Decision Support System*. To more accurately analyse the recommendations made, a more time would be required for those opportunities already selected and for a greater number of new ones to also be selected and progress to market. Following this, a more in-depth analysis can be conducted.

V. Discussion and Conclusion

Based on the *Decision Support System* presented, several conclusions can be drawn. The underlying structure used [11], delivered the process required for companies such as the SME for the investigation of innovation opportunities. Using this in combination with the ethnographic process for this work, several enhancements and additions were made to the information capture process to increase the overall company knowledge in relation to an opportunity. This structure also highlighted the requirement for the decision point to come after the capture of information, using defined scoring methods. The advantage of this is that decisions can be made based on like-for-like information due to each opportunity having the same points researched.

Using the defined scoring methods, the same attributes from different potential opportunities can be directly compared after conversion into a numerical form on the same normalised scale. This can deliver an understanding of where certain opportunities are stronger than others. Secondly, it is very flexible for the company, as any attribute can be scored using the outlined methods. Therefore, only the information that is important to the company is analysed. The approach also diminishes the impact of subjectivity on the final score. By defining the review process to be one of three methods, the results found from different points of view should be very similar; meaning consistent results can be achieved irrespective of who is conducting the review. Bias and personal influence can also be minimised as the final score is not created based on discussion but rather the generation of numerical scores. However, there is the chance for outliers in the scoring process, more commonly seen from those from unsuitable backgrounds or skillsets.

These scoring methods individually deliver significant capabilities to the decision-making process by converting all attributes to the same scale for direct comparison. This is extended further through the addition of information certainty. This allows for the calculated score to be effectively weighted down, depending on the confidence of the Reviewer in the information presented. The advantage this delivers is that untrustworthy information will not have the same level of impact on the calculation of the scores and ranking as that from a reputable source. This achieves a greater level of control over the score and ranking and reduces the influence of poor information.

The scores calculated, and weighting values entered are then combined using the Weighted Sum Model. This simpler approach allows for the utilisation of calculated values and measures representing the company in place of weights, to result in a final score. The advantage of this is the visibility of the scores calculated and therefore the final position in the ranking, delivering traceability.

With the final score and ranking calculated via the defined scoring methods, certainty values and the Weighted Sum Model, a threshold can be applied. This reflects the company's position, as the decision threshold value can be set at the appropriate level. For companies with limited resources, such as SMEs [9], this threshold level can be increased such that potential development projects have to display a higher level of certainty of success before considering them. This threshold completes the recommendations made by this *Decision Support System* by indicating those opportunities that should be taken forwards for a selection process. This can be implemented by any SME in a similar position through stages of capturing information, defining their company position, profiling the Reviewers, scoring the information and certainty and applying a threshold to the final score and ranking.

Concluding, we could firstly say that the *Comparative* method demonstrates increased sensitivity in relation to the scores, due to the number of positions possible during use. However, due to the defined nature of the normalisation process, these scores are converted into a more consistent ranking in comparison to those of a similar background. This is representative of a real-life application whereby those reviewing the same information would be assigned this due to their experience and background. Finally, the recommendations delivered are understandable and trustworthy within the environment where this *Decision Support System* was created. In addition, those opportunities recommended to be taken forwards displayed reasonable levels of success given the ability of the SME to fund their development.

There can be seen to be several ways this *Decision Support System* has deliver impact to the SME and has potential to the wider field. To the SME, the internal product assessment procedure has been changed, to include the structure demonstrated by the *Decision Support System*. This restructures their information capturing efforts in relation to innovation opportunities, the review of this information, and the decision processes. Altogether this has delivered a more professional assessment process over the conventional ad-hoc approach commonplace with SMEs without burdening them with unnecessary activities. To the wider field, this *Decision Support System* and its information capture method can deliver several improvements. The defined information capturing process results in directly comparable opportunities due to the same attributes for each being understood. These can then be reviewed by a defined scoring method, irrelevant of their type. The calculation method offers simplistic creation of a representative score for the opportunity, based on the results of the scoring methods and the representatives of a company. Overall, this results in a complete modelling and assessment of opportunities to hand. Therefore, the approach outlined in this work forms a practical method to investigate, evaluate and select from available opportunities to direct a company's innovation activities.

ACKNOWLEDGMENT

This work was supported by the Systems Centre and the EPSRC funded Industrial Doctorate Centre in Systems (Grant EP/G037353/1) and Imetrum Limited.

REFERENCES

[1] D. Pashley, T. Tryfonas, A. Crossley, and C. Setchell, "Scoring Methods to Enable Bespoke Portfolio Management," in *ICONS 2017 : The Twelfth International Conference on Systems Scoring*, 2017, pp. 54–61.

[2] R. Mitchell, R. Phaal, and N. Athanassopoulou, "Scoring methods for prioritizing and selecting innovation projects," *PICMET 2014 - Portl. Int. Cent. Manag. Eng. Technol. Proc. Infrastruct. Serv. Integr.*, no. 2001, pp. 907–920, 2014.

[3] A. N. Kiss and P. S. Barr, "New Product Development Strategy Implementation Duration and New Venture Performance: A Contingency-Based Perspective," *J. Manage.*, pp. 1–26, 2014.

[4] K. R. Jespersen and R. Bysted, "Implementing New Product Development: a Study of Personal Characteristics Among Managers," *Int. J. Innov. Manag.*, vol. 20, no. 3, pp. 1–23, 2016.

[5] D.-J. Lim and T. R. Anderson, "Technology trajectory mapping using data envelopment analysis: the ex ante use of disruptive innovation theory on flat panel technologies," *R&D Manag.*, no. 1973, p. n/a-n/a, 2015.

[6] M. G. Kaiser, F. El Arbi, and F. Ahlemann, "Successful project portfolio management beyond project selection techniques: Understanding the role of structural alignment," *Int. J. Proj. Manag.*, vol. 33, no. 1, pp. 126–139, 2015.

[7] M. Abbassi, M. Ashrafi, and E. Sharifi Tashnizi, "Selecting balanced portfolios of R&D projects with interdependencies: A cross-entropy based methodology," *Technovation*, vol. 34, no. 1, pp. 54–63, 2014.

[8] E. Tapinos, R. G. Dyson, and M. Meadows, "Does the balanced scorecard make a difference to the strategy development process?," *J. Oper. Res. Soc.*, vol. 62, no. 5, pp. 888–899, 2011.

[9] R. McAdam, R. Reid, and M. Shevlin, "Determinants for innovation implementation at SME and inter SME levels within peripheral regions," *Int. J. Entrep. Behav. Res.*, vol. 20, no. 1, pp. 66–90, 2014.

[10] G. D'Aniello, A. Gaeta, M. Gaeta, M. Lepore, F. Orciuoli,

and O. Troisi, "A new DSS based on situation awareness for smart commerce environments," *J. Ambient Intell. Humaniz. Comput.*, vol. 7, no. 1, pp. 47–61, 2016.

[11] D. Pashley, T. Tryfonas, A. Crossley, and C. Setchell, "A Directed Research Approach for repeatable SME decision making," *J. Syst. Sci. Syst. Eng.*, no. Under review at time of submission.

[12] S. Lahlou, S. Le Bellu, and S. Boesen-Mariani, "Subjective Evidence Based Ethnography: Method and Applications," *Integr. Psychol. Behav. Sci.*, vol. 49, no. 2, pp. 216–238, 2015.

[13] K. Kashimura, Y. Tsukada, T. Kawasaki, H. Kitagawa, and Y. Maruyama, "Design approach based on social science for social innovation business," *Hitachi Rev.*, vol. 63, no. 9, pp. 548–559, 2014.

[14] R. L. Baskerville and M. D. Myers, "Design ethnography in information systems," *Inf. Syst. J.*, vol. 25, no. 1, pp. 23–46, 2015.

[15] A. Ghezzi, "Revisiting business strategy under discontinuity," *Manag. Decis.*, vol. 51, no. 7, pp. 1326–1358, 2013.

[16] S. F. Slater, E. M. Olson, and C. Finnegan, "Business strategy, marketing organization culture, and performance," *Mark. Lett.*, vol. 22, no. 3, pp. 227–242, 2011.

[17] S. Soltanizadeh, S. Z. A. Rasid, N. M. Golshan, and W. K. W. Ismail, "Business strategy, enterprise risk management and organizational performance," *Manag. Res. Rev.*, vol. 39, no. 9, pp. 1016–1033, 2016.

[18] K. A. Bentley, T. C. Omer, and N. Y. Sharp, "Business strategy, financial reporting irregularities, and audit effort," *Contemp. Account. Res.*, vol. 30, no. 2, pp. 780–817, 2013.

[19] F. Lieder and T. L. Griffiths, "When to use which heuristic: A rational solution to the strategy selection problem," *Proc. 37th Annu. Conf. Cogn. Sci. Soc.*, vol. 1, no. 3, pp. 1–6, 2015.

[20] M. Y. Brannen and C. J. Voisey, "Global Strategy Formulation and Learning From the Field : Three Modes of Comparative Learning and a Case," *Glob. Strateg. J.*, vol. 2, pp. 51–70, 2012.

[21] L. Bucciarelli, "A Review of Innovation and Change Management: Stage Model and Power Influences," *Univers. J. Manag.*, vol. 3, no. 1, pp. 36–42, 2015.

[22] C. Baden-Fuller and S. Haefliger, "Business Models and Technological Innovation," *Long Range Plann.*, vol. 46, no. 6, pp. 419–426, 2013.

[23] S. F. Slater, J. J. Mohr, and S. Sengupta, "Radical product innovation capability: Literature review, synthesis, and illustrative research propositions," *J. Prod. Innov. Manag.*, vol. 31, no. 3, pp. 552–566, 2014.

[24] J. L. Hervas-Oliver, C. Boronat-Moll, and F. Sempere-Ripoll, "On Process Innovation Capabilities in SMEs: A Taxonomy of Process-Oriented Innovative SMEs," *J. Small Bus. Manag.*, vol. 54, no. April 2015, pp. 113–134, 2016.

[25] C. F. Cheng, M. L. Chang, and C. S. Li, "Configural paths to successful product innovation," *J. Bus. Res.*, vol. 66, no. 12, pp. 2561–2573, 2013.

[26] D. A. Norman and R. Verganti, "Incremental and Radical Innovation: Design Research vs. Technology and Meaning Change," *Des. Issues*, vol. 30, no. 1, pp. 78–96, 2014.

[27] W. E. Baker, J. M. Sinkula, A. Grinstein, and S. Rosenzweig, "The effect of radical innovation in/congruence on new product performance," *Ind. Mark. Manag.*, vol. 43, no. 8, pp. 1314–1323, 2014.

[28] A. D. Henriksen and A. J. Traynor, "A practical R & D project-selection scoring tool," *{IEEE} Trans. Eng. Manag.*, vol. 46, no. 2, pp. 158–170, 1999.

[29] R. C. McNally, S. S. Durmuşoğlu, and R. J. Calantone, "New product portfolio management decisions: Antecedents and consequences," *J. Prod. Innov. Manag.*, vol. 30, no. 2, pp. 245–261, 2013.

[30] P. Patanakul, "Key drivers of effectiveness in managing a group of multiple projects," *IEEE Trans. Eng. Manag.*, vol. 60, no. 1, pp. 4–17, 2013.

[31] R. Sperry and A. Jetter, "Theoretical framework for managing the front end of innovation under uncertainty," *PICMET Portl. Int. Cent. Manag. Eng. Technol. Proc.*, pp. 2021–2028, 2009.

[32] M. Martinsuo, "Project portfolio management in practice and in context," *Int. J. Proj. Manag.*, vol. 31, no. 6, pp. 794–803, 2013.

[33] Q. Tian, J. Ma, J. Liang, R. C. W. Kwok, and O. Liu, "An organizational decision support system for effective R&D project selection," *Decis. Support Syst.*, vol. 39, no. 3, pp. 403–413, 2005.

[34] H. Eilat, B. Golany, and A. Shtub, "Constructing and evaluating balanced portfolios of R&D projects with interactions: A DEA based methodology," *Eur. J. Oper. Res.*, vol. 172, no. 3, pp. 1018–1039, 2006.

[35] S. Coldrick, P. Longhurst, P. Ivey, and J. Hannis, "An R&D options selection model for investment decisions," *Technovation*, vol. 25, no. 3, pp. 185–193, 2005.

[36] K. Katz and T. Manzione, "Maximize Your 'Return on Initiatives' with the Initiative Portfolio Review Process," *Haarvard Bus. Rev.*, pp. 14–16, 2008.

[37] A. Wilkinson, M. Mayer, and V. Ringler, "Collaborative futures: Integrating foresight with design in large scale innovation processes-seeing and seeding the futures of Europe," *J. Futur. Stud.*, vol. 18, no. 4, pp. 1–26, 2014.

[38] R. Miller, "Learning, the Future, and Complexity. An Essay on the Emergence of Futures Literacy," *Eur. J. Educ.*, vol. 50, no. 4, pp. 513–523, 2015.

[39] M. Silva, "Thinking Outside the Triangle: Using Foresight in Project Environments to Deliver a Resilient Tomorrow," *IPMA Expert Semin. 2016*, pp. 1–14, 2016.

[40] B. V. Smith and M. G. Ierapepritou, "Modeling and optimization of product design and portfolio management interface," *Comput. Chem. Eng.*, vol. 35, no. 11, pp. 2579–2589, 2011.

[41] et all Rogério dos Santos Alves; Alex Soares de Souza, "Case Study: An Intelligent Decision- Support System," *Igarss 2014*, vol. 20, no. 1, pp. 1–5, 2014.

[42] A. Arbussa, A. Bikfalvi, and P. Marquès, "Strategic agility-driven business model renewal: the case of an SME," *Manag. Decis.*, vol. 55, no. 2, pp. 271–293, 2017.

[43] M. W. Staniewski, R. Nowacki, and K. Awruk, "Entrepreneurship and innovativeness of small and medium-sized construction enterprises," *Int. Entrep. Manag. J.*, vol. 12, no. 3, pp. 861–877, 2016.

[44] N. Lee, H. Sameen, and M. Cowling, "Access to finance for innovative SMEs since the financial crisis," *Res.*

Policy, vol. 44, no. 2, pp. 370–380, 2015.
[45] Y. Liao and J. Barnes, "Knowledge acquisition and product innovation flexibility in SMEs," *Bus. Process Manag. J.*, vol. 21, no. 6, pp. 1257–1278, 2015.
[46] V. Kokotovich and C. P. Killen, "Enhancing Design Project Review Board Effectiveness Through a Visual Collaborative Approach," *Int. Conf. Coop. Des. Vis. Eng.*, pp. 118–125, 2016.
[47] N. O'Regan, M. Sims, and A. Ghobadian, "High Performance: Ownership and Decision-making in SMEs," *Manag. Decis.*, vol. 43, no. 3, pp. 382–396, 2005.
[48] Z. Turskis, E. K. Zavadskas, J. Antucheviciene, and N. Kosareva, "A Hybrid Model Based on Fuzzy AHP and Fuzzy WASPAS for Construction Site Selection Methodology," *Int. J. Comput. Commun. Control*, vol. 10, no. 6, pp. 873–888, 2015.
[49] J. Davis, a MacDonald, and L. White, "Problem-structuring methods and project management: an example of stakeholder involvement using Hierarchical Process Modelling methodology," *J. Oper. Res. Soc.*, vol. 61, no. 6, pp. 893–904, Apr. 2010.
[50] J. Daniels, P. W. Werner, and a. T. Bahill, "Quantitative methods for tradeoff analyses," *Syst. Eng.*, vol. 4, no. 3, pp. 190–212, 2001.

APPENDICES

Login Screen

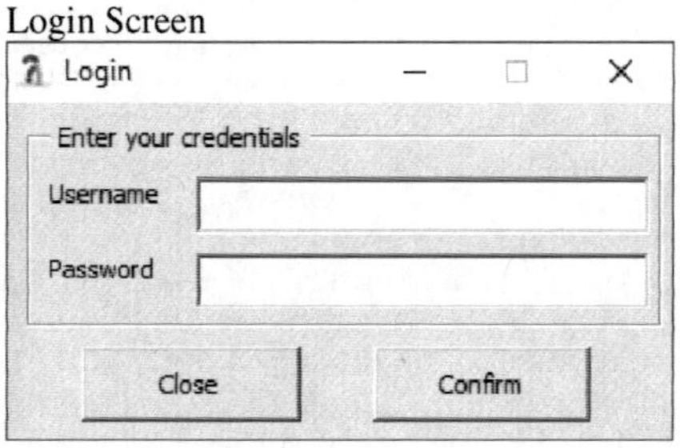

Admin class user home

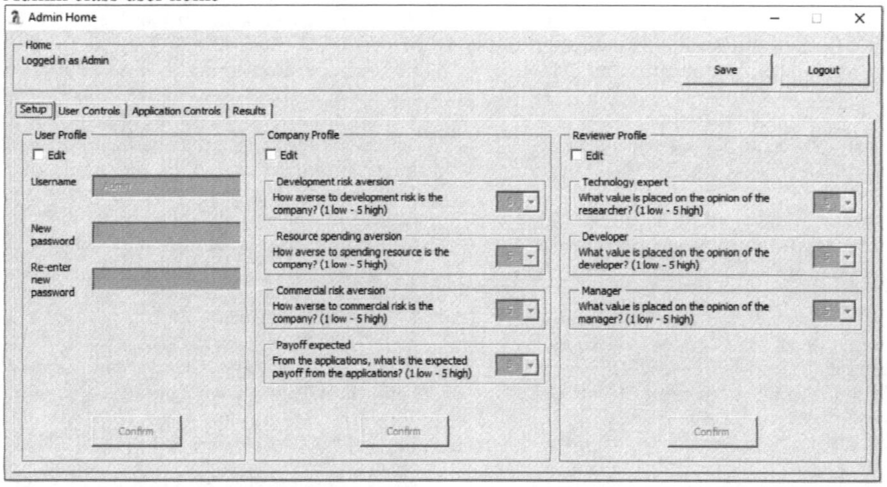

Reviewer class user home

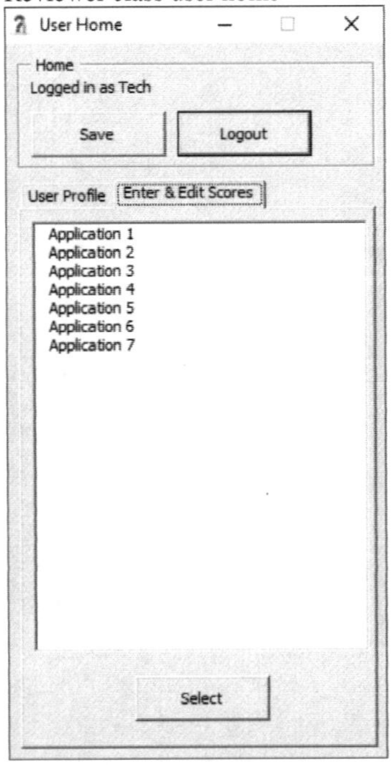

Scoring screen

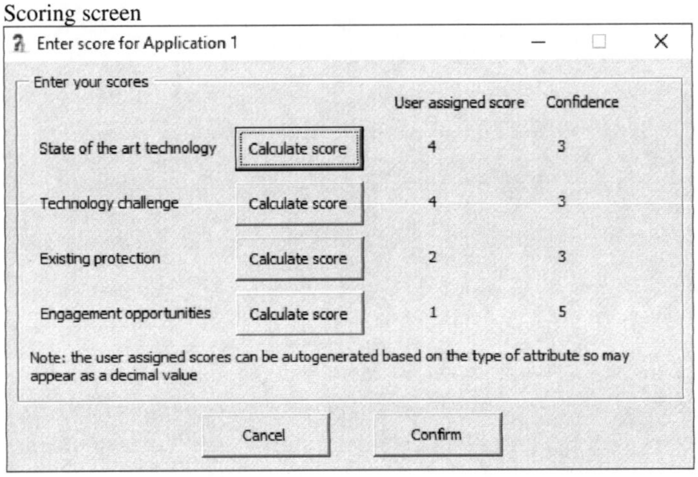

Results breakdown

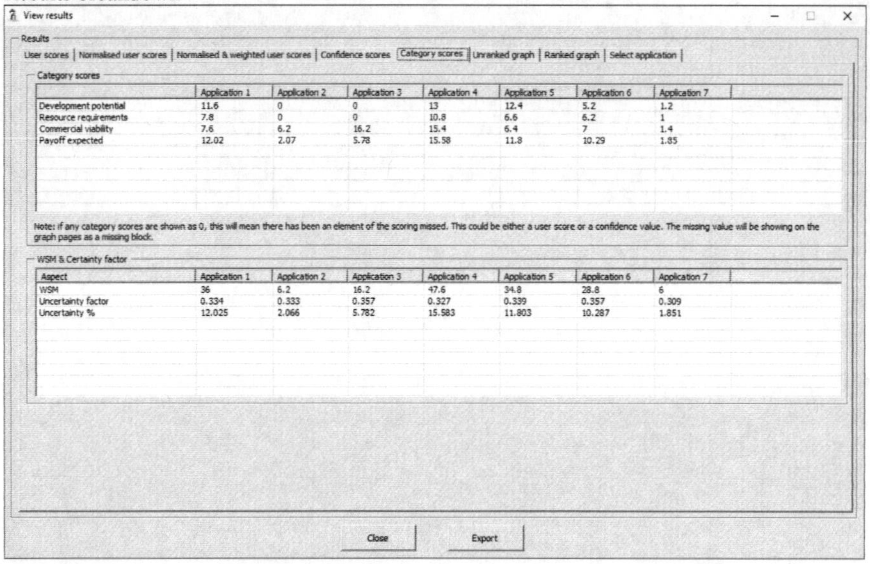

Results export

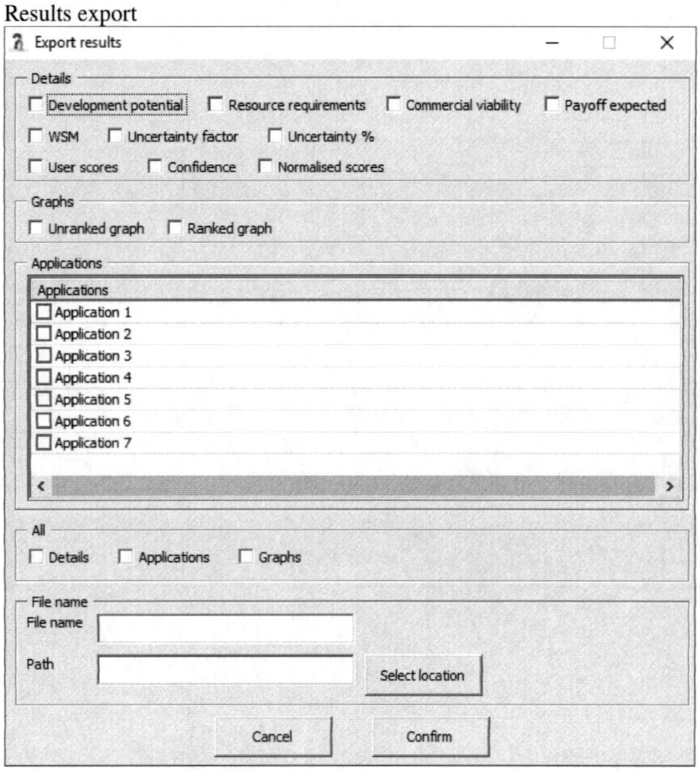

Coding Collaboration Process Automatically: Coding Methods Using Deep Learning Technology

Kimihiko Ando
Cloud Service Center
Tokyo University of Technology
Tokyo, Japan
email:ando@stf.teu.ac.jp

Chihiro Shibata
School of Computer Sciences
Tokyo University of Technology
Tokyo, Japan
email:shibatachh@stf.teu.ac.jp

Taketoshi Inaba
Graduate School of Bionics, Computer and Media Sciences
Tokyo University of Technology
Tokyo, Japan
email:inaba@stf.teu.ac.jp

Abstract— **In Computer Supported Collaborative Learning (CSCL) research, gaining a guideline to carry out appropriate scaffolding by analyzing mechanism of successful collaborative interaction and extracting indicators to identify groups where collaborative process is not going well, can be considered as the most important preoccupation, both for research and for educational implementation. And to study this collaborative learning process, different approaches have been tried. In this paper, we opt for the verbal data analysis; the advantage of this method is that it enables quantitative processing while maintaining qualitative perspective, with collaborative learning data of considerable size. However, coding large scale educational data is extremely time consuming and sometimes goes beyond men's capacity. So, in recent years, there have also been attempts to automate complex coding by using machine learning technology. In this background, with large scale data generated in our CSCL system, we have tried to implement automation of high precision coding utilizing deep learning methods, which are derived from the leading edge technology of machine learning. The results indicate that our approach with deep learning methods is promising, outperforming the machine learning baseline. But the prediction accuracy could be improved by constructing coding schemes and models more sensitive to the context of collaboration and conversation. Therefore, we propose a new coding scheme that can represent the context of learning more comprehensively and accurately at the end of this paper for the next research.**

Keywords-CSCL; leaning analytics; coding scheme; deep learning methods.

I. INTRODUCTION

This article is an extended version of a conference paper presented at eLmL 2017, the Ninth International Conference on Mobile, Hybrid and On-line Learning [1]. It introduces more information on the theoretical background of this study and especially a new coding scheme, based on the experiment results.

A. *Analysis of collaborative process*

One of the greatest research interests in the actual Computer Supported Collaborative Learning (CSCL) research is to analyze its social process from a social constructionist viewpoint, and key research questions are as follows: how knowledge and meanings are shared within a group, what types of conflict, synchronization and adjustment of opinions occur, and how knowledge is constructed from discussions. And answering to these questions enables to develop more effective scaffolding methods and CSCL system and tools.

In earlier researches at initial stage of CSCL, the focus was on each individual within a collaborating group, and the main point of interest had been how significantly a personal learning outcome was affected by characteristic types of a group (such as group size, group composition, learning tasks, and communication media) [2]. However, it gradually became clear that those characteristics are complexly connected and intertwined with each other, and showing causal relation to a specific result was extremely difficult. From the 1990s, the interest in CSCL research had moved away from awareness of the issue on how a personal learning is established within a group, to attempting to explain the process by clarifying the details of group interactions when learning is taking place within a group [3].

However, attempting to analyze collaborative process goes beyond merely shifting a research perspective; it also leads to fundamental re-examination of its analytical methodology. In other words, this involves a shift from quantitative analysis to qualitative analysis. Naturally, there are useful data among quantitative data saved within CSCL system, such as the number of contributions within a group, the number of contributions by each group member, and in some cases contribution attributes obtained from system interface (sentence opener), but those are very much a mere surface data. The most important data for analysis are contributions in chats, images/sounds within tools such as Skype, and various outputs generated in the process of collaborative learning; for analysis of those, ethnomethodologies such as conversation analysis and video analysis have been invoked [4][5].

However, those researches by their very nature tend to be in-depth case studies of collaborative activities with a limited number of groups and have the disadvantage of not at all being easy to derive a guideline that has a certain level of universality and can be applicable in other contexts. Therefore, researches have been carried out using verbal data analysis method that carry out coding from a perspective of linguistic or collaborative learning activities on a certain volume of language data generated in collaborative learning and analyzing them [6][7][8]. The advantage of this method is that it enables quantitative processing while maintaining qualitative perspective, with collaborative learning data of considerable size as the subject, while coding them manually is an extremely time consuming task, which goes sometimes beyond men's capacity. For example, Persico et al. developed a technological tool which helps the tutors to code the contributions in chats and displays quantitative information about the qualitative information and coding data [9]. However, given that the coding procedure itself remains manual in most existing studies [10][11], there is an insurmountable limit in front of big data. Hence, we seek an automatic coding technique for a large scale collaborative learning data with deep learning methods.

B. *Educational data and Learning Analytics*

With the progress of educational cloud implementation in educational institutions, data generated in Learning Management System (LMS), e-learning, Social Network Service (SNS), Massive Open Online Course (MOOC) and others are increasing rapidly, and a new research approach called Learning Analytics (LA) that tries to gain knowledge that would lead to support of learning and educational activities by analyzing those educational big data is becoming more active [12][13]. Big educational data obtained from CSCL system integrated in educational cloud at a campus, such as conversation data, submitted documents and images/sounds of learning activities, will certainly become a subject for analysis in the near future: therefore, it is believed that we are coming into a time when it is necessary to seriously examine a new possibility of collaborative learning research as LA. Due to such background, in this research we have reconstructed CSCL system that has been operating in a campus server for the last five years as a module within Moodle, which is a LMS within the campus cloud, and have already structured an environment that can be operated within the campus and collect/analyze collaborative learning data.

C. *The goal and purpose of this study*

The goal of our research is to analyze large-scale collaborative data from the perspective of LA as described above and discover the mechanism of activation and deactivation of collaborative activity process which could not be gained from micro level case studies up to now. Furthermore, this research, based on its results, aims to implement supports in authentic learning/educational contexts, such as real-time monitoring of collaborative process and scaffolding to groups that are not becoming activated.

In this paper, as the first step towards this goal, we present work in progress, which attempts to develop an automation technique for coding of chat data and verifies its accuracy. To be more specific, a substantial volume of chat data is coded manually, and has a part of that learnt as training data in deep learning methods, which are derived from the leading edge technologies for machine learning; afterwards, automatic coding of the raw data is carried out. For validation of accuracy, the effectiveness of using deep learning methods is assessed by comparing accuracy against Naive Bayes and Support Vector Machines, which are baselines of machine learning algorithm used in existing studies that carried out automatic coding by machine learning.

D. *Structure of this paper*

This paper is structured as follows. In Section II, we present the related work. The Section III describes our datasets and coding scheme. The approach with deep learning methods for automatic coding is discussed in Section IV. Then, our experiment and results from our evaluation are described in Section V. In Section VI, taking account of experimental results, we propose a new coding scheme. Section VI concludes the paper.

II. Related Work

Since deep learning can often outperform existing machine learning methods, such as SVMs, it has been applied in various research areas, such as image recognition and natural language processing [14]. Text classification is an important task in natural learning processing, for which various deep learning methods have been exploited extensively in recent studies. A structure called a CNN has been applied for text classification using word- or character-level modeling [15][16]. LSTM [17] and gated recurrent units (GRUs) [18] are popular structures for RNNs. Both structures are known to outperform existing models, such as n-grams, and thus are widely available as learning models for sequential data like text. RNNs are also applied to text classification in various ways [19][20]. For instance, Yang et al. used a bidirectional GRU with attention modeling by setting two hierarchical layers that consist of the word and sentence encoders [19].

In the field of CSCL, some researchers have tried to apply text classification technology to chat logs. The most representative studies would be Rosé and her colleagues' works [21][22][23]. For example, they applied text classification technology to a relatively large CSCL corpus that had been coded by human coders using the coding scheme with multiple dimensions, developed by Weinbeger and Fisher [22][24]. McLaren's Argunaut project took a similar approach: he used online discussions coded manually to train machine-learning classifiers in order to predict the appearance of these discussions characteristics in the new e-discussion [25]. However, it should be pointed out that all these prior studies rely on the machine learning techniques before deep learning studies emerge.

III. Data and Coding Scheme

In this section, we explain how we collected our dataset and what coding scheme we adopted to categorize the dataset.

A. Data Description

Our dataset obtained through chat function within the system, comes from conversations among students while carrying out online collaborative learning in university lectures using CSCL, which had been previously developed by the researchers of this study [26].

This CSCL is used without face to face contact; therefore, these data are all from occasions when unacquainted and separated students formed groups within lecture halls at the campus. And within the system all names of students are shown in nicknames, so that even if students knew each other they would not recognize each other.

The overview of CSCL contributions data used in this research is shown in Table I. The number of lectures is seven and all classes of these lectures form groups of three to four; in fact, there are a lot of data that we could not process by coding them in this research. Learning times vary depending on the class, from 45 to 90 minutes. In total, the dataset contains 11504 contributions; there are 202 groups from all the classes, with 426 participating students; since students attend multiple classes, the number of participating students are smaller than the product of number of groups and number of students in a group.

Table II shows a conversation example of chat. This is a conversation example of three students.

TABLE I. CONTRIBUTIONS DATA USED IN THIS STUDY

Number of Lectures	7 Lectures
Member of Groups	3-4 people
Learning Time	45-90 mintutes
Number of Groups	202 groups
Number of Students	426 students

TABLE II. CONVERSATION EXAMPLE (TRANLATION FROM JAPANESE)

Talker	Contents
D	Where do you want to change?
E	That's right … I guess, first of all, we definitely need to change the question, and then, what about the well-formed formula?
D	How is it that changes only the third line of the question?
D	Regarding the well-formed formula, it's the final part after ⊃.
E	That's good idea.
F	I agree. How do we want to change that?

B. Coding scheme

In accordance with our manual for code assignment, one code label is assigned to one contribution in a chat. There are 16 types of code labels as shown in Table III, and one of those labels is assigned for all cases.

All labels in our dataset are coded by two people; the coincidence rate between the labels assigned was 67%. However, when we reviewed the resultant coding data, it was discovered that there were duplicated labels for some contributions, and some labels had variances depending on the coder; therefore, after conferring among us, we unified labels and re-coded the contributions. The resultant number of labels assigned is shown in Table III. Concordance rate is 82.3% and this is a high concordance rate with 0.800 Kappa coefficient, and we consider this to be sufficiently practical for use as an educational dataset in deep learning methods. Fig. 1 shows the frequencies of the labels in the dataset. Nine labels describe more than 90% of occurrences; label occurrences appear to have a long-tail distribution. The main purpose of this study is to learn and infer these labels from posted contributions.

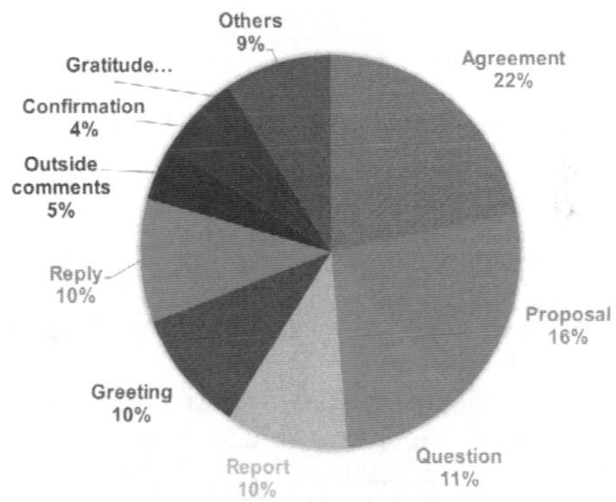

Figure 1. Ratio of each conversational coding labels

IV. Approach –Deep Learning

In recent years, deep learning technology has led to dramatic developments in the field of artificial intelligence. Deep learning is a general framework of learning methods that use neural networks with millions of weight parameters. The weights in neural networks are optimized so that their output coincides with labels in the given data. With the recent development of parallel computing using Graphics Processing Units (GPUs) and optimization algorithms, machines are able to learn large numbers of parameters from large datasets at realistic costs.

To try automatic coding, we adapt three types of deep neural network (DNN) structures: a convolutional neural network (CNN) based model and two bidirectional Long short-term memory (LSTM) based models, LSTM and Sequence-to-Sequence (Seq2Seq). The first and second models take only a single contribution as input and cannot refer to context information in the conversation. Conversely, the Seq2Seq model can capture context information by using

TABLE III. List of labels

Label	Meaning of label	Contribution example	Number of times used
Agreement	Affirmative reply	I think that's good	5033
Proposal	Conveying opinion, or yes/no question	How about five of us here make the submission?	3762
Question	Other than yes/no question	What shall we do with the title?	2399
Report	Reporting own status	I corrected the complicated one	2394
Greeting	Greeting to other members	I'm looking forward to working with you	2342
Reply	Other replies	It looks that way!	2324
Outside comments	Contribution on matters other than assignment contents	My contribution is disappearing already; so fast!	1049
	Opinions on systems and such	A bug	
Confirmation	Confirm the assignment and how to proceed	Would you like to submit it now?	949
Gratitude	Gratitude to other members	Thanks!	671
Switchover	A contribution to change event being handled, such as moving on to the next assignment	Shall we give it a try?	625
Joke	Joke to other members	You should, like, learn it physically? :)	433
Request	Requesting somebody to do some task	Can either of you reply?	354
Correction	Correcting past contribution	Sorry, I meant children	204
Disagreement	Negative reply	I think 30 minute is too long	160
Complaint	Dissatisfactions towards assignments or systems	I must say the theme isn't great	155
Noise	Contribution that does not make sense	?meet? day???	143

a pair of sentences as its input, which represent source and replay contributions.

A. CNN-based model

The CNN-based model uses the network architecture proposed by Kim et al. (Fig. 2). Before training, all words in the data are converted to word vectors. Word vectors are often obtained by pre-training using another external dataset. In this study, we implemented two types of word vectors: 1) vectors obtained by applying word2vec (the skipped gram model with negative sampling) to all Japanese text in Wikipedia, and 2) randomly initialized vectors that are tuned simultaneously with the CNN.

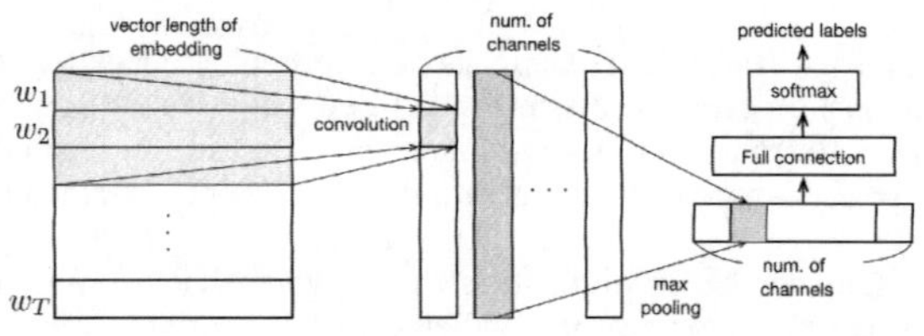

Figure 2. CNN-based model

B. Bidirectional LSTM-based model

An LSTM is a recurrent neural networks (RNNs) that is carefully constructed so that it can capture long-distance dependencies in sequential data. Generally speaking, an RNN consists of input vector x_t and output vector y_t for each time t. To obtain the output $y_{\{t\}}$, the previous output vector $y_{\{t-1\}}$ is fed to the neural network along with the current input vector x_t. The LSTM has another hidden vector, c_t, called the *state vector* in addition to the input and output vectors. While the state vector is also output from the neural network, it is computed to track long-distance relations through a function called a *forget gate*, which is designed to decide whether the state vector should be changed. We feed word vectors into the two-layer LSTM network sequentially in both the forward and reverse directions. After all words in a contribution are input, both output vectors are concatenated and fed into the two-layer fully-connected network and the softmax layer to obtain classification results. Fig. 3 illustrates this architecture.

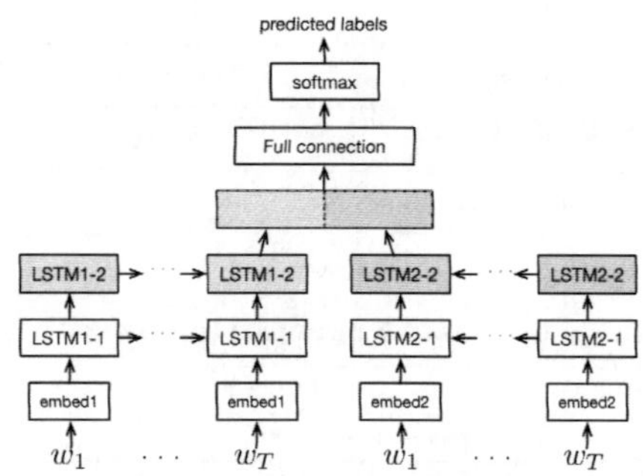

Figure 3. Bidirectional LSTM-based

C. Bidirectional Seq2Seq-based model

Each contribution is a part of a conversation; therefore, to classify labels more accurately, we must account for conversational contexts. To do this, we convert all contributions in conversations into pairs of *source* and *reply* contributions (Table IV). Even if a user posts a contribution that does not explicitly cite another, we assume that it cites a previous contribution. We also suppose that the first contribution of each conversation cites the empty string. To construct a model that regards the source contribution as a conversational context and the reply as a representation of the user's intention, we use the Seq2seq framework. Seq2seq [27] was originally proposed as a neural model using RNNs for machine translation, and later applied to other tasks, such as conversational generation [28]. It consists of two separate LSTM networks, called the encoder and decoder. We use two-layer LSTM networks for both the encoder and decoder. Words are sequentially fed in both the forward and reverse directions. Output vectors from decoders are concatenated and fed into the two-layer fully-connected network and the softmax layer (Fig. 4).

TABLE IV. Examples for source and replay contributions

Source (u)	Replay (w)	Label
(None)	How about five of us here make the submission?	**Proposal**
(None)	I must say the theme isn't great.	**Com-plaint**
How about five of us here make the submission?	It sounds great!	**Reply**
I must say the theme isn't great.	If we had another hour, we could change it…	**Agree-ment**
It sounds great!	Thanks!	**Gratitude**

V. Evaluation

A. Data Preprocessing

For each contribution, we trimmed sentences beginning with the symbol ">," which were automatically generated by the system. Since all the data consist of Japanese text, morphological analysis was needed. We split texts into words using a tool called MeCab [29]. Replacing low-frequency words with "unknown," the vocabulary size was decreased to approximately 4,000. Each contribution was given two labels annotated by different people; we removed contributions that were assigned two different labels. We used 90% of the remaining 8,015 contributions as training data and 10% as test data. The accuracy of the learning result for each model is measured with the test data.

B. Baseline Methods

For comparison, we used three classifiers; Naive Bayes, a linear support vector machine (SVM), and an SVM with a radial basis function (RBF) kernel. We also used two types of feature sets: unigrams only and unigrams and bigrams. For the SVM classifiers, in order to improve the classification accuracy, input vectors were obtained by normalizing zero-one vectors whose elements represent occurrences of unigrams or bigrams.

C. Model Parameters and Learning

Model parameters, such as the vector sizes of layers, are determined as follows. Both the size of word embedding and the size of the last fully connected layer are 200 for all models. We set the patch size of the convolutional layer in the vertical direction to 4 and the number of channels to 256 for the CNN-based models. We set the size of both LSTM layers to 800 for the LSTM and Seq2Seq models. The set of parameters were needed to be chosen so that their prediction accuracy of the model will not be reduced, and at the same time, the computational cost of learning is in the range of reasonable time. Generally, the vector size of LSTM layers is needed to be increased for better prediction accuracy when it is inappropriately small. On the other hand, if it is sufficiently large, increasing their size is almost in vain for better accuracy. For instance, if we set it larger than that of our setting, say 1000 or 2000, we will get almost the same value of accuracy as the result of the experiment. Thus, we empirically decided it so as to achieve the nearly optimal accuracy and to minimize computational cost. Meanwhile, we need to carefully choose the vector size of the last fully connected layer. Our model easily suffers from over fitting if we set it too large. On the other hand, if we set it too small, our model is suffered from the lack of the expression capability. Thus, we should set it moderately; not so small to

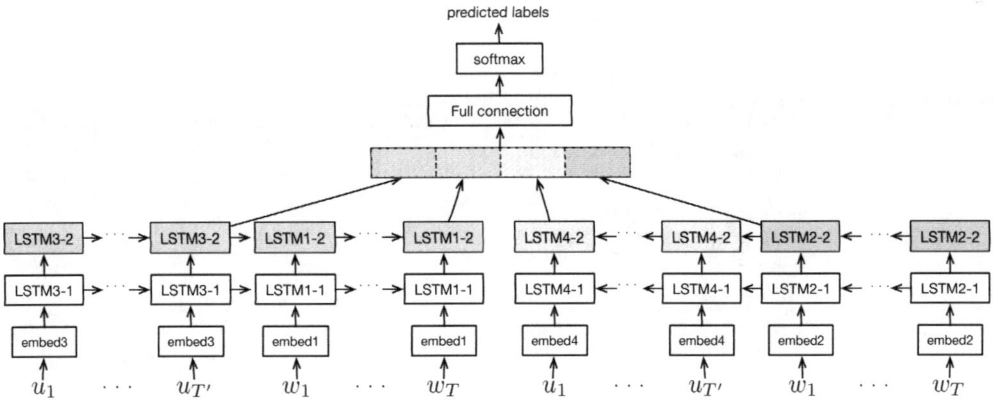

Figure 4. Bidirectional Seq2Seq-based model

have the sufficient capability to learn accurately, and not so large to avoid the over fitting problem. We obtained 200 as an appropriate value for the vector size of the last layer through several experiments.

Models are learned by stochastic descent gradient (SDG) using an optimization method called Adam. To avoid overfitting, iteration was stopped at 10 epochs for the LSTM-based methods and 30 epochs for the CNN-based methods. Due to the fluctuation in accuracy results between epochs, we took the average of the last 5 epochs to measure the accuracy of each model. To prevent overfitting, dropout was applied to the last and second-last fully connected layers. Figure 5 shows the learning curves of the CNN-based model with Wikipedia and the bi-directional Seq2Seq-based model. The y-axis shows the accuracy on the test data. As the figure shows, the accuracy converges approximately after around 10 epochs for the Seq2Seq-based model. On the other hand, it converges after around 30 epochs. The numbers of epochs that are needed for convergence largely depend on the models.

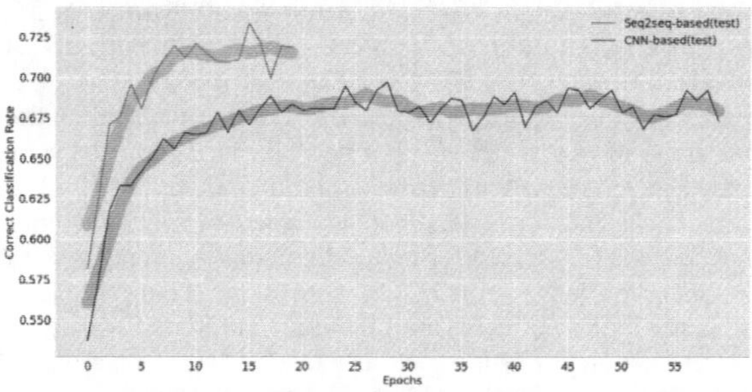

Figure 5. Learning curves of Seq2Seq-based and CNN-based models

D. *Experimental Results*

Table V shows the accuracies of the three DNN models and baseline methods. Overall, the DNN models outperform the baselines, even as the SVMs maintain their high performance. Among baseline methods, the SVM with the RBF kernel achieved the highest accuracy. For the CNN-based models, using word vectors trained using the Wikipedia data slightly enhanced accuracy. For the LSTM-based models, bidirectional processing yielded slightly higher accuracy than single-directional processing.

TABLE V. PREDICTIVE ACCURACIES FOR BASELINES AND DEEP-NEURAL-NETWORK MODELS

Naïve Bayes		SVM(Linear)		SVM(RBF Kernel)	
unigram	*uni+bigram*	*unigram*	*uni+bigram*	*unigram*	*uni+bigram*
0.554	0.598	0.642	0.659	**0.664**	0.659

CNN		LSTM		Seq2Seq	
with wikipedia	*w.o. wikipedia*	*single-direction*	*bidirection*	*bidirection*	*bidir. w. interm.*
0.686	0.677	0.676	0.678	**0.718**	0.717

There was no significant difference in the accuracies of the CNN model using Wikipedia and the bidirectional LSTM model. Both of these methods outperformed the best of SVMs by 1-2%.

The Seq2Seq model outperformed other methods clearly; the best of SVMs by 5-6% and other DNN models by 3-4%.

The kappa coefficient for the bidirectional LSTM model was 0.63, which is sufficiently high. However, to automatically comprehend and judge the activities of users from only the labels inferred by machines, the kappa coefficient must be improved. By using the Seq2Seq model, which is able to capture the contextual information from the source or the adjacent contribution, the kappa coefficient was improved to 0.723.

Hereafter, we analyze the misclassification of each label individually. The precision and recall for each label are shown in Table VI. Of the ten most frequent labels, the precision of "Greeting" predictions were highest (F1: 0.94) and that of "Agreement" was the second highest (F1: 0.83).

TABLE VI. PRESITION AND RECALL FOR EACH LABEL (RESULT OF BI-DIRECTIONAL LSTM)

Label	Presition	Recall	F1-Value
Agreement	0.85	0.81	0.83
Proposal	0.73	0.74	0.73
Question	0.75	0.8	0.77
Report	0.64	0.62	0.63
Greeting	0.94	0.94	0.94
Reply	0.62	0.46	0.53
Outside Commnets	0.17	0.47	0.25
Confirmation	0.58	0.74	0.65
Gratitude	0.67	0.67	0.67

"Question" was also predicted with high accuracy (F1: 0.77). These results are consistent with our intuition, as both seem to be easy to infer from the contributions themselves, without knowing their context. In contrast, as Table VI shows, the label "Reply" was hard for our model to predict. That performed worst with respect to the recall, tending to be misclassified as an "Agreement", "Proposal" or "Report," as shown in the confusion matrix (Fig. 6). This can be solved if richer context in neighboring contributions is used as input to classifiers in addition to the source contribution.

VI. NEW CODING SCHEME

As indicated in some case that Replay may include a meaning of Agree in the coding scheme based on speech acts used in the current study, the fact that the definition of one label may sometimes overlap the definition of another label has become a factor making it difficult to assign a label always with accuracy and reliability just in artificial intelligence coding but also in manual coding as well. In addition to these technical problems, more importantly, labels based on speech acts which express the linguistic characteristics of the conversation are insufficient for the analysis of the learning process. With this single linguistic scheme, one can not clearly realize whether members of a group engage in activities to solve the task, how members

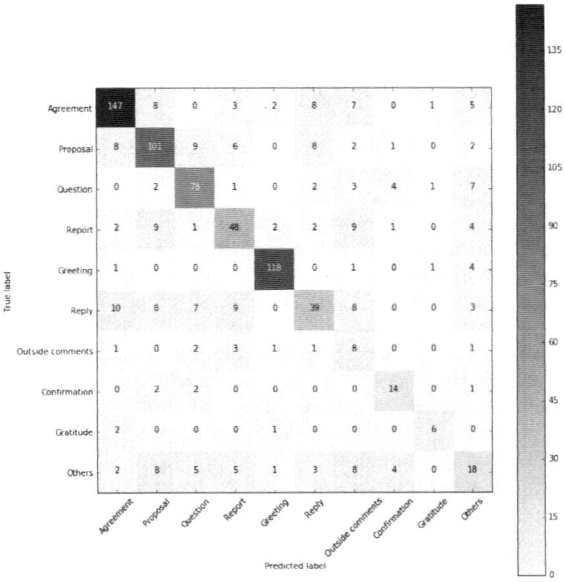

Figure 6. Confusion matrix for the Seq2S2q model.

coordinate each other in terms of task division, time management, etc. during their collaboration, how each member constructs his argument, how members discuss and negotiate each other. From those described above, we propose a new coding scheme so that the automated coding accuracy will improve and that we may understand more accurately and globally collaborative process.

Our new coding scheme is constructed based on the multi-dimensional coding scheme proposed by Weinberger et Fischer who try to analyze whole samples of discourse corpora on multiple process dimensions and "better understand how specific processes of computer-supported collaborative learning contribute to and improve individual acquisition of knowledge" [24]. As shown in Table VII, our scheme consists of five dimensions, while Winberger and Fischer's one has four dimensions without Coordination dimension. We provide labels basically regarding a statement in a chatting as a unit similarly to way we used in the study. In addition, while such values as number of statements are provided as Participation dimension labels, those in other four dimensions are provided by selecting one label from among multiple labels. In other words, since one label is given for each dimension for one statement, a plurality of labels will be assigned to one statement. Therefore, the coding work with this scheme is extremely complicated and takes a lot of time, but the merit of automated coding is even greater. Each dimension is described in detail below.

A. Participation dimension

As shown in Table VIII, Participation dimension is for measuring participation frequency in argumentation. Since this dimension is defined as quantitative data mainly including number of statements, number of letters of statements, time for and interval of statements, there is no need for neither manual nor artificial intelligence coding, requiring a coding just by statistical processing on a database.

Even though Participation dimension labels are capable of analyzing quantitatively different aspects of participation in conversations since they work on specific number of statements or the like, they are incapable of qualitatively analyzing such as whether the contribution has contributed to problem solving.

TABLE VII. NEW CODING SCHEME

Dimension	Description
Participation	Frequency of participation in argumentation
Epistemic	How to be directly involved in problem solving
Argumentation	Ideal assertion in argumentation
Social	How to cope with others' statements
Coordination	How to coordinate to advance discussion smoothly

B. Epistemic dimension

This dimension represents whether each statement is directly related to problem solving as a task and the labels are classified as shown in the table below depending on contents of statements. Labels of this dimension are provided to all statements.

Weinberger and Fischer's scheme has 6 categories to code epistemic activities which consist in applying the theoretical concepts to case information. But, as shown in Table IX, we set only two categories here, because we want to give generality that we can handle as many problem solving types as possible.

TABLE VIII. PARTICIPATION DIMENSION

Category	Description
Number of statements	Number of statements of each member during sessions
Number of letters of a statement	Number of letters during a single speech
Time for statement	Time used for a statement
Interval of statements	Time elapsed since last statement
Statements distribution	Standard deviation of each member within a group

TABLE IX. LABELS IN EPISTEMIC DIMENSION

Label	Description
On Task	Statements directly related to problems
Off Task	Statements without any relationship with problems

"On Task" here indicates such statements which are directly related with assigned problem solving and statements with any of contents described below are regarded as "Off Task."

- Statements asking meaning of problems and how to advance them
- Statements to allocate tasks
- Statements regarding the system

Labels in Epistemic dimension are regarded to be the most basic ones for qualitative analysis since they represent whether they are directly involved in problem solving. For example, it is understood that almost no effort has been made on a problem if there is less "On task" labels.

Besides, Argumentation and Social dimension labels as referred to in the next section and beyond are provided only if Epistemic dimension is "On Task" and those in coordination dimension are provided only if Epistemic dimension is "Off Task."

C. Coordination dimension

Labels of Coordination dimension are provided only if Epistemic dimension labels are "Off Task" and the statements are not directly but indirectly involved in problems. While a list of Coordination dimension labels is shown in Table X, labels are provided not to all of statements of "Off task" but only one label is provided to any statement which falls under the label. For responses to statements to which Coordination dimension labels are provided, those in the same Coordination dimension are provided.

"Task division" here refers to a statement to decide who to work on which task requiring division of tasks for advancing problem solving. "Time management" is a statement to coordinate degree of progress in problem solving, and for example, such statements fall under the definition that "let's check it until 13 o'clock," and "how has it been in progress?" "Meta statement" refers to a statement for clarifying what the problem is when intention and meaning of the problem is not understood. "Technical coordination" refers to questions and opinions about how to use the CSCL System.

TABLE X. LABELS OF COORDINATION DIMENSION

Label	Description
Task division	Allotment of tasks
Time management	Check of temporal and degree of progress
Meta statement	Questions to ask meaning of problems
Technical coordination	How to use the system, etc.

Since Coordination dimension labels are provided to statements for executing problem solving smoothly, it is believed to be possible to predict progress in arguments by analyzing the timing that the labels were provided. In case of less Coordination dimension labels recognized, it is also predicted that smooth relationships have not been built up within the groups.

In a case that a lot of these labels have been provided in many groups, on the other hand, it is assumed that there is some sort of defect in contents of the problems or systems.

In addition, it should be noted that this dimension is not set in Weinberger and Fischer's scheme.

D. Argument dimension

Labels of Argument dimension are provided to all statements when Epistemic labels are "On Task", indicating attributes such as whether each statement includes the speaker's opinion and whether the opinion is based on any ground. Labels of this dimension are provided to just one statement content without considering whether any ground was described in other statement.

A list of Argument dimension labels is shown in Table XI. Here, presence/absence of grounds is determined whether any ground to support the opinion is presented or not but it does not matter whether the presented ground is reliable or not. A qualified claim represents whether it is asserted that presented opinion is applied to all or part of situations to be worked on as a task. "Euphemism" indicates such statements with low confidence rating that presented opinion is just a prediction or shows only possibility. "Non-Argumentative moves" refer to statements without including any opinion and simple questions are also included in this tag.

Labels in Argument dimension are capable of analyzing the logical consistency of statement contents. For example, if a statement is filled just with "Simple Claim" it is assumed as a superficial argument.

In comparison with Weinberger and Fischer's scheme, we introduce a new label "Euphemism". But we do not set for now the categories of macro-level dimension in which single arguments are arranged in a line of argumentation such as arguments, counterarguments, reply, for the reason that it seems difficult that the automatic coding by deep learning methods for this macro dimension works correctly.

TABLE XI. LABELS IN ARGUMENT DIMENSION

Label	Description
Simple Claim	Simple opinion without any ground
Qualified Claim	Opinion based on a limiting condition without any ground
Grounded Claim	Opinion based on grounds
Grounded and Qualified claim	Opinion with limitation based on grounds
Euphemism	Unconfident and ambiguous opinion
Non-argumentative moves	Statement without containing opinion (including questions)

E. Social dimension

Labels in Social dimension are provided when Epistemic code is "On task" but they are provided not to all statements "On task" but to a statement which conforms to Epistemic code. This dimension represents how each statement is related to those of other members within the group. Therefore, it is required to understand not only a statement but also the previous context. A list of this dimension labels is shown in Table XII.

TABLE XII. CODE OF SOCIAL DIMENSION

Label	Description
Externalization	Externalization: No reference to other's opinion
Elicitation	Questionning the learning parner or proviking a reacion from the learning partner
Quick consensus building	Prompt consensus formation
Integration-oriented consensus building	Consensus formation in an integrated manner
Conflict-oriented consensus building	Consensus forming based on a confrontational stance

"Externalization" here refers to a statement without reference to those of others and it is provided mainly to statements as a point of argument origin such as in the beginning of argument on certain topic. "Elicitation" is provided to such statements which require others to extract information such as questions.

From its property as a statement to be made in response to other's opinion, "Consensus building" is classified into the following three labels. "Quick consensus building" is provided to a statement aiming at achieving prompt agreement with other's opinion. In particular, it is provided to a case to agree without delivering any specific opinion. "Integration-oriented consensus building" is provided to statements with an intention to achieve agreement with other's opinion while adding its own opinion. "Conflict-oriented consensus building" is provided to statements which adopt a confrontational stance or request revision against other's opinion.

A sub-dimension called as "Refer" in Social dimension represents which statement is referred to in the statement coded as "Consensus building". Labels in "Refer" dimension are provided without exception only if Social dimension labels belong to "Consensus building."

Since Social dimension labels represent relationship with others, it is possible to estimate how lively discussions were conducted or whose opinion in the group was respected by analyzing Social dimension labels. For example, arguments including a lot of "Quick consensus building" are assumed to be a result obtained just by taking a delivered opinion directly with almost no profound discussion.

F. Each coding and Learning toward artificial intelligence

In the new coding scheme, "Participation" dimension labels are automatically generated from statement logs, whereas other labels require manual coding by a coder in order to build up training data for deep learning and test data. Further, labels to be provided are decided by selecting from any of the dimensions of "Argumentation", "Social" and "Coordination" depending on a result of "Epistemic" labels. Therefore, coder provides "Epistemic" labels based on analysis of "Participation" dimension labels. Subsequently, "Argumentation" and "Social" dimension labels are provided if the "Epistemic labels are "On task." In addition, in a case that "Social" dimension labels belong to "Consensus building", statement number is provided as "Refer" since there exists reference source statement without exception. In a case that "Epistemic" labels are "Off task", those in "Coordination" dimension are provided.

VII. SUMMARY AND FUTURE WORK

This section recapitulates the findings of this study and suggests briefly some future issues.

A. Summary

As the first step to analyze collaborative process of big educational data from the perspective of LA, we tried to automate time-consuming coding task by using deep learning methods.

First, we developed a coding scheme based on the speech acts, coded manually for the remarks, and created training data and test data for deep learning. Next, three DNN models, that is, CNN-based model, LSTM-based model, Seq2Seq-based model were constructed for automatic coding, and their accuracy of automatic coding was verified. In addition, we also compared accuracy with SVMs, which are the baselines of classical machine learning. The result was promising; our approach, particularly, Seq2Seq model outperformed other methods clearly; the best of SVMs by 5-6% and other DNN models by 3-4%. It seems that this model could obtain almost the same predictive accuracy with other coding schemes than ours, for the reason that our coding scheme is sufficiently complex with 16 labels, based not on the surface information, but on the contextual significance of each contribution.

B. Future work

As for the future research directions, we may have two approaches to pursue.

The first approach is about DNN models. To improve prediction accuracy, it may be effective to introduce other network structures such as memory networks [30] instead of DNNs that consist of RNNs and CNNs. Memory networks make a vector from conversation by taking weighted mean of vectors of all sentences. Those weights play a role of attention since they correspond to importance of each sentence. In addition, the context of conversation should be considered. To capture context more precisely, it may be necessary to construct more complex models that take multiple preceding contributions as input vectors.

The second and most important approach concerns coding scheme. Our scheme, based on speech acts, was sufficiently complex, but not global. In order to more accurately and comprehensively grasp various collaborative learning activities such as individual cognitive process, social cognitive process, coordination among members, it will be necessary to construct a coding scheme which is more sensitive to details of interaction and social cognitive process of learning. Therefore, we proposed a new coding scheme with five dimensions, namely the participation dimension, the epistemic dimension, the coordination dimension, the argument dimension, the social dimension. With this new scheme, we are coding all the datasets again to constitute training data and test data for deep learning, in order to verify if this scheme contributes to a more precise understanding of the collaborative process and to improve the accuracy of automatic coding by our DNN models.

ACKNOWLEDGMENT

This work was supported by JSPS KAKENHI Grant Number 26350289 and 16K01134. We also thank to Ryo Yoshinaka for his thoughtful comments.

REFERENCES

[1] C. Shibata, K. Ando, and T. Inaba, "Towards Automatic Coding of Collaborative Learning Data with Deep Learning Technology," The Ninth International Conference on Mobile, Hybrid, and On-line Learning, 2017, pp. 65-71.

[2] G. Stahl, T. Koschmann, and D. Suthers, "Computer-supported collaborative learning," In The Cambridge handbook of the learning science, K. Sawyer, Eds. Cambridge university press, pp. 479-500, 2014.

[3] P. Dillenbourg, P. Baker, A. Blaye, and C. O'Malley, "The evolution of research on collaborative learning," In Learning in humans and machines: Towards an interdisciplinary learning science, P. Reimann and H. Spada, Eds. Oxford: Elservier, pp. 189-211, 1996.

[4] T. Koschmann, "Understanding understanding in action," Journal of Pragmatics, 43, pp. 435-437, 2011.

[5] T. Koschmann, G. Stahl, and A. Zemel, "The video analyst's manifesto (or The implications of Garfinkel's policies for the development of a program of video analysis research within the learning science)," In Video reseach in the learning sciences, R. Goldman, R. Pea, B. Barron and S. Derry, Eds. Routledge, pp. 133-144, 2007.

[6] M. Chi, "Quantifying qualitative analyses of verbal data : A pratical guide ," Journal of the Learning Science, 6(3), pp. 271-315, 1997.

[7] A. Meier, H. Spada, and N. Rummel, "A rating scheme for assesseing the quality of coputer-supported collaboration processes," International Jounal of Computer Suppported Collaborative Learning, 2, pp. 63-86, 2007.

[8] H. Jeong, "Verbal data analysis for understanding interacitons," In The International Handbook of Collaborative Learning, C. Hmelo-Silver, A. M. O'Donnell, C. Chan and C. Chin, Eds. Routledge, pp. 168-183, 2013.

[9] D. Persico, F. Pozzi, and L. Sarti, "Monitoring collaborative activities in computer supported learning," Distance Education, 31(1), pp. 5-22, 2010.

[10] L. Lipponen, M. Rahikainen, J. Lamillo, and K. Hakkarainen, "Patterns of participation and discourse in elementary students'computer-supported collaborative learning," Learning and Instruction, 13, pp. 487-509, 2003.

[11] S. Schrire, "Knowledge building in asynchronous discussion groups: Going beyond quantitative analysis," Computer & Education 46, pp. 49-70, 2006.

[12] 1st Internationa Conference on Learning Analytics and Knowledge. [Online]. Avaiable from: https://tekri.athabascau.ca/analytics/, Nov. 29, 2017.

[13] B. R. Schaun and P. S. Inventado, "Educational data mining and learning analytics," In Learning Analytics, J. A. Larusoon and B. White, Eds. Springer, pp. 61-75, 2014.

[14] Y. LeCun, Y. Bengio, and G. Hinton, "Deep learning," Nature, 521(7553), pp. 436-444, 2015.

[15] Y. Kim, "Convolutional neural networks for sentence classification," arXiv preprint arXiv:1408.5882, 2014.

[16] X. Zhang, J. Zhao, and Y. LeCun. "Character-level convolutional networks for text classification," In Proceedings of the 28th International Conference on Neural Information Processing Systems (NIPS2015), pp. 649-657, 2015.

[17] S. Hochreiter and J. Schmidhuber, "Long short-term memory," Neural Computation, 9(8), pp.1735-1780, 1997.

[18] J. Chung, C. Gulcehre, K. Hyun Cho, and Y. Bengio, "Empirical Evaluation of Gated Recurrent Neural Networks on Sequence Modeling," arXiv preprint arXiv:1412.3555, 2014.

[19] Z. Yang et al., "Hierarchical Attention Networks for Document Classification," In Proceedings of the 2016 Conference of the North American Chapter of the Association for Computational Linguistics (NAACL2016), Human Language Technologies, 2016.

[20] D. Tang, B. Qin, and T. Liu, "Document modeling with gated recurrent neural network for sentiment classification," In Proceedings of the 2015 Conference on Empirical Methods in Natural Language Processing (EMNLP2016), pp. 1422–1432, 2015.

[21] C. Rosé et al., "Towards an interactive assessment framework for engineering design project based learning," In Proceedings of DETC2007, 2007.

[22] C. Rosé et al., "Analyzing collaborative learning processes automatically: Exploiting the advances of computational linguistics in computer-supported collaborative learning," International Journal of Computer Supported Collaborative Learning, 3(3), pp. 237-271, 2008.

[23] G. Gweon, S. Soojin, J. Lee, S. Finger and C.Rosé, "A framework for assessment of student project groups on-line and off-line," In Analyzing Interactions in CSCL: Methods, Approaches and Issues, S. Putambekar, G.Erkens and C. Hmelo-Silver Eds. Springer, pp. 293-317, 2011.

[24] A. Weinberger and F. Fischer, "A frame work to analyze arugmetative knowledge construciton in computer-supported learning," Computer & Education, 46(1), pp. 71-95, 2006.

[25] B. McLaren, O. Scheuer, M. De Laat, H. Hever and R. De Groot, "Using machine learning techniques to analysze and support mediation of student e-discussions," In Proceedings of artificial intelligence in education, 2007.

[26] T. Inaba and K. Ando. "Development and Evaluation of CSCL System for Large Classrooms Using Question-Posing Script," International Journal on Advances in Software, 7(3&4), pp. 590-600, 2014.

[27] D. Bahdanau, K. Cho, and Y. Bengio, "Neural machine translation by jointly learning to align and translate," arXiv preprint arXiv, pp.1409.0473, 2014.

[28] O. Vinyals and Q. V. Le, " A Neural Conversational Mode," arXiv preprint arXiv:1506.05869, (ICML Deep Learning Workshop 2015), 2015.

[29] T. Kudo, "MeCab: Yet Another Part-of-Speech and Morphological Analyzer". http://mecab.sourceforge.net/, Nov 29, 2017.

[30] S. Sukhbaatar, A. Szlam, J. Weston and R. Fergus, "End-to-end Memory Networks," Proceedings of the 28th International Conference on Neural Information Processing Systems, pp. 2440-2448, 2015.

A Cost-Benefit Method for Business Rules Normalization

Koen Smit
Digital Smart Services
HU University of Applied Sciences Utrecht
Utrecht, the Netherlands
koen.smit@hu.nl

Martijn Zoet
Optimizing Knowledge-Intensive Business Processes
Zuyd University of Applied Sciences
Sittard, the Netherlands
martijn.zoet@zuyd.nl

Abstract— **This paper presents a cost/benefit analysis method for the normalization of business rules. To determine the economic benefit of business rules normalization three variables are addressed: 1) the number of anomalies a rule set endures, 2) the storage space a rule set requires and the 3) deterioration of rules in response time. The approach is evaluated by means of an experiment, based on mortgage data of an international bank. Results show that the method is useful for determining when to normalize business rule sets; the method enables business rules analysts to produce more cost-effective business rules architectures. In this paper, we re-address and - present our earlier work [1], yet we extended the previous research with more detailed descriptions of the related literature, findings, and results, which provides a grounded basis from which further research on business rules normalization can be conducted.**

Keywords-Business Rules; Decision Management; Normalization; Cost-Benefit Analysis

I. INTRODUCTION

Good decision making is a key denominator for a corporation's competitiveness [2]. Therefore, organizations are increasingly urged to make fast and accurate decisions. At the same time, decisions are becoming more and more complex, affecting maintainability and transparency. Decisions can be formulated by means of business rules [3][4]. A business rule is defined by Morgan [5] as: "*a statement that defines or constrains some aspects of the business intending to assert business structure or to control the behavior of the business.*" To realize changes within an organization's decision-making process, an organization should be able to maintain the aforementioned asserts and it should be able to adapt its business rules efficiently and effectively to realize changes within its decision-making process [6]. In order to realize this, information systems, such as expert systems, knowledge management systems, case based reasoning systems, fuzzy expert systems and business rules management systems have been built for and adopted by organizations [7].

Research on the management of business rules has been conducted since the mid-1960's [7][8]. Distinct research streams have emerged, focusing on the following three subjects: 1) subject transformation, 2) platform transformation, and 3) business rule model transformation [9]. Subject transformation research focuses on processes, methods and information systems used for mining and cleansing decision sources, such as regulations, organizational policies, laws, documents and databases. Platform transformation research focuses on the use of information technology for the deployment, execution and monitoring of business rules. Important research topics in this stream are: 1) algorithms for faster and easier execution, 2) business rules architectures, and 3) business rules engines [10][11][12]. Business rule model transformation research focuses on verification, validation and improvement of existing business rules. To verify business rules, a formal grammar notation and/or a set of constructs is applied. A grammar notation describes how a business rule should be constructed or formulated. An example of a standardized business rules grammar is the Semantics of Business Vocabulary and Business Rules [13].

Despite the accumulation of literature, there is a surprisingly scarce amount of research that examines methods and processes to factor business rules [3]. Factoring entails the process of dividing business rules, and therefore decisions, in more comprehensible structural elements to increase maintainability and transparency [14]. Research that has focused on this subject is "single language oriented" [9][3][15]. Since a relatively high number of business rules modelling languages exist within scientific and professional literature, a factoring procedure per language is not desired from the viewpoint of the authors. Furthermore, current research does not provide guidelines to financially quantify the value of factoring business rules [9]. As far as the authors are aware, no method exists that is business rules modelling language-independent in combination with quantifying the financial benefits of factoring business rules. An example is the work of [15], which solely focuses on achieving the third normal form while factoring business rules, without investigating whether this is financially optimal. Given the fact that organizations invest large amounts of money for implicitly managing business rules, a valid question is whether and when an explicit factoring procedure is economically beneficial. For example, a business rule set, which only changes or is executed twice a year might, from an economic perspective, be better off in an un-factored form. Taken previous statements into account, the following research question arose: "*How can business rules be factored such that economic beneficial manageability is realized?*" Following Van Thienen and Snoeck's [16] research on factoring decision tables and Zoet's [3] research on factoring business rules, relational theory is adopted to factor business rules.

The current study extends previous research by developing a factoring method that incorporates mainstream rule modeling languages and guidelines to determine the cost and revenue of (re-)factored business rules. A factoring method is developed and validated by means of an experiment based on case study data at a large international bank. The results showed that our method is effective in determining the economic costs and benefits.

In section two, a discussion is provided on the theoretical foundations of factoring business rules in terms of relational theory, normalization and economic factors. This is followed by the construction of the method in section three. In section four, a demonstration of the application of the method on mortgage decision making at a large international bank is provided. The paper is concluded, in section five, with the study's core findings, contributions as well as its limitations.

II. Background and Related Work

There are few methods available to (re-)factor business rules [3]. Currently, two different methods are described: one by Van Thienen and Snoeck [16] and one by Zoet et al. [9]. Van Thienen and Snoeck's [16] method has two underlying assumptions; 1) business rules are specified in decision tables and 2) relational theory is the basis for normalizing business rules. Guidelines are proposed to factor decision tables, thereby improving maintainability. However, instead of formulating one common procedure they proposed multiple exceptions to the normal form. These exceptions are an implicit result of the foundation of their research, namely the use of decision tables. The second method proposed by Zoet et al. [9] also takes relational theory into account. Moreover, this method distinguishes itself by applying one common procedure, which can be used for several languages. Similar to previous studies, this paper also applies relational theory as underlying foundation.

The definition of the term relational as used in this paper is adopted from the mathematical domain, more specifically from the relational algebra theory [17]. Relational algebra theory has received a lot of attention during the last four decades, since it is popularized by Codd [17] for database normalization. The basic idea of the relational algebra theory involves that a relationship (R) can exist of a given set of elements (Sn), visualized as follows: R = (S1, S2, ..., Sn) [17]. The elements (Sn) can be condition- or conclusion-facts. Most authors [17][18] represent element sets by applying two-dimensional arrays. In order to apply relational theory on business rules, one must be able to translate business rules to sets of relationships. Previous research has answered the question [9] whether current business rule modelling languages can be translated to unified views by applying relational algebra theory. Based on representational difference analysis, the authors show that the six most common business rules languages can be transformed to sets of relations [19][20]. The six languages, that were examined during this study are: If-Then business rules [21], Decision Tables [22][16], Decision Trees [23], Score Cards [24], Event, Condition & Action Business Rules [25], and Event Condition Action Alternative Business Rules [26]. By translating business rules to relations between specific sets of elements, normalization is made possible. Normalization is the process of removing partial dependencies and transitive dependencies [17][18].

III. Method Construction

A detailed explanation of the business rules normalization procedure can be found in [9]. However, to ground our research, a summary of the normalization procedure is provided in sub-section A. Subsequently, in sub-section B, the cost reduction analysis method for business rules normalization is described.

A. Business Rules Normalization Procedure

The process for business rules normalization consists of three activities. The results of these activities are 1) the transformation of business rules to the proper relational structure, and 2) the removal of partial and 3) the removal of transitive dependencies. The latter is realized by applying the third normal form, while the second normal form deals with partial dependencies and the 1st normal form deals with achieving the proper structure for business rules.

The first normal form is realized by duplicating the original business rules equally often as the amount of conclusion-facts that exist. In other words, all of the duplicated rules exist of all condition- and conclusion-fields. The difference between the original and new tables is that only one of the original conclusion-fields is now still a conclusion-field while the others are condition-fields. In order for a relation to be in the second normal form, all condition-facts must be functionally dependent on a conclusion-fact and adhere to the first normal form. Condition-facts, which are not fully dependent on the conclusion-fact must be deleted or added to another relationship. The second normal form reveals whether condition-facts are included that actually do not contribute to a conclusion. To realize the third normal form in business rule sets, condition-facts that are not fully dependent on the conclusion-fact (but on another condition fact) should be removed and added to a new relation. The new relation contains the removed condition-facts, as well as the conclusion-fact to which they are related. A relationship is established between two sets of relations by means of a secondary decision. After applying the third normal form, all specified relations do not contain any repeating groups, partial dependencies and transitive dependencies anymore.

To visualize the normalization procedure a decision tree can be used [27]. A decision tree consists of two types of nodes: 1) normalization decision nodes (squares) and 2) end nodes (circles), for example see Fig. 1. A normalization decision node represents the decision to further normalize the relationship. From a normalization decision node, two types of branches can emerge: 1) a stop branch, and 2) a normalization branch. A stop branch emerges when further normalization is not needed, consequently leading to an end node. When further normalization is needed, two or more normalization branches emerge from the decision node. These branches lead to other decision nodes representing the newly normalized relationships.

End nodes do not have further identification information, whereas normalization decision nodes do. Each node starts with the capital letter R, which is an abbreviation for relationship. The digit before the decimal point shows the number of the relationship. In case two digits are included before the comma, it designates a relationship resulting from another relationship. Furthermore, the digit after the decimal point indicates in what normalization form the relationship resides. In our example (see Fig. 1), the node R1,2 means that relationship 1 is in the second normal form. Moreover, the nodes R11,3 and R12,3 are both in the third normal form and are a relationship resulting from R1,2.

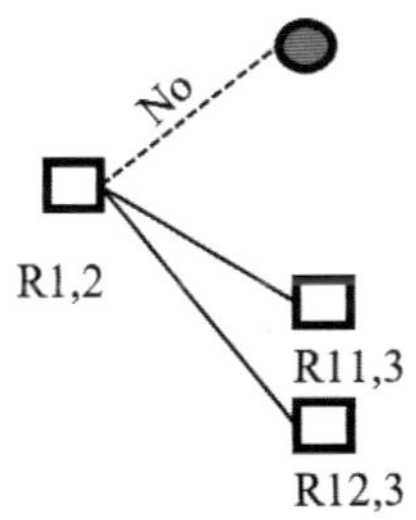

Figure 1. Decision Tree for Normalization

To demonstrate the business rules normalization procedure, a decision is normalized, which is based on the case study material that was collected, along the lines of the earlier work on the normalization of business rules by Zoet et al. [9]. In this example a process is considered in which the eligibility of a mortgage request is determined by the bank, see Fig. 2. The first step of the procedure is to determine the scope of the decision to normalize. During the process, visualized in Fig. 2, two analytical tasks are executed; 1) determine mortgage request eligibility and 2) discuss mortgage details with mortgage advisor. In this section, the focus is on the first analytical task. During this activity the eligibility of the mortgage request will be determined based on multiple criteria with regards to the personal situation of the applicant, the financial situation of the applicant, and the employment situation of the applicant. Based on the values of these criteria the mortgage request is either approved or rejected. When the mortgage request is approved, the applicant is invited to discuss mortgage details with a mortgage advisor from the bank.

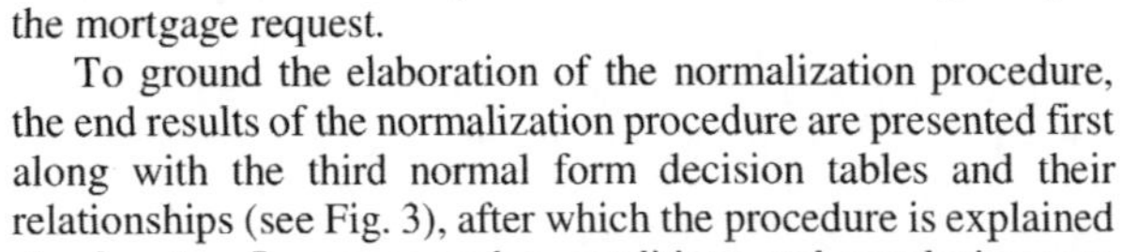

Figure 2. Determination process for the eligibility of mortgage requests

Now that the scope of the normalization procedure for this case is determined, the next step comprises the elicitation of the facts and their relationships used to determine the eligibility of the mortgage request.

To ground the elaboration of the normalization procedure, the end results of the normalization procedure are presented first along with the third normal form decision tables and their relationships (see Fig. 3), after which the procedure is explained step-by-step. In our examples, conditions and conclusions are shown without instantiated values. This is due to the fact that the case has to be reported in an anonymous way.

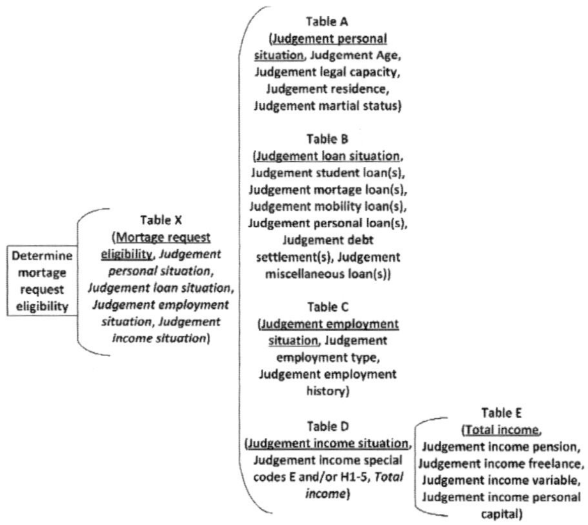

Figure 3. Overview of the normalized decision tables (derivation structure)

The elicitation of the facts and their relationships used to determine the eligibility of the mortgage request can be done in several ways. First, if the organization has already made the conditions (facts) explicit, written down in text or in a specific representation (i.e., decision trees, decision tables, domain models), this can serve as a starting point. When this is not the case, backward chaining can be applied to elicitate the facts and their relationships. With regards to our sample case, three decision tables were already present, see Fig. 4.

Table A: Judgement personal situation

Conditions				Conclusions
Judgement age	Judgement legal capacity	Judgement residence	Judgement marital status	Judgement personal situation
Value	Value	Value	Value	Value

Table B: Judgement loan situation

Conditions			Conclusions
Judgement student loan(s)	Judgement mortgage loan(s)	Judgement mobility loan(s)	Judgement loan situation
Value	Value	Value	Value
Judgement personal loan(s)	Judgement debt settlement(s)	Judgement miscellaneous loan(s)	
Value	Value	Value	

Table C: Judgement employment situation

Conditions				Conclusions	
Judgement income pension	Judgement income freelance	Judgement income variable	Judgement income Personal capital	Judgement income situation	Judgement employment situation
Value	Value	Value	Value	Value	Value
Judgement income special codes E and/or H1-5	Total income	Judgement employment type	Judgement employment history		
Value	Value	Value	Value		

Figure 4. Original and un-normalized decision tables

The next step of the procedure focuses on establishing the first normal form. The first normal form requires that every relation only contains one conclusion fact. In our case study this means that Table A and B comply with the requirement of the first normal form. Table C contains multiple conclusions and therefore needs to be transformed to comply with the first normal form. The transformation comprises the creation of two identical copies of Table C with the two different conclusion facts separated, one per table in Fig. 5.

Table C: Judgement employment situation

Condition				Conclusion
Judgement income pension	Judgement income freelance	Judgement income variable	Judgement income Personal capital	Judgement income situation
Value	Value	Value	Value	Value
Judgement employment history	Judgement employment type	Total income	Judgement income special codes E and/or H1-5	
Value	Value	Value	Value	

Condition				Conclusion
Judgement income pension	Judgement income freelance	Judgement income variable	Judgement income Personal capital	Judgement employment situation
Value	Value	Value	Value	Value
Judgement employment history	Judgement employment type	Total income	Judgement income special codes E and/or H1-5	
Value	Value	Value	Value	

Figure 5. First normal form decision tables

Table C: Judgement employment situation

Conditions		Conclusion
Judgement employment type	Judgement employment history	Judgement employment situation
Value	Value	Value

Table D: Judgement income situation

Conditions			Conclusion
Judgement income pension	Judgement income freelance	Judgement income variable	Judgement income situation
Value	Value	Value	Value
Judgement income personal capital	Judgement income special codes E and/or H1-5	Total income	
Value	Value	Value	

Figure 6. Second normal form decision tables

The second normal form is established when all relationships comply with the requirement for the first normal form, and additionally, when all conditions that are not fully dependent on the conclusion fact are removed. This is achieved by determining which of the conditions are irrelevant when formulating the conclusion and deleting these. In our case study, this affects all conditions labeled with the '*income*' statement that contribute to the '*Judgement income situation*' conclusion. The same holds for both the conditions '*Judgement employment type*' and '*Judgement employment history*', which contribute to the '*Judgement employment situation*' conclusion. This results into the following relationships, shown in Fig. 6.

The third normal form requires that all conditions only lead to the conclusion and do not derive another condition present in the decision. All conditions that are not fully dependent on the conclusion must be removed and added to a new decision. This is done by determining what conditions are not a determinant of the conclusion, but actually from another conclusion. In our case, the conditions '*Judgement income pension*', '*Judgement income freelance*', '*Judgement income variable*' and '*Judgement income personal capital*' from Table D are determining another conclusion, namely '*Total income*' and are therefore removed and defined as a separate decision (calculation), see Fig. 7, table E. All relationships are now specified in the third normal form, see Fig. 7.

Table C: Judgement employment situation

Conditions		Conclusion
Judgement employment type	Judgement employment history	Judgement employment situation
Value	Value	Value

Table D: Judgement income situation

Conditions		Conclusion
Judgement income special codes E and/or H1-5	Total income	Judgement income situation
Value	Value	Value

Table E: Calculate Total income

Conditions				Conclusion
Judgement income pension	Judgement income freelance	Judgement income variable	Judgement income personal capital	Total income
Value	Value	Value	Value	Value

Figure 7. Third normal form decision tables

B. *Cost Reduction Analysis Method for Business Rules Normalization*

Currently, in most normalization procedures the decision to normalize is generally based on intuitive flair. It remains uncertain whether the normalization effort is economically beneficial. For example, from an economic perspective, a business rule set, which only changes twice a year may not be beneficial to normalize.

Lee [28] and Westland [27] have conducted research towards the cost reduction of database normalization. Cost reductions realized by database normalization are 1) decreased machine time and 2) decreased data-inconsistencies (avoiding loss of business). The three main drivers of cost reduction are a) reduced anomalies, b) reduced storage requirements, and c) deteriorated response time. Anomalies that occur to data are: update-anomalies, insert-anomalies and deletion-anomalies

[17]. Previous research has shown that database normalization principles can be applied to business rule sets [9]. Taken previous statement into account, the following question arose: "*Can the cost reduction model for database normalization be adopted for business rules normalization?*"

Before adopting and adapting the model for business rules normalization, first the fit between the database determinants and business rules determinants has to be investigated. First, both business rules and data are updated, deleted, and inserted. Second, previous research [28] has shown that business rules normalization can also lead to fewer storage requirements, such as the case is with database normalization. Thirdly, deteriorated response time is an important issue since decision making in organizations is becoming increasingly complex with, for example, predictive analytics. As such, the formulas proposed by Lee [28] are adopted. However, before the formulas can be applied, the variables need to be adapted towards business rules. The remainder of this section will discuss the formulas provided by Lee altered towards business rules.

The cost reduction realized by normalization is calculated in four phases; 1) cost reduction due to reduced anomalies, 2) cost reduction due to reduced storage space, 3) cost increase due to increased join processing, and 4) comparing cost reduction due to reduced anomalies and cost reduction due to reduced storage space with the cost increase due to increased join processing.

Let ϕ be the cost reduction due to reduced anomalies, see also (1). ϕ is defined as:

$$\phi = \sum_{M=1}^{Nu} \alpha_M^U \lambda_M^U \acute{\omega}_M^U + \sum_{M=1}^{Ni} \alpha_M^I \lambda_M^I \acute{\omega}_M^I + \sum_{M=1}^{Nd} \alpha_M^D \lambda_M^D \acute{\omega}_M^D \tag{1}$$

Where Nu, Ni, and Nd are the number of updates, number of inserts and number of deletions, respectively, λ_M^U, λ_M^I and λ_M^D denote the frequency of the m'th update, the m'th insertion and the m'th deletion. The average number of business rules affected by the update, insertion and deletion are denoted by $\acute{\omega}_M^U$, $\acute{\omega}_M^I$ and $\acute{\omega}_M^D$. Furthermore, α_M^U, α_M^I and α_M^D denote the cost for each insert, update and deletion.

Let ψ be the cost reduction due to reduced storage space, see also (2). ψ is defined as:

$$\psi = B\acute{\omega} - B_x\,\acute{\omega}_x - B_y\acute{\omega}_y \tag{2}$$

Where B represents the storage cost per business rule in the current normalized situation. B_x and B_y denote the storage cost per business rule in the normalized situation + 1. The number of business rules stored in the current normalization situation is depicted by $\acute{\omega}$, while the normalized situation + 1 is depicted by $\acute{\omega}_x$ and $\acute{\omega}_y$.

Let Ω be the cost increase due to increased join processing, see also (3). Ω is defined as:

$$\Omega = \sum\nolimits^{\emptyset}_{\substack{M=1 \\ x,y\in o^m}} \ddot{\Upsilon}_m\, \mu_m\, \acute{\omega}_x\, \acute{\omega}_y \tag{3}$$

Where $\emptyset$ is the number of joins required to determine the conclusion of a specific decision. $\ddot{\Upsilon}_m$ denotes the cost per execution per business rule for join M. Moreover, μ_m represents the frequency of join M. The number of business rules in the business rule sets that are joined are expressed by $\acute{\omega}_x$ and $\acute{\omega}_y$. The business rule sets (x and y) between which the join M is realized, is denoted by $x, y, \in o^m$. Let O be the cost reduction from normalization form R (R1,2) to normalization form R+1 (R11,3). Summarizing, $O = \phi + \psi \geq \Omega$. O can be either positive or negative [3], [16]. If O is positive, then normalization should be applied.

IV. Experiment Setup

In our validation, an experiment on case study data is applied. This allows us to use data from an actual case while fully controlling the execution of the method and input variables. The method is applied to a mortgage decision of an Anonymous International Bank (AIB). Our choice to select this case study setting was based on two theoretical criteria. Firstly, the case had to provide a proper amount of business rules used to take a decision. The mortgage decision at AIB consisted of 1479 facts (conditions and conclusions), and 665 individual business rules. Secondly, the organization had to be willing to provide the financial details needed to perform the calculations. AIB agreed to this, however, with two conditions. The first condition implied that their name and financial data were altered when it would be published. The second condition entailed that the applied business rule sets were not completely published.

Figure 8. Photo impression 1 of normalized business rules

The evaluation, by means of conducting an experiment, was divided into three phases. Phase one was used to make the researchers familiar with the case parameters, by analyzing 133-pages with descriptions of decisions for completeness and accuracy. This phase resulted in the identification of multiple gaps. With the help of additional documentation and experts these gaps have been fixed. During the second phase, the business rules have been normalized according to our method. This normalization was done on paper, after which the results were presented on a big wall (see Fig. 8 and Fig. 9). During the normalization, additional gaps were identified. These gaps have been marked with "post-its", see Fig. 8 and Fig. 9. Again, with the help of additional documentation and experts, these gaps have been resolved.

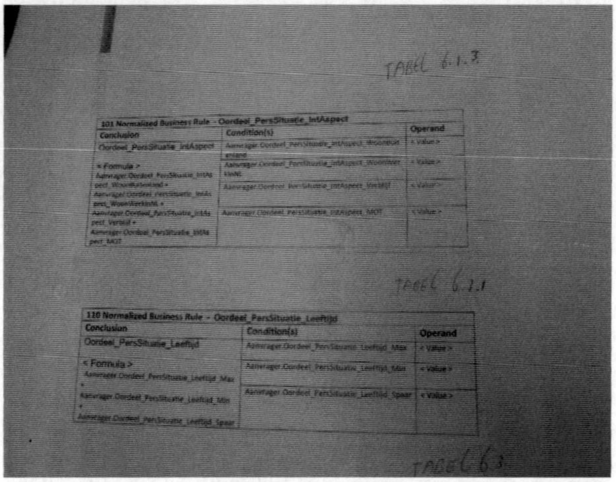

Figure 9. Photo impression 2 of normalized business rules

V. APPLICATION OF THE METHOD

To ground our method, three example scenarios are presented and elaborated. First, the determination of the cost reduction from normalization form R to normalization form R+1 for the business rule set "*personal situation of applicant*" is explained. It is part of the case described in the previous section. The data used in these examples are derived from the collected case data.

A. *Example one – small part of the mortgage case (positive benefits)*

The business rule set exists of 10 facts, 1 conclusion fact and 9 condition facts; see the left side of Fig. 10. The question that needs to be answered before normalizing this business rule set is: "*Does normalizing the business rule set from R to R+1 realize a cost reduction?*"

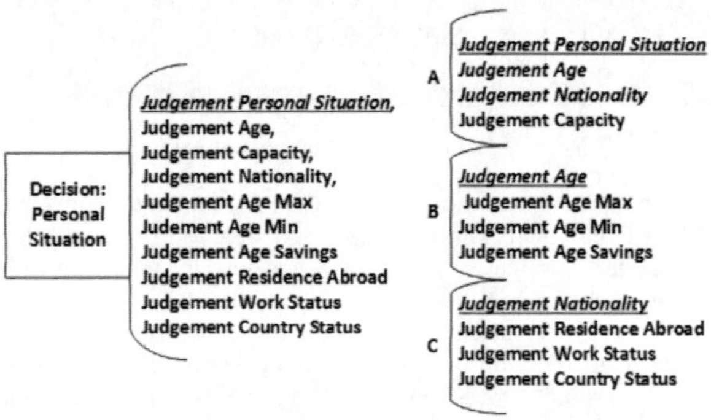

Figure 10. Normalization from the second to the third normal form

The decision personal situation is only affected by update and insert anomalies. For example, the facts "*judgment age*" and "*judgment age savings*" are updated regularly. Insert anomalies occur when new type of rules for age determination are inserted. The application of the method exist out of four phases 1) determine benefits in terms of reduced anomalies, 2) determine savings of storage requirements and 3) determine effect on response time, and 4) comparing cost reduction due to reduced anomalies and cost reduction due to reduced storage space with the cost increase due to increased join processing.

During phase one, three steps can be distinguished. *Step one:* determine the amount of update, insert and deletion operations on a specific business rule set. In our case, "update judgment age rules" and "insert age determination rules". For each identified operation type, it should be determined if the operation is affected by anomalies. If anomalies do not occur, normalization is not needed at all. If anomalies do occur, the frequency of each operation type and the number of business rules that are affected should be determined, this corresponds to step *two*. In this specific case $\lambda_1^U = 7$ (/per 2 weeks), and $\lambda_2^U = 6$ (/ per 2 weeks). Additionally, the number of business rules affected by each update needs to be determined. In this specific case $\acute{\omega}_1^U = 2$ and $\acute{\omega}_2^U = 1.5$. During step *three*, the cost of an anomaly should be determined. In this case, the cost of a person that adjusts the specific business rules $\alpha_1^U = €35.00$ per instance and $\alpha_2^U = €52.50$ per instance, see also (4). So, the total benefit due to reduced number of anomalies is:

$$\phi = (35 * 7 * 2) + (52.5 * 6 * 1.5) = €962.50 \quad (4)$$

The first step of phase two is to determine the results of the transformation in terms of business rule sets. In this case, one business rule set (personal situation) is divided into three business rule sets, namely: 1) judgment personal situation, 2) judgment age, and 3) judgment nationality. The results of the normalization are shown in Fig. 10. For each business rule set, the number of business rules must also be determined, in this case, respectively, $\acute{\omega} = 20$, $\acute{\omega}_x = 2$, $\acute{\omega}_y = 3$, $\acute{\omega}_z = 6$. During the second step, the cost per stored business rule must be determined. This needs to be determined for the current situation as well as for the post normalization situation. This information was retrieved from the information technology department, in this case, respectively, $B = €4$, $B_X = €0.5$, $B_y = €0.5$ and $B_z = €0.5$. Duplications are removed, thereby decreasing the number of individual business rules, see also (5). The total benefit due to reduced storage space is:

$$\psi = 20 * 4 - 2 * 0.5 - 3 * 0.5 - 6 * 0.5 = €74.50 \quad (5)$$

To form a decision, two joins are required in the new situation, so $\emptyset = 2$. The cost for each join $\ddot{Y}_m = 0.015$. The execution frequency of the join is 4000 per two weeks (μ_m), see also (6). The additional cost due to additional join operations (Ω) is therefore:

$$\Omega = 0.015 * 4000 * (2 + 3 + 6) = €660.00 \quad (6)$$

In conclusion, further normalization for the decision personal situation is recommended since:

$$(\phi = €962.50 + \psi = €74.50) > \Omega = €660.00$$

Assume a situation where λ_1^U = 7(/per 2 weeks), λ_2^U= 6 (/ per 2 weeks) are decreased to λ_1^U = 2(/per 2 weeks), λ_2^U = 2 (/ per 2 weeks). Applying these changes reduces ϕ from €962.50 to €446.25, which changes O from (ϕ = €962.50 + ψ = €73.00) > Ω = €660.00 to (ϕ = €446.25 + ψ = €73.00) < Ω = €660.00, in which case further normalization would not realize a cost reduction.

The above example has shown a situation in which normalization leads to cost reduction and therefore the normalization should occur. By changing two parameters, it is demonstrated that normalization would lead to a negative cost reduction, and therefore an increase in cost. Based on this, normalization should not be performed. To demonstrate such a situation another example is discussed in the next paragraph.

B. *Example two – (negative benefits)*

In this example, slightly altered case characteristics are defined as input for the formulas used to determine economic fit of further normalization of the decision "*Determine nationality code*". This decision is utilized to determine the code of the nationality of the applicant, for all products and services that the AIB Bank offer. Again, applying the method starts with determining the amount of update, insert and deletion operations on a specific business rule set, which is λ_1^U = 1 (/per 6 months), and λ_2^U = 2 (/ per 6 months), and λ_3^U = 1 (/per 6 months). These low amount of update, insertion, and deletion modifications are explained by the fact that the list of recognized countries by the UN, which the AIB bank adheres to, is rarely altered. Furthermore, the number of business rules affected by each update need to be determined, which is $\acute{\omega}_1^U$ = 2, $\acute{\omega}_2^U$ = 2, and $\acute{\omega}_3^U$ = 2.

Lastly, the cost of an anomaly, which represents the total cost to repair the business rule set to a state without the anomaly, should be determined. In this case, the cost of a person that adjusts the specific business rules α_1^U = €1.00 per instance. α_2^U = €2.00 per instance and α_3^U = €1.00 per instance. The costs are relatively low as modifying the list of country codes is a simple task for the AIB bank information specialist. The costs for insertion type modifications are doubled as a new country needs to be registered with several meta-data fields, which is not the case with regards to update and deletion type modifications.

With regards to storage space, the number of business rules must be determined, which is in this case $\acute{\omega}$ = 25, $\acute{\omega}_x$= 10, and $\acute{\omega}_y$= 10. Normalization of the decision to the first normal form leads to the removal of five redundant business rules. Additionally, the cost per stored business rule must be determined, in this case B = €0.75, B_X = €0.5, B_y = €0.5 and B_z = €0.5. In this particular case, the storage costs are €0.75 in the un-normalized form.

With regards to additional costs due an increase of join operations, the amount of joins to form a decision need to be determined, which is $\emptyset$ = 1. The cost for each join $\ddot{Y}_m$ = 0.00015. The execution frequency of the join is 500.000 per month (μ_m). The execution frequency is relatively high, which is caused by the generality of the decision and underlying business rules. Therefore, this particular decision is utilized in many other services by the AIB (i.e., different financial products like insurances and investment options) to determine the country of origin of an applicant.

To normalize from the un-normalized form to the first normal form, again the 1) total benefit due to reduced anomalies is calculated, see (7):

$$\phi = (1 * 1 * 2) + (2 * 2 * 2) + (1 * 1 * 2) = €12.00 \quad (7)$$

2) the total benefit due to reduced storage space, see (8):

$$\psi = 250 * 0{,}75 - 10 * 0.5 - 10 * 0.5 = €87.50 \quad (8)$$

3) the additional cost due to additional join operations, see (9):

$$\Omega = 0.00015 * 500.000 * (10 + 10) = €1.500{,}00 \quad (9)$$

Further normalization for the decision 'Determine nationality code' is not recommended since:

$$(\phi = €12 + \psi = €87.50) < \Omega = €1.500{,}00$$

C. *Example three – normalization of the decision "Judgement Age"*

Lastly, the method is demonstrated by evaluating the normalization steps with regards to the decision "*Judgement Age*". To ground the normalization, first the transformations from the 0th to 1st normal form, from the 1st to the 2nd normal form, and from the 2nd to the 3rd normal form are shown in Fig. 11.

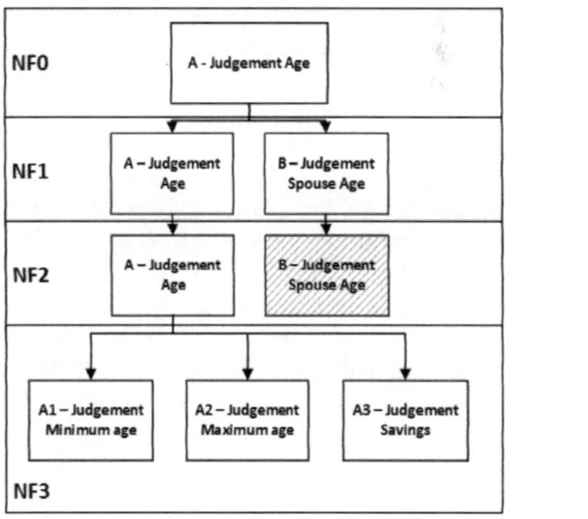

Figure 11. Normalization mapping of the decision "*Judgement Age*" of the mortgage case

First, the variables with regards to anomalies, storage space, and join operations need to be determined. In this specific case $\lambda_1^U = 70$ (/per 2 weeks), $\lambda_2^U = 70$ (/ per 2 weeks), and $\lambda_3^U = 70$ (/ per 2 weeks). Additionally, the number of business rules affected by each operation are $\acute{\omega}_1^U = 6$, $\acute{\omega}_2^U = 6$, and $\acute{\omega}_3^U = 6$. In this case, the cost of a person that adjusts the specific business rules α_1^U = €2.50 per instance, α_2^U = €2.50 per instance, and α_3^U = €2.50 per instance.

With regards to storage space, the number of business rules must be determined, which in this case is $\acute{\omega} = 54$, $\acute{\omega}_x = 54$, and $\acute{\omega}_y = 54$, where the latter two represent the tables that are copied as part of the normalization into the first normal form. Additionally, the cost per stored business rule must be determined, in this case B = €0.75, B_X = €0.5, B_y = €0.5 and B_z = €0.5. In this particular case, the storage costs are €0.75 in the un-normalized form, and €0.5 in the first, second and third normal form.

With regards to additional costs due an increase of join operations the amount of joins to form a decision need to be determined, which is $\emptyset = 1$ in case of the first normal form. The cost for each join $\ddot{Y}_m = 0.00015$. The execution frequency of the join is 5.000 per month (μ_m). Applying the method starts from the un-normalized decision table "*Judgement Age*" that includes all fact types in one single table towards the first normal form, see (10), (11) and (12):

$$\phi = (2.5 * 70 * 6) + (2.5 * 70 * 6) + (2.5 * 70 * 6) = \text{€ } 3.150{,}00 \quad (10)$$

$$\psi = 54 * 0.75 - 54 * 0.5 - 54 * 0.5 = \text{€ } \text{-}13.50 \quad (11)$$

$$\Omega = 0.00015 * 10000 * (54 + 54) = \text{€ } 162.00 \quad (12)$$

Further normalization for the decision "*Judgement Age*" is recommended since:

$$(\phi = \text{€}3.150.00 + \psi = \text{€-}13.50) > \Omega = \text{€}162.00$$

Normalization from the un-normalized decision table to the first normal form results in the creation of two separate decision tables, A "*Judgement Age*" and B "*Judgement Spouse*". The normalization of the case to the second normal form is continued. In this situation, only one join ($\emptyset = 1$) is required to derive a conclusion for the decision "*Judgement Age*". Furthermore, normalizing table A results in the removal of 18 business rules. Normalizing table B results in the removal of 52 business rules. The fact that 18 and 52 business rules were removed had the following reason. Analysis of the case showed that only six condition facts and one conclusion fact are related to table A. Furthermore, only two conditions and one conclusion fact are related to table B. Again, the same formulas are applied, see (13), (14) and (15):

$$\phi A = (2.5 * 70 * 6) + (2.5 * 70 * 6) + (2.5 * 70 * 6) = \text{€}3.150{,}00$$
$$\phi B = (2.5 * 70 * 6) + (2.5 * 70 * 6) + (2.5 * 70 * 6) = \text{€}3.150{,}00 \quad (13)$$

$$\psi = (54 + 54) * 0.5 - 36 * 0.5 = \text{€}36.00 \quad (14)$$

$$\Omega = 0.00015 * 10000 * (36 + 2) = \text{€}57.00 \quad (15)$$

Further normalization of both decisions are recommended since:

$$(\phi = \text{€}6.300.00 + \psi = \text{€}37{,}00) > \Omega = \text{€}56.00$$

The case is normalized to the second normal form since the benefits of the normalization are greater than the costs ($(\phi + \psi) > \Omega$). Normalizing tables A and B, which are in the second normal form, towards the third normal form results in the creation of an additional three tables. Table A will split into table A1 "*Judgement Minimum Age*", A2 "*Judgement Maximum Age*", and A3 "*Judgement Savings*". In the third normal form table A1 will contain 2 business rules, table A2 will contain 3 business rules and table A3 will contain 3 business rules as well. Table B will remain as is. To derive a conclusion for the decision "*Judgement Age*", two joins ($\emptyset = 2$) are required in the third normal form. Furthermore, normalization towards the third normal form results in a decrease of possible anomalies per type of operation. Also, the average number of affected business rules are reduced due to the reduced number of business rules in the tables due to normalization. Normalization from the second to the third normal form results in the following situation, see (16), (17) and (18):

$$\phi = (2.5 * 30 * 4) + (2.5 * 30 * 4) + (2.5 * 30 * 4) = \text{€}900.00 \quad (16)$$

$$\psi = (36 + 2) * 0.5 - (2 * 0.5 - 3 * 0.5 - 3 * 0.5) = \text{€}15.00 \quad (17)$$

$$\Omega = 0.00015 * 15000 * (2 + 3 + 3) = \text{€}18.00 \quad (18)$$

When transforming table B from the first to the second normal form it automatically adheres to the third normal form. Therefore, no further normalization can be applied. Further normalization for table A is recommended since:

$$(\phi = \text{€}900.00 + \psi = \text{€}15.00) > \Omega = \text{€}18.00$$

The resulting derivation structure for the decision "*Judgement Age*" in the context of its parent decision "*Judgement Personal Situation*" is depicted in Fig. 12.

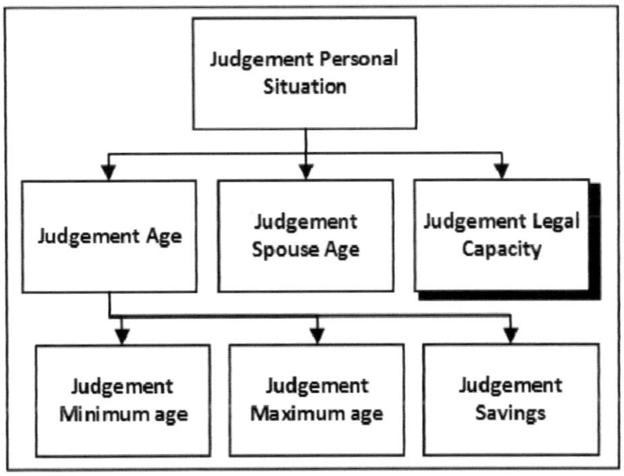

Figure 12. Normalization mapping of the decision "*Judgement Age*" of the mortgage case

VI. Experiment Validity

Internal validity threats, when conducting controlled experiments, can be classified into eight categories: 1) selection, 2) history, 3) maturation, 4) regression, 5) attrition, 6) testing, 7) instrumentation, and 8) additive and interactive effect of threats to internal validity [29]. We can ensure that the learning effect was not present during our case. Given the fact that all four subjects who have participated in the experiment already had executed the business normalization procedure before. Furthermore, the economical beneficially calculation itself was made explicit in Excel and required the respondents only to enter the variables. We cannot exclude learning during the transformation of the case information to the relational representation. Selection, history, maturation, attrition, instrumentation and additive and interactive effects of threats to internal validity are mitigated due to the application of a controlled experiment.

Outcomes of an experiment can vary when subjects, tasks or the environment changes. External validity is concerned with the extension of variations on such changes [29]. Our results were obtained from one decision: a mortgage decision. Therefore, we cannot claim that our conclusions are generally applicable. However, the answer to the research question itself is not influenced by the fact that only one case has been analyzed. Our experiment has been applied outside the project life cycle of AIB. We do not consider this as a threat to environmental validity since the entire procedure can be repeated during normal project life cycles.

VII. Conclusion, Discussion and Future Research

Business rules are a key denominator for a corporation's competitiveness. Thereby, the management of such business rules is increasingly becoming more important. However, business rules are becoming more and more complex affecting maintainability and transparency. In order to properly structure business rules, normalization is applied. Normalization increases control over insertion, update and deletion anomalies affecting storage requirements and response time. Currently, the normalization procedure does not take the costs and benefits of normalization into account but is based on intuitive flair. Therefore, we defined the research question: *How can business rules guiding decisions be factored such that economic beneficial manageability is realized?*

We presented a cost/benefit formula, which output provides guidelines for normalizing business rules. To determine the normalization business case, three variables were addressed 1) the number of anomalies a business rule set endures, 2) the storage space a business rule set requires, and the 3) deterioration in response time due to an increased amount of joins. By means of an experiment based on case study data from an international bank, we have shown the applicability of the model. Results show the importance of properly normalized decisions and what role the cost and benefit analysis plays in this. On the one hand, modelers should attempt to properly factor business rules. To achieve this factoring, the three normalization forms can be applied. On the other hand, practitioners should take cost and benefits of the organization into account when applying such normalizations forms. Currently, the transformation of the business rules is performed manually. However, in future research we aim to develop an approach that applies an algorithm to re-write (transform) business rules for applying the method presented in this paper. Furthermore, future research should also focus on further validating the method presented in this paper using more cases, and ideally, cases from different industries in various sizes to improve its generalizability.

From a practical perspective, our study provides product engineers, business rules modelers and (business) decision modelers with a method that can be used to normalize business rules based on an economic rationale. This rationale comprises the fit between storage space utilization, anomaly management and execution costs. The method will enable organizations to guard, on the one hand, execution costs and, on the other hand, performance of business rules.

The factor of speed to decide to normalize business rules is becoming increasingly important. Un-normalized business rules have a higher execution speed then normalized business rules, due to the additional join that have to be created. For a mortgage decision the reduction in speed is not that important since a few seconds extra doesn't affect the outcome for clients. For different decisions in banking, these few extra seconds (or mili- or microseconds) are a challenge. An example of an area where such decisions can be found is High Frequency Trading (HFT). Therefore, business rules in this area are usually not normalized. An interesting direction for future research would be to identify types or patterns of decisions that have an economic benefit for normalization and those that do not.

In this paper we focus on the normalization of decisions based on economic incentive. However, economic incentive is not the only factor that can affect the choice whether to normalize or not to normalize. For example, with the arrival of the GDPR regulation in May 2018 [30], transparency becomes an important factor for banks and other organizations. Normalization has an effect on the understandability (and therefore transparency) of the decision [31]. Therefore, the formula to normalize a decision and underlying business rules should be extended by a factor that takes into account transparency.

The current normalization procedure is based on relational algebra theory. However it focusses on highly explicit business rules. This means that the business rules are known upfront and can be fully written down. Other forms of decision logic that are based on relational algebra are Machine Learning algorithms and Neural networks. The method might apply machine learning and neural networks. However, the formulae needs to be properly adapted for such changes. This will be part of future research as well as taking into account the privacy factor for neural networks.

REFERENCES

[1] M. Zoet and K. Smit, "An Economic Approach to Business Rules Normalization," in *Proceedings of the Ninth International Conference on Information, Process, and Knowledge Management*, 2017, pp. 1–6.

[2] M. W. Blenko, M. C. Mankins, and P. Rogers, "The Decision-Driven Organization," *Harv. Bus. Rev.*, vol. 88, no. 6, pp. 54–62, Jun. 2010.

[3] M. Zoet, *Methods and Concepts for Business Rules Management*, 1st ed. Utrecht: Hogeschool Utrecht, 2014.

[4] R. G. Ross, "The business rule approach," *Computer (Long. Beach. Calif).*, vol. 36, no. 5, pp. 85–87, 2003.

[5] T. Morgan, *Business rules and information systems: aligning IT with business goals*. Addison-Wesley Professional, 2002.

[6] M. L. Nelson, R. L. Rariden, and R. Sen, "A lifecycle approach towards business rules management," in *Proceedings of the 41st Annual Hawaii International Conference on System Sciences*, 2008, pp. 113–123.

[7] S. Liao, "Expert system methodologies and applications—a decade review from 1995 to 2004," *Expert Syst. Appl.*, vol. 28, no. 1, pp. 93–103, Jan. 2004.

[8] A. Kovacic, "Business renovation: business rules (still) the missing link," *Bus. Process Manag. J.*, vol. 10, no. 2, pp. 158–170, 2004.

[9] M. Zoet, P. Ravesteyn, and J. Versendaal, "A structured analysis of business rules representation languages : Defining a normalisation form," *Proc. 22nd Aust. Conf. Inf. Syst.*, p. Paper 20, 2011.

[10] D. Arnott and G. Pervan, "A critical analysis of decision support systems research," *J. Inf. Technol.*, vol. 20, no. 2, pp. 67–87, 2005.

[11] I. Graham, *Business rules management and service oriented architecture: a pattern language*. John wiley & sons, 2007.

[12] M. L. Nelson, J. Peterson, R. L. Rariden, and R. Sen, "Transitioning to a business rule management service model: Case studies from the property and casualty insurance industry," *Inf. Manag.*, vol. 47, no. 1, pp. 30–41, Jan. 2010.

[13] Object Management Group, "Semantics of Business Vocabulary and Business Rules (SBVR) - V1.0," 2008.

[14] E. Eessaar, "The database normalization theory and the theory of normalized systems: finding a common ground," *Balt. J. Mod. Comput.*, vol. 4, no. 1, pp. 5–33, 2016.

[15] B. Von Halle and L. Goldberg, *The Decision Model: A Business Logic Framework Linking Business and Technology*. CRC Press, 2009.

[16] J. Vanthienen and M. Snoeck, "Knowledge factoring using normalisation theory," *Int. Symp. Manag. Ind. Corp. Knowl.*, pp. 27–28, 1993.

[17] E. F. Codd, "A relational model of data for large shared data banks," *Commun. ACM*, vol. 13, no. 6, pp. 377–387, 1970.

[18] W. Kent, "A Simple Guide to Five Normal Forms in Relational Database Theory," *Commun. ACM*, vol. 6, no. 2, pp. 120–125, 1983.

[19] M. Hubank and D. Schatz, "Identifying Differences in Mrna Expression by Representational Difference Analysis of Cdna," *Nucleic Acids Res.*, vol. 22, no. 5, pp. 5640–5648, 1994.

[20] M. zur Muehlen and M. Indulska, "Modeling languages for business processes and business rules: A representational analysis," *Inf. Syst.*, vol. 35, no. 4, pp. 379–390, Jun. 2010.

[21] R. Rivest, "Learning Decision Lists," *Mach. Learn.*, vol. 2, no. 3, pp. 229–246, 1987.

[22] R. Kohavi, "The Power of Decision Tables," in *Proceedings of the 8th European Conference on Machine Learning*, 1995, pp. 174–189.

[23] J. Boyer and H. Mili, *Agile business rule development: Process, Architecture and JRules Examples.* Springer Berlin Heidelberg, 2011.

[24] D. A. Morrow, E. M. Antman, A. Charlesworth, R. Cairns, S. A. Murphy, and E. de Lemos, J. A. Braunwald, "Timi Risk Score for St-Elevation Myocardial Infarction: A Convenient, Bedside, Clinical Score for Risk Assessment at Presentation," *Circulation*, vol. 10, no. 2, pp. 2031–2037, 2000.

[25] U. Dayal, A. P. Buchmann, and D. R. McCarthy, "Rules are objects too: a knowledge model for an active, object-oriented database system," in *Proceedings of the International Workshop on Object-Oriented Database Systems*, 1988, pp. 129–143.

[26] T. Heimrich and S. Günther, "Enhancing Eca Rules for Distributed Active Database Systems," in *NODe 2002 Web- and Database-Related Workshops*, 2003, pp. 199–205.

[27] C. Westland, "Economic Incentives for Database Normalization," *Inf. Process. Manag.*, vol. 28, no. 5, pp. 647–662, 1992.

[28] H. Lee, "Justifying Database Normalization: A Cost/Benefit Model," *Inf. Process. Manag.*, vol. 31, no. 1, pp. 59–67, 1995.

[29] W. R. Shadish, T. D. Cook, and D. T. Campbell, *Experimental and quasi-experimental designs for generalized causal inference*. Wadsworth Cengage learning, 2002.

[30] European Commission, "Protection of personal data - GDPR," 2017. [Online]. Available: http://ec.europa.eu/justice/data-protection/ [Accessed: 14-Aug-2017].

[31] B. Goodman and S. Flaxman, "EU regulations on algorithmic decision-making and a 'right to explanation,'" in *ICML workshop on human interpretability in machine learning (WHI)*, 2016.

Semantic Behavior Modeling and Event-Driven Reasoning for Urban System of Systems

Maria Coelho and Mark A. Austin
Department of Civil and Environmental Engineering,
University of Maryland, College Park, MD 20742, USA
E-mail: memc30@hotmail.com; austin@isr.umd.edu

Mark Blackburn
Stevens Institute of Technology,
Hoboken, NJ 07030, USA
E-mail: mblackbu@stevens.edu

Abstract—**Modern urban infrastructure systems are defined by spatially distributed network structures, concurrent subsystem-level behaviors, distributed control and decision making, and interdependencies among subsystems that are not always well understood. The study of the interdependencies within urban infrastructures is a growing field of research as the importance of potential failure propagation among infrastructures may lead to cascades affecting multiple urban networks. There is a strong need for methods that can describe the evolutionary nature of "system-of-systems" (SoS) as a whole. This paper presents a model of system-level interactions that simulates distributed system behaviors through the use of ontologies, rules checking, message passing mechanisms, and mediators. We take initial steps toward the behavior modeling of large-scale urban networks as collections of networks that interact via many-to-many association relationships. The prototype application is a collection of families interacting with a collection of school systems. We conclude with ideas for scaling up the simulations with Natural Language Processing.**

Keywords-Systems Engineering; Ontologies; Behavior Modeling; Mediator; Network Communication.

I. Introduction

This paper is concerned with the development of modeling abstractions, procedures, and prototype software for the behavior modeling of urban systems of systems with ontologies, rules and message passing mechanisms. It builds upon our previous work [1], [2] on distributed systems behavior modeling with semantic web technologies.

A. Problem Statement

The past century has been marked by outstanding advances in technology (e.g., the Internet, smart mobile devices, cloud computing) and the development of urban systems (e.g., transportation, electric power, waste-water facilities and water supply networks, among others) whose individual resources and capabilities are pooled together to create new, more complex systems that offer superior levels of performance, extended functionality and good economics. While end-users applaud the benefits that these systems of systems afford, model-based systems engineers are faced with a multitude of new design challenges that can be traced to the presence of heterogeneous content (multiple disciplines), network structures that are spatial, multi-layer, interwoven and dynamic, and behaviors that are distributed and concurrent.

Large-scale urban systems do not follow a standard cradle-to-grave lifecycle. Instead, the constituent domains within a city evolve over extended periods of time in response to external forces (e.g., the need for economic expansion) and disruptive events (e.g., the need for planning of relief actions in response to a natural disaster). In both cases, planning of urban operations is complicated by the large scale of modern cities, the large number of constituent behaviors, and multiple dimensions of interdependency among physical, cyber and geographic systems [3]. These facts are what makes cities "system of systems," rather than just systems, and they change the very nature of systems design and management. For example, in order for the communication among the participating urban domains to occur in an orderly and predictable way, designers need to pay attention to the boundaries (or interfaces) of domains [4]. Similar concerns exit for the replacement of aging infrastructure. In his article on the topic of complex system failure "How Complex Systems Fail," Cook discusses how complex systems are prone to catastrophic failure, due to the impractical cost of keeping all possible points of failure fully protected, and even identifying them all [5]. When part of a system fails, or perhaps an unexpected combination of localized failures occurs, there exists a possibility that the failure will cascade across interdisciplinary boundaries to other correlative infrastructures, and sometimes even back to the originated source, thus making highly connected systems more fragile to various kinds of disturbances than their independent counterparts. Figure 1 presents an overview of some generic interdependencies among key infrastructure sectors: oil and natural gas, electricity, transportation, water, and communications.

B. Scope and Objectives

In order to understand how cascading failures might be best managed, it is necessary to have the ability to model events and the exchange of data/information at the interdependency boundaries, and to model their consequent effect within a subsystems boundary. This points to a strong need for new capability in modeling and simulation of urban infrastructure systems as system-of-systems, and the explicit capture of infrastructure interdependencies. We envision such a system having an architecture along the lines shown in Figure 2, and eventually, tools such as OptaPlanner [7] providing strategies for real-time control of behaviors, assessment of domain resilience and planning of recover actions in response to severe events. This paper presents a model of distributed system-level behaviors based upon the combined use of ontologies, rules checking, and message passing mechanisms, and explores

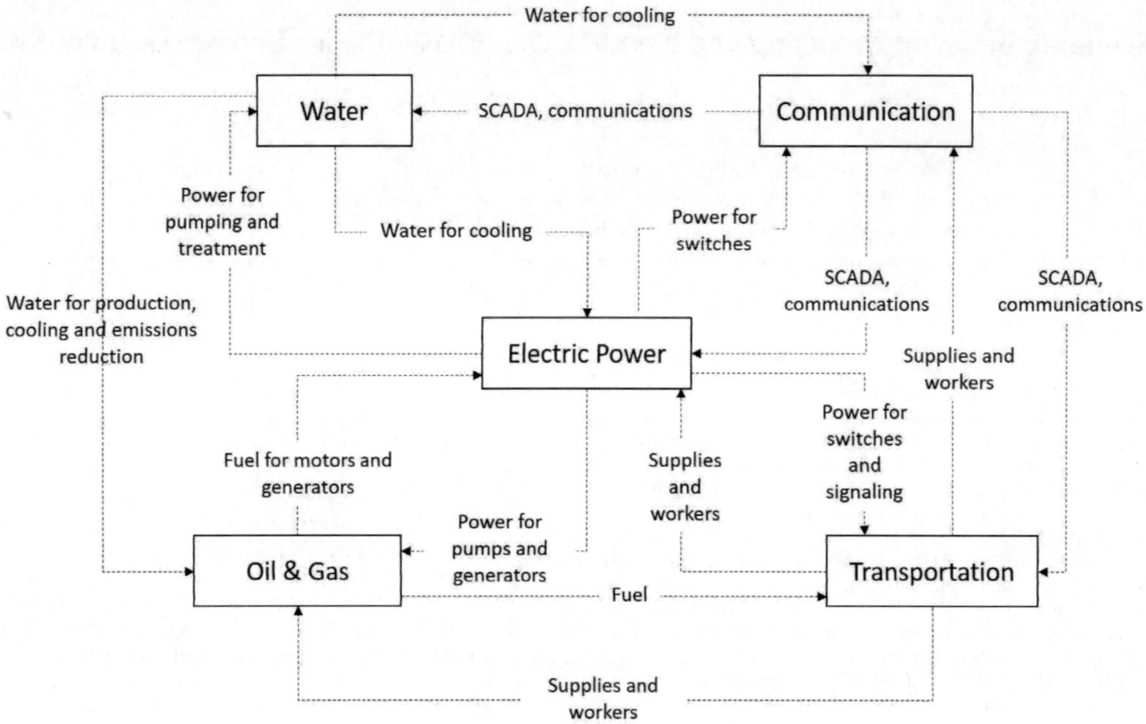

Figure 1. Illustration of the interdependent relationship among different infrastructures [6].

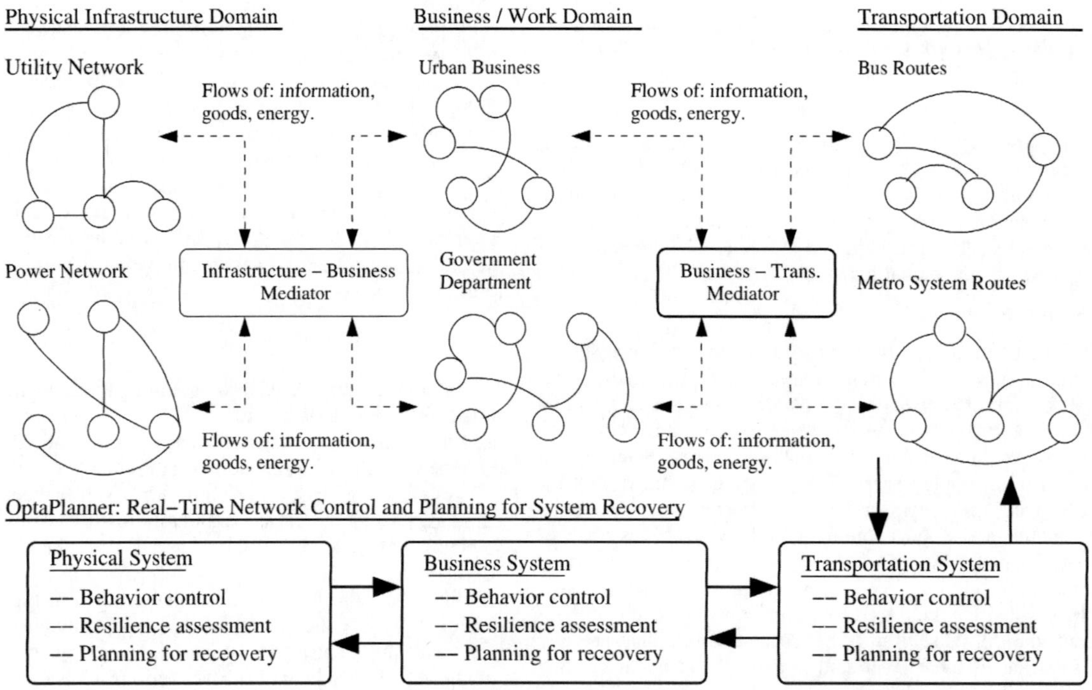

Figure 2. Architecture for multi-domain behavior modeling with many-to-many associations.

opportunities for modeling urban systems as collections of discipline-specific (or community) networks that will dynamically evolve in response to events. As illustrated in Figure 2, each community will have a graph that evolves according to a set of community-specific rules, and subject to satisfaction of constraints. The contributions of this paper are three-fold:

Contribution 1. We provide a framework for modeling concurrent, directed communication between all entities composing a system. The architecture builds upon the framework presented by Austin et al. [2], and in particular, extends the distributed behavior modeling capability from one-to-one association relationships among communities to many-to-many association relationships among networked communities.

As illustrated in Figure 3, one-to-one association relationships can be modeled with exchange of messages in a point-to-point communication setup.

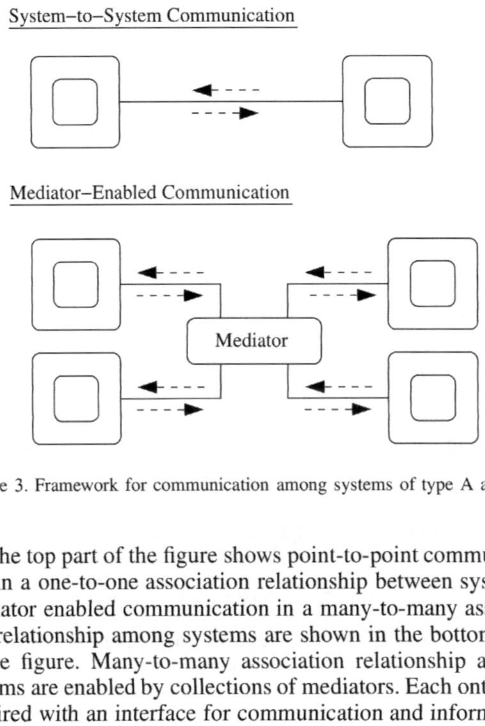

Figure 3. Framework for communication among systems of type A and B.

The top part of the figure shows point-to-point communication in a one-to-one association relationship between systems. Mediator enabled communication in a many-to-many association relationship among systems are shown in the bottom half of the figure. Many-to-many association relationship among systems are enabled by collections of mediators. Each ontology is paired with an interface for communication and information exchange with other ontologies. From a communications standpoint, this architectural setup is simpler than what is commonly found in multi-hop routing of messages in wireless sensor networks.

Contribution 2. We employ a novel use of software design patterns and Apache Camel [8] [9], to allow communication management in the urban system of systems framework. The visitor design pattern is also implemented to allow for data retrieval.

Contribution 3. We explore mechanisms for incorporating notions of space and time in event-driven reasoning processes for urban decision making.

The remainder of this paper proceeds as follows: Section II covers related research that has been done in critical infrastructure simulation. Section III explains how Semantic Web technologies [10] can be employed for semantic modeling and rule-based reasoning. Section IV explains the advantages of constructing a model with time and space reasoning. Section V describes several aspects of our work in progress, including: (1) Distributed system behavior modeling with ontologies and rules, and (2) Use of mediators for behavior modeling of distributed systems having many-to-many association relationships among connected networks. We describe the software architecture for an experimental platform for assembling ensembles of community graphs and simulating their discrete, event-based interactions. In Section VI we exercise this capability with an application involving collections of families interacting with multiple school systems. Domain-specific ontologies are developed for family and school system domains, which, in turn, import spatial (geometry) ontologies and rules [11] [12]. We conclude with ideas for scaling up the simulations with Natural Language Processing (NLP).

II. Related Work

A. Critical Infrastructure

Experience over the past decade with major infrastructure disruptions, such as the 2011 San Diego blackout, the 2003 Northeast blackout, and Hurricane Irene in 2011, has shown that the greatest losses from disruptive events may be distant from where damages started. For example, Hurricane Katrina disrupted oil terminal operations in southern Louisiana, not because of direct damage to port facilities, but because workers could not reach work locations through surface transportation routes and could not be housed locally because of disruption to potable water supplies, housing, and food shipments [13]. Interdependencies constitute a significant dimension for understanding system vulnerability. Examples of vulnerabilities where systems could be brought down are an important basis for identifying interdependencies and focusing on those that are critical. Using data provided by references [14], [15] and [16], Table I provides some examples of faults that propagate through interdependency relationships of different critical infrastructure sectors.

In its October 1997 report to the U.S. President, the President's Commission on Critical Infrastructure Protection identified the nation's eight critical infrastructures. It recognized the importance that interdependencies play in their continuous and reliable operation, as well as the increased security concerns and risks associated with them [17]. Although interdependencies are a complex and difficult problem to analyze, over the past twenty years increased effort by the operational, research and development, and policy communities has led to improvements in our ability to identify and understand interdependencies among infrastructures, and their influence on infrastructure operations and behavior. As a case in point, Rinaldi and co-investigators [3] have proposed a multi-dimensional taxonomy to frame the major aspects of interdependencies: types of interdependencies, infrastructure environment, coupling and response behavior, infrastructure characteristics, types of failures, and state of operations. These dimensions point to the need for development of a comprehensive architecture for interdependency modeling and simulation. Many models and simulations exist for individual

	Energy: Oil and Gas	Energy: Electricity	Transportation	Water	Communication
Energy: Oil and Gas		No fuel to operate power plant motors and generators	No fuel to operate transport vehicles	No fuel to operate pumps and treatment. Gas pipeline failure located beneath roads may contaminate water pipeline also located beneath roads	No fuel to maintain temperatures for equipment; no fuel to backup power
Energy: Electricity	No electricity for extraction and transport (pumps, generators, control systems)		No power for traffic lights, rail systems, street lights. Passengers may be trapped inside trains. Air transport may become compromised due to to the loss of communications and unlit runways.	No electric power to operate pumps and treatment leading to potential water quality issues and pumping issues in buildings. No power to operate flood protection systems.	No energy to run cell towers and other transmission equipment
Transportation	Delivery of supplies and workers interruption	Delivery of supplies and workers interruption		Delivery of supplies and workers interruption	Delivery of supplies and workers interruption
Water	No water available for production, cooling, and emissions reduction	No water available for production, cooling, and emissions reduction. Water pipeline failure located beneath roads may damage power lines located beneath and above roads	No water for vehicular operation. Water pipeline failure located beneath roads may interrupt traffic.		No water available for equipment cooling. Water pipeline failure located beneath roads may damage cables and underground wiring also located beneath roads, and above ground networks aligned with roads
Communication	Inability to detect breakages and leaks. Remote control of operations interruption	Inability to detect and maintain operations and electric transmission	Inability to identify and locate disabled vehicles, rails, and roads. No provision of user service information.	Inability to detect and control water supply and quality	

TABLE I. Summary of urban faults propagated by interdependencies between critical infrastructure systems.

infrastructure behavior, but simulation frameworks that allow for the coupling of multiple interdependent infrastructures to address infrastructure protection, mitigation, response, and recovery issues are only beginning to emerge.

B. Urban Interdependence Simulators

Pederson et al. [18] have compiled a survey on contemporary research on critical infrastructure modeling and simulation. This study showed a wide variety of ideas proposed in recent years, and observed that the vast majority of these recently implemented frameworks are based on agent-based technology. In an effort to overcome some of the limitations associated with agent-based frameworks, such as scalability and distorted results, Rahman et al. [19] proposed a new type of framework for simulating infrastructure interdependencies. The proposed model captures physical interdependencies among different critical infrastructures using precise mathematical expression. Each entity and interaction between infrastructures is mapped to a single equivalent semantic. In this way, components defined in physical layer can interact with the decision making layer through event forwarding mechanisms.

C. Urban System Ontologies

A detailed discussion the use of ontologies in urban development projects can be found in Falquet, Metral, Teller and Tweed [20]. Ontologies have been developed for the geographic information sector, to model interconnections (mediators) among urban models, and to describe urban mobility processes. Extensive studies have been conducted on the development of ontologies for the geography markup language (GML) and CityML, the XML markup language for cities [21].

As part of the recent interest in Smart Cities, researchers have proposed so-called smart city ontologies. A close examination reveals that they contain an exhaustive list of things you might find in a smart city, and proposals for relationships among things, but are otherwise not smart at all.

Our viewpoint is that ontologies (including classes and their associated data and object properties) need to be developed alongside rules, and that the resulting semantic modeling systems need to be executable and capable of event-driven processing. A notable effort in this direction is the DogOnt ontology and rules for statechart behavior modeling of devices in home automation [22].

III. Semantic Modeling and Rule-based Decision Making

A. Framework for Semantic Modeling

Model-based systems engineering development is an approach to systems-level development in which the focus and primary artifacts of development are models, as opposed to documents. As engineering systems become increasingly complex the need for automation arises [23]. A tenet of our work is that methodologies for strategic approaches to design will employ semantic descriptions of application domains, and use ontologies and rule-based reasoning to enable validation of requirements, automated synthesis of potentially good design solutions, and communication (or mappings) among multiple disciplines [24] [25] [26].

The upper half of Figure 4 complements Figure 2, and pulls together the different pieces of the proposed architecture for distributed system behavior modeling with ontologies, rules, mediators and message passing mechanisms. On the left-hand side, the textual requirements are defined in terms of mathematical and logical rule expressions for design rule checking. Engineering models will correspond to a multitude of graph structure and composite hierarchy structures for the system

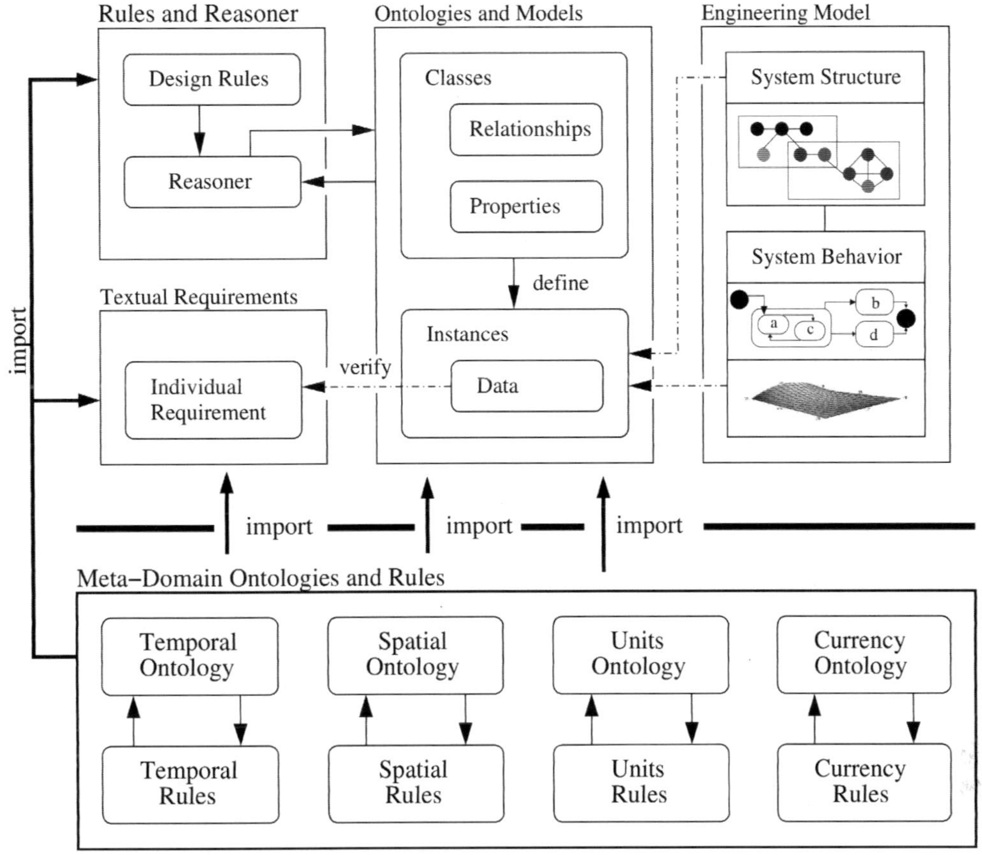

Figure 4. Framework for implementation of semantic models using ontologies, rules, and reasoning mechanisms (Adapted from Delgoshaei, Austin and Nguyen [12]).

structure and system behavior. Behaviors will be associated with components. Discrete behavior will be modeled with finite state machines. Continuous behaviors will be represented as the solution to ordinary and partial differential equations. Ontology models and rules will glue the requirements to the engineering models and provide a platform for simulating the development of system structures, adjustments to system structure over time, and system behavior. In a typical application, collections of ontologies and rules will be developed for the various domains (see, for example, Figures 1 and 2) that participate in the system structure and system behavior models.

The use of Semantic Web technologies for rule checking has several key benefits [27], [28]: (1) Rules that represent policies are easily communicated and understood, (2) Rules retain a higher level of independence than logic embedded in systems, (3) Rules separate knowledge from its implementation logic, and (4) Rules can be changed without changing source code or the underlying model. A rule-based approach to problem solving is particularly beneficial when the application logic is dynamic (i.e., where a change in a policy needs to be immediately reflected throughout the application) and rules are imposed on the system by external entities. Rules can be developed to resolve situations of conflict and/or competing objectives – such strategies use notions of fairness to prevent deadlocks in the system operation. All three of these conditions apply to the design and management of urban systems.

B. Working with Jena and Jena Rules

Our experimental software prototypes employ Apache Jena and Jena Rules. Apache Jena [29] is an open source Java framework for building Semantic Web and linked data applications. Jena provides APIs (application programming interfaces) for developing code that handles RDF (resource description framework), RDFS, OWL (web ontology language) and SPARQL (support for query of RDF graphs). The Jena rule-based inference subsystem is designed to allow a range of inference engines or reasoners to be plugged into Jena. Jena Rules is one such engine.

Jena Rules employs facts and assertions described in OWL to infer additional facts from instance data and class descriptions. As we will soon see in the case study example, domain-specific ontologies can import and use multi-domain (or cross-cutting) ontologies, rules can be distributed among domains (which is at odds with ideas within the Semantic Web community that ontologies should be tightly coupled to ontologies), and rules can be written to respond to events that involve (or affect) reasoning among multiple domains. Such inferences result in event-driven structural transformations to the semantic graph model.

Jena also provides support for the development of builtin functions that can link to external software programs and streams of data sensed in the real world, thereby extending its reasoning capability beyond what is possible with the basic data types provided in OWL.

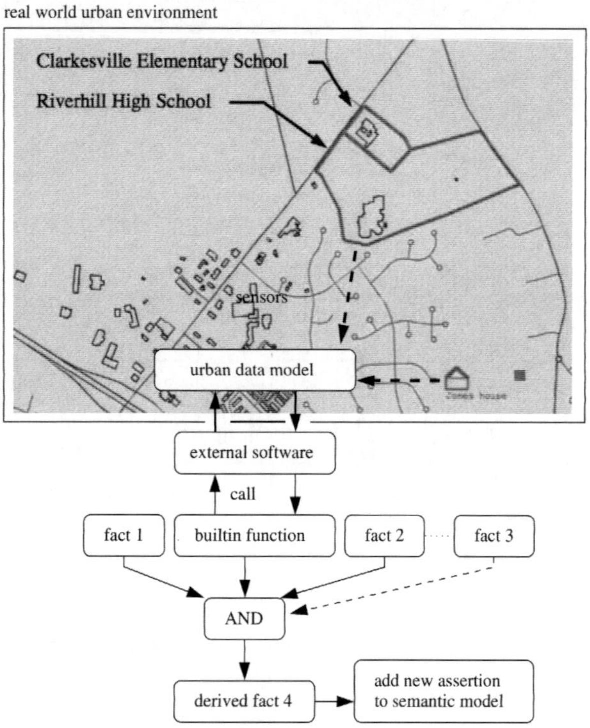

Figure 5. Framework for forward chaining of facts and results of builtin functions to new assertions (derived facts).

Figure 5 shows, for example, the essential details for forward and backward chaining driven by data collected from an urban setting. To combat the lack of support for complex data types, such as those needed to represent data for spatial and temporal reasoning, we adopt a strategy of embedding the relevant data in character strings, and then designing builtin functions and external software that can parse the data into spatial/temporal models, and then make the reasoning computations that are required.

C. Data-Driven Generation of Semantic Models

In order to build the semantic models presented in Figure 4, there needs to be a pathway from the specification of ontologies and rules to population of the semantic graphs with individuals representing various forms of urban data.

As illustrated along the left-hand side of Figure 6, the process begins with development of software for an abstract ontology model (i.e., AbstractOntologyModel). AbstractOntologyModel contains software for the domain-neutral specification and handling of ontologies and rules. Domain-specific Jena Models are an extension of the abstract model. They are

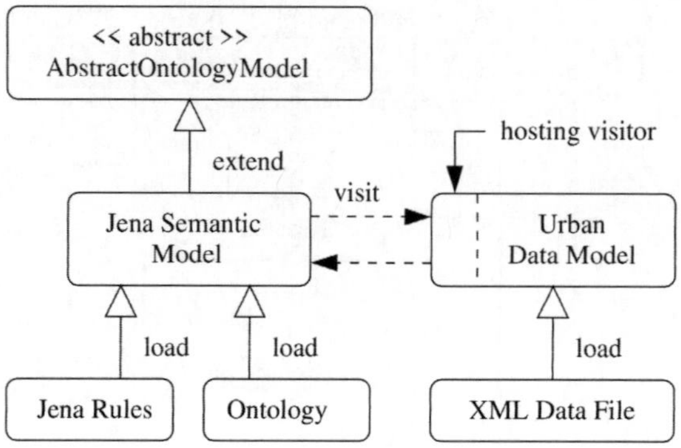

Figure 6. Data-driven approach to generation of individuals in semantic graphs.

capable of systematically assembling semantic graphs, transforming the graph structure with rules, and querying the graph structure. Next, data is imported into Java Object data models using JAXB, the XML binding for Java. After the ontologies and rules have been loaded into the Jena Semantic Model, the semantic model creates instances of the relevant OWL ontologies by visiting the urban data models and gathering information on the individuals within a particular domain. Once the data has been transferred to the Jena Semantic Model and used to create an ontology instance, the rules are applied.

It is important to note that while Figure 6 implies a one-to-one association relationship between semantic graphs and data, in practice a semantic graph model might visit multiple data models to gather individuals.

IV. Reasoning with Time and Space

Urban decision making processes are nearly always affected by notions of time and space, which have universal application across domains.

A. Reasoning with Time

Temporal logic describes how a system changes over time, and apply when we want to know not what is true, but when? For example, temporal logic allows us to determine if the schools shown in Figure 5 have an age beyond their working lifetime, and if the young residents of the house are old enough to attend the local schools.

Formal theories for reasoning with points and intervals of time are covered by Allen's temporal interval calculus [30], [31]. Notions of (calendar) time are supported as a data type in Jena. Ontologies of time can be loaded into Jena. Procedures for reasoning about points and intervals of time can be implemented in Jena Rules.

B. Reasoning with Space.

Spatial logic is concerned with regions and their connectivity, allowing one to address issues of the form: what is true, and where? Figure 5 shows, for example, the border for two schools and a house in the local neighborhood. Spatial reasoning mechanisms allows us to verify if the schools share a boundary and/or if the house is within the school zone.

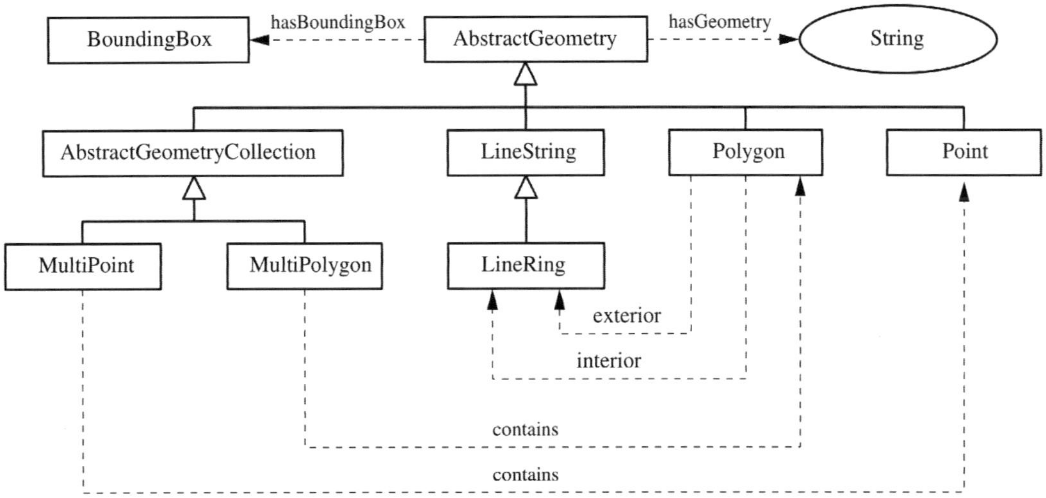

Figure 7. Abbreviated representation of spatial (geometry) ontology and associated data and object properties.

Formal theories for reasoning with space – points, lines, and regions – are covered by region connected calculus [32]. A robust implementation of two-dimensional spatial entities and associated reasoning procedures is provided by the Java Topology Suite (JTS) [33].

An important detail of implementation implied by Figure 5 is the need for backend reasoning procedures associated with JTS to operate independently of the source domains. This is achieved with the spatial (geometry) ontology and associated data and object properties shown in Figure 7. High-level classes – abstract concepts – are provided for entities that represent singular geometry (e.g., AbstractGeometry) and groups of entities (e.g., AbstractGeometryCollection). Specific types of geometry (e.g,, Polygon, MultiPoint) are organized into a hierarchy similar to the Java implementation in JTS. The high-level class AbstractGeometry contains a Datatype property, hasGeometry, which stores a string representation of the JTS geometry. For example, the abbreviated string "POLYGON ((0 0, 0 5, ... 0 0))" shows the format for pairs of (x,y) coordinates defining a two-dimensional polygon. Within Jena Rules, families of builtin functions can be developed to evaluate the geometric relationship between pairs of spatial entities (e.g., to determine whether or not a point is contained within a polygon) and return a boolean result. The latter is fact in the reasoning process shown in Figure 5.

C. Reasoning with Time and Space.

Logics for time and space can be combined allowing one to address issues of the form: We want to know when and where something will be (or has been) true? Spatio-temporal reasoning procedures in geoinformatics can be used for predictive (i.e., looking forward in time) and historical (i.e., looking back in time) purposes. For example, Figure 5 shows there are now two schools in our geographical area of interest. But what about 50 years ago – perhaps it was farmland back then?

V. Distributed System Behavior Modeling

A. Distributed System Behavior Modeling

Urban systems have decentralized system structures. No decision maker knows all of the information known to all of the other decision makers, yet as a group, they must cooperate to achieve system-wide objectives. Communication and information exchange are important to the decision makers because communication establishes common knowledge among the decision makers which, in turn, enhances the ability of decision makers to make decisions appropriate to their understanding, or situational awareness, of the system state, its goals and objectives. While each of the participating disciplines may have a preference toward operating their urban domain as independently as possible from the other disciplines, achieving target levels of performance and correctness of functionality nearly always requires that disciplines coordinate activities at key points in the system operation. This is especially important for the planning of relief actions in response to natural disasters.

Until very recently infrastructure management systems did not allow a manager of one system to access the operations and conditions of another system. Therefore, emergency managers would fail to recognize this interdependence of infrastructures in responding to an incident, a fact recognized by The National Strategy for the Physical Protection of Critical Infrastructures and Key Assets [34]. In such situations, where there is no information exchange between interdependent systems, interdependencies can lead to cascading disruptions throughout the entire system in unexpected, undesirable and costly ways. The objective of this research effort is to explore opportunities for overcoming these limitations.

B. Software Architecture

Figure 8 shows the software architecture for distributed system behavior modeling for collections of graphs that have dynamic behavior defined by ontology classes, relationships among ontology classes, ontology and data properties, listeners, mediators and message passing mechanisms. The abstract

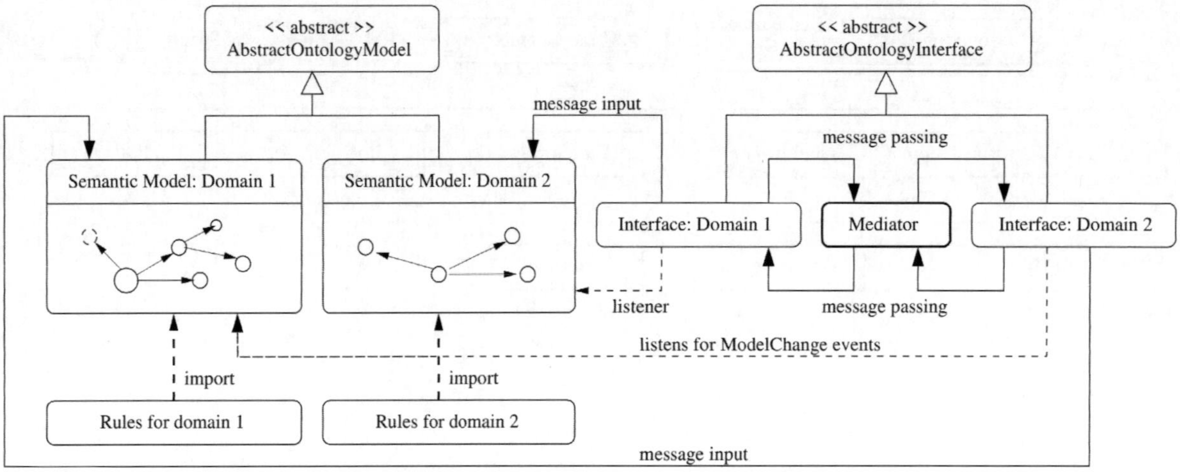

Figure 8. System architecture for distributed system behavior modeling with ontologies, rules, mediators and message passing mechanisms.

ontology model class contains concepts common to all ontologies (e.g., the ability to receive message input).

Domain-specific ontologies are extensions of the abstract ontology classes. They add a name space and build the ontology classes, relationships among classes, properties of classes for the domain. In an urban setting, individual domain ontologies may be constructed for infrastructure systems such as water, communications, oil and gas, transportation, and electric power systems shown in Figure 1. Instances (see Figure 4) are semantic objects in the domain. By themselves, the ontologies provide a framework for the representation of knowledge, but otherwise, cannot do much and really aren't that interesting. This situation changes when domain-specific rules are imported into the model and graph transformations are enabled by formal reasoning and event-based input from external sources.

C. Distributed Behavior Modeling with Ontologies and Rules

Distributed behavior modeling involves multiple semantic models, multiple sets of rules, mechanisms of communication among semantic models, and data input, possibly from multiple sources. We provide this functionality in our distributed behavior model by loosely coupling each semantic model to a semantic interface. Each semantic interface listens for changes to the semantic domain graph and when required, forwards the essential details of the change to other domains (interfaces) that have registered interest in receiving notification of such changes. They also listen for incoming messages from external semantic models. Since changes to the graph structure are triggered by events (e.g., the addition of an individual; an update to a data property value; a new association relationship among objects), a central challenge is design of the rules and ontology structure so that the interfaces will always be notified when exchanges of data and information need to occur. Individual messages are defined by their subject (e.g., report receipt confirmation), a source and a destination, and a reference to the value of the data being exchanged. The receiving interface will forward incoming messages to the semantic model, which, in turn, may trigger an update to the graph model. Since end-points of the basic message passing infrastructure are common to all semantic model interfaces, it makes sense to define it in an abstract ontology interface model.

VI. Case Study Problem

Whilst there are a number of definitions for critical national infrastructure, from a city perspective the concept of critical infrastructure is not well defined. Boyes et al. [35] proposed that criticality in a city's context addresses elements necessary for the delivery of essential services to the populace who are resident and/or work in the city and that impact is focused at city rather than national level. The critical infrastructure must encompass both the citys normal operating state, and its ability to the basic facilities, services, and installations needed for the functioning of a community or society. This includes transportation and communications systems, water and power lines, and public institutions including schools, post offices and prisons.

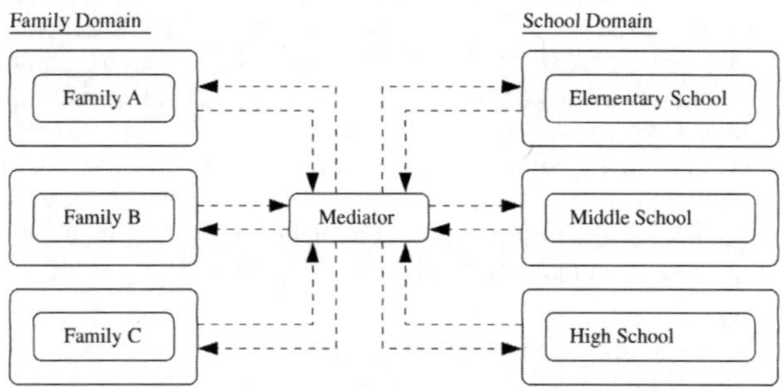

Figure 9. Framework for communication among multiple families and schools enabled by a mediator.

To illustrate the capabilities of our experimental architecture, we now present the essential details of a simulation framework for event-driven behavior modeling of a critical urban system: education. In this case study set up, a multiplicity of families interact with schools embedded in an urban environment. Interactions among groups of families and schools is governed by ontologies, rules, and exchange of information as messages, which pass through and are managed by a mediator (see Figure 9). The decision making framework includes reasoning with spatial attributes of families and schools, and time-driven events.

A. Scenario for Family-School System Behavior Modeling

We now illustrate the capabilities of the proposed modeling abstractions by working step by step through the following scenario of interactions between families and the school system: (1) Determine eligibility for enrollment, (2) Complete enrollment form, (3) Receive enrollment confirmation, (4) Report period starts, (5) Send reports home, and (6) Receive parent signature. Evaluation of Step 1 involves combinations of spatial and temporal reasoning. Steps 2 through 6 focus on the exchange and processing of message among the participating urban domains.

Figure 10 is a detailed view of the connectivity relationships and flows of data/information in the family-school case study scenarios. The enrollment process involves an exchange of data from a family to the corresponding school in which the child should enroll. Then, and some point later in time, the school system sends a school report home.

B. Framework for Family-School-Urban Interactions

We begin by abstracting the urban components of the problem from consideration, and simply focus on the model for family school interactions.

Figure 11 shows a schematic of the schools in the Columbia-Clarksville Area (shown on left) and fictitious school zone boundaries (shown on right-hand side). As every parent knows, the enrollment process involves the exchange of specific information between schools and families. The school system only allows enrollment of students who meet the age requirements, and live within the school zone jurisdiction. Once the child is accepted the school system takes over. They decide when school reports will be sent home, and if the child is entitled to school bus service. Some of these determinations are done by comparing spatial entities, such as family addresses, school addresses, and school zone boundaries. Addresses are defined by latitude and longitude coordinates; therefore, a simple calculation using the latitudes and longitudes of two addresses can determine the distance between them. Similarly, school zones are defined by a collection of latitude and longitude coordinates that compose a polygon geometric shape. Any algorithm that solves the point-in-polygon (PIP) problem can determine if the address lies within the school zone boundaries. This work uses OpenStreetMap tool to retrieve the latitudes and longitudes necessary for the these comparisons. Figure 10 is an instantiation of the concepts introduced in Figure 8 and shows the software architecture for a family-school interaction.

C. Instantiating Semantic Models with Data

In this problem setup, the information to be exchanged between ontologies is stored as key/value pairs in XML datafiles. The key (e.g. "first name", "citizenship", etc.) identifies, and is used to retrieve the values (e.g., "Mark", "New Zealand", etc.). Textual content stored in the XML datafiles is extracted and instantiated as class instances in the data model. Our prototype implementation employs JAXB technology for the creation of data models as shown in Figure 12. We then systematically visit each element of the data model (the code is implemented as a visitor software design pattern) and create instances of the ontology classes. The latter are called Individuals), and they are laden with the data from XML files.

D. Family and School System Ontologies

Our application employs OWL to define ontologies as collections of classes, data and object properties, and the relationships among them.

Figure 13 shows the relationship between classes in the family ontology. Male, Female, Child and Student are subclasses of class Person. The class Boy is a subclass of class Male. The class Person has properties that get inherited by all subclasses such as hasAge, hasWeight, hasBirthdate, hasFamilyName, has FirstName, hasSocialSecurityNo, hasCitizenship. The class Student has properties associated with school enrollment, such as livesInSchoolZoneOf, attendsPreschool, attendsSchool, attend sElementarySchool, attendsMiddleSchool, attendsHighSchool, and hasReportFrom. The class family has property hasFamilyName, and the class Address has proper ties hasLatitude and hasLongitude. Other properties such as hasFamilyMember, belongsToFamily, hasFather, hasSon, hasDaughter, and hasAddress define relation ships that hold between objects.

In the same fashion, an ontology can be constructed for the school system. Figure 14 shows the relationship between classes in a school ontology. Elementary School, Middle School and High School are subclasses of School. Grades 1 through 12 are subclasses of Grade. A school has properties that get inherited by all school subclasses such as hasName. A grade also has properties that get inherited by all grade subclasses such as hasEnrollment. A student has properties similar to the ones dened in the classes Person and Student in the family ontology such as hasFirstName, hasFamilyName, hasBirthDate, hasAge, hasSocialSecurityNo, attendsElemntarySchool, attendsMiddleSchool, attendsHighSchool, and hasReport. In addition, it also has properties such as eligibleForSchoolBus and willArriveLate. The class Address also follows the same pattern of the family ontology, with properties hasLatitude and hasLongitude. The classes Calendar and Event are included in this ontology to provide temporal behavior modeling capabilities. The class Event has properties hasStartTime and hasEndTime. The class Bus has property hasArrivalTime. Other properties such as hasGrade, hasStudent, isInGrade, hasStudentAddress, hasSchoolAddress, hasBus, livesInSchoolZoneOf and hasEvent define relationships that can hold between objects.

E. Family and School System Rules

By themselves ontologies cannot model the dynamic evolution of objects, properties and relationships. Consider the family ontology, some of the data remains constant over time (e.g., birthdates), while other data is dynamic (e.g., attending preschool). However, when coupled with a set of domain-specific rules, ontological representations enable graph transformations. In our application, we use Jena Rules to define

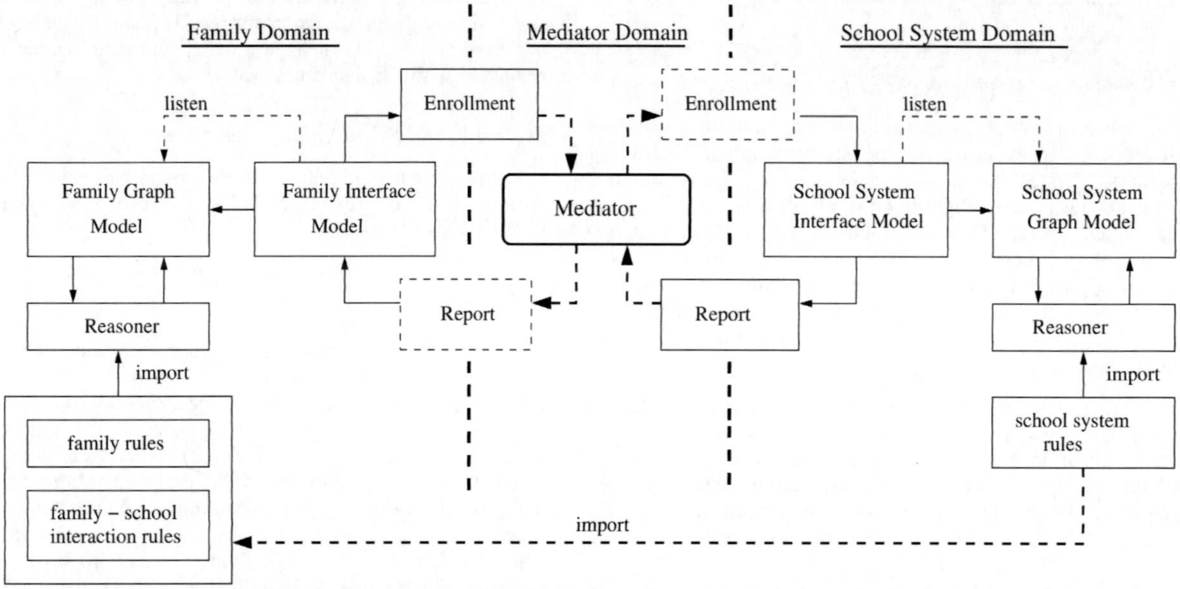

Figure 10. Software architecture for distributed behavior modeling in the family-school case study.

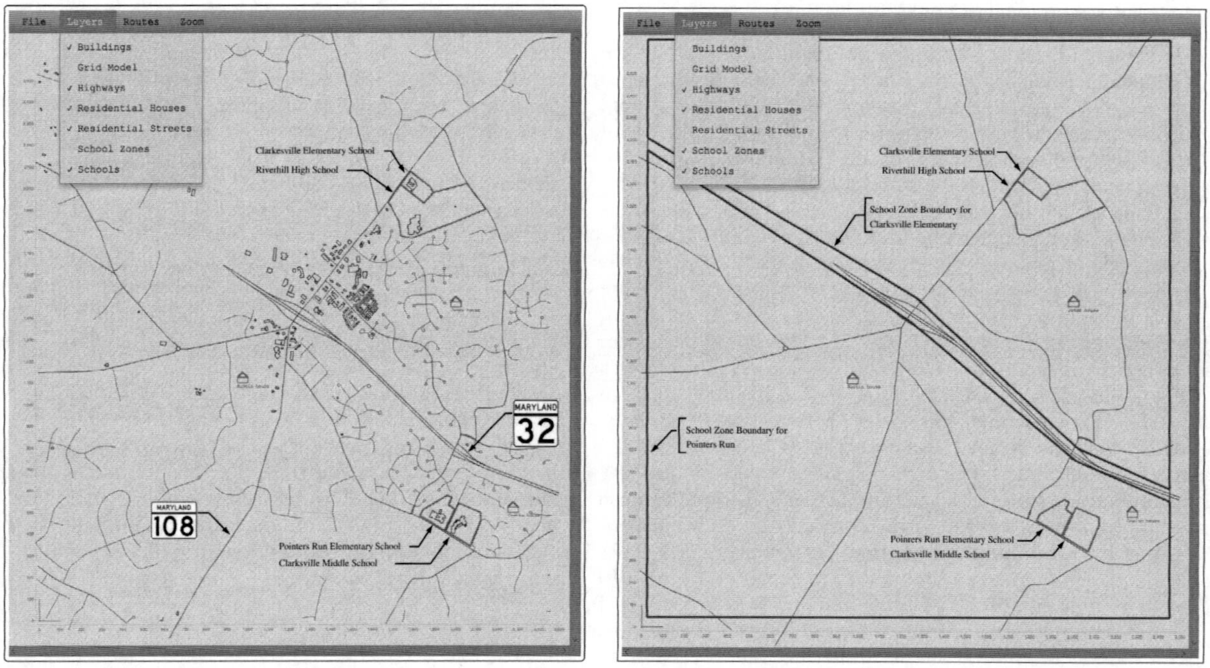

Figure 11. Graphical interface for behavior modeling of family-school-urban geography system dynamics. The school and school zones correspond to the Columbia-Clarksville Area, Maryland, USA.

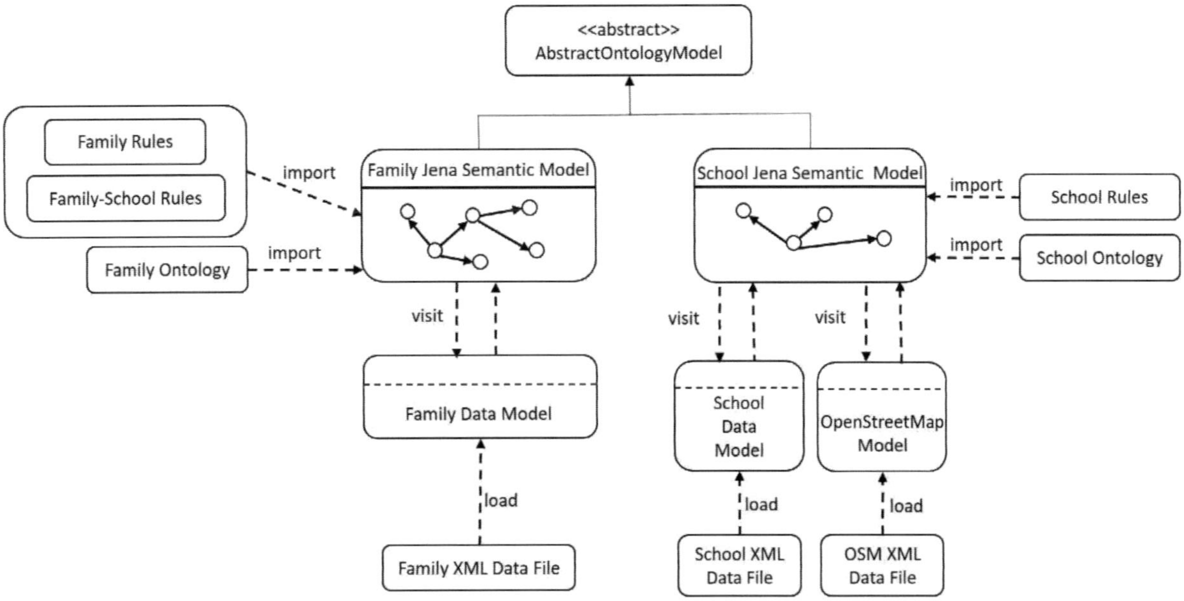

Figure 12. Generation of family and school semantic models, with input from the family data file, the school system data file, and data from OpenStreetMap.

domain-specific rules.

Figure 15 contains an abbreviated list of Jena rules for identifying relationships and properties within a family semantic model. The combination of ontologies and ontology rules is extremely powerful in scenarios where ontology graphs are dynamic. Suppose, for example, that a boy Sam was born December 10, 2007. Given a birthdate and the current year, a built-in function getAge() computes Sam's age. An age rule defined using Jena Rules determines whether or not a person is also a child. Therefore, the behavior modeling for the family system is defined by the set of rules governing graph transformations. Graph transformation can occur due to input (e.g., family graph changes because a new child is born) or time (e.g., the family graph changes because a specific member is no longer a child).

Figure 16 contains an abbreviated list of Jena rules for event-driven transformation of the School Semantic Model. Rules are provides for attendance, progression through the grades, timing of school reports, eligibility for transportation services and event induced alerts. Transformations in the semantic graph structure can also be induced by a variety of temporal and spatial factors. From a family perspective, individuals such as Sam are modeled as instances of the classes Boy, Male and Child. From a school perspective, Sam is eligible to become a student when he is between the ages of 5 and 18, and his family lives within the defined school zone. School reporting periods are events defined by intervals of time on an academic calendar. When a built-in function getToday() determines that the current time falls within one of the "reporting intervals" school reports are sent home. Similarly, the built-in function getDistance() computes the the distance between Sam's home address and the school address, and a rule determines whether or not he is eligible for school bus service. Each of these entities triggers a change in the school semantic graph.

F. Rules for Family-School System Interaction

So far the family and school rule systems have been completely decoupled and one might think that they operate independently. In reality, a small set of rules that govern family behavior are defined by the school system and distributed to individual families in the family system. As illustrated in Figure 17, rules for family-school system interaction define the grades that are appropriate for each age and the schools (e.g., elementary, middle, high) that will be attended. In practice, the family-school interaction rules are loaded into the family system alongside the regular family system rules. The former will inform Sam's family when he is now old enough to attend regular school by triggering a change to the family graph. This change, in turn, will trigger the school enrollment process for Sam to start preschool.

Family-school system interactions are also affected by spatial concerns. In particular, a child can only enroll in a particular school if he/she has a home address the lies within its school zone. From a geometric standpoint (see Figure 7), this test is equivalent to verifying that the home address (a geographic point) is contained within the school zone (a geographic polygon). JTS can easily handle this computation. In practice, however, resolving this issue is complicated by the fact that the home address and school zone are contained in different models. Thus, a strategy is needed whereby a family can query the school system for details on the school zone and do the point-in-polygon computation on the family model, or, the child's address is part of the enrollment package and the school verifies spatial eligibility on the school system side. In either case, a simple Jena rule can retrieve details of the point and polygon in a string format – see the top right-hand side of Figure 7 – and a Jena built-in function working with JTS

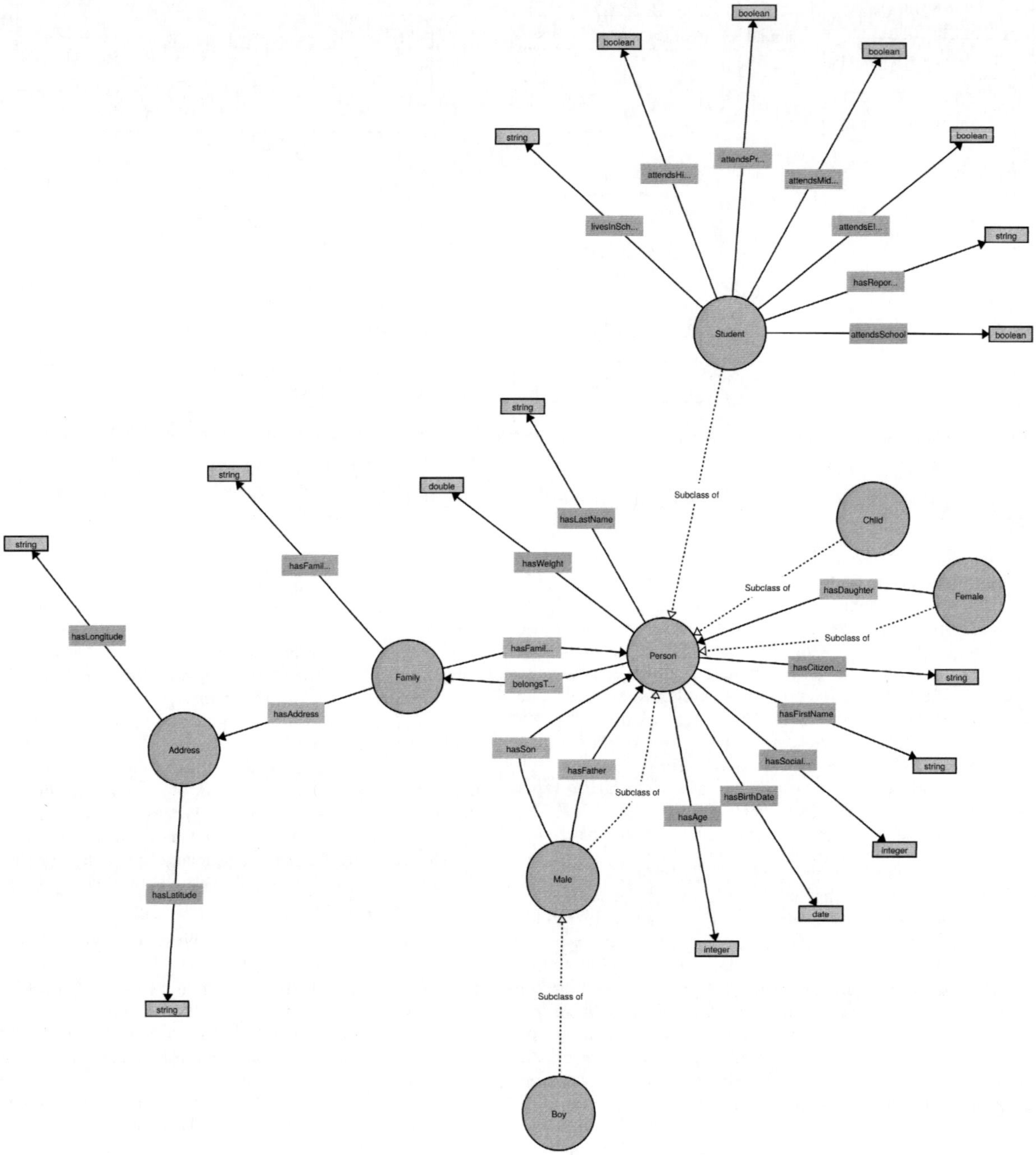

Figure 13. Family ontology diagram with classes, properties, and relationships among classes and properties.

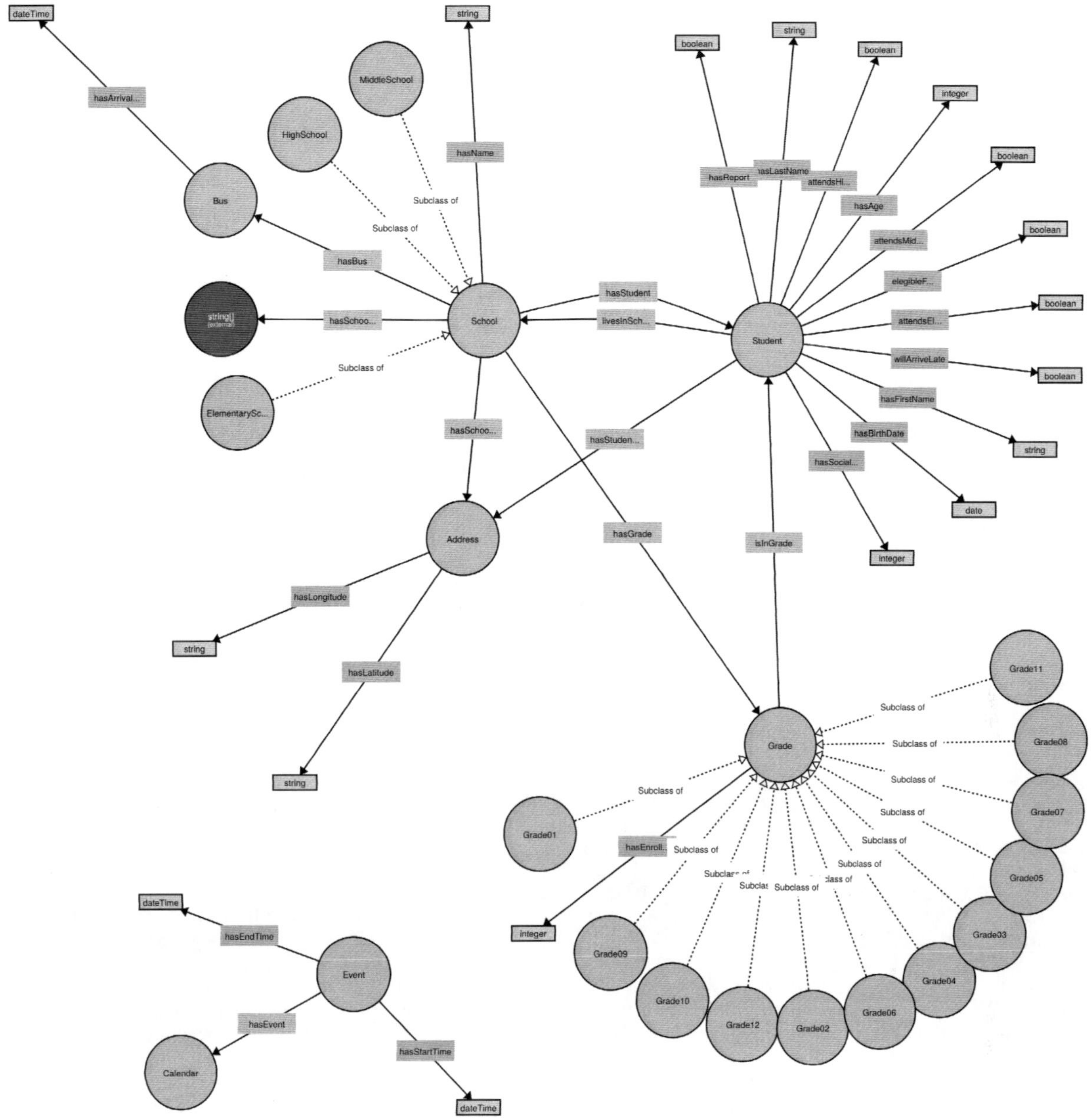

Figure 14. School system ontology diagram with classes, properties, and relationships among classes and properties.

can evaluate the point-in-polygon containment.

G. Mediator Design

When the number of participating applications domains is very small, point-to-point channel communication between interfaces is practical. Otherwise, an efficient way of handling domain communication is by delegating the task of sending and receiving specific requests to a central object. In software engineering, a common pattern used to solve this problem is the Mediator Pattern.

As illustrated in Figures 2 and 3, the mediator pattern defines a object responsible for the overall communication of the system, which from here on out will be referred as the mediator. The mediator has the role of a router, it centralizes the logic to send and receive messages. Components of the system send messages to the mediator rather than to the other components; likewise, they rely on the mediator to send change notifications to them [36]. The implementation of this pattern greatly simplifies the other classes in the system; components are more generic since they no longer have to contain logic to manage communication with other components. Because other

```
@prefix af:  <http://www.isr.umd.edu/family#>.
@prefix rdf: <http://www.w3.org/1999/02/22-rdf-syntax-ns#>.

// Rule 01: Propagate class hierarchy relationships

[ rdfs01: (?x rdfs:subClassOf ?y), notEqual(?x,?y),(?a rdf:type ?x) -> (?a rdf:type ?y) ]

// Rule 02: Family rules

[ Family: (?x rdf:type af:Family) (?x af:hasFamilyMember ?y) -> (?y af:belongsToFamily ?x) ]

// Rule 03: Identify a person who is also a child

[ Child: (?x rdf:type af:Person) (?x af:hasAge ?y) lessThan(?y, 18) -> (?x rdf:type af:Child) ]
[ UpdateChild: (?x rdf:type af:Child) (?x af:hasBirthDate ?y) getAge(?y,?b) ge(?b, 18) -> remove(0) ]

// Rule 04: Identify a person who is also a student

... Student rules removed ...

// Rule 05: Compute and store the age of a person

[ GetAge: (?x rdf:type af:Person) (?x af:hasBirthDate ?y) getAge(?y,?z) -> (?x af:hasAge ?z) ]

[ UpdateAge: (?a rdf:type af:Person) (?a af:hasBirthDate ?b) (?a af:hasAge ?c)
  getAge(?b,?d) notEqual(?c, ?d) -> remove(2) (?a af:hasAge ?d) ]

// Rule 05: Set father-son and father-daughter relationships

[ SetFather01: (?f rdf:type af:Male) (?f af:hasSon ?s)-> (?s af:hasFather ?f)]
[ SetFather02: (?f rdf:type af:Male) (?f af:hasDaughter ?s)-> (?s af:hasFather ?f)]
```

Figure 15. Abbreviated list of Jena rules for transformation of the Family Semantic Model.

components remain generic, the mediator has to be application specific in order to encapsulate application-specific behavior. One can reuse all other classes for other applications, and only need to rewrite the mediator class for the new application.

H. Working with Apache Camel

Looking to the future, we envision a full-scale implementation of distributed behavior modeling (see Figure 1) having to transmit a multiplicity of message types and content, with the underlying logic needed to deliver messages possibly being a lot more complicated than send message A in domain B to domain C. In our preliminary work [1] the mediator capability was simplified in the sense that domain interfaces were assumed to be homogeneous. But looking forward, this will not always be true. Cities are transitioning from an industrial- to information-age fabric, where highly efficient communication networks are employed to minimize the importance of time constraints and relieve the need for urban congestion. Information and Communication Technologies (ICT) have become a significant part of information-age cities. ICT can be found at many levels, ranging from the collection of data from ordinary daily tasks (e.g. traffic monitoring), to informing managerial tasks that involve decision-making based on the monitored data (e.g. electricity and water management; education and health; climate change monitoring) [37]. Typically, each of the smart systems and sensors has specific requirements, processes and outputs. The flow and variety of urban data captured by these smart systems and sensors is only going to grow and diversify in years to come. This situation points to a strong need for new approaches to the construction and operation of message passing mechanisms.

One promising approach that we will explore in this work is Apache Camel [8] [9], an open source Java framework that focuses on making Enterprise Integration Patterns (EIP) accessible through carefully designed interfaces, base objects, commonly needed implementations, debugging tools and a configuration system. It joins together messaging start and end points, allowing for the transferring of messages from different sources to different destinations. Figure 18 shows, for example, a platform infrastructure for behavior modeling of three connected application (networked) domains. In addition to basic content-based routing, Apache Camel provides support for filtering and transformation of messages. The latter is an essential feature to future cities, where heterogeneous domain interfaces will need to produce and consume messages that are not always in the same language or format.

A project developed in 2015 by Abdellatif Bouchama has successfully implemented Apache Camel for data transfer in an urban scenario. The project demonstrates how to improve urban air quality by gathering real time data from cities in France, and adding value to it by using Apache Camel to process the data and notifying users of the system [38]. Apache Camel can also be congured to receive data from Twitter, Facebook, Open Weather Map and many other web environments [39] of interest to an urban model. A study

```
@prefix af:  <http://www.isr.umd.edu/school#>.
@prefix rdf: <http://www.w3.org/1999/02/22-rdf-syntax-ns#>.

// Rule 01: Propagate class hierarchy relationships

... Class hierarchy rules removed ...

// Rules 02: Elementary school rules

[ EnterElementarySchool: (?x rdf:type af:Student) (?y rdf:type af:ElementarySchool)
     (?x af:hasBirthDate ?a) getAge(?a,?b) ge(?b, 6) le(?b, 10) ->
     (?x af:attendsElementarySchool af:True) (?y af:hasStudent ?x)]

[ LeaveElementarySchool: (?x rdf:type af:Student) (?x af:hasBirthDate ?a)
     (?x af:attendsElementarySchool af:True) (?y af:hasStudent ?x)
     getAge(?a,?b) ge(?b, 10) -> remove(2) ]

[ GradeOne: (?x rdf:type af:Student) (?x af:hasBirthDate ?a)
          getAge(?a,?b) equal(?b, 6) -> (?x af:isInGrade af:Grade01) ]

... Rules for Grades 2 through 5 removed ...

// Rules 05: If today is report period, send school report

[ GenerateReport: (?x rdf:type af:Event) (?y rdf:type af:Student) (?z rdf:type af:School)
      (?z af:hasStudent ?y) (?x af:hasStartTime ?t1) (?x af:hasEndTime ?t2) getToday(?t3)
      lessThan(?t3,?t2) greaterThan(?t3,?t1) -> (?y af:hasReport af:True)  ]

// Rules 06: School transporation service rules

[ ESTransportationService: (?x rdf:type af:Student) (?y rdf:type af:ElementarySchool)
      (?y af:hasStudent ?x) (?x af:hasStudentAddress ?k) (?y af:hasSchoolAddress ?z)
      (?k af:hasLatitude ?l1) (?k af:hasLongitude ?l2) (?z af:hasLatitude ?l3) (?z af:hasLongitude ?l4)
      getDistance(?l1,?l2,?l3,?l4,?d) greaterThan(?d,1000) -> (?x af:isElegibleForSchoolBus af:True)  ]

// Rules 07: If bus is late, send alert to parents

[ DelayAlert: (?x rdf:type af:School)(?y rdf:type af:Bus)(?z rdf:type af:Student) (?x af:hasBus ?y)
             (?y af:hasArrivalTime ?t) greaterThan(?t,"2020-09-20T03:00:00"^^xsd:dateTime)
             (?x af:hasStudent ?z) (?z af:isElegibleForSchoolBus af:True) -> (?z af:willArriveLate af:True) ]
```

Figure 16. Abbreviated list of Jena rules for transformation of the School Semantic Model. Middle and high school rules for grade assignment and use of transportation services are not shown.

performed in 2017 by Oliveira et al., investigated the use of an intelligent middleware, containing Apache Camel, to support data capture and analysis techniques to inform urban planning and design. Results were reported from a "Living Campus" experiment at the University of Melbourne, Australia, focused on a public learning space case study. Local perspectives, collected via crowd sourcing, are combined with distributed and heterogeneous environmental sensor data [37].

I. Extension 1: Using Apache Camel as a Mediator

In the first extension, communication among the family and school communities is handled by a mediator built using Apache Camel. Figure 9 is the network setup for three families interacting with elementary, middle and high schools. Every component of the system (i.e., families and schools) register in a JDNI Registry as bean components. Once a family member reaches a certain age, the age rules associated with the family system will trigger a school enrollment form to be sent to the mediator in the form of an XML file, with source, subject and destination attributes. The mediator logic routes the message according to its content, more specifically the destination attribute value and sends it to the matching bean in the registry. Similarly, once the system calendar reaches a certain date, the reporting rules associated with the school system will trigger a school report to be sent to the mediator. The messaging design allows the school enrollment form to be received only by the school of interest, and not broadcasted to the entire school system. Likewise, this design allows the school reports to be sent only to the student's family. This mediator logic design is known as point-to-point channel, and it ensures that only one listener consumes any given message. The channel can have multiple listeners that consume multiple messages concurrently, but the design ensures that only one of them can successfully consume a particular message. Using this approach, listeners do not have to coordinate with each other; coordination could be complex, create a lot of communication overhead, and increase coupling between otherwise independent receivers.

J. Extension 2: Failure Simulation

The second case study extension examines computational support for simulating failures in the distributed system oper-

```
@prefix af:  <http://www.isr.umd.edu/family#>.
@prefix rdf: <http://www.w3.org/1999/02/22-rdf-syntax-ns#>.

// Rules 01: Children of age 4 and 5 attend preschool

[ EnterPreSchool: (?x rdf:type af:Student) (?x af:hasBirthDate ?a) getAge(?a,?b) ge(?b, 4)
   le(?b, 5) -> (?x af:attendsPreSchool af:True) ]

[ LeavePreSchool: (?x rdf:type af:Student) (?x af:hasBirthDate ?a) (?x af:attendsPreSchool af:True)
   getAge(?a,?b) ge(?b, 6) -> remove(2) ]

// Rules 02: Children aged 6 through 10 attend elementary school

... Rules for attending Elementary school removed ...

// Rules 03: Children aged 11 through 13 attend middle school ....

... Rules for attending Middle school removed ...

// Rules 04: Children aged 14 through 17 attend high school ....

... Rules for attending High school removed ...

// Rules 05: Children aged 6 through 18 attend regular school ....

... Rules for attending school removed ...
```

Figure 17. Jena rules for family-school system interactions at the preschool level. Rules for interactions among elementary, middle, and high schools and families are not shown.

ation. As already noted in Section I, complex urban systems always run on degraded mode, which means at some point failure and loss of urban system functionality is an inevitable fact. A resilient urban system recovers quickly and continues operating. In order to show how the architecture proposed by this work can contribute to a resilient complex system design, we introduce failure within the family and schools interaction simulation. The school rules defines which students are eligible for school bus service (a spatial decision), and by what time such students should be delivered back to their parents after school (a temporal schedule). Now imagine that a school bus is running late. The boolean property willArriveLate will be set to True. The school's semantic model interface will identify the corresponding update to the semantic graph, and in response, send an alert to the families of students in the late bus in the form of a message. The mediator will match the message destination, with each of the families' semantic model interface and forward the message. The family semantic model interface will identify the message type (i.e., late bus alert), and could potentially trigger changes to the semantic model graph to accommodate their own schedule. While this urban scenario seems urealistically simple, it captures the essense of safety and security concerns facing young urban residents. If communication among the participating parties is not handled properly and in a timely manner, uncertainties in situational awareness can easily trigger the involvement of other related systems, such as the police department.

VII. Discussion

Our vision for future (more advanced) uses of Apache Camel in behavior modeling of urban environments is focused on its ability to integrate interfaces from multiple disciplines that may not speak and understand the same language. Today, Civil Engineers are faced with the challenge of designing systems that transmit and consume a multiplicity of message types and content. Looking into the future, this challenge will be aggravated by the growth of ICT presence in urban settings. Apache Camel avoids vulnerabilities introduced by the growing flow and variety of urban data being transmitted, and allows for more resilient message passing mechanisms in urban scenarios.

VIII. Conclusions and Future Work

This paper has focused on the design and preliminary implementation of a message passing infrastructure needed to support communication in many-to-many association relationships connecting domain-specific networks.

Our long-term research objective is computational support for the design, simulation, and validation of models of distributed behavior in real-world urban environments. The family-school distributed behavior model is merely a starting point. We anticipate that the end-result will look something like Figure 2, and provide strategies for real-time control of behaviors, assessment of domain resilience, and planning of recovery actions in response to severe events. Models of urban data and system state will be coupled to tools for spatial and temporal reasoning, and will synchronize with layers of domain-specific visualization (not shown in Figure 2). In order to drive the design and validation of domain rules, and rules for exchange of messages between domains, we will design and simulate a series of progressively complicated urban case study problems.

Our future work will investigate opportunities for linking

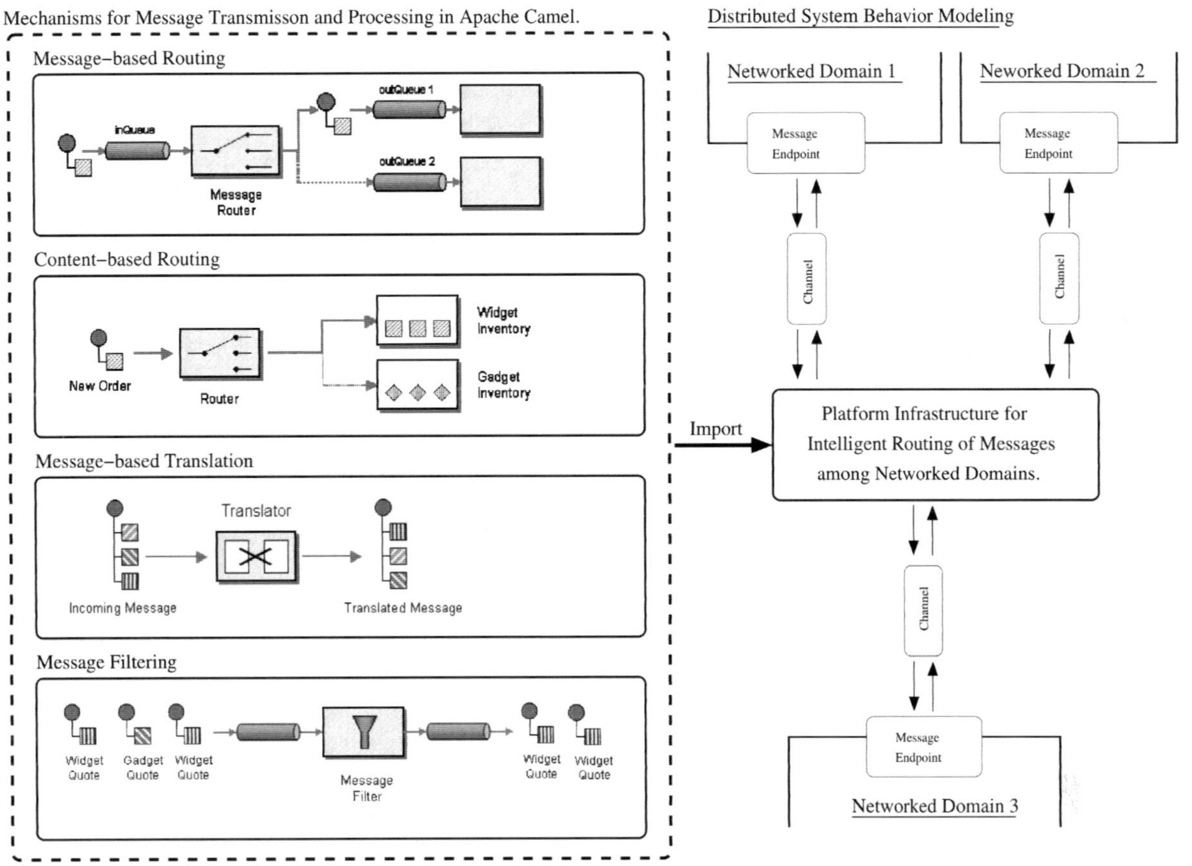

Figure 18. Platform infrastructure for distributed behavior modeling and intelligent communication (message passing) among networked domains.

of our simulation framework to tools for optimization and trade-off analysis. Such tools would allow decision makers to examine the sensitivity of design outcomes to parameter choices, understand the impact of resource constraints, understand system stability in the presence of fluctuations to modeling parameter values, and potentially, even understand emergent interactions among systems.

Lastly, a potential extension to the presented work, is in the development of ontologies. As it is presented in this work, the construction of ontologies is based on the data available from the XML datafiles, but this process is done manually. When modeling complex urban systems, this approach may become troublesome. A necessary step forward would be to implement Natural Language Processing (NLP) for the semi-automated identification of knowledge provided by the datafiles.

REFERENCES

[1] M. Coelho, M.A. Austin, and M. Blackburn, "Distributed System Behavior Modeling of Urban Systems with Ontologies, Rules and Many-to-Many Association Relationships," The Twelth International Conference on Systems (ICONS 2017), April 23-27 2017, pp. 10–15.

[2] M. A. Austin, P. Delgoshaei, and A. Nguyen, "Distributed Systems Behavior Modeling with Ontologies, Rules, and Message Passing Mechanisms," in Thirteenth Annual Conference on Systems Engineering Research (CSER 2015), Hoboken, New Jersey, March 17-19 2015, pp. 373–382.

[3] S.M. Rinaldi, J.M. Peerenboom, and T.K. Kelly, "Identifying, Understanding, and Analyzing Critical Infrastructure Interdependencies," IEEE Control Systems Magazine, vol. 21, December 2001, pp. 11–25.

[4] S. Selberg, and M.A. Austin, "Toward an Evolutionary System of Systems Architecture," in 18th Annual International Symposium of The International Council on Systems Engineering (INCOSE 2008), Utrecht, The Netherlands, July 15-19 2008.

[5] R. I. Cook, "How Complex Systems Fail." Cognitive Technologies Laboratory, University of Chicago, Chicago IL., 1998.

[6] J. Gao, X. Liu, D. Li, and S. Havlin, "Recent Progress on the Resilience of Complex Networks," Energies, vol. 8, 2015, pp. 12 187–12 210.

[7] OptaPlanner (2016), A Constraint-Satisfaction Solver. For details, see: https://www.optaplanner.org (Accessed, Jan 4., 2017).

[8] C. Ibsen, J. Antsey, and Z. Hadrian, Camel in Action. Manning Publications Company, 2010.

[9] G. Hohpe and B. Woolf, Enterprise Integration Patterns: Designing, Building and Deploying Message Passing Solutions. Addison Wesley, 2004.

[10] T. Berners-Lee, J. Hendler, and O. Lassa, "The Semantic Web," Scientific American, May 2001, pp. 35–43.

[11] P. Delgoshaei, M. A. Austin, and D. A. Veronica, "A Semantic Platform Infrastructure for Requirements Traceability and System Assessment," The Ninth International Conference on Systems (ICONS 2014), February 2014, pp. 215–219.

[12] P. Delgoshaei, M. A. Austin, and A. Pertzborn, "*A Semantic Framework for Modeling and Simulation of Cyber-Physical Systems*," in International Journal On Advances in Systems and Measurements, Vol. 7, No. 3-4, December, 2014, pp. 223–238., 2014.

[13] C.A. Myers, T. Slack, and J. Singelmann, "Social Vulnerability and Migration in the Wake of Disaster: The case of Hurricanes Katrina and Rita," Population and Environment, vol. 29, 2008, pp. 271–291.

[14] R. Zimmerman and C. E. Restrepo, "Analyzing Cascading Effects within Infrastructure Sectors for Consequence Reduction." 2009 IEEE International Conference on Technologies for Homeland Security, HST 2009, Waltham, MA. , 2009.

[15] Association of Bay Area Governments (ABAG), "Water System and Disasters." 2009-2010 Update of the ABAG-Led Multi-Jurisdictional Local Hazard Mitigation Plan for the San Francisco Bay Area, 2009.

[16] M. Hogan, "Anytown: Final Report." London Resilience Team, London, England, 2013.

[17] C. Robert T. Marsh, "Critical foundations: Protecting america's infrastructures - the report of the president's commission on critical infrastructure protection," Tech. Rep., October 1997. [Online]. Available: https://www.fas.org/sgp/library/pccip.pdf

[18] P. Pederson, D. Dudenhoeffer, S. Hartley, and M. Permann, "Critical infrastructure interdependency modeling: A survey of us and international research," Tech. Rep., August 2006. [Online]. Available: https://inldigitallibrary.inl.gov/sites/sti/sti/3489532.pdf

[19] H. Rahman, M. Armstrong, D. Mao, J. Marti, "I2Sim: A matrix-partition based framework for critical infrastructure interdependencies simulation," IEEE Canada Electric Power Conference, 2008, pp. 1–8.

[20] G. Falquet, C. Metral, J. Teller, and C. Tweed, Ontologies in Urban Development Projects. Springer, 2005.

[21] "OpenGIS Geography Markup Language Encoding Standard (GML). See http://www.opengeospatial.org/standards/gml (Accessed December 1, 2017)."

[22] D. Bonino, and F. Corno, DogOnt - Ontology Modeling for Intelligent Domotic Environments. Berlin, Heidelberg: Springer Berlin Heidelberg, 2008, pp. 790–803.

[23] M. A. Austin and J. S. Baras, An Introduction to Information-Centric Systems Engineering. Toulouse, France: Tutorial F06, INCOSE, June 2004.

[24] M. A. Austin, V. Mayank, and N. Shmunis, "Ontology-Based Validation of Connectivity Relationships in a Home Theater System," 21st International Journal of Intelligent Systems, vol. 21, no. 10, October 2006, pp. 1111–1125.

[25] ——, "PaladinRM: Graph-Based Visualization of Requirements Organized for Team-Based Design," Systems Engineering: The Journal of the International Council on Systems Engineering, vol. 9, no. 2, May 2006, pp. 129–145.

[26] N. Nassar and M. A. Austin, "Model-Based Systems Engineering Design and Trade-Off Analysis with RDF Graphs," in 11th Annual Conference on Systems Engineering Research (CSER 2013), Georgia Institute of Technology, Atlanta, GA, March 19-22 2013, pp. 216–225.

[27] Q.H. Mahmoud, "Getting started with the Java Rule Engine API (JSR 94): Toward Rule-Based Applications," Sun Microsystems, 2005, For more information, see http://java.sun.com/developer/technicalArticles/J2SE/JavaRule.html (Accessed, March 10, 2008).

[28] G. Rudolf, "Some Guidelines For Deciding Whether To Use A Rules Engine," 2003, Sandia National Labs. For more information see http://herzberg.ca.sandia.gov/guidelines.shtml (Accessed, March 10, 2008).

[29] Apache Jena:, "An Open Source Java framework for building Semantic Web and Linked Data Applications. For details, see https://jena.apache.org/," 2016.

[30] J.F. Allen, "Maintaining Knowledge about Temporal Intervals," Communications of the ACM, vol. 26, no. 11, 1983, pp. 832–843.

[31] ——, "Towards a General Theory of Action and Time," Artificial Intelligence, vol. 23, no. 2, 1984, pp. 123–154.

[32] D.A. Randell, Z. Cui, and A.G. Cohn, "A Spatial Logic based on Regions and Connectivity," 1994, Division of Artificial Intelligence, School of Computer Studies, Leeds University.

[33] Java Topology Suite (JTS). See http://www.vividsolutions.com/jts/ (Accessed August 4, 2017).

[34] White House (2003), The National Strategy for the Physical Protection of Critical Infrastructures and Key Assets. Washington, DC.

[35] T. W. H. Boyes, R. Isbell, "Critical infrastructure in the future city - developing secure and resilient cyber-physical systems," in Critical Information Infrastructures Security - 9th International Conference, CRITIS 2014, Limassol, Cyprus, October 13-15, 2014, Revised Selected Papers, 2014, pp. 13–23.

[36] S. Stelting and O. Maassen, Applied Java Patterns. SUN Microsystems Press, Prentice-Hall, 2002.

[37] E.A. Oliveira, M. Kirley, T. Kvan, J. Karakiewicz, and C. Vaz, Distributed and Heterogeneous Data Analysis for Smart Urban Planning. Berlin, Heidelberg: Springer Berlin Heidelberg, 2015, pp. 37–54.

[38] A. Bouchama, The IoT in the Service of the Environment using Apache Camel & JBoss A-MQ. For details, see: http://bushorn.com/iot-service-environment-using-apache-camel-jboss-mq/ (Accessed, Jul 1., 2017).

[39] Apache Camel (2017), Components Included. For details, see: http://camel.apache.org/components.html (Accessed, Jul 1., 2017).

A Method for the Analysis of the Nano- and Micromorphology of Printed Structures on Flexible Polymer Films

Analysis of the cross section of inkjet-printed conductive traces on PET film substrates based on ultramicrotome sectioning and SEM imaging.

Martin Ungerer[1], Waldemar Spomer[1], Irene Wacker[2], Rasmus Schröder[2,3], Ulrich Gengenbach[1]

[1] Institute for Applied Computer Science (IAI), Karlsruhe Institute of Technology (KIT), Eggenstein-Leopoldshafen, Germany

[2] Centre for Advanced Materials (CAM), University Heidelberg, Heidelberg, Germany

[3] CellNetworks, BioQuant, University Hospital Heidelberg, Heidelberg, Germany

e-mail: ungerer@kit.edu

Abstract—**The development of smart sensor systems, wearables or internet of things devices necessitates new fabrication technologies. The challenge is to meet requirements such as low-cost, flexibility, reproducibility and capability for large area fabrication. Fabricating conductive microstructures on polymer films by additive processes like inkjet printing has become increasingly important for these applications in the last decade. Additive processes are potentially more ecofriendly than conventional electronics fabrication processes but printing has still not reached wider implementation in industry. One of the potential reasons is the still insufficient reliability of printed components that must sustain electrical, thermal, mechanical and chemical stress. This reliability of printed products is influenced by a vast number of factors and process parameters. The impact of a certain parameter on the product's reliability can so far not be defined precisely. Besides functional testing, the examination of cross sections of printed structures can lead to a more detailed understanding of their morphology and may entail information for the optimization of the fabrication process. Regarding the requirements, the nano- and microstructure of printed structures has to be analyzed. In the present work, a method is described for the investigation of nano- and microstructures of inkjet-printed conductive traces on polymer substrates by means of scanning electron microscopy of cross sections prepared by ultramicrotome sectioning.**

Keywords-Inkjet-printing; silver nanoparticle ink; polyethylene terephthalate; sintering; ultramicrotome sectioning; imaging by scanning electron microscopy; cross section of conductive traces; microstructure; nanoparticle density.

I. INTRODUCTION

Currently, printing of electronically functional components represents an important field of study in regard of which not only fabrication processes have to be investigated but also methods for the analysis of the reliability of printed devices [1]. In the last decade, printing technologies have become more and more important in research and development for flexible electronics [2]. The objective is to replace conventional subtractive fabrication processes of printed circuit board (PCB) manufacturing by additive processes. Printing processes can be used to fabricate conductive structures, as well as more complex electronic components on flexible polymer films.

The analysis of inkjet-printed conductive structures on polymer substrates in terms of morphology and nanostructure is essential for the assessment of reliability and reproducibility in printed electronics [1]. Established preparation methods for nanostructure analysis are Focused Ion Beam (FIB) milling and ultramicrotome sectioning.

A. *Preparation methods for analyzing cross sections of printed structures on polymer films*

In FIB milling the material is being etched by a beam of focused Gallium ions, with removal rates of a few μm^3/minute and a depth resolution in the range of 5 nanometres [3]. Usually, the FIB instrument is combined with a scanning electron microscope (SEM), so that the new by FIB etching prepared sample surface can be immediately imaged (FIBSEM). Repeated FIB etching and imaging allows inspection of sample volumes, but still on a very limited scale. Moreover the impact of the Gallium ions may, depending on the sample material, create severe damage on and below the milled surface [3]. This includes local amorphization, heating damage and Ga implantation. Chain scission, cross-linking and chain shrinkage have been observed, effects which may transform the structure and crystallinity of polymers [4]. Another aspect is that repeating etching and imaging steps in a FIBSEM the prepared sample surface is continuously being destroyed with the next etching step, hence lost for other imaging modalities.

Ultramicrotome sectioning means embedding the sample in a polymer and cutting thin slices, called sections, with a diamond knife. Section width is limited by the width of the diamond knife, which may reach up to several millimetres. Thus, ultramicrotome sectioning is applicable for structural elucidation of larger volumes than FIB milling. Its depth resolution is however limited by the minimum section thickness achievable for the given combination of sample and embedding material, typically 30 to 200 nm. After cutting the sections float on the water surface of the knife boat behind the diamond knife edge from where they can be picked up and transferred onto the substrate (glass cover slip, silicon wafer, TEM-grid). Depending on the substrate the sections are then available for different imaging modalities such as light microscopy, SEM or transmission electron microscopy (TEM). Proper embedding of the sample is a challenge; the embedding material stiffness should be compatible with the stiffness of the sample. Distortion of the nanostructure of the sample, e.g., swelling of porous materials due to embedding has to be avoided [4]. Loosely connected particles in the sample may be detached and smeared across the section during cutting. Moreover, mechanical stresses during cutting may lead to deformations and structural alterations.

Melo compares FIB milling and ultramicrotome sectioning for sample preparation for analytical microscopy of the cathode layer of a polymer electrolyte fuel cell and shows the drawbacks of FIB milling and the challenges for ultramicrotome sectioning [4].

The requirements for sample preparation for the structural elucidation of printed electronic structures fabricated in our lab are

- potential for larger sample volumes (a few hundred microns up to a few millimetres width/depth and up to a hundred microns thickness)
- analysis of the samples with different imaging modalities (light microscopy and electron microscopy)

Hence, ultramicrotome sectioning has been selected as method for sample preparation for analysis of printed traces.

B. Functional printing vs. conventional PCB fabrication

A number of printing technologies were transferred from the realm of graphic printing to electronics manufacturing in the last decade. Manufacturing processes can be categorized into processes for mass production and processes for single part or small series production. In the same way, printing processes can be also classified with regard to process productivity. Conventional printing processes based on printing tools (stencils, print cylinders) are well suited for large-scale production whereas, tool-less, non-impact printing processes are more suited to individual part up to small series manufacturing and research applications [5] [6].

Conventional, subtractive PCB fabrication requires a complex process sequence with electroplating, lithography and etching steps based on a fair amount of toxic chemicals. Printing processes usually need one single additive fabrication step followed by an additional curing process in order to create conductive traces on a substrate [7] [8]. Thus, material usage is optimized and the toxic waste accumulated in subtractive processing is eliminated [9]. Printing allows faster, cleaner, cheaper and more environmentally friendly fabrication of PCB's than conventional processes [8]. Additionally, printing enables large area processing of flexible polymer substrates at low temperatures and ambient conditions [10].

The implementation of printing processes for a desired electronic function in microstructure resolution demands careful selection of the three main process components - ink, substrate and printing system. These components have to be precisely tuned to get optimum conditions for realizing features with high reproducibility [5].

C. Ink materials

There exists a number of ink materials to realize electronic functions like resistors, capacitors [11] or transistors [12]. A fundamental element in printed electronics however are conductive traces [7]. They have to provide high conductivities in order to minimize power loss. Currently, there are two main ink types for printing conductive traces available. One type are metal organic decomposition (MOD) inks, with oxidized metal ions as main component [13]. The most prevalent type are nanoparticle inks, where the particles are dispersed in solvents and stabilized by an organic capping agent against agglomeration [14].

Due to their high conductivity, silver-based inks are most widely used [9]. For printed silver nanoparticle traces a conductivity of about 10 % of bulk silver is applicable for many applications [15].

Typically, the particle size of such inks can be found in the range of 10 to 80 nm. Small nanoparticle sizes are desirable, as the nanoparticle size severely influences the curing process, due to melting point depression; the smaller the particles, the lower the melting point compared to the bulk material [16] [17].

D. Printing substrate materials

For printed flexible electronic applications low cost polyethylene terephthalate (PET) substrates are widely used. The base materials have a glass-transition temperature (T_g) of 78 °C and a melting point of 255 °C [18] [19]. Commercially available PET films, e.g., Melinex® ST from DuPont Teijin Films are often used in printed electronic applications. Such PET substrates are thermoplastic semi-crystalline polymer films whose maximum working temperature for printing and sintering processes (T_{max}) of about 150 °C is largely independent of their T_g due to a heat-stabilization [18] [19] [20]. Semi-crystalline polymer films have better resistances against solvents than amorphous polymers [20].

E. Inkjet-printing

Drop-on-demand (DoD) piezo inkjet printing is the most widespread non-impact printing principle in the field of printed electronics [10]. It allows direct, mask-less and vectorial printing of layouts on flexible polymer films [5]. The layouts are created by computer-aided design (CAD) tools. With regard to printability the interaction between print head and ink is of crucial importance. Relevant ink parameters are viscosity, surface energy, density, particle size and particle stability [7] [8]. In order to prevent print head nozzle clogging a particle diameter of less than 1 % of the nozzle diameter is recommended [21].

Inkjet-printing often produces non-uniform, low edge quality and non-reproducible morphology compared to conventional electronics fabrication processes [22] [23]. In order to obtain an optimum line quality, the important printing parameters that need to be controlled are the droplet velocity (v_d), the frequency of droplet generation (f_d), the distance between two adjacent droplets (d_d) on the substrate, the substrate temperature (T_s) and substrate surface properties [24] [25].

F. Curing of printed structures

After the printing process, the resulting structures must be cured in order to get the desired electrical conductivity [15]. First, the ink solvent has to be evaporated; then, the organic stabilizing shell has to be removed. During sintering, a percolation-based network of conductive paths is established due to sporadic agglomeration of particles [15]. At higher temperatures, sintering necks improve the conductivity, the coalescence of the particles leads to a higher metal density of the printed feature [26]. High conductivities have been achieved by means of an oven sintering regime with 30 minutes or more at temperatures above 250 °C [2].

Despite the lower melting point of nanoparticles compared to the bulk material, a sintering regime required for such an increased conductivity is not compatible with many of the widely used low-cost polymer substrates, e.g., PET [27].

Therefore, low temperature sintering methods are taken into consideration that allow either sintering at room temperature (commonly known as chemical sintering) or selective sintering where only the printed structure that needs to be cured is heated while the substrate stays at moderate temperatures [2]. Selective sintering methods are photonic flash sintering, laser sintering, plasma sintering, microwave sintering and electrical current sintering [2] [15].

Chemical sintering comprises, among other methods, sintering triggered by additives in the ink, embedded in the substrate material or coated on its surface [28].

G. Properties of printed structures

In view of the manifold applications of printed structures, such as conductors and passive components, not only their electrical characteristics must be considered, but also their mechanical and chemical properties. Printed conductive traces have to withstand mechanical, chemical und thermal stresses that can influence their inherent porous nanostructure and thereby impair the reliability. Particularly, adhesion to the substrate, bendability and fatigue resistance are important properties of printed structures for applications on flexible polymer substrates. Sintering conditions substantially influence mechanical properties, such as fatigue resistance [29].

H. Hybrid electronics

To date, many electronic functional elements besides conductive traces such as resistors, capacitors, transistors, organic light emitting diodes (OLED), organic photovoltaics (OPV) and sensors have been realized by printing technologies. However, it is currently not possible to achieve the performance of silicon electronic devices; e.g., the switching frequencies of printed transistors are still several orders of magnitude lower than their silicon counterparts.

Moreover, highly integrated circuits such as microcontrollers cannot yet be realized by printing. Therefore, a hybrid approach for the fabrication of more complex electronic systems on flexible polymer substrates seems to be an interesting solution in the medium term to overcome the still low performance of printed complex elements [30] [31]. Marjanović et al. define hybrid electronic integration as the combination of printed components and surface-mount technology (SMT) devices on foils [30].

For demonstration of a hybrid intralayer-integration approach, the conductive trace structure of a flip-flop circuit shown in [31] was first printed with silver nanoparticle ink on a PET film.

Then SMT components were connected to the conductive traces with silver flake based conductive adhesive. Figure 1 shows the realized flip-flop circuit. Tests with these circuits indicated that the system is sensitive to mechanical stress such as bending. Either the conductive adhesive that connects the SMT components fails or the conductive traces crack or delaminate from the substrate. In order to improve the structure's resistance to mechanical stress, the microstructure of the printed traces has to be investigated, as it directly affects the mechanical properties of the printed feature and is of high importance for reliable circuits [32].

After this introduction to hybrid electronics based on functional printing, in Section II, the materials and methods are described that were used for realizing test structures. In Section II.A, the analysis method is outlined, in Section II.B, the test structure is described, in Section II.C, the applied inkjet printer, the silver ink and the PET substrate are presented. Section II.D illustrates the printing process and Section II.E the sample preparation that is needed for the analysis of the cross sections. In Section III, the results of the printing process (Section III.A), the sample preparation (Section III.B) and the SEM analysis of the fabricated cross sections (Section III.C) are outlined. Finally, Section IV gives a conclusion and an outlook.

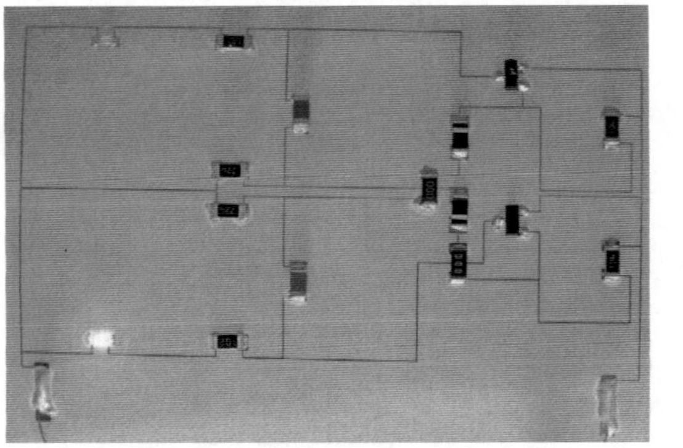

Figure 1. Flip-flop circuit with printed conductive traces and mounted SMT-components

II. Materials and Methods

A. Analysis workflow

The method for the analysis of the nano- and microstructure of printed structures on flexible polymer films demonstrated in the present paper is based on a workflow composed of the process steps for sample preparation, the ultrathin sectioning and the analysis itself. Figure 2 shows the workflow of this method. After printing and curing of a test structure on a flexible polymer substrate, rectangular samples were taken. These samples were embedded into an epoxy resin and cured subsequently. Afterwards, the resulting sample blocks were trimmed and sectioned with the ultramicrotome. Scanning electron microscopy (SEM) images were taken from the sections and analyzed afterwards.

B. Test structure

A test structure was defined for the electrical and mechanical evaluation of the properties of different ink-substrate-printer-combinations and different processing parameters. The test structure conceived for electrical and mechanical characterization consists of a 45 mm long conductive trace (L) that connects two contact pads each having a length (B) of 7 mm and a width (T) of 2 mm. Figure 3 shows the geometry of the test structure (top) and some inkjet-printed samples (bottom).

C. Materials

The printer used for printing the test structures is based on a custom-built piezo-driven four-axis positioning system NAMOSE. It has a working space of 400 mm x 150 mm x 40 mm, a repeatability of less than 1 µm and a maximum speed of 200 mm/s [5]. The NAMOSE system is controlled by a Beckhoff-CX2040 with TwinCAT, programmable logic controller (PLC) and numerical control (NC) axis controlling. For inkjet-printing, the positioning system is equipped with a piezo-electrically driven single nozzle Microfab print head (MJ-AL-01-50-8MX) with an orifice diameter of 50 µm [5]. A NC-task synchronizes the droplet frequency (f_d) with the axis velocity (v), while the droplet distance (d_d) is maintained at its set point. Furthermore, the NAMOSE system is equipped with a

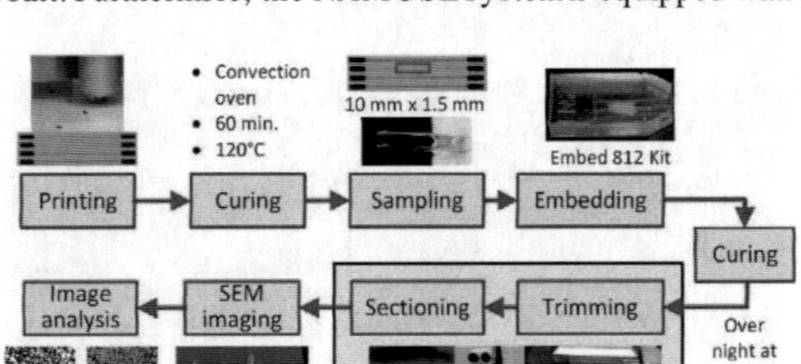

Figure 2. Workflow for the analysis of printed structures

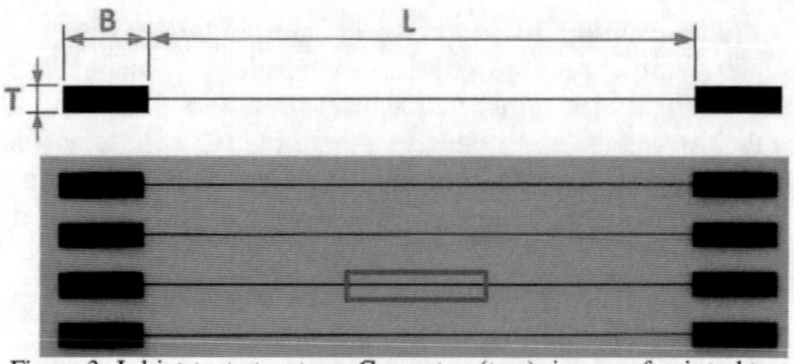

Figure 3. Inkjet test structure. Geometry (top), image of printed test structures (bottom), specimen geometry for sectioning (red box)

heated vacuum chuck and an optical observation system for controlling and adjusting droplet formation.

The silver-nanoparticle ink DGP 40LT-15C (Advanced Nano Products (ANP)) was purchased from Sigma Aldrich (736465 ALDRICH). The ink has a solid content of 30 - 35 wt % of silver nanoparticles of less than or equal to 50 nm diameter, a surface tension of 35 - 38 mN/m, a viscosity of about 10 - 17 mPa·s and is designed for application on polymer films. The manufacturer recommends a curing regime with 30 - 60 minutes at 120 - 150 °C. The main solvent of the ink is triethylene glycol monoethyl ether (TGME) [33]. The ink contains polyvinylpyrrolidone (PVP) as capping agent that leads to an electrostatic stabilization of the nanoparticles [14].

In the present work, two different PET-films were used as substrates. The 125 µm thick Melinex® ST506™ from DuPont Teijin Films is optimized for printed electronics. Both sides of this film are pre-treated for improved adhesion of inks [19]. The NB-TP-3GU100 from Mitsubishi Paper Mills is a 135 µm thick PET-film that is optimized for inkjet-printing of conductive structures based on silver nanoparticle dispersions. Due to its optimized nanoporous single side coating, it provides fast drying of water-based inks [34]. The thickness, morphology and the surface chemistry of this coating are not further specified by the supplier.

D. Printing samples

Test structures were printed on both substrates using the ink DGP 40LT-15C. The piezo-inkjet-device was actuated with a standard trapezoidal waveform. Figure 4 left illustrates the applied waveform. Figure 4 right shows the resulting droplet formation. For all samples, the waveform parameter t_{rise} was 3.0 µs, t_{dwell} was 28.0 µs and t_{fall} 3.0 µs.

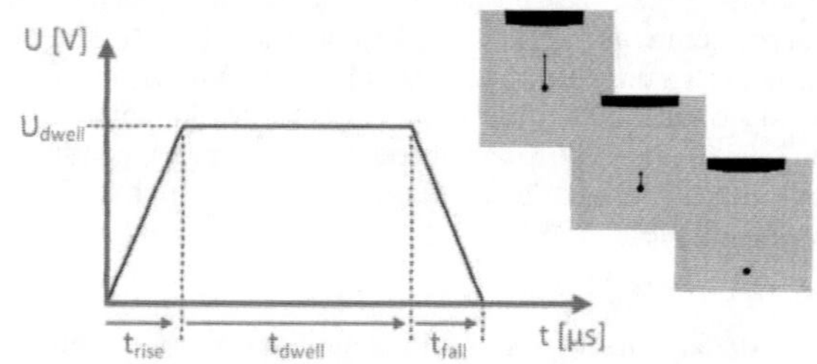

Figure 4. Waveform parameters and droplet formation

TABLE I. PRINTING PARAMETERS

sample	substrate	d_d [µm]	T_S [°C]	v [mm/s]
A	Melinex® ST506™	147	80	50
B	Melinex® ST506™	13	80	50
C	NB-TP-3GU100	31	RT	10
D	NB-TP-3GU100	1	RT	10

For the samples A, C and D, U_{dwell} was 38.0 V. For sample B, U_{dwell} was 35.0 V.

Table I shows the printing parameters for four different samples. After printing, the samples were cured in a convection oven (Memmert UP 500) for about 60 min. at 120 °C.

After curing, the width of the central part of the test structure (see the red box in Figure 3) was measured by optical microscopy and image processing with the DIPLOM software that was developed at the KIT Institute for Applied Computer Science (IAI). The image processing yields the line width and its standard deviation which can be used as an indicator of the line edge quality.

E. Sample preparation for SEM-analysis

For analyzing the cross section in the central area of the printed traces, about 10 mm long and 1.5 mm wide rectangular specimen were cut from the printed test structures (see the red box in Figure 3).

As it is not possible at ambient conditions, to directly cut the flexible polymer with an ultramicrotome without delamination of the ink, the printed samples need to be embedded into a polymer in order to achieve proper sections. Two different specimens were embedded parallel to each other into one embedding mould.

As embedding resin, the Embed 812 Kit from Electron Microscopy Sciences was used. The filled embedding moulds were cured over night at 60 °C in a convection oven.

After polymerization, the resulting blocks with the embedded samples were removed from the moulds and then prepared for ultramicrotome sectioning. For this purpose, the blocks were trimmed in a Leica Ultracut 7 ultramicrotome using a standard glass trimming knife. Then, sections of 100 nm and 200 nm thickness were cut with the same instrument but with a Diatome Ultra 35° knife at ambient conditions. The knife boat was filled with double-distilled water during the cutting process. To avoid electrostatic charging of the sample, a Diatome static line 2 ionizer was used. The cut sections are floating on the water surface of the knife boat, where they can be subsequently picked up and placed on a silicon wafer for imaging in the scanning electron microscope (SEM).

For SEM imaging, an Ultra 55 (Carl Zeiss Microscopy, Oberkochen, Germany) was used. Particle density in the SEM images of the cross sections was measured with the software package Fiji [35].

Figure 5 illustrates the approach to determine the particle density by image segmentation. The threshold for the segmentation was manually selected for different details of a SEM-image of a cross section. The particles density in the sectional plane was calculated for each detail.

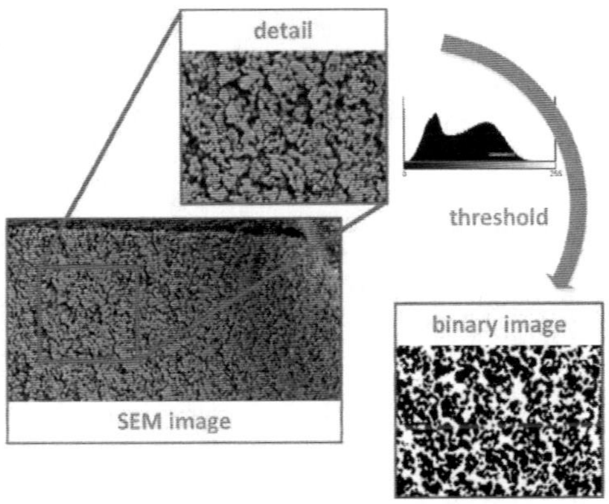

Figure 5. Determination scheme of the nanoparticle density

III. RESULTS AND DISCUSSION

A. Printing and curing

In a preliminary test, it was found that the behavior of the ink after deposition at room temperature is completely different on the two different substrates. Although the initial wetting seems to be good, printing on the Melinex® ST506™ substrate is followed by a continuous parasitic spreading combined with a resulting shape similar to a coffee-ring effect. This results in very flat, broad and fringed traces, with poor edge quality. The nanoporous coating of the PET-film from Mitsubishi Paper Mills avoids this ink spreading over a broad range of droplet-distances d_d. A considerable trace height can be achieved, even for narrow traces. Optimizing the droplet-distance (d_d), it is even possible to print continuous traces with a width of less than the diameter of a single droplet. Figure 6 shows microscope images of this preliminary test. The printing parameters were the same for both substrates: the jetting frequency (f_d) was 2000 Hz, the axis speed (v) was 100 mm/s and the droplet-distance (d_d) results in 50 µm. The silver trace on Melinex® ST506™ (see Figure 6 left) shows a poor edge quality, a width of about 1180 µm and a height in the range of about 100 nm, whereas the trace printed on NB-TP-3GU100 (see Figure 6 right) has a good edge quality at a width of about 88 µm and a height of about 1140 nm.

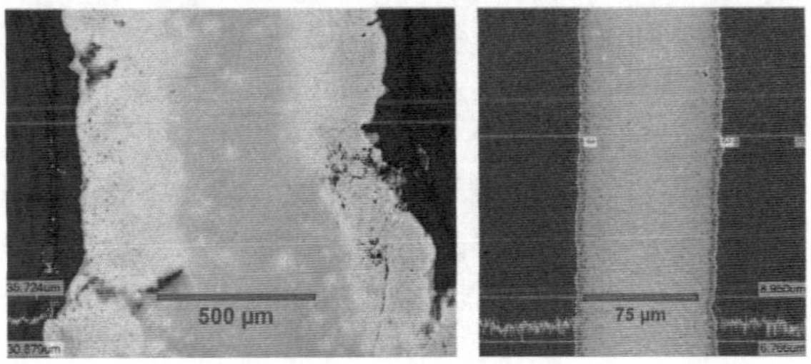

Figure 6. Microscope images of printed silver ink traces at room temperature on Melinex® ST506™ (left) and on NB-TP-3GU100 (right)

In further tests, it was found that printing on Melinex® ST506™, with 80 °C substrate temperature results in much better trace quality. This parameter was maintained for all subsequent tests with this substrate.

Concerning the sintering in a convection oven, an irreversible warping of the NB-TP-3GU100 can be observed when heating above T_g of PET. This warpage potentially induces an initial strain into the printed structures, which may lead to damages such as cracks and delamination. A possible explanation for this effect could be different thermal expansion coefficients of the single-side nanoporous coating and the PET bulk material. The Melinex® ST506™ substrate does not show such an effect.

B. *Ultramicrotome sectioning*

Figure 7 shows the block with the embedded specimens (left, a and b), the top of the block during trimming with the glass knife (center, c) and a section directly after cutting (right).

200 nm sections can be cut reproducibly but with a significant wrinkling of the embedding material along the edges of the embedded specimens (see Figure 7 right, d and e). Lower section thicknesses led to delamination between specimen and embedding resin due to this wrinkling.

Different cutting directions were evaluated with respect to the sample orientation in the block: perpendicular, parallel and at an angle to the embedded substrate plane. Figure 8 shows typical results indicating the effect of the cutting direction (red arrows).

When cutting is performed perpendicular to the substrate plane, the interface between the ink and the substrate is being compressed and can therefore not be used for further investigation of the interface. Additionally, this section shows many wrinkles and dominant knife marks (see Figure 8 left). In contrast, sections obtained when cutting parallel to the substrate plane, show less wrinkles and knife marks (see Figure 8 center). It is assumed that this cutting direction introduces fewer mechanical stresses to the interface between ink and substrate. The sections obtained, when cutting at an angle of about 26° to the substrate plane, were also acceptable (see Figure 8 right). The embedded NB-TP-3GU100 substrate (see Figure 8 a and c) produces much more wrinkles than the Melinex® ST506™ (see Figure 8 b and d). We suppose that Melinex® film is harder than the Mitsubishi film due to its heat and surface

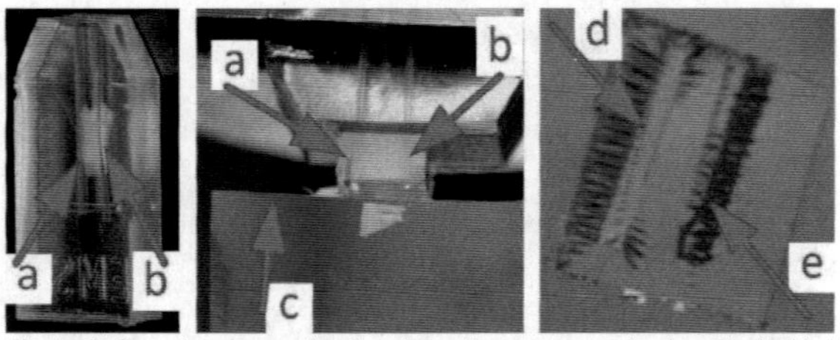

Figure 7. Sample preparation by ultramicrotome sectioning. Embedded specimens (a and b), trimming (center) with a glass knife (c) and 200 nm thin section floating on the water in the knife boat (right); Wrinkling of the embedding material along the edges of the embedded specimens (d and e)

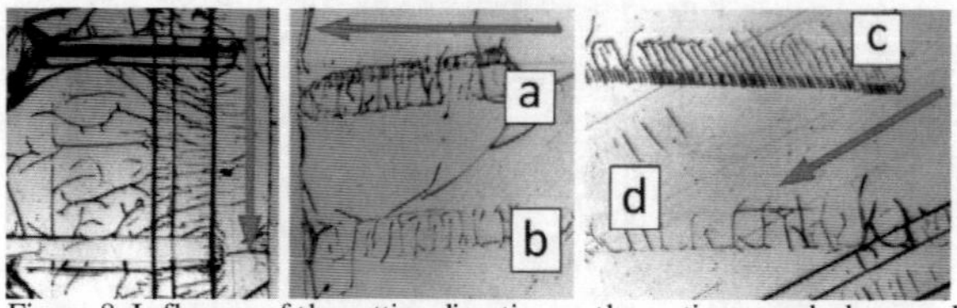

Figure 8. Influence of the cutting direction on the section morphology and the specimens (a and c: NB-TP-3GU100; b and d: Melinex® ST506™). Perpendicular (left), parallel (center) and 26° (right) to substrate plane (arrows indicate cutting direction)

treatment. This can explain why the sections of NB-TP-3GU100 specimen show a stronger wrinkling than the Melinex® substrate.

C. *SEM analysis and image segmentation*

Despite varying the cutting direction, a certain degree of section wrinkling was unavoidable. This led to a degradation of the sections in terms of cracks. Sometimes delamination occurred in the section while cutting. Figure 9 shows a section from a NB-TP-3GU100 substrate cut parallel to the substrate plane (I). It can be seen that the substrate was torn during the cutting process (see Figure 9 I) and the printed ink delaminates from the coated substrate at the locations of the wrinkles (II and III).

Nevertheless, there are enough regions suitable for further analysis (compare Figure 9 II and III), since the cutting preserved the nanostructure of the cross section.

Table II summarizes some of the results obtained from the analysis of images from SEM and optical microscopy of the printed samples.

Using the SEM-images, the line width was measured in the cross sections. It can be seen that there is a discrepancy between both results for the line width. For the samples B and D, the discrepancy is stronger than for the other samples. The samples B and D were taken from the line ends, where a decrease in line width can be detected for both samples via optical microscopy. Therefore, the line widths measured using the SEM-images cannot be compared to the line width obtained from the optical scanning of the printed and

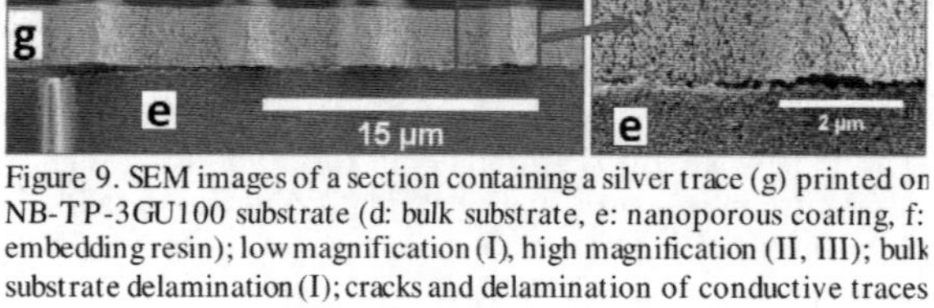

Figure 9. SEM images of a section containing a silver trace (g) printed on NB-TP-3GU100 substrate (d: bulk substrate, e: nanoporous coating, f: embedding resin); low magnification (I), high magnification (II, III); bulk substrate delamination (I); cracks and delamination of conductive traces (II, III)

TABLE II. RESULTS

Sample	Line width (REM, section) [µm]	Line width (opt., middle) [µm]	Ink layer thickness (REM) [nm]	Cutting angle [°]
A	155,2	205,1 +/- 4,4	182,2 +/- 18	5,9
B	273,2	607,74 +/- 93	1705,0 +/-24	25,6
C	84,5	98,0 +/- 2,8	840,0 +/- 85	5,6
D	393,6	612,6 +/- 8	3719 +/- 20	28,9

sintered lines (as described in Section II.D).

In the case of the samples A and C that were taken from the middle of the lines, both values for the line width can be compared. For A, the line width measured from the REM-image is about 76 % of the line width calculated from the optical scanning data. For the sample C, this value is about 86 %. For both substrates, there is a wrinkling induced "shrinkage" of the measured line width in the range of 14 to 24 % of the line width due to the ultramicrotome-cutting process at an angle of about 6° between the cutting direction and the substrate's surface. The wrinkles coming out of the section plane are the results of that process. Table II also shows the results of the measurements of the ink layer thickness by SEM-image-analysis.

The ratio of the ink layer thickness and the line width is about 0.09 % for the narrow line printed on Melinex® ST506™ (sample A). This ratio is about 0.86 % for a narrow line printed on NB-TP-3GU100 (sample C). The wide line on Melinex® ST506™ achieves a ratio of ink layer thickness and line width of about 0.28 % (sample B) whereas this ratio is about 0.61 % for NB-TP-3GU100 (sample D). The actual cutting angles for all four samples are also given in Table II.

Figure 10 shows the cross section of the samples B (I) and D (II). The full low magnification cross section for each sample can be seen on the top, a detail image can be found on the bottom for each sample. Using such high magnification images from SEM the particle density of each

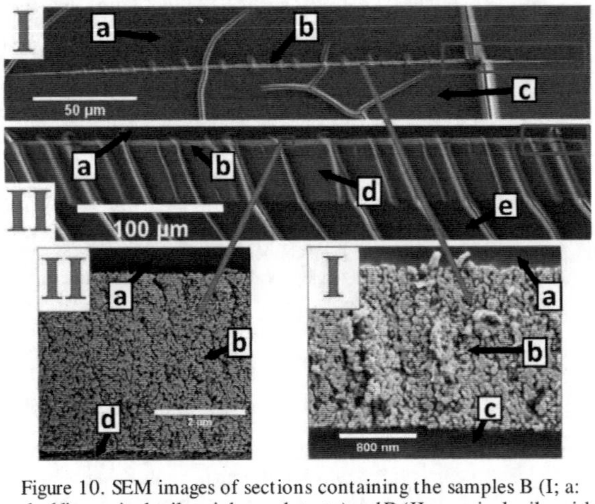

Figure 10. SEM images of sections containing the samples B (I; a: embedding resin, b: silver ink, c: substrate) and D (II; a: resin, b: silver ink, d: nanoporous coating, e: bulk substrate); low magnification (top) and high magnification images (bottom)

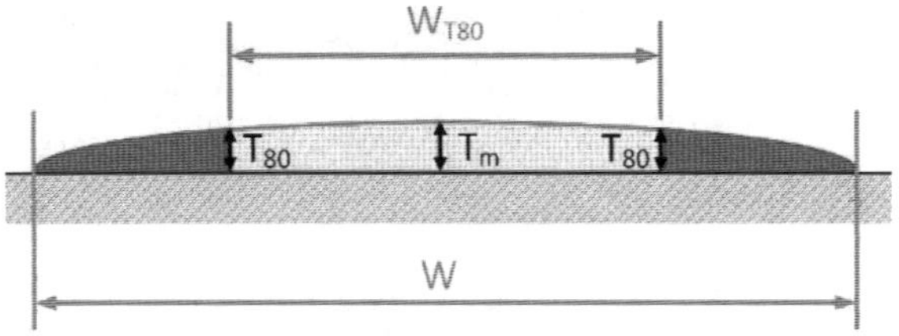

Figure 11. Off leveling of the cross section of a printed line towards its edges. T_m: ink layer thickness measured in the middle of the cross section; T_{80}: 80 % of the ink layer thickness T_m; W: line width; W_{T80}: width of the cross section segment for which the ink layer thickness is greater or equal to T_m

sample according to the procedure described above has been determined. The particle density of the conductive traces calculated for all four samples was between 58 % and 65 %. The particle density is slightly higher for structures printed on Melinex® ST506™ than on Mitsubishi NB-TP-3GU100. For the samples A and B the particle density is about 65 % and 61 %, respectively. In the case of the samples C and D, the particle density was calculated to about 60 % and 58 %.

Moreover, from these SEM images, it can be derived that the cross section of the traces printed on Melinex® ST506™ tapers off towards the line edges (see the blue box in Figure 10 I). In contrast, the height of the silver trace on NB-TP-3GU100 only decreases close to the edges (see the blue box in Figure 10 II). An off leveling ratio of the line's thickness towards its edges was determined for the different samples. Figure 11 illustrates the determination of the off leveling ratio. The ink layer thickness was measured in small steps starting in the middle of the cross section moving towards the edges. The two points T_{80} where the ink layer thickness falls below 80 % of the ink layer thickness in the middle of the cross section T_m delimit the segment W_{T80} of the cross section. Formula (1) defines the off leveling ratio OL.

$$OL = \frac{W - W_{T80}}{W} \cdot 100\,\% \qquad (1)$$

The obtained value gives an impression of the ink layer thickness across the line width. It can be seen, that the off leveling is stronger for the substrate Melinex® ST506™ than for the NB-TP-3GU100. For the sample B, the off leveling ratio is about 43.8 %, for the sample C, it is 24.4 % and for the sample D, the off leveling ratio is 24.6 %. The off leveling ratio seems to be characteristic for a given substrate (compare values for samples B and D) and independent of the line width (compare values for samples C and D).

Figure 12 shows SEM images of the samples A (I) and C (II). In the segment at the bottom of Figure 12 it can be seen that the ink layer thickness of the sample C (II) is higher than for sample A.

Figure 13 shows SEM images of one section containing both samples B and D. It can be seen that the wrinkling is stronger for the NB-TP-3GU100 substrate than for the Melinex® ST506™. In can be supposed that Melinex® ST506™ is stiffer than NB-TP-3GU100 and that the embedding resin is more or less as hard as Melinex®

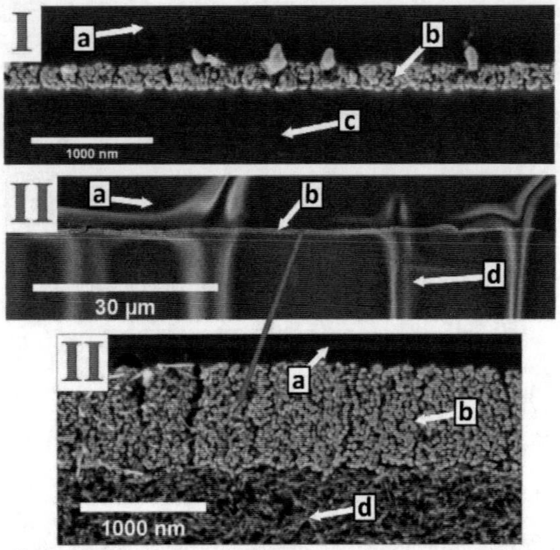

Figure 12. SEM images of sections containing the samples A (I; a: embedding resin, b: silver ink, c: substrate) and C (II; a: resin, b: silver ink, d: nanoporous coating); low magnification (top and bottom), high magnification (middle)

ST506™. This finding confirms the observation described above (Section III.B).

Moreover, Figure 13 I shows that in sample A larger silver particles have been ripped out of the conductive trace and are smeared into the embedding resin. This indicates that the embedding and cutting process have to be further optimized. Using different SEM- and optical microscope images, the the substrate thickness has been measured. For Melinex® ST506™ a substrate thickness of 127.9 µm +/- 2.0 µm was determined. The Mitsubishi NB-TP-3GU100 has a thickness of 138.2 +/- 2.5 µm, whereof the nanoporous layer is 38.3 µm +/- 1.0 µm.

The comparatively high thickness of this layer supports the hypothesis stated above (Section III.A) that this might be the main reason for the warping of the substrate after thermal sintering. There was no indication for sectioning or embedding process related changes of substrate thickness,

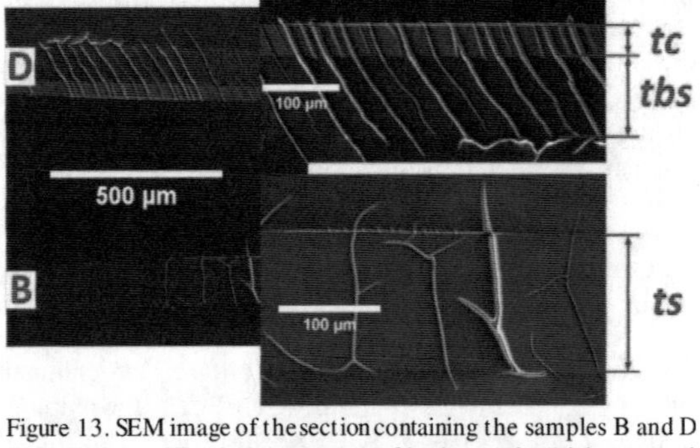

Figure 13. SEM image of the section containing the samples B and D (left, low magnification), segments of both samples (right top and bottom, tc: thickness of the coating, tbs: thickness of the bulk substrate, ts: thickness of the entire substrate; higher magnification)

neither for the bulk substrate nor for the porous coating. With proper cutting parameters (angle between cutting direction and substrate plane) the influence on the ink layer thickness should be minimal. Section wrinkling due to stiffness incompatibilities between substrate and embedding materials is probably the only remarkable deformation of the samples during the whole sectioning process.

IV. Conclusion and Outlook

A method was outlined for analyzing the nano- and microstructure of inkjet printed conductive traces on different polymer substrates using ultramicrotome sectioning and SEM imaging. Our results confirm the finding by Melo [4]. The sections produced showed wrinkling along the substrate plane partially leading to delamination. This may result from stiffness differences between the substrate material and the embedding resin, a parameter to be optimized in further investigations. Despite the resulting delaminations, there were enough regions that could be used for investigation of the nanoparticle network of the printed conductive traces. This indicates that with properly optimized embedding and cutting parameters, the described scheme is a promising method for analyzing thermal, mechanical and chemical influences on the morphology of printed metal nanoparticle inks and on the interface between substrate and ink.

Acknoledgments

The authors thank Dr. Tim Scharnweber from the KIT Institute for Biological Interfaces (IBG1) for granting access to the laser-scanning microscope.

References

[1] M. Ungerer, W. Spomer, L. Veith, A. Fries, C. Debatin, I. Wacker et al., "Analysis of the cross section of inkjet-printed conductive tracks on PET films," ACHI 2017: The Tenth International Conference on Advances in Computer-Human Interactions, Nice, France. March 19 - 23, 2017, pp. 162–168.

[2] J. Perelaer and U. S. Schubert, "Novel approaches for low temperature sintering of inkjet-printed inorganic nanoparticles for roll-to-roll (R2R) applications," Journal of Materials Research, Vol. 28, No. 4, 2013, pp. 564–573. doi:10.1557/jmr.2012.419.

[3] J. Gierak, "Focused Ion Beam nano-patterning from traditional applications to single ion implantation perspectives," Nanofabrication, Vol. 1, No. 1, 2014. doi:10.2478/nanofab-2014-0004.

[4] L. G. de A. Melo, A. P. Hitchcock, V. Berejnov, D. Susac, J. Stumper and G. A. Botton, "Evaluating focused ion beam and ultramicrotome sample preparation for analytical microscopies of the cathode layer of a polymer electrolyte membrane fuel cell," Journal of Power Sources, Vol. 312, 2016, pp. 23–35. doi:10.1016/j.jpowsour.2016.02.019.

[5] M. Ungerer, U. Gengenbach, A. Hofmann and G. Bretthauer, "Comparative and systemic analysis of digital single nozzle printing processes for the manufacturing of functional microstructures," Proc. MikroSystemTechnik Kongress (MST 2015): MEMS, Mikroelektronik, Systeme, Karlsruhe. 10/26/2015 - 10/28/2015.

[6] J. Lessing, A. C. Glavan, S. B. Walker, C. Keplinger, J. A. Lewis and G. M. Whitesides, "Inkjet Printing of Conductive

Inks with High Lateral Resolution on Omniphobic "RF Paper" for Paper-Based Electronics and MEMS," Advanced Materials, Vol. 26, No. 27, 2014, pp. 4677–4682. doi:10.1002/adma.201401053.
[7] H.-H. Lee, K.-S. Chou and K.-C. Huang, "Inkjet printing of nanosized silver colloids," Nanotechnology, Vol. 16, No. 10, 2005, p. 2436. doi:10.1088/0957-4484/16/10/074.
[8] Y. Kawahara, S. Hodges, N.-W. Gong, S. Olberding and J. Steimle, "Building Functional Prototypes Using Conductive Inkjet Printing," IEEE Pervasive Comput., Vol. 13, No. 3, 2014, pp. 30–38. doi:10.1109/MPRV.2014.41.
[9] T. Öhlund, A. Schuppert, B. Andres, H. Andersson, S. Forsberg, W. Schmidt et al., "Assisted sintering of silver nanoparticle inkjet ink on paper with active coatings," RSC Advances, Vol. 5, No. 80, 2015, pp. 64841–64849. doi:10.1039/C5RA06626C.
[10] S. H. Ko, H. Pan, C. P. Grigoropoulos, C. K. Luscombe, J. M. J. Fréchet and D. Poulikakos, "All-inkjet-printed flexible electronics fabrication on a polymer substrate by low-temperature high-resolution selective laser sintering of metal nanoparticles," Nanotechnology, Vol. 18, No. 34, 2007, p. 345202. doi:10.1088/0957-4484/18/34/345202.
[11] M. Mikolajek, A. Friederich, C. Kohler, M. Rosen, A. Rathjen, K. Krüger et al., "Direct Inkjet Printing of Dielectric Ceramic/Polymer Composite Thick Films," Advanced Engineering Materials, Vol. 17, No. 9, 2015, pp. 1294–1301. doi:10.1002/adem.201400451.
[12] T. T. Baby, M. Rommel, F. von Seggern, P. Friederich, C. Reitz, S. Dehm et al., "Sub-50 nm Channel Vertical Field-Effect Transistors using Conventional Ink-Jet Printing," Advanced Materials, Vol. 29, No. 4, 2017. doi:10.1002/adma.201603858.
[13] J. Perelaer, R. Jani, M. Grouchko, A. Kamyshny, S. Magdassi and U. S. Schubert, "Plasma and Microwave Flash Sintering of a Tailored Silver Nanoparticle Ink, Yielding 60% Bulk Conductivity on Cost-Effective Polymer Foils," Advanced Materials, Vol. 24, No. 29, 2012, pp. 3993–3998. doi:10.1002/adma.201200899.
[14] H. Andersson, A. Manuilskiy, T. Unander, C. Lidenmark, S. Forsberg and H.-E. Nilsson, "Inkjet Printed Silver Nanoparticle Humidity Sensor With Memory Effect on Paper," IEEE Sensors J., Vol. 12, No. 6, 2012, pp. 1901–1905. doi:10.1109/JSEN.2011.2182044.
[15] J. Niittynen, R. Abbel, M. Mäntysalo, J. Perelaer, U. S. Schubert and D. Lupo, "Alternative sintering methods compared to conventional thermal sintering for inkjet printed silver nanoparticle ink," Thin Solid Films, Vol. 556, 2014, pp. 452–459. doi:10.1016/j.tsf.2014.02.001.
[16] G. L. Allen, R. A. Bayles, W. W. Gile and W. A. Jesser, "Small particle melting of pure metals," Thin Solid Films, Vol. 144, No. 2, 1986, pp. 297–308. doi:10.1016/0040-6090(86)90422-0.
[17] P. Buffat and J.-P. Borel, "Size effect on the melting temperature of gold particles," Phys. Rev. A, Vol. 13, No. 6, 1976, p. 2287. doi:10.1103/PhysRevA.13.2287.
[18] W. A. MacDonald, "Engineered films for display technologies," J. Mater. Chem., Vol. 14, No. 1, 2004, p. 4. doi:10.1039/b310846p.
[19] DuPont Teijin Films, "Product Information Melinex® ST506™," 2012. http://www.koenig-kunststoffe.de/produkte/melinex/melinex-r-st506.pdf, accessed 23 December 2017.
[20] W. A. MacDonald, M. K. Looney, D. MacKerron, R. Eveson, R. Adam, K. Hashimoto et al., "Latest advances in substrates for flexible electronics," Journal of the Society for Information Display, Vol. 15, No. 12, 2007, pp. 1075–1083. doi:10.1889/1.2825093.
[21] S. Magdassi, "Ink Requirements and Formulations Guidelines," In: S. Magdassi, Ed., The chemistry of inkjet inks, World Scientific Pub. Co, Singapore, Hackensack, N.J, 2010, pp. 19–41.
[22] D.-H. Lee, K.-T. Lim, E.-K. Park, J.-M. Kim and Y.-S. Kim, "Optimized ink-jet printing condition for stable and reproducible performance of organic thin film transistor," Microelectronic Engineering, Vol. 111, 2013, pp. 242–246. doi:10.1016/j.mee.2013.03.177.
[23] G. Li, R. C. Roberts and N. C. Tien, "Interlacing method for micro-patterning silver via inkjet printing," Proc. IEEE 13th Sensors Conference, Valencia, Spain. 2/11/2014 - 5/11/2014, pp. 1687–1690.
[24] F. Molina-Lopez, D. Briand and N. F. de Rooij, "All additive inkjet printed humidity sensors on plastic substrate," Sensors and Actuators B: Chemical, 166–167, 2012, pp. 212–222. doi:10.1016/j.snb.2012.02.042.
[25] D. Soltman and V. Subramanian, "Inkjet-printed line morphologies and temperature control of the coffee ring effect," Langmuir the ACS journal of surfaces and colloids, Vol. 24, No. 5, 2008, pp. 2224–2231. doi:10.1021/la7026847.
[26] I. Reinhold, C. E. Hendriks, R. Eckardt, J. M. Kranenburg, J. Perelaer, R. R. Baumann et al., "Argon plasma sintering of inkjet printed silver tracks on polymer substrates," Journal of Materials Chemistry, Vol. 19, No. 21, 2009, pp. 3384–3388. doi:10.1039/B823329B.
[27] J. Perelaer, M. Klokkenburg, C. E. Hendriks and U. S. Schubert, "Microwave Flash Sintering of Inkjet-Printed Silver Tracks on Polymer Substrates," Advanced Materials, Vol. 21, No. 47, 2009, pp. 4830–4834. doi:10.1002/adma.200901081.
[28] S. Magdassi, M. Grouchko, O. Berezin and A. Kamyshny, "Triggering the sintering of silver nanoparticles at room temperature," ACS nano, Vol. 4, No. 4, 2010, pp. 1943–1948. doi:10.1021/nn901868t.
[29] B.-J. Kim, T. Haas, A. Friederich, J.-H. Lee, D.-H. Nam, J. R. Binder et al., "Improving mechanical fatigue resistance by optimizing the nanoporous structure of inkjet-printed Ag electrodes for flexible devices," Nanotechnology, Vol. 25, No. 12, 2014, p. 125706. doi:10.1088/0957-4484/25/12/125706.
[30] N. Marjanović, "Hybrid electronics systems by CSEM," Proc. 8th International Exhibition and Conference for the Printed Electronics Industry (LOPEC 2016): Technical Conference, München, 2016.
[31] U. Gengenbach, Markus Dickerhof, Liane Koker, Jörg Nagel, Ingo Sieber, Georg Schwartz et al., "A toolbox for multifunctional multilayer printed systems," Proc. MikroSystemTechnik Kongress (MST 2015): MEMS, Mikroelektronik, Systeme, Karlsruhe. 10/26/2015 - 10/28/2015.
[32] S. Merilampi, T. Laine-Ma and P. Ruuskanen, "The characterization of electrically conductive silver ink patterns on flexible substrates," Microelectronics Reliability, Vol. 49, No. 7, 2009, pp. 782–790. doi:10.1016/j.microrel.2009.04.004.
[33] Advanced Nano Products (ANP), "Nano-Silver Ink for Inkjet Printing," 2017. http://anapro.com/eng/product/silver_inkjet_ink.html, accessed 27 February 2017.
[34] Mitsubishi Paper Mills, "Technical Data Sheet: Mitsubishi Nano Benefit Series NB-TP-3GU100," 2014. https://www.mitsubishi-paper.com/fileadmin/user_upload/PrePress/downloads/silver_nano/PET_Film_NB-TP-3GU100.pdf, accessed 23 December 2017.

[35] J. Schindelin, I. Arganda-Carreras, E. Frise, V. Kaynig, M. Longair, T. Pietzsch et al., "Fiji: an open-source platform for biological-image analysis," Nature Methods, Vol. 9, No. 7, 2012, pp. 676–682. doi:10.1038/nmeth.2019.

International Journal on Advances in Intelligent Systems, vol 10 no 3 & 4, year 2017, http://www.iariajournals.org/intelligent_systems/

Framework for Knowledge-Based Fault Detection and Diagnostics in Multi-Domain Systems: Application to Heating Ventilation and Air Conditioning Systems

Parastoo Delgoshaei
Department of Civil and Environmental Engineering,
University of Maryland, College Park, MD 20742, USA
E-mail: p.delgoshaei@gmail.com

Mark A. Austin
Department of Civil and Environmental Engineering,
and Institute for Systems Research,
University of Maryland, College Park, MD 20742, USA
E-mail: austin@isr.umd.edu

***Abstract*—State-of-the-art fault detection methods are equipment and domain specific and non-comprehensive. As a result, the applicability of these methods in different domains is very limited and they can achieve significant levels of performance by having knowledge of the domain and the ability to mimic human thinking in identifying the source of a fault with a comprehensive knowledge of the system and its surroundings. This paper presents a comprehensive semantic framework for fault detection and diagnostics (FDD) in systems simulation and control. Our proposed methodology entails of implementation of the knowledge bases for FDD purposes through the utilization of ontologies and offers improved functionalities of such system through inference-based reasoning to derive knowledge about the irregularities in the operation. We exercise the proposed approach by working step by step through the setup and solution of a fault detection and diagnostics problem for a small-scale heating, ventilating and air-conditioning (HVAC) system.**

Keywords-Fault Detection and Diagnostics; Heating Ventilating and Air-Conditioning (HVAC); Inference-Based, Knowledge Base, Ontologies; Reasoning.

I. Introduction

This paper is concerned with the development of ontology and rule-based modeling abstractions, procedures, and prototype software for automated fault detection and diagnostic (FDD) analysis of condition-based maintenance in multi-domain systems (e.g., buildings, health monitoring, power plants and aviation systems). The article builds upon our previous work [1]–[3] on behavior modeling and analysis of engineering systems with semantic web technologies.

A. Problem Statement

Automated fault detection and diagnostic (FDD) techniques provide a means of detecting unwanted conditions (i.e., "faults") in systems by recognizing deviations in real-time or recorded data values from expected values, and then diagnosing the causes leading to the faults. Automated fault detection and diagnostic (FDD) techniques provide mechanisms for condition-based maintenance of engineered systems (e.g., buildings, health monitoring, power plants and aviation systems). Proper implementation of FDD can enable pro-active identification and remediation of faults before they become significantly deleterious to the safety, security, or efficiency of the operating system.

Within the building sector, degraded or poorly-maintained equipment currently accounts for 15 to 30 % of energy consumption in commercial buildings [4]. Approximately 50 to 67 % of air conditioners (residential and commercial) are either improperly charged or have airflow issues [5] and [6]. Faulty heating, ventilating, air conditioning, and refrigeration (HVAC&R) systems contribute to 1.5 to 2.5 % of total commercial building consumption [7]. Much of this energy usage could be prevented by utilizing automated condition-based maintenance. During the last decade, considerable research has focused on the development of FDD methods for HVAC&R systems. This work has been driven, in part, by the historically less-than-optimal operation of many state-of-the-art HVAC systems. Yet, in spite of recent advances in building simulation, automation and control (see the arrangement of ontologies, rules, reasoning and simulation software in Figure 1), automatic methods for FDD of building systems remain at a relatively immature stage of development. As a result, we require more advanced FDD techniques that leverage the untapped capabilities of building automation integrated with methods in artificial intelligence and semantic modeling. These interdisciplinary FDD systems can benefit from utilizing knowledge repositories for storing automation/simulation data and the inference-based reasoning techniques to obtain additional higher information, such as sensors location, equipment service area.

B. Objectives and Scope

This paper describes a framework for knowledge-based fault detection and diagnostics in multi-domain systems, with a focus on applications to HVAC Systems. In a departure from state-of-the-art developments in ontology engineering, which place a priority on the development and testing of ontologies alone, our objective is to create a modeling framework that supports: (1) concurrent data-driven development of domain models, ontologies and rules, and (2) inference-based reasoning for detection of faults and their causes. The proposed method employs the Web Ontology Language (OWL) [8] and Jena API [9] for the development of semantic models (ontologies and rules) spanning the building, mechanical equipment, sensor, fault detection and diagnostics (FDD), occupant and weather domains. Support for spatial reasoning among entities is provided at the meta-domain level.

The remainder of this paper proceeds as follows: Section

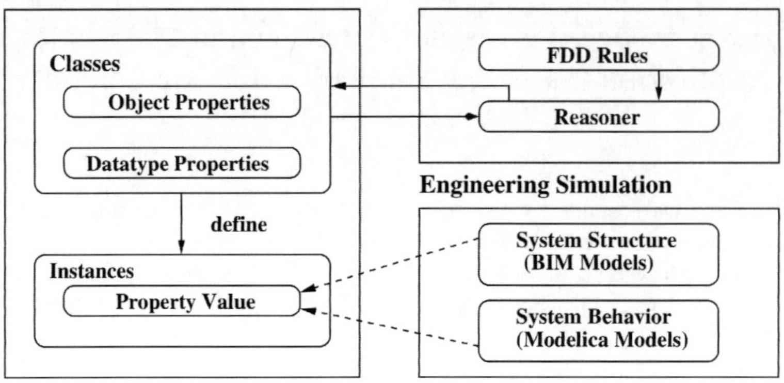

Figure 1. Architecture of engineering simulations connected to semantic models (ontologies and rules) reasoners for fault detection and diagnostic analysis (Adapted from Delgoshaei, Austin and Pertzborn [2]).

II describes related work in FDD. Section III contains a brief introduction to the uses of the Semantic Web and its enabling technologies. The proposed methodology is described in Section IV. Sections V and VI cover: (1) the meta-domain and domain-specific ontologies and rules, respectively, and (2) a step-by-step procedure for detection and analysis of system faults. Section VII presents a case study problem that involves detection of faults in a simple building – procedures for reasoning across multiple domains are presented. Finally, the conclusions of this study and a discussion of next steps is presented in Section VIII.

II. Related Work

Recent advances in building automation technologies provide a means for sensing and collecting the data needed for software applications to automatically detect and diagnose faults in buildings. During the past few decades a variety of FDD techniques have been developed in different domains, including model-based, rule-based, knowledge-based, and simulation-based approaches. Katipamula and Brambley summarizes FDD research for HVAC systems [4]. Their work also describes different fundamental FDD methods under the two main categories of model-based and empirical (history-based) approaches. The major difference is in the nature of the knowledge used to formulate the diagnostics. Model-based diagnostics evaluate residuals between actual system measurements and *a priori* models (e.g., first principle models). Data-driven empirical strategies, on the other hand, do not require *a priori* models. The models used in model-based methods can be quantitative or qualitative. Quantitative models represent the requisite *a priori* knowledge of the system in terms of mathematical equations, typically as explicit descriptions of the physics underlying system components. Qualitative models, conversely, combine concepts such as descriptive "states" and "rules" into statements that are axiological instead of mathematical, expressing operational correctness or desirability through an axiology, a value system, appropriate to each physical application. As a result, the building system operation can be continuously classified as being either faulty or not faulty.

Rule-based strategies are one example of qualitative model-based FDD methods. Rules can be based on first principles or they can be inferred from historical experiments, but in either case they represent expert qualitative knowledge that no purely quantitative representation could model. The first diagnostic expert systems for technical fault diagnosis were developed at MIT by Scherer and White [10]. Since then, diagnostic systems have evolved from rule-based to model-based and expert systems approaches. Semantic models offer a means for the representation of distributed and explicit knowledge and provide ways through inference-based rules to derive implicit knowledge. Berners-Lee and co-workers [11] points out to the benefits of ontology usage for knowledge representation, and utilizing high-level reasoning capabilities in the area of agent-based control solutions. Exploitation of semantics and ontologies in the area of agent-based engineering systems has become one of the hot topics recently. The main reason behind this trend is the success and promotion of Semantic Web technologies to enable languages that are both machine and human processable. Semantic Web-based applications have been developed in the areas of health care [12], biology [13], [14], and transportation [15]. In the area of fault detection and diagnostics, Batic [16] has developed an ontology-based fault detection and diagnosis systems and tested it on airport ontologies to detect the high level irregularities in the operation of airport heating/cooling plants. Also, Schumann [17] highlights the potential impacts of artificial intelligence techniques such as ontologies on tackling the challenges in obtaining a unified diagnosis framework. The benefit of this approach is that ontologies are an essential technology guaranteeing data and information interoperability in heterogeneous and content-rich environments [18] which is at heart of comprehensive fault detection and diagnostic methods.

III. The Semantic Web

A. Semantic Models

Semantic models consist of ontologies, graphs of individuals (specific instances), and inference-based rules in the form of *if <conditions> then <consequences>*. Together, these entities and mechanisms allow for the construction and execution of domain-specific knowledge bases.

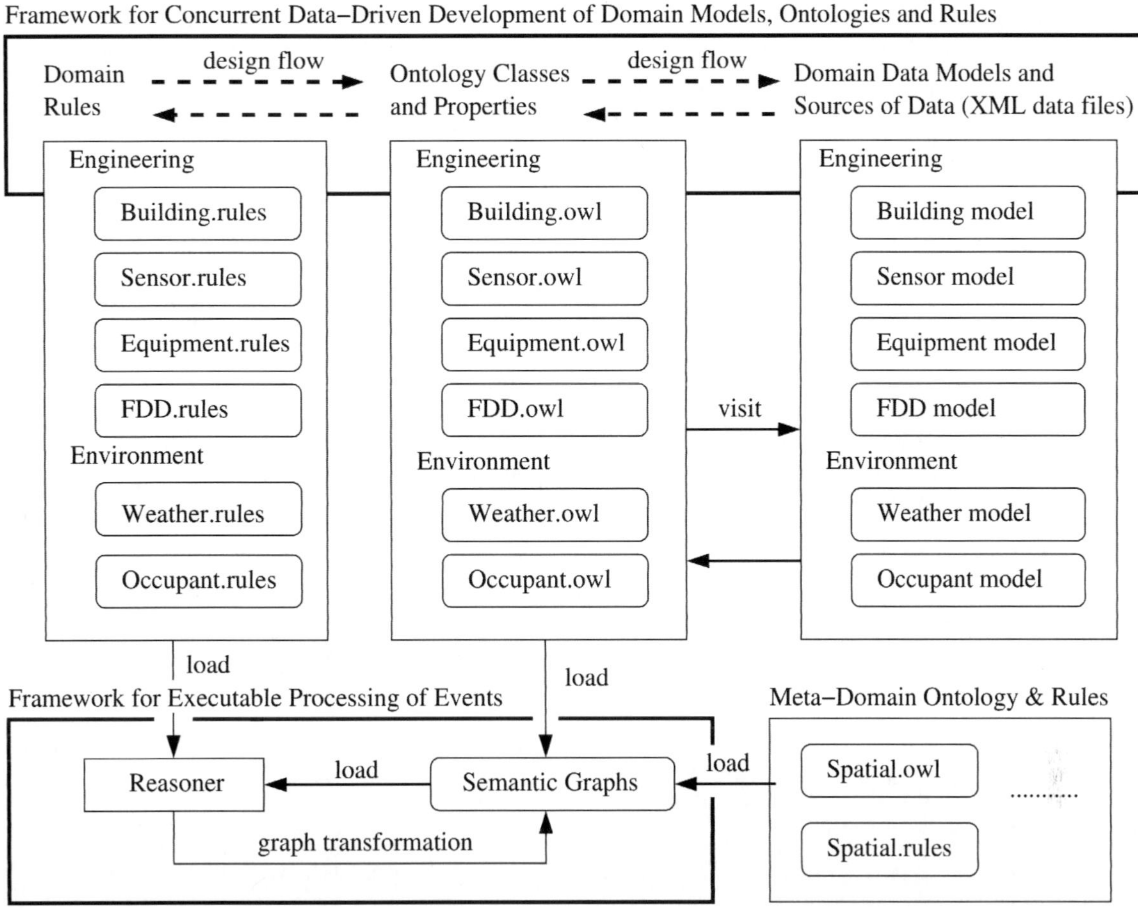

Figure 2. Proposed architecture for: (1) concurrent data-driven development of domain models, ontologies and rules, and (2) executable processing of events.

Ontologies: An ontology is a formal and explicit representation of the concepts, referred to as "classes" (e.g., cooling coil, valve), and their interrelationships in a domain. The classes may have attributes that are stored as a simple data type properties" (e.g., coil setpoint). Support for semantic relationships between classes is provided by object properties (e.g., a coil has as a valve). For the representation of domains where there are many variations to be represented, but common data properties among those variants, ontology languages provide support for the organization of similar concepts into hierarchies, and support for propagation of data and object properties through hierarchies via inheritance mechanisms. We may wish to state, for example, that a cooling coil is a type of coil. In this hierarchy, the class cooling coil is a subclass of the class coil. And the class coil is superclass of the class cooling coil. The details of the classes, data properties and object properties can be summarized as follows:

- **Classes**: Valve, Cooling Coil
- **Datatype properties**: coilTemperature (double), isClosed (Boolean), coilSetpoint(double)
- **Object Property**: hasValve

Individuals: Individuals are instances of ontology concepts, and their purpose is to represent the data in a domain, e.g.,

- **Individuals**: ValveI, ValveII, Ccoil, Hcoil
- **Storing individuals**: ¡Hcoil hasValve ValveII¿

One common syntax for representing facts about a domain is the triple structure <subject, predicate, object>.

Inference Rules: Inference rules and their associated reasoning mechanisms provide a way derive new information based on the existing data stored in the ontology in the form of: if <conditions> then <consequent>. For example, the script:

```
Logical Rule:

(?coil rdf:Type coil) (?coil setPoint ?sp)
(?coil coilTemperature ?cp) equal(?cp,?sp)
(?coil hasValve ?valve)  -> (?valve isClosed true)

Stored individuals : <Hcoil hasValve ValveII>
                     <Ccoil coilTemperature 35>
                     <Ccoil coilSetpoint  35>
Inferred Knowledge: <ValveII  isClosed true>
```

takes existing facts and rule that covers the setpoint and temperature of a coil to infer that a valve is closed.

A key benefit of semantic modeling frameworks is that the ontologies and rules are human readable, yet they can also be compiled into code that is executable on machines.

IV. METHODOLOGY

A. Architecture Framework

In state-of-the-art development of semantic models, a common strategy is to provide classes and data properties for all possible configurations within a domain, as well as linkage to related domains. For example, in the integrated model-centric engineering ontologies (IMCE) developed at JPL (Jet Propulsion Laboratory) during the 2000-2010 era [19], [20], the electrical engineering ontology (i.e., electrical.owl) imports the mechanical engineering ontology (i.e., mechanical.owl). Both the electrical and mechanical engineering ontologies import a multitude of foundation ontologies (e.g., analysis.owl, mission.owl, base.owl, project.owl, time.owl) and make extensive use of multiple inheritance mechanisms in the development of new classes. The result is ontologies containing more than two hundred classes, with some classes containing three or four dozen data and object properties. Notions of "simplicity in system design" through modularity of semantic models (e.g., bundling of ontologies and rules) do not seem to exist.

In a first step toward mitigating these complexities, we propose a semantic modeling framework (see Figure 2) that supports: (1) concurrent data-driven development of domain models, ontologies and rules, and (2) executable processing of incoming faults. Instead of creating ontologies and then developing a few rules for validation of model properties, our goal is to put the development of data, ontologies and rules on an equal footing. A key advantage of this approach is that it forces designers to provide semantic representations for data that are needed in decision making, and increases the likelihood that data not needed for decision making will be left out. Rules will be developed for verification of domain properties and processing of faults through reasoning with data sources, possibly from multiple domains. Implementation of the latter goal leads to semantic graphs that will dynamically adapt to the consequences of incoming data and events (e.g., changing occupant locations and weather events) acting on the system.

Our second strategy is to minimize the use of multiple inheritance in the specification of OWL ontologies and, instead, explore opportunities for replacing inheritance relationships by object property relations. In order for the architectural framework to be both scalable and adaptable to changing external conditions, the ontologies will need to be modular, and the rules will need to act both within a domain and across domains.

B. Working with Jena and Jena Rules

Our prototype software implementation makes extensive use of Apache Jena and Jena Rules. Apache Jena [9] is an open source Java framework for building Semantic Web and linked data applications. Jena provides APIs (application programming interfaces) for developing code that handles RDF (resource description framework), RDFS, OWL (web ontology language) and SPARQL (support for query of RDF graphs). The Jena rule-based inference subsystem is designed to allow a range of inference engines or reasoners to be plugged into Jena. Jena Rules is one such engine.

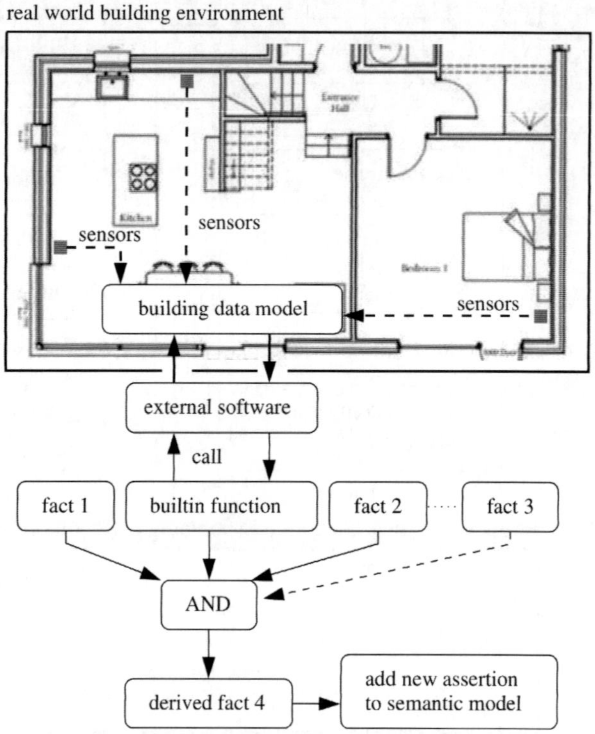

Figure 3. Framework for forward chaining of facts and results of builtin functions to new assertions (derived facts).

Jena Rules employs facts and assertions described in OWL to infer additional facts from instance data and class descriptions. As illustrated in Figure 3, it also provides support for the development of builtin functions that can link to external software programs and streams of data sensed in the real world. For the implementation of the vision implied by Figure 2, particularly support for spatial and temporal reasoning, the latter turns out to be crucially important because, by default, OWL only provides builtin datatype support for numbers (i.e., float and double), booleans (i.e., to represent true and false) and character strings (i.e., string). To combat the lack of support for complex data types, such as those needed to represent data for spatial and temporal reasoning, we adopt a strategy of embedding the relevant data in character strings, and then designing builtin functions and external software that can parse the data into spatial/temporal models, and then make the reasoning computations that are required.

C. Data-Driven Approach to Generation of Individuals in Semantic Graphs

In the proposed framework semantic models are the composition of ontologies, rules and data.

Figure 4 illustrates a data-driven approach to the generation of individuals in semantic graphs.

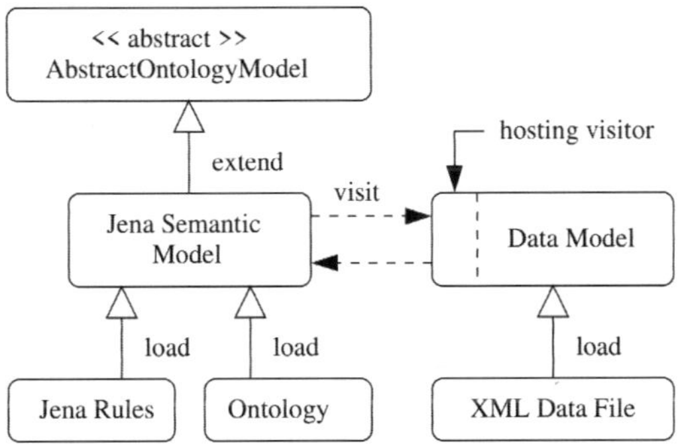

Figure 4. Data-driven approach to generation of individuals in semantic graphs.

First, data is imported into Java Object data models using JAXB, the XML binding for Java. After the ontologies and rules have been loaded into the Jena Semantic Model, the semantic model creates instances of the relevant OWL ontologies by visiting the data model and gathering information on the individuals within a particular domain (e.g., building, sensor, occupant). Once the data has been transferred to the Jena Semantic Model and used to create an ontology instance, the rules are applied.

V. Meta-Domain Ontologies and Rules

Meta-domain ontologies and rules have universal application across domains, and include concepts such as time, space, physical units and currency. This study employs spatial reasoning to determine the relationship of sensor and occupants to geometric entities such as rooms and building zones.

A. Spatial Ontology and Rules

Spatial logic is concerned with regions and their connectivity, allowing one to address issues of the form: what is true, and where? Formal theories for reasoning with space – points, lines, and regions – are covered by region connected calculus [21]. A robust implementation of two-dimensional spatial entities and associated reasoning procedures is provided by the Java Topology Suite (JTS) [22].

Spatial Ontology and Rules for Spatial Reasoning. Figure 5 shows an abbreviated representation of our experimental spatial (geometry) ontology and associated data and object properties. High-level classes – abstract concepts – are provided for entities that represent singular geometry (e.g., AbstractGeometry) and groups of entities (e.g., AbstractGeometryCollection). Specific types of geometry (e.g,, Polygon, MultiPoint) are organized into a hierarchy similar to the Java implementation in JTS. The high-level class AbstractGeometry contains a Datatype property, hasGeometry, which stores a string representation of the JTS geometry. For example, the abbreviated string "POLYGON ((0 0, 0 5, ... 0 0))" shows the format for pairs of (x,y) coordinates defining a two-dimensional polygon. This feature allows a semantic model to visit a domain data model, and gather a complete description of the two-dimensional geometry.

Within Jena Rules, families of builtin functions can be developed to evaluate the geometric relationship between pairs of spatial entities (e.g., to determine whether or not a point is contained within a polygon). Figure 6 shows, for example, the Jena Rule that identifies the room in which a sensor is placed. An English translation of the rule fragments is as follows: If (?r) is a room with geometry (?rg) and string representation (?rjts), and (?s) is a sensor with geometry (?sg) and string representation (?sjts), then the builtin function getPointInPolygon(?sjts,?rjts,?t) will determine if the sensor (point geometry) is inside the room (polygon geometry) and return the result as a boolean (?t). If (?t) is true, then the sensor is inside the room and a new relationship (?s bld:isInRoom ?r) is created. A similar rule would be written to establish the relationship between sensors and HVAC zones.

VI. Domain Ontologies and Rules

The domain-specific ontologies and rules are organized into two groups: (1) engineering ontologies and rules, and (2) surrounding environment ontologies and rules. In Figures 7 through 13 we use red rectangles with heavy dashed edges to highlight the classes that participate in the rule checking and/or the case study problem presented in Section VII. For a complete description of the ontologies used in this study we refer the interested reader to Delgoshaei and Austin [23].

A. Engineering Ontologies and Rules

The engineering ontologies and rules cover four domains: (1) buildings, (2) mechanical equipment, (3) sensors, and (4) procedures for fault detection and diagnosis.

Building Ontology and Rules. The prototype building ontology and rules (see Figures 7 and 8) provide computational support for the representation of two-dimensional floorplan geometry, modeling relationships between elements of floorplan geometry and sensors, zones for HVAC control, and building elements such as doors, windows and walls. The latter are modeled as subclasses of a component that has geometry described by a JTS string.

Connections to the mechanical equipment and occupancy domains are achieved through data properties for the building environment state; see, for example, hasRoomSetpoint and isOccupied. Object properties record the relationship of a room to relevant HVAC zones and sensors. Windows have the boolean data property isOpen to record whether or not a particular window is open. As we will soon in the case study problem, this parameter plays a pivotal role in diagnostic analysis of the causes leading to a fault in mechanical equipment.

The prototype software implementation has one rule for determining the spatial relationship among zones of the building. The rule systematically retrieves the JTS geometry of each zone, verifies they are not equal, and then uses the builtin function getPointInPolygon() to verify their geometric relationship. As previously noted, these backend computations are handled by the Java Topology Suite software [22].

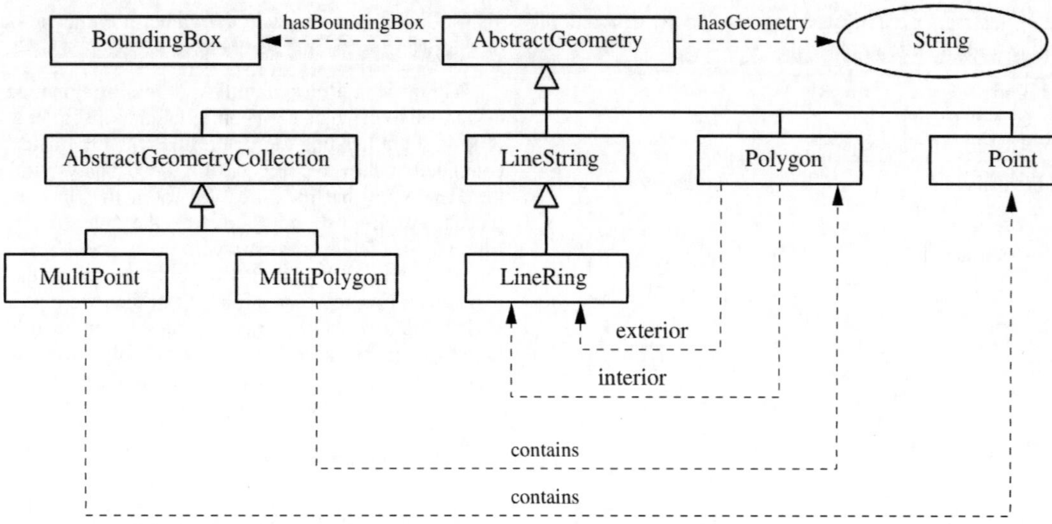

Figure 5. Abbreviated representation of spatial (geometry) ontology and associated data and object properties.

Jena Rules

```
// Rule to check if a sensor is inside a room ...

[ BuildingRule01: (?r rdf:type bld:Room) (?r bld:hasGeometry ?rg) (?rg geom:hasGeometry ?rjts)
                  (?s rdf:type sen:Sensor) (?s sen:hasGeometry ?sg) (?sg geom:hasGeometry ?sjts)
                  getPointInPolygon(?sjts,?rjts,?t)
                  equal(?t, "true"^^xs:boolean) -> (?s bld:isInRoom ?r)]
```

Figure 6. Rules to determine the rooms in which sensors have been placed.

Mechanical Equipment Ontology and Rules. Figures 9 and 10 illustrate the concepts (i.e., ontology classes), properties (i.e., data and object properties) and rules governing the operation and identification of faults in mechanical systems equipment. In practice, datatype property values associated with the various ontologies will be set from streams of data either performed by a simulation tool (e.g. EnergyPlus, Dymola, TRNSYS) [24]–[26], or perhaps from measurements taken in a real building, working in conjunction with BACnet protocols [27] and a co-simulation middleware.

The semantic graph shown in Figure 9 is quite broad, covering concepts from chillers and fans to zones. The scope of our investigation focuses on faults associated with valves, coils and air handling units. Basic rules (see Figure 10) are provides for: (1) controlling the flow in a valve, (2) determining if a valve is leaky, and (3) identifying situations where the normal operational status of a valve is false. Thus, we are able to determine that when a cooling coil valve is faulty, the associated air handling unit is also faulty.

Sensor Ontology and Rules. Figure 11 shows the classes and properties in our experimental sensor ontology. Our goal is to provide computational support for modeling: (1) sensor operation, including when a sensor reading might be outside an acceptable working range, and (2) determining the location of a sensor relative to the environment in which it is embedded. These objectives are achieved with three classes: Sensor, Measurement, and the external class Geometry.

Support for modeling various types of sensor (e.g., temperature sensor, flow sensor, and CO2 sensor) is provided through the definition of specialized sensor classes that subclass Sensor. The class Measurement has data properties to keep track of the current sensor value, the time, and the units associated with the measurement.

Two sensor rules (see Figures 6 and 12) are supported: (1) To determine if a sensor reading is beyond the acceptable range, (2) To determine the room in which the sensor is located. The first rule uses the classes Sensor and Measurement and associate properties. The second rule uses the classes Sensor and Geometry.

Fault Detection and Diagnostic Ontologies, Rules, and Procedures. The fault detection and diagnostic (FDD) ontology (see Figure 13) captures the knowledge needed for: (1) identifying that a fault exists, and (2) systematically diagnosing the fault to find the root causes. The main classes in this process are State, Fault, Hypothesis and Evidence. State is a high-level state representation that has data values – see, for example, the boolean properties hasExpectedValue and hasCurrentValu – common to many types of state representation.

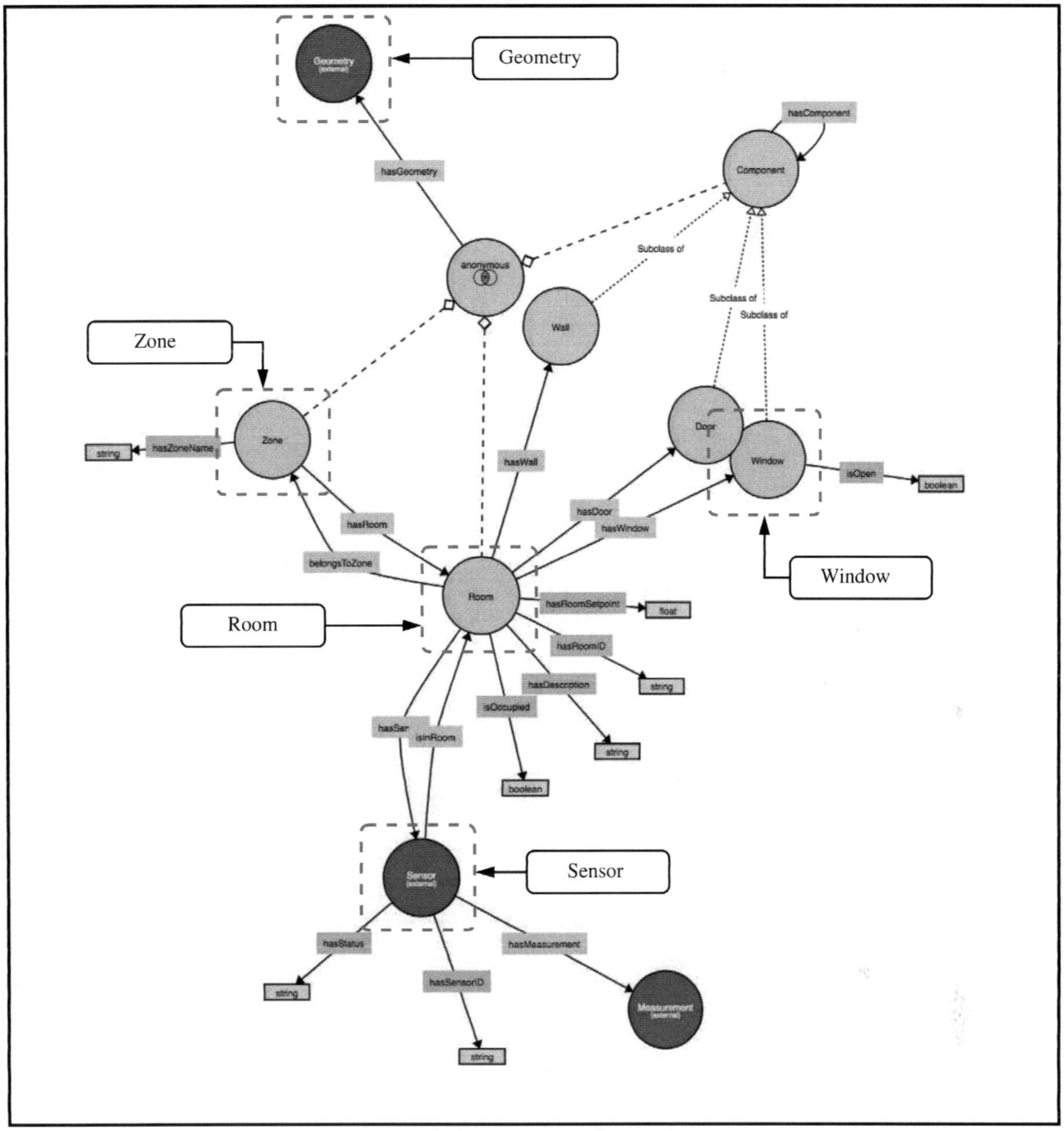

Figure 7. Schematic of building ontology classes and properties.

Jena Rules

```
// Rule to check if two zones intersect ...

[ BuildingRule02: (?r1 rdf:type bld:Zone) (?r1 bld:hasGeometry ?r1g) (?r1g geom:hasGeometry ?r1jts)
                  (?r2 rdf:type bld:Zone) (?r2 bld:hasGeometry ?r2g) (?r2g geom:hasGeometry ?r2jts)
                  notEqual( ?r1jts, ?r2jts ) getPointInPolygon( ?r1jts, ?r2jts, ?t)
                  equal(?t, "true"^^xs:boolean) -> (?r1 bld:intersects ?r2)]
```

Figure 8. Rule for Zone Intersect.

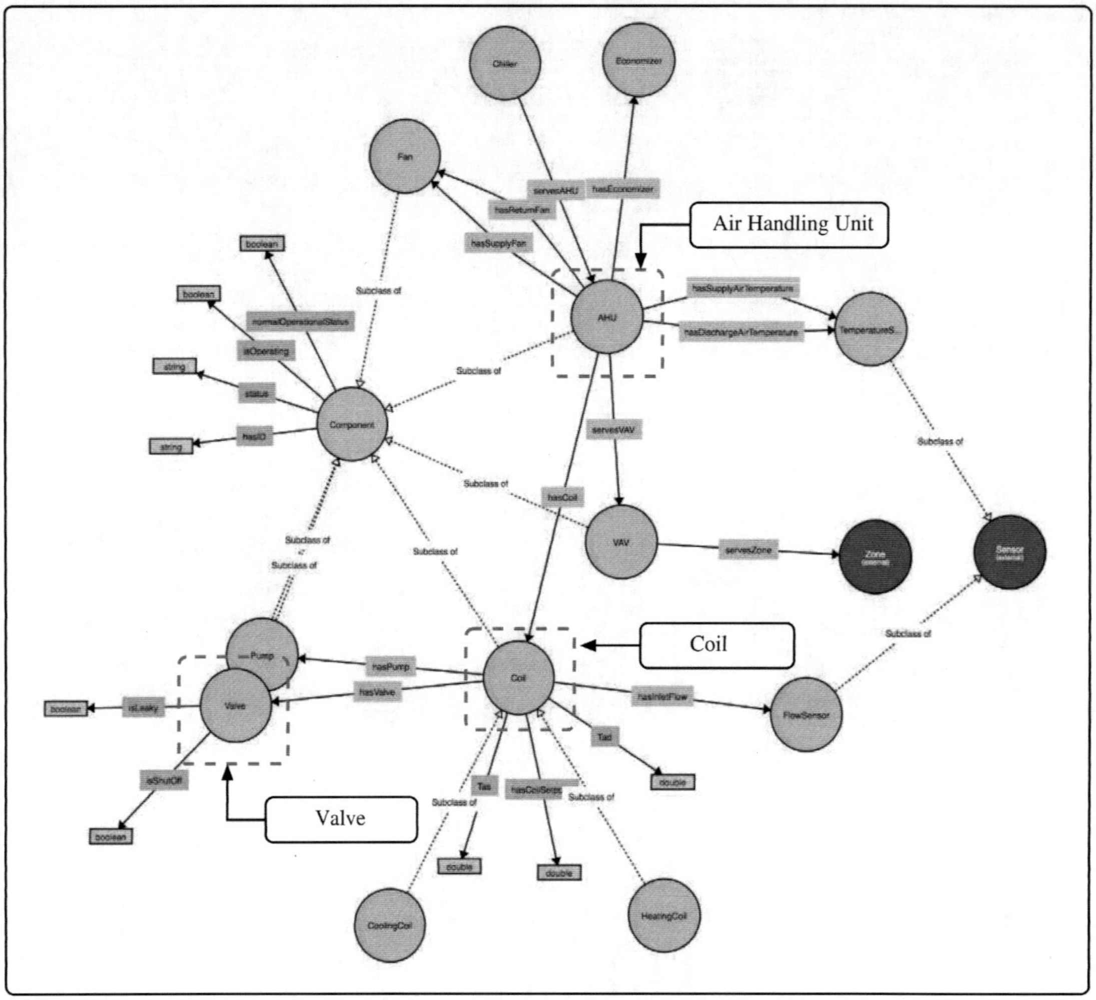

Figure 9. Schematic of equipment ontology classes and properties.

Jena Rules

```
// Close the valve when the coil temperature is the same as coil setpoint.

[ EquipmentRule01: (?coil rdf:type eq:Coil) (?coil eq:hasCoilSetpoint ?sp)
                   (?coil eq:hasCoilTemperature ?cp) equal(?sp,?cp) (?coil eq:hasValve ?valve) ->
                   (?valve eq:isShutOff "true"^^xs:boolean) print('valve is shut')]

// If the valve is shut, the temperature of the air that passes through the coil
// has to be the same. Otherwise, the valve is leaky

[ EquipmentRule02: (?hwv rdf:type eq:Valve) (?hwv eq:isShutOff "true"^^xs:boolean)
                   (?c rdf:type eq:Coil)(?c eq:hasValve ?hwv) (?c eq:Tad ?t1)
                   (?c eq:Tas ?t2) notEqual(?t2 ?t1) -> (?hwv eq:isLeaky "true"^^xs:boolean)
                   (?hwv eq:hasNormalOperationalStatus "false"^^xs:boolean) print('valve is Leaky')  ]

// If the a valve fails, the AHU fails too ...

[ EquipmentRule03: (?hwv rdf:type eq:Valve) (?AHU eq:hasCoil ?c) (?c eq:hasValve ?v)
                   (?v eq:hasNormalOperationalStatus "false"^^xs:boolean) ->
                   print('AHUMalfunction') (?AHU eq:hasNormalOperationalStatus "false"^^xs:boolean)]
```

Figure 10. Rules for establishing the operational status and simple operations of mechanical equipment.

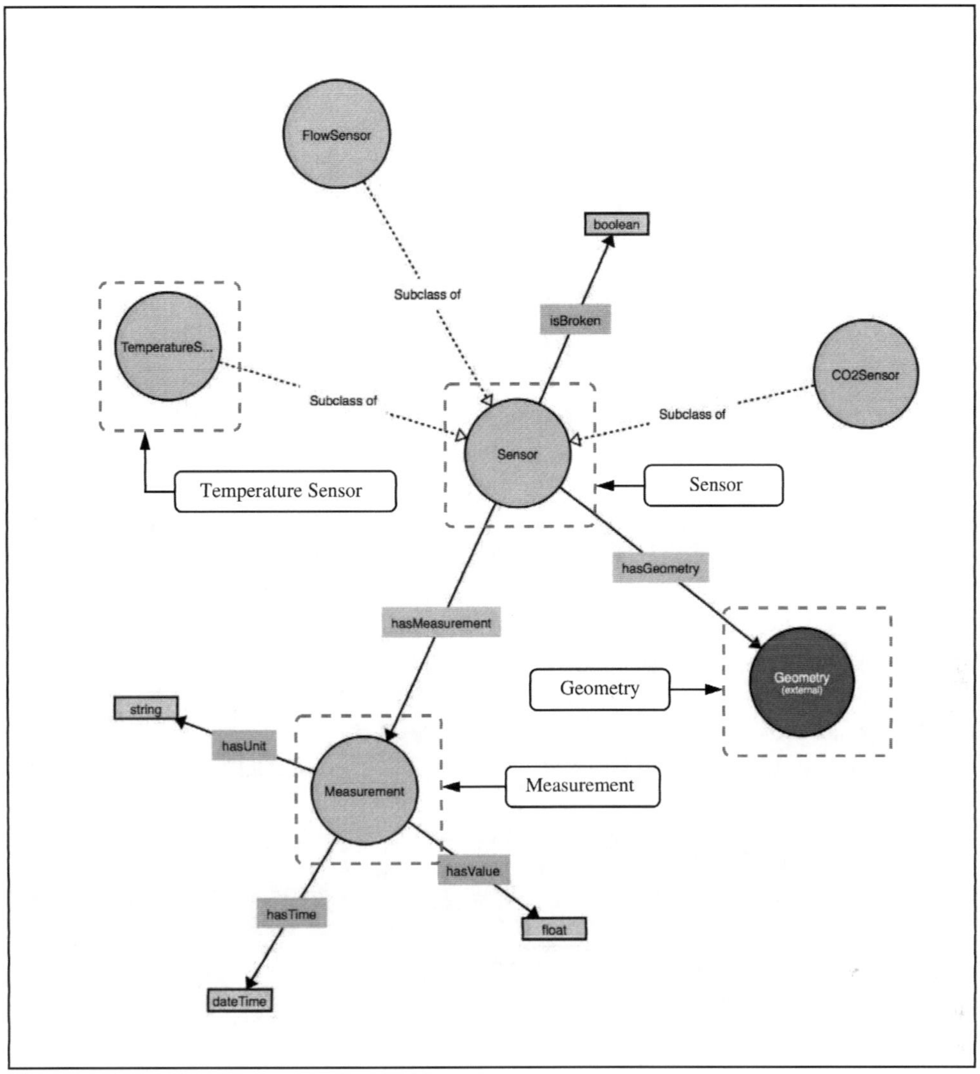

Figure 11. Sensor ontology classes and properties.

Jena Rules

```
// Simple rule to check if a sensor is broken ...

[ SensorRule01: (?s rdf:type sen:Sensor) (?s sen:hasMeasurement ?m) (?m sen:hasValue ?r)
                isOutOfRange(?m ?t) -> (?s sen:isBroken ?t) ]
```

Figure 12. Rule for Zone Intersect.

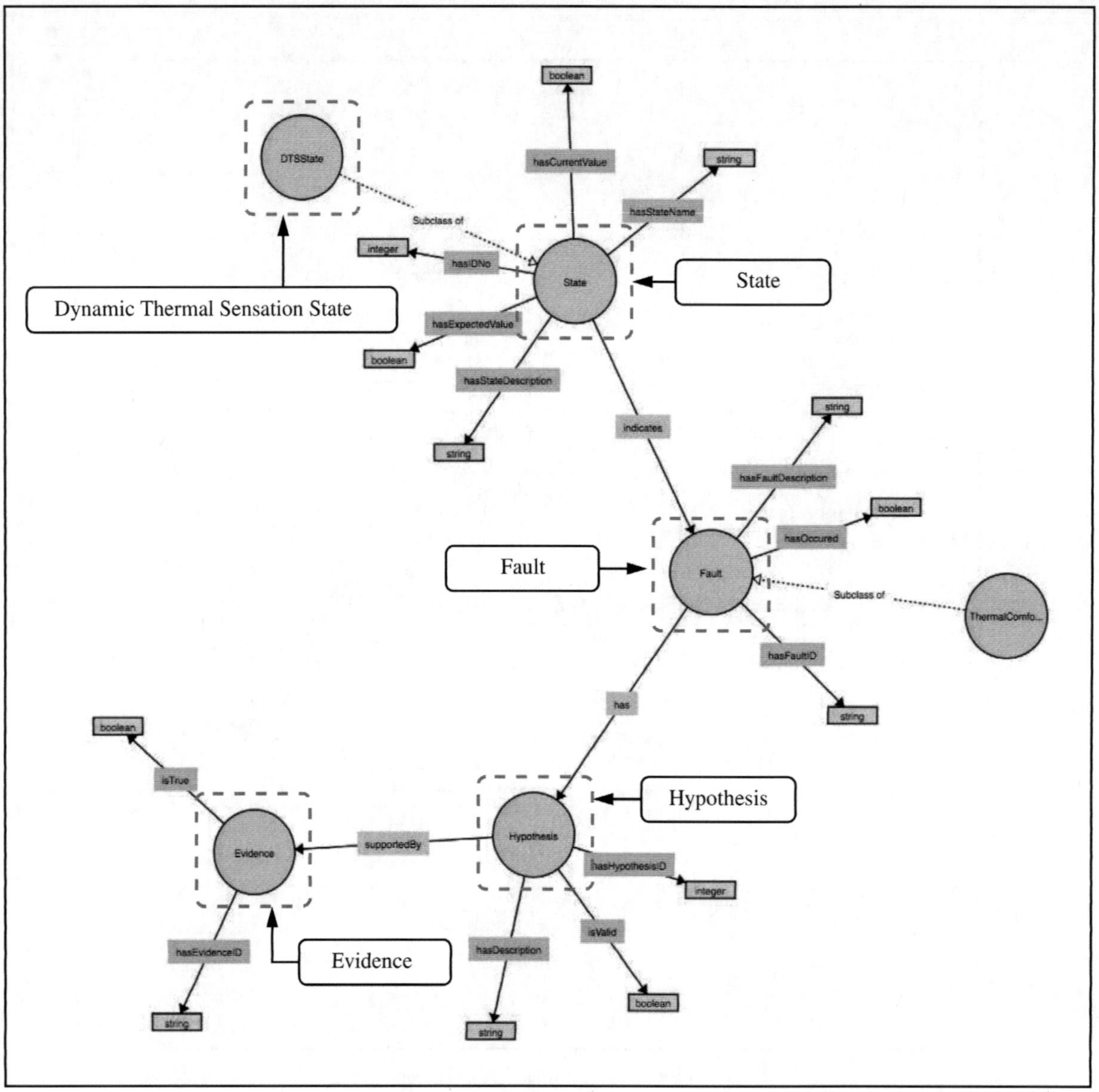

Figure 13. Fault detection and diagnostic ontology classes and properties.

Jena Rules

```
// General purpose rule for recording when a fault has occurred.

[FDDRule01: (?st rdf:type fdd:State) (?st fdd:hasCurrentValue ?csv)
            (?st fdd:belongsToFault ?F) (?st fdd:hasExpectedValue ?esv)
            notEqual(?csc,?esv) -> (?F fdd:hasOccured ''true'')   print('faultoccured')]
```

Figure 14. Rule for detecting a faulty state.

Jena Rules

```
// Determine romm in which an occupant is located.

[ OccupantRule01: (?r rdf:type bld:Room) (?o rdf:type occ:Occupant)
                  (?o occ:hasOccupantGeometry ?og) (?og geom:hasGeometry ?ojts)
                  (?r bld:hasGeometry ?rg) (?rg geom:hasGeometry ?rjts)
                  getPointInPolygon(?ojts,?rjts,?t) equal(?t, "true"^^xs:boolean) ->
                  (?r bld:hasOccupant ?o) print(?o,'OccupantisInRoom',?r,?t)]

// When positive values of DTSIndex are greater than 0.3, an occupant is not comfortable.

[ OccupantRule02: (?oc rdf:type occ:Occupant) (?oc occ:hasDTSIndex ?v) greaterThan(?v,0.3)
                  (?oc occ:hasDTSState ?dts)  -> print(?oc,'isComfortable' "false"^^xs:boolean)
                  (?oc occ:isComfortable "false"^^xs:boolean)
                  (?dts fdd:hasCurrentValue "false"^^xs:boolean)]
```

Figure 16. Rule for occupants location and thermal comfort.

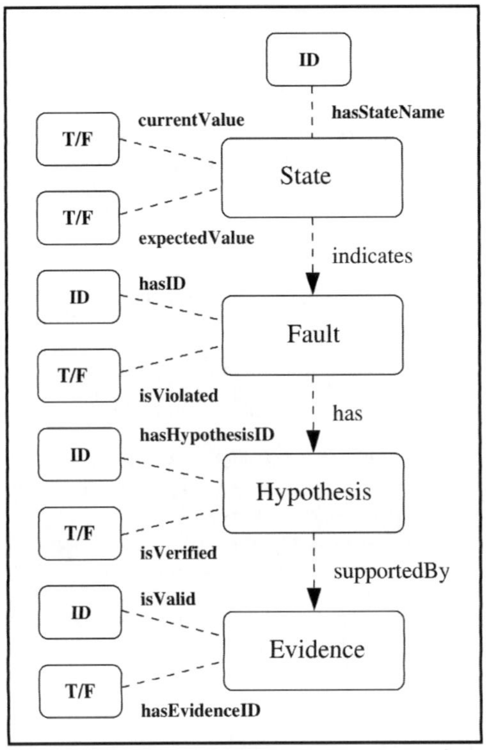

Figure 15. Flow chart for identification of faults and identification and verification of hypotheses and supporting evidence.

Our experimental FDD ontology also supports DTSState, a subclass of State, designed to represent states associated with dynamic thermal sensation (DTS).

Figure 15 is a flowchart for fault detection and the identification and verification of relevant hypotheses and supporting evidence. The step-by-step procedure for detecting a fault and diagnosing its causes corresponds to a traversal through the classes State, Fault, Hypothesis and Evidence. A fault is indicated when the current and expected values of a state are in conflict. Each fault has a hypothesis that needs to be supported by evidence. The evaluation procedure works backwards. Verification of the evidence is a prerequisite to validating a hypothesis. In an implementation of the procedure, data properties indicate whether or not a fault has been verified, whether or not an hypothesis has been verified, and whether or not supporting evidence is valid. This procedure is mirrored by set of rules shown in Figure 14.

B. Surrounding Environment Ontologies and Rules

The surrounding environment ontologies and rules include model support for the building occupants and weather phenomena.

Occupant Ontology and Rules. While several studies [28], [29] have recently identified the importance of including inhabitants as an integral part of simulation and control of energy systems and indoor environments, present-day procedures rely on predetermined occupancy schedules and/or empirical estimates based on sensors. For fault detection and diagnostic analysis of mechanical equipment in buildings, solutions are complicated by the strong coupling of human presence, comfort and behavior, to details of the building state (e.g., whether or not a window is open) and surrounding environment (e.g., what side of the building is in the sun).

Figure 16 takes a first step toward the development of rules for modeling and evaluation of occupant location and thermal comfort. The occupant ontology (see reference [23] for details) expands upon the work of Mahdavi and Taheri [30], and considers four subcategory problems: (1) location, (2) actions (e.g., open/close window), (3) attitudes (e.g., thermal sensation) and (4) preferences in terms of temperature and moisture of the air. Occupant location is modeled as point geometry in the building.

Weather Ontology and Rules. Based upon the work of Staroch [31], the weather ontology and rules cover concepts such as Weather Phenomenon, Weather Report, and Weather State. The weather state is composed of different Weather phenomenon class holds the physical attributes regarding the weather such as the temperature, pressure, solar radiation, wind

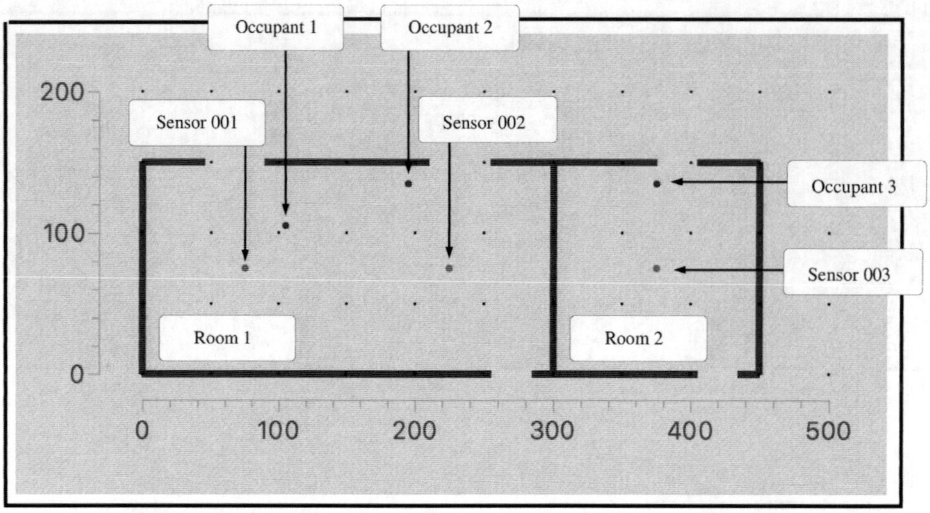

Figure 17. Plan view of two-room building architecture, sensors, and building occupants.

and cloud. Weather data is obtained from current Weather [32], a free and open source API (application programming interface) that provides access to historical as well as current and future forecast weather data from an online server. A Weather report can include data about the current weather or a forecast, specified in terms of start time and duration. For example, a medium range weather report has duration of more than 3 hours, with a start time of less than 12 hours into the future. Weather rules use current temperature values to identify a frosty and heat temperature conditions. For example, a Frost temperature condition occurs when observed temperature is below 0 C. A Heat temperature condition occurs when observed temperature is above 30 C. Similar intervals of temperature range can be defined for cold, below room temperature (at least 10 C and less than 20 C), and so forth.

VII. Case Study Problem

To examine capabilities of the framework for knowledge-based fault detection and diagnostic analysis, this section presents a case study test problem where faults in HVAC equipment are triggered by occupant discomfort in a conditioned space. The case study shows how heterogeneous data and knowledge from a variety of sources and domains can be integrated into a single semantic graph, how ontologies and rules can work together to detect the existence of a fault, and then diagnose the causes by systematically considering hypotheses and the supporting evidence.

A. Problem Description

Figure 17 is a plan view of the case study problem setup, consisting a small two-room building architecture, three sensors and three building occupants. Not shown is the mechanical equipment responsible for conditioning the room temperature and achieving acceptable levels of occupant comfort. The mechanical equipment consists of an air handling unit (AHU). The AHU has a coil (i.e., for heating and cooling). The water temperature that flows to the coil is managed by a valve.

Three rules are responsible for the operation and classification of faults in the mechanical equipment:

- Close the valve when the coil temperature is the same as coil setpoint.
- If the valve is shut, the temperature of the air that passes through the coil has to be the same. Otherwise, the valve is leaky
- If the a valve fails, the AHU fails too.

One measure to evaluate thermal comfort for the occupants is through computing the thermal sensation as a function of environmental factors such as outdoor and indoor temperature and some personal factors such as clothing levels. A dynamic model to compute thermal sensation (DTS) index to was introduced by Chen and co-workers [33]. According to thermal sensation scale suggested by ASHRAE [34], an acceptable range for occupancy comfort is the interval $[-0.3, 0.3]$. By comparing the current and expected values in a DTS state, the rules in Figure 14 will infer the existence of a faulty state, and then systematically examine the evidence associated with each hypothesis to find a root cause.

B. Snapshot of Semantic Graph Model Assembly

Figure 18 shows a snapshot of the building, equipment, sensor, weather, and FDD ontologies integrated together, and populated with system data. The semantic graph model contains instances of ontologies (individuals), relationships among individuals (often spanning domains), and data values associated with various individuals.

From a fault detection and diagnostics standpoint, the main points to note are as follows:

- Occupant 1 is located in Room 1.
- Room 1 has window, a temperature sensor (Sensor 001), and a carbon dioxide sensor (Sensor 002). HVAC services are provided to Room 1 by air handling unit

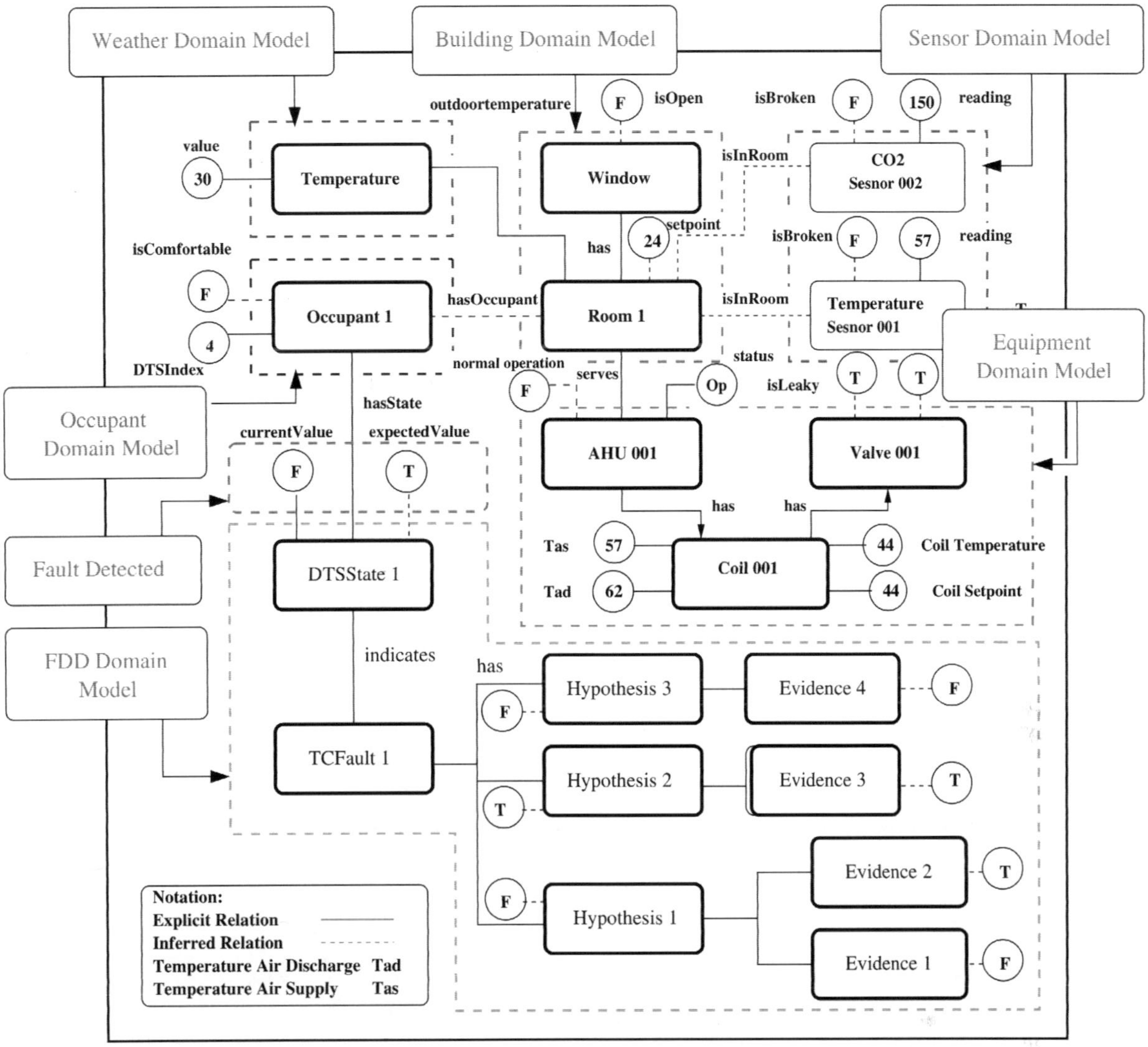

Figure 18. Snapshot of fully assembled semantic graph model. The data values will be computed and filled by the rules.

TABLE I. Instances of states, hypotheses, and evidence for identifying the cause for abnormal occupant thermal comfort value.

Class	Individual	Description
State	DTSState 1	The DTS index in between $[-0.3, 0.3]$.
Fault	TCFault 1	The DTS index lies outside the interval $[-0.3, 0.3]$ when the air-handling unit is operating.
Evidence	Evidence 1	The CO2 sensor reading is above the normal range the and that shows the window is open.
	Evidence 2	The outdoor temperature is greater than room setpoint.
	Evidence 3	A sensor's reading is outside the range that indicates the sensor is broken.
	Evidence 4	A component is AHU is malfunctioning that results in an abnormal operation of AHU.
Hypothesis	Hypothesis 1	Warm outside air is leaking into the room through an open window –> Supported by Evidence 1 and Evidence 2.
	Hypothesis 2	The serving air-handling unit has abnormal operation. –> Supported by Evidence 3.
	Hypothesis 3	The room sensor that provides feed-back to AHU reaching its target setpoint is broken –> Supported by Evidence 4.

Jena Rules

```
// Evidence Rule 01: A window is open base on C02 concentration in the room.
// -------------------------------------------------------------------------

[ EvidenceRule01: (?cs rdf:type sen:CO2Sensor) (?cs bld:isInRoom ?room)
            (?r bld:hasWindow ?w)(?cs bld:hasReading ?m) lessThan(?m,600)
            greaterThan(?m,400) (?e fdd:hasEvidenceID ?n)  equal("1"^^xs:integer,?n) ->
            (?w building:isOpen "true"^^xs:boolean) (?e fdd:isTrue "true"^^xs:boolean)  ]

// Evidence Rule 02: Outside temperature is warmer than the setpoint.
// -------------------------------------------------------------------------

[ EvidenceRule02: (?r rdf:type bld:Room) (?r bld:hasSetpoint ?sp)
                (?t rdf:type we:Temperature) (?t we:hasTemperatureValue ?tv)
                greaterThan(?tv,?sp) equal("2"^^xs:integer,?n) (?e rdf:type fdd:Evidence)
                (?e fdd:hasEvidenceID ?n) -> (?e fdd:isTrue "true"^^xs:boolean)  ]

// Evidence Rule 03: Temperature sensor in a room is broken.
// -------------------------------------------------------------------------

[EvidenceRule03: (?ts rdf:type sen:TemperatureSensor) (?ts bld:isInRoom ?room)
               (?ts bld:isBroken ?t)  equal(?t, "true"^^xs:boolean)  equal("3"^^xs:integer,?n)
               (?e rdf:type fdd:Evidence)
               (?e fdd:hasEvidenceID ?n ->(?e fdd:isTrue "true"^^xs:boolean) ]

// Evidence Rule 04: Malfunction is in the Air Handling Unit.
// -------------------------------------------------------------------------

[EvidenceRule04: (?AHU rdf:type eq:AHU) (?v eq:hasNormalOperationalStatus "false"^^xs:boolean)
               equal(?t, "true"^^xs:boolean)  equal("4"^^xs:integer,?n)
               (?e rdf:type fdd:Evidence)->  (?e fdd:isTrue "true"^^xs:boolean) ]

// FDD Rule 02: Indicate when thermal comfort in a conditioned room has expected value.
// ------------------------------------------------------------------------------------

[FDDRule02: (?AHU rdf:type eq:AHU)(?AHU eq:servesRoom ?r)(?r bld:hasOccupant ?oc)
          (?oc occ:hasDTSState ?dts) (?AHU eq:status ?s)
          equal(?s "Operating") -> print('Expected DTS',?oc)(?dts fdd:hasExpectedValue "true"^^xs:boolean)]
```

Figure 19. Fault detection diagnostic rules for operation of a heating coil and for checking evidence 3 and evidence 4.

AHU 001. AHU 001 has a coil (Coil 001); Coil 001 has a valve (Valve 001).

- The datatype property for AHU001 "normal Operation" is set to false. This setting is based on the system data and the result of equipment rules 01 through 03 being triggered.
- The setpoint temperature for Room 1 is 24 C, but the current temperature reading for Sensor 001 is 57 C.
- OccupantRule02 sets the "isComfortable" datatype property for Occupant1 to "false" as the result of a DTSindex value of 4.
- Occupant 1 has dynamic thermal sensation (DTS) state DTSState 1. DTSState 1 indicates a thermal comfort fault (TCFault1), which will be diagnosed by looking at three hypotheses and their supporting evidence.
- The relationship between Hypotheses 1 through 3 and supporting evidence is shown along the bottom of Figure 18. Users may query the semantic graph to find the correct hypotheses and valid supporting evidence.

C. Test Problem Scenario and Hypothesis Evaluation Procedure

The test problem scenario assumes that the numerical value of occupant thermal comfort in a conditioned room has fallen outside the acceptable range. This is detected by FDD Rule 01. With this scenario in place, any one of three hypotheses could potentially be true. To correctly identify the correct hypothesis, the system requires to reason among the facts and identify the evidence existing in different domains,

- The outdoor temperature is higher than the setpoint (weather) and the window in the room is open (building, sensor, weather).
- The air-handling unit is malfunctioning (mechanical equipment),
- The room sensor providing feed-back to the air-handling unit to reach its target setpoint is broken (sensor).

As a result, this task will require comprehensive reasoning over multiple domains and identifying the supporting evidence to the most probable hypothesis. To achieve this, we used the proposed framework and implemented ontologies for weather, building, occupant, sensor and equipment domains. The ontologies are populated with data. However, in general this data will be obtained from simulations or real buildings.

D. Synthesis of Multi-domain Rules

Table I describes the instances for key concepts of FDD ontology as they apply to the test case problem, and explains details of the individuals for FDD ontology. For the case study problem, the chain of dependency relationships between hypotheses and supporting evidence is as follows:

- Hypothesis 1 is that warm outside air is leaking into the room through an open window. Evaluation of this hypothesis is supported by execution of two evidence rules, EvidenceRul01 and EvidenceRule02.
- Hypothesis 2 is that the serving air-handling unit has abnormal operation. Evaluation of this hypothesis is supported execution of EvidenceRule03.
- Hypothesis 3 states that the room sensor that provides feedback to AHU reaching its target setpoint is broken. Supporting evidence is provided by the execution of EvidenceRule04.

Figure 19 presents the fault detection diagnostic rules for: (1) Operation of a heating coil, (2) Checking evidence 3 and evidence 4, and (3) Detecting when the thermal comfort in a conditioned room matches its expected value.

E. Multi-domain Rule Evaluation

Figure 20 shows a snapshot of multi-domain evaluation and forward chaining of rules. From an evaluation standpoint, the eight rules can be clustered into two pathways, the first focusing on fault detection and the second focusing on diagnostic investigation of probable causes, represented as hypotheses and supporting evidence.

Fault Detection: The first pathway identifies the existence of a fault and is covered by rules 1 through 4:

- Rule 01: Use OccupantRule01 (see Figure 16) to determine when an occupant is located in a room.
- Rule 02: Use FDDRule02 (see Figure 19) to determine the expected comfort of an occupant.
- Rule 03: Use OccupantRule02 (see Figure 16) to determine the current comfort of an occupant.
- Rule 04: Use OccupantRule02 (see Figure 16) to compute when a fault has occurred.

determine in which room an occupant is located and whether or not the current value of occupant comfort matches the expected value of comfort. In the snapshot, activation of Rule 01 determines that: Occupant1 is located in Room1. A separate execution would also determine that Occupant2 is also located in Room1. Activation of Rule 02 is based upon the output of Rule 01, state data from the building domain, the relationship of the air handling unit to Room1. In the snapshot trace, the output of Rule 02 states that DTSState for Occupant1 is true and that Occupant1 has a DTSIndex of 4. A fault occurs when there is a discrepancy between the current and expected values of comfort (see F7 and F9), as indicated by the values of current and expected values of DTSState.

Fault Diagnostics: By systematically examining hypotheses and supporting evidence, the second pathway diagnoses the causes of a fault. For the scenario outlined in Figure 20, this procedure is covered by rules 5 through 8:

- Rule 05: Use EquipmentRule01 (see Figure 10) to determine if a valve is shut.
- Rule 06: Use EquipmentRule02 (see Figure 10) to determine if the coil has failed.
- Rule 07: Use EquipmentRule03 (see Figure 10) to determine whether or not the air handling unit has failed.
- Rule 08: If EvidenceRule04 (see Figure 19) evaluates to true then Hypothesis 3 is true.

The rule for determining whether or not the valve is shut takes input values from the Coil001 CoilSetpoint (44) and CoilTemperature (44) (see F12 and F13), and checks to verify that the coil has a valve. In our scenario, the rule output (F14) is true, indicating that Valve001 is shut, and hence in Rule 06 normal operation evaluates to false. A simple check to verify that the coil belongs to air handling unit AHU001 generates the conclusion that normal operation of the AHU is false (see F19). Finally, input from the room occupancy test and a test to verify that AHU001 is connected to Room1, leads to the conclusion Evidence 4 is supported and Hypothesis 3 is valid. Finally, we note that except for the room occupancy information feeding into Rule 08, the fault detection and diagnosis pathways operate independently.

VIII. Conclusions and Future Work

We have proposed in this paper a knowledge-based framework for fault detection and diagnostics. The underlying process closely mimics the "thinking process" that humans follow in identifying and diagnosing the causes of a fault. Thus, the steps of gathering data for the participating domains, populating ontologies with individuals, and using rules to detect and diagnose faults and their causes is easy for humans to understand and generally applicable to other domains (e.g., building energy, automotive, health care) for FDD purposes. Capabilities of the prototype implementation has been demonstrated by working step by step through the procedure of detecting and diagnosing the source of faults in an HVAC system.

Key advantages of this approach include: (1) it is decoupled from the system simulation, (2) it is comprehensive, and (3) it is scalable. In fact, the process for expanding an application to include new domains as they come along is very straight forward. The inference-based rules are guaranteed to check at anytime a changed occurred in a an ontology resulting in event-driven fault detection and diagnostic. Finally, inference-based rules provide mechanisms in capturing chain effects that exists in the nature of system failure – for example, if a valve is not

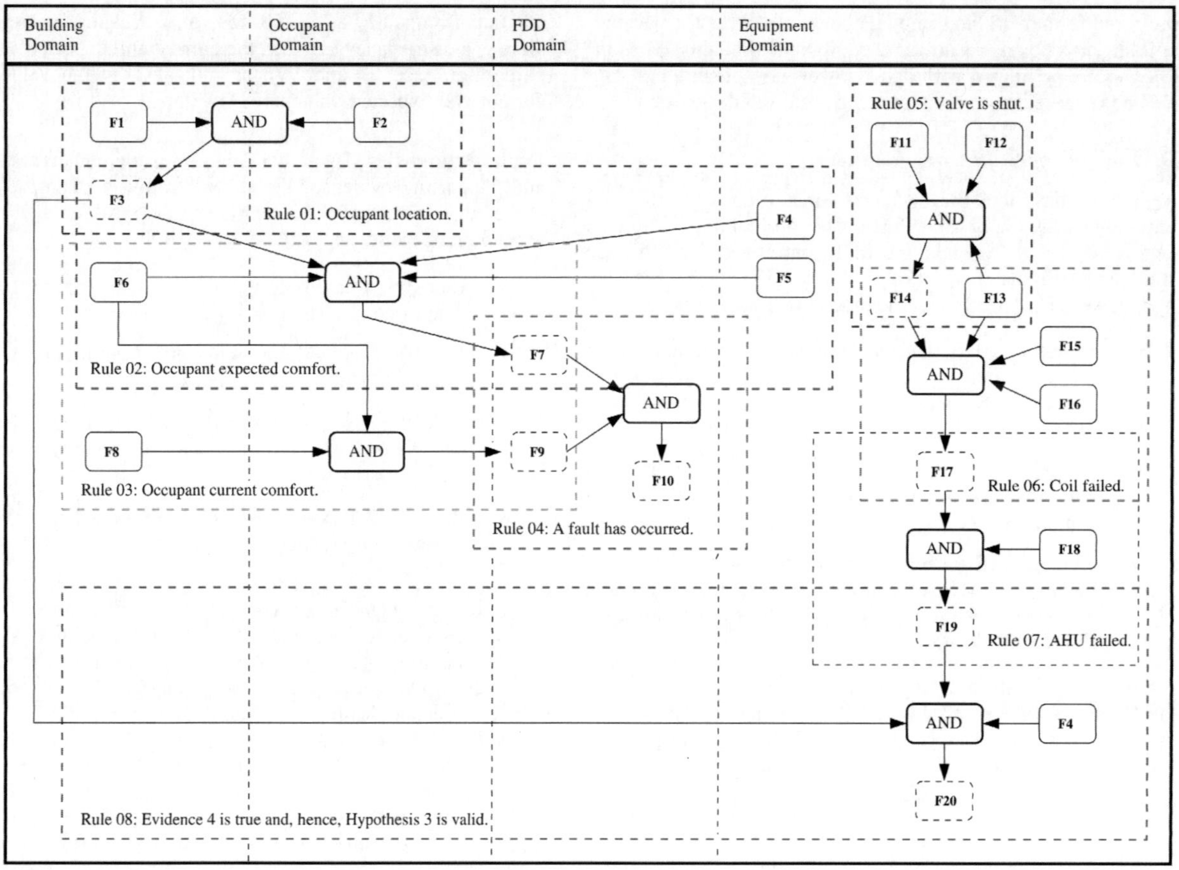

Legend:

F1 = Room hasGeometry
F2 = Occupant hasGeometry
F3 = Room1 has Occupant1
F4 = AHU001 serves Room1
F5 = AHU001 status operating
F6 = Occupant1 hasState DTSState
F7 = DTSState expectedValue true
F8 = Occpant1 hasDTSIndex 4
F9 = DTSState currentValue false
F10 = DTSState indicates DTSFault
F11 = Coil001 CoilSetpoint 44
F12 = Coil001 CoilTemperature 44
F13 = Coil001 hasValve Valve001
F14 = Valve001 isShut true
F15 = Coil001 Tas 62
F16 = Coil001 Tad 57
F17 = Valve001 isShut normalOperation false
F18 = AHU001 hasCoil Coil001
F19 = AHU001 normalOperation false
F20 = Evidence1 isValid true

Figure 20. Snapshot of multi-domain evaluation and forward chaining of rules.

operational, the evidence that AHU is not operating properly also holds true.

In our prototype implementation, the small two-room building model extracted data from a custom "system data model" currently under development. We expect that a more mature version of this ontology would extract semantic information from instances of building information models (BIM) such as the Industry Foundation Class (IFC). Future work will also include deployment in real building systems. We anticipate that the proposed methodology will be integrated into building automation systems (BAS) and support investigations where analytic built-in functions are implemented in the condition part of inference-based rules. These functions will perform time-history analyses to identify a faulty state for the system. We anticipate a trend where formal approaches to analysis are used to irregularities in building performance, which are indicators of possible system faults. Moreover, we will investigate strategies for taking control actions based on recognized faults of the system.

IX. Acknowledgment

The first author was supported by a fellowship award from the NIST Graduate Student Measurement Science and Engineering (GMSE) Program.

References

[1] P. Delgoshaei, M.A. Austin, and D. Veronica, "Semantic Models and Rule-based Reasoning for Fault Detection and Diagnostics: Applications in Heating, Ventilating and Air Conditioning Systems," The Twelfth

International Conference on Systems (ICONS 2017), April 23-27 2017, pp. 48–53.

[2] P. Delgoshaei, M. A. Austin and A. Pertzborn, "A Semantic Framework for Modeling and Simulation of Cyber-Physical Systems," International Journal On Advances in Systems and Measurements, vol. 7, no. 3-4, December 2014, pp. 223–238.

[3] M.A. Austin, P. Delgoshaei and A. Nguyen, "Distributed System Behavior Modeling with Ontologies, Rules, and Message Passing Mechanisms," Procedia Computer Science, vol. 44, 2015, pp. 373 – 382, 2015 Conference on Systems Engineering Research. [Online]. Available: http://www.sciencedirect.com/science/article/pii/S1877050915002951

[4] S. Katipamula and M. R. Brambley, "Review Article: Methods for Fault Detection, Diagnostics, and Prognostics for Building SystemsA Review, Part I," HVAC&R Research, vol. 11, no. 1, 2005, pp. 3–25.

[5] J. A. Siegel and C. P. Wray, "An Evaluation of Superheat-based Refrigerant Charge Diagnostics for Residential Cooling Systems/Discussions," ASHRAE Transactions 108(1), 2002, p. 965.

[6] W. Kim and J. E. Braun, "Impacts of refrigerant charge on air conditioner and heat pump performance," in Impacts of Refrigerant Charge on Air Conditioner and Heat Pump Performance, July 10–15 2010, pp. 2433–2441.

[7] M. Wiggins and J. Brodrick, "Emerging Technologies: HVAC Fault Detection," ASHRAE Journal, April 2012, pp. 78–80.

[8] OWL:, "Web Ontology Language Overview, W3C Recommendation from February, 2004. For details, see http://www.w3.org/TR/owl-features/ (Accessed, April 2017)."

[9] Apache Jena, "An Open Source Java Framework for building Semantic Web and Linked Data Applications, Accessible at https://jena.apache.org (Accessed on 12/12/16)," 2016.

[10] W. T. Scherer and C. C. White, A Survey of Expert Systems for Equipment Maintenance and Diagnostics. Boston, MA: Springer US, 1989, pp. 285–300.

[11] T. Berners-Lee, J. Hendler and O. Lassila, "The Semantic Web," Scientific American, May 2001, pp. 35–43.

[12] T. Q. Dung and W. Kameyama, Ontology-based Information Extraction and Information Retrieval in Health Care Domain, ser. Lecture Notes in Computer Science (including subseries Lecture Notes in Artificial Intelligence and Lecture Notes in Bioinformatics), 2007, vol. 4654 LNCS, pp. 323–333.

[13] C. Taswell, "DOORS to the Semantic Web and Grid with a PORTAL for Biomedical Computing," IEEE Trans Inf Technol Biomed, vol. 12, no. 2, 2008, pp. 191–204.

[14] P. Lord, S. Bechhofer, M. D. Wilkinson, G. Schiltz, D. Gessler, D. Hull, C. Goble, and L. Stein, Applying Semantic Web Services to Bioinformatics: Experiences Gained, Lessons Learnt. Berlin, Heidelberg: Springer Berlin Heidelberg, 2004, pp. 350–364.

[15] D. Corsar, D. Milan, P. Edwards, and J. D. Nelson, The Transport Disruption Ontology. Lecture Notes in Computer Science, vol 9367, Springer, 2015, pp. 329–336.

[16] M. Batic, N. Tomasevic and S. Vranes, "Ontology-based Fault Detection and Diagnosis System Querying and Reasoning Examples," in ICKDDM 2015 : 17th International Conference on Knowledge Discovery and Data Mining, vol. 2, no. 1. International Science Index, Industrial and Manufacturing Engineering, 2015.

[17] S. Schumann, J. Hayes, P. Pompey and O. Verscheure, "Adaptable Fault Identification for Smart Buildings," in 2011 AAAI Workshop (WS-11-07), 2011.

[18] M. Merdan, "Knowledge-based Multi-Agent Architecture Applied in the Assembly Domain," Ph.D. Dissertation, Vienna University of Technology, 2009.

[19] T. Bayer, D. Dvorak, S. Friedenthal, S. Jenkins, C. Lin and S. Mandutianu, "Foundational Concepts for Building System Models," in SEWG MBSE Training Module 3, see http://nen.nasa.gov/web/se/mbse/documents, California Institute of Technology, CA, USA, 2012.

[20] D.A. Wagner, M.B. Bennett R. Karban, N. Rouquette, S. Jenkins and M.o Ingham, "An Ontology for State Analysis: Formalizing the Mapping to SysML," in Proceedings of 2012 IEEE Aerospace Conference, Big Sky, Montana, March 2012.

[21] D.A. Randell, Z. Cui, and A.G. Cohn, "A Spatial Logic based on Regions and Connectivity," 1994, Division of Artificial Intelligence, School of Computer Studies, Leeds University.

[22] Java Topology Suite (JTS). See http://www.vividsolutions.com/jts/ (Accessed August 4, 2017).

[23] P. Delgoshaei, and M.A. Austin, "Framework for Knowledge-Based Fault Detection and Diagnostics in Multi-Domain Systems: Application to HVAC Systems," Institute for Systems Research, University of Maryland, College Park, MD 20742, USA, Tech. Rep. 2017-4, November 2017.

[24] D.B. Crawley, L.K. Lawrie, F.C. Winkelmann, W.F. Buhl, Y.J. Huang, C.O. Pedersen, R.K. Strand, R.J. Liesen, D.E. Fisher, M.J. Witte and J. Glazer, "EnergyPlus: Creating a New-Generation Building Energy Simulation Program," Energy and Buildings, vol. 33, no. 4, 2001, pp. 319 – 331, Special Issue: {BUILDING} SIMULATION'99.

[25] S.A. Klein, W.A. Beckman, et al., 1994, TRNSYS: A Transient Simulation Program, Engineering Experiment Station Report 38-12, University of Wisconsin, Madison.

[26] "TRNSYS: The Transient Energy System Simulation Tool. See: http://www.trnsys.com/ (Accessed September 8, 2017)." 2017.

[27] 2004, BACnet: A Data Communication Protocol for Building Automation and Control Networks, ANSI/ASHRAE 135.

[28] Y. Agarwal, B. Balaji, R. Gupta, J. Lyles, M. Wei and T. Weng, "Occupancy-Driven Energy Management for Smart Building Automation," in Proceedings of the 2nd ACM Workshop on Embedded Sensing Systems for Energy-Efficiency in Building (BuildSys 2010), Zurich, Switzerland, November 3-5 2010, pp. 1–6.

[29] J. Lu, T.Sookoor, V. Srinivasan, G. Gao, B. Holben, J. Stankovic, E. Field and K. Whitehouse, "The Smart Thermostat: Using Occupancy Sensors to Save Energy in Homes," in Proceedings of the 8th ACM Conference on Embedded Networked Sensor Systems (SenSys 2010), Zurich, Switzerland, November 3-5 2010, pp. 211–224.

[30] A. Mahdavi and M. Taheri, "An Ontology for Building Monitoring," Journal of Building Performance Simulation, October 2016, pp. 1–10.

[31] P. Staroch, "A Weather Ontology for Predictive Control in Smart Homes," 2013, M.S. Thesis in Software Engineering and Internet Computing, Vienna University of Technology.

[32] Weather API. See https://openweathermap.org/api (Accessed September 14, 2017).

[33] X. Chen, and Q. Wang, and J. Srebric, "Occupant Feedback-based Model Predictive Control for Thermal Comfort and Energy Optimization: A Chamber Experimental Evaluation," Applied Energy, vol. 164, 2016, pp. 341 – 351.

[34] 2010, ASHRAE Standard 552010 Thermal Environmental Conditions for Human Occupancy, American Society of Heating, Refrigerating and Air-Conditioning Engineers.

Spectrum Sharing Transforms Mobile Broadband Networks Towards Markets

Analysis of Sharing Economy Antecedents for Recent Spectrum Sharing Concepts

Seppo Yrjölä
Nokia
Oulu, Finland
e-mail: seppo.yrjola@nokia.com

Marja Matinmikko
University of Oulu
Oulu, Finland
e-mail: mmatinmi@ee.oulu.fi

Miia Mustonen
VTT Technical Research Centre of Finland
Oulu, Finland
e-mail: miia.mustonen@vtt.fi

Petri Ahokangas
Oulu Business School
Oulu, Finland
e-mail: petri.ahokangas@oulu.fi

Abstract—**The exponential growth of wireless services with diversity of devices and applications depending on connectivity has inspired the research community to come up with novel concepts to improve the efficiency of spectrum use. Recently, several spectrum sharing system concepts have been introduced and widely researched to cope with spectrum scarcity, though, to date, only a few have reached the policy and standardization phase. Moreover, only a subset of these concepts has gained industry interest with pre-commercial deployments and lucrative business model characteristics. This paper analyzes sharing economy business antecedent factors of the three topical regulatory approaches for spectrum sharing: global TV White Space (TVWS), Licensed Shared Access (LSA) from Europe, and Citizens Broadband Radio Service (CBRS) from the US. A comparison is made between these concepts to identify similarities and differences for developing a successful scalable sharing concept. Key factors for a sharing economy enabled scalable business model are introduced including platform, reduced need for the ownership, leverage of underutilized assets, adaptability to different policy regimes, trust, and value orientation. The results indicate that all analyzed sharing concepts meet basic requirements to scale, TVWS radically lowering entry barrier, LSA leveraging key existing assets and capabilities of mobile network operators, and CBRS extending the business model dynamics. By reducing the costs of spectrum coordination, spectrum sharing concepts will lead to an overall shift from hierarchies towards more use of markets to coordinate economic activity related to spectrum assets. The Sharing Economy and Markets and Hierarchies frameworks provide a dynamic framework for analyzing and developing the spectrum sharing business models.**

Keywords-business model; cognitive radio; markets and hierarchies; sharing economy; spectrum sharing.

I. INTRODUCTION

We have seen the exponential growth of wireless services, applications and devices, requiring connectivity. Furthermore, the number of mobile broadband (MBB) subscribers and the amount of data consumed is set to grow significantly, leading to increasing spectrum demand discussed in the COCORA 2017 [1]. Both the European Commission (EC) [2] and the US President's Council of Advanced Science & Technology (PCAST) [3] have recently emphasized the need for novel thinking within wireless industry to cope with the growing capacity crunch in spectrum allocation, utilization and management. The prominence of dynamic spectrum access and spectrum sharing has been emphasized in improving the efficiency of the spectrum utilization through balancing across domains with different spectrum dynamics. For any spectrum sharing framework to emerge and scale, close cooperation between research, regulation and across industry domains is essential. The collaboration between research and industry is essential in validating enabling platforms, technologies and innovations. The spectrum regulation and standardization has played a central role in enabling current multibillion business ecosystems: For the MBB via exclusive Quality of Service (QoS) spectrum usage rights, and at the same time for the unlicensed wireless local area network (Wi-Fi) ecosystem drawing from the public spurring innovations. Without sound and sustainable business models for all the key industry stakeholders, new concepts will not become deployed in a large scale.

To date, only few of the Dynamic Spectrum Access (DSA) concepts from research have crossed the threshold into policy domain. Furthermore, several spectrum sharing concepts supported by National Regulatory Authorities (NRA) and standardization have not to date scaled up in the wireless services market, the TV White Space (TVWS) being the latest example. After a decade of profound unlicensed TVWS concept research, standardization and trials in the US [4] and the UK [5] with their key learnings, license and database based sharing models have recently emerged and are under regulatory discussion, standardization and pre-commercial trials. The most prominent novel spectrum sharing concepts are the Licensed Shared Access (LSA) [6] from Europe and the three-tiered Citizens Broadband Radio Service (CBRS) from the US [7].

For all the three spectrum sharing concepts there is no prior work available regarding their business model design comparative analysis. An initial evaluation of the general spectrum sharing concept from the business modeling point of view can be found in [8]. Business modelling for the TVWS network was discussed in [9], and the LSA focused strategy and business model analysis in [10][11]. Business model typology and scalability analysis for the LSA and the CBRS were done in [12]. We extend that work by focusing on analyzing and comparing the viability and attractiveness of all three spectrum sharing concepts using sharing economy [13] antecedent factors and markets and hierarchies analytic framework [14]. This paper investigates:

1) How do recent spectrum sharing concepts support the antecedents for business model scalability in the sharing economy framework?

2) How spectrum sharing concepts can be positioned in the markets and hierarchies analytic framework?

The rest of the paper is organized as follows. First, the TVWS, the LSA and the CBRS sharing concepts are introduced in Section II. Theoretical backgrounds for the sharing economy and the markets and hierarchies analytic frameworks are introduced in Section III. The business model characteristics and the sharing economy antecedents for the TVWS, the LSA, and the CBRS spectrum sharing concepts are derived and analyzed in Section IV. Implications to ecosystem and market – hierarchy positioning are summarized in Section V. Finally, conclusions are drawn in Section VI.

II. Overview of Recent Spectrum Sharing Concepts

This section presents the three prominent spectrum sharing frameworks and system model concepts under discussion in regulatory domain: the TVWS, the LSA and the CBRS. The common intention of the concepts is to improve spectrum usage efficiency by allowing new users to access a spectrum on the space or time basis when not being used by the incumbent system(s) currently holding the spectrum usage rights. Detailed description and the status of the TVWS, the LSA, the CBRS, and the concepts and technologies, under continuous revision can be found for example in [4][5], [15][16], and [17][18], respectively.

A. TV White Space (TVWS)

In this section, the opportunistic TV White Space concept utilizing terrestrial broadcasting Ultra High Frequency (UHF) spectrum is discussed in general level. TVWS standardization is spread to several organizations around the world, and there is no single dominant standard, technology or solution to date. In addition to Wi-Fi IEEE 802.11 standards based technologies focused on in this paper, also other radio technologies like the Long Term Evolution (LTE) and the Worldwide Interoperability for Microwave Access (WiMAX) have been experimented for the TVWS.

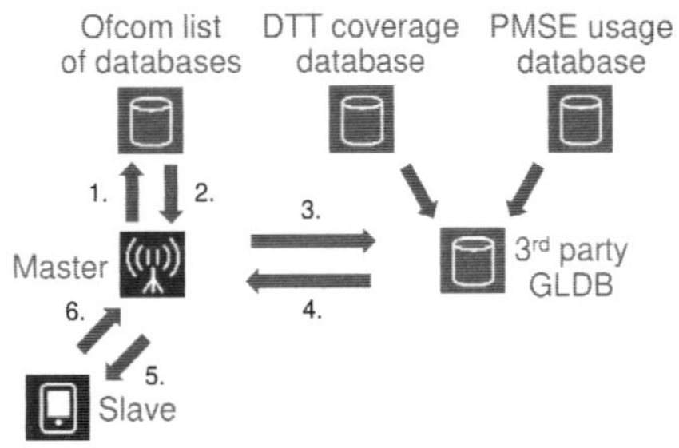

Figure 1. Overview of TV White Spaces framework in the UK.

The TVWS aims to improve spectrum efficiency through utilizing the unused and underutilized spectrum in space and time based on databases. In this concept, license-exempt *White Space Devices* (WSDs) obtain the available channel information via a certified *Geo-Location Database* (GLDB), which optimizes the effective reuse of the spectrum, and ensures interference free operation for the incumbent licensed users. The GLDB stores and periodically updates TV licensees' Digital Terrestrial TV (DTT) network infrastructure and channel occupancy information, and in the case of the UK, the Program Making and Special Events (PMSE) service usage data. In the operations phase, to access the TVWS spectrum, *WSD base stations* (BS) reports locations to a GLDB, which computes and returns the available TV channels for WSDs. Figure 1 depicts an overview of the TVWS framework, and how access to white spaces based on the GLDB would work in the UK case. In the preparatory phase, the GLDB will deploy the basic operational dataset provided by the Office of Communications (Ofcom) consisting of DTT coexistence data, location agnostic data, PMSE data, and unscheduled adjustments data. A master WSD would first consult a list of DBs provided by Ofcom hosted Website. Then, it would select its preferred GLDB from the list, and send to it its location and device parameters. The GLDB would then return details of the allowed frequencies and power levels [5].

In the US, the FCC has finalized the TVWS regulation [19], followed by the Infocomm Development Authority (IDA) of Singapore [20] in 2014 and Ofcom from the UK in 2015 [5]. The ECC prepared European level technical framework in the European Conference of Postal and Telecommunications (CEPT) FM53 working group [21]. The TVWS regulatory frameworks to date have been unprotected and license-exempt, applicable for deploying the most prominent TVWS Wi-Fi version of IEEE 802.11af [22]. The FCC has temporarily certified several companies including Google, Microsoft, and Spectrum Bridge as geolocation database operators. In UK, Fairspectrum, Nominet UK, Sony Europe, and Spectrum Bridge are qualified to provide database services for the TVWS. The first use cases of the TVWS in the US have been fixed Wireless Internet Service Provisioning (WISP) for rural communities and industry verticals, where another connection technology, typically Wi-Fi, is needed between the User Equipment (UE) and the TVWS Customer Premises Equipment (CPE).

B. Licensed Shared Access (LSA)

The EC communication based on an industry initiative promoted spectrum sharing across wireless industry and diverse types of incumbents [23]. In 2013, the Radio Spectrum Policy Group (RSPG) of the EC defined LSA as [2] "*a regulatory approach aiming to facilitate the introduction of radio communication systems operated by a limited number of licensees under an individual licensing regime in a frequency band already assigned or expected to be assigned to one or more incumbent users. Under the LSA framework, the additional users are allowed to use the spectrum (or part of the spectrum) in accordance with sharing rules included in their rights of use of spectrum, thereby allowing all the authorized users, including incumbents, to provide a certain QoS.*"

The recent development in policy, standardization and architecture has focused on applying the LSA to leverage scale and harmonization of the Third Generation Partnership Project (3GPP) ecosystem. This would enable MBB systems to gain shared access to additional harmonized spectrum assets not currently available on exclusive basis, particular the 3GPP band 40 (2.3-2.4 GHz) as defined by the CEPT [24]. The European Telecommunications Standards Institute (ETSI) introduced related system reference, requirements and architecture documents [16][25][26] from the standardization perspective. In the LSA concept, the incumbent spectrum user, such as a PMSE video link, a telemetry system, or a fixed link operator, is able to share the spectrum assigned to it with one or several LSA licensee users according to a negotiated *sharing framework* and *sharing agreement*. The LSA model guarantees protection from harmful interference with predictable QoS for both the incumbent and the LSA licensee.

The LSA architecture consists of two new elements to protect the rights of the incumbent, and for managing dynamics of the LSA spectrum availability shown in Figure 2: the *LSA Repository* (LR) and the *LSA Controller* (LC). The LR supports the entry and storage of the information about the availability, protection requirements and usage of spectrum together with operating terms and rules. The LC located in the LSA licensee's domain grants permissions within the mobile network to access the spectrum based on the spectrum resource availability information from the LR. The LC interacts with the licensee's mobile network in order to support the mapping of LSA resource availability information (LSRAI) into appropriate radio transmitter configurations via Operation, Administration and Management (OAM) tools, and to receive the respective confirmations from the network. The LSA system for 2.3-2.4 GHz band has been validated in field trials in Finland, Italy and France. Architecture, implementation and field trial results are presented, e.g., in [27] – [30].

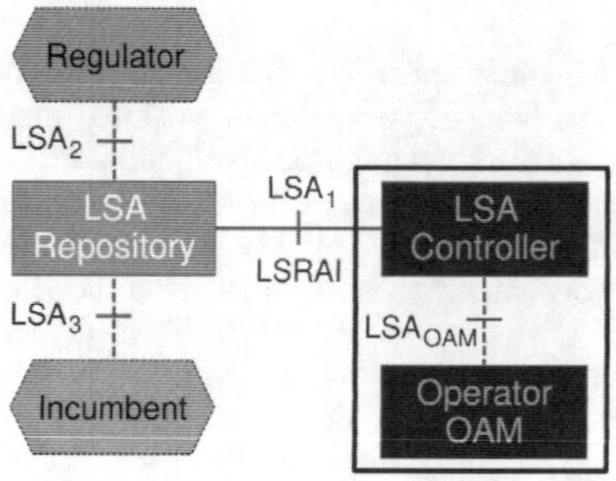

Figure 2. The LSA architecture reference model.

The second use case currently being considered in European regulation is the application of LSA to the 3.6-3.8 GHz band [31]. For this band, the incumbent usage is less dynamic, and the LSA band availability is guaranteed in the license area for a known period. This allows extension to more innovative use cases, such as local networks using small cells, as there is no need for additional frequency resource or existing infrastructure to support dynamic handover. The ETSI Reconfigurable Radio Systems Technical Committee (ETSI RRS) initiated a feasibility study "temporary spectrum access for local high-quality wireless networks" [32] in 2017 to study LSA evolution towards 5G spectrum, localization of spectrum for novel 5G use cases, and to enable horizontal sharing and sub-licensing for efficient use of the spectrum assets.

C. Citizens Broadband Radio Service (CBRS)

As the LSA policy discussion started in Europe, in the US the CBRS concept started to gain interest as a complementary spectrum management approach. In the US, the PCAST report [3] in 2012 suggested a dynamic spectrum sharing model as a new tool to the US wireless industry to meet the growing crisis in spectrum allocation, utilization and management. The key policy messages of the document were further strengthened in 2013 with Presidential Memorandum [33] stating "*...we must make available even more spectrum and create new avenues for wireless innovation. One means of doing so is by allowing and encouraging shared access to spectrum that is currently allocated exclusively for Federal use. Where technically and economically feasible, sharing can and should be used to enhance efficiency among all users and expedite commercial access to additional spectrum bands, subject to adequate interference protection for Federal users.*"

In Figure 3, the US three-tier authorization framework with the FCC's spectrum access models for 3550-3650MHz and 3650-3700MHz spectrum segments are illustrated. While the general CBRS framework could be applied to any spectrum and between any systems, the current regulatory efforts in the Federal Communications Commission (FCC) are concentrated on the 3550-3700 MHz band as the first use case [7].

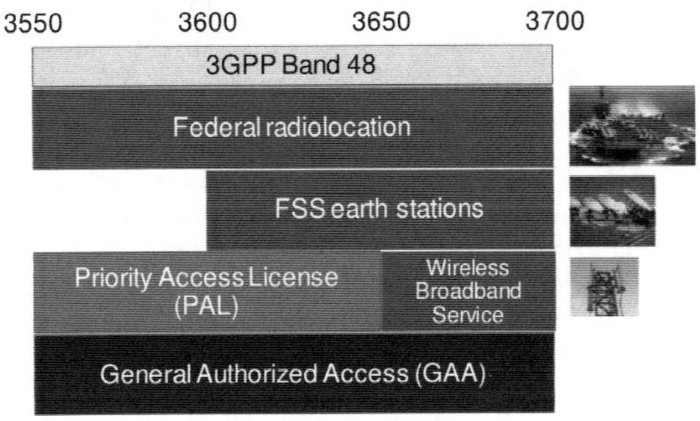

Figure 3. The US 3-tiered CBRS spectrum access model and band plan.

The standardization process for the CBRS is ongoing in the Wireless Innovation Forum (WinnForum) [18], and for the specific spectrum band in the 3GPP [34]. The three tiers depicted in Figure 3 are:

1) *Incumbent Access* (IA) layer consists of the existing primary operations including authorized federal users and Fixed Service Satellite (FSS) earth stations. The IA is protected from harmful interference from the CBRS users by geographic exclusion zones and interference management conducted by the dynamic *Spectrum Access System* (SAS),

2) *Priority Access* (PA) layer includes critical access users like hospitals, utilities, governmental users, and non-critical users, e.g., Mobile Network Operators (MNOs). PA users receive short-term priority authorization (currently, a three-year authorization is considered) to operate within designated geographic census track with Priority Access Licenses (PALs) in 10 MHz unpaired channel. PALs will be awarded with competitive bidding, and with ability to aggregate multiple consecutive PALs and census tracks in order to obtain multi-year rights and to cover larger areas. Any entity eligible to hold a FCC license could apply for a PAL and is protected from harmful interference from the General Authorized Access (GAA) layer.

3) *General Authorized Access* layer users, e.g., residential, business and others, including Internet service providers are entitled to use the spectrum on opportunistic *license-by-rule* regulatory basis without interference protection. In addition to the 50% GAA spectrum availability floor specified to ensure nationwide GAA access availability, the GAA could access unused PA frequencies. GAA channels are dynamically assigned to users by a SAS. The addition of the third tier is intended to maximize spectrum utilization, and to extend usage from centralized managed BSs to stand-alone GAA access points.

The SAS dynamically determines and assigns PAL channels and GAA frequencies at a given geographic location, controls the interference environment, and enforces exclusion zones to protect higher priority users as well as takes care of registration, authentication and identification of user information. In 2016, the FCC finalized rules for CBRS [7], and introduced the *light-touch leasing* process to make the spectrum use rights held by PALs available in secondary markets. Under the light-touch leasing rules, PA Licensees are free to lease any portion of their spectrum or license outside of their *PAL protection area* (PPA) without the need for the FCC oversight required of partitioning and disaggregation. This allows lessees of PALs to provide targeted services to geographic areas or quantities of spectrum without additional administrative burden. Coupled with the minimum availability of 80 MHz GAA spectrum in each license area, these rules will provide the increased flexibility to serve specific or targeted markets. Furthermore, the FCC will let market forces determine the role of a SAS, and as such, stand-alone exchanges or a SAS-managed exchanges are permitted.

The *CBRS devices* (CBSDs) are fixed or portable BSs or access points, or networks of such, and can only operate under the authority and management of a centralized SAS, which could be multiple as shown in Figure 4. Both the PA and the GAA users are obligated to use only certified the FCC approved CBSDs, which must register with a SAS with information required by the rules, e.g., operator identifier, device identification and parameters, and location information. In a typical MNO deployment scenario, the CBSD is a managed network comprising of the *Domain Proxy* (DP) and Network Management System (NMS) functionality. The DP may be a bidirectional information routing engine or a more intelligent mediation function enabling flexible self-control and interference optimizations in such a network. In addition to larger MNO-operated MBB networks, DP enables combining, e.g., the small cells of a shopping mall or sports venue to a virtual BS entity that covers the complete venue. The DP can also provide a translational capability to interface legacy radio equipment in the 3650–3700 MHz band with an SAS to ensure compliance with the FCC rules. A, MNO could utilize a DP and/or operator-specific SAS in protecting commercially sensitive details of their network deployment data. In the dialog between industries [35], the FCC and the main incumbent user, United States Department of Defense (DoD), it is assumed that in addition to informing database approach, there is a need to introduce a Non-Informing Approach, requiring *Environmental Sensing Capability* (ESC).

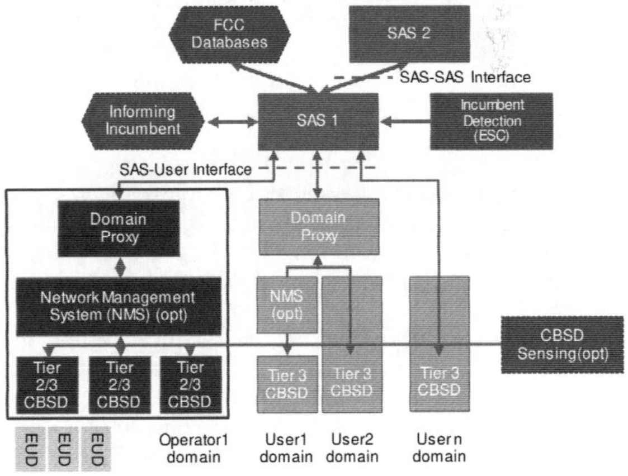

Figure 4. The US 3-tiered 3 CBRS concept and functional architecture.

The ESC architecture and implementation scenarios discussed include a dedicated sensing network for a SAS, collaborative sensing by commercial network BSs, or their combination. According to the FCC rules [7], the SAS must either confirm suspension of the CBSD's operation or its relocation within 300 seconds after the ESC detection communication, or other type of notification from the current federal user of the spectrum band.

The White House aims to expand wireless innovation in spectrum sharing further through identifying an additional 2 GHz of federal owned spectrum below 6 GHz for future commercial sharing [35]. The success of the CBRS is critical to future federal–commercial spectrum sharing. Moreover, the FCC has already proposed the use of the three-tier model and the SAS for 5G in several cmWave and mmWave bands.

III. Business Model and Sharing Economy Antecedents

Development of business models for spectrum sharing can benefit from the previous work on business models in the Internet business domain. Scalable business model analysis has been developed by Amit and Zott [36] as a model of e-business based on four independent dimensions: efficiency, complementarities, lock-in, and novelty. Rappa [37] classified the Web-based business models as brokerage model, advertising model, information-intermediary model, merchant model, manufacturer direct model, affiliate model, community model, subscription model, and utility and hybrid models. Bouwman et al. [38] differentiate in their business model analysis business model effects: organizational structure, services, technology, revenue, and environmental factors: regulation, technology, market. Hallowell [39] stated a scalability paradox that while the reduction of scalability is often caused by human intervention, the competitive advantage based on differentiation is also gained by human intervention. Stampfl identified and categorized the antecedents of business model scalability into five mutually exclusive factors in the explorative business model scalability model [40], which Stephany adapted into his sharing economy definition [41].

Next, the theoretical frameworks used to analyze how business models and their key elements could evolve and scale in response to novel spectrum sharing models are introduced.

A. *Business Models and Ecosystems*

Business models in general are built to exploit a business opportunity [42], in connection with the company and its external business environment [43]. In order to gain and sustain competitive advantage, companies must continuously develop and renew their business models. In the development of any new spectrum sharing concept, it is essential to consider the underlying business opportunities and the business model elements that are attractive and feasible for all the key stakeholders. Authors in [44] define business model in general as a framework across three analytical building blocks: a) focus of the business (activities that provide the basis for value creation and capture), b) locus of the business (i.e., defining the potential and scalability of business), and c) modus of business (simplicity and dynamism of business). The discussed spectrum sharing concepts confront the MBB and the wireless industry with strategic environmental changes, such as emerging competitive market structures, policy and regulatory changes as well as technology complexity, which all require companies to adapt or reinvent one or more aspects of their business model designs within their ecosystem.

Ecosystems [45] are created and emerge around synergistic value co-creating and co-capturing activity-systems between stakeholders. Based on the ideas of Moore [45], stakeholders of the ICT specific businesses have started to discuss digital business ecosystems that comprise the converged information and communications technology networks, social networks and knowledge networks. Contemporary research on digital business ecosystems is mostly technology and platform focused, but authors in [46] argued that software components, applications and services could be regarded as digital "species" in global competitive selection process. Regulation, technology and business co-evolve within ecosystemic settings.

B. *Business Model Saclability*

Potential for scalability is an important aspect when developing a business model, and synchronizing it to the respective business opportunity is crucial. The scalability of the business model and its key elements has been shown to be the primary driver for the venture growth [47], and the attractor towards venture capital investments [48]. Vertical scalability approach scales-up a system by adding more resources into the system nodes, while the horizontal scale-out approach adds more nodes to the complete system. Stampfl [40] identified and categorized the antecedents of business model scalability into five mutually exclusive factors in the explorative business model scalability model: technology, cost and revenue structure, adaptability to different legal regimes, network effects, and user orientation.

The emerging *sharing economy framework* has leveraged these scalability factors with focus on resource efficiency and on-demand platform [49]. Through studying recent early adopters of the framework, Stephany [41] defined sharing economy as "*the value in taking the underutilized assets and making them accessible online to a community, leading to a reduced need for ownership of those assets*." Furthermore, the framework originated from collaborative individual peer-to-peer community consumption has lately evolved to corporations and governments participating the ecosystem as buyers, sellers or lenders [50]. Proposed sharing economy antecedent factors used in assessing business model characteristics of the spectrum sharing concepts are:

a) *Platform for online, on-demand accessibility,*

b) *Reduced need for the ownership,*

c) *Utilization of underutilized assets,*

d) *Adaptability to different legal and policy regimes,*

e) *Communities and trust, and*

f) *Value creation and user orientation.*

Each of these antecedent factors relate to the specificities of the focus, locus and modus of the business in question.

C. *Market and Hierarchies*

The basis of all business activities is the transformation of resources and capabilities into goods and services. The goods dominant logic views services in terms of a type of intangible goods whereas the service-dominant logic considers service – a process of using one's resources for the benefit of and in conjunction with another party – as the fundamental purpose of economic exchange. Value creation in service dominant logic stems from the use of internal and external resources and overcoming the internal and external resistance for co-creating and co-capturing value in exchange. The service dominant logic together with the resources/capabilities discussion extends nicely to future mobile broadband businesses in large that are characterized with increasing sharing of resources from spectrum to infrastructure with various business models.

Economies have traditionally considered to have two basic mechanisms for coordinating the flow of assets or services through adjacent steps in the value chain: markets and hierarchies, depicted in Figure 5 [14].

Malone [14] studied the change in how firms and markets organize flow of goods and services. He defines *hierarchies* as "Visible Hand" that coordinate the flow of goods through adjacent steps by controlling and directing it at higher level in the managerial hierarchy within a firm and its value chain. Typically, in hierarchies, production costs are relatively high, and *coordination costs* low. These coordination costs consider the costs of gathering information, negotiating contracts, and protecting against the risks of "opportunistic" bargaining [52]. Coordination costs are a part of the *transaction costs* that cover all costs that are involved in making and carrying out a transaction between two parties or more [53]. On the other hand, *markets* can be defined as "Invisible Hand" coordinating the flow through supply and demand forces and external transactions between firms and individuals.

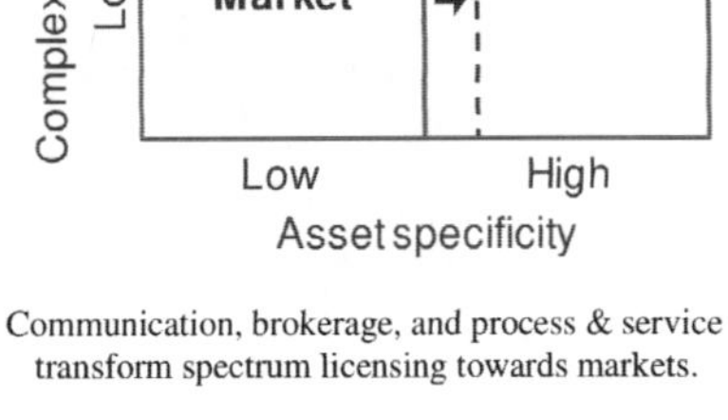

Figure 5. Communication, brokerage, and process & service integration transform spectrum licensing towards markets.

Coordination cost of the markets are relatively high, and production costs low. Naturally, variants of the two pure relationships exist, but can usually be categorized as primarily one or the other.

Figure 5 illustrates Malone's Market-Hierarchy analytic framework [14]. *Complexity of product description* can be defined as amount of information needed to specify the attributes of a product in enough detail to allow a buyer to make a selection. Because highly complex product description requires more information exchange, they also increase coordination cost advantage of hierarchies over markets. *Asset specificity* measures the extent to which investments made to support a particular transaction have a higher value to that transaction than would have if they were redeployed for any other purpose. Specificity relates, e.g., to single function, location, skills, time or lengthy process of development in close collaboration with suppliers.

IV. Analysis of the Spectrum Sharing Concepts

The three spectrum sharing models, the TVWS, the LSA, and the CBRS, introduced and discussed in Section II are next analyzed and compared against the sharing economy criteria presented in Section III. The summary of the sharing economy antecedent analysis is given in Table I.

A. *Platform*

Sharing economy business models are hosted through platforms and automatized processes across connectivity, content, context and commerce layers that enable a more precise, real-time measurement of available capacity, and the ability to dynamically making that capacity accessible. From commerce perspective, platform is a business based on enabling value-creating interactions between external producers and consumers. Platform provides an open, participative infrastructure for these interactions and sets governance conditions for them.

At the connectivity layer, this dynamic adaptability to short-term changes, and automatic configuration of radio infrastructure and user equipment is the key differentiator to static sharing concepts, e.g., in the Industrial, Scientific and Medical (ISM) spectrum bands. The global 3GPP ecosystem with scale and harmonization will be the common technology scalability factor for the LSA and the CBRS approaches, while the TVWS has heritage on the Institute of Electrical and Electronics Engineers (IEEE) Wi-Fi ecosystem at the ISM bands.

Compared to the LSA and the CBRS, regulatory and standardization actions for the TVWS have been concluded. However, to date the TVWS platform has not reached a tipping point, despite support from several major IT companies providing the GLDB. Interference constraints and strict technical requirements entail dedicated radio designs. Furthermore, radio ecosystem has not scaled due to scattered standardizations, lack of mobile operators' interest, and the lack of certainty for the long-term availability of white spaces.

TABLE I. SPECTRUM SHARING BUSINESS MODEL ANTECEDENT FACTORS.

Antecedents	Sharing model		
	TVWS	***LSA***	***CBRS***
a) Platform	+ Technology platform standardized and may thus be adopted quickly - Based on evolving technologies scores on flexibility, but may lack scale and harmonization - Interference constraints and strict technical requirements requires specialized radios - Uncertainty of spectrum assets has limited interest of major technology vendors and MNOs.	+ Utilizes existing 3GPP ecosystem assets and scale + Network management system automatization based spectrum control function (LC) + Simple repository function (LR) fullfills static and semi-static use cases + Protects and leverages MNOs infrastructure investments	+ Extend 3GPP ecosystem to unlicensed and standalone LTE unlicensed + Dense urban deployments have additional utility and infra assets to share, e.g., fixed optical infra - Requires new intelligent and near real time SAS and ESC sensing functions. - New capabilities in big data & spectrum analytics needed to manage horizontal interference, co-existence and transactions - New spectrum band and introduced dynamism impacts BS and UE radios
b) Reduced need for the ownership	+ Offers access to practically free spectrum + Scores well in terms of efficiency of frequency bands utilization and rapidity of access - Unlimited number of users administratively imposed, rather than voluntarily chosen	+ Enables faster access to lower cost capacity spectrum without coverage obligations + Protects the turf on existing MNO infra with radio upgrades +/- Based on traditional exclusive licensing model with relatively high up front license payment + Expands sharing into other assets, e.g., with local venue owners	+ Unbundles investment in spectrum, network infrastructure and services + Spectrum access with low initial annuity payments + Access to local spectrum driven by business needs, when and where + Expands sharing into other assets, e.g., with local venue owners.
c) Utilization of underutilized assets	- Future availability of the shared UHF spectrum assets is uncertain particularly in dense urban areas - Heterogeneous incumbent users and TV channels properties - Non-guaranteed QoS may limit scope of services	+ Availability of spectrum assets dependent on regulation, currently LSA considerd for 2.3 GHz and 3.6 GHz spectrum band. + MNO connectivity model as is + Differentiation through extra data capacity and high speed enabling QoS and QoE pricing + Option to expand to capacity wholesale service	+ For MNOs low cost offloading + Nomadic Wi-Fi type of Internet access on dense urban environment hot spots + PAL – GAA tier flexibility + Spectrum and small cell hosted solution (SCaaS) + Enables new vertical segments: IoT - Concerns over the QoS predictability particularly with and at GAA layer and neighboring users across census tracks - Transaction costs increase in early development with increased complexity
d) Adaptability to different legal and policy regimes	+/- Regulated and standardized the US and Europe / UK with variants, e.g., in Singapore and Canada. + Low administrative burden + Low entry barrier enables quick access to the market	+ Legal certainty and security with existing regulatory framework + Requires a harmonized framework in regional standardization and regulation in order to reach economies of scale + Initial European focus but very generic concept adaptable to other regimes - National regulation with incumbent ecosystem	+ Low administrative burden with low entry barrier on GAA - Uncertainty with short PA license term and GAA with opportunistic access only - Need regulation and standardization with incumbent ecosystem (DoD) - Initially US federal specific, need adaptability to other regimes
e) Communities and trust	+ Geo-location database is trust vehicle to protect incumbent users' QoS - Heterogeneous GLDB operators in terms of services and business models - Rules out the possibility of decentralized agreement over accepted interference levels - The tragedy of the commons - Business model uncertainty limits incentives to invest	+ Trust in predictability of QoS and pragmatic incumbent protection build on binary agreements and implemented in LR. + Protection of LSA licensee business critical information quaranteed + Use existing consumer ownership on connectivity with existing known services for lock-in + Small cell ecosystem could introduce new players & shared asset opportunities	+ Trust implemented using the SAS + Internet giants 'innovation' ecosystems to trigger communities + Customer data ownership on apps and services for customer lock-in + Small cell ecosystem introduces new players and shared asset opportunities +/- Complemented by sensing as defense incumbents lack of trust in GLDB - Protection of MNOs business sensitive information assets in SAS uncertain - DoD OPSEC requirements
f) Value and user orientation	+ Main current use case is to provide Internet to rural unserved areas + Free spectrum facilitates local niche services, e.g., for various IoT vertical start-ups +/- Spectrum market related new value-added service opportunity for database providers utilizing positive network externality - Unlicensed users' QoS not protected - Requires special user equipment	+ Clear business model as is + Additional capacity to serve customers with improved QoS and QoE + Customer experience management as a tool for value differentiation + Can open the market to new players with local licenses	+ Flexible regulatory framework allows facilitates introduction of innovative local business model designs + Local and Internet players offer differentiation based on user knowledge. + Enables heterogeneous segments, e.g., consumers, enterprises, IoT + Introduces new roles: SAS admin, broker and sensing + Local services, e.g., media broadcasting and advertisement

The deployment of the LSA system will require relatively minor changes to the existing mobile broadband infrastructure. MNOs can utilize existing network off-the-shelf, and build additional LSA controller as an added Self Organizing Network (SON) functionality on top of the OAM system. In the LSA system, envisaged for the 2.3-2.4 GHz band, spectrum control is inside the MNO domain, and diffusion towards cognitive networks, in large, could be retained within MNOs control. Furthermore, the LR has low complexity compared other sharing concepts as sharing will be static or semi-static and binary between the incumbent and the licensee.

In the CBRS model with higher dynamics, the third opportunistic GAA layer and sensing function will require a more complex SAS system. In managing a higher volume of dynamic transactions, big data analytics capabilities of Internet players could become of need and bring competitive advantage. In the radio access side, higher dynamics in the spectrum control across the PA and the GAA layers and operator service areas will necessitate advanced spectrum analytics and horizontal co-existence management. Furthermore, with tight response time requirements this could also affect radio design of BSs. On the other hand, the PAL and the GAA layers with the common SAS will offer opportunities to common markets for licensed and licensed-by-rule equipment, and services across customer segments. Higher frequency and the small cell focus layer enables CBRS operators to utilize their fixed optical infra assets in backhauling. In addition to this, the GAA layer has an optimal opportunity to leverage emerging LTE unlicensed and Wi-Fi ecosystems to scale and complement LTE operator and stand-alone solutions.

B. Reduced Need for Ownership

The second factor deals with the superior value proposition and transactions that offer access over ownership, and ability to realize more choices with rapidity and lower initial costs. Sharing economy are spawning a variety of efficient new as-a-service (aaS) business models.

In the unlicensed TVWS concept, only device authorization is needed before starting operations on practically free spectrum, which radically lowers the entry barrier compared to two other concepts. Unlimited number of users are administratively imposed, rather than voluntarily chosen. Concept scores well in terms of efficiency of frequency bands utilization and rapidity of access. In the UK TVWS concept, the unlicensed approach is complemented with a licensed option for devices that must be manually configured.

The LSA concept offers lower cost spectrum without coverage obligations, with QoS guaranteed by licensing. For a greenfield operator, the up-front investment in spectrum license combined with needed infrastructure continues to set an entry barrier. Therefore, the second use case of LSA on the band 3.6-3.8 GHz envisaged for more local licenses and deployment without need for existing mobile infrastructure or specific network management tools provides opportunities that are more prominent for new entrants. Extra capacity could in addition offer a scale-out opportunity with a wholesale service. The PAL operator in the CBRS could deploy similar kind of business model designs.

The CBRS three-tiered regulatory approach can disruptively unbundle investment in spectrum, network infrastructure and services, and transform spectrum sharing further towards markets. Access to low cost spectrum with lower initial annuity payments for spectrum rights enables local 'pro-competitive' deployments, and further expands sharing mechanism for infra resources between operators. Furthermore, the light-touch leasing process will make the spectrum use rights held by a PA licensee available in secondary markets. The CBRS concept has potential on a longer term to reduce the need for parallel network infrastructure when spectrum, and related radio access infra assets are tradable, and hosted and shared on-demand and as-a-Service.

C. Utilization of Underutilized Assets

Access and deployment of the underutilized assets on-demand is essential to generate continuous revenue early. The value of the shared spectrum resources is highly dependent on the availability, liquidity and predictability.

Future availability of the shared TVWS spectrum assets is uncertain particularly in the dense urban areas. In rural area, TVWS operators are optimally positioned to create revenues from savings in spectrum costs, extended coverage and increased relative capacity. Coverage has potential to extend the customer base, while capacity could increase the Average Revenue Per User (ARPU). On the other hand, non-guaranteed QoS, heterogeneous incumbent users, and TV channel properties limit usability and the scope of services of the shared resources.

In the LSA approach, a sharing framework and binary sharing agreement negotiated between regulator, incumbent and licensee guarantee QoS and statistically known availability in advance. The LSA sharing framework could be initiated on a voluntary basis, but the regulator also may impose it. Availability of spectrum assets is highly dependent on the regulation, and the LSA was studied in the context of 2.3 GHz spectrum band as the starting point. The second use case currently under discussion is the 3.6-3.8 GHz band, in which case the predictability of spectrum availability is even higher, as dynamic changes in spectrum availability do not occur. Similar predictability is possible for the second tier PAL operator in the CBRS. Utilizing extra capacity established MNOs could create differentiating value proposition around QoS and Quality of Experience (QoE), and have option to expand to capacity wholesale and hosting services.

While the third opportunistic GAA layer offers the unlicensed Wi-Fi ecosystem type innovation environment, the availability, and particularly the QoS is not guaranteed. This has limited MNOs interest, based on traditional business models with need for the high upfront investments. On the other hand, both traditional MNOs and alternative operators could use the GAA layer with free spectrum resource for offloading and nomadic Wi-Fi type of Internet access. On dense urban environment, new business model designs and revenue structures could emerge combining spectrum with other shared assets, e.g., small cell hosted solution as-a-service (SCaaS), advertisement & transaction based models, and enabling new vertical segments within Internet of Things (IoT). Furthermore, the three-tier model offers network operators unprecedented flexibility and scalability through the ability for to move between the PA and the GAA tiers. This allows for the use of much shorter leasing periods, one to three years, without requiring a lessee to forgo their investment if their lease does not renew via simply converting from PA to GAA tier. For a new market entrant, this enables to try out their new service utilizing the GAA tier without having to invest in spectrum with future option to choose to buy a PA license when / where needed depending on the market and interference protection needs. In the system level, this flexibility and scalability between tiers combined with the secondary market provisions will improve spectrum efficiency in capacity, and particularly in value as spectrum can be regularly re-allocated to the most valuable use. The complexity of the CBRS introduces new independent or integrated roles to the ecosystem related to SAS administration, sensing operator and future spectrum broker that could increase deployment costs in early development. New technology introduction should be continuously assessed in relation with added complexity and deployment costs.

D. *Adaptability to Different Legal and Policy Regimes*

The harmonization of spectrum management is indispensable to unlock a wide range of positive externalities throughout the entire value chain. Scalability of all sharing concepts could be limited by fragmented national incumbent use cases, related different incumbent protection mechanisms, and regulatory differences affecting repository/database and spectrum management system architectures and implementations.

The TVWS concept is regulated and standardized the US and Europe / the UK with variants, e.g., in Singapore and Canada. While having a negative impact on the platform scale, the low administrative burden approach of the TVWS offers low entry barrier to the market.

Existing European LSA regulatory framework offers legal certainty and security with relatively high initial administrative burden. This protects the turf for established players, but limits the scalability through high entry barrier during the early macro deployments on the 2.3 GHz band. While the LSA offers visibility and predictability needed for high up-front investments in spectrum and infrastructure, both the CBRS and the TVWS regulatory approaches are pro-competitive targeting to lower administrative burden and entry barrier. The higher frequency small cell use cases of the LSA envisage opportunities that are more prominent for new entrants, and similar kind of business model designs than the PAL layer in the CBRS.

The CBRS will have advantage on leveraging the common US market. Sharing concepts in Europe require a harmonized framework in regional standardization and regulation to reach economies of scale. The regulatory and standardization actions needed with regulated or highly political incumbents' ecosystem (like defense, media and broadcasting) will potentially limit the scalability of all the frameworks. Uncertainty is introduced with the short PA licensing terms, and the GAA with opportunistic access only.

E. *Communities and Trust*

Making spectrum accessible is not enough; the underutilized assets need to move within the community. The trust is the trigger of collaborative shared consumption that makes the system grow and scale. The creation of a critical mass ecosystem with positive network effects is important for all three approaches with new context model based spectrum administrator and broker roles.

The TVWS concept rules out the possibility of decentralized agreement over accepted interference levels and is prone to the *tragedy of the commons* as number of competitive users grows. Heterogeneous GLDB operators in terms of services and business models may have additional negative impact to the community and the trust factor.

The repository or database is the vehicle to accomplish trust in all the models. Trust in the predictability of QoS and pragmatic incumbent protection is built on binary agreements and implemented in LSA Repository. In the CBRS, the database approach is complemented by the ESC for defense incumbents. Additional challenge for the CBRS is protection of MNOs business critical information assets in a SAS, and to meet stringent DoD's Operational Security (OPSEC) requirements.

In network externalities, business model designs represent a co-opetitive situation between MBB, wireless Internet and Internet domains. TVWS operators leverage their niche through tailoring according to local customer segment they serve benefiting of extended coverage. Furthermore, particularly in rural use cases, communication bit rates could be increased to level that enables access to Internet and media services to new user group.

In case LSA licensees have existing infrastructure and dedicated resources in other mobile bands, they can utilize their connectivity scale and customer base to achieve instant critical mass, and use existing consumer ownership on connectivity for lock-in. New entrants in the case of LSA and CBRS could build their critical mass and lock-ins using Internet 'innovation' ecosystems, and consumer and customer data ownership on apps and services.

Shared spectrum local small cell deployments in all the sharing concepts scale out ecosystems from legal and real estate aspects to radio planning and site camouflaging, as small cells will attach to structures and building assets not owned by traditional operator. This creates additional opportunities for sharing and collaboration between operators and various specialist companies like infrastructure owners and providers, real estate and street furniture owners, utility service companies and backhaul providers.

F. *Value Creation and User Orientation*

Sharing economy platforms create reciprocal economic value. Simplicity of the offer built around user knowledge driven 'demand pull' is critical in differentiating with existing service, as well as in scaling new spectrum sharing enabled services.

In the TVWS concept, unlicensed users' QoS is not protected. To date, the primary commercial 'niche' use case has been the non-competitive Fixed Wireless Access (FWA) WISP, in which a single GLDB serves a set of unlicensed WSDs belonging to local WISP providing Internet access to unserved rural areas. Free spectrum facilitates local niche services, e.g., for various IoT vertical start-ups. FWA use cases need specialized devices seen as extra complexity by users.

MNOs could utilize the surplus LSA spectrum in strengthening customer satisfaction through fulfilling existing need pull with familiar services and simplicity of the offer built on existing customer data via customer experience management tools. In general, spectrum sharing technologies should only be visible to end user through benefits offered in availability, coverage, capacity, data rates, or as decreased service costs. Both the LSA and the CBRS can also facilitate introduction of innovative local business model designs. For MNOs, they enable differentiation opportunities in serving more heterogeneous customer segments, e.g., consumers and enterprises, and for alternative type operators like Internet players faster efficient access to new systems and services. Local and Internet players are uniquely positioned to offer differentiation around existence of their extensive user knowledge. On one hand, operators prefer specialized services, or enhanced QoS traffic delivery for a fee to content, application, or over-the-top service providers. New entrants from Internet domain, in particular, on the GAA layer would like to see broadband as a utility, transparent and non-exclusive basis.

In addition to providing mandatory spectrum availability information brokerage, the LSA repository, the SAS, and the GLDB administrators can capture value through selling advanced information regarding the quality of the shared spectrum based on information from both the incumbents and other sharing users. These value-added services will be framed by regulatory action, and their value will increase with the number of service users, creating a positive network externality. On the other hand, for operators the added complexity of the spectrum management can be seen as increased transaction and opportunity costs.

V. Implication: Toward Markets for Spectrum Sharing Business Evolution

In this section, the analysis of spectrum sharing concepts discussed in Section IV are summarized using the markets and hierarchies analytic framework, presented in Section III. The summary of the anticipated changes into the mobile broadband ecosystem is depicted in Figure 6 and market-hierarchy positioning in Figure 7.

A. Value Creation and Capture Mechanism Transformation in the Ecosystem

As a continuation to the sharing economy analysis, we used the concepts of ecosystems and business model to provide a framework regarding the resources, business model, value and trust, shown in Figure 6. Specific attention in the framework is paid to value creation and capture mechanisms and their evolution over time.

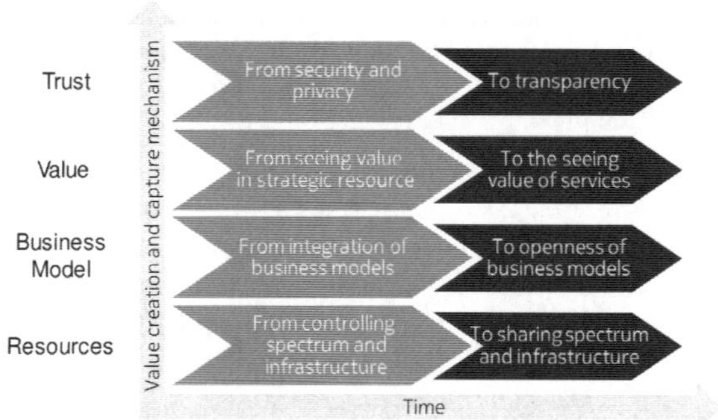

Figure 6. Value creation and capture mechanism transformation in the ecosystem.

At resource level, a clear transition from controlling spectrum and infrastructure toward sharing of spectrum and infrastructure assets can be observed. At the business model level, it could be expected that that the role of openness in business models would gain in importance. Regarding value, the spectrum sharing appears to conform more the "value from service" -approach than what traditionally has been the case in the industry. In the value creation process, firms may work as an integrator, collaborator, transaction broker or bridge provider, and correspondingly take care of resource configuration microprocesses like streamlining, sorting, resource crowdsourcing or continuous testing. The theme trust was seen to play a crucial role in the spectrum sharing and future 5G business ecosystem in large. The security and privacy concerns remain in providing services from the customers' perspective, but the role of transparency within the ecosystem was seen as becoming more pronounced.

There can be seen two developmental processes ongoing towards spectrum sharing and 5G. On one hand, MNOs are striving for technologies that enable more efficient use of existing spectrum assets, such as Carrier Aggregation (CA), Multiple-Input and Multiple-Output (MIMO) antenna technologies, and LTE on unlicensed spectrum concepts. On the other hand, regulators on their part strive to increase the amount of available spectrum. Both streams of action influence the value of spectrum, either from technological cost perspective or through new stakeholders entering the ecosystem. From conceptual perspective, these aforementioned developmental processes give us a layered view on value creation and capture. Accepting that business models are the devices for creating and capturing value, both *openness* and *integration* of business models are essential elements for understanding the ongoing dynamics toward 5G. Sharing of resources, whether spectrum or infrastructure, influences both integration of different players' business models and the required degree and type of openness of these business models, and in turn having an impact of the value creation and capture achieved within the ecosystem. At the second layer, where regulators strive to increase the amount of available spectrum for 5G, also the different types of operators such as existing MNOs or upcoming micro-operators [53] that could offer local services, influence value creation. However, the creation of trust, that also influences value creation and capture, is a more multifaceted issue as it cannot only be created through regulative control: it requires also a certain level of openness that needs to be adopted within the future 5G ecosystems.

B. *Positioning of the Spectrum Sharing Concepts in the Markets and Hierarchies Analytic Framework*

As discussed in Section III, there are three major forces transforming industries towards markets through reducing asset specificity and complexity of product description: communication, brokerage, and integration [14]. Based on the recent platform economy research [55], spectrum sharing markets can be seen to provide the several benefits compared to hierarchies in the communication and IT domain. Markets scale more efficiently by eliminating gatekeepers and utilizing network effects, unlocking new sources of value creation and supply, and providing superior marginal economics of production and distribution. Moreover, commerce platforms de-links ownership of assets from the value it creates, and aggregates unorganized markets with lower transaction costs.

We used the concepts of sharing economy and markets and hierarchies to provide a framework regarding the positioning of the spectrum sharing concepts as depicted in Figure 7. We argue that all the six sharing economy antecedent factors have positive effect in transforming towards markets. Complexity of product description is seen to be lowered particularly by platform, adaptability and value creation and user orientation antecedents. Assets specificity, on the other hand, is impacted by reduced need for the ownership, utilization of underutilized assets, and communities and trust. As a summary, resulted positioning of the analyzed spectrum sharing concepts is depicted in the Figure 7. In *asset specificity*, the high site specificity of the TVWS concepts impacts it's low score. For the LSA, the time specificity of the availability of the spectrum limits it's market characteristics. On the other hand, the CBRS score well due to scalable and flexible three-tiered model, fine-grained spectrum allocation in time and location, and the sub-leasing option that enables vertical disintegration.

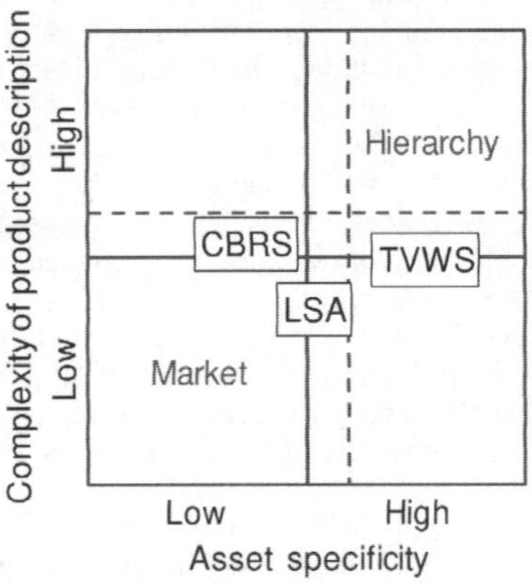

Figure 7. The positioning of the spectrum sharing concepts in the markets and hierarchies analytic framework.

Low *complexity* of product description favors the LSA, which builds on existing licensing regulatory regime with guaranteed QoS, predictability and legal certainty. TVWS on the other hand, stems from most mature regulatory and standardization landscape globally, and the simplicity of offer to specific niche use case. The CBRS extends the offer to heterogeneous local use cases and service providers. Though, the flexibility and dynamism of the CBRS result in increased system complexity at early deployment phase.

VI. CONCLUSION AND FUTURE WORK

Recently, several spectrum sharing system concepts have been introduced and widely studied to cope with spectrum scarcity, though to date only a few has developed into pre-commercial deployments. This paper discussed business model characteristics and sharing economy scalability criteria, and evaluated recent spectrum sharing concepts, the TV Whites Space, the European Licensed Shared Access and the US Citizens Broadband Radio Service, with respect to these criteria.

For a spectrum sharing concept to be adopted, it is essential not just to develop technology enablers to meet regulatory criteria but also to provide a scalable business model design for all the stakeholders. Harmonization and scalability of the platform and automation of processes will drive economies of scale and trigger early market opening. The model must be able to offer superior value proposition that offer access over ownership and ability to realize more choices with lower initial transactions costs compared to exclusive models. Value of the shared spectrum resources are highly dependent on its availability, liquidity and the predictability. Access, resource orchestration and configuration of the underutilized assets on-demand is essential to generate continuous revenue early. Scalability of all sharing concepts could be highly impacted by fragmented national incumbent use cases, related different incumbent protection mechanisms and regulatory differences. Trust is the trigger of all collaborative shared consumption that makes system grow and scale. The creation of a critical mass ecosystem with positive network effects is important for all three approaches with new database spectrum administrator and broker roles. Simplicity of the offer built around user knowledge driven 'demand pull' is critical in value differentiation for existing services as well as in scaling new spectrum sharing enabled services.

By reducing the costs of spectrum coordination, spectrum sharing concepts will lead to an overall shift from hierarchies towards more use of markets to coordinate economic activity related to spectrum assets. This transition is triggered by communication, brokerage, and integration enablers from technology, policy and business domains that reduce asset specificity and complexity of product description.

The analysis indicates that the TVWS concept actively promoted by the US and the UK administrations, benefits from practically free spectrum and low entry barrier. However, to date the level of market acceptance has remained low mainly due to uncertainties related to the available spectrum assets, platform scale, and predictability. Moreover, unlicensed non-guaranteed QoS has limited the scope of services and business model designs. The LSA provides high predictability and certainty for both the incumbent and the LSA licensee, leverages existing platforms and capabilities, and preserves low impact to the ecosystem and business models. The opportunistic third tier of the CBRS concept lowers entry barrier to new alternative operators, scale out ecosystem with new roles, and foster service innovation particularly. Similarly, the higher frequency small cell use cases of the LSA envisages more flexible and scalable opportunities for new entrants, and novel business model designs. On the other hand, introduced dynamism will increase system complexity, and requires novel technology enablers in building trust and ensuring pragmatic predictability in the spectrum management platform while minimizing additional transaction costs.

At resource level, a clear transition from controlling spectrum and infrastructure toward sharing of spectrum and infrastructure assets can be observed. At the business model level, it could be expected that that the role of openness in business models would gain in importance, and the spectrum sharing appears to conform more the "value from service" - approach than what traditionally has been the case in the industry. We argue that all the six sharing economy antecedent factors have positive effect in transforming towards markets. Complexity of product description is seen to be lowered particularly by platform, adaptability and value creation and user orientation antecedents. Assets specificity, on the other hand, is impacted by reduced need for the ownership, utilization of underutilized assets, and communities and trust.

The sharing economy and market and hierarchies analytic theories provide a dynamic framework for analyzing and developing the spectrum sharing business models. In the future, spectrum sharing concept business modelling studies will need to be expanded to cover novel ecosystem roles and stakeholders in resource orchestration and configuration. In particular, co-operative business model with traditional mobile network operators and local alternative micro-operators will be an important aspect to research.

ACKNOWLEDGMENT

This work is supported by Tekes – the Finnish Funding Agency for Technology and Innovation. The author would like to acknowledge the 5thGear CORE++ and uO5G project consortia.

REFERENCES

[1] S. Yrjölä, M. Matinmikko, M. Mustonen, and P. Ahokangas, "Analysis of Sharing Economy Antecedents for Recent Spectrum Sharing Concepts," In Proc. The Seventh International Conference on Advances in Cognitive Radio (COCORA), Venice, pp. 1-10, 2017.

[2] RSPG Opinion on Licensed Shared Access. RSPG13-538, Radio Spectrum Policy Group, Nov. 2013.

[3] The White House, Realizing the Full Potential of Government-Held Spectrum to Spur Economic Growth, President's Council of Advisors on Science and Technology (PCAST) Report, July 2012.

[4] FCC, Second Memorandum Opinion and Order (FCC 08-260), FCC, Washington, DC, USA, Sep. 2010.

[5] Ofcom, Statement on Implementing TV White Spaces. [Online] Available from: http://stakeholders.ofcom.org.uk/binaries/consultations/white-space-coexistence/statement/tvws-statement.pdf 2017.11.06

[6] ECC, Licensed Shared Access (LSA), ECC Report 205, Feb. 2014.

[7] FCC, FCC 16-55: The Second Report and Order and Order on Reconsideration finalizes rules for innovative Citizens Broadband Radio Service in the 3.5 GHz Band (3550-3700 MHz). [Online]. Available from: https://apps.fcc.gov/edocs_public/attachmatch/FCC-16-55A1.pdf 2017.11.06

[8] J. Chapin and W. Lehr, "Cognitive radios for dynamic spectrum access - The path to market success for dynamic spectrum access technology," IEEE Commun. Mag., vol. 45, no. 5, pp. 96-103, 2007.

[9] Y. Luo, L. Gao, and J. Huang, "Business Modeling for TV White Space Networks, " IEEE Commun. Mag., vol. 53, pp. 82 – 88, 2015.

[10] P. Ahokangas, M. Matinmikko, S. Yrjölä, H.Okkonen, and T. Casey,""Simple rules" for mobile network operators' strategic choices in future spectrum sharing networks," IEEE Wireless Commun., vol. 20, no. 2, pp. 20-26, 2013.

[11] P. Ahokangas et al., "Business models for mobile network operators in Licensed Shared Access (LSA)," IEEE International Symposium on Dynamic Spectrum Access Networks (DYSPAN), pp. 263 – 270, 2014.

[12] S. Yrjölä, P. Ahokangas, and M. Matinmikko, "Evaluation of recent spectrum sharing concepts from business model scalability point of view," IEEE International Symposium on Dynamic Spectrum Access Networks (DYSPAN), pp. 241-250, 2015.

[13] A. Sundararajan, "The Sharing Economy: The End of Employment and the Rise of Crowd-Based Capitalism," MIT Press, May 2016.

[14] T. Mallone, J. Yates, and R. Benjamin, "Electronic Markets and Electronic Hierarchies," Communications of the ACM vol. 30, no. 6, pp. 484-497, 1987.

[15] M. Mustonen et al., "Cellular architecture enhancement for supporting the European licensed shared access concept," IEEE Wireless Commun., vol. 21, no. 3, pp. 37 – 43, 2014.

[16] ETSI, System Architecture and High Level Procedures for operation of Licensed Shared Access (LSA) in the 2300 MHz-2400 MHz band. TS 103 235, 2015.

[17] M. Sohul, M. Yao, T. Yang, and J. Reed, "Spectrum Access System for the Citizen Broadband Radio Service," IEEE Commun. Mag., vol. 53, no. 7, pp. 18-25, 2015.

[18] The WINNF Spectrum Sharing Committee, "SAS Functional Architecture," [Online]. Available from: http://groups.winnforum.org/d/do/8512 2017.11.06

[19] FCC, White Spaces. [Online]. Avaialable from: http://www.fcc.gov/topic/white-space 2017.11.06

[20] Info-Communications Development Authority of Singapore. "Regulatory framework for TV White Space operations", June 2014.

[21] CEPT, the regulatory framework for TV WSD (White Space Devices) using a geolocation database and guidance for national implementation, ECC report 236, May 2015.

[22] IEEE Standards Association. "Part 11: Wireless LAN Medium Access Control (MAC) and Physical Layer (PHY) Specifications, Amendment 5: Television White Spaces (TVWS) Operation", 2013.

[23] EC, Promoting the shared use of radio spectrum resources in the internal market, COM (2012) 478, European Commission, Sept. 2012.

[24] CEPT, Harmonised technical and regulatory conditions for the use of the band 2300-2400 MHz for Mobile/Fixed Communications Networks (MFCN), CEPT, ECC Decision (14)02, June 2014.

[25] ETSI, Mobile Broadband services in the 2300-2400 MHz frequency band under Licensed Shared Access regime. ETSI TR 103.113, 2013.

[26] ETSI, System requirements for operation of Mobile Broadband Systems in the 2300 MHz -2400 MHz band under LSA. ETSI TS 103 154, 2014.

[27] M. Matinmikko et al., "Cognitive radio trial environment: First live authorized shared access-based spectrum-sharing demonstration," IEEE Veh. Technol. Mag., vol. 8, no. 3, pp. 30-37, 2013.

[28] S. Yrjölä et al., "Licensed Shared Access (LSA) Field Trial Using LTE Network and Self Organized Network LSA Controller," Wireless Innovation Forum European Conference on Communication technologies and Software Defined Radio (WInnComm-Europe), pp. 68-77, Oct. 2015.

[29] Italy, "World's first LSA pilot in the 2.3-2.4 GHz band," Input contribution to ECC PT1 #51, ECC PT1(16)028, Jan. 2016.

[30] RED Technologies, "Ericsson, RED Technologies and Qualcomm Inc. conduct the first Licensed Shared Access (LSA) pilot in France," [Online]. Available from: http://www.redtechnologies.fr/news/ericsson-red-technologies-and-qualcomm-inc-conduct-first-licensed-shared-access-lsa-pilot-france 2017.11.06

[31] ECC PT1, "Operational guidelines for spectrum sharing to support the implementation of the current ECC framework in the 3 600-3 800 MHz range", ECC PT1(16)82 Annex 20, Apr. 2016.

[32] ETSI RRS, DTR/RRS-0148: Feasibility study on temporary spectrum access for local high-quality wireless networks, Early draft 0.0.6, June 2017.

[33] The White House, Expanding America's Leadership in Wireless Innovation, Presidential Memorandum, June 2013.

[34] The 3GPP R4-168006: Relevant requirements for Band 48 introduction in 36.104, TSG-RAN4 Meeting #80bis, Ljubljana, Slovenia, Oct. 2016.

[35] FCC, Amendment of the Commission's Rules with Regard to Commercial Operations in the 3550-3650 MHz Band, FCC, Docket 12-354, 14-49, 2014.

[36] R. Amit and C. Zott, "Value creation in e-business," Strategic Management Journal, vol. 22, no. 6/7, pp. 493-520, 2001.

[37] M. A. Rappa, "The utility business model and the future of computing services," IBM Systems Journal, vol. 43, no. 1, pp. 32-42, 2004.

[38] H. Bouwman and I. MacInnes, "Dynamic business model framework for value Webs," in the Proceedings of the 39th Hawaii International Conference on System Sciences, Hawaii, USA, vol. 2, p. 43, Jan. 2006.

[39] R. Hallowell, "Scalability: the paradox of human resources in e-commerce," International Journal of Service Industry Management, vol. 12, no. 1, pp. 34-43, 2001.

[40] G. Stampfl, R. Prügl, and V. Osterloh, "An explorative model of business model scalability," Int. J. Product Development, vol. 18, nos. 3/4, pp. 226-248, 2013.

[41] A. Stephany, The Business of Sharing: Making it in the New Sharing Economy, Palgrave and Macmillan, 2015.

[42] C. Zott and R. Amit, "Business model design: An activity system perspective. Long Range Planning, vol. 43, no. 2-3, pp. 216-226, 2010.

[43] D. Teece, "Business models, business strategy and innovation," Long Range Planning, vol. 43, no. 2-3, pp. 172-194, 2010.

[44] A. Onetti, A. Zucchella, M. V. Jones, and P. P. McDougall-Covin, " (2012) Internationalization, innovation and entrepreneurship: business models for new technology-based firms. J Manag Gov, vol 16, pp. 337-368, 2012.

[45] J. F. Moore, "Predators and prey: a new ecology of competition," Harvard business review, vol. 71, no. 3, pp. 75-83, 1993.

[46] J. Wang and P. D. Wilde, "Evolution-generated communications in digital business ecosystems", IEEE Conference on Cybernetcis and Intelligent Systems, pp. 618-623, 2008.

[47] L. Berry, V. Shankar, J. Parish, S. Cadwallader, and T. Dotzel, "Creating new markets through service innovation," MIT Sloan Management Review, vol. 47, no. 2, pp. 56-63, 2006.

[48] N. Franke, M. Gruber, D. Harhoff, and J. Henkel, "Venture capitalists' evaluations of startup teams: trade-offs, knock-out criteria, and the impact of VC experience," Entrepreneurship: Theory & Practice, vol. 32, no. 3, pp. 459-483, 2008.

[49] S. Choudary, M. Van Alstyne, and G. Parker, "Platform Revolution: How Networked Markets Are Transforming the Economy--And How to Make Them Work for You," John Wiley & Sons, Inc., Mar. 2016.

[50] A. Sundararajan, "From Zipcar to the Sharing Economy" HBR, June 2013.

[51] O. E. Williamson, "Markets and Hierarchies," Free Press, New York, 1975.

[52] O. E. Williamson, "The economics of organization: The transaction cost approach. Am. J. Sociol., vol. 87, no. 3, pp. 548-575, 1981.

[53] D. C. North, "Transaction costs, institutions, and economic performance," San Francisco, CA: ICS Press, 1992.

[54] M. Matinmikko, M. Latva-aho, P. Ahokangas, S. Yrjölä, and Timo Koivumäki, "Micro operators to boost local service delivery in 5G," Wireless Personal Communications journal, Springer, May 2017.

[55] M. Van Alstyne, G. Parker, and S. Choudary, "Pipelines, Platforms, and the New Rules of Strategy," Harvard Business Review, vol. 94, no. 4, pp. 54-62, 2016.

Development of a Support System for Japanese Extensive Reading:

An evaluation of the system by learners

Teiko Nakano
Shobi Universiy
Saitama Japan
e-mail: t-nakano@b.shobi-u.ac.jp

Abstract—**This paper reports on a study of a support system for Japanese extensive reading. The purpose of this system is to provide Japanese graded readers and an environment where learners can learn by themselves. The system contains video clips that replace teachers, boards that display other learners' comments, and personal pages that display progress of the learners. From the results of a post-questionnaire and the logs of the system left by participants, the usefulness of the system is analyzed.**

Keywords-online library; Japanese graded readers; reading habits; digital books.

I. Introduction

Considering that most learners of foreign languages are studying outside the countries where the target language is used, an online library of graded readers is useful for providing learning materials. Such an online library is beneficial for learners who learn abroad from the standpoints of time and cost. Especially, those learners without teachers will find it beneficial. However, currently, there is no system of Japanese extensive reading that is available to independent learners outside the classroom. Therefore, this study has designed and developed a support system for Japanese extensive reading, in which an online library is installed. In the eLmL2017, we reported the extensive reading support system for independent learners of Japanese [1].

Extensive reading is part of an approach for teaching English to speakers of other languages to build vocabulary and develop reading comprehension [2] [3] [4] [5]. Extensive reading has not been a common approach in education programs because it is time consuming and qualitatively different compared with existing reading courses that are typically offered; however, through the development of a module that can hold students accountable for their reading [5], extensive reading outside the classroom has been made possible. The module is used for managing learners' records. As a solution to the problem of teachers who cannot take time to have students read during the class, this study has developed a support system for them in order to be able to make enough time for their students to read study materials on the systems outside of the classroom. In addition to that, we have implemented blended type lessons of extensive reading [7] [8] [9]. Using the system, teachers can have learners read books on the system as homework and can use classroom time for post reading activities. Learners can read books on their devices at any time.

However, considering that learners can choose when and how to learn, extensive reading can be thought of as autonomous learning [10]. Therefore, this study aims to include all learners not only those studying with teachers and has developed a support system for Japanese extensive reading based on the system that supported blended type lessons. On the system, video clips and a comment board were used, and in addition, the progress of all users was displayed anonymously to let the learners who studied independently feel the presence of other learners. The results of a post-questionnaire and the amount of reading done confirmed the usefulness of those facilities.

Moreover, a reading community on Facebook was tested as a post-reading activity. However, it was suggested that membership in the ER FB group was an important indicator of participation in FB discussions. The effect of ER FB group membership on FB commenting and the effect of the comment board of the self-ER support system were almost the same in that they encouraged learners to read by making them aware of the presence of other learners. These results indicate that an ER FB group is not necessary, but that a comment board is useful in the self-ER support system. Therefore, the study concluded that the post-reading activities on Facebook were not essential [1]. Based on feedback from the questionnaire on the eLmL2017, we improved the system and it was released to the public in August 2017. In this current system, a "Personal Page" that shows users' reading histories was added to motivate learners to continue reading, and the way of displaying the results of the "Questions and Questionnaire" was improved.

As an evaluation of the current system, from the results of the post-questionnaire and the logs on the system left by users surveyed by the author, this paper discusses the following questions:

(1) whether the personal page and the improvements were useful in encouraging learners to read,

(2) whether the digital reading materials were useful for learners to read extensively,

(3) whether the extensive reading support system is useful for independent learners on learning Japanese.

In Section II, the design of this system and how it has evolved will be discussed. Then, in Section III, the methodology of this study will be explained. In Section IV, the usefulness of this system based on the results of a post-questionnaire and the logs on the system left by participants will be examined. In Section V, the study will be concluded.

II. A Support System for Extensive Reading

First, we will introduce the previous study. Then, we will explain the scheme of the current system indicating the points that were improved. Lastly, we will show the information that can be collected from the logs left by users.

A. *Outline of Previously Used System*

Fig. 1 shows a schematic of the support system for Japanese extensive reading, which has two purposes and functions. First, the system supports blended extensive reading lessons (blended-ER support system), which are designed for teachers who provide such lessons [7] [8] [9]. Second, it is a support system for learners who study by themselves (self-ER support system) [1]. This system was designed to facilitate learning outside the classroom, and provides an online library of Japanese graded readers (hereafter referred to as JGR) so that learners can learn autonomously. The function that the two systems have in common is called "ER Lab," which is mainly composed of "Libraries" and "Questions and Questionnaire". When users submit their replies to the "Questions and Questionnaire", the system recognizes that the users have read the books and displays their scores of the "Questions" and their replies to the "Questionnaire" on the "Progress" page under their IDs. Moreover, the system calculates the amount read by the users and displays the top three users on the top of the "Progress" page. Also, their replies to the "Questionnaire" are aggregated and the average scores are calculated. Then, on the "Evaluation" page, these scores are displayed in the form of the choices available on the questionnaire on each title (for example, a score of 3.8/5 may be "This book is interesting").

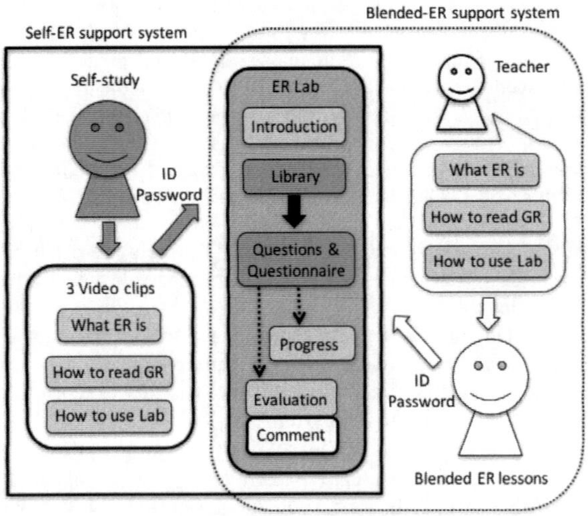

Figure 1. Schematic of a Support System for Japanese Extensive Reading.

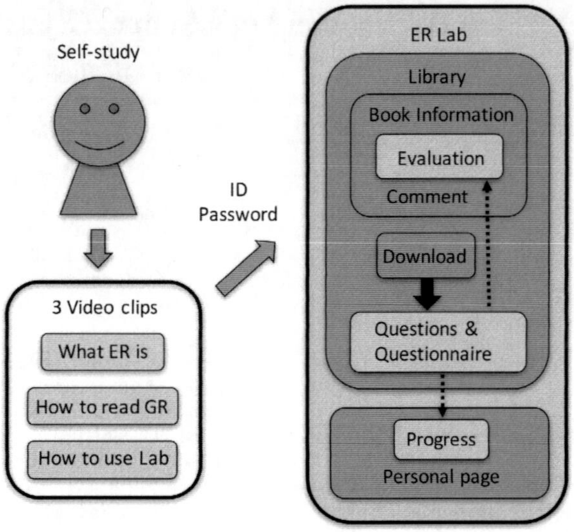

Figure 2. Schematic of a Current Self-ER Support System.

In the blended-ER support system, the teacher explains extensive reading, how to read graded readers, and how to use the ER Lab. The teacher can also provide post-reading activities, such as initiating discussions about the readings. A blended ER lesson using the blended-ER support system was implemented, and the availability of the system was confirmed [7].

In contrast, the self-ER support system was designed for learners to learn independently through the system, without teachers. In this system, video clips are used in place of the teacher's explanation so that learners can receive the same information as students in the blended-ER support system. It is recognized that, despite limitations, Video-Based Learning represents an effective learning method that can replace teacher-led learning approaches [11]. Additionally, a comment board that allowed users to write their impressions of the books that they had read was added to the ER Lab to ensure that learners were aware of the presence of other learners. It was expected that knowing how much other learners had read would promote reading among learners visiting the comment board [12].

B. *Current System*

Fig. 2 shows a schematic of the current self-ER support system. Before login, users watch three video clips on the "Top" page of the system (see Fig. 3). Video clips are used to teach "what extensive reading is," "how to read graded readers" and "how to use ER Lab". The time required to watch each video clip is around 2 minutes.

The ER Lab is composed of the "Library" and a new page called the "Personal Page" for each user. The "Library" contains *SAKURA,* which is a small collection of JGRs divided into eight levels from A to H (beginner to upper intermediate levels) [13]. A vocabulary level test that judges the appropriate level of *SAKURA* for learners to start reading from is under development [14] [15].

Figure 3. TOP page.

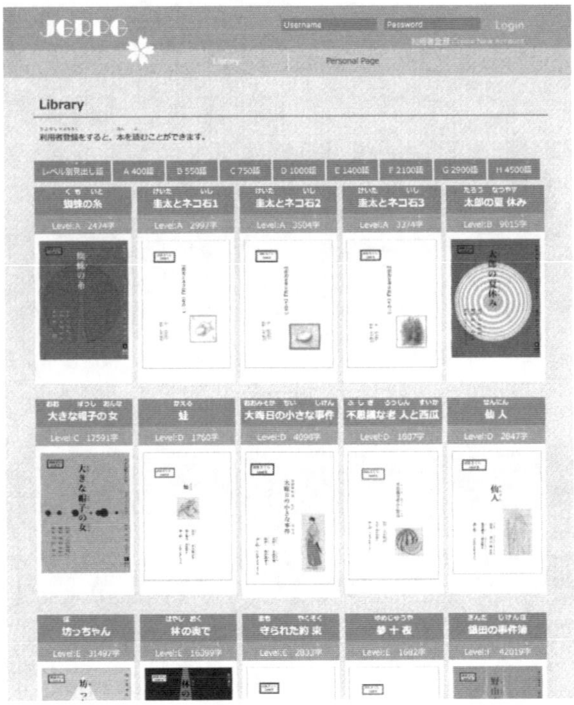

Figure 4. Library

Figure 5. Book Information Page on each Title

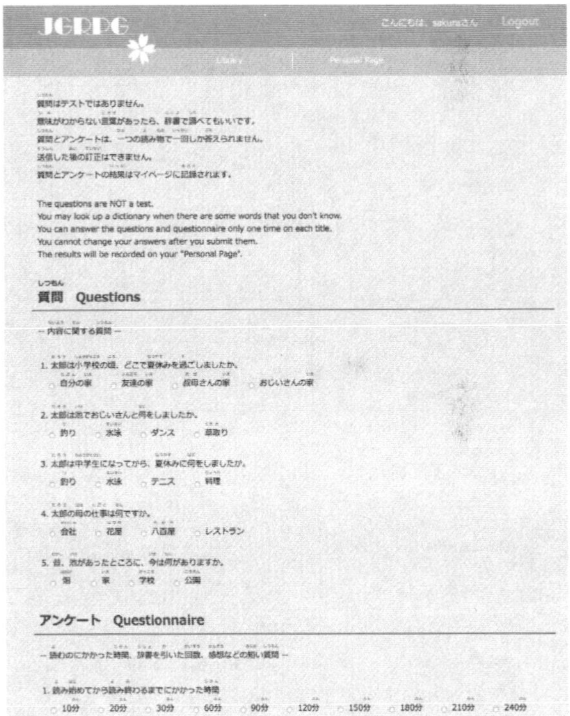

Figure 6. Questions and Questionnaire

In the library, the cover of each title is lined up with the number of letters (Chinese characters and Japanese phonetic alphabet) starting from the easiest level (see Fig. 4). By clicking the cover of the book, an information page on each title will appear (see Fig. 5). On the right side of the cover, the author, the original book, and the number of letters are displayed. Below this information, the page provides recommendation stars (1-5), which represent how interesting other users felt the book to be. Also, a brief introduction written by the rewriter of the book that was displayed separately in the former system is included here.

Below this information, the download button is displayed. Users can choose from three types of digital book; "ePub", "mobi", or "html". If users choose "html", they can read the book on the page. After downloading the digital file, a "Questions and Questionnaire" button will appear so that users cannot see the questions before they read the story.

Figure 7. Comment Board

The "Questions and Questionnaire" page consists of "Questions" about the stories and a "Questionnaire" about their reading experience (see Fig. 6). In the "Questions" part, participants are required to answer five questions about the book they had read. Each question has four answer choices to gauge their reading comprehension. In the "Questionnaire" part, participants are required to complete a questionnaire. Therein, they evaluate the length, difficulty, contents of the story and illustrations, and are asked to report the frequency of dictionary usage using a five-point Likert scale. Besides these questions, users are asked how long they had spent reading and which device they had used to read. In the final part of the "Questionnaire", there is a space where users can write their impressions about a given story if they choose to.

Users may leave comments on each story. At the bottom of the information page on each title, these comments are displayed under their ID, not their name, together with the users' responses to the questionnaire on length, difficulty, and interest (Fig. 7). To prevent users knowing the end of a story before reading it, they can only see other users' comments after they have submitted their replies to the "Questions and Questionnaire".

Fig. 8 shows the "Personal Page". On the Personal page, users' registration data (nickname, place of residence, first language, date of registration) is displayed at the top. Below

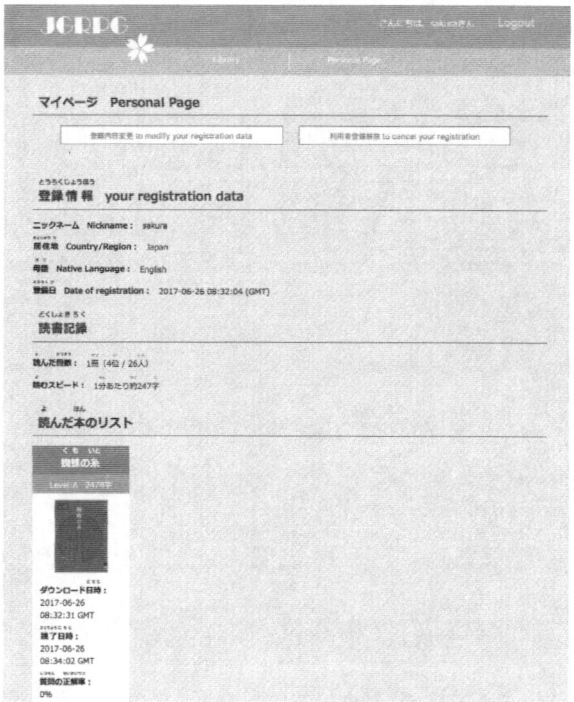

Figure 8. Personal Page

the registration data, both their rank among all users regarding the number of letters they had read, and also their average reading speed are displayed. It is because "to read quickly" is one of the important points of extensive reading [16]. Reading speed is calculated from their answers to the questionnaire and the number of letters in the book they had read. A list of the books they had read is displayed at the bottom. When users click the books displayed in their list of books read, their answers to the questions and the correct answers to the questions on each book will appear. Also, the replies to the "Questionnaire" are displayed on the "Personal Page".

As mentioned in chapter 1, in this study, the way of displaying the answers to the "Questions and Questionnaire" has been improved. The "Progress" page that shows the ranking of the amount that users have read has been eliminated. Instead, on the "Personal Page", each user can see where he or she is ranked according to how much they have read. In the previous study [1], some participants were motivated to read more by seeing how much progress others had made. However, some participants did not want to see how much other participants had read or how well they had answered the questions about the books. Therefore, in the current system, this data remains private. Moreover, their average reading speed, that is calculated from their answers to the questionnaire, is displayed simultaneously. It was considered that showing a user's progress would motivate them to continue reading.

C. *Logs Left by Users*

The administrator can collect the records or logs left by users when they registered, which contain the following data:

1) Registration data: Users' nickname, first language, place of residence, and self-assessment of their Japanese level (beginner, intermediate, advanced)

2) Date and time the file was downloaded and kind of the file (ePub, mobi, html)

3) Date and time the answers were submitted

4) Moreover, the administrator can collect the data below from users' questions and questionnaires:

a) Five questions about the books that they had read. Each question has four answer choices to gauge their reading comprehension

b) Users' evaluation, using five-point Likert scale, of the length (short 1 – long 5), difficulty (easy 1- difficult 5), contents of the story (boring 1 – interesting 5) and illustrations (not helpful 1 – helpful 5)

c) Frequency of dictionary usage（never, 1 – 3 times, 4 -6 times, 7 -9 times, 10 times or more）

d) How long users had spent reading（10 minutes, 20 minutes, 30 minutes, 60 minutes, 90 minutes, 120 minutes, 150 minutes, 180 minutes, 210 minutes, 240 minutes, 300 minutes, 360 minutes）

e) The type of device they had used to read（PC, Smartphone, Tablet, Other）

f) Their impressions of the stories

TABLE I. PARTICIPANTS' JAPANESE PROFICIENCY

		Average	Standard Deviation
Vocabulary	Upper	84	4.7
	Lower	63	11.5
Grammar	Upper	87	7.5
	Lower	67	10.5

III. METHOD

In this section, first, we will introduce the participants and then, explain the methodology of the study. Lastly, we will show the post-questionnaire.

A. *Participants*

Nineteen international students (8 male and 11 female) at a Japanese university participated in this study. Their ages ranged from 20 to 31 (average 22.7). Their home countries included China (8), Vietnam (5), Malaysia (2), Korea (2), Hong Kong (1), and Nepal (1). As for the first language of the participants, 11 participants spoke languages that use Chinese characters, while 8 spoke languages that do not. To ascertain participants' Japanese abilities, the Simple Performance-Oriented Test (SPOT) and a vocabulary assessment were administered. SPOT was used to assess grammar [17]. A vocabulary part of a Japanese language proficiency test was used to assess vocabulary. The results of these tests are shown in Table I. In both columns, the upper group represents nine participants, the lower group, ten participants. The participants on the lower group had widely different scores. Although participants who do not use Chinese characters tend to get lower scores in vocabulary, six participants in the upper group of both in vocabulary and grammar (SPOT) were the same individuals. Therefore, in chapter 4, participants are divided into upper group (nine persons) and lower group (ten persons) by total scores of vocabulary and grammar.

B. *Procedure*

The procedures were as follows:

1) After watching the video clips on the "Top" page and registering as users of the system, participants could log into the ER Lab using their user IDs and passwords.

2) Participants read books from the library on their devices. They were recommended to start reading from the lower level of SAKURA. ER Lab was used for a week.

3) Participants answered questions about the story that they had read, and completed a questionnaire to evaluate the book. They were then invited to write their comments about the story.

4) Participants answered the post-questionnaire on the last day of reading.

C. Post-Questionnaire

In the post-questionnaire, participants were asked as follows:

1) Did you feel the video clips were useful?

If yes, please choose your reason from A, B and C (You can choose any number).

a) I could understand the explanation without reading.

b) The video clips motivated me to read the books because they were amusing.

c) Other (Please write a comment)

If no, please write your reason.

2) Did you feel the five questions about the books in the "Library" were useful?

If yes, please choose your reason from A, B and C (You can choose any number).

a) I could check my understanding about books.

b) Aiming for a high score in the questions motivated me to understand the story.

c) Other (Please write a comment)

If no, please write your reason.

3) Did you feel it was useful to display "Other users' comments" in the Library?

If yes, please choose your reason from A, B and C (You can choose any number).

a) Knowing other users' opinions was interesting.

b) Knowing other users' opinions motivated me to read more.

c) Other (Please write a comment)

If no, please write your reasons.

4) Did you feel it was useful to display the "Ranking" on the "Personal Page"?

If yes, please choose your reason from A, B and C (You can choose any number).

a) Knowing my rank was enjoyable.

b) Knowing my rank moivated me to read more.

c) Other (Please write a comment)

If no, please write your reason.

5) Did you feel it was useful to display your "Reading Speed" on the "Personal Page"?

If yes, please choose your reason from A, B and C (You can choose any number).

a) Knowing my speed of reading was fun.

b) Knowing my speed of reading motivated me to read more.

c) Other (Please write a comment)

If no, please write your reason.

6) Did you feel "A List of the Books you had read" was useful?

If yes, please choose your reason from A, B and C (You can choose any number).

a) I will not forget the books I had read

b) The list motivated me to read more.

c) Other (Please write a comment)

If no, please write your reason.

7) Which devices did you use most to read digital books?

a) PC

b) Smartphone

c) Tablet

d) Other (Please write a comment)

8) Do you prefer paper books or digital books and why? Please choose one from A, B or C.

a) Paper books

b) Digital books

c) I do not mind

Please write why you chose A, B, or C.

9) Were there any differences in your reading habits regarding the time or place you read digital books compared to when you read paper books in the past?

10) If you answered "yes" in (9), how it affected your reading habits regarding time and place. Which is the most frequent when you read on paper books.

a) Time of day : 6:00-12:00, 12:00-18:00, 18:00-22:00, 22:00-5:00

b) Place : home, in the train, outside of home, university (includes library), a public library

c) If there is another difference, please write in detail.

11) What time of the day and where you read the digital books on the ER Lab.

a) Time of day : 6:00-12:00, 12:00-18:00, 18:00-22:00, 22:00-5:00

b) Place : home, in the train, outside of home, university (includes library), a public library

12) What do you think the strong points of the graded readers is? (You can choose more than two)

a) I can read books without a dictionary.

b) I can read quickly.

c) Kana is written on the right side of the kanji.

d) Japanese literature is rewritten in easy Japanese.

e) I think that it helps to improve my reading ability.

f) Other (Please write a comment)

13) What do you think the weak points of the graded readers is? (You can choose more than two)

a) Vocabulary is too repetitious.

b) The stories are too long.

c) The stories are too short.

d) The stories are too simple.

e) Other (Please write a comment)

14) If there is something that you prefer to have or to improve, please write.

IV. Results and Discussion

From the results of the post-questionnaire and the logs left by participants, here we will discuss the research questions. First, we will discuss the functions of the current self-ER support system. Next, we will discuss the usefulness of digital books. Lastly, we will discuss the usefulness of this system on learning Japanese.

A. *Usefulness of the Current Self-ER Support System*

From the results of questions (1) to (6) of the post-questionnaire, we will discuss the usefulness of the functions of the current self-ER support system.

1) Video Clips

All the responses to question (1) "Did you feel the video clips were useful?" were positive. Fourteen participants chose "I could understand the explanation without reading" and five participants chose "the video clips motivated me to read books because they were amusing". To understand the explanation without reading is important for beginners. Since all users must watch video clips before they log into the ER Lab, reading on the ER Lab that the video clips are amusing will encourage them to read.

2) Library

All the responses to question (2) "Did you feel the five questions about the books in the "Library" were useful?" were positive. Seventeen participants chose "I could check my understanding about books" and two participants chose "It became the motivation while reading".

In the current system, the comment board was moved inside the library. To question (3) "Did you feel it was useful to display "Other users' comments in the "Library"?", seventeen participants responded positively. Ten participants chose "Knowing other users' opinion motivated me to read more" and nine participants chose "Knowing other users' opinion is interesting". However, one participant commented "Although it is useful to look, it might bother someone who wants to read casually". This participant did not notice that writing comments is optional. The reasons for the response "No" were "There was no comment" and "I did not notice it". Making it easier to see the comments might be beneficial.

3) Personal Page

To question (4) "Did you feel it was useful to display the "Ranking" on the "Personal Page"?", seventeen participants responded positively. Twelve participants chose "Knowing my rank was enjoyable" and four participants chose "Knowing my rank motivated me to read more". Two participants wrote "I could confirm the book I had read". The reason for the response "No" was "I do not care," which is not negative.

All the responses to question (5) "Did you feel it was useful to display your "Reading speed" on the "Personal Page"?" were positive. Fifteen participants chose "Knowing my speed of reading was fun" and five participants chose "Knowing my speed motivated me to read more".

All the responses to question (6) "Did you feel "A List of the Books you had read" was useful?" were positive. Nine participants chose "I will not forget the books I had read", eight participants chose "The list motivated me to read more". Other reasons were "I could confirm the book I read", "It would be convenient to find the book when I read the book again" and "It would be enjoyable".

On the "Video Clips" and the "Library", the above-mentioned positive responses were given by participants the same as in the previous study [1]. On the "Personal page" that was newly added to the current system, there were also no negative responses. Knowing their progress motivated most of the participants to read more. It is considered that displaying the amount the user read and reading speed is useful to make learners be aware of the important points of extensive reading, that is, "read more" and "read quickly".

B. *Usefulness of Digital Books for Extensive Reading*

From the results of questions (7) to (11) of the post-questionnaire, we will discuss the usability of the digital books.

Table II shows the device and the file format when participants read digital books. "Device" is the answer to

TABLE II. DEVICES, FILES AND PREFERENCES

ID	Device	file	Preference
1	Smartphone	html	Paper
2	PC	html	Paper
3	Smartphone	html	Paper
4	Smartphone	html	Digital
5	Smartphone	ePub	I do not mind
6	Smartphone	html	Paper
7	Smartphone	ePub	Digital
8	Smartphone	html	Digital
9	Smartphone	html	Paper
10	Smartphone	html/ePub	I do not mind
11	Smartphone	html	I do not mind
12	PC	html	Digital
13	Smartphone	ePub	Digital
14	PC	html	Paper
15	Smartphone	html	Digital
16	Smartphone	ePub/html	I do not mind
17	Smartphone	html	Paper
18	PC	html	Digital
19	Smartphone	ePub	Digital

TABLE III. READING HABITS ON PAPER AND DIGITAL BOOKS

ID	Japanese	Reading Habits			Place and Time (%)			
		Preference	Habit	Paper	Home	Train	Univ	Outside
10	104	DP	differ	U	0	100	0	0
4	118	D	differ	U	0	100	0	0
5	125	DP	differ	U	8	33	50	8
16	131	DP	same		57	43	0	0
18	133	D	differ	H	33	67	0	0
7	140	D	same		26	47	27	0
12	140	D	same		100	0	0	0
19	141	D	differ	H	0	100	0	0
17	143	P	same		10	90	0	0
15	147	D	same		100	0	0	0
1	154	P	differ	H	0	67	0	33
8	158	D	same		100	0	0	0
9	160	P	differ	H	44	24	0	31
2	161	P	differ	U	100	0	0	0
11	168	DP	differ	H	0	100	0	0
3	172	P	same		96	0	4	0
13	176	D	same		40	0	60	0
14	179	P	same		100	0	0	0
6	188	P	differ	H	0	100	0	0

question (7). "File" is the results of the logs left by participants. "Preference" is the answer to question (8).

Although all the participants had smartphones, fifteen participants used smartphones and four participants used PCs when they read digital books. For the files to read digital books, fifteen participants downloaded "html", six participants downloaded "ePub" and no participants downloaded "mobi". The reason is perhaps that in the video clip instruction, using "html" for reading digital books is recommended if the user had never used "ePub" or "mobi".

To the question (8) "Do you prefer paper books or digital books and why?", eight participants chose "digital", seven participants chose "paper", and four participants chose "I do not mind". The reason for choosing digital was "it is convenient". Other reasons were "Digital book is good for heavy books" and "Paper books do not have functions to display other users' comments or reading speed".
The reason for choosing "I do not mind" was "both have good points". As the participants who downloaded "ePub" prefer digital books, it is considered that the participants who prefer paper had not been accustomed to using digital books. For the reason of preferring paper, "paper is good to memorize contents because I can leave a note on it", "paper is not bad for one's eyes", "paper is good to concentrate on reading" were given. However, most participants gave the same reason they preferred paper.

Next, we will compare paper books and digital books regarding the time or place used. Table III shows reading habits and preference for paper books and/or digital books. The two left hand columns show participant's information. "Japanese" means Japanese language proficiency and shows total scores of vocabulary and grammar. The three center columns show preference and habits of reading books. In the column "Preference", "D" means digital book, "P" means paper book, and "DP" means that the participant chose "I do not mind".

The results of question (9) "Were there any differences in your reading habits regarding the time or place you read digital books compared to when you read paper books in the past?" is shown in the column, "habits". The results of question (10) "How it affected your reading habits regarding time and place? Which is the most frequent when you read on paper books?" is shown in the column, "paper". "H" means home. "U" means university that includes university library. The four right hand columns show the rate of the place and time when participants read digital books in this experiment. "Outside" means participants were outside of their homes. The numeral value shows the percentage of the total time spent for reading based on the logs left by participants at each place answered in the results of question (11). Preference shown in Table II is reprinted. The table is displayed in ascending order of Japanese language proficiency.

To question (9), ten participants answered "There were differences between paper and digital in their reading habits regarding time and place". For the place where the ten participants read books most frequently, six of the ten participants answered "home" and four of the ten participants answered "university". The participant with ID-2 answered that he usually read at the university library, although he had read at home in this experiment. The participants with ID-4, ID-5 and ID-10 had read in the train or other places outside. From these results, it appears that the most different point in reading habits between paper and digital was place when reading. The time of day for reading tended to differ depending on the place. The participants read in the morning or in the evening at home, and they read outside their home in the day time. On the other hand, the nine participants who answered "There was no difference between paper and digital in their reading habits regarding time and place" usually read digital books. In this experiment, The participants with ID-3, ID-8, ID-12, ID-14, ID-15 and ID-16 read mostly at home, the participant with ID-7 and ID-17 read mostly on the train, and the participant with ID-13 read mostly read at her university.

From this result, it could be said that the learners who usually read paper books at home or university (classroom or library) would have more chances to read digital books with their smartphones anywhere and anytime. Therefore, the participants with ID-4 and ID-5 who usually read at the university library answered that there was an advantage to digital books. A digital library would be more convenient because they could borrow books anywhere.

These results support the usefulness of the current system. Although we need more research on their reading habits, it was interesting that the participants who got higher scores tend to prefer paper over digital in Table III. We suppose that the participants who prefer paper were accustomed to reading paper books. We also suppose that the participants who did not have the habit of reading might read more if they could use digital books.

C. *Japanese Extensive Reading on ER Lab*

In the previous study [1], the group that scored lower on vocabulary and grammar read more books than the upper group. We suppose that one of the reasons was because the experimenter recommended the participants to start reading from the lower levels. The participants who belonged to the upper group gave some comments like "If I was given something that was appropriate to my level, I would have read more". Therefore, in this study, the experimenter did not recommend participants to start reading from the lower levels, although the video clips recommended users to start reading from the lower level.

Table IV shows the levels of the book that was read by participants based on the logs left by participants. In this study, the higher scoring group (upper group) both on vocabulary and grammar read more books than the lower group. All the participants except ID-16 in the lower group started reading from the lowest level. However, four participants in the upper group did not read the lowest level. Three in the four participants started reading from the fourth lowest level, D. Moreover, the participants in the upper group read the books in F level, which was not read by the lower group. This result supports the method of extensive reading "students select what they want to read" proposed by Day and Bamford [4].

TABLE IV. LEVELS OF THE BOOKS PARTICIPANTS READ

ID	Japanese	A		B	C	D				E				F		
10	104	■		■		■										
4	118	■														
5	125	■	■	■		■	■	■				■				
16	131					■	■			■						
18	133	■	■			■										
7	140	■	■	■	■	■						■	■			
12	140	■		■	■	■	■									
19	141	■					■									
17	143	■	■	■												
15	147	■				■	■									
1	154	■	■													
8	158	■				■				■						
9	160	■	■	■	■	■	■	■	■	■	■	■	■	■	■	■
2	161	■	■													
11	168						■								■	
3	172			■	■	■	■	■		■	■	■			■	■
13	176	■				■	■	■	■	■						
14	179					■				■						
6	188					■	■			■	■		■			

TABLE V. ADVANTAGES OF JGR

Japanese proficiency					Strong points of JGR				
ID	Kanji-use	Grammar	Vocabulary	Speed	Quick	Kanji	Literature	Dictionary	Ability
14	not	92	87	69	○				
16	not	81	51	75		○	○	○	○
19	not	81	60	107	○	○	○		
7	not	90	49	115				○	
8	use	78	80	118	○	○	○		
13	use	91	84	147		○	○	○	
18	not	75	58	157	○	○	○	○	○
11	use	86	82	161		○		○	
3	use	83	89	174			○		○
15	not	86	61	201		○			○
17	not	87	55	214		○		○	
4	use	59	59	247	○		○		
12	use	69	71	297	○		○		
2	use	79	82	309		○	○		
9	not	84	76	334	○	○		○	
5	use	57	69	368	○			○	
1	use	73	81	412	○		○		
10	use	51	53	442	○	○			
6	use	98	89	565	○			○	

Next, the results of question (12) "What do you think the strong points of the graded readers is?" is shown in Table V with the participants' information. "Speed" shows the number of letters read per minute. It was calculated by the number of the letters in the book they read and the time they spent for reading the books from the logs left by them. The data in Table V is shown in ascending order of reading speed. In the five right hand columns, "Quick" represents "I can read quickly", "Kanji" represents "Kana is written on the right side of the kanji", "Literature" represents "Japanese literature is rewritten in easy Japanese", "Dictionary" represents "I can read books without a dictionary", and "Ability" represents "I think that it helps to improve my reading ability". In the five left hand columns, "Kanji-user" represents whether they use Kanji in their first language.

The participants with lower reading speed tended to be those who do not use Kanji in their first language. The participants with higher reading speed tended to choose "I can read quickly". The participants who chose "Kana is written on the right side of the kanji" included both participants who use Kanji and who do not use Kanji in their first language. This result found that JGRs are also useful for the participants who use Kanji in their first language because the pronunciation of Kanji in Japanese is different from that in Chinese. Moreover, from the result that the number of the participants who chose "Japanese literature is rewritten in easy Japanese" was ranked third, we could find the beneficial point of graded readers that are rewrites of literature whose copyright has expired. Three of the four participants who chose "I think that it helps to improve my reading ability" were those who do not use Kanji in their first language and belonged to the lower group.

For the results of question (13) "What do you think the weak points of the graded readers are?", nine participants chose "Vocabulary is too repetitious", six participants chose "It was too simple". These are the character of graded readers. One participant answered "there is no weak point". On the other hand, three participants answered "it was not user-friendly on a smartphone" and "it would be convenient if I could read it on some application instead of "html"". To trace these problems, some improvement might be needed in the explanations in the video clips that recommended "html" if the user had never used "ePub" or "mobi".

To question (14) "If there is something that you prefer to have or to improve, please write", the following responses were given:

"It is wonderful that Japanese literature was rewritten in easy Japanese for learners." (ID-8)

"I would like to read some interesting stories that are written in more advanced vocabulary and grammar." (ID-3)

"I would like to improve my reading ability using this system." (ID-15)

"It would be better if there are a few more questions in "Questions" about the stories." (ID-14)

"It would be better if the story had been written horizontally (especially on smartphones)." (ID-8, ID-15)

Although most of the books are written horizontally, novels in Japanese are written vertically. Going forward, we need to consider whether writing JGR horizontally would be more learner friendly.

V. CONCLUSION

In this study, the current self-ER support system was evaluated from the results of the post-questionnaire and the logs on the system left by users surveyed by the author. Knowing one's progress on their personal pages helped participants to enjoy reading and motivated them to read more. The advantage of the self-ER support system is that it can provide digital books for learners outside the classroom at minimal cost and no waiting time. The online library of JGRs has the potential to provide the opportunity to make time to read for learners who cannot find the time to read. Moreover, the results confirmed that independent learners without teachers could start Japanese extensive reading by using the system. Further work is needed to increase the number of JGRs and to add a vocabulary level test that can judge the appropriate level of JGR for learners to start reading from.

ACKNOWLEDGMENT

This work was supported by JSPS KAKENHI Grant Number 15k02650.

REFERENCES

[1] T. Nakano, "Development of a Support System for Japanese Extensive Reading: Supporting learners' autonomous learning outside the classroom," *Proceedings of eLmL 2017,* 13-16.

[2] S. D. Krashen, "Some new evidence for an old hypothesis," Paper presented at the Georgetown Round Table for Lanuguage and Linguistics. April, 1992.

[3] P. Nation, "The language learning benefits of extensive reading," The Language Teacher. 21, 5, pp. 13-16, 1997.

[4] R. R. Day and J. Bamford, "Extensive reading in the second language classroom," Cambridge: Cambridge University Press, 1998.

[5] T. Huckin and J. Coady. "Incidental vocabulary acquisition in a second language," SSLA. 21, pp. 181-193, 1999.

[6] T. Robb and M. Kano, "Effective extensive reading outside the classroom: A large-scale experiment," Reading in a Foreign Language, vol. 25, No. 2, pp. 234–247, Octover 2013.

[7] T. Nakano, Introduction of extensive reading using electronic teaching materials, *Shobi University Sogoseisaku Ronshu* 17, pp.137–144, 2013.

[8] T. Nakano, "Implementing Extensive Reading in Japanese as L2 Environment: A Case Using Facebook to Build a Reading Community", Proceedings of The Third World Conference on Extensive Reading, Chap. 8, pp. 69-78. [Online]. Sept. 2015, Available from: http://erfoundation.org/wordpress/ [retrieved: August 2017]

[9] T. Nakano, "Extensive Reading for Second Language Learners of Japanese in Higher Education: Graded Readers and Beyond," *The Reading Matrix*, Vol.16, No. 1, pp. 119-132. [Online]. Available from: http://readingmatrix.com/ [retrieved: August 2017]

[10] N. Aoki, "Examining Definitions of Learner Autonomy," Handai Nihongo Kenkyu 10, pp.129-148, Mar. 1998. [Online]. Available from: http://hdl.handle.net/11094/8114. [retrieved: August 2017]

[11] M. A. Chatti, M. Marinov, O. Sabov, R. Laksono, Z. Sofyan, A. M. F. Yousef, and U. Schroeder, "Video annotation and analytics in CourseMapper," *Smart Learning Environments* 3(1), 10, 2016.

[12] N. Kuga, T. Nakano, Y. Cong, J. Jung, and S. Mayekawa, "A Study of Social Facilitation Effect on e-Learning," *Proceedings of e-Learn* 2006, 1659-1664, 2006.

[13] B. Reynolds, T. Harada, M. Yamagata, and T. Miyazaki, "Towards a framework for Japanese graded readers: Initial research findings," *Papers of the Japanese Language Teaching Association in honor of Professor Fumiko KOIDE*, Vol.11, pp.23–40, 2003.

[14] T. Harada, K. Mikami, and T. Nakano, "Tadoku no tame no goi level test kaihatu ni kansuru kenkyu: nihongo no tadoku

wo hajimeru gakushusha no tameni," *Proceedings of the International Conference on Japanese Language Education*, p.154, Nagoya, August 2012.

[15] K. Mikami, T. Harada, and T. Nakano, "Tadoku no tame no goi level test: kokunaigai deno test shiko kekka to kongo no kadai," *Proceedings of the 23rd Conference of the Japanese Language Teaching Association in honor of Professor Fumiko KOIDE*, Tokyo, pp.34-35, July 2014.

[16] C. Nuttall, Teaching reading skills in a foreign language, Macmillan, Oxford, 2005.

[17] N. Kobayashi, "SPOT: Measuring Japanese language ability," *The 31th annual meeting of the Behaviormetric Society of Japan,* 110–113, 2003.

Evaluation of Similarity Measures for Shift-Invariant Image Motif Discovery

Sahar Torkamani and Volker Lohweg
inIT – Institute Industrial IT
Ostwestfalen-Lippe University of Applied Sciences
Liebigstr. 87, D-32657 Lemgo, Germany
Email: {sahar.torkamani, volker.lohweg}@hs-owl.de

Abstract—**The rapid growth of optical imaging technologies increased the access and collection of data, which boosts the demand of data and knowledge discovery. This is a fast growing topic in several industry and research areas. Nowadays, a large number of images and signals must be analysed in order to gain and learn proper knowledge. Detecting images with similar contents without specifying an image, recently attracts the researches in image processing domain. Motif discovery in image processing aims to tackle the problem of deriving structures or detecting regularities in image databases. Most of the motif discovery methods solve this problem by converting images into one dimensional time series in a pre-processing step and then applying a motif discovery on these one dimensional time series for image motifs detection. Nevertheless, this conversion might lead to information loss and also the problem of inability to discover shifted and multi-scale image motifs of different size. Contrary to other approaches, here, a method is proposed to find image motifs of different size in image data sets by employing images in original dimension (2D) without converting them to one dimensional time series. The proposed approach consists of three steps: Mapping or transformation, feature extraction and measuring similarities. First, images are inspected by the Complex Quad Tree Wavelet Packet transform, which provides broad frequency analysis of an image in various scales. Next, statistical features are extracted from the wavelet coefficients. Finally, image motifs are detected by measuring the similarity of the features applying various similarity measures. Here, the performance of six similarity measures are benchmarked in details. Moreover, the efficiency of the proposed method is demonstrated on a data set with images from diverse applications such as hand gesture, text recognition, leaf and plant identification, etc. Additionally, the robustness of this method is examined with the image data overlaying with distortions such as noise and blur.**

Keywords–Motif discovery; Image processing; Wavelet transformation.

I. INTRODUCTION

The accelerated growth of digital computation, telecommunication and imaging technologies results in a flood of information and data. These data are obtained in various forms such as text, graphics, pictures, videos or integrated multimedia. Such data are valuable if efficient information can be acquired from them. This issue is addressed by data mining and machine learning tasks. These tasks can be categorised into clustering, classification, anomaly detection and *motif discovery* [1].

Information such as number of clusters or classes, prototype patterns/images for each class or providing an image query to find, is necessary for such tasks [2]. The problems of clustering or classifying images as well as finding a query image in an image database are fairly known problems, which have been investigated during last decades [3]–[5]. The problem of deriving structures or detecting regularities in image databases is rather new topic and investigated by researchers [6]. This new topic is called motif discovery and aims to detect frequently repeated unknown images in a database without any prior information. The term motif has its roots in genetics and DNA sequences. A sequence motif in a DNA is a widespread amino-acid sequence pattern, which shows a biological significance [7]. In time series data mining, the term motif was first triggered by Patel et al. [8].

Motif discovery recently applied in image processing applications with various image databases. The aim of the image motif discovery is also to detect similar images and shapes within an image database without prior information. Such images are called *image motifs*. Fig. 1 aims to enhance the role of image motifs by given examples of some petroglyphs that are gathered in the USA [9]. The study of such petroglyphs is important for anthropologists, since these images show the spread of cultures and people. Therefore, detecting similar images that captured in different locations are in concerns for anthropologists. As depicted in Fig. 1, the images (a) and (c) captured in Capitol reef are similar to (b) and (d) that are obtained in Nine Mile Canyon [10]. Consequently, anthropologists are interested to discover such images (image motif) in a petroglyph image data set [9].

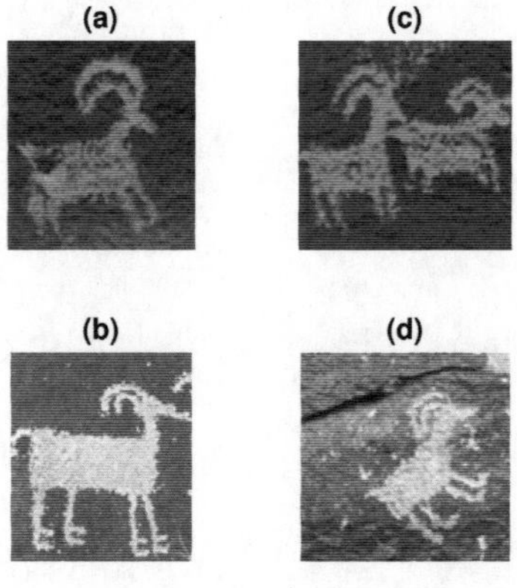

Figure 1. Examples of petroglyphs from Capitol reef and Nine Mile Canyon in Utah, USA [10]. Images (a) and (c) are from Capitol reef, and images (b) and (d) are captured in Nine Mile Canyon.

Detecting motifs add valuable insights about the problem under investigation to the user. Huge research effort has been performed on this topic [6], [11]. However, most of the image motif discovery methods detect motifs by converting images into one-dimensional time series and then attempt to find motifs in such data by operating a motif discovery algorithm. This converting might lead to information loss and also the problem of inability to detect shifted and multi-scale motifs of different size [9]. Correspondingly, a method is proposed to find shifted and multi-scale motifs of different size in image data sets by applying the images in original dimension without converting them to one dimensional time series [1], [9].

This contribution is the extend version of the article published in [1]. Detailed information about the approach and comprehensive results are provided in this work. The proposed approach is benchmarked also with the distorted test cases in order to obtain the robustness of this method. This paper is structured as follows: the related work in motif discovery for image data type is described in Section II. Section III explains the proposed approach. The evaluation and the obtained results are illustrated in Section IV. At the end, a conclusion and the future work are indicated in Section V.

II. Related Work

Over the past decades, image and shape analysis have attracted several researchers and been a matter for discussion. Huge amount of research has been performed in several image processing tasks such as clustering, classification, query by content, segmentation, etc. [4], [12]–[15]. Recently, a new topic namely motif discovery in image and shape analysis is added to this research area. Motif discovery has evoked the interest in several researches, who aimed to link time series data mining tasks and issues to the image and shape analysis domain [6], [9], [16]. For instance, Barone et al. [17] studied the problem of classifying ordered sequences of digital images.

The first approach in image motif discovery is proposed by Xi et al. [9]. The authors detected image motifs in image data sets by representing an image or a shape in a one dimensional time series. This method extracts a time series from the contour of an image. The main problem of such an approach is that transforming a two dimensional data to a one dimensional might lead to information loss. Moreover, the image should be segmented in order to obtain the shapes in it.

The same procedure as in [9] is applied by Chi et al. [18] in order to detect image motifs in face image data sets. The term shapelet was introduced by Ye and Keogh [16]. Shapelets are a discriminative subsequence of the time series, which is considered instead of analysing the whole time series. Ye and Keogh [9] as well as Grabocka et al. [19] extended the proposed approach in [9]. After transforming an image to a one dimensional representation, shapelets are analysed to detect motifs. The performance of these methods is promising, but these approaches transform the data to a one dimensional time series. Caballero and Aranda [20] proposed an effective shape-based image retrieval system for leaf images. This contour descriptor reduces the number of points for the shape representation considerably.

Rakthanmanon and his colleagues [21] handled this problem by detecting motifs in images without representing them into a one dimensional signal. They, first, segmented the tested images using a sliding window of a fixed size, then the similarity between these segments are measured by the generalised Hough transform [22]. The fixed size of the sliding window is one of the disadvantages of this method. Since, a fixed size sliding window results in inability of detecting motifs with various proportions. En et al. [23] followed a similar approach, nevertheless they employed sliding windows with varying sizes of 20, 40, 80, and 160 pixels.

In our first approach [24], motifs in an image data base are discovered in their original dimension without converting them to time series. Images are decomposed into several frequency scales by the dual tree complex wavelet transform (DTCWT) [25], next features are extracted from the wavelet coefficients and finally motif images are found by measuring the similarity of their features. However, further experiments showed that the DTCWT is shift tolerance and not shift invariant [26]. For this reason, in this work, an approach is proposed, which is based on a shift-invariant feature extraction method for motif discovery (SIMD), given in [26]. This method is applied as core in our approach and explained in the following section. Additionally, this contribution is an extended version of the paper presented in [1] with comprehensive experiments.

III. Proposed Approach

The proposed motif discovery algorithm combines two research areas: pattern recognition and motif discovery. Motif discovery algorithms mainly consist of a representation and a similarity measure step. In this contribution, feature extraction step, which mostly applies in pattern recognition tasks, is added to the procedure of the approach depicted in Fig. 2.

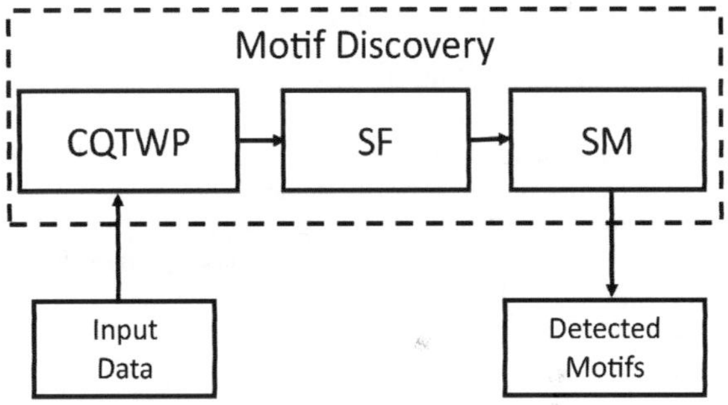

Figure 2. The proposed approach; CQTWP is the Complex Quad Tree Wavelet Packet; SF is the statistical features and SM represents similarity measures.

First, images are transformed by the *Complex Quad Tree Wavelet Packet* (CQTWP) into a broad frequency scales. Wavelets have several properties such as: ability to analyse data into different frequency scales, flexible time-frequency resolution and prefect reconstruction. Wavelet transformations proved their performance in signal and image processing applications [27]–[29]. In the second step, features are extracted from the normalised wavelet coefficients. At last, motifs are discovered by measuring the similarity between features using various distance measures. Before explaining these steps in details, some notations and useful definitions used in this paper are described in the following.

A. Definitions and Notations

Definition 1 (Image). *A digital image $X_{m,n}$ is represented in a 2D discrete space as a $m \times n$, $m, n \in \mathbb{N}$ matrix:*

$$X_{m,n} = \begin{pmatrix} x_{1,1} & x_{1,2} & \cdots & x_{1,n} \\ x_{2,1} & x_{2,2} & \cdots & x_{2,n} \\ \vdots & \vdots & \ddots & \vdots \\ x_{m,1} & x_{m,2} & \cdots & x_{m,n} \end{pmatrix}.$$

Images can vary in their size and the applications they are captured from.

Definition 2 (Image Motif). *An image motif in an image data base is a pair of images $(X_{m,n}, Y_{p,q})$, where $m, p \in \mathbb{N}$ are the number of rows and $n, q \in \mathbb{N}$ are the number of columns, so that $distance(X, Y)$ is the smallest among all possible pairs* [9].

Function $distance(\mathbf{X}, \mathbf{Y})$ is a distance similarity measure.

Definition 3 (1st-Image Motifs). *Given an image data base $D = X^i, i = 1, 2, ..., N,\ N \in \mathbb{N}$, the most significant image motif in D is the image X^j that has the highest amount of matches. This image motif is called the 1st-Image Motif.*

Definition 4 (K-Image Motifs). *The K-th most significant image motif in D is the image X^k with the kth highest amount of image matches.*

B. Complex Quad Tree Wavelet Packet Transform

1) 1D-CQTWP: The CQTWP is proposed to overcome the drawbacks of the DTCWT. It is an extended version of the DTCWT [25] and it consists of two wavelet packet trees (WPT) working parallel to each other. "WPT A" represents the real part and "WPT B" provides the imaginary part of the signal. A graphical representation of the "*1D-WPT A*" is given in Fig. 3, where $\downarrow 2^e$ and $\downarrow 2^o$ depict the even and odd down-sampling. The low and high-pass filters are denoted by ${}^s g_a$ and ${}^s h_a$, for $s \in \mathbb{N}$. Parameter s represents the scale of the decomposition. The wavelet coefficients are given by ${}^s c_i$ for $i \in [0, 4^s]$.

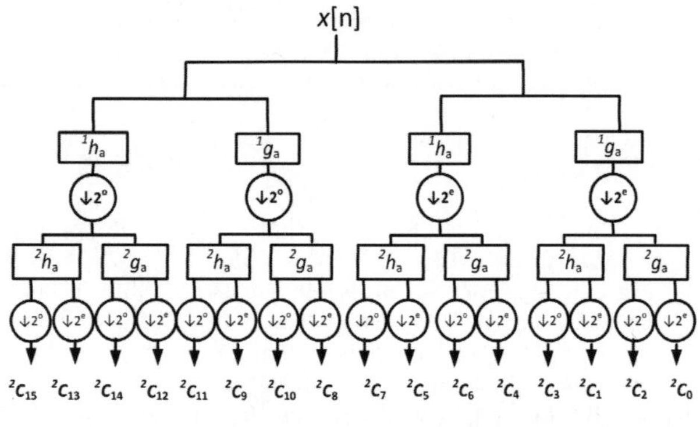

Figure 3. First wavelet packet filter bank of a two scale CQTWP. The second wavelet packet is obtained by replacing the filters ${}^1g_a$ and ${}^1h_a$ with ${}^1g_b$ and ${}^1h_b$ for the first scale and ${}^2g_a$ and ${}^2h_a$ with ${}^2g_b$ and ${}^2h_b$ for the second scale.

The low and high-pass filters applied in CQTWP are similar to the filters of DTCWT. The filters of the DTCWT satisfy the conditions required for having an analytic and complex wavelet transforms [25]. An analytic representation of a signal is achieved if and only if the filters of the CQTWP form a Hilbert pair [25], [26].

Definition 5. *Wavelets ψ_a and ψ_b with the following property*

$$\Psi_a(j\omega) = \begin{cases} -j\Psi_b(j\omega), & \omega > 0, \\ j\Psi_b(j\omega), & \omega < 0, \end{cases}$$

are called the Hilbert pair, *where $\Psi(j\omega)$ is the Fourier transform of $\psi(t)$.*

Consequently, the response of each branch of the "WPT A" and the corresponding branch of the "WPT B" forms a Hilbert pair and therefore, the CQTWP is approximately analytic in each sub band. Besides obtaining complex wavelet coefficients, the analytic representation has advantages such as reduction of aliasing.

To accomplish wavelets with Hilbert form, they must be designed by the following theorem:

Theorem 1 (Half-sample delay [30]). *Wavelets ψ_a and ψ_b form a Hilbert pair, if the filters ${}^s g_a$ and ${}^s g_b$ satisfy the condition,*

$${}^sG_a(e^{j\omega}) = {}^sG_b(e^{j\omega})e^{-j\frac{\omega}{2}}. \tag{1}$$

Eq. (1) can be presented in terms of the magnitude and phase functions:

$$|{}^sG_a(e^{j\omega})| = |{}^sG_b(e^{j\omega})|, \quad \angle{}^sG_a(e^{j\omega}) = \angle{}^sG_b(e^{j\omega}) - \frac{1}{2}\omega, \tag{2}$$

which is the so-called "half-sample delay" *condition between two low-pass filters ${}^s g_a$, ${}^s g_b$.*

Proof. Proof is represented by Selsnick in [30]. □

Based on the half-sample delay theorem, the scaling low-pass filters must be offset from one another by a half sample. This is the necessary and sufficient condition for two wavelets to form a Hilbert transform pair, proved by Yu and Ozkaramanli [31].

Definition 6 (q-shift filters [32]). *Kingsbury's solution for design such suitable filters is called* "q-shift", *which satisfies the "half-sample delay" condition given in Theorem* 1, *where the low-pass filters are set as*

$${}^sg_a[n] = {}^sg_b[M - 1 - n]. \tag{3}$$

Here, $M \in \mathbb{N}^+$ is the even length of filter ${}^s g_b$, which is supported on $0 \le n \le M - 1$.

In order to achieve the half-sample delay theorem, at each scale the filters of WPT A translated by 2^s must be fall midway between the translated filters of WPT B. However, this condition leads to have filters in the first scale that have one sample delay difference. All the filters are real, orthonormal and are obtained by the design given by Abdelnour [33] and Kingsbury [32]. In the first scale, the filters have the even-length of 10 [33] and in the scale greater than one, filters have the even-length of 14 [32].

The wavelet and scaling functions of the CQTWP are defined as:

Definition 7. *Let $\psi_{a,2J+1}(t)$, $\psi_{a,2J+3}(t)$, $\psi_{b,2J+1}(t)$, $\psi_{b,2J+3}(t)$ and $\phi_{a,2J}(t)$, $\phi_{a,2J+2}(t)$, $\phi_{b,2J}(t)$, $\phi_{b,2J+2}(t)$ be the wavelet and scaling functions of the CQTWP. The wavelet and scaling functions in "WPT A", $\forall n \in \mathbb{N}$ are given by*

$$
\begin{aligned}
{}^{s+1}\psi_{a,2J+1}(t) &= \sqrt{2}\sum_{n=0}^{M} {}^{s}h_a[n]\ {}^{s}\phi_{a,2J}(2t-n),\\
{}^{s+1}\psi_{a,2J+3}(t) &= \sqrt{2}\sum_{n=0}^{M} {}^{s}h_a[n]\ {}^{s}\phi_{a,2J+2}(2t-n+1),\\
{}^{s+1}\phi_{a,2J}(t) &= \sqrt{2}\sum_{n=0}^{M} {}^{s}g_a[n]\ {}^{s}\phi_{a,2J}(2t-n),\\
{}^{s+1}\phi_{a,2J+2}(t) &= \sqrt{2}\sum_{n=0}^{M} {}^{s}g_a[n]\ {}^{s}\phi_{a,2J+2}(2t-n+1).
\end{aligned}
$$

Parameter $J = 2j$ where $0 \leq j < 2^s \cdot (s-1)$, and $s \in \mathbb{N}$ is number of scales, and $M \in \mathbb{N}^+$ is the length of the filters.

For "WPT B" the wavelet and scaling functions are defined in the same manner, but the high-pass filter ${}^{s}h_a$ and the low-pass filter ${}^{s}g_a$ are replaced by ${}^{s}h_b$ and ${}^{s}g_b$ respectively. All filters are causal so ${}^{s}h_{a,b}[n] = 0$ and ${}^{s}g_{a,b}[n] = 0$ for $n < 0$.

The wavelet and scaling coefficients of the CQTWP for the "*WPT A*" are defined in Def. 8.

Definition 8. *Coefficients of the CQTWP for the "WPT A" are given by ${}^{s}C[n] = \{\ {}^{s+1}C_{2J}[n],\ {}^{s+1}C_{2J+1}[n],\ {}^{s+1}C_{2J+2}[n],\ {}^{s+1}C_{2J+3}[n]\}$ and obtained by*

$$
\begin{aligned}
{}^{s+1}C_{2J}[n] &= \sum_{k=0}^{M+Len-1} {}^{s}g_a[k]\ {}^{s}C_j[2n-k],\\
{}^{s+1}C_{2J+1}[n] &= \sum_{k=0}^{M+Len-1} {}^{s}h_a[k]\ {}^{s}C_j[2n-k],\\
{}^{s+1}C_{2J+2}[n] &= \sum_{k=0}^{M+Len-1} {}^{s}g_a[k]\ {}^{s}C_j[2n+1-k],\\
{}^{s+1}C_{2J+3}[n] &= \sum_{k=0}^{M+Len-1} {}^{s}h_a[k]\ {}^{s}C_j[2n+1-k].
\end{aligned} \tag{4}
$$

where $Len = length({}^{s}C_j)$, $J = 2j$, and $0 \leq j < 2^s \cdot (s-1)$. Similarly, the wavelet and scaling coefficients of the "WPT B" are obtained by replacing the high and low-pass filters ${}^{s}h_a$ and ${}^{s}g_a$ to ${}^{s}h_b$ and ${}^{s}g_b$. These coefficients are depicted by ${}^{s}D[n] = \{\ {}^{s+1}D_{2J}[n],\ {}^{s+1}D_{2J+1}[n],\ {}^{s+1}D_{2J+2}[n],\ {}^{s+1}D_{2J+3}[n]\}$.

Beside comprehensive frequency analysis, the CQTWP has another advantage of being shift-invariant [26].

Definition 9 (shift-invariant). *The* shift-invariant *is defined by studying the wavelet coefficients of every scale $s \in \mathbb{N}$ from both the original and translated signal. This means if $x[n]$ and $x[n-S]$ are respectively the original and translated signal shifted by $S \in \mathbb{Z}$, then the corresponding wavelet coefficients are given by ${}^{s}C[n]$ and ${}^{s}C[n,S]$. Let the wavelet transformation be presented by $x[n] \mapsto {}^{s}C[n]$, then this transformation must satisfy $x[n-S] \mapsto {}^{s}C[n,S]$, where ${}^{s}C[n,S] = {}^{s}C[n-S]$.*

The shift-invariant property is obtained by decomposing a non-shifted and a shifted version of the input signal in each scale. Thus, the wavelet and scaling functions of the CQTWP select both even and odd samples of the signal in order to detect the occurred shift. The results of this property is identical wavelet coefficients for both the original signal and its shifted versions. The shift invariance property is proved by the following corollary:

Corollary 2. *Assume $x[n]$ is a discrete signal and let $S_{e/o} \in \mathbb{Z}$ be shifts occurred on signal $x[n]$, where $S_{e/o}$ can be even or odd. The CQTWP wavelet coefficients of $x[n-S_e]$ and $x[n-S_o]$ from "WPT A" in scales s, are depicted by ${}^{s}C'_e[n,S_e]$ and ${}^{s}C'_o[n,S_o]$, given by:*

$$
\begin{aligned}
{}^{s}C'_{e/o}[n,S_{e/o}] = \{\ & {}^{s+1}C'_{2J}[n,S_{e/o}],\ {}^{s+1}C'_{2J+1}[n,S_{e/o}],\\
& {}^{s+1}C'_{2J+2}[n,S_{e/o}],{}^{s+1}C'_{2J+3}[n,S_{e/o}]\},
\end{aligned}
$$

and for "WPT B" are provided by

$$
\begin{aligned}
{}^{s}D'_{e/o}[n,S_{e/o}] = \{\ & {}^{s+1}D'_{2J}[n,S_{e/o}],\ {}^{s+1}D'_{2J+1}[n,S_{e/o}],\\
& {}^{s+1}D'_{2J+2}[n,S_{e/o}],{}^{s+1}D'_{2J+3}[n,S_{e/o}]\},
\end{aligned}
$$

Then, the following equations hold

$$
\begin{cases}
\forall\ x[n-S_e], & \begin{cases} {}^{s}C[n] = {}^{s}C'_e[n-\lfloor \frac{S_e}{2^s} \rfloor], \\ {}^{s}D[n] = {}^{s}D'_e[n-\lfloor \frac{S_e}{2^s} \rfloor]. \end{cases} \\
\\
\forall\ x[n-S_o], & \begin{cases} {}^{s}C[n] = {}^{s}C'_o[n-\lfloor \frac{S_o}{2^s} \rfloor], \\ {}^{s}D[n] = {}^{s}D'_o[n-\lfloor \frac{S_e}{2^s} \rfloor]. \end{cases}
\end{cases} \tag{5}
$$

Proof. Proof is given in Appendix A. □

For simplicity, the odd and even wavelet and scaling functions of "WPT A" are denoted by $\psi_{a,e}(t) = \psi_{a,2J+1}(t)$ and $\psi_{a,o} = \psi_{a,2J+3}(t)$; and $\phi_{a,e} = \phi_{a,2J}(t)$, $\phi_{a,o} = \phi_{a,2J+2}(t)$. The functions of "WPT B" are represented in the same manner.

2) 2D-CQTWP: It is able to expand the CQTWP to a higher dimension. The 2D-CQTWP analyses an image into various frequency bands. The structure of two scales decomposition of the "*2D-WPT A*" is depicted in Fig. 4(b), where both low and high-pass filtered sub bands decomposed further. This property results in a more flexible and broad frequency decomposition of the images.

The first scale of the 2D-CQTWP is similar to the 2D-discrete wavelet transform [34], where an image is decomposed into four sub bands namely LL_1, LH_1, HL_1 and HH_1, cf., Fig. 4(a). However, in the first scale, the 2D-CQTWP has two LL, two LH, two HL and two HH sub bands obtained from both "*2D-WPT A*" and "*2D-WPT B*".

The product of the low-pass function $\phi_a()$ along the first dimension (row) and the low-pass function $\phi_a()$ along the second dimension (column) results in LL_1. LH_1 is the product of the low-pass function $\phi_a()$ along the first dimension and the high-pass function $\psi_a()$ along the second dimension. Similarly, the HL_1 and HH_1 are labelled, and the index 1 determines the decomposed scale. The same procedure is performed on each sub band in order to obtain the second scale coefficients.

The wavelet and scaling functions of the 2D-CQTWP are defined as:

Definition 10. *The "2D-WPT A" of the 2D-CQTWP is characterised by twelve wavelets and four scaling functions.*

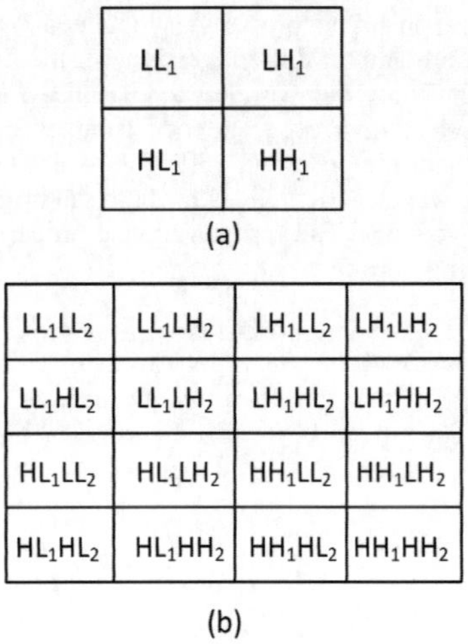

Figure 4. Structure of two scales decomposition of the "*2D-WPT A*": (a) the first scale decomposition, (b) the second scale decomposition.

The 2D-wavelet $\psi(x,y) = \psi(x)\psi(y)$ is associated with the row-column implementation of the wavelet transform. The wavelet functions for the wavelet packet tree A are given by

$$\psi_{a,1}(x,y) = \phi_{a,e}(x)\psi_{a,e}(y), \qquad \psi_{a,4}(x,y) = \phi_{a,e}(x)\psi_{a,o}(y),$$
$$\psi_{a,2}(x,y) = \psi_{a,e}(x)\phi_{a,e}(y), \qquad \psi_{a,5}(x,y) = \psi_{a,e}(x)\phi_{a,o}(y),$$
$$\psi_{a,3}(x,y) = \psi_{a,e}(x)\psi_{a,e}(y), \qquad \psi_{a,6}(x,y) = \psi_{a,e}(x)\psi_{a,o}(y).$$

The rest of the wavelet functions are obtained similarly. The scaling functions are defined as

$$\phi_{a,1}(x,y) = \phi_{a,e}(x)\phi_{a,e}(y), \qquad \phi_{a,2}(x,y) = \phi_{a,e}(x)\phi_{a,o}(y),$$
$$\phi_{a,3}(x,y) = \phi_{a,o}(x)\phi_{a,e}(y), \qquad \phi_{a,4}(x,y) = \phi_{a,o}(x)\phi_{a,o}(y).$$

The wavelet and scaling functions of the "2D-WPT B" are given accordingly.

The wavelet and scaling coefficients of the 2D-CQTWP for the "2D-WPT A" are given by

Definition 11. *Coefficients of the 2D-CQTWP for the "2D-WPT A" are given by ${}^{s}C[x,y] = \{\ {}^{s+1}C_{2J}[x,y],\ {}^{s+1}C_{2J+1}[x,y], ...,\ {}^{s+1}C_{2J+11}[x,y]\}$ and obtained by*

$$\begin{aligned}
{}^{s+1}C_{2J}[x,y] &= {}^{s}C_j[x,y] * {}^{s}g_a[2x]\ {}^{s}g_a[2y],\\
{}^{s+1}C_{2J+1}[x,y] &= {}^{s}C_j[x,y] * {}^{s}g_a[2x+1]\ {}^{s}g_a[2y],\\
&\ \vdots\\
{}^{s+1}C_{2J+5}[x,y] &= {}^{s}C_j[x,y] * {}^{s}g_a[2x]\ {}^{s}h_a[2y],\\
{}^{s+1}C_{2J+6}[x,y] &= {}^{s}C_j[x,y] * {}^{s}g_a[2x]\ {}^{s}h_a[2y+1],\\
&\ \vdots\\
{}^{s+1}C_{2J+14}[x,y] &= {}^{s}C_j[x,y] * {}^{s}h_a[2x]\ {}^{s}h_a[2y],\\
{}^{s+1}C_{2J+15}[x,y] &= {}^{s}C_j[x,y] * {}^{s}g_a[2x+1]\ {}^{s}g_a[2y+1].
\end{aligned}$$

Parameter $s \in \mathbb{N}$ is the number of scales and parameter $J = 8j$ is the index of the coefficient nodes, whereby for $s = 1$, $j = 0$ and for $s > 1$, $0 \leq j < 4^s$. The wavelet coefficients for the "2D-WPT B" are computed similarly and denoted by ${}^{s}D[x,y] = \{\ {}^{s+1}D_{2J}[x,y],\ {}^{s+1}D_{2J+1}[x,y], ...,\ {}^{s+1}D_{2J+15}[x,y]\}$.

The 2D-CQTWP has the same properties of the one dimensional CQTWP.

3) Selection of the Best Nodes: Decomposing the data in each scale leads to the number of nodes which grows exponentially in each wavelet packet tree. Therefore, selecting the nodes with the most information content reduces the amount of redundant and unnecessary information. Every node of the wavelet packet tree A and B has a potential to be chosen as a proper node, which provides meaningful information for feature extraction. In order to select the best nodes, a method is applied, which is based on the algorithm introduced in [35] for the discrete wavelet packet and its concept is established by an additive cost function.

Definition 12 (Cost function [35]). *A cost function CF that maps the sequences $\{x_i\}_{i=1}^{N}$ to real numbers considers as additive, if $CF(\{x_i\}) = \sum_{i=1}^{N} g(x_i)$ for some $g : \mathbb{R} \rightarrow \mathbb{R}$ and for all $\{x_i\}_{i=1}^{N}$.*

An entropy-based cost function is considered here.

Definition 13 (Entropy-based cost function). *The entropy-based cost function for the wavelet packet "WPT A" is denoted by $W_H({}^{s}C[n])$ and obtained by*

$$W_H({}^{s}C[n]) = -\sum_{n=1}^{N} E_c[n] \log(E_c[n]),$$

where $({}^{s}C[n])$ is the wavelet coefficients defined in Def. 8, and the normalized energy is given by $E_c[n] = \frac{({}^{s}C[n])^2}{\sum_n ({}^{s}C[n])^2}$. The entropy-based cost function for the wavelet packet "WPT B" is obtained by replacing ${}^{s}C[n]$ with ${}^{s}D[n]$.

The normalized energy of the wavelet coefficients applied in the above definition allows to adjust and compare coefficients from different scales. The algorithm for detection the best node, Algorithm 1, has the following steps:

Algorithm 1 Best Nodes Selection
Input: Entropy-based cost function $W_H({}^{s}C[n])$
Output: Best nodes

```
for s = s − 1 : 1 do
    for j = 0 : 2^s do
        J = 2j
        if W_H(^s C_j[n]) < W_H(^{s+1} C_{2J}[n]) + ... + W_H(^{s+1} C_{2J+7}[n]) then
            ^s BN_j = (^s C_j[n]) is selected as best node.
        else
            W_H(^s C_j[n]) = W_H(^{s+1} C_{2J}[n]) + ... + W_H(^{s+1} C_{2J+7}[n])
        end if
    end for
end for
```

The best nodes selection algorithm computes the entropy-based cost function for each coefficients node upwards from the scale s to the first scale. The same approach applies for the 2D-CQTWP transform.

C. Feature Extraction

Feature extraction plays an important role in pattern recognition applications, and it helps to reduce the size of the data. Since, features present the special characters of the data, it is important that they are detectable under changes in proportion, location or even under noise circumstances. A proper feature extraction method must be able to generalise over differences within a class (intra-class) and determine the variations between various classes (inter-class).

In the second step, from wavelet coefficients features must be extracted. But before extracting features, it is necessary to normalise the coefficients of each scale. The normalisation is performed because the proposed method is able to analyse images of various size, therefore the wavelet coefficients have also different size. Thus, normalisation allows to rescale all the coefficients in order to compare them. The normalised histogram of the wavelet coefficients is denoted by $H(p)$ and is given by

$$H(p) = \frac{1}{v \cdot u} \cdot h(p),$$

where $u, v \in \mathbb{N}$ determine the size of the matrix coefficients and parameter p is number of the histogram bins. The rate in each bin is presented by $h(p)$.

The first four statistical moments [36], namely, mean value, variance, skewness and kurtosis are extracted from the wavelet coefficients in both wavelet packet trees. As 2D-CQTWP is shift-invariant, then these features have identical values even in the case of shift occurrence in the data.

Additionally, the energy of the wavelet coefficients is considered as another feature. Since the CQTWP is shift-invariant, the energy of the wavelet coefficients and their shifted ones are similar. Moreover, according to the Parseval's theorem the energy of the signal or image is preserved in the coefficients and as described in Section III-B1, the scaling and wavelet functions of the CQTWP are orthonormal, which satisfy the Parseval's theorem.

D. Similarity Measures

In order to detect image motifs, the similarity between their features must be measured. In general, similarity measures can be divided into four groups: shape-based, edit-based, model-based and feature-based methods [6].

Shape-based distance similarity measures compare the total shape of the signals or images. Members of the Minkowski distance family [37], and Dynamic Time Warping (DTW) [37] belong to this group of measures. Here, the two members of the Minkowski distance or L_p-distance namely, Euclidean distance (ED) and Canberra distance (CD) are applied. Both of these measures have linear computational time complexity $O(n)$, and are metric. The Euclidean distance is obtained by setting $p = 2$ in L_p-distance. This measure is also known as L_2-distance. Besides the advantages of the Euclidean distance, results of this similarity measure are not promising, when performing directly on the data, in the case of outliers. The Canberra distance is actually a weighted version of Manhattan distance or L_1-distance, and is useful in the case of ranking lists or results. DTW matches various sections of a signal by warping of the time axis, or finding the proper alignment. This similarity measure is more flexible than Euclidean or Canberra distance although its time-complexity is $O(n^2)$. Apart from its quadratic computational time complexity, still DTW is one of the most popular approaches for measuring similarity/dissimilarity.

Edit-based similarity measures compare two signals according to the minimum number of operations needed to transform one signal or feature vector into another one. Such operations are insertion, deletion, and substitution. These methods are also known under Levebshtein distances [38]. Examples of these similarity measures are Edit Distance [38], and the Longest Common SubSequence(LCSS) [39]. The Edit distance method is usually applied on the string data sets. This can be seen as one disadvantage for this method. If $s_1 =$'Hello' and $s_2 =$'Have' are two strings, then the Editdistance$(s_1, s_2) = 4$. Since 4 operations must be done: replace(e,a), replace(l,v), replace(l,e) and delete(o).

LCSS aims to detect the characteristic segment between two time series by looping over all possible Edit distances.

Definition 14 (Longest Common SubSequence). *The LCSS of two time series $x[n] = (x_1, x_2, ..., x_N)^T$ and $y[n] = (y_1, y_2, ..., y_M)^T$ of lengths $N, M \in \mathbb{N}$ is denoted by LCSS(x, y) and computed by* [39]

$$LCSS = \begin{cases} 0 & \text{if } N = 0 \text{ or } M = 0, \\ LCSS(rest(x), rest(y)) + 1 & \text{if } dist(x_1, y_1) \leq \epsilon, \\ \max(LCSS(rest(x), y), LCSS(x, rest(y))) & \text{else,} \end{cases}$$

where the threshold $0 < \epsilon < 1$ should be defined in advance, in order to show if two elements match. The $dist()$ function is defined by $dist(x_1, y_1) = |x_1 - y_1|$ and $rest(x)$ defines the remaining sequence of x.

The main problem of the LCSS is being sensitive to noise. Similar to the Euclidean and Canberra distance, the time-complexity of the Edit distance is $O(n)$. LCSS for $n \in \mathbb{N}$ number of time series or sequences performs in $O(2^n)$.

Typically model-based methods use prior knowledge about the model that generated the data sets. These methods compute the similarity between data sets by first modelling one data set and then examine the likelihood that other data sets are also generated by the same model. Methods such as Hidden Markov Models (HMM) [40] and Autoregressive Moving Average model (ARMA) [41] belong to this group. Since these methods need prior knowledge about the data, they are not applied in this work.

Feature-based methods measure the similarity between different data sets based on the obtained sets of features. In these methods, first features are derived from the data and then distance measures are applied to capture patterns. Likelihood ratio [42] is a measure belongs to the feature-based methods.

Definition 15 (Likelihood ratio LR). *Given the two time series $x[n] = (x_1, x_2, ..., x_N)^T$ and $y[n] = (y_1, y_2, ..., y_N)^T$ with periodograms a_i and b_i respectively, the likelihood ratio between them is determined by* [42]

$$LR(X(\omega), Y(\omega)) = 4 \sum_{i=1}^{k} \{2 \log(a_i + b_i) - \log a_i - \log b_i\},$$

where $X(\omega)$ and $Y(\omega)$ are the DFT of the time series $x[n]$ and $y[n]$. Periodogram a_i is obtained by $a_i = p_i^2 + q_i^2$, where (p_i, q_i) are Fourier coefficients of the time series $x[n]$.

The class of shape-based similarity measures usually is considered as another candidate for feature-based similarity measures. The edit-based measures can be also utilized as feature-based similarity measures. Since, feature extraction belongs to the process of our approach, the performance of feature-based similarity measures are tested in this work.

IV. Experiments and Results

In this section, the results of the proposed method are described. All the tests are executed on Windows 10 with a AMD Ryzen 5 1600 core processor and 16GB RAM. The codes are performed by MATLAB R2017a [43].

A test case image data base with different images is considered, which is sent as input data to the proposed approach. The experiments followed the procedure given in Fig. 2. To evaluate the performance of the proposed approach, different validation principles are performed, given in Section IV-A. After that, the captured results of image motif discovery are presented in Section IV-C. The experiments are executed in two parts: the first part is performed on the test case images without any added distortions. In the second part of experiments, two types of noise are added to the data. Finally, the test images are distorted by effects such as blurring.

A. Validation Principles

As described in Section III-C, different features are extracted from the normalised histogram of the wavelet coefficients. The quality of the selected features is measured by the linear discriminant analysis (LDA) algorithm [2], [44].

There are various validation methods to analyse the performance of a method. Here, the outcome of the investigations is benchmarked by the quality measures explained in the following section.

1) Linear Discriminant Analysis: Linear Discriminant Analysis (LDA) is a supervised method, which projects the features from the samples of the two or more classes onto a lower dimensional space with good class separability in order to avoid over-fitting and computational costs reduction. This method projects a data set into a lower dimensional space with good class separability.

Given samples from two motif groups, C_1 and C_2, LDA's aim is to find the direction $W = (w_1, w_2, ..., w_N)$ such that when the data are projected onto W, the motif examples of each group are as perfectly separated as possible:

$$F_{prj} = W^T F,$$

where $F = (f_1, f_2, ..., f_N)$ is the vector of the objects and F_{prj} is a scalar that samples in F are projected onto.

To be able to obtain a good projection vector, a measure for separation between the projections must be defined. The arithmetic mean value of the vector F and its projected one F_{prj} are given by [2]

$$\mu = \frac{1}{N}\sum_{i=1}^{N} f_i, \qquad \widetilde{\mu} = \frac{1}{N}\sum_{i=1}^{N} W^T f_i.$$

One possibility is to consider the distance between the projected means of each motif group, but this option is not a proper measure since it does not consider the standard deviation within each motif group.

Fisher proposed a solution to maximise a function that represents the difference between the means, normalised by a measure of the within-class (group or cluster) scatter. For each motif group, the scatter is defined as [2]

$$\widetilde{\sigma_i} = \sum_{F_{prj} \in C_i} (F_{prj} - \widetilde{\mu_i})^2,$$

where parameter $i \in \mathbb{N}$ is the number of motif groups (here $i = 2$). The Fisher linear discriminant is determined by [2]

$$J(W) = \frac{|\widetilde{\mu_1} - \widetilde{\mu_2}|^2}{\widetilde{\sigma_1^2} + \widetilde{\sigma_2^2}}.$$

Thus, LDA searches for a projection where the motifs belonging to the same group are very close to each other, and the motifs of various groups are as farther apart as possible [2]. Therefore, to estimate the efficiency of the extracted features, the classification error by LDA is considered here. This error is denoted by e where $0 \leq e \leq 1$. The less the error, the better is merit of the features. If the data can be separated linearly and correctly, the error will be 0, and if the whole data cannot be classified linearly and correctly, then the error has its maximum amount of 1.

2) Quality Measures: An image motif which matches all the images in the target class and no other images out of that class, is considered as a perfect motif. To qualify a motif matching an image, four possibilities of the confusion matrix are available; namely, true positive rate (TP), false negative rate (FN), true negative rate (TN), and false positive rate (FP). Parameter (TP) represents a positive example that is also predicted positive. A positive example with a false prediction shows by (FP). (TN) depicts a negative example when the prediction is also negative. Finally, (FN) is a result of having a positive prediction for a negative example [2].

The results of the proposed algorithm are evaluated by the following quality measures [2]: Correct motif discovery rate CR, Sensitivity Sn, Precision Pr and F-Measure $F - M$.

Definition 16 (Correct motif discovery rate). *This rate expresses the performance of the algorithm. It is given by*

$$CR = \frac{n^+}{N},$$

where $N \in \mathbb{N}$ is number of all motifs and n^+ is number of correctly detected motifs.

Definition 17 (Sensitivity). *Sensitivity measures the capacity of images of the target class correctly matched by the motif. This measure is also denoted by recall.*

$$Sn = \frac{TP}{TP + FN},$$

where $Sn \in [0,\ 1]$ and the optimal case is $Sn = 1$.

Definition 18 (Precision). *This measure provides the fraction of images of the target class that are matched by the motif and the images that are not correctly matched by the motif.*

$$Pr = \frac{TP}{TP + FP},$$

where $Pr \in [0,\ 1]$. In other words, Pr relates the number of correct detected motifs to all positive determined motifs with the optimal case of $Pr = 1$.

Definition 19 (F-Measure). *F-Measure considers both precision and sensitivity and is determined by*

$$F - M = 2 \cdot (\frac{Pr \cdot Sn}{Pr + Sn}).$$

The best value for F-Measure is 1 and the worst is 0.

B. Test Case

The test image data base consists of images from diverse applications and domains like hand gesture, leaf identification [45], [46], and text and object recognition. Fig. 5 represents some images of four groups. All the images have various size and scale, to analyse the performance of the proposed method. Since, both images of fixed and variable size can be analysed in this work.

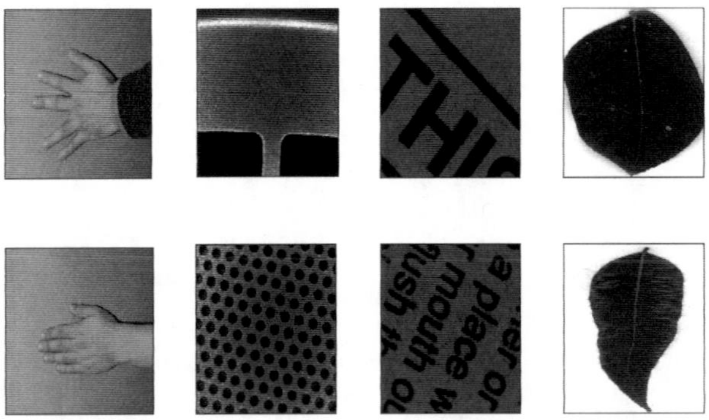

Figure 5. Data set of different images captured from various applications.

Top inserted image motifs or the most occurred images are the pictures of hands and leaves, which are depicted in Fig. 6. In order to demonstrate the shift-invariant property of the 2D-CQTWP in feature space, images such as given in Fig. 6 (a-d) are considered. These images are the shifted version of the image (a), and image (e) is the rotated version of image (a). Images (f-j) are different leaf types with various size and shape. The number of test images is increased from 280 to 2202 images. From these figures, 400 images are the inserted motif images.

C. Results and Evaluation

The proposed method starts with a pre-processing step, where all the images are converted in grey-scale, since the colour information is not required.

Next, all the images are sent to the main part of the method namely to the 2D-CQTWP transform. As explained, the 2D-CQTWP is able to decompose the images into various signals (up to $s = \log_2^{(m \times n)}$). In this work, the wavelet coefficients of the second scale are selected, since the amount of noise is usually reduced in the second scale for the noisy data. The best nodes with the highest information content are selected from these scales, according to the algorithm 1.

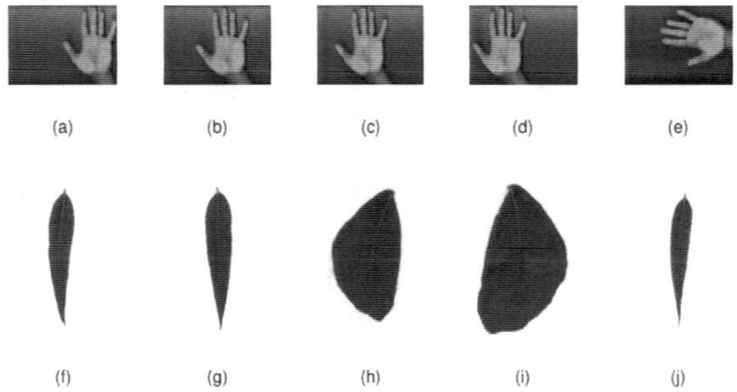

Figure 6. Images of hands and leaves. Images (b-d) are the shifted version of image (a); Image (e) is the rotated version of image (a). Images (f-j) are various sorts of leaves.

As the test case consists of images of various size, the wavelet coefficients have also different size. Therefore, the normalised histograms of the selected wavelet coefficients are calculated. Fig. 7 is the graphical representation of the normalised histogram of the HL sub band coefficients of "2D-WPT A" from the images depicted in Fig. 5.

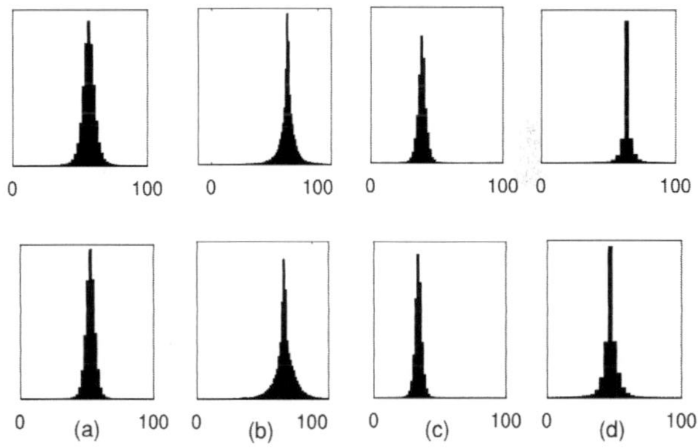

Figure 7. Normalised histogram of the HL sub band coefficients, obtained from the corresponding images from Fig. 5 (a-d).

According to Fig. 7, the histograms of wavelet coefficients from the two depicted images in each group (a), (b), (c) and (d) are similar to each other but different to the histograms of other groups. This helps to determine the variations between various motif classes (inter-class).

In order to represent the shift-invariant property of the 2D-CQTWP, the hand images in upper subfigures of Fig. 8 are considered. The position of the hand is shifted in these images. Based on the 2D-CQTWP transform the wavelet coefficients and therefore, the normalised histograms of these images must be identical to each other. As illustrated, the normalised histograms are all identical to each other, which shows the shift-invariant property of the 2D-CQTWP. The normalised histograms depicted in Fig. 8 are obtained from the HL sub band coefficients of the hand images in Fig. 6 (a)-(d).

After determining the normalised histograms from the wavelet coefficients, the five stated features are extracted from

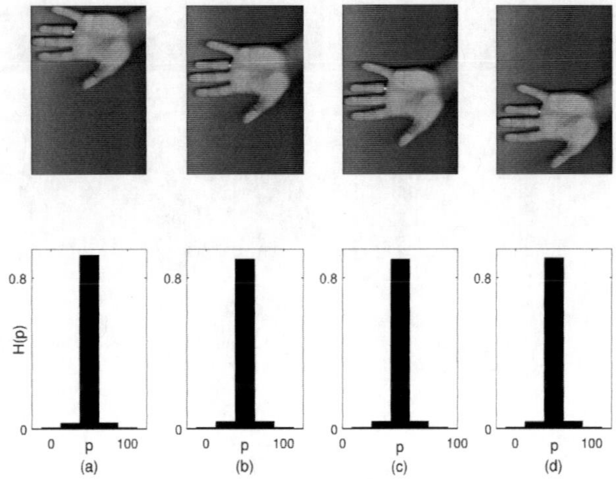

Figure 8. (a) a hand pattern; (b) shifted version of image in (a); (c) and (d) represent the normalised histograms of the HL sub band coefficients from images (a) and (b).

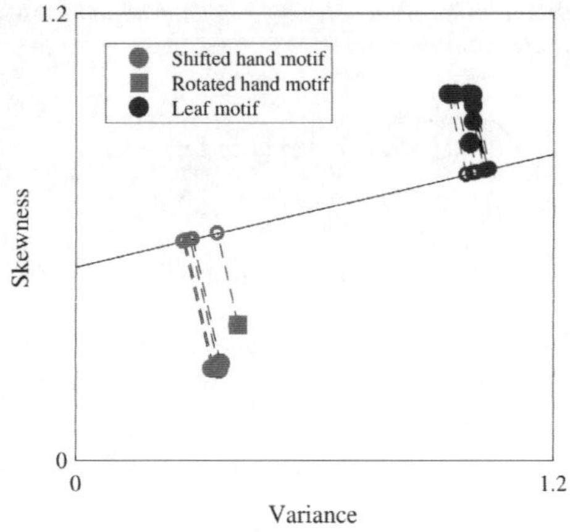

Figure 9. LDA projection of the two features from some of the hand and leaf image motifs; the distance between features within an image motif group is as minimum as possible and the distance between features of different image motif groups is large enough. Red circle markers represent the shifted images of the hand where the red square marker depicts the rotated image of the hand. Blue circle markers demonstrate the leaves images.

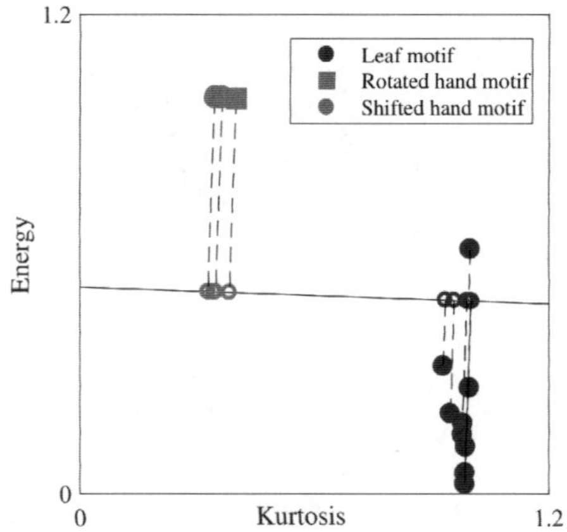

Figure 10. LDA projection of the kurtosis and energy features from some of the hand and leaf image motifs; the images of both groups can be easily separated. Red circle and square markers represent the shifted and rotated image of the hand. Blue circle markers demonstrate the leaves images.

them. The efficiency of these features are investigated by the linear discriminant analysis (LDA) algorithm [2], [44]. The experiments show that for most of the tested features the minimum error is $0 \leq e \leq 0.01$. Furthermore, the distance between feature clusters is as great as possible, which facilitates the grouping.

The result of the LDA projection of the two extracted features (skewness and variance) from the image motifs in Fig. 6 is given in Fig. 9. As demonstrated, the distance between the two groups is large enough in order to separate them correctly. Moreover, the distance between features belonging to the same image motif group (represented on the projection line) is minimised.

The features of the first four hand images are as close as possible to each other and their projection on the projection line is at the same position. This also depicts a graphical representation of the shift-invariant property of the 2D-CQTWP transform. These images are depicted by the circle red marker. Nevertheless, the projection of the features extracted from the rotated image (illustrated by the square red marker) is not at the same position of other hand images. This illustrates that the 2D-CQTWP is nearly rotation invariant, but still we are able to detect this image motif and separate it from other image motifs.

Another example is presented in Fig. 10, where similar to the Fig. 9 the features (energy and kurtosis) of the first four hand images are as close as possible to each other and their projection on the projection line is at the same position. On the contrary to Fig. 9, in Fig. 10 the projection of the features extracted from the rotated image (illustrated by the square red marker) is closer to the position of other hand images.

In the last step, the similarity between feature values is measured by the Euclidean, Canberra and Edit distance, and also by the Dynamic Time Warping, the Longest Common SubSequence measures and the Likelihood ratio.

The results of these measures the are given Table I. The best performance is obtained by the Canberra distance and the LCSS provided the inadequate results (under 0.5). The LR measure is applied only on the wavelet coefficients of the images with the fixed size, since this measure is unable to compare images of various size and also the periodogram of the extracted features does not provide any useful information.

From 400 image motifs, Euclidean distance and DTW are able to detect respectively 327 and 322 motif images. The Edit distance and LCSS distinguished 244 and 139 motif images. Number of 154 image motifs are identified by the LR measure. It should be noticed that for the LR measure only 250 inserted motifs are tested, as these images have the same size. The

TABLE I. Results of detected motifs considering the best selected wavelet nodes, CR: Correct motif discovery rate, F-M: F-Measure, Sn: Sensitivity, Pr: Precision; ED: Euclidean distance, DTW: Dynamic Time Warping, CD: Canberra distance, Edit: Edit distance, LCSS: Longest common subsequence, and LR: Likelihood ratio.

Similarity Measure	CR	Sn	Pr	F-M
ED	0.812	0.812	0.820	0.816
DTW	0.807	0.807	0.794	0.801
CD	0.927	0.927	0.913	0.920
Edit	0.617	0.617	0.601	0.609
LCSS	0.344	0.344	0.339	0.341
LR	0.625	0.625	0.615	0.627

maximum amount of 370 image motifs is detected by the CD similarity measure.

As mentioned, the most repeated image motif is the hand images. All the tested similarity measures are able to detect this image motif as the 1st-Image motif. The highest amount F-Measure is obtained by the Canberra and the Euclidean distance measures, which confirms the accuracy of these measures.

In the experiments given in the last contribution [1], the best motif discovery rate was achieved by the Euclidean distance (correct motif discovery = 0.861), and the Canberra and DTW measures performed in the same manner. Here, by increasing the size of the data set the performance of the Canberra distance improves since this measure involves some standardisation across the two observations being compared rather than simply adding the distance differences. The DTW achieves the lower results than the Euclidean distance by increasing the size of the data. This issue is also mentioned in [47], where the authors showed that by increasing the size of the data, the Euclidean distance outperforms the DTW measure. Moreover, by selecting the nodes with the best information content the performance of these similarity measures is increased.

In order to test the robustness of the proposed method, the same experiments are performed by adding noise to the test images. The test case is overlaid with two different types of noise namely Gaussian and Salt & Pepper [48], cf., Fig. 11. The Gaussian noise is the most occurring noise in images. It has the same discrete probability density function as the normal distribution.

$$p[X] = \frac{1}{\sigma\sqrt{2\pi}} e^{\frac{-(X-\mu)}{2\sigma^2}},$$

where $X(m,n)$ is the original image (grey-scaled) and μ and σ are the mean value and the standard deviation. Thus, the values of the noise are Gaussian-distributed.

The Salt & Pepper noise does not corrupt the whole image, instead some pixel values of the image are changed. The damaged image by Salt & Pepper looks like that several black and white dots scattered on the image. The Salt & Pepper noise can be simply modelled by

$$p[X = X_N] = 1 - \alpha,$$
$$p[X_N = max] = \alpha/2,$$
$$p[X_N = min] = \alpha/2,$$

where $X(m,n)$ is the original image and $X_N(m,n)$ is the image altered by the Salt & Pepper noise. The *min* and *max* are the minimum and maximum image values (for 8-bit images $min = 0$ and $max = 255$), and $0 \leq \alpha \leq 1$ is the probability that a pixel is corrupted. By the discrete probability density equals to $1-\alpha$, the pixels stay unchanged and with probability $\alpha/2$, the pixels are changed to the largest or smallest values [48]. The added Gaussian and Salt & Pepper noise to the images are respectively 20dB and 13dB.

The performance of the proposed motif discovery algorithm under the influence of noise and applying the above similarity measures is given in Tables II-III.

TABLE II. Detected motifs from test images overlaid with the Gaussian noise, CR: Correct motif discovery rate, F-M: F-Measure, Sn: Sensitivity, Pr: Precision; ED: Euclidean distance, DTW: Dynamic Time Warping, CD: Canberra distance, Edit: Edit distance, LCSS: Longest common subsequence, and LR: Likelihood ratio.

Similarity Measure	CR	Sn	Pr	F-M
ED	0.781	0.781	0.769	0.775
DTW	0.781	0.781	0.769	0.775
CD	0.835	0.835	0.822	0.829
Edit	0.601	0.601	0.592	0.596
LCSS	0.329	0.329	0.324	0.326
LR	0.590	0.590	0.584	0.586

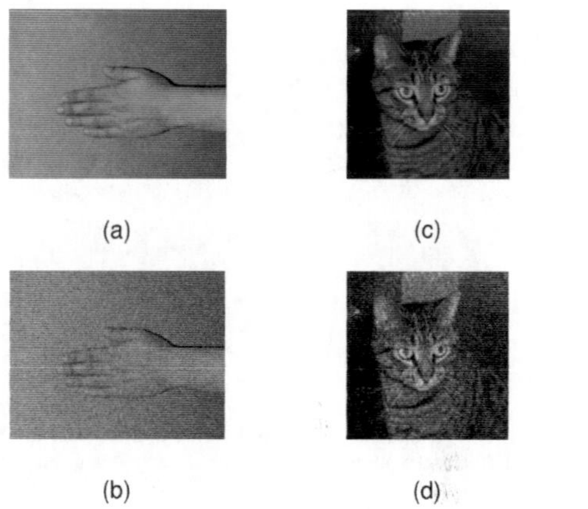

Figure 11. Example of the tested images overlaid with the Gaussian and Salt & Pepper noise. Images (a) and (c) are original images, and images (b) and (d) are images overlaid respectively with the Salt & Pepper and the Gaussian noise.

As stated, the performance of the LCSS is very poor under the noise circumstances, and it provides under 50% correct motif discovery rate. The best outcome is obtained by the Canberra distance in all three cases. The rest of the similarity measures provide the similar performance. As the CQTWP transform reduces the amount of noise, the performance of most of these similarity measures stays alike, but in general the correct motif discovery of the noisy test data is lower than the original test data (without noise). The Euclidean and Canberra distances and the DTW measure are more robust to noise than the Edit distance and LCSS measure. The outcomes of the LR measures is only obtained from images of the equal size.

TABLE III. Evaluating results of detected motifs under Salt & Pepper noise, CR: Correct motif discovery rate, F-M: F-Measure, Sn: Sensitivity, Pr: Precision; ED: Euclidean distance, DTW: Dynamic Time Warping, CD: Canberra distance, Edit: Edit distance, LCSS: Longest common subsequence, and LR: Likelihood ratio.

Similarity Measure	CR	Sn	Pr	F-M
ED	0.732	0.732	0.721	0.727
DTW	0.748	0.748	0.736	0.742
CD	0.832	0.832	0.820	0.826
Edit	0.565	0.565	0.557	0.551
LCSS	0.326	0.326	0.354	0.340
LR	0.527	0.527	0.519	0.523

Image blurring [49] is another distortion occurs by an optical system. Fig. 12 is a graphical representation of this effect. The same experiments are carried out on the test case with blurred images and the outcome is given in Table IV.

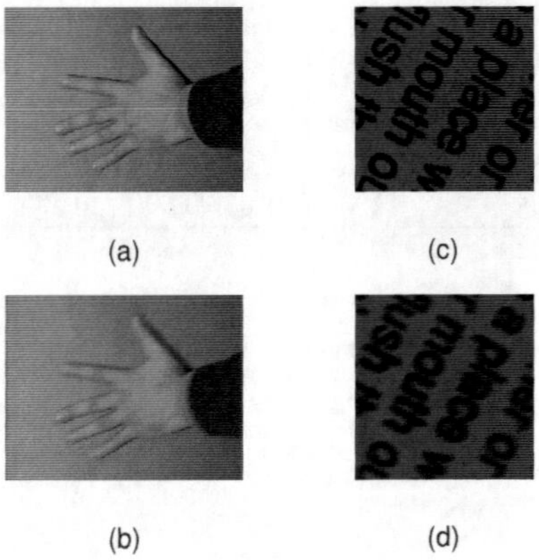

Figure 12. Image blurring effect. Subfigures (b) and (d) are the blurred images, figures (a) and (c) are the original images.

TABLE IV. Evaluating results of detected motifs under image blurring effect, CR: Correct motif discovery rate, F-M: F-Measure, Sn: Sensitivity, Pr: Precision; ED: Euclidean distance, DTW: Dynamic Time Warping, CD: Canberra distance, Edit: Edit distance, LCSS: Longest common subsequence, and LR: Likelihood ratio.

Similarity Measure	CR	Sn	Pr	F-M
ED	0.794	0.794	0.792	0.793
DTW	0.807	0.807	0.794	0.801
CD	0.786	0.786	0.774	0.780
Edit	0.421	0.421	0.415	0.418
LCSS	0.331	0.331	0.326	0.329
LR	0.606	0.606	0.619	0.613

The highest correct motif discovery rate is obtained by the DTW measure (CR=0.807). The Euclidean distance outperforms the Canberra distance, since the Canberra distance is very sensitive to the values close to zero.

The performance time for each of these similarity measures that took to detect image motifs is given in Table V and Fig. 13, where the number of the image motifs is increased up to 2000 images.

TABLE V. Evaluating the performance time took by the applied similarity measures ;ED: Euclidean distance, DTW: Dynamic Time Warping, CD: Canberra distance, Edit: Edit distance, LCSS: Longest common subsequence,, and LR: Likelihood Ratio.

Measures	ED	DTW	CD	Edit	LCSS	LR
Run-Time(s)	0.09	3.28	0.05	10.28	29.15	3.94

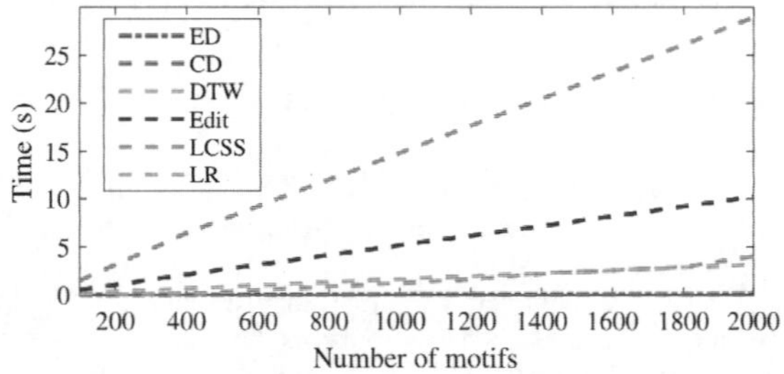

Figure 13. Performance time of the proposed method applying different similarity measures while increasing the size of the data. ED: Euclidean distance, DTW: Dynamic Time Warping, CD: Canberra distance, Edit: Edit distance, LCSS: Longest common subsequence, and LR: Likelihood Ratio.

As the size of the data increases, the performance takes longer. Among these similarity measures, Canberra distance was the fastest one with 0.05 s and the LCSS was the slowest measure with 29.15 s. The DTW and LR have similar execution time.

V. Conclusion and Outlook

In order to handle the drawbacks of existing methods, in this contribution an approach for detecting image motifs is proposed. This method overcomes the existing limitation by considering both fixed and variable size. Moreover, the tested images are not transformed to a one dimensional representation form, thus no information is lost.

This image motif discovery method is performed within three steps: In the first step, the Complex Quad Tree Wavelet Packet transform (CQTWP) analyses the images in various frequency scales. In this work, images are decomposed up to the second scale, since the amount of noise is mostly decreased at this scale. The nodes with the highest information are chosen in order to reduce the amount of redundant information and increase the execution time. The CQTWP consists of two wavelet packets working parallel to each other. Besides the advantages of wavelet transformations, the CQTWP transform has an efficient property of being shift-invariant. Also, its ability for approximately analytic representation is helpful in order to reduce aliasing.

In the second step, features are extracted from the normalised histograms obtained from the wavelet coefficients. These features are the first four statistical moments, and the energy of the wavelet coefficients. Since motif discovery is an unsupervised task, there is no information about the tested images. Consequently, the statistical features are applied in this work, but depending on the task it is possible to employ other types of features. The efficiency of these features is benchmarked with the linear discriminant analysis (LDA) algorithm [2].

In the last step, motifs are detected by measuring the similarity between their feature values. Six different similarity measures are applied here. The performance of the proposed method and these similarity measures are evaluated by different quality measures. The highest amount of correct motif discovery rate is achieved by the Canberra distance. The Euclidean distance and DTW provide the second best correct motif discovery. By increasing the size of the data, the performance of the Canberra distance improves while the performance of the DTW decreases. The Euclidean distance provides better results than the DTW in the case of larger test cases. The Canberra distance includes the standardisation of the differences between various test data and therefore, it provides the higher correct motif discovery rate compared with the Euclidean distance.

All the experiments carried out with the test cases that are overlaid with noise and blurring effects. These distortions are added to the data to measure the robustness of the proposed method. The best outcome is obtained by the Canberra distance and the LCSS provided the lowest result. The correct motif discovery of the noisy test data is lower than the original test data (without noise). However, as the CQTWP transform decreases the amount of noise, the results obtained from these similarity measures in the case of noisy data are still proper. In case of image blurring, the Euclidean distance executed robuster than the Canberra distance, since the Canberra distance is sensible to the values near zero.

From these similarity measures, the Canberra and Euclidean distance were the fastest one, and the Longest Common SubSequence has the lowest execution time among all.

In the future approach, our aim is to examine other cost functions or approaches to detect the proper nodes of the 2D-CQTWP with the best information content. The approach applied here, is based on the entropy-based cost function, nevertheless other cost functions such as energy or variance can be applied as well. Investigation in effects of image rotation for image motif discovery is another concept, which has to be regarded in the future work. Finally, discovery of motifs within various images without segmenting these images, is the last issue that must be considered in outlook.

ACKNOWLEDGMENT

This research is partly supported by the International Graduate School of Intelligent Systems in Automation Technology (ISA), which is run by scientists of the Faculty of Computer Science, Electrical Engineering and Mathematics and the Faculty of Mechanical Engineering of the University of Paderborn and the Institute of Industrial Information Technologies (inIT) of the Ostwestfalen-Lippe University of Applied Sciences.

APPENDIX A

Proof: The coefficients of signal $x[n-S_{e/o}]$ for both odd and even shifts are given in following:

1. Even Shifts. If $x[n-S_e]$ where the shift $S_e = 2m,\ \ m \in \mathbb{Z}$ then CQTWP's coefficients ${}^{s+1}C'_{2J}[n,S_e]$ and ${}^{s+1}C'_{2J+1}[n,S_e]$ are able to detect the shift. Thus,

$$\begin{aligned}
{}^{s+1}C'_{2J}[n,S_e] &\overset{S_e=2m}{=} \sum_{k=0}^{M+Len-1} {}^{s}g_a[k]\ {}^{s}C'_j[2n-2m-k] = \\
&= \sum_{k=0}^{M+Len-1} {}^{s}g_a[k]\ {}^{s}C'_j[2(n-m)-k] = {}^{s+1}C_{2J}[n-m], \\
{}^{s+1}C'_{2J+1}[n,S_e] &\overset{S_e=2m}{=} \sum_{k=0}^{M+Len-1} {}^{s}h_a[k]\ {}^{s}C'_j[2n-2m-k] = \\
&= \sum_{k=0}^{M+Len-1} {}^{s}h_a[k]\ {}^{s}C'_j[2(n-m)-k] = {}^{s+1}C_{2J+1}[n-m],
\end{aligned} \tag{6}$$

where $Len = length({}^{s}C_j)$ and $M \in \mathbb{N}^+$ is the length of the filters.

2. Odd Shifts. If $x[n-S_o]$ where the shift $S_o = 2m+1,\ \ m \in \mathbb{Z}$ then CQTWP's coefficients ${}^{s+1}C'_{2J+2}[n,S_o]$ and ${}^{s+1}C'_{2J+3}[n,S_o]$ are able to detect the shift. Thus,

$$\begin{aligned}
{}^{s+1}C'_{2J+2}[n,S_o] &\overset{S_o=2m+1}{=} \\
&= \sum_{k=0}^{M+Len-1} {}^{s}g_a[k]\ {}^{s}C'_j[2n+1-2m-1-k] = \\
&= \sum_{k=0}^{M+Len-1} {}^{s}g_a[k]\ {}^{s}C'_j[2(n-m)-k] = {}^{s+1}C_{2J}[n-m], \\
{}^{s+1}C'_{2J+3}[n,S_o] &\overset{S_o=2m+1}{=} \\
&= \sum_{k=0}^{M+Len-1} {}^{s}h_a[k]\ {}^{s}C'_j[2n+1-2m-1-k] = \\
&= \sum_{k=0}^{M+Len-1} {}^{s}h_a[k]\ {}^{s}C'_j[2(n-m)-k] = {}^{s+1}C_{2J+1}[n-m].
\end{aligned} \tag{7}$$

Similarly, the coefficients for the second wavelet packet "*WPT B*" are obtained. ∎

REFERENCES

[1] S. Torkamani and V. Lohweg, "Shift-invariant motif discovery in image processing," in The Seventh International Conference on Performance, Safety and Robustness in Complex Systems and Applications; Special track MAIS: Machine Learning Algorithms in Image and Signal Processing. IARIA, 2017.

[2] E. Alpaydın, Introduction to Machine Learning, 2nd ed. Cambridge: The MIT Press, 2010.

[3] N. M. A. S. Khan, S. A. and N. Riaz, "Gender classification using image processing techniques: A survey," in 2011 IEEE 14th International Multitopic Conference. IEEE, 2011, pp. 25–30.

[4] M. G. K. J. C. S. Nath, S. S. and N. Dey, "A survey of image classification methods and techniques," in International Conference on Control, Instrumentation, Communication and Computational Technologies (ICCICCT). IEEE, 2014, pp. 554–557.

[5] S. Gangwar and R. P. Chauhan, "Survey of clustering techniques enhancing image segmentation process," in 2015 Second International Conference on Advances in Computing and Communication Engineering. IEEE, 2015, pp. 34–39.

[6] P. Esling and C. Agon, "Time-series data mining," vol. 45. ACM, 2012, pp. 1–34.

[7] M. K. Das and H.-K. Dai, "A survey of dna motif finding algorithms," BMC bioinformatics, vol. 8 Suppl 7, 2007, p. 21.

[8] K. E. L. J. Patel, P. and S. Lonardi, "Mining motifs in massive time series databases," in Proceedings IEEE International Conference on Data Mining. IEEE, 2002, pp. 370–377.

[9] K. E. W. L. Xi, X. and A. Mafra-Neto, "Finding motifs in a database of shapes," in Proceedings of the 2007 SIAM international conference on data mining. SIAM, 2007, pp. 249–260.

[10] D. Crowther and M. Thompson, "Geology.com-petroglyph photo gallery," 2005-2017. [Online]. Available: http://geology.com/articles/petroglyphs/more-petroglyphs.shtml

[11] S. Torkamani and V. Lohweg, "Survey on time series motif discovery," in Journal: Wiley Interdisciplinary Reviews: Data Mining and Knowledge Discovery. Article ID: WIDM1199, 2017.

[12] H. R. X. N. L. H. Hu, W. and S. Maybank, "Image classification using multiscale information fusion based on saliency driven nonlinear diffusion filtering," IEEE Transactions on Image Processing, vol. 23, no. 4, 2014, pp. 1513–1526.

[13] N. M. Zaitoun and M. J. Aqel, "Survey on image segmentation techniques," Procedia Computer Science, vol. 65, 2015, pp. 797–806, Elsevier.

[14] G. Azzopardi and N. Petkov, Eds., Computer Analysis of Images and Patterns: 16th International Conference, CAIP 2015, Valletta, Malta, September 2-4, 2015 Proceedings, Part I. Springer International Publishing, 2015.

[15] B. K. Gayathri and P. Raajan, "A survey of breast cancer detection based on image segmentation techniques," in 2016 International Conference on Computing Technologies and Intelligent Data Engineering (ICCTIDE'16). IEEE, 2016, pp. 1–5.

[16] L. Ye and E. Keogh, "Time series shapelets: A new primitive for data mining," in Proceedings of the 15th ACM SIGKDD International Conference on Knowledge Discovery and Data Mining, ser. KDD '09. ACM, 2009, pp. 947–956.

[17] C. M. F. Barone, P. and R. March, "Segmentation, classification and denoising of a time series field by a variational method," Journal of Mathematical Imaging and Vision, vol. 34, no. 2, Jun 2009, pp. 152–164.

[18] F. Y. C. H. Chi, L. and Y. Huang, "Face image recognition based on time series motif discovery," in IEEE International Conference on Granular Computing. IEEE, 2012, pp. 72–77.

[19] S. N. W. M. Grabocka, J. and L. Schmidt-Thieme, "Learning time-series shapelets," in Proceedings of the 20th ACM SIGKDD International Conference on Knowledge Discovery and Data Mining, ser. KDD '14. ACM, 2014, pp. 392–401.

[20] C. Caballero and M. C. Aranda, "Wapsi: Web application for plant species identification using fuzzy image retrieval," Advances on Computational Intelligence, 2012, pp. 250–259, Springer.

[21] Z. Q. Rakthanmanon, T. and E. Keogh, "Mining historical documents for near-duplicate figures," in IEEE 11th International Conference on Data Mining. IEEE, 2011, pp. 557–566.

[22] D. H. Ballard, "Generalizing the hough transform to detect arbitrary shapes," Pattern recognition, vol. 13, no. 2, 1981, pp. 111–122, elsevier.

[23] P. C. N. S. En, S. and L. Heutte, "Segmentation-free pattern spotting in historical document images," in 13th International Conference on Document Analysis and Recognition (ICDAR). IEEE, 2015, pp. 606–610.

[24] D. H. Torkamani, S. and V. Lohweg, "Multi-scale motif discovery in image processing," in Workshop on Probabilistic Graphical Models, Heidelberg, Germany, Oct 2015.

[25] B. R. G. Selesnick, I. W. and N. G. Kingsbury, "The dual-tree complex wavelet transform," Signal Processing Magazine, IEEE, vol. 22, no. 6, 2005, pp. 123–151.

[26] S. Torkamani and V. Lohweg, "Shift-invariant feature extraction for time-series motif discovery," in 25. Workshop Computational Intelligence, ser. Schriftenreihe des Instituts für Angewandte Informatik - Automatisierungstechnik am Karlsruher Institut für Technologie, vol. 54. KIT Scientific Publishing, 2015, pp. 23–45.

[27] L. Q. Z. S. Li, T. and M. Ogihara, "A survey on wavelet applications in data mining," ACM SIGKDD Explorations Newsletter, vol. 4, no. 2, 2002, pp. 49–68, ACM.

[28] G. A. K. G. Chaovalit, P. and Z. Chen, "Discrete wavelet transform-based time series analysis and mining," ACM Computing Surveys (CSUR), vol. 43, no. 2, 2011, p. 6, ACM.

[29] S. A. T. S. M. L. Y. Y. C. S. C. I. S. S. Y. J. S. Meng, T. and P. Iyengar, "Wavelet analysis in current cancer genome research: A survey," IEEE/ACM Transactions on Computational Biology and Bioinformatics, vol. 10, no. 6, 2013, pp. 1442–1459, ACM.

[30] I. W. Selesnick, "Hilbert transform pairs of wavelet bases," IEEE Signal Processing Letters, vol. 8, no. 6, 2001, pp. 170–173.

[31] R. Yu and H. Ozkaramanli, "Hilbert transform pairs of orthogonal wavelet bases: Necessary and sufficient conditions," IEEE Transactions on Signal Processing, vol. 53, no. 12, 2005, pp. 4723–4725, IEEE.

[32] N. Kingsbury, "Design of q-shift complex wavelets for image processing using frequency domain energy minimization," in Proceedings International Conference on Image Processing, vol. 1. IEEE, 2003, pp. I–1013.

[33] A. F. Abdelnour and I. W. Selesnick, "Symmetric nearly shift-invariant tight frame wavelets," IEEE Transactions on Signal Processing, vol. 53, no. 1, 2005, pp. 231–239, IEEE.

[34] C. S. Burrus, R. A. Gopinath, and H. Guo, Introduction to wavelets and wavelet transforms: A primer. Upper Saddle River and NJ: Prentice Hall, 1998.

[35] M. V. Wickerhauser, "Lectures on wavelet packet algorithms," in Lecture notes, INRIA. Citeseer, 1991, pp. 31–99.

[36] H. Niemann, Pattern analysis and understanding. Springer Science & Business Media, 2013, vol. 4.

[37] M. M. Deza and E. Deza, Encyclopedia of distances. Springer, 2009.

[38] V. I. Levenshtein, "Binary codes capable of correcting deletions, insertions and reversals," in Soviet physics doklady, vol. 10, 1966, p. 707.

[39] M. Paterson and V. Dancik, Longest common subsequences. Springer Berlin Heidelberg, 1994, vol. 841.

[40] Z. Guoqing and D. Wei, "An HMM-based hierarchical clustering method for gene expression time series data," in IEEE Fifth International Conference on Bio-Inspired Computing: Theories and Applications (BIC-TA). IEEE, 2010, pp. 219–222.

[41] Y. Xiong and D.-Y. Yeung, "Time series clustering with ARMA mixtures," Pattern Recognition, vol. 37, no. 8, 2004, pp. 1675–1689, Elsevier.

[42] B. A. J. Janacek, G. J. and M. Powell, "A likelihood ratio distance measure for the similarity between the Fourier transform of time series," in Advances in Knowledge Discovery and Data Mining: 9th Pacific-Asia Conference, PAKDD 2005, Hanoi, Vietnam. Springer Berlin Heidelberg, 2005, pp. 737–743.

[43] MathWorks, "MATLAB," 2017, last access: 31.08.17. [Online]. Available: https://de.mathworks.com/products/matlab.html

[44] C. Bayer, M. Bator, U. Mönks, A. Dicks, O. Enge-Rosenblatt, and V. Lohweg, "Sensorless drive diagnosis using automated feature extraction, significance ranking and reduction," in 18th IEEE Int. Conf. on Emerging Technologies and Factory Automation (ETFA 2013). IEEE, 2013, pp. 1–4.

[45] M. B. Stegmann and D. D. Gomez, "A brief introduction to statistical shape analysis," 2002, informatics and Mathematical Modelling, Technical University of Denmark, DTU.

[46] M. A. R. S. Silva, P. F. B. and da Silva R. A., "UCI machine learning repository: Leaf data set," 2014. [Online]. Available: https://archive.ics.uci.edu/ml/datasets/Leaf

[47] M. A. D. H. T. G. S. P. Wang, X. and E. Keogh, "Experimental comparison of representation methods and distance measures for time series data," 2013, pp. 1–35, data Mining and Knowledge Discovery.

[48] C. Boncelet, "Image noise models," in The Essential Guide to Image Processing. Elsevier, 2009, pp. 143–167.

[49] W. Burger and M. J. Burge, Principles of digital image processing. Springer, 2009.

Platform As A Service Development Cost & Security

Aspen Olmsted
College of Charleston
Department of Computer Science, Charleston, SC 29401
e-mail: olmsteda@cofc.edu

Abstract— **In this paper, we investigate the problem of development costs in Platform-as-a-Service (PaaS) cloud-based systems. We develop a set of tools to analyze the size of code executed to support features in the PaaS. In this research, we specifically focus on stable, open source platforms to ensure as much of an equivalent offering from each platform with a distinction made between PaaS and Platform Infrastructure as a Service (PIaaS). The focus of the paper is on the features both functional and non-functional provided to the developer that is not provided by traditional network operating systems. On the functional side, we look at features provided by the platform to assist the developer in programming tasks the software must do. On the non-functional side, we look at security defenses the platform provides to protect the end users data. Our study demonstrates a savings cost of nearly thirteen million dollars to develop the application services provided by a typical PaaS.**

Keywords-PaaS; cloud computing; CRM

I. INTRODUCTION

In this work, we investigate the problem of estimating the cost of developer services provided by a platform-as-a-service (PaaS) cloud-based system. In traditional client-server architectures, developers expend considerable effort developing functionality that is not specific to the business domain where the application will operate in. This work builds on our earlier work on development effort estimation [1].

Cloud computing has traditionally been made up of three broad categories of offerings:

- Software as a Service (SaaS) – This category includes applications that run in a Web browser and do not require any local software or hardware besides a Web browser and an Internet connection. Examples of software in this category include Google Docs [2] and Microsoft Office 365 [3].
- Infrastructure as a Service (IaaS) – This category includes virtualization software that allows an operating system to be run in the cloud. Typically, the user will pick a hardware configuration and install an operating system into the virtual hardware configuration. IaaS was designed to free the user from the purchase of hardware and allow for easy hardware upgrades. Examples of IaaS offerings are Amazon EC2 [4] and Rackspace [5].
- Platform-as-a-Service (PaaS) – This category includes pre-built components that a developer can use when developing a cloud application. The goal of PaaS is to allow the developer to focus on the development of a solution for the business functions rather than software functions that span many application domains. A good example of PaaS is force.com where the developer is provided many of the essential parts of an application out of the box.

Over the years, software development has matured to allow the developer to spend a larger percentage of their development time on the business problem instead of the infrastructure for the application. In the early days of programming, each instruction the programmer wrote matched an instruction in the hardware. The late 1980s and 90s were dominated by 3rd generation languages such as C, PASCAL, and ADA where each instruction written by the developer was compiled to many machine instructions. The first decade and a half, of the 21st century, have been dominated by bytecode compiled languages which have runtime engines that execute the code on different hardware platforms. The Java Runtime Engine (JRE) and the Microsoft .NET Runtime Engine (.NET) are the most dominant examples of the bytecode engines that free the developer from thinking about the underlying hardware. PaaS is the next evolution in freeing up the developers' times, so they can focus on the problem they are trying to solve instead of the technical plumbing required for the solution.

The organization of the paper is as follows. Section II describes the related work and the limitations of current methods. In Section III, we document typical services provided. Section IV analyzes different PaaS providers and the services they provide. Section V explores the alternative costs to develop the individual services. We give a motivating example in Section VI. In Section VII, we look at software security defenses as provided by the different platforms. We conclude and discuss future work in Section VIII.

II. RELATED WORK

The NIST (National Institute of Standards) definition of "cloud computing" defines PaaS as "the capability provided to the consumer [...] to deploy onto the cloud infrastructure consumer-created or acquired applications created using programming languages, libraries, services, and tools supported by the provider. The consumer does not manage or control the underlying cloud infrastructure including network, servers, operating systems, or storage, but has control over the deployed applications and possibly configuration settings for the application-hosting environment" [6]. In the same document, they define SaaS and IaaS similarly to our definitions in the introduction.

Kolb and Wirtz [7] investigate ways to construct applications for the cloud that are portable across different

PaaS providers. Their work assumes lower level services compared to the offerings than our work. We are less interested in maintenance costs to move platforms as we are in startup costs for greenfield Engineering. In software engineering, greenfield engineering occurs when you are starting from scratch or are re-engineering your product on a different architectural paradigm in which you cannot port your current code base.

Baliyan and Kumar [8] explore how services provided by a PaaS provider affect the software development lifecycle (SDLC). Again, in their work, they consider just a few services. In our work, we think about many more services. The larger perspective on service would have an even greater impact on their work.

In our model of services, end users can create new objects, new forms for data entry and new reports to display the data in both detail and aggregate form as well as new dashboards. Ng [9] looks at PaaS as a model for deploying end-user programming through a model of Tasks. The programming model provided by the platforms in our study has demonstrated success in allowing end users to extend the application.

Boehm, Clark, Horowitz, Westland, Madachy, and Selby [10] developed an algorithm to estimate effort for a software engineering project. The algorithm uses variables that represent a programmer's experience and programming expertise required in the project. For this study, we used the "nominal" value for each variable to get an average cost. Madachy [11] provides an online tool to calculate the effort including maintenance over the life of the software.

III. PAAS SERVICES

With PaaS, the developer does not need to be concerned with the operating system on which the specified platform runs. For example, the platform will provide a service to save a file, and the developer does not need to worry about what operating system the platform is running. We group the service offerings into two distinct categories:

A. *Infrastructure Services*

- Node Configuration – This service allows the end user to modify configuration settings to allow the system to scale to handle larger or smaller workloads by adding or removing nodes, storage or Central Processing Units (CPUs). This service allows the implementation to start with minimal hardware to save costs during start-up. Additional resources can then be added as the application user base grows without the need to re-engineer the application.
- Load Balancing – This service allows the end user to setup multiple systems to ensure uptime when loads are higher, or network partitions occur. Each system is an exact replica, and the load will be distributed across the replicas. The application will need to be designed properly for replication. The system must also not store resources in a specific replica as each request could be sent to a different replica. Both persisted data and session state should be stored in the database server.
- Logging – The logging service allows an audit log to be enabled to help diagnose application and platform issues. The service should allow the log to be toggled on and off so that space is not wasted when an audit is not needed. Ideally, there will be different granularity of audits available, such as errors, warnings, and information.
- Database – The database service allows the application data to persist across executions of the application. Traditionally, this has been a relational database such as Oracle [12] or MySQL [13] but may also be a NoSQL [14] database that is better at distribution. The database service should provide: create, read, update and delete (CRUD) services and potentially transaction support.
- Scheduled Jobs – This service allows bulk operations to be scheduled at specific and recurring intervals. Example jobs include sending out bulk emails, updating de-normalized database fields and communicating with external systems. Often, this service is delivered through a cronjob interface where jobs can be scheduled down to the specific second of each hour.

B. *Application Services*

- Authentication – The authentication service provides a way to define users and allow authentication in the application being developed. Ideally, this would provide both the administrative tool for creating users and groups along with the user interface with which the end users interact to authenticate themselves. The service should provide multifactor authentication which incorporates information the end user knows along with someplace they are or something they have.
- Authorization – The authorization service provides a way to define which users can see different data, forms, and reports in the application. The authorization service should provide an administrative tool to assign access permission to both users and groups to objects created in the system. The objects should be both standard objects and custom objects defined by the developer and end users.
- Rule Engine – A rule engine allows for customization of correctness rules at implementation time. Business rules control

organization policies that may change often and should not be coded in the software solution.

- Workflow – This service provides for several discrete application steps to be sequenced together. Often, a human interaction (approval) is part of the workflow.
- Bulk Email – Bulk email allows for email marketing with proper adherence to email spam rules [15]. Bulk email may be used for attracting or recruiting new customers in addition to confirming transactions with current customers.
- Importing – An importing feature allows the end user to import new instances of objects into the platform. Ideally, this would allow data from several different data formats including Comma-Separated Values (CSV) and Microsoft Excel workbook. The tool should provide a validation step so that imported data does not corrupt the current database.
- Exporting – An exporting feature allows the end user to dump instances of the objects into an external file such as a comma-separated value (CSV) or Microsoft Excel workbook. The tool should allow a query by example (QBE) where novice users can visually build export queries and see the results in the application.
- Activity tracking – Activity tracking allows for linking of phone calls, emails, meetings, and notes to objects persisted by the application. Activities may originate in an external system with an interface to the new system that is being built. An example could be a Web browser extension that allows emails in a Web email application to be linked to a related activity to an object in the new system.
- Object Customization – Object customization allows end users to add additional data to be collected in the application without changing the source code. Most enterprise systems require some form of customization either through integration to external systems or enhancements to specific features in the current system. Object customization allows the end user to make the changes without needing the software to be modified at each individual enterprise.
- New Object Creation – New object creation services allow end users to define new objects to store data that is collected in the application. Like with object customization, new object creation can be used to customize the software without changing the source code. Often, the new objects need to relate to a current object in the system. These related objects should seamlessly be displayed in the user interface.
- Detail View – The detail view renders the object details based on the configured layout. The detail view also renders one-to-many related data. The related data is often rendered in tabs.
- Edit View – The edit view renders an editable object screen based on the configured layout. The edit view is used to modify one specific object and potentially related objects.
- Data Update – The data update service provides a CRUD interface to a backend data store. The data update service abstracts the vendor specifics of the back-end data store services and allows business rule hooks to fire on the CRUD operations.

TABLE I. APPLICATION SERVICES BY PLATFORM

Service	Salesforce	Zoho	SugarCRM	SuiteCRM	vTiger	Heroku
Authentication	✓	✓	✓	✓	✓	✓
Authorization	✓	✓	✓	✓	✓	
Rule Engine	✓		✓			
Workflow	✓	✓	✓	✓	✓	
Bulk Email	✓	✓	✓	✓	✓	
Activity tracking	✓	✓	✓	✓	✓	
Object Audit	✓		✓	✓	✓	
Importing	✓	✓	✓	✓	✓	
Exporting	✓	✓	✓	✓	✓	
Object Customization	✓	✓	✓	✓	✓	
New Object Creation	✓	✓	✓	✓	✓	
User Interface Customization	✓	✓	✓	✓	✓	
Multi-Select Fields	✓	✓	✓	✓	✓	
Report Display	✓	✓	✓	✓	✓	
Report Creation	✓	✓	✓	✓	✓	
Dashboard Display	✓	✓	✓	✓	✓	
Dashboard Creation	✓	✓	✓	✓	✓	
Web-services	✓	✓	✓	✓	✓	
Mobile Application	✓	✓	✓		✓	
Partner Portal	✓					
Customer Portal	✓		✓	✓	✓	
Anonymous Sites	✓					✓
Price per user/month	$25	$35	$65	N/A	N/A	N/A

- User Interface Customization – The user interface customization service allows for forms in the application to be modified by the end users without changing the source code. This is often required to allow implementations to vary slightly by collecting custom data.
- Multi-Select Fields – Multi-select fields are a way to simplify end-user customizations. A multi-select field represents an easy way to store a one-to-many relationship of data without the need of adding new objects. Multi-select fields also save on the number of tuples stored in the system. Often, cloud providers charge for data storage based on the number of tuples [16].
- Report Display – The report display service allows execution of pre-defined reporting queries. The report display should prompt the user with replaceable run-time parameters and be exportable to PDF and spreadsheet formats. Ideally, there would be a scheduling service through which the report parameters would be based on the run date. For example, a start date parameter should be replaced based on an offset from the date the report is run.
- Report Creation – The report writer service allows both the developer and the end users to define management information system (MIS) reports that can be run and customized by the changing of run-time parameters. Typically, this includes both tabular reports that group rows of records with aggregate calculations and cross-tab reports that aggregate values based on the intersection of the row and column.
- Dashboard Display – The dashboard display service renders dashboard charts and allows them to be refreshed automatically. The dashboard is a graphical display of a metric the organization wants to measure.
- Dashboard Creation – Dashboards allow both the developer and the end users to define graphical dashboards that allow visualization of data stored in the application. Dashboards typically are bar or pie charts and are updated several times an hour.
- Mobile Application – A mobile application allows end users to perform CRUD operations on objects stored in the application without the need of creating custom mobile applications. Similar to the detail and edit view services above, any object in the system should be visible and editable.
- Partner Portal – A partner portal is a service to provide pages, forms, reports and dashboards to authenticated users with a lower training level. Typically, these are users that use the application infrequently compared to an employee.
- Customer Portal – A customer portal is a service to provide custom pages and forms to authenticated users with no training required. The service is intended for customer self-service sites where the customer can identify themselves and perform transactions.
- Anonymous Sites – The anonymous site service allows development of pages and forms to unauthenticated users. This is typically the part of an organizations website where customers do not need to identify themselves.

IV. Platform Analysis

In this study, we analyze several PaaS providers including Salesforce [17], Zoho CRM [18], SugarCRM [19], SuiteCRM [20], vTiger [21] and Heroku [22]. We chose the first five platforms because they each provide many of the services we discussed in detail. The last platform was added to show the difference between PaaS and PIaaS offerings. Each of the first five PaaS offerings was developed as a customer relationship management (CRM) system. The CRM vertical market software space requires integration with enterprise resource planning (ERP) systems. This integration requirement led the CRM vendors to develop their products as platforms instead of simply vertical market products. TABLE II shows the distributed services offered by each platform. Note the load balancing service is marked for the three PHP [23] platforms since the state of the session is stored in the database. Having the session state stored in the database allows additional business tier servers to be added to the configuration in the cloud. Though only Heroku has a graphical user interface (GUI) to manage node configuration, the PHP solutions can be hosted by an IaaS provider that provides the feature. TABLE II shows the application services offered by each platform. The final row shows a cost per user

TABLE II. DISTRIBUTED SERVICES BY PLATFORM

Service	Salesforce	Zoho	SugarCRM	SuiteCRM	vTiger	Heroku
Node Configuration						✓
Load Balancing			✓	✓	✓	
Logging	✓		✓	✓	✓	✓
Database	✓	✓	✓	✓	✓	✓
Scheduled Jobs	✓	✓	✓	✓	✓	

if the PaaS provider is providing both the infrastructure and application services.

V. Effort Study

To calculate the effort savings provided by the different PaaS service providers, we calculated the source lines of code (SLOC) in a stable platform release. For this study, we choose to use the SuiteCRM [20] system as our model. SuiteCRM is open source software, so we had access to the source code developed to provide the platform.

SuiteCRM is written in the PHP programming language using a MySQL database as its persistence layer. Using the debugger extension xDebug [24], we are able to trace all lines of code executed on the server when interacting with the application. xDebug plugs into the server-side execution of the code and creates a trace file with these lines of code. We developed tooling to parse the trace file and store the data in a MySQL database based on the function executed.

Due to the nature of Web application architectures, a single round trip from the Web browser to the Web server will often execute two distinct sets of functionalities. For example, when a user enters their login credentials, the POST to the server authenticates the user and then executes the code to display the homepage of dashboards. Our tooling allows a trace to add to or subtract from the functional cost. In the earlier example, we trace the combined functionality and then subtract the individual functionality of building the home screen.

For the study, we wanted the cost for local application software engineers in the Charleston, SC area. We recognize the cost for software developers changes from region to region but have an applied local example helps us present the work. The Bureau of Labor Statics [25] estimated the average cost for an application software engineer is $96,200/year. Hadzima [26] estimates the cost of an employee's benefits and taxes at between 25% and 40% of base salary. On top of the salary cost, the employer must pay for rent for an office space, equipment, recruitment, training, etc. For our study, we are estimating the hourly cost of $71.50 for an application programmer's time. In TABLE III, we show the estimated cost to pay an application programmer in the Charleston, SC area to redevelop the functionality provided by the service. For the study, we choose a specific platform that provided us with the source code so we could put a developer cost to the different services provided by PAAS providers. We analyzed SuiteCRM and looked at the source lines of code (SLOC). SuiteCRM stores the service source code in module folders on the file systems. We counted the executable lines of code and compared to the executed lines of code from the trace. Each trace represented a slightly higher number of lines of code because of shared libraries. We felt it was not appropriate to count all the shared lines of code per service, but we also felt it was not appropriate to ignore them completely. We decided to take the average between the two-line counts. We plugged the average number into the Constructive Cost Model (COCOMO) II formula [27] with our local application programmer cost of $71.50 per hour. The fifth column in TABLE III shows the cost per service and the total cost of all services. We eliminated a few services from the study as the source code was not available. Note the table does not show the cost of the infrastructure services. The infrastructure services can be provided by an IaaS provider if the development is done to leverage the services.

TABLE III. COST PER SERVICES

Service	SLOC	Trace	Average	CoCoMoII
Authentication/ Authorization	1156	1437	1297	$ 590,131
Workflow	954	1146	1050	$ 467,789
Bulk Email	702	1054	878	$ 384,246
Activity tracking	1178	1302	1240	$ 561,674
Object Audit	656	873	765	$ 330,225
Importing	1654	1857	1756	$ 823,478
Exporting	945	1246	1096	$ 490,375
Object Customization	2164	2874	2519	$ 1,224,557
New Object Design	1474	1826	1650	$ 768,981
Detail View	291	464	378	$ 152,095
Edit View	1828	464	1146	$ 515,031
Data Updates	656	989	823	$ 357,860
User Interface Customization	2073	2482	2278	$ 1,096,353
Multi-Select Fields	402	512	457	$ 187,395
Report Display	1912	2356	2134	$ 1,020,384
Report Creation	2957	3345	3151	$ 1,566,362
Dashboard Display	1342	1672	1507	$ 696,016
Dashboard Creation	1874	2198	2036	$ 968,972
Web-services	986	1822	1404	$ 643,884
Total				$ 12,845,808

VI. Motivating Example

Imagine a software company wants to offer a new software solution to medium-sized entertainment venues such as local theaters, museum or minor league sporting attractions. Typically, the development stakeholders hold a tremendous amount of knowledge about the application domain they want to develop a solution for, but may not have either the knowledge or resources to develop the entire application architecture to deploy their application to the cloud. In fact, we would argue that they should hire programmers that can focus development on the domain-specific problems. In this example, the domain-specific problems include selling tickets from a limited inventory. The inventory may be assigned seats, general admission seats or some combination. There is also often a great deal of Management Information Systems (MIS) reports that are standard for the industry. These reports must be specified, developed and tested by the development team along with the software functionality for the data entry functions.

By leveraging a platform, the developers are able to spend their programming energy focused on the domain specific logic instead of application code that is standard across all business applications. This will reduce the costs, risks and the time to market.

VII. Platform Security

When a software application is built a set of functional requirements and non-functional requirements are normally created to help the developers to understand the expectations of the software. The functional requirements specify what the software must, and the non-functional requirements specify what must be true for the lifecycle of the software and the data created by the application. Most of our study to this point has focused on the functional requirements. Non-functional requirements tend to fall into three main categories:

- Performance and Concurrency – Non-functional requirements in this category specify how quickly the software must respond or how many simultaneous users the system must be able to support. A great example of this type of non-functional requirement is seen when looking at the construction of the healthcare.gov website in the United States [28]. The healthcare.gov website was developed to allow citizens of the United States to purchase individual health care through an online exchange. The system had a non-functional requirement of fifty thousand concurrent patrons. During the first week of the launch, the system was unusable because the non-functional requirement was not sufficient for the usage of two hundred and fifty thousand users.
- Data Correctness Constraints – Non-functional requirements in the data correctness constraint category include all the traditional relational database constraints including unique tuple identifiers, foreign key relationships and attribute domain values. A good example of this type of constraint from our motivating example above would be that every discounted ticket must be linked to a valid customer.
- Security – Non-functional security requirements tend to be less specific. We have briefly touched on authentication and authorization in our work above. Beyond those categories, almost every software application has a non-stated non-functional requirement that the software should not allow a malicious user to use the software in an unintended fashion.

Some of the service offerings compared in TABLE IV help with the first category of non-functional requirements. Specifically, the load balancing service is designed to allow the implementers to add additional server nodes to scale up the application to support more concurrent users.

For the broad category of non-functional requirement, we called security; we want to think about several different vulnerabilities and how a platform helps us to minimize or eliminate that vulnerability. We will think about the vulnerabilities in three categories:

- Injection Vulnerabilities – Injection vulnerabilities include attacks where either the malicious user can inject code into an application's page, or the malicious user is able to inject additional or altered database commands into a current database query.
- Forgery vulnerabilities – Forgery vulnerabilities allow an application to use the credentials the current operating user to gain access to an external resource.
- Redirection Vulnerabilities – Redirection vulnerabilities allow a malicious user to modify the URL that an application goes to after an action. This modification will often allow the malicious user to leverage the other two types of vulnerabilities.

A. *Platform Injection Attacks*

There are two types of injection attacks that a platform should protect an application from Cross-Site Scripting (XSS) and SQL injection. Cloud-based applications dynamically generate the user interface code (HTML, JavaScript, and CSS) that is rendered in a web browser. This is done through the cloud platform's server-side programming language. The application will read data from the data store; parameters are passed in the request for the page and session state information is used to decide what code is placed into the user interface.

XSS is an injection vulnerability that exists when a malicious user can insert unauthorized JavaScript, HTML or other active content into an application's user interface page. When an operator views the page, the malicious code executes and affects or attacks the operator. For example, a malicious script can hijack the operator's session, submit unauthorized transactions as the operator, steal confidential information or simply deface the user interface of the application.

XSS attacks occur when operator input is reflected back in the user interface of an application page. This vulnerability stems from the poor separation between the code context and the user data. This poor separation allows the user input to be executed as code. There are three different types of XSS attacks that vary in the method in which the malicious payload is injected into the application and subsequently processed by the application.

- Stored XSS – This type of XSS attack occurs when the malicious input is permanently stored in the clouds data store and the code is reflected back to the user in a vulnerable application user interface page. A simple example where this type of attack often occurs in an application that displays a directory listing that shows users on the system. Any data stored in a user profile is stored in the cloud database and reflected back in the user interface listing.

- Reflected XSS – This type of XSS attack occurs when the malicious input is sent to a server and reflected back to the user on the response page. With this type of attack, the malicious user needs to convince the operator to click a hyperlink that has the malicious input connected to the link as a parameter. An example of a reflected XSS attack would be a hyperlink with JavaScript code in the parameter that attempts a Cross-Site Request Forgery (CSRF) to the hosted application.

- DOM-based XSS – This type of XSS attack occurs when a malicious payload is executed as a result of modifying the web page's document object model (DOM) in the operator's browser. The original application page is not modified, but the client-side code executes in a different way because of the changes in the DOM. In this case, the attack is done client side completely and not in the cloud. Many security techniques cannot detect this type of attack if the malicious input doesn't reach the cloud.

The second category of injection attack the platform should assist the developer in defending against is SQL injection. With SQL injection, a dynamically built database query is modified based on the input parameters of the operator to either expose private data or modify current data. Often, SQL injection attacks that modify data are a combination of both injection attack categories. The data being modified includes XSS code that will be rendered back to future users of the application.

B. Platform Injection Defence

When the server-side programming code merges either data from the database, a request parameter or a session variable, it needs to escape the variable, so any malicious code is no longer executable. There are three different types of user interface code that are vulnerable to injection attacks:

- HTML – The HTML represents the structure of the user interface page. This is the main area where merge fields are inserted by the server-side code.

TABLE IV. XSS ENCODING DEFENCES BY PLATFORM

Encoding Defense	Salesforce	Zoho	SugarCRM	SuiteCRM	vTiger	Heroku
Automatic HTML	✓	✓				
Disable Automatic	✓					
Programmable HTML	✓		✓	✓	✓	
Programmable JavaScript	✓					

- CSS – The CSS represents the style of the user interface page. It is infrequent that merge fields are inserted into the CSS, but it is possible and often an overlooked vulnerability.
- JavaScript – The JavaScript represent the client-side executable code. Again, it is infrequent that merge fields are inserted into the JavaScript, but it is also possible and also an overlooked vulnerability.

The defense for the XSS vulnerabilities in all three contexts is to encode the merge field so that malicious code is not executed. This follows the standard security mantra of "trust no-one." Do not trust parameters from the operator, do not trust data from the data store and do not trust variables from the session state. TABLE IV shows a comparison of the XSS encoding defenses provided by the platforms analyzed in our study. The first row of the table is for platforms that will allow all HTML to be encoded automatically. This is probably the best solution as it is not left to the programmer to remember not to trust the users. Unfortunately, sometimes the programmer needs to deal with the data directly, and automatic encoding causes issues. The second row from TABLE IV shows the platforms that allow the automatic encoding to be turned off on individual forms. The last two rows of TABLE IV show the programmatic functionality provided by the platform to the programmer. Programmable HTML encoding is a function in the library the developer must call and use the sanitized results returned from the function. Programmable JavaScript encoding is a function in the library the developer must call whenever a merge field is assigned to a JavaScript variable. This ensures that the malicious user did not inject additional JavaScript after the variable value.

The vulnerability with SQL injection stems from the developer programmatically building up of a SQL command by concatenating strings. The merge fields are typical values inserted between single quotes in the string. The platform defenses for the SQL injection attempt to sanitize the values appended to the string command. TABLE V shows the SQL injection defenses provided by the platforms in our study. The first defense in the study allows the programmer to encode the single quotes so that the merge field cannot turn a single value into a second command. The second defense in

TABLE V. SQL INJECTION DEFENCES BY PLATFORM

Defense	Salesforce	Zoho	SugarCRM	SuiteCRM	vTiger	Heroku
Single Quote Encoding	✓		✓	✓	✓	
Bind Variables	✓	✓				
No Command Execution	✓	✓				✓
No Modifiable Statements	✓					

TABLE V is a method that allows the merge field to be bound to a specific data type. This second method provides greater flexibility and protection. The last two defenses included in TABLE V stem from the legacy of the data store. If the data store is a traditional relational database in the cloud, there are vulnerabilities carried forward to the cloud. New solutions for cloud applications can protect against these vulnerabilities. Traditional relational databases allowed command execution on the server through the database engine. At implementation time, all databases could have this feature turned off, but the "No Command Execution" defense means the cloud provider removed this vulnerability. The final defense in TABLE V is if the cloud provider only provides an object-relational management (ORM) interface for data manipulation. This protects the systems by not allowing SQL injection attacks to modify the date.

C. *Platform Redirection Vulnerabilities and Defence*

Applications built in the cloud often follow a model-view-controller (MVC) design pattern. MVC allows your application to separate the user interface, the data that is persisted in the data store and the flow control of the application. We have already discussed security vulnerabilities in the user interface and the data store. With cloud architectures, an application's controller will often base the navigation in the application on a merge field from the user's request, session state or a database value. As seen with the user interface and database vulnerabilities, this can lead to problems.

In the best-case scenario, a malicious user can use the open redirect to open a page with a movie or cartoon on it. In the worst case, the malicious user can open a page that has an XSS or CSRF attack on it. There are three major defenses for open redirect attacks:

- Hardcode the URL – This defense limits the flexibility of the application by insisting that the programmer hardcode every URL in the controller.
- Local Only – This defense limits the flexibility by only allowing redirects to the same host and application.
- Whitelist – This defense requires the organization to build a list of acceptable URLs to redirect to.

TABLE VI. REDIRECT DEFENCES BY PLATFORM

Defense	Salesforce	Zoho	SugarCRM	SuiteCRM	vTiger	Heroku
Hardcoded flow		✓				
Local Only						
Whitelist						

Unfortunately, TABLE V shows the limited platform support for these three defenses. Only the Zoho CRM has any support, and it is because there is no programmatic access on the server side. With the Zoho CRM, custom objects follow the same flow for inserts, saves, deletes and cancellation. This lack of support leaves the programmers to implement the architecture strategy chosen for the product. Platform providers could make this easier by implementing a platform URL whitelist per application or by limiting the location for the redirects to local URLs only.

D. *Platform Forgery Vulnerabilities and Defence*

Modern web browsers allow the end user to have many tabs open in a single web-browser with cookies shared among browser tabs. This leads to a vulnerability called CSRF. As an example, imagine we have logged into a bank portal in one tab of my web browser. Typically, a website will write a cookie to identify the session on the server so future requests from my web-browser will not need to authenticate myself. If a malicious piece of code is running in another tab on the same browser, it can send a request to the bank website using the same cookie and gain access to my financial data. This example tries to make it clear that malicious code can gain access to data that should not be available to the malicious user, and CSRF allows the malicious user access to do just this. There are many less nefarious examples where the CSRF is attacking the same application and gaining access to or modifying data, not on the current user interface. Figure 1 shows a sequence diagram where malicious code gains access to an application called yourapp.com. In the scenario, a valid operator named Fred opens a web-browser tab to visit a

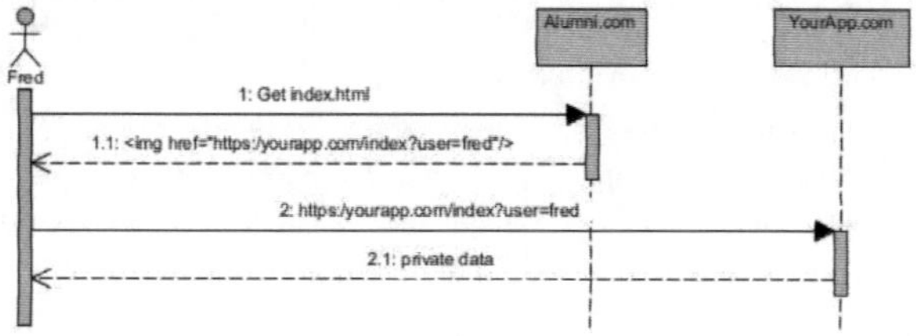

Figure 1.CSRF Attack

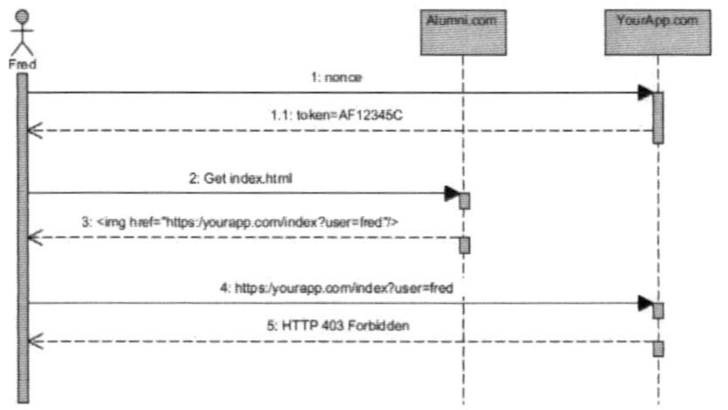

Figure 2.CSRF Defense

website named alumni.com. Alumni.com has an XSS injection where an image has a CSRF attack in the link for the image. When Fred clicks on the image, the malicious code uses his validated credentials on yourapp.com to gain access to private data.

There are two main defenses against CSRF, and both of the defenses require server-side validation of the request, allowing an even stronger defense.

- Server Side CSFR Tokens – In this defense the server generates a token per response. If the token is not returned with the follow-up request, then the request is considered a forgery and rejected.
- Refer Check – A standard header in the HTTP protocol is the REFER value. The refer value gives the URL of the page where the current request came from.

In Figure 2 we see a sequence diagram that modifies the earlier scenario to include a server-side CSFR token. The original request returns a token that needs to be included in the follow-up request. Typically, this is a hidden form field, so when the form has submitted the value of the tag is included in the HTTP post. If the HTML form code is returned by the server in one tab and the user toggles to another tab to visit another website, this tab will not have access to the one-time token.

TABLE VII shows the two types of CSRF defenses as implemented by the different platforms. As we saw with the open re-direct defenses, much more work can be done by the PaaS providers to make it easier for the application developers to focus on the business problem they are trying to solve. None of the providers apply both protections which would increase the protections for the applications with little work on the developer.

TABLE VII. CSRF DEFENCES BY PLATFORM

Defense	Salesforce	Zoho	SugarCRM	SuiteCRM	vTiger	Heroku
Server Side CSFR Tokens	✓	✓	✓			
Refer Check						

E. Platform Clickjacking Vulnerabilities and Defence

Clickjacking is an application vulnerability used by attackers to fool valid users into thinking that they are interacting with one object while they are actually interacting with a different object altogether. In a clickjacking-injected user interface, the malicious user shows content to the user while another form is on top of the content with a transparent layer. When interacting with the clickjacking user interface, the operators think they are clicking buttons corresponding to the bottom layer, while in reality, they are interacting with buttons on the hidden form on top. There are two common attacks that utilize clickjacking:

- Cursorjacking – This attack tricks operators into enabling the webcam and microphone on their machine through the Flash runtime engine.
- Lifejacking – This attack involves sharing or liking links on Facebook.

A common defense used to prevent clickjacking is called frame-busting. Frame-busting code is included on every page that stops a malicious user from loading your application in an iFrame. If the code detects the page is loaded in a frame, it will prevent the page from loading.

Another clickjacking defense is to use a relatively new HTTP header called X-FRAME-OPTIONS. This header is supported in all the latest web-browser version. The header defends the page in a similar way to the frame-busting code. The X-FRAME-OPTIONS header can be set to one of three values:

- DENY – This value does not allow the page from loading in a frame.
- SAMEORIGIN – This value allows the page to load in a frame only if the origin is the same as the content.
- ALLOW-FROM – This value allows the page to load in a frame only from a specific URL.

TABLE VIII shows the clickjacking defenses by each of the PaaS providers in our study. As we have seen with the past few attack defenses, the service providers have a long way to go to defend the platforms properly.

TABLE VIII. CLICKJACKING DEFENCES BY PLATFORM

Defense	Salesforce	Zoho	SugarCRM	SuiteCRM	vTiger	Heroku
Frame-busting	✓					
X-FRAME-OPTION	✓					

VIII. CONCLUSION

In this paper, we analyzed the programming effort required to reproduce services provided by a cloud PaaS provider. Our solution utilizes two methods to estimate the number of lines of code required for a service: SLOC and an execution trace. We utilize an average of the two methods to apply the COCOMO II costing algorithm. Our study demonstrates removing the need to develop the application services provided by the PaaS providers leads to a cost savings of nearly thirteen million dollars.

We also looked at non-functional services provided by the platform. In some cases, the platforms provided significant non-functional services; but in other cases, the platforms could do a much better job of providing the necessary protection.

In this research, we focused on application services provided by a PaaS, and future work needs to study the infrastructure services costs and the application development knowledge required to leverage the provided distribution services.

IX. ACKNOWLEDGEMENTS

We would also like to thank Kaitlyn Fulford who assisted on the earlier work this research has built upon.

REFERENCES

[1] A. Olmsted, "Platform As A Service Effort Reduction," in *CLOUD COMPUTING 2017 : The Eighth International Conference on Cloud Computing, GRIDs, and Virtualization*, Athens, Greece, 2017.

[2] Google, "About Google Docs," 2017. [Online]. Available: https://www.google.com/docs/about/. [Accessed 10 Feb. 2017].

[3] Microsoft, "Office products," 2017. [Online]. Available: https://products.office.com/en-us/products. [Accessed 10 Feb. 2017].

[4] Amazon Web Services, Inc, "Amazon Elastic Compute Cloud - Virtual Server Hosting," 2017. [Online]. Available: https://aws.amazon.com/ec2/. [Accessed 10 Feb. 2017].

[5] Rackspace, "Rackspace.com - Rackspace® Managed Cloud," 2017. [Online]. Available: https://www.rackspace.com/. [Accessed 10 Feb. 2017].

[6] P. Mell and P. Grance, "The NIST Definition of Cloud," 09 2011. [Online]. Available: http://nvlpubs.nist.gov/nistpubs/Legacy/SP/nistspecialpublication800-145.pdf. [Accessed 07 Sep. 2016].

[7] S. Kolb and G. Wirtz, "Portability in Platform as a Service," in *2014 IEEE 8th International Symposium on Service Oriented System Engineering*, Oxford, United Kingdom, 2014.

[8] N. Baliyan and S. Kumar, "Towards Software Engineering Paradigm for," in *2014 Seventh International Conference on Contemporary Computing*, Noida, India, 2014.

[9] J. Ng, "Extending the Cloud From an App Development Platform into a Tasking Platform," in *2015 IEEE World Congress on Services*, New York, NY, 2015.

[10] B. Boehm, B. Clark, E. Horowitz, C. Westland, R. Madachy and R. Selby, "Cost models for future software life cycle processes: COCOMO 2.0," *Annals of Software Engineering*, vol. 1, no. 1, p. 57–94, 1995.

[11] M. Ray, "COCOMO II - Constructive Cost Model," 2016. [Online]. Available: http://csse.usc.edu/tools/COCOMOII.php. [Accessed 07 Sep. 2016].

[12] Oracle, "Oracle Database," 2017. [Online]. Available: https://www.oracle.com/database/index.html. [Accessed 10 Feb. 2017].

[13] Oracle, "MySQL Database," 2017. [Online]. Available: https://www.mysql.com/. [Accessed 10 Feb. 2017].

[14] Wikimedia Foundation, Inc, "NoSQL," 2017. [Online]. Available: https://en.wikipedia.org/wiki/NoSQL. [Accessed 10 Feb. 2017].

[15] Wikimedia Foundation, Inc, "Email spam," 2017. [Online]. Available: https://en.wikipedia.org/wiki/Email_spam. [Accessed 10 Feb. 2017].

[16] A. Olmsted and G. Santhanakrishnan, "Cloud Data Denormalization of Anonymous Transactions," in *Cloud Computing*, Rome, Italy, 2016.

[17] Salesforce.com, inc, "Run your business better with Force.," 2006. [Online]. Available: http://www.salesforce.com/platform/products/force/?d=70130000000f27V&internal=true. [Accessed 03 Feb. 2016].

[18] Zoho Corporation Pvt. Ltd, "Zoho CRM is ready," 2016. [Online]. Available: https://www.zoho.com/crm. [Accessed 07 Sep. 2016].

[19] SugarCRM, "Discover a different kind of CRM," 2016. [Online]. Available: http://www.sugarcrm.com/. [Accessed 07 Sep. 2016].

[20] SalesAgility, "SuiteCRM – CRM for the world," 2016. [Online]. Available: https://suitecrm.com/. [Accessed 07 Sep. 2016].

[21] vTiger, "Grow sales, improve marketing ROI, and deliver great customer service," 2016. [Online]. Available: https://www.vtiger.com/. [Accessed 07 Sep. 2016].

[22] Salesforce, "Cloud Application Platform," 2016. [Online]. Available: https://www.heroku.com/. [Accessed 07 Feb. 2016].

[23] The PHP Group, "About PHP," 2017. [Online]. Available: http://php.net/. [Accessed 10 Feb. 2017].

[24] D. Rethans, "Xdebug - Debugger and Profiler Tool for PHP," 2016. [Online]. Available: www.xdebug.org. [Accessed 07 Sep. 2016].

[25] Bureau of Labor Statisics, "Occupational Employment Statistics," 2016. [Online]. Available: http://www.bls.gov/oes/current/oes_16700.htm. [Accessed 07 Sep. 2016].

[26] J. Hadzima, "How Much Does An Employee Cost?," [Online]. Available: http://web.mit.edu/e-club/hadzima/how-much-does-an-employee-cost.html. [Accessed 07 Sep. 2016].

[27] R. Madachy, "COCOMO II - Constructive Cost Model," [Online]. Available: http://csse.usc.edu/tools/COCOMOII.php. [Accessed 10 Feb. 2017].

[28] T. Mullaney, "Obama adviser: Demand overwhelmed HealthCare.gov," The USA Today, 5 Oct 2013. [Online]. Available: https://www.usatoday.com/story/news/nation/2013/10/05/health-care-website-repairs/2927597/. [Accessed 10 May 2017].

Why We Need Static Analyses of Service Compositions

Fault vs. Error Analysis of Soundness

Thomas M. Prinz and Wolfram Amme
Course Evaluation Service and Chair of Software Technology
Friedrich Schiller University Jena
Jena, Germany
e-mail: {Thomas.Prinz, Wolfram.Amme}@uni-jena.de

***Abstract*—The programming of classic software systems is well-supported by integrated development environments. They are able to give immediate information about syntax and some logic failures. Although service compositions are widely used within modern systems, such a support for building service compositions is expandable. In this paper, we plead for the creation of an integrated development environment for service compositions, which enables immediate failure feedback during the development. To this end, there is a need for new research activities on occurring failures and how they can be found. Since most current failure finding techniques are based on dynamic approaches, e. g., state space exploration, we show in a case study on soundness that the application of dynamic techniques is not a suitable solution for integrated development environments. In most cases, they are either too time consuming or their output does not lead easily to the root of a failure. As a result, we suggest new advanced (static) analyses of service compositions. To accentuate that pleading, the paper demonstrates a static analysis tool, *Mojo*, which can be used to check soundness and to get detailed fault diagnostics. With the help of this tool, it was possible to compare the behaviour of dynamic and static analysis techniques in a practical context. For this, a benchmark of real world service compositions was checked regarding soundness with a state space-based (dynamic) and a compiler-based (static) tool. Altogether, the case study and the comparison in a practical context show that dynamic analyses are not suitable for development support. Static analyses should be used instead.**

Keywords–Service Composition; Analysis; Case Study; Mojo; Soundness.

I. Introduction

The development of *service compositions* (aka *work-flows*) is an error-prone task just like the development of software systems. For example, only approx. 46 % of compositions of a real world benchmark have a comprehensible behaviour, as will be shown later in this paper. Whereas integrated development environments (IDEs) exist for the development of software systems, the tool support for the development of service composition is expandable at this time. That is surprising since there is a substantial common ground between both: There is data information passed through variables and there is a flow graph, which represents the structure. However, most tools for service compositions cover only their modelling and execution. They do *not* support the creation of *correct* compositions.

As an example, Figure 1 shows a service composition (taken from the conference version of this paper [1]). The composition handles the logic during the execution of a survey and follows the notation and semantics of the *Business Process Model and Notation* (BPMN) [2]. Typically, the execution begins at the *start node*. Then, the execution reaches a *task/service node*, which loads the survey at first. After the task node, the execution reaches a *fork node*. A fork node produces parallelism so that all outgoing edges are followed by a *control flow*.

One control flow of the fork node follows the lower edge to a further service, which handles the inputs of the survey. Subsequently, it reaches a *join node*, which synchronizes parallel control flows. Since another control flow has not reached the other incoming edge of the join node yet, the current flow has to wait.

The other control flow produced by the fork follows the upper outgoing edge. It loads the current page and reaches a *merge node*. A merge node combines sequential control flows. After the merge is executed, the flow arrives at a *split node*. The split node decides, which outgoing edge the flow follows. Either the flow goes to the upper edge and loads the next page, or it executes the task node at the right hand side and loads the previous page of the survey. If the previous page is loaded, the flow reaches another merge node, which guides the flow to a node visited previously. Therefore, the composition contains a cycle.

If the split node decides to load the next page, then the flow arrives a further split node. It decides whether the survey is finished or not. If the survey is finished, the control flow reaches the join node like the other flow before. Now, the join node can be executed and a conclusion will be shown. Eventually, the survey is finished when it reaches the *end node*.

As mentioned, we expected a wide development support during the creation of the composition of Figure 1 since the research on service-oriented architectures has passed its 20th anniversary. However, it is hard to find tools that give immediate development support. For this missing support, there are two possibilities, which exclude each other: Either there is some research, which seriously supports the development, but it is not used in the tools. Or, there is no such research and, therefore, the tools need qualified research results for that support.

We found some research approaches to *verify* service

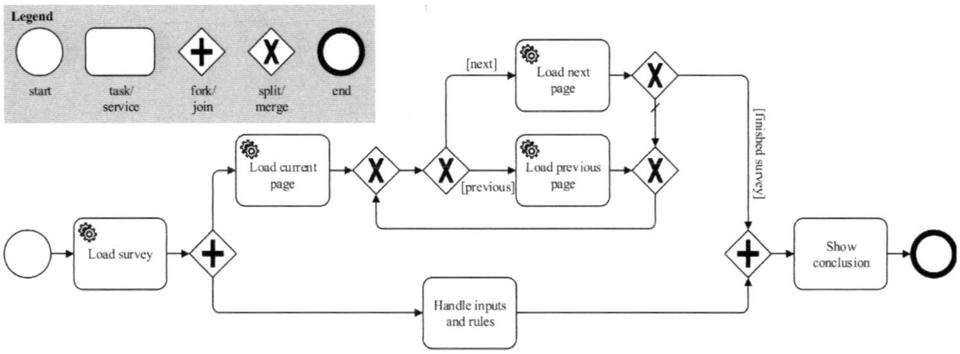

Figure 1. A service composition, which handles the logic of the execution of a survey.

compositions in form of business processes in the literature. A large number of those approaches concentrate on the verification of the *soundness* property [3] requiring that a service composition cannot run into *deadlocks* or in undesired double executions of services (*lacks of synchronization*). Since the soundness property is defined on the runtime behaviour of the composition, most algorithms search for undesired behaviour in a simulation. That means, they regard the *state space* of the composition, whereas the state space defines all possible reachable states.

State space-based algorithms perform *dynamic* analyses of service compositions since each found error can actually appear at runtime. However, as each error is a malformed reachable state, which has a *cause* within the service composition, finding exactly that cause given a specific error is a hard task.

Imagine, a developer extends the composition of Figure 1 to the one of Figure 2, i. e., the developer adds a new service, which delivers additional information (e. g., when the survey was started). The developer does it in a composition tool with a state space-based algorithm. After performing the algorithm, an error message is displayed and the tool visualizes the malformed state — a deadlock — directly into the composition (cf. Figure 2, illustrated by the black dots, *tokens*, which represents the control flows). As the tool does provide the *error* only and *not its cause* (the *fault*), the developer has to search the cause of the deadlock. However, there is not a classic cause of that deadlock since it happens because of a possible previous lack of synchronization, i. e., the double execution of the same nodes (illustrated by grey dots in the figure). If the composition contains additional nodes and becomes complexer, it be harder to detect the cause of that error in the composition. It seems that dynamic approaches are too imprecise and time consuming to support the development of service compositions seriously.

In this paper, we will demonstrate that problem in a case study on soundness with dynamic analyses relating to classical software testing terms. Furthermore, we will accentuate that problem by a direct comparison of dynamic and static analysis techniques in the field of user support. As a case example for a dynamic analysis technique, state space exploration is used throughout the paper. For static analyses, our own proposals for checking soundness are used. They search for faults of deadlocks and lacks of synchronization instead of errors [4][5][6][7]. We refer to our techniques as *fault finding*. The comparison is done in a practical application of both techniques in form of the tools *LoLA* (state space exploration) and our analysis tool *Mojo* (fault finding).

As the result of this paper, it can be shown why it is better to use static analysis techniques for tool support during development instead of dynamic analyses. As a consequence, we plead for more research of static analyses for service composition.

This paper is structured as follows: At first, it introduces the field of verifying service compositions by taking a look on the state of the art (see Section II). Afterwards, a more formal and language independent model for service compositions will be explained — the *workflow graphs* (see Section III). Subsequently, in Section IV, it shows within a case study on soundness that dynamic analysis approaches are not suitable to give profitable tool support. Based on this case study, further practical considerations are done in Section V by a direct comparison of a dynamic and a static approach. Eventually, this paper closes with a summary in Section VI, which will support the notion that it is important to use static analyses instead of dynamic ones during composition development. Furthermore, it shows possible future work.

II. State of the Art

The *soundness* analysis of service compositions, especially in the case of *workflows* and *processes*, has a long tradition. It appears firstly in the work of van der Aalst [3] in the year 1995. To this day, several different notions of soundness were introduced. The interested reader can find them in Puhlmann [8] and van der Aalst et al. [9].

In this paper, we have chosen the classic notion of soundness. There are several approaches, which try to classify whether a workflow is sound or not. The first known algorithm was introduced by van der Aalst [3]. It is based on the rank theorem [10], which can be solved in cubic time complexity regarding the size of the workflow graph

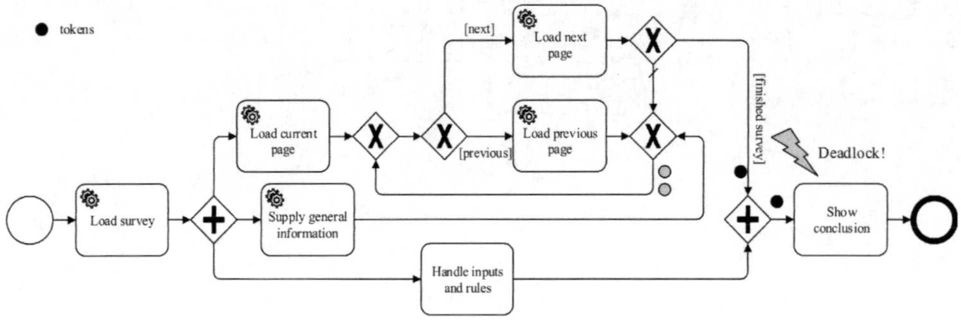

Figure 2. A malformed service composition of the service of Figure 1.

[11]. However, this approach does not give any diagnostic information, *where* or *why* the workflow graph is unsound [12]. For this reason, other approaches were developed, which we classify into three main approaches: (1) Model checking, (2) graph decomposition, and (3) pattern and compiler-based approaches.

A. Model Checking

The dominating approach in workflow verification is *state space exploration* [13]. In state space exploration, each possible execution step of a workflow will be considered (the state space). If during the consideration there is an execution step, which contains an error, the analysis will be stopped and the erroneous state inclusive a so-called *trace* will be returned. The analysis will be stopped since some (even small) workflows have a very large (sometimes arbitrary large) state space and a complete examination of the state space would take too much time or will not end. This fact is called the state space explosion problem [14]. To counteract this problem, arbitrary growing states are replaced with a neutral element. The resulting state space is called *Coverability Tree* [15], but its size is still exponential large with regard to the entire workflow.

Therefore, Lohmann and Fahland refined the state space approach by performing some graph reductions [16]. They also tried to explain why errors happen in processes, however, there work never reached a final state and there are still open issues unfortunately.

Finished graph reduction techniques, which consider the state space of processes too, are used by the tools Woflan [17] and LoLA [18]. The *Low Level Petri Net Analyzer* (LoLA) serves as general model checking tool for Petri nets. It performs graph reduction techniques and state space exploration. The verification property to prove (e. g., soundness) must be given as formal equation. Then, LoLA checks whether each state in the state space fits to the propery.

Woflan seems to be the most complete analysis tool for workflows and is based on workflow nets and state space exploration. Besides soundness it checks other quality criteria. This is done by reducing the entire workflow iteratively. If the result of this reduction is trivial, the workflow is sound. Otherwise, Woflan decides with the *S-coverability* [10] whether it can give diagnostic information or not. If the workflow is not S-coverable, it is unsound, however, it is unknown whether there is a deadlock or a lack of synchronization. If the workflow is S-coverable, a state space exploration has to check the soundness property. That results in an exponential runtime of Woflan.

Besides state space exploration there are other model checking approaches to check soundness for workflows. Sadiq and Orlowska have introduced the *instance graphs*, which are subgraphs and represent possible execution traces [19]. Eshuis and Kumar use this approach to find erroneous instance graphs with integer programming [20]. That gives enough diagnostic information to repair a workflow. However, the workflows have to be acyclic and the integer program has an exponential worst-case runtime.

B. Graph Decomposition

Since model checking techniques have their limits in performance and failure diagnostic, other approaches were considered. A prominent approach is the decomposition of the workflow into smaller subgraphs. Chrząstowski-Wachtel et al. use this approach and offer a new concept of representing workflows at the same time: The representation as a tree [21]. They propose to construct a workflow starting by the root and adding child nodes iteratively. Then, the workflow is sound by construction. However, such a structured construction of workflows is not used in practice since most workflows should represent unstructured service compositions or real-world business processes.

The derivation of a tree structure starting by an unstructured workflow was done by Vanhatalo et al. [22][23]. They split the entire workflow into fragments (subgraphs) with one ingoing and one outgoing edge — a *Single-Entry-Single-Exit* (SESE) fragment. Since this splitting into SESE fragments results in a hierarchy of fragments, they can be visualized as a tree: The *Process Structure Tree* (PST). Each fragment can be analysed separately by replacing subfragments with a single edge. Simple fragments are analysed by performing some rules and heuristics. Complex fragments cannot be handled, however, alternative soundness approaches can be applied. That approach reduces the size of the graphs to consider, allows the finding of one error per fragment, and has a linear asymptotic runtime [24]. But it is incomplete regarding soundness.

C. Pattern and Compiler-based Approaches

Actually, SESE decomposition is a compiler-based approach since it considers the workflow without simulation and it was already applied for compilers by Johnson et al. [25][26]. Besides typical compiler approaches, there is a growing number of approaches considering *patterns* in the last years.

Dongens et al. began with pattern approaches by defining two relations called *causal foot prints* [27]. On the base of this foot prints, they find three (anti) patterns for deadlocks and lacks of synchronization. However, it is not sure that an anti pattern means that the workflow is really unsound.

Another pattern-based approach was introduced by Favre and Völzer [12]. They define two relations for deadlocks and lacks of synchronization too. With a kind of dataflow analysis, the information needed by the relations are propagated through the workflow. The approach results in good diagnostic information and has a polynomial asymptotic runtime. However, the pattern approach only works for acyclic workflows.

Based on anti-patterns, Favre et al. proposed another approach [28][29]. The used anti-patterns are similar to those of Dongens et al. and can be applied to workflows with cycles. If a workflow contains such an anti-pattern, then the workflow is unsound. In the case of incorrectness, additional analyses are started to supply diagnostic information. The diagnostic information are very good, but the runtime behaviour is quintic and it is only possible to detect one error at once.

We proposed a compiler-based approach in [4][5][6][7]. Instead of considering the errors of deadlocks and lacks of synchronization, we investigated their faults by starting our analyses from different entry points of the workflow — a partial analysis. This makes it possible to detect *potential* errors behind others. Based on this partial analysis, we introduced two new techniques: One for detecting faults of deadlocks and a second for detecting faults of lacks of synchronization.

For deadlocks, we observed that in sound workflows, a node never jams obviously. It never jams since its execution is guaranteed every moment, the execution reaches it. We figured out that a node never has a deadlock when on each path to this node another node guarantees its execution. Otherwise, there is the potential for a deadlock.

Our second technique considers faults of lacks of synchronization. At first, we observed that parallelism must occur before the manifestation of a lack of synchronization obviously. Each of the parallel control flows can meet each other first, where two paths starting from the start of the parallelism meet at first. We call them *meeting points*. If all meeting points are synchronization nodes (join nodes), we cannot run into a lack of synchronization. Otherwise, there is a potential for a lack of synchronization.

Both techniques have in common that they are complete regarding soundness. Furthermore, they find the causes of deadlocks and lacks of synchronization in a bi-quadratic asymptotic runtime (depending on the number of edges in the workflow). As result, exact diagnostic information are provided and it is possible to detect faults behind faults.

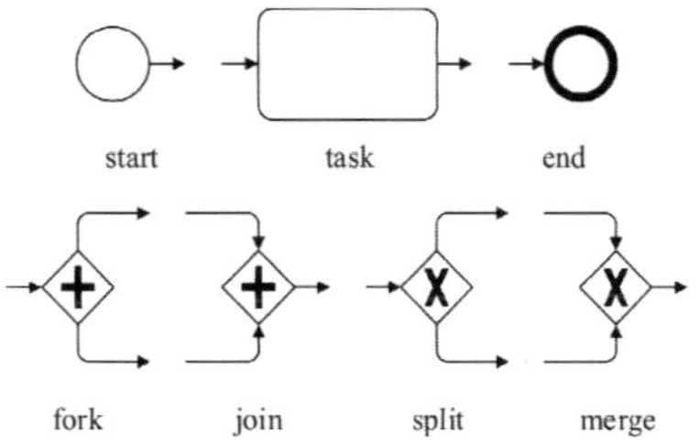

Figure 3. Notations for start, end, task, fork, join, split, and merge nodes.

At this time, we believe that our approach is the best one helping to build sound service compositions.

III. Preliminaries

There are different languages and notations to describe service compositions and business processes. Popular examples of those languages are BPMN [2], the *Business Process Execution Language* (BPEL) [30], and the *Yet Another Workflow Language* (YAWL) [31]. In research, however, the general concepts of those composition languages are simplified to describe service compositions in a language independent way. For this purpose, two notions are used: The *workflow nets* introduced by van der Aalst [3][13] and the *workflow graphs* of Sadiq and Orlowska [19]. Whereas the former uses the notions of Petri nets [32], the latter are similar to control flow graphs of the theory of compiler construction. Since we believe that workflow graphs are easier to understand and to illustrate, we use workflow graphs throughout this paper to represent service compositions.

In general, a workflow graph is a *directed graph* consisting of *nodes* and *edges*. Each of the workflow graph nodes is either a *task*, a *fork*, a *join*, a *split*, a *merge*, the unique *start*, or the unique *end* node; where all nodes of the same type have the same appearance and semantics, i. e., how they are executed. Rules define how the nodes are connected. They depend on the kind of node: The start node has no incoming but exactly one outgoing edge, whereas the end node has exactly one incoming but no outgoing edge. Each task node is reached and leaved by exactly one edge. A split and fork node has exactly one incoming edge and at least two outgoing edges. Merges and joins are reached by at least two incoming edges and can be leaved by one outgoing edge. For the visualization of workflow graphs, we use the same notations as the BPMN standard [2]. For this reason, start and end nodes are visualized as (thick) circles. Tasks are illustrated as simple rounded rectangles. Split and merge nodes are visualized by diamonds with crosses. Eventually, diamonds with pluses are used to illustrate fork and join nodes (cf. Figure 3).

The different visualizations mark the different semantics of the nodes. Usually (e.g., from Vanhatalo et al. [22]), the semantics of the nodes are described as a *token game* known from Petri net semantics [32]. In token games, the numbers of *tokens* on the edges are used to describe a single execution situation (a *state*). In each state there is a number

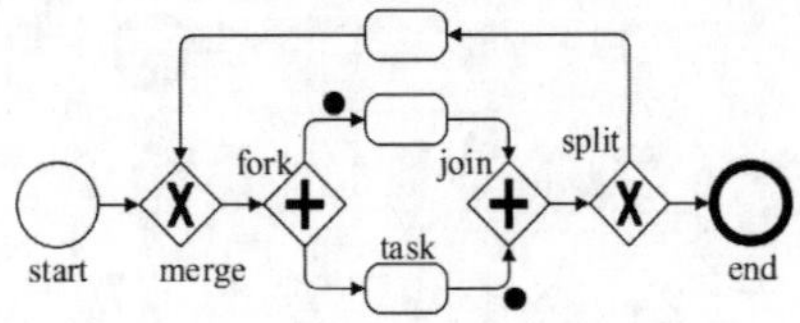

Figure 4. A simple workflow graph within an execution state.

of tokens assigned to each edge. There are two important states of workflow graphs: (1) The initial state and (2) the termination state. Within the initial state, only the single outgoing edge of the start node carries a token, whereas within the termination state only the single incoming edge of the end node carries a token. Throughout this paper, we use black dots on edges to illustrate tokens in a state. Figure 4 shows such a state of a simple workflow graph.

In each state (except the termination state), there should be some nodes, which are *executable*, i. e., their functionality can be performed. After the *execution* of a node, the state changes (a *state transition*). A sequence of state transitions is an execution sequence of the workflow graph and we can say, that the last state of the sequence is *reachable* by each other state of the sequence [22].

As mentioned before, whether a node is executable and what happens after the execution of this node is defined by its type. The start and end node have no special semantics. Therefore, they are only used to mark the start and end of a workflow graph. Each node, except a join node, is executable once there is at least one token on one of its incoming edges. A task node takes a token from its incoming edge and puts it back to its outgoing edge. Split and merge nodes perform non-deterministic choices instead: Split nodes take a token from their incoming edge and put a single token to one of their randomly chosen outgoing edges; whereas merge nodes take one token from one randomly chosen incoming edge (with a token) and put a token to their outgoing edge. Eventually, fork and join nodes handle parallelism. Fork nodes take a token from their incoming edge and put a token on each outgoing edge. However, join nodes are only executable if each of their incoming edges has at least one token. If a join node is executed, a token is removed from each incoming edge and a single new token is placed on its outgoing edge. Figure 5 summarizes the execution semantics.

As explained in the introduction of this paper, we consider the notion *soundness* [3][19] as correctness criterion of service compositions. A workflow graph is called *sound* if neither a *deadlock* nor a *lack of synchronization* is reachable from the initial state. A *deadlock* is a non-termination state, in which no node is executable. A *lack of synchronization* is a state in which at least one edge carries more than one token.

Figure 6 shows a typical and simplified deadlock state. The join node in the figure (the right node with the plus) will never be executed since it needs another token on its lower incoming edge. A typical lack of synchronization is

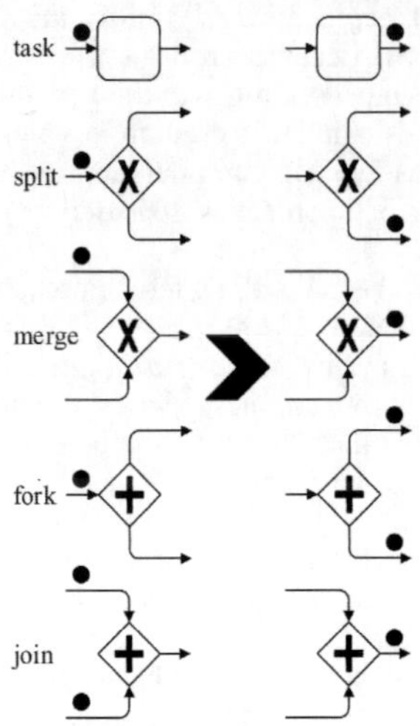

Figure 5. The execution of the different kind of nodes.

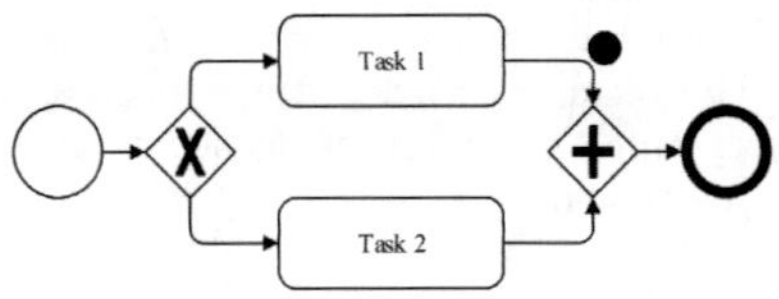

Figure 6. A deadlock.

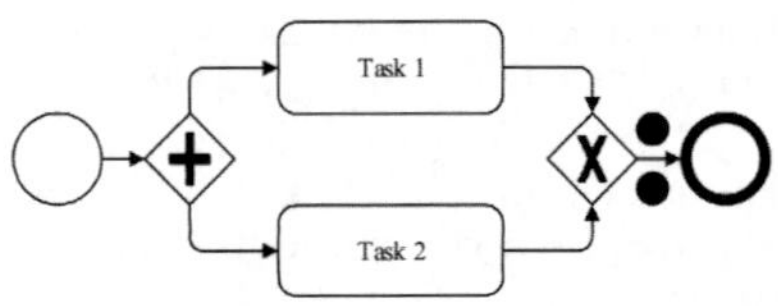

Figure 7. A lack of synchronization.

illustrated in Figure 7. The outgoing edge of the merge node carries two tokens. This is possible since both tokens produced by the left fork node will never by synchronized.

IV. Consideration of Dynamic Analyses for Workflow Development

If an execution of a workflow graph results in a deadlock or lack of synchronization, the graph's behaviour is not well defined and comprehensible. So, it is beneficial to know whether a workflow graph is sound or not. This can be easily answered by the usage of dynamic analysis techniques like state space exploration.

State space exploration dominates the literature in process verification up to the present date. It indicates whether the workflow graph is sound. Furthermore, the developer gets a *failure trace*, or more precisely, a path within the state space from the initial to the erroneous state.

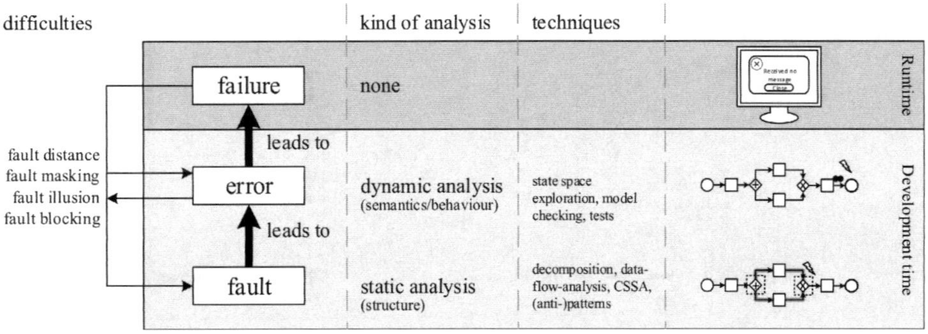

Figure 8. Overview of the connections between failures, errors, and faults.

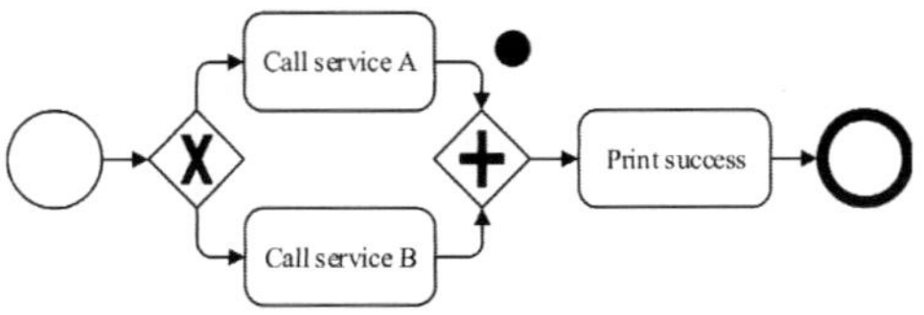

Figure 9. The success message is never printed leading to a failure.

The strength of such dynamic analyses are that new correctness criteria can be defined and checked easily. This makes it possible to use the same dynamic analysis technique for different verification problems and to add new analyses very fast. This is useful to guarantee the delivery of correct software products. However, as mentioned in the introduction, dynamic analysis techniques have their weaknesses during development time since they answering rarely, *why* a workflow graph runs into a deadlock and a lack of synchronization. But a developer needs to know, *why* some wrong behaviours happen to repair and to avoid them.

In the following, we reinforce these weaknesses by showing that dynamic analysis techniques lead to a time expensive and hard troubleshooting when we try to identify the causes of wrong workflow graph behaviours. For this, we consider a case study on dynamic analyses regarding typical *terms of software testing* (taken from [33]). We use this vocabulary since we talk about the development of workflows like software. Furthermore, these terms make it possible to evaluate the located errors and how they can be used for troubleshooting. In addition, the following comparisons motivate the usage of service composition specific static analyses. An overview of the terms and their interdependencies is illustrated in Figure 8.

A. Failures, Errors, and Faults

In software testing, there are different terms with different meanings for wrong execution states of a program. A state is called a *failure* if a user of the program sees an undesired behaviour or result [33]. For example, in the workflow graph in Figure 9, we see that the last task — the printing of the success message — will not be executed since the composition runs into a deadlock in the join node. Therefore, the user is informed by the missing success message that there is a failure.

Such a failure is the manifestation of an incorrect development of the composition. This manifestation is called an *error* [33]. For example, the process developer may know why the user does not see the success message, as the developer may identify that the execution blockades. The reason, *why* the execution blockades, is called a *fault*. A fault is the wrong human action during the development of the service composition [33].

Obviously, to repair an erroneous service composition, a developer has to know the fault instead of errors and failures. If the developer knows only the error or the failure, it has to derive the fault from the diagnostic information.

Considering the previous term definitions, each dynamic analysis technique always results in an error since it searches within the different execution possibilities of a workflow graph instead at the workflow graph itself. As a result, the developer has to derive the real fault after each dynamic analysis, to be able to repair the composition. However, this derivation of the fault is a difficult task since errors can be *masked* or *disguised*. Furthermore, the developer may underestimate the possible *distance* between the error and the fault, thus disregarding an origin early in the composition. All those different difficulties are considered in the following sub sections.

B. Fault Distance

The *distance* between a fault and its error is known as the passed time or passed program instructions until a fault results in an error [34]. The workflow graph in Figure 10 has some bigger subgraphs, which are folded as services D and E for reasons of lack of space. After the subgraph D is executed, the workflow graph will end in a deadlock state as the join on the right-hand side cannot be executed. Naturally, a developer would now search the corresponding fault near the error. Since a lot of time has passed and the workflow graph is complex owing to the subgraphs D and E, it is very difficult to identify the fault. A natural and simple correlation is that the difficulty of finding corresponding faults of errors grows with their distances.

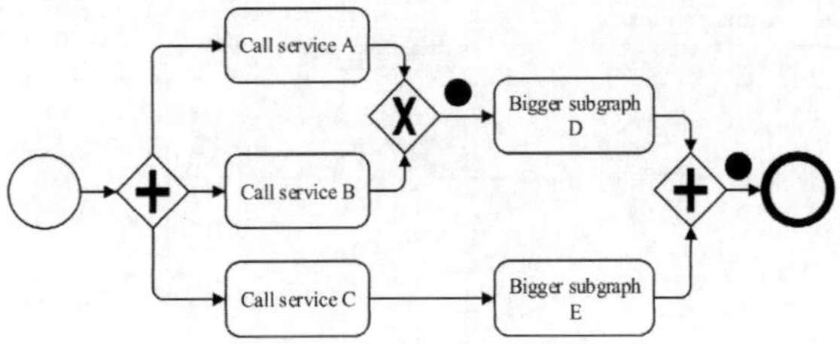

Figure 10. The distance between the fault and its error may be large.

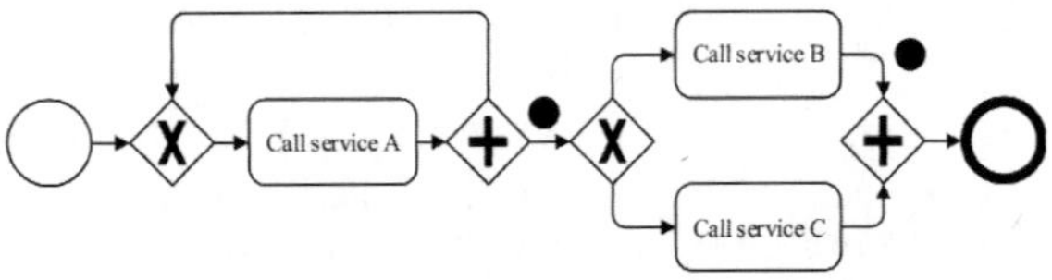

Figure 11. One fault masks another fault so that the failure may disappear.

C. Fault Masking

Fault masking is the situation, in which one fault prevents the detection of another fault [33]. This leads to much difficulty as the faults do not necessarily cause a visible failure. Furthermore, it may happen that one fault is repaired by another one.

An example of fault masking in the context of service compositions is illustrated in Figure 11. The first part of the workflow graph (the loop) results in a lack of synchronization, whereas the second part has an obvious deadlock. However, the first part produces an endless number of tokens so that the previous lack of synchronization always prevents the latter deadlock at runtime. A dynamic approach would now result in a lack of synchronization only — it is not able to detect the deadlock as it does not appear at runtime. To this end, the first fault has to be repaired *before* the deadlock appears within a dynamic approach. This makes the correction of a service composition more time expensive since a necessary analysis has to run for each error at least.

D. Fault Illusion

Fault illusion is not a classic term of software testing. We introduce it at this point, because such a situation is not accurately described by the existing terms. Figure 12 exemplifies this illusion with a workflow graph. Currently, that workflow graph is within a deadlock state since there is no node, which can be executed.

A dynamic analysis technique could provide this deadlock state. However, if the developer of the service composition takes a closer look at the workflow graph, it will not find a good fitting fault of the deadlock. This happens for the reason that the deadlock is caused by a lack of synchronization: The left-hand side fork node has two upper outgoing control flows that are not synchronized by a join node. Only a merge node combines both flows, which possibly results in a lack of synchronization on its outgoing

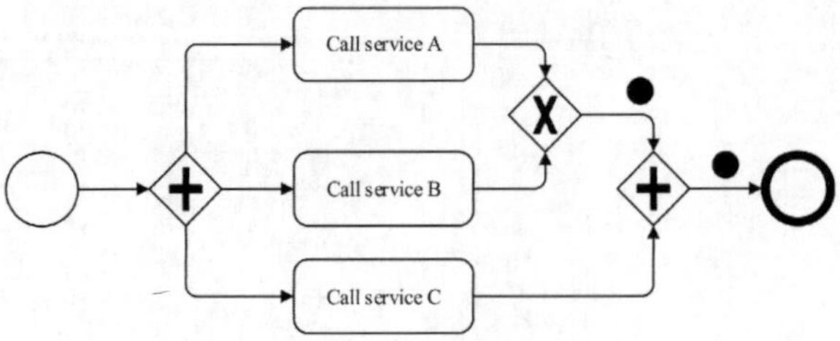

Figure 12. One error produces another error so that there is the illusion of a fault, which does not exists.

edge. Nevertheless, if, e. g., service A needs much more time than service B, the control flow of service B reaches the join node on the right-hand side before the control flow, which performs service A. Because of this, the join node can be executed before the lack of synchronization appears. Then, however, the workflow graph runs into a deadlock although there is the fault of a wrong control flow synchronization.

So, in short, a fault illusion is the appearance of an error although the faults of other errors cause it. The finding of such a fault illusion is a very hard task in big service compositions. In this context, dynamic analysis techniques are not suitable for fault identification.

E. Fault Blocking

Fault blocking is the condition, in which a fault blocks the further failure detection [35]. Since software testing aims at detecting the presence of errors only, *fault blocking* is not bad. However, when it is the goal to find as many errors as possible, fault blocking makes the fault detection time expensive since a necessary analysis has to run at least for each error (which can be an arbitrary large number, e.g., in the case of lacks of synchronization). It is easy to see that it is not possible to detect errors *after* a deadlock in dynamic approaches since there is no further reachable state. As a result, it is not possible to detect all *errors*, let alone *faults*, within a service composition with dynamic approaches.

Another difficulty of fault blocking is that one error may result in another error. This is linked to fault illusion. In Figure 13, we see a simple workflow graph, in which a split node causes (local) deadlocks in the upper and lower join nodes. However, as we can also see, the deadlock of the lower join node is caused by the deadlock of the upper one, i. e., if the upper join node would be a merge node, the deadlock of the lower join node disappears. Therefore, the deadlock of the lower join node is the result of the blocking of a control flow of the upper join node. Since a dynamic error finding approach like state space exploration may return the deadlock of the lower join node, it is hard to find its fault.

F. Discussion

In summary, dynamic approaches are dependable analyses considering soundness *verification* of workflows. They decide trusty whether a workflow is sound or not. However, the case study has shown their weaknesses as tool support for workflow developers seriously. The typical problems

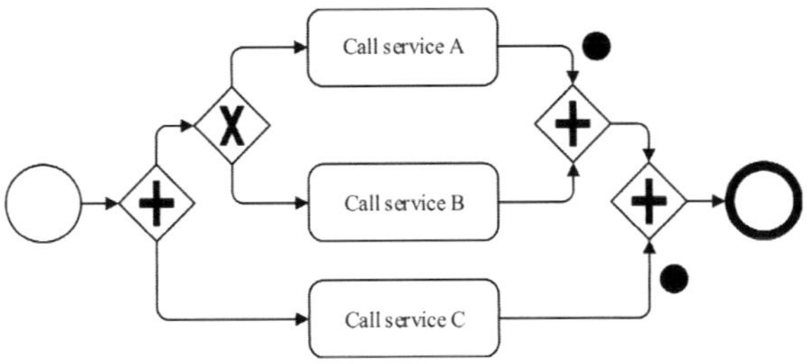

Figure 13. One error blocks another error.

of fault distance, blocking, masking, and illusion complicate the derivation of the fault knowing only the error significantly. They make dynamic approaches inefficient and imprecise. As a result of this case study, to support developers, other tools must be provided.

V. Direct Comparison of Dynamic and Static Analyses

The consideration of dynamic analyses during workflow development showed their weaknesses relating to support the developer seriously. To strengthen this result, we show in this section that problem-specific static analyses have advantages over more general *dynamic* ones. Since the argumentation in the last section is based on a *theoretic* consideration of dynamic approaches verifying soundness, we want to show that these theoretic considerations have relevance in practice. Therefore, we have developed a tool *Mojo*, which uses our static fault finding techniques. Since there are tools like *LoLA* [18] allowing dynamic soundness checks of service compositions, *Mojo* round off the palette of tools by a complete static approach. This makes it possible to compare dynamic and static approaches for soundness checking for the first time.

In this section, we introduce our tool *Mojo* at first. Afterwards, we use *Mojo* to compare static and dynamic analysis techniques.

A. *The Analyser* Mojo

Mojo is a research static analyser, which is freely available and can be downloaded on GitHub [36]. It allows the writing of own analyses, which can be applied as extensions to the system. Conceptionally, *Mojo* is part of our idea of a system for the development and execution of workflows [37], simplified illustrated in Figure 14. In the current state of build, it covers a part of the system's producer side.

On the *producer side* (the static analyser), the *parser* reads the service composition (alias workflow). During the reading, it checks the structure of the input. Afterwards, the *transformer* takes the syntactically correct workflow and transforms it into an intermediate representation (*IR*). *Mojo* uses the notion of workflow graphs as IR. The IR is an abstract format and hides special properties of the entire modelling language, e. g., of BPMN. The *Business Process Executation Language* (BPEL) is difficult to use as IR since it is a structured language whereas most workflows are unstructured.

After the creation of the IR, the composition is checked regarding some semantic properties. An example of such a semantic property is the introduced notion of soundness. If the *semantic analyser* finds faults, the system informs the developer such that the developer can repair the workflow. Otherwise, if the workflow is already correct, it will be encoded and stored within a file or workflow repository.

Besides the producer side, the system even consists of a *consumer side*. The consumer side is a virtual machine. It reads a composition from a file or repository and rebuilds the IR. Furthermore, the *verifier* checks the IR regarding its semantics. This revised check of semantics is necessary to exclude the possibility of manipulations on the IR. With the help of *annotations*, the check can be sped up significantly. In conclusion, the virtual machine executes the workflow and does some runtime analyses in some cases.

Detailed information about our whole system of compiling and executing workflows are available in [37]. An overview about the static analyser and virtual machine can be found in preceding papers [38] and [6].

As mentioned before, the tool *Mojo* can be interpreted as a first version of the producer side of our proposed system. Since *Mojo* is not closed in its functionality and the implementation and testing of new analyses is time-consuming in the context of service compositions, *Mojo* was implemented with the concept of extensions. Extensions (or plugins) allow the easy integration of new analyses and can be used by other researchers without changing the core application. For this, it defines extension points as interfaces, which have to be used to write own plugins. At the moment, extension points for new input languages and new analyses are defined.

In *Mojo*, the order of the performed analyses are defined by *analysis plans*. An analysis plan structures the necessary stages to guarantee correct analyses. In some cases, such a stage can be a complex analysis plan again consisting of different stages. For that reason, *Mojo* follows a classic compiler architecture.

An overview about the current version of *Mojo* is illustrated in Figure 15. The input is possible via files in the languages *Petri Net Markup Language* (PNML) [39] and *BPMN* [2], or directly via programmatic defined workflow graphs. There exist two predefined plugins to enable the input languages PNML and BPMN. Each of these plugins consists of a parser and a transformer.

Afterwards, the resulted workflow graphs can be analysed using the analysis plans. Typical stages of such an analysis plan are a dominance and post dominance analysis [40][41] as well as the determination of the causes of deadlocks and lacks of synchronization. The analysis plan, which should be used, can be defined as a parameter of the tool. Since each analysis plan has a unique number, the precise selection of an analysis plan is easy.

The analysis plan with number 0 performs a soundness inspection with our fault finding techniques explained in previous work [4][5][7] and in Section II. Therefore, (1) Mojo uses a complete static analysis based on well-known compiler theory, (2) it is the first implementation of our soundness checking algorithms, and (3) it finds development

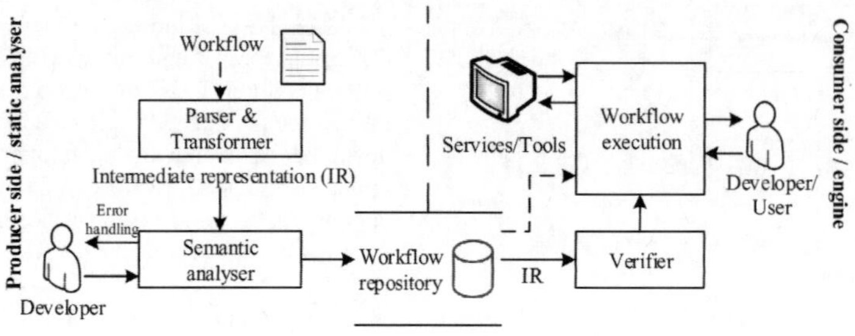

Figure 14. Overview of a system for the development and execution of workflows (taken and simplified from [37]).

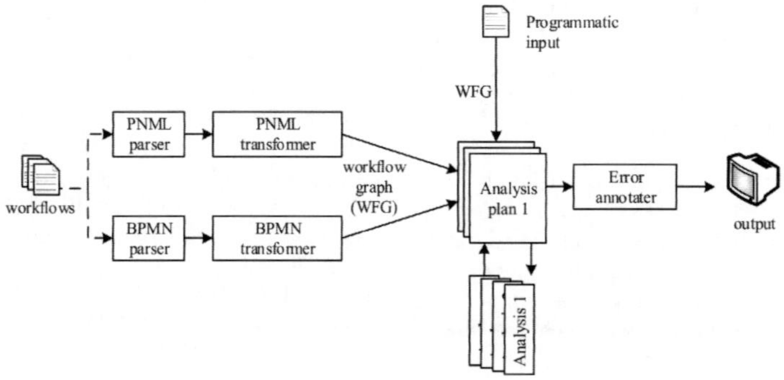

Figure 15. Structure of the static analyser *Mojo*.

faults instead of runtime errors. The found faults will be registered and annotated to the workflow graph. It is possible to get a textual fault output or to use a graphical visualization when *Mojo* is integrated in a workflow modelling tool. Such a tool is the *Activiti BPMN 2.0 Designer*[42], which we have modified to allow analyses with *Mojo*. Figure 16 shows the application of *Mojo* in *Activiti*.

In this application, *Mojo* performs analyses without a visible delay in each modification step of the workflow. Furthermore, the faults can be visited in two modes: (1) The overview mode and (2) the detailed mode. In the overview mode (1), all faults are visualized within the workflow with reduced information. Thus, it is possible to get an overview of the faults within the composition. In the detailed mode (2), the user selects a fault and gets all detailed diagnostic information. That visualizes the fault more precisely to the developer and it should be easier to repair the workflow.

B. Comparison

After the introduction of the tool *Mojo*, it is possible to practically compare the application of static and dynamic analysis approaches for soundness in service compositions. As a typical example of dynamic approaches, we use the state space exploration tool *LoLA*. For static analyses, our compiler-based tool *Mojo* is considered. Both tools were used to study how they perform for real-world service compositions. These service compositions were taken from a business process library [43].

Before we can consider the results of the study, the evaluation settings have to be explained at first. Afterwards, three examples of compositions from the library are considered in detail. For these three compositions, the dynamic approach leads to different results than a static approach in practice. Subsequently to this detailed consideration, we give an overview of the results and differences of static and dynamic analyses of all service compositions of the considered library. At the end, the evaluation shows that a detailed fault analysis has not to be expensive regarding the invested time.

1) Settings: For quantitative statements of evaluation, a large number of test cases is necessary to minimize the effect of irrelevant influencing factors. In the context of soundness checking of workflows, a library of real world business processes of the *IBM WebSphere Business Modeler*[44] is used. That library contains $1,368$ processes (i. e., workflows) and is separated into five benchmarks: A (282 workflows), $B1$ (288 workflows), $B2$ (363 workflows), $B3$ (421 workflows), and C (32 workflows). Thereby, the benchmarks $B1$ to $B3$ describe ongoing improved and developed workflows.

Originally, the library was provided by IBM Zurich. However, the official support was stopped. A more simple parsing and usage is possible in the standardized PNML format. PNML describes Petri nets in a simple syntax with transitions, places and arcs. The workflows are available in the context of the work of Fahland et al. [45][46], who compared different soundness checkers in year 2011. For our evaluation, we have used these PNML files.

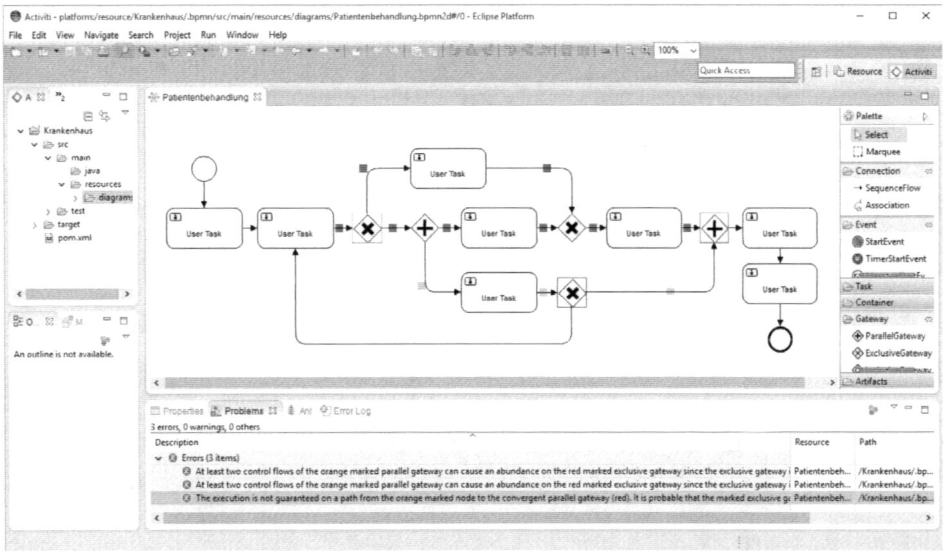

Figure 16. Integration of *Mojo* in the Activiti BPMN 2.0 Designer.

We have considered the PNML workflow library with two tools: (1) The previous introduced tool *Mojo* [5] and (2) the state space-based tool *LoLA* [18]. *LoLA* requires the Petri nets to be in a special, proprietary file format. The needed files can be downloaded inclusive an installation guide on [45].

The runtime system for the evaluation was a typical computer with a 64 bit *Debian GNU/Linux 9.0 (stretch)* operating system. The Linux kernel was *4.8.0-2-amd64 x86_64*. The computer used a 4-core *Intel©Core*^{TM}*i5-4570* CPU with 3.2 GHZ frequency and 8 GB main memory. Since *Mojo* is implemented in Java, we run an OpenJDK runtime environment in version *1.8.0_111* with 2 GB heap space.

2) Examples: In our first evaluation setting, we consider some workflows of the library that show remarkable differences between *LoLA* and *Mojo*. We have reduced the complexity of these compositions so that we can illustrate them in the context of this paper.

The first workflow, we consider in more detail, has the name *a.s00000031__s00001361* and is part of benchmark *A*. The reduced version of this workflow is illustrated in Figure 17 *a)*.

LoLA finds exactly one deadlock (error) for this workflow. It detects it in one of the upper both join nodes depending on the strategy of state space exploration. Furthermore, *LoLA* is able to give a failure trace to that error. In the figure, we have illustrated this trace with the help of tokens, which contain numbers where, e. g., the number 2 describes the position of all tokens in the second state.

In contrary, *Mojo* finds the causes of two potential deadlocks and one potential lack of synchronization (cf. Figure 18 *a)*). That means, *Mojo* finds a structural fault that may lead to a lack of synchronization which *LoLA* cannot detect. In this case, it is impossible to find the potential lack of synchronization with the help of a state space-based approch since there is no state in the whole state space, in which an edge contains more than two tokens. However, if we assume that both upper join nodes should actually be executed correctly, then the lack of synchronization is possible — the static approach of *Mojo* discovers faults behind other faults and ignores the problem of fault blocking.

Furthermore, the static approach of *Mojo* provides all faults with a lot of detailed diagnostic information. Figure 19 shows a possible description of one of the deadlocks of the example, which helps a developer to repair the composition.

In conclusion to the first remarkable composition, the static approach gives more help to the developer than the state space-based approach of *LoLA*.

The second workflow to consider with name *b2.s00000793__s00006437* of benchmark *B2* is shown in Figure 17 *b)*. In this example, the state space-based approach finds a lack of synchronization and a deadlock. The lack of synchronization is possible after the merge node since two parallel flows can execute that node at the same time. However, if they are run asynchronously, the failure trace of Fig. 17 *b)* is possible containing a deadlock in the join node.

If we consider the same workflow with the static approach of *Mojo*, we find only the cause of one lack of synchronization because the merge node cannot synchronize two parallel control flows (cf. Figure 18 *b)*). Since the deadlock found by *LoLA* results from a lack of synchronization, the static approach does not find it. That behaviour helps the developer since the deadlock is a fault illusion. In conclusion, for this second remarkable case, the static approach shows its benefits since fault illusions are ignored.

The last example shows similarities to the previous one.

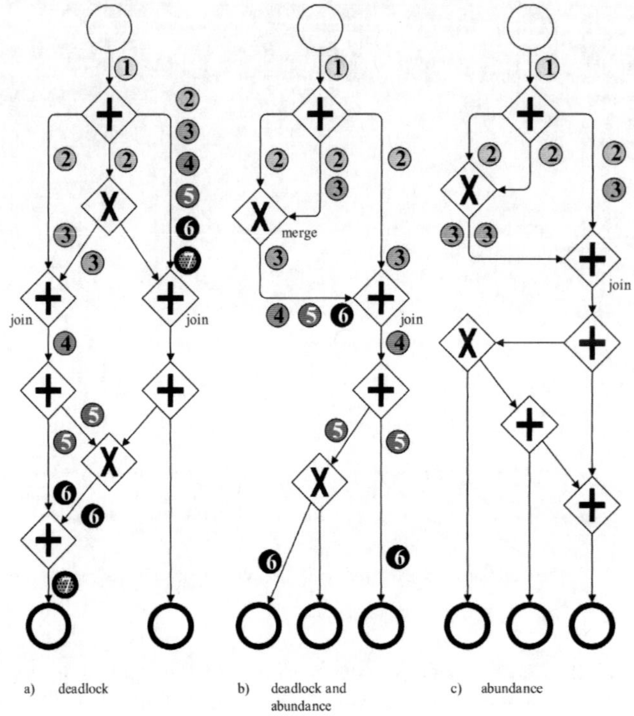

Figure 17. Workflows with noteworthy differences between *LoLA* and *Mojo*: The *LoLA* output.

It has the name *b1.s00000115__s00003189* and is part of benchmark $B1$ (Figure 17 *c)*). Although the example has the same basic structure as the previous workflow, *LoLA* results only in one lack of synchronization, i. e., a deadlock in the upper join node is not reached in the state space. Maybe, the differences in the structures lead to those different results. This could be supported by the fact that *LoLA* stops its error detection after a first error is found — a case of fault blocking. As a consequence, the result of state space-based approaches depends on the strategy and, sometimes, on pure coincidence.

Instead, *Mojo* shows the same behaviour and, furthermore, finds the fault of a potential deadlock in the lower join node (cf. Figure 18 *c)*). That means, fault blocking and fault illusion does not have a chance to occur in static approaches.

As summary of the consideration of the three different workflows of the benchmark, state space-based and static compiler-based approaches show different results. For the three considered examples, a static approach shows more benefits since fault illusions and fault blocking are ignored, the results are transparent, and it provides detailed diagnostic information.

3) Benchmark: It is of interest whether the observations of the last sub section hold in general. For this, we have compared the results of *Mojo* and *LoLA* for the whole workflow library.

Table I shows the number of faults (*not* errors!) found by *Mojo* for the different benchmarks. In total, *Mojo* has found $4,007$ faults. That means, each workflow contains approx. 2 to 3 faults on average. Furthermore, on average a workflow contains more causes for potential lacks of synchronization than deadlocks.

Table I. Number of *faults* found by *Mojo*.

	Deadlocks	Lacks of synchronization
A	140	170
B1	273	720
B2	326	948
B3	289	1,056
C	24	61
Sum	1,052	2,955
Total		4,007

Our expectation was that *LoLA* finds more errors than *Mojo* faults, because an arbitrary number of errors could be derived from one single fault. However, Table II shows a different picture: Only, $1,137$ errors (*not* faults!) were found by *LoLA*. That means, *LoLA* does only find approx. a quarter of the number of errors than *Mojo* faults. One reason for this behaviour is that *LoLA* can find only up to one error per analysis since it stops its state exploration after a first error is found. As *LoLA* performs two separated analyses for the deadlock and lack of synchronization detection, two errors are the maximum.

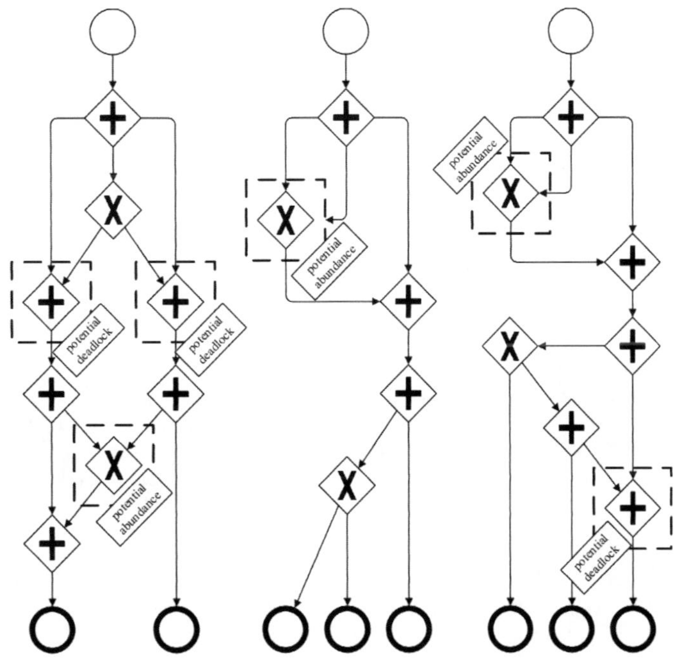

a) deadlock and abundance   b) abundance   c) deadlock and abundance

Figure 18. Workflows with noteworthy differences between *LoLA* and *Mojo*: The *Mojo* output.

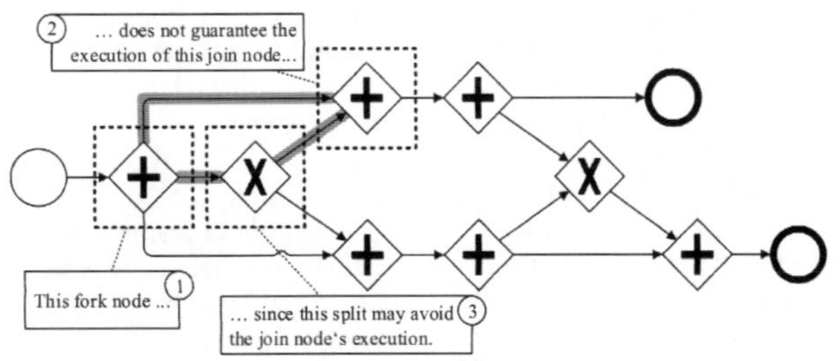

Figure 19. Detailed fault diagnostic with *Mojo*.

Table II. Number of *errors* found by *LoLA*.

	Deadlocks	Lacks of synchronization
A	97	68
B1	81	200
B2	84	238
B3	83	262
C	10	14
Sum	355	782
Total		1,137

On closer inspection of the differences between *LoLA* and *Mojo*, for 3 workflows *LoLA* finds one lack of synchronization as well as one deadlock. *Mojo*, however, finds only causes of lacks of synchronization for them (cf. example *b)* of Figure 17). For these workflows, the deadlocks are the result of lacks of synchronization as explained before. Such a behaviour could be the case for many workflows, however, since *LoLA* stops its state space exploration after the first found error, they are hard to identify.

For 171 workflows, *Mojo* finds causes of lacks of synchronization and deadlocks; in comparison, *LoLA* reaches only lacks of synchronization (cf. example *c)* of Figure 17). In 205 cases, *LoLA* finds no lack of synchronization since a deadlock blocks the occurrence of a lack of synchronization at runtime (cf. example *a)* of Figure 17). However, *Mojo* finds both: Lacks of synchronization as well as deadlocks.

All those cases strengthen our hypothesis that the static

Table III. Number of sound and unsound workflows with *Mojo* and *LoLA*.

	Total	*Mojo* sound	*Mojo* unsound	*LoLA* sound	*LoLA* unsound
A	282	152	130	152	130
B1	288	107	181	107	181
B2	363	161	202	161	202
B3	421	207	214	207	214
C	32	17	15	15	17
Summe	1,386	644	742	642	744

soundness approach used by *Mojo* has many advantages over the state space-based approach of *LoLA*.

We also have checked whether a static approach can be used for pure soundness checking. Therefore, we have checked whether *Mojo* and *LoLA* detects the same sound and unsound workflows in the library. Furthermore, we have counted the total number of sound and unsound workflows. Table III shows the results of this aggregation for *Mojo* (left) and *LoLA* (right).

As it turned out, *Mojo* and *LoLA* mark the same workflows as sound except for two of them. *Mojo* marks both as sound, *LoLA* as unsound. They have the names *c.s00000042__s00001033* and *c.s00000042__s00001050* and are part of benchmark C. This can also be observed in Table III on the differences between the total number of sound and unsound workflows. We considered both compositions in detail and worked out that both workflows are unconnected. Since *Mojo* was implemented as a tool, which supports the *development* of workflows, it must be able to handle unconnected workflows. For this, it builds a connected workflow using the semantics of BPMN. After a long inspection of both workflows, we could not find any fault. Since we do not know how *LoLA* handles unconnected workflows, we assume that this fact is the origin of the divergence of both tools. As a consequence, the results of Fahland et al. [46] should be handled with care since they consider the same process library and the tool LoLA too.

In summary, we see that the usage of static analysis approaches has benefits in the context of soundness verification. It results in a more detailed fault overview ignoring difficulties like fault illusion and fault blocking.

4) Time Behaviour: In the last step of our evaluation, we want to take a look on the time behaviour of both tools since it is possible that static approaches are more time expensive than dynamic techniques. To be used in an IDE, analyses should be fast such that they can be performed during each modification step of a program or, in our case, of a service composition. Figure 20 shows the distribution of the analysis times of *Mojo* and *LoLA* in two histograms. As we can see in the figure, *Mojo* spends for approx. $95\,\%$ of the workflows less than two milliseconds to find the faults of deadlocks and lacks of synchronization. It needs $0.03\,[ms]$ in the best, $0.25\,[ms]$ in the median, and $24.5\,[ms]$ in the worst case. In summary, *Mojo* works very fast with the workflows of the library and can be used without a noticeable latency.

LoLA spends a bit more time for its analysis of the workflows (bottom histogram). Nearly 67% of the workflows need approx. $5\,[ms]$ to be analysed with *LoLA*. Almost all workflows ($99\,\%$) of the library can be analysed within 5 to 10 milliseconds. In the minimum, *LoLA* needs $5.26\,[ms]$, in the median $5.78\,[ms]$, and in the maximum $17.97\,[ms]$ for the analysis of a single workflow.

In total, *Mojo* spends 818 milliseconds to check all $1,386$ workflows. *LoLA* uses $8,238$ milliseconds instead and is, therefore, approx. 10 times slower than *Mojo*. Although it is slower than *Mojo*, it has a respectable time and can also be used without any visible latency. However, as shown in this evaluation, the usage of a static analysis as used by *Mojo* has more advantages than a state space-based approach as used by *LoLA*.

VI. Conclusion and Future Work

The major advantages of well-known analyses used in modern IDEs for software development are the extensive diagnostic information and the possibility to find potential failures along the whole program. We have shown in a case study that dynamic analysis techniques can result in an imprecise and time consuming error detection. Though, most analyses for service compositions do use dynamic error finding techniques as motivated in the state of the art. But dynamic techniques can only find first appearing errors since afterwards the program is within a dirty state. This makes it difficult and inefficient to repair a defect composition. Furthermore, the case study showed that *dynamic analysis techniques are not suitable as immediate tool support during the development of service compositions*. This fact was strengthen by a direct comparison of dynamic and static analyses. The comparison was done with our static fault finding technique and the dynamic state space exploration. The static analysis techniques give detailed and precise fault information throughout a whole process, whereas the dynamic analysis techniques are only suitable for which they were made for: Verification, i. e., checking whether a verification criterion holds or not. So, dynamic error finding techniques like state space exploration have some serious disadvantages during the reparation of malformed service compositions.

The introduced tool *Mojo* shows the strengthen of applying *static* analyses during the creation of workflows. The analyses cannot only be performed in each modification step of the service composition, they also give detailed diagnostic information about the faults. For this reason, *Mojo* is the first tool that can be used profitable as an extension to a service composition modeller making the modeller to a first IDE. We believe that there are many other composition-specific problems, which can be avoided by static analyses.

Although there is a substantial common ground between the creation of service compositions and a software product, there are some serious differences making the adaptation of static analyses from classical software development to service compositions difficult: (1) In most cases, service compositions are developed by the use of visual modelling languages, e. g., *BPMN* and Event-driven process chains [47]. Visually modelled compositions often result in unstructured workflow graphs, e. g., approx. $60\,\%$ of all real world processes taken from IBM Zurich [43] are unstructured. Un-

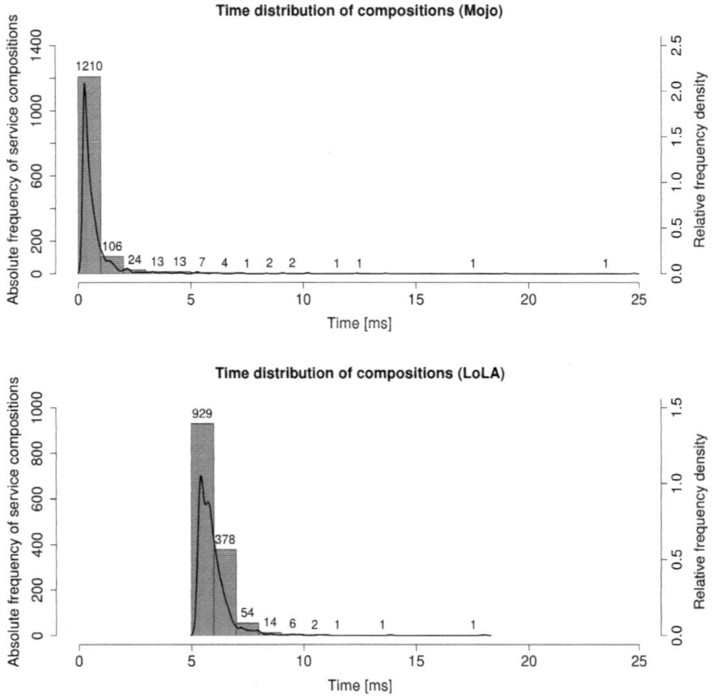

Figure 20. Distribution of analysis times for *Mojo* (top) and *LoLA* (bottom).

fortunately, most known fast analysis algorithms of compiler theory work only for structured graphs.

(2) A second major difference between the development of software systems and service compositions is the ability to model explicit parallelism within service compositions. Since most algorithms for program analysis cannot be applied to parallel programs, they must be adapted [48]. Lee et al. [49] introduced the *Concurrent Static Single Assignment* (CSSA) form, making it possible to use algorithms of sequential programs for parallel software. Unfortunately, the building of the CSSA form requires knowledge about possible race conditions to ensure high quality analysis results. The derivation of race conditions, however, is inefficient for unstructured workflow graphs so far [49].

In summary, we plead for an adaptation of fast and well-known analysis techniques of modern IDEs to the development of service compositions. Furthermore, we argue for the development of new static analysis techniques especially for service compositions to solve composition-specific problems. In this context, we also plead for a first real compiler for service compositions, which enables those analyses as well as the transformation of service compositions into runnable applications [37]. The practical benefits of such an approach were demonstrated by the introduction of the analysis tool *Mojo* and its usage in an evaluation of the soundness checking of real world service compositions.

REFERENCES

[1] T. M. Prinz and W. Amme, "Why We Need Advanced Analyses of Service Compositions," in SERVICE COMPUTATION 2017: The Ninth International Conferences on Advanced Service Computing, Athens, Greece, February 19–23, 2017. Proceedings, pp. 48–54.

[2] Object Management Group (OMG), "Business Process Model and Notation (BPMN) Version 2.0," OMG, Jan. 2011, standard. [Online]. Available: http://www.omg.org/spec/BPMN/2.0

[3] W. M. P. van der Aalst, "A class of Petri nets for modeling and analyzing business processes," Eindhoven University of Technology, Eindhoven, Netherlands, Computing Science Reports 95/26, 1995, Technical Report.

[4] T. M. Prinz and W. Amme, "Practical Compiler-Based User Support during the Development of Business Processes," in Service-Oriented Computing - ICSOC 2013 Workshops - CCSA, CSB, PASCEB, SWESE, WESOA, and PhD Symposium, Berlin, Germany, December 2-5, 2013. Revised Selected Papers, pp. 40–53.

[5] T. M. Prinz, N. Spieß, and W. Amme, "A First Step towards a Compiler for Business Processes," in Compiler Construction - 23rd International Conference, CC 2014, Held as Part of the European Joint Conferences on Theory and Practice of Software, ETAPS 2014, Grenoble, France, April 5-13, 2014. Proceedings, pp. 238–243.

[6] T. M. Prinz, R. Charrondière, and W. Amme, "Geschäftsprozesse kompiliert - Wichtige Unterstützung für die Modellierung," in Proceedings 18. Kolloquium Programmiersprachen und Grundlagen der Programmierung, KPS 2015, Pörtschach am Wörthersee, Austria, pp. 476–491.

[7] T. M. Prinz, "Entwicklung von kontrollflussbasierten Methoden und Techniken für einen benutzerfreundlichen Entwurf von sicheren Geschäftsprozessen," Ph.D. dissertation, Friedrich-Schiller-

Universität, Jena, Germany, Oct 2017.

[8] F. Puhlmann, "Soundness Verification of Business Processes Specified in the Pi-Calculus," in On the Move to Meaningful Internet Systems 2007: CoopIS, DOA, ODBASE, GADA, and IS, OTM Confederated International Conferences CoopIS, DOA, ODBASE, GADA, and IS 2007, Vilamoura, Portugal, November 25-30, 2007, Proceedings, Part I, pp. 6–23.

[9] W. M. P. van der Aalst, K. M. van Hee, A. H. M. ter Hofstede, N. Sidorova, H. M. W. Verbeek, M. Voorhoeve, and M. T. Wynn, "Soundness of workflow nets: classification, decidability, and analysis," Formal Aspects of Computing, vol. 23, no. 3, May 2011, pp. 333–363.

[10] J. Desel and J. Esparza, Free Choice Petri Nets, ser. Cambridge Tracts in Theoretical Computer Science, C. van Rijsbergen, S. Abramsky, P. H. Aczel, J. W. de Bakker, J. A. Goguen, Y. Gurevich, and J. V. Tucker, Eds. Cambridge, Great Britain: Cambridge University Press, 1995, no. 40.

[11] P. Kemper and F. Bause, "An Efficient Polynomial-Time Algorithm to Decide Liveness and Boundedness of Free-Choice Nets," in Application and Theory of Petri Nets 1992, 13th International Conference, Sheffield, UK, June 22-26, 1992, Proceedings, pp. 263–278.

[12] C. Favre and H. Völzer, "Symbolic Execution of Acyclic Workflow Graphs," in Business Process Management - 8th International Conference, BPM 2010, Hoboken, NJ, USA, September 13-16, 2010. Proceedings, pp. 260–275.

[13] W. M. P. van der Aalst, "Verification of Workflow Nets," in Application and Theory of Petri Nets 1997, 18th International Conference, ICATPN '97, Toulouse, France, June 23-27, 1997, Proceedings, pp. 407–426.

[14] A. Valmari, "The State Explosion Problem," in Lectures on Petri Nets I: Basic Models, Advances in Petri Nets, the volumes are based on the Advanced Course on Petri Nets, held in Dagstuhl, September 1996, pp. 429–528.

[15] T. Murata, "Petri Nets: Properties, Analysis and Applications," Proceedings of the IEEE, vol. 77, no. 4, Apr. 1989, pp. 541–580.

[16] N. Lohmann and D. Fahland, "Where Did I Go Wrong? - Explaining Errors in Business Process Models," in Business Process Management - 12th International Conference, BPM 2014, Haifa, Israel, September 7-11, 2014. Proceedings, pp. 283–300.

[17] H. M. W. E. Verbeek, T. Basten, and W. M. P. van der Aalst, "Diagnosing Workflow Processes using Woflan," The Computer Journal, vol. 44, no. 4, Sep. 2001, pp. 246–279.

[18] K. Schmidt, Application and Theory of Petri Nets 2000: 21st International Conference, ICATPN 2000 Aarhus, Denmark, June 26–30, 2000 Proceedings. Berlin, Heidelberg: Springer Berlin Heidelberg, 2000, ch. LoLA A Low Level Analyser, pp. 465–474.

[19] W. Sadiq and M. E. Orlowska, "Analyzing Process Models Using Graph Reduction Techniques," Information Systems, vol. 25, no. 2, Apr. 2000, pp. 117–134.

[20] R. Eshuis and A. Kumar, "An integer programming based approach for verification and diagnosis of workflows," Data & Knowledge Engineering, vol. 69, no. 8, Mar. 2010, pp. 816–835.

[21] P. Chrząstowski-Wachtel, B. Benatallah, R. Hamadi, M. O'Dell, and A. Susanto, "A Top-Down Petri Net-Based Approach for Dynamic Workflow Modeling," in Business Process Management, International Conference, BPM 2003, Eindhoven, The Netherlands, June 26-27, 2003, Proceedings, pp. 336–353.

[22] J. Vanhatalo, H. Völzer, and F. Leymann, "Faster and More Focused Control-Flow Analysis for Business Process Models Through SESE Decomposition," in Service-Oriented Computing - ICSOC 2007, Fifth International Conference, Vienna, Austria, September 17-20, 2007, Proceedings, pp. 43–55.

[23] J. Vanhatalo, H. Völzer, and J. Koehler, "The Refined Process Structure Tree," Data & Knowledge Engineering, vol. 68, no. 9, Sep. 2009, pp. 793–818.

[24] J. E. Hopcroft and R. E. Tarjan, "Dividing a Graph into Triconnected Components," SIAM Journal on Computing, vol. 2, no. 3, Sep. 1973, pp. 135–158.

[25] R. Johnson, D. Pearson, and K. Pingali, "Finding regions fast: Single entry single exit and control regions in linear time." Cornell University, Ithaca, NY, Ithaca, NY, USA, Tech. Rep. TR 93-1365, Jul. 1993.

[26] R. Johnson, D. Pearson, and K. Pingali, "The Program Structure Tree: Computing Control Regions in Linear Time," in Proceedings of the ACM SIGPLAN'94 Conference on Programming Language Design and Implementation (PLDI), Orlando, Florida, USA, June 20-24, 1994, pp. 171–185.

[27] B. F. van Dongen, J. Mendling, and W. M. P. van der Aalst, "Structural Patterns for Soundness of Business Process Models," in Tenth IEEE International Enterprise Distributed Object Computing Conference (EDOC 2006), 16-20 October 2006, Hong Kong, China, pp. 116–128.

[28] C. Favre, "Detecting, Understanding, and Fixing Control-Flow Errors in Business Process Models," Ph.D. dissertation, ETH Zürich, Zürich, Switzerland, 2014, DISS. ETH NO 22266.

[29] C. Favre, H. Völzer, and P. Müller, "Diagnostic Information for Control-Flow Analysis of Workflow Graphs (a.k.a. Free-Choice Workflow Nets)," in Tools and Algorithms for the Construction and Analysis of Systems - 22nd International Conference, TACAS 2016, Held as Part of the European Joint Conferences on Theory and Practice of Software, ETAPS 2016, Eindhoven, The Netherlands, April 2-8, 2016, Proceedings, pp. 463–479.

[30] M. B. Juric, B. K. Mathew, and P. Sarang, Business Process Execution Language for Web Services: An Architects and Developers Guide to BPEL and BPEL4WS, second edition ed., ser. From Technologies to Solutions, M. Little and D. Shaffer, Eds. Birmingham, UK: Packt Publishing Ltd., Jan. 2006.

[31] W. M. P. van der Aalst and A. H. M. ter Hofstede, "YAWL: Yet Another Workflow Language," Information Systems, vol. 30, no. 4, Jun. 2005, pp. 245–275.

[32] C. A. Petri, "Communication with Machines (Kommunikation mit Maschinen)," Ph.D. dissertation, Faculty for Mathematics and Physics, Technische Hochschule Darmstadt, Bonn, Jul. 1962.

[33] A. Avizienis, J. Laprie, B. Randell, and C. E. Landwehr, "Basic Concepts and Taxonomy of Dependable and Secure Computing," IEEE Transactions on Dependable and Secure Computing, vol. 1, no. 1, 2004, pp. 11–33.

[34] I. Sommerville, Software Engineering, 8th ed. Munich, Germany: Pearson Studium, Apr. 2007.

[35] M. A. Friedman and J. M. Voas, Software Assessment: Reliability, Safety, Testability, 1st ed., ser. New Dimensions In Engineering Series. New York, USA: John Wiley & Sons, Inc., Aug. 1995, vol. Book 16.

[36] T. M. Prinz, "GitHub – mojo.core," website, visited on July 18th, 2017. [Online]. Available: https://github.com/guybrushPrince/mojo.core

[37] T. M. Prinz, T. S. Heinze, W. Amme, J. Kretzschmar, and C. Beckstein, "Towards a Compiler for Business Processes - A Research Agenda," in SERVICE COMPUTATION 2015: The Seventh International Conferences on Advanced Service Computing, pp. 49–54.

[38] T. M. Prinz, "Proposals for a Virtual Machine for Business Processes," in Proceedings of the 7th Central European Workshop on Services and their Composition, ZEUS 2015, Jena, Germany, February 19-20, 2015., pp. 10–17.

[39] M. Weber and E. Kindler, "The Petri Net Markup Language," in Petri Net Technology for Communication-Based Systems - Advances in Petri Nets, pp. 124–144.

[40] R. T. Prosser, "Applications of Boolean Matrices to the Analysis of Flow Diagrams," in Papers Presented at the December 1-3, 1959, Eastern Joint IRE-AIEE-ACM Computer Conference, pp. 133–138.

[41] E. S. Lowry and C. W. Medlock, "Object Code Optimization," Communications of the ACM, vol. 12, no. 1, Jan. 1969, pp. 13–22.

[42] Alfresco Software, Inc, "Activiti bpm software home," website, visited on July 18th, 2017. [Online]. Available: https://www.activiti.org/

[43] IBM, "IBM Research - Zurich: Computer Science," website, visited on January 30th, 2017. [Online]. Available: http://www.zurich.ibm.com/csc/bit/downloads.html

[44] IBM Corporation, "IBM - Software - IBM Business Process Manager," website, visited on July 18th, 2017. [Online]. Available: http://www-03.ibm.com/software/products/de/modeler-basic

[45] service-technology.org, "service-technology.org/publications," website, visited on July 18th, 2017. [Online]. Available: http://www.service-technology.org/publications/fahlandfjklvw_2009_bpm/

[46] D. Fahland, C. Favre, J. Koehler, N. Lohmann, H. Völzer, and K. Wolf, "Analysis on Demand: Instantaneous Soundness Checking of Industrial Business Process Models," Data & Knowledge Engineering, vol. 70, no. 5, May 2011, pp. 448–466.

[47] G. Keller, M. Nüttgens, and A.-W. Scheer, "Semantic Process Modelling Based on "Event-driven Process Chains (EPC)" (Semantische Prozessmodellierung auf der Grundlage "Ereignisgesteuerter Prozessketten (EPK)")," Institut für Wirtschaftsinformatik, Saarbrücken, Germany, Veröffentlichungen des Instituts für Wirtschaftsinformatik 89, 1992, Technical Report. [Online]. Available: http://www.iwi.uni-sb.de/iwi-hefte/heft089.zip

[48] S. P. Midkiff and D. A. Padua, "Issues in the Optimization of Parallel Programs," in Proceedings of the 1990 International Conference on Parallel Processing, Urbana-Champaign, IL, USA, August 1990. Volume 2: Software., pp. 105–113.

[49] J. Lee, S. P. Midkiff, and D. A. Padua, "Concurrent Static Single Assignment Form and Constant Propagation for Explicitly Parallel Programs," in Languages and Compilers for Parallel Computing, 10th International Workshop, LCPC'97, Minneapolis, Minnesota, USA, August 7-9, 1997, Proceedings, pp. 114–130.

Recognition of Similar Marble Textures through Different Neural Networks with De-correlated Input Data

Short Paper

Irina Topalova
Faculty of German Engineering Education and Industrial Management
Technical University of Sofia, Bulgaria
Sofia, Bulgaria
itopalova@abv.bg

Magdalina Uzunova
Department Mathematics
University of Architecture, Civil Engineering and Geodesy
UACEG
Sofia, Bulgaria
magi.uzunova@abv.bg

***Abstract*— The automated recognition of marble slab surface textures is an important task in the contemporary marble tiles production. The simplicity of the applied methods corresponds with fast processing, which is important for real-time applications. In this research a supervised learning of a multi-layered neural network is proposed and tested. Aiming at high recognition accuracy, combined with simple pre-processing, the neural network is trained with different alternating input training sets including combination of high correlated and de-correlated input data. The de-correlated input data are also used for training of a self-organized map neural network, aiming to prove the efficiency of the pre-processing method also for unsupervised neural networks. The obtained good results in the recognition stage are represented, compared and discussed. Further research is proposed.**

Keywords- MLP neural network; SOM neural network; texture recognition; pre-processing; de-correlation

I. INTRODUCTION

This article is a continuation of the study by the same authors and published at the conference "IARIA/ ICAS'2017", Barcelona, Spain [1]. The automated recognition of marble slab surfaces is an important factor for increasing the production efficiency. The prerequisite for that is to apply reduced hardware equipment and simple software methods to obtain fast processing in real-time work. Taking into account these requirements, the achieved recognition accuracy is very important especially in the case of similar marble surface textures. Finding the appropriate input data transformations would facilitate the next recognition step. Thus, the choice of simple texture parametrical descriptions and their interclass de-correlation in the pre-processing stage is an essential question. The next one is the right choice of an appropriate trained adaptive recognition structure.

In this research a simple hardware structure combined with a supervised learning of a multi-layered neural network (NN) is proposed and tested. Two different types of texture descriptions are used for training the network. Aiming high recognition accuracy, combined with simple pre-processing, the NN is trained with these alternating input training sets including combination of high correlated and de-correlated input data.

The obtained results, when training the network with a single type and with different types of alternating input training sets are represented. The obtained good results in the recognition stage even for similar textures are represented and discussed. Further research is proposed.

In Section II, the state of the art is represented, together with a discussion about disadvantages of the listed methods concerning the obtained results. In Section III, the selected pre-processing method is explained and the used system components are described. Section IV contains the experimental conditions and results, along with comparative discussions. In Section V, the conclusions and future work are defined.

II. RELATED WORKS

There are many related research proposals for recognition of similar, different shaded or hardly distinguishable marble textures. One of the often investigated proposals for extraction of texture feature descriptions is the statistical, instead of structural methods. In [2], the authors represent texture-based image classification using the gray-level co-occurrence matrices (GLCM) and self-organizing map (SOM) methods. They obtain 97.8 % accuracy and show the superiority of GLCM+SOM over the single and fused Support-Vector-Machine (SVM), over the Bayes classifiers using Bayes distance and Mahalanobis distance. To identify the textile texture defects, the authors in [3], propose also a method based on a GLCM feature extractor. The numerical simulation shows error recognition of 91%. The authors in [4], investigate marble slabs with small gradient of colors and hardly-distinguishable veins in the surface. They apply a faster version of a Co-occurrence matrix to form a feature vector of *mean, energy, entropy, contrast* and *homogeneity,* for each of the three color channels. Thus they constitute a NN input feature vector of 15 neurons and the designed network presents 15 neurons in the input layer. In this case the authors claim high-speed processing and recognition accuracy of 80-92.7%. Another known approach for texture segmentation and classification using NN as recognition structure, is the implementation of Wavelet transform over the image and feeding the network with a feature vector of Wavelet coefficients [5][6]. Training a hierarchical NN structure with texture histograms and their second derivative is also announced as giving good recognition accuracy [7]. Recently, the authors of [8] have published a color balancing model for texture recognition and implementation of convolutional neural networks (CNN). Their approach includes texture images acquired under several different lighting conditions. Since the neural network can be trained inefficiently when the training set is not big enough, some authors offer appropriate variations in the learning stage in order to obtain good recognition results [9]. These authors offer an alternative to the full training procedure, adapting an already trained network to a new classification, by additional training only a chosen subset of parameters. The authors of [10] offer color texture descriptors that measure local contrast. These descriptors are less sensitive than the colors themselves to variations in illuminance. The same authors enhanced their method by proposing a novel colour space where changes in illumination are even simplified [11]. J. M. P. Batista presents a method for classification of color marble textures, using logistic regression, first order fuzzy Takagi-Sugeno system, based on the clustering algorithms and Fuzzy C-Means [12].

Considering the explicated data, we could formulate some disadvantages of the approaches given above. The obtained accuracy of 97.8% in [2] is only for textures that are not very similar, i.e. they are not overlapping in the parametrical feature space. The use of GLCM needs high computations and even faster version of a Co-occurrence matrix as given in [4], needs computations multiple times over the whole image for each of the three colors. The calculation of Wavelets is also a time-consuming operation. Using hierarchical NN structure, feeding different NNs [7], with different input feature vectors, would be more complicated, particularly for real-time applications in different hardware platforms. The obtained accuracy is high, but not approaching 100%. The authors of [8] apply a complex approach without taking into account that different lightening for the same textures results in the translation of the histogram of the image along the X axis, without substantially altering its shape. If the translated histogram is used as an input vector on a suitable neural network, it will be able to make a translational invariant recognition. Changes in the texture histogram and along the Y axis have to be taken into account as they are influenced by the contrast changes between the local segments. In this way the algorithm would be greatly simplified. The approach given in [9] requires additional training by choosing appropriate subset of texture parameters, which would complicate the algorithm. The authors of [10][11] propose simplified descriptors that are less sensitive to variations in illuminance, but it still requires significant computing resources. The study given in [12] applies a complex method of recognizing marble textures but achieves a relatively low accuracy of 83.54% and there is a need to speed up the algorithm, because it gives 1.3 sec per marble texture.

Thus, the important source of optimization for the recognition method lies in a simplification of the pre-processing stage /the input feature vector and in finding a Method and System Development more efficient training method along with reducing the NN nodes. In this section, a motivation for choosing the proposed input training sets is given, along with a description of the system components.

A. Selecting a Pre-processing Method

Complying with the finding that NN training would be more efficient, when applying different types of intra class input data [13][14], we choose to training a single MLP Back-propagation NN alternating with two types of input vectors. The first one is the calculated first derivative dH(g)/dg of the corresponding normalized grey level (g) texture histogram H(g). As we test marble tiles with similar textures, the obtained inter class vectors are high correlated, which will "embarrass" the NN class-separation capabilities. However, we use this training set because it reflects the vertical H(g) axis changes. To compensate the high inter class correlation, we investigated different types of simple mathematical transformations over the H(g), to find de-correlated input training vectors. In our case, U = Exp(k.H(g)) gave the best reduction of the inter class correlation coefficient. It was chosen for second input training set. So, the MLP NN is trained with these alternating input training sets including combination of high correlated and de-correlated input data. The de-correlated input data are also used for learning of a SOM neural network, aiming to prove the efficiency of the pre-processing method also for unsupervised neural networks, verifying the good impact of the de-correlated input data on the training facility.

B. System Components

The proposed test system includes one smart camera *NI 1742(300dpi)* with triggered infrared lighting, software Vision Builder for Automated inspection [15] AI'14 (VB for AI) and Neuro-System V5.0 - shown in Figure 1. The images are taken at the same distance with the same spatial resolution. The system works in two modes - off-line or training and on-line, or recognition and classification. In both modes, first the contrast quality for the captured images is improved in *VB for AI,* applying simple lookup logarithmic power square function, followed by the corresponding pre-processing of the two types of training sets. In off-line /or training mode/, the two types of calculated training sets of all classes are applied to the inputs of the proposed neural network structures (MLP or SOM). The training process ends with the result - two matrices of weighting coefficients $\mathbf{W}_{MLP}$ and $\mathbf{W}_{SOM}$. In on-line /or test mode - recognition and classification/ the same operations are performed for each test sample, but the input data only "go" through the saved (after the training), weight matrixes $\mathbf{W}_{MLP}$ or $\mathbf{W}_{SOM}$. The results are given to *VB for AI* for visualization and preparation for extraction through standard interfaces.

III. EXPERIMENTS AND RESULTS

In this section, the details of the pre-processing stage are given, along with a description of the MLP NN and of the SOM NN training. Also, the choice of the NN parameters is explained. In the end of the section, the achieved results are shown and a comparative analysis is represented. The pre-processing stage is presented in subsection A, the MLP and

SOM NN's training methods are explained in subsections B and C respectively.

A. Pre-processing Stage

The experiments are carried out for nine marble tiles/classes with similar textures given in Figure 3. The color images are transformed to grey level images applying the method (R+B+G)/3, which will reduce and average the color channel information. It is a loss of information, but it will simplify the further calculations. Calculating different color histograms or any color model parameters (as Hue color parameters), aiming to prepare different input vectors for MLP NN and SOM NN, would require a much more complex NN structures.

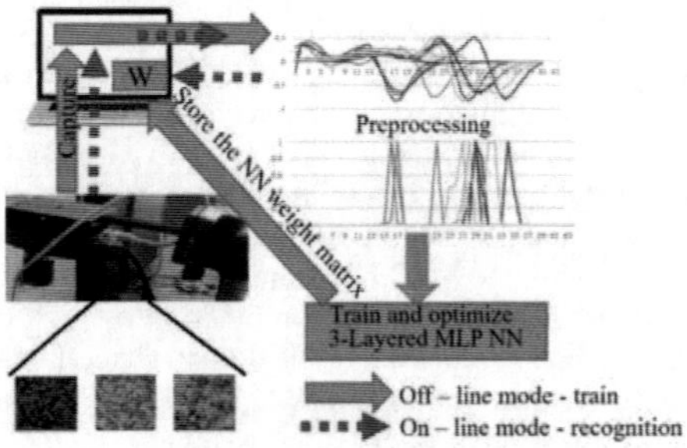

Figure 1. System components

In our case, this loss of information is compensated by using de-correlated input data as Exp(k.H(g)). To evaluate the similarity between samples of

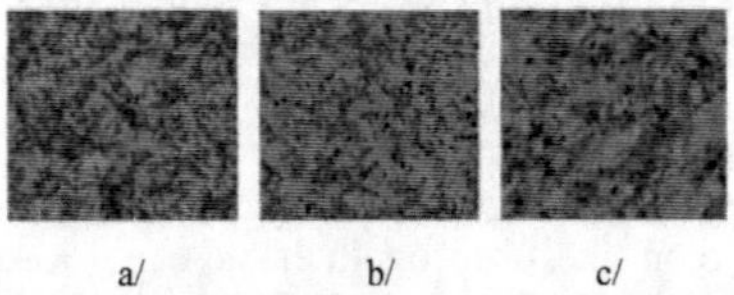

a/ b/ c/

Figure 2. Grey level marble tiles – a/-class1, b/-class2, c/-class3

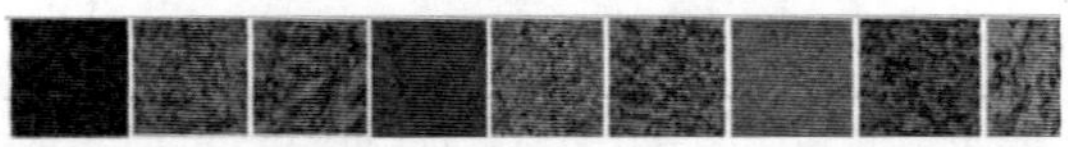

1 2 3 4 5 6 7 8 9

Figure 3. All tested classes of similar marble textures

classes i, j for different input NN feature vector descriptions, the correlation coefficient r_{ij} is calculated according to [16]. Points 1 to 4 of X axis in Figure 4 show the correlation between some exemplars of classes 1 and 2, points 5 to 8 - the correlation between exemplars of classes 2 and 3, points 9 to 12 - the correlation between exemplars of classes 1 and 3, shown in Figure 3. As the coefficient r_{ij} for H(g) varies in the range (-0.24;0.96), it shows very high similarity between classes 2 and 3. That is the reason for searching additional transformations over H(g), to achieve low inter class correlation and better separation between the classes. Thus, the input training vectors will facilitate the NN generalizing capabilities. As the normalized $H(g)/H_{max}(g)$ variables are in the range (0;1), the function U= Exp(k.H(g)), where k $\in$ **R**,

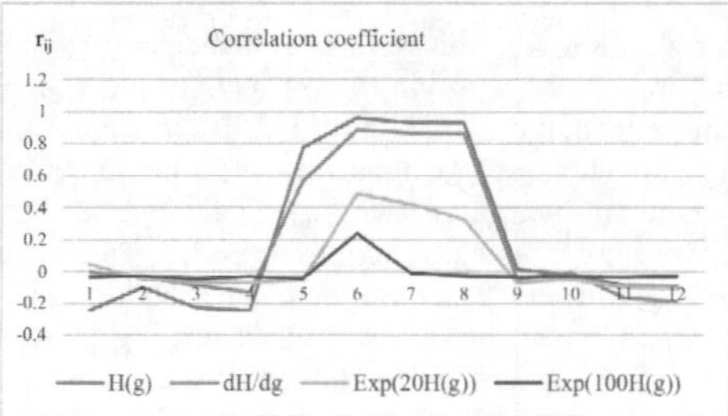

Figure 4. Correlation coefficient r_{ij} for different input training sets

will be suitable. We choose this function because the correlation coefficient is not invariant about this transformation. Good separable descriptions are obtained when choosing proper values for k (k=10 k=20, k= -10, etc.). With k=100, i.e., for U=Exp(100.H(g)), we achieve the best de-correlation results, shown in Figure 4, where r_{ij} varies in the range (-0.036;0.24). For the normalized H(g) values given in Figure 5, the calculated U are represented in Figure 6. As the function U has a smoothing effect over H(g), it also reduces the sharpness of vertical changes in H(g). To conserve and even increase these informative areas we use dH(g)/dg as additional NN training set. It also gives better r_{ij} than H(g). The training set of dH(g)/dg is shown in Figure 7.

B. Training Method for MLP NN

The decision plane consists of a 3-layered MLP NN, trained with well-known Backpropagation algorithm [17]. The input layer is connected with 45 dH(g)/dg and U=Exp(100.H(g)) sampled values over the histograms, according to the requirements for signal/histogram reconstruction, proved by Shannon sampling theorem [18]. This sampling allows a reduction of the input vector. Both types of vectors are applied alternative to the NN input layer nodes. By training of MLP NN we want to obtain "softer" transitions or larger regions, where the output stays

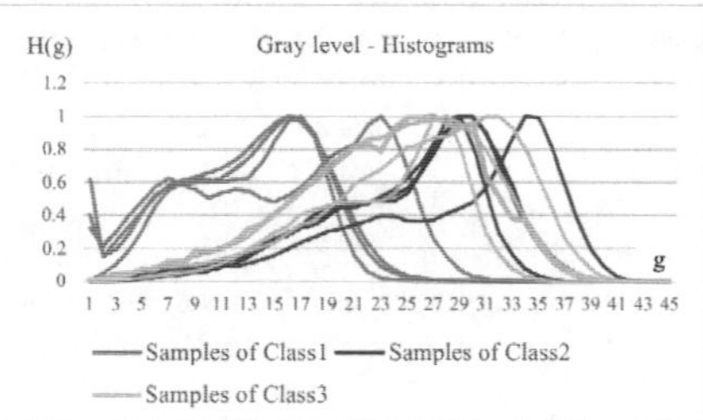

Figure 5. Normalized histogram values H(g) for samples of classes1, 2, 3

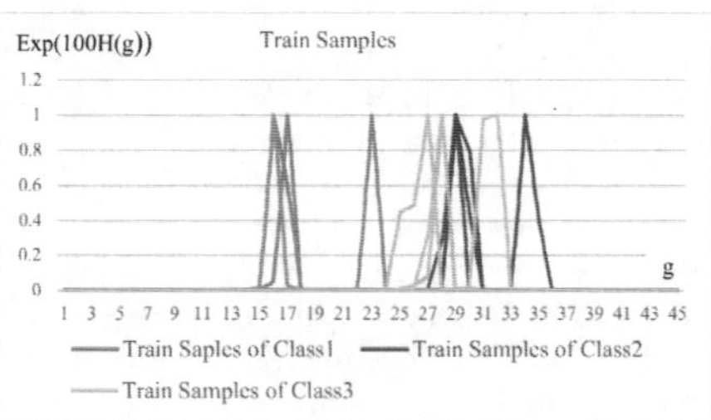

Figure 6. Training Exp(100.H(g)) values for the samples of classes1, 2, 3

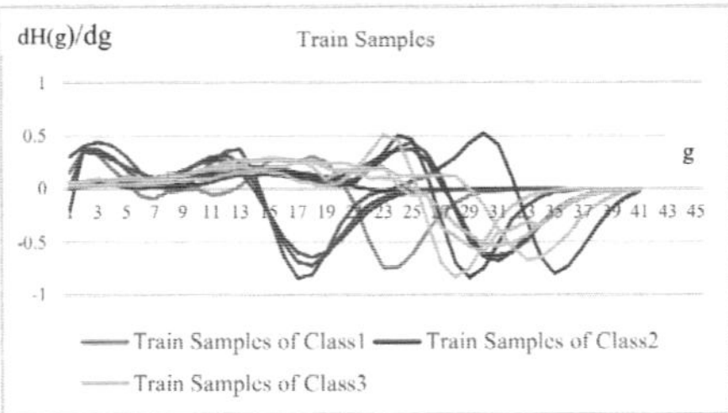

Figure 7. Training dH(g)/dg values for the samples of classes1,2 and 3

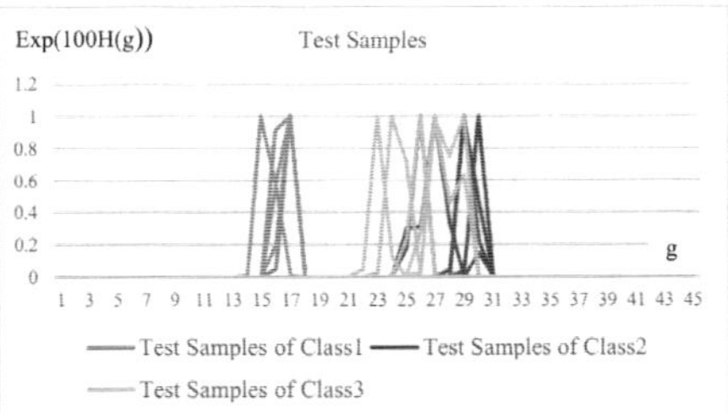

Figure 8. Test Exp(100.H(g)) values for the samples of classes1,2 and 3

near to "1" or "-1" (using tangent hyperbolic as activation function). The training in off-line mode was repeated to find the optimized MLP NN structure according to the method given in [6]. We obtained the best fitting structure with 18 hidden layer neurons and 3 output neurons, corresponding to the three trained classes. Figures 5 through 8 represent respectively H(g), training dH(g)/dg, training Exp(100.H(g)) and test Exp(100.H(g)) values for four samples of each class. The achieved output neuron values when recognizing samples of classes 1, 2 and 3 are shown in Figures 9, 10 and 11. Figure 12 shows the output neuron values for recognition of all test amples of the three classes. The proportion of 60%-7%-33%: (60 training samples, 7 verification samples, 33 test samples of each class) between training, cross validating and testing set of the general sample number is used in the research [17]. The 60% of the samples for each class were randomly given to the MLP NN for training with 20 samples of each class. To some of the training exemplars Motion Blur or Gaussian Noise is added. Motion Blur is added to simulate the effect of smoothing and blurring the images, when they are moving on a conveyer belt. The value of 9Pix Motion Blur corresponds to an image resolution of 300 dpi or 118 Pix/cm, to 25 m/min linear velocity of the conveyer belt and to 1/500 sec camera exposure time. The same conditions but for 1/300 exposure time correspond to 15Pix Motion Blur and for 1/200 exposure time corresponds to 25 Pix Motion Blur. Gaussian Noise 2%, 3% or 9Pix Motion Blur to three of the training samples of each class was added. To five of the test samples for each class was added Gaussian Noise between 3 and 5% or Motion Blur between 10 and 15%. The training process terminated when a Mean Square Error (MSE) of 0.01 was obtained. The recognition accuracy is calculated as (1 - Number of false recognized samples/Number of all test

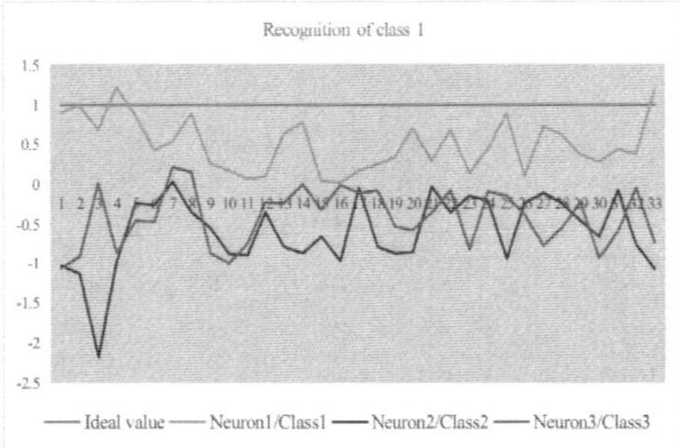

Figure 9. Output neuron values for recognition of class1 samples

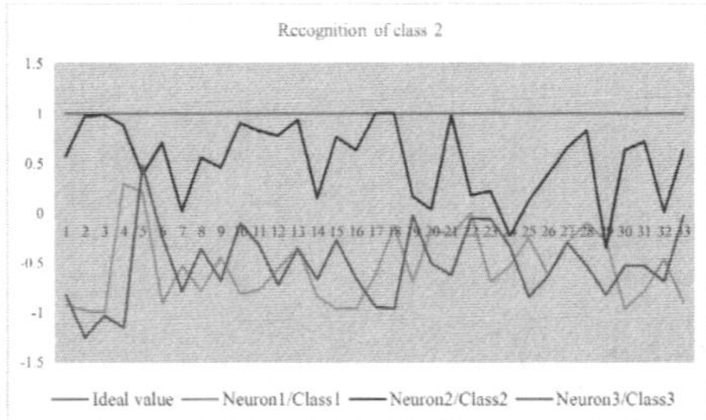

Figure 10. Output neuron values for recognition of class2 samples

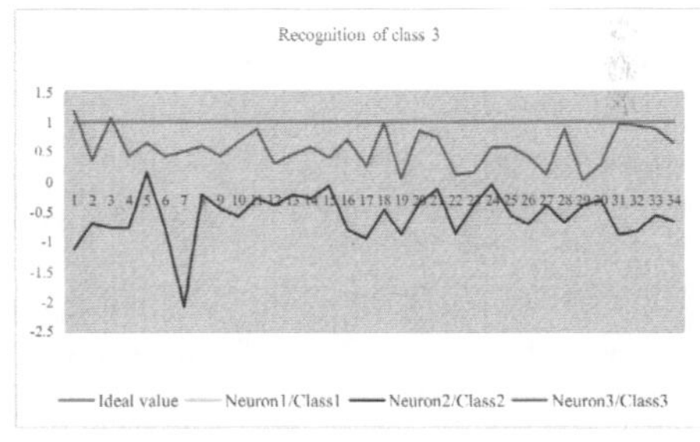

Figure 11. Output neuron values for recognition of class3 samples

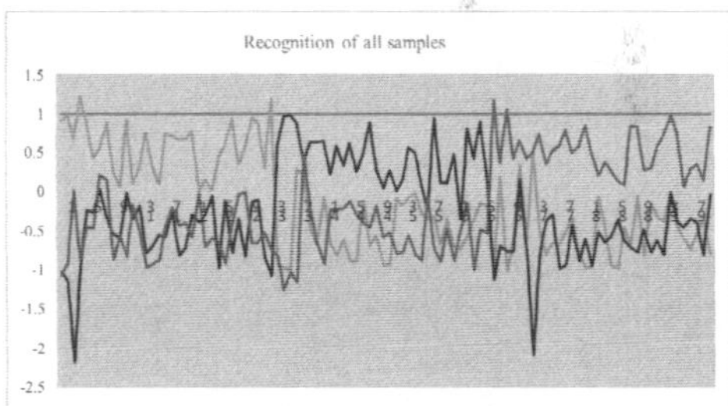

Figure 12. Output neuron values for recognition of all 33 test amples of the three classes

samples of each class) x 100 [%] and is given in Table I. The results are given for three different training modes: first case - training the NN only with dH(g)/dg; second case – training only with Exp(100.H(g)); third – training alternatively with both dH(g)/dg and Exp(100.H(g)). The best recognition

TABLE I. RECOGNITION ACCURACY FOR ALL TESTED SAMPLES

Recognition Accuracy [%]	Recognized classes 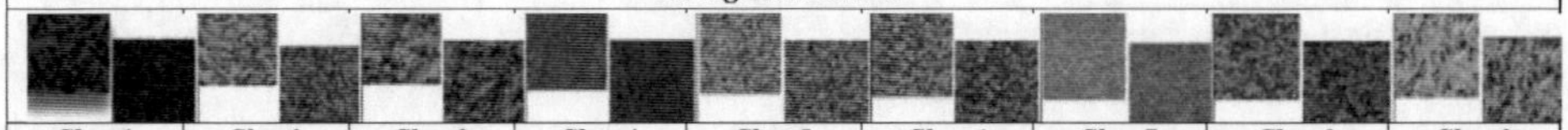								
	Class1	*Class2*	*Class3*	*Class4*	*Class5*	*Class6*	*Class7*	*Class8*	*Class9*
Case 1-*dH/dg*	5/**84.8%**	7/ **78.8%**	8/ **75.7%**	5/**84.8%**	8/ **75.7%**	8/ **75.7%**	5/**84.8%**	7/ **78.8%**	6/ **81.8%**
Case 2-E*xp(100.H(g))*	3/ **90.9%**	6/ **81.8%**	6/ **81.8%**	3/ **90.9%**	5/ **84.8%**	6/ **81.8%**	4/ **87.8%**	5/ **84.8%**	3/ **90.9%**
Case 3-MLP-alternately (dH/dg; Exp(100.H(g))	1/ **97%**	2/ **94%**	1/ **97%**	1/ **97%**	3/ **90.9%**	3/ **90.9%**	1/ **97%**	2/ **94%**	1/ **97%**
Case 4-SOM200 Exp(100.H(g)	0/ **100%**	2/ **94%**	2/ **94%**	0/ **100%**	1/ **97%**	1/ **97%**	0/ **100%**	2/ **94%**	0/ **100%**

accuracy between 94% and 100% is obtained in the third case. The output results are extracted through *VB for AI* in different conventional interface formats as Modbus, RS 232 and GigE Vision Standard. Table II shows the comparative results concerning recognition accuracy and real-time execution. They are related to the research given in [6][7] where the same images were tested, but applying pre-processing with Wavelets (DWT) and DCT over grey image histograms. Almost the same recognition accuracy was achieved as with DWT, but with a simplified NN structure (only 18 neurons in the hidden layer) because of simple pre-processing method providing at the same time de-correlation of the NN input training data. In the case of alternately training with dH/dg; Exp(100.H(g), the execution time is about three times reduced.

C. *Training Method for SOM NN*

To prove the efficiency of the pre-processing method also for unsupervised neural networks, verifying the good impact of the de-correlated input data on the training facility, a SOM NN is trained with the same and only with the U=Exp(100.H(g)) values. Here we apply the Kohonen

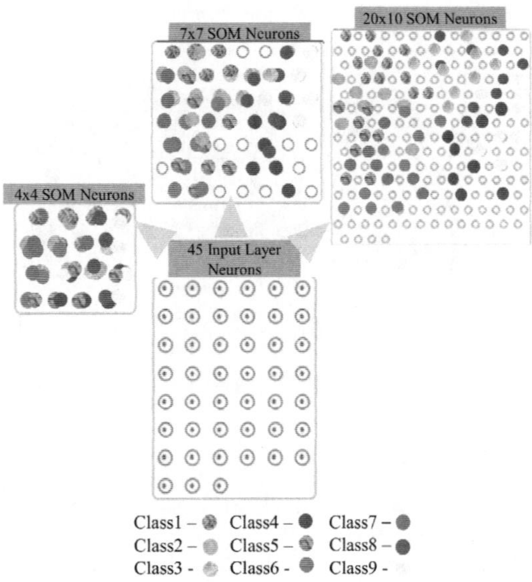

Figure 13. Test results in SOM NN structure with different grid size

SOM algorithm [19] with a topology shown in Figure 13. We use 45 Input neurons and different number of SOM neurons, in series with 4x4, 7x7 and finally with 20x10 neurons. The size of the SOM grid is determined empirically, considering the recommendations given by the Kohonen himself [19]. It stands that the size of the SOM grid array must roughly correspond to the major dimension of the distribution of the Input data [20]. As the reducing the real-time execution is desirable when applying the methods for real-time applications we begin the training with a small size of SOM grid (4x4) and increase this number (7x7) until good recognition accuracy in the test phase is achieved (20x10). We choose a hexagonal SOM grid. These network was trained with initial *learning rate* of 0.06, initial *neighbourhood size* of 200 and *neighbourhood decay amount* of 0.5. Figure 13 represents the test results for the 9 classes. It is visible that the small grid gives bad results with high overlapping of recognized samples, but increasing the size to 20x10 neurons gives very good clustering. In the best case only two samples of class 2 overlap with one sample of class 5 and class 6. Also one sample of class 3 overlaps with two samples of class 8. When calculating the recognition accuracy over the whole number of test samples of all 9 classes, i.e. 9x33=297, with only 8 false clustered samples, it gives 97.3% accuracy. Table I and Table II reflect the obtained recognition accuracy and execution time also for the tested SOM NN. It is distinct that the SOM gives also very high accuracy along with simple pre-processing and in

TABLE II. COMPARATIVE RESULTS FOR RECOGNITION ACCURACY AND REAL-TIME EXECUTION

Method	Number of hidden neurons	MSE [%] / Learning Rate for SOM	Recognition accuracy [%]	Real-time execution [ms]
MLP-Histogram	50	0.16	85	578
MLP-DCT	50	0.01	95	638
MLP-DWT	25	0.16	100	649
MLP-alternately (dH/dg; Exp(100.H(g))	18	0.01	97-100	247
SOM-Exp(100.H(g)	200 SOM Neurons	1.23E-321	94-100	112

addition gives shorter execution time in comparison to MLP NN. The most recent results obtained by the authors in [12] are 1.3 sec per marble texture, with relatively low recognition accuracy of 83.54%. Comparing the results achieved in terms of computing performance and accuracy, we could say that the presented method offers significantly better performance.

IV. CONCLUSION

In this research, a simple method for recognition of similar marble tiles with high correlated histograms is proposed and tested for nine texture classes. High recognition accuracy is obtained under very simple calculations in the pre-processing stage. Calculation of dH(g)/dg and Exp(100.H(g)) is a very simple single operation over H(g). Training the MLP NN with both – slightly de-correlated inter class data as dH(g)/dg, thus conserving the local changes of H(g) between neighbors g, and strong de- correlated data as Exp(100.H(g)) is a prerequisit to obtain very good recognition results and makes it possible to implement this method in different real-system systems. The choice of only one NN with a relatively small number of neurons, instead of a hierarchical NN structure and the simple processing, allows method implementation in real-time systems. It is also interesting to find analog transformations for good NN input data de-correlation. The achievment of high recognition accuracy in shorter execution time for SOM NN, by the same de-correlated input data proves the generalization of the proposed method. It is also interesting to find analog transformations for good NN input data de-correlation.

In future work, the method will be tested for more classes with similar textures also for other type of textures, to generalize the results. For example, the study can also be applied to similar textures on wooden surfaces. Another interesting idea for us is to first apply only SOM NN, to group / categorize in advance the proposed de-correlated data, after which the values of SOM neurons are submitted as inputs to the MLP network. In this way, it would be possible to precisely distinguish small local variations in textures, such as minor defects.

REFERENCES

[1] I.Topalova and M. Uzunova, "Neural Network Structure with Alternating Input Training Sets for Recognition of Marble Surfaces," IARIA/ ICAS'2017 – the Thirteenth International Conference on Autonomic and Autonomous Systems, ISBN: 978-1-61208-555-5, May, pp.40-44, Barcelona, Spain, 2017.

[2] C. W. D. Almeida, R.M.C.R. de Souza, and A. L. B. Candeias, "Texture Classification Based on a Co-Occurrence Matrix and Self-Organizing Map," IEEE International Conference on Systems Man & Cybernetics, University of Pernambuco, Recife, pp. 2487-2491, 2010.

[3] G. A. Azim and S. Nasir, "Textile Defects Identification Based on NNs and Mutual Information," International Conference on Computer Applications Technology (ICCAT), Sousse Tunisia, pp. 1-8, 2013.

[4] J. M. C. de-V. Alajarin, T. Balibrea, and M. Luis, "Marble Slabs Quality Classifcation System using Texture Recognition and NNs Methodology," ESANN'1999 proceedings - European Symposium on Artificial NNs, Bruges, Belgium, pp. 75-80, 1999.

[5] D. Feng, Z. Yang, and X. Qiao, "Texture Image Segmentation Based on Improved Wavelet NN," LNCS, Springer, Heidelberg, vol. 4493, pp. 869–876, 2007.

[6] I. Topalova, "Automated Marble Plate Classification System Based on Different NN Input Training Sets and PLC Implementation," IJARAI – International Journal of Advanced Research in Artificial Intelligence, Volume1, Issue2, pp. 50-56, 2012.

[7] I. Topalova, "Recognition of Similar Wooden Surfaces with a Hierarchical NN Structure," SAI/ IJARAI – International Journal of Advanced Research in Artificial Intelligence, Volume 4, Issue10, pp. 35-39, 2015.

[8] S. Bianco, Cl. Custano, P. Napolitano, and R. Schettini, "Improving CNN-Based Texture Classification by Color Balancing," Journal of Imaging, 27 July, 2017.

[9] A.S. Razavian, H. Azizpour, J. Sullivan, and S. Carlsson, "CNN features off-the-shelf: An astounding baseline for recognition", Proceedings of the 2014 IEEE Conference on Computer Vision and Pattern Recognition Workshops (CVPRW), Columbus, OH, USA, 23–28 June, 2014.

[10] C.Cusano, P. Napoletano, and R. Schettini, "Combining local binary patterns and local color contrast for texture classification under varying illumination," J. Opt. Soc. Am. A, 31, 1453–1461, 2014.

[11] C. Cusano, P. Napoletano, and R. Schettini, "Local Angular Patterns for Color Texture Classification," New Trends in Image Analysis and Processing – ICIAP 2015 Workshops. Murino, V., Puppo, E., Sona, D., Cristani, M., Sansone, C., Eds.; Springer International Publishing: Cham, Switzerland, pp. 111–118, 2015.

[12] J. M. P. Batista, "Marble Polished Stones Automatic Classification," Universidade de Lisboa, Portugal, November, 2015.https://fenix.tecnico.ulisboa.pt/downloadFile/1126295043834456/Resumo_Alargado.pdf, last access – 20.11.2017.

[13] B. Widrow and S. Stearns, "Adaptive Signal Processing," Prentice-Hall, Inc. Englewood Cliffs, N.J. 07632, pp.36-40, 2004.

[14] R. C. Gonzalez and R. E Woods, "Digital Image Processing," 3rd Edition, Prentice Hall, India, 2008.

[15] Vision Builder AI, User Manuel, Copyright © 2013, pp. 45-58, 2013.

[16] E. W. Weisstein, "Correlation Coefficient," From MathWorld, A Wolfram Web Resource. Available from: http://mathworld.wolfram.com/CorrelationCoefficient.html, 2017.

[17] Neuro Solutions, Copyright © 2014, NeuroDimension, pp. 67-79, 2015.

[18] St. W. Smith, "The Scientists and Engineer's Guide to Digital Signal Processing," Book, Copyright © 1997-2011 by California Technical Publishing, 2011.

[19] Sh. M. Guthikonda, "Kohonen Self-Organizing Maps," Wittenberg University, pp.8-10, December, 2005.

[20] T. Kohonen and T. Honkela, "Kohonen network," Scholarpedia. Retrieved 2012-09-24, 2012.

iaria journals

www.iariajournals.org

International Journal On Advances in Intelligent Systems
issn: 1942-2679

International Journal On Advances in Internet Technology
issn: 1942-2652

International Journal On Advances in Life Sciences
issn: 1942-2660

International Journal On Advances in Networks and Services
issn: 1942-2644

International Journal On Advances in Security
issn: 1942-2636

International Journal On Advances in Software
issn: 1942-2628

International Journal On Advances in Systems and Measurements
issn: 1942-261x

International Journal On Advances in Telecommunications
issn: 1942-2601

International Academy, Research,
and Industry Association (IARIA)
412 Derby Way
Wilmington, DE 19810

ISBN 978-1-5108-5647-9

9 781510 856479

CURRAN ASSOCIATES INC.
proceedings.com